THE OFFICIAL (ISC)² CISSP® CBK® REVIEW SEMINAR

STUDENT HANDBOOK
Version 10.0

(ISC)²®

SECURITY TRANSCENDS TECHNOLOGY℠

World Headquarters
Jones & Bartlett Learning
40 Tall Pine Drive
Sudbury, MA 01776
978-443-5000
info@jblearning.com
www.jblearning.com

Jones & Bartlett Learning Canada
6339 Ormindale Way
Mississauga, Ontario L5V 1J2
Canada

Jones & Bartlett Learning International
Barb House, Barb Mews
London W6 7PA
United Kingdom

Jones & Bartlett Learning books and products are available through most bookstores and online booksellers. To contact Jones & Bartlett Learning directly, call 800-832-0034, fax 978-443-8000, or visit our website, www.jblearning.com.

Production Credits
Chief Executive Officer: Ty Field
President: James Homer
SVP, Chief Operating Officer: Don Jones, Jr.
SVP, Chief Technology Officer: Dean Fossella
SVP, Chief Marketing Officer: Alison M. Pendergast
SVP, Chief Financial Officer: Ruth Siporin
SVP, Curriculum Solutions: Christopher Will
VP, Manufacturing and Inventory Control: Therese Connell
Editorial Management: High Stakes Writing, LLC, Editor and Publisher: Lawrence J. Goodrich
Reprints and Special Projects Manager: Susan Schultz
Associate Production Editor: Tina Chen
Composition: Richard B. Whiteman, Pixel Works
Cover Image: © the International Information Systems Security Certification Consortium, Inc. (ISC)²®.
Printing and Binding: Malloy, Inc.
Cover Printing: Malloy, Inc.

ISBN: 978-1-4496-2216-9

6048
Printed in the United States of America
15 14 13 12 11   10 9 8 7 6 5 4 3 2 1

Table of Contents

(ISC)²®

Dear CISSP Candidate,

I would like to thank you for choosing to take advantage of (ISC)²'s Official CISSP CBK Review Seminar in anticipation of becoming a certified member of our organization. This official course will provide a comprehensive review of the necessary topics and deepen your knowledge of information security. Your efforts this week will be an integral part of preparing yourself to attain the CISSP certification.

Your choice to become an (ISC)² certified professional comes at a momentous time for the industry as information security has become a top priority in both the public and private sectors with professionals in demand like never before. To illustrate this demand, in a 2010 survey of nearly 3,000 (ISC)² members worldwide, 52.8 percent received salary increases amid a global recession in 2009 and 53.3 percent of those with hiring responsibilities responded that they were looking to hire new employees in 2010. By becoming a certified (ISC)² member, you are taking an important step toward securing your own future in this industry.

By becoming a member of (ISC)², you are also joining the elite ranks of the largest not-for-profit membership body of certified information security professionals worldwide. The prestige of the organization continues to grow as our members hold top information security positions throughout government agencies, organizations and corporations around the world.

As a member, you also will enjoy access to exclusive (ISC)² professional education and networking opportunities, infosecurity events and webinars, along with the quarterly *InfoSecurity Professional* magazine and *(ISC)² Journal*, all offered free or with extensive discounts.

While I know the exam is demanding, rest assured the certification will be well worth your efforts. By taking the Official CISSP CBK Review Seminar, you will be able to leverage the course materials provided along with the expertise of your qualified (ISC)² instructor to best prepare for the CISSP examination. I wish you the best of luck in the seminar and on your journey to becoming a CISSP.

Thank you.

Sincerely,

W. Hord Tipton, CISSP-ISSEP, CAP, CISA
Executive Director
(ISC)²

CISSP®
Candidate Information Bulletin

Effective Date: January 2009

Certified Information Systems Security Professional (CISSP®)

Candidate Information Bulletin

Effective Date: 1 January 2009

This Candidate Information Bulletin provides the following:

- exam blueprint to a limited level of detail that outlines major topics and subtopics within the domains which are listed in alphabetical order,
- suggested reference list,
- description of the format of the items on the exam, and
- basic registration/administration policies.

Applicants must have a minimum of five years of direct full-time security professional work experience in two or more of the ten domains of the (ISC)² CISSP® CBK® or four years of direct full-time security professional work experience in two or more of the ten domains of the CISSP® CBK® with a four-year college degree. Only one year experience exemption is granted for education.

CISSP professional experience includes:

- Work requiring special education or intellectual attainment, usually including a liberal education or college degree.
- Work requiring habitual memory of a body of knowledge shared with others doing similar work.
- Management of projects and/or other employees.
- Supervision of the work of others while working with a minimum of supervision of one's self.
- Work requiring the exercise of judgment, management decision-making, and discretion.
- Work requiring the exercise of ethical judgment (as opposed to ethical behavior).
- Creative writing and oral communication.
- Teaching, instructing, training and the mentoring of others.
- Research and development.
- The specification and selection of controls and mechanisms (i.e., identification and authentication technology) (does not include the mere operation of these controls).
- Applicable titles such as officer, director, manager, leader, supervisor, analyst, designer, cryptologist, cryptographer, cryptanalyst, architect, engineer, instructor, professor, investigator, consultant, salesman, representative, etc. Title may include programmer. It may include administrator, except where it applies to one who simply operates controls under the authority and supervision of others. Titles with the words "coder" or "operator" are likely excluded.

Certified Information Systems Security Professional (CISSP®)

Candidate Information Bulletin

Effective Date: 1 January 2009

Access Control

Overview

Access Control is the collection of mechanisms that permits managers of a system to exercise a directing or restraining influence over the behavior, use, and content of a system. It permits management to specify what users can do, which resources they can access, and what operations they can perform on a system.

The candidate should fully understand access control concepts, methodologies and implementation within centralized and decentralized environments across the enterprise's computer systems. Access control techniques, detective and corrective measures should be studied to understand the potential risks, vulnerabilities, and exposures.

Key Areas of Knowledge

- ☑ Control access by applying the following concepts/methodologies/techniques
- ☑ 1. Policies
- ☑ 2. Types of controls (preventive, detective, corrective, etc.)
- ☑ 3. Techniques (e.g., non-discretionary, discretionary and mandatory)
- ☑ 4. Identification and Authentication
- ☑ 5. Decentralized/distributed access control techniques
- ☑ 6. Authorization mechanisms
- ☑ 7. Logging and monitoring
- ☑ Understand access control attacks
- ☑ Assess effectiveness of access controls

Certified Information Systems Security Professional (CISSP®)

Candidate Information Bulletin

Effective Date: 1 January 2009

Application Development Security

Overview

Application Security refers to the controls that are included within systems and applications software and the steps used in their development. Applications refer to agents, applets, software, databases, data warehouses, and knowledge-based systems. These applications may be used in distributed or centralized environments.

The candidate should fully understand the security and controls of the systems development process, system life cycle, application controls, change controls, data warehousing, data mining, knowledge-based systems, program interfaces, and concepts used to ensure data and application integrity, security, and availability.

Key Areas of Knowledge

- ☑ Understand and apply security in the system life cycle
- ☑   1. Systems Development Life Cycle (SDLC)
- ☑   2. Maturity models
- ☑   3. Operation and maintenance
- ☑   4. Change management
- ☑   5. Perform risk analysis
- ☑ Understand the application environment and security controls
- ☑   1. Security of the application environment
- ☑   2. Security issues of programming languages
- ☑   3. Security issues in source code (e.g., buffer overflow)
- ☑   4. Configuration management
- ☑ Assess the effectiveness of application security
- ☑   1. Certification and accreditation
- ☑   2. Auditing and logging
- ☑   3. Corrective actions

Certified Information Systems Security Professional (CISSP®)
Candidate Information Bulletin
Effective Date: 1 January 2009

Business Continuity and Disaster Recovery Planning

Overview

The Business Continuity and Disaster Recovery Planning domain addresses the preservation of the business in the face of major disruptions to normal business operations. BCP and DRP involve the preparation, testing and updating of specific actions to protect critical business processes from the effect of major system and network failures.

Business Continuity Plans counteract interruptions to business activities and should be available to protect critical business processes from the effects of major failures or disasters. It deals with the natural and man-made events and the consequences if not dealt with promptly and effectively.

Business Impact Assessment determines the proportion of impact an individual business unit would sustain subsequent to a significant interruption of computing or telecommunication services. These impacts may be financial, in terms of monetary loss, or operational, in terms of inability to deliver.

Disaster Recovery Plans contain procedures for emergency response, extended backup operation and post-disaster recovery should a computer installation experience a partial or total loss of computer resources and physical facilities. The primary objective of the Disaster Recovery Plan is to provide the capability to process mission-essential applications, in a degraded mode, and return to normal mode of operation within a reasonable amount of time.

The candidate will be expected to know the difference between business continuity planning and disaster recovery; business continuity planning in terms of project scope and planning, business impact analysis, recovery strategies, recovery plan development, and implementation. The candidate should understand disaster recovery in terms of recovery plan development, implementation and restoration.

Certified Information Systems Security Professional (CISSP®)

Candidate Information Bulletin

Effective Date: 1 January 2009

Key Areas of Knowledge

- ☑ Understand business continuity requirements
- ☑   1. Develop and document project scope and plan
- ☑ Conduct business impact analysis
- ☑   1. Identify and prioritize critical business functions
- ☑   2. Determine maximum tolerable downtime and other criteria
-       3. Assess exposure to outages (e.g., local, regional, global)
- ☑   4. Define recovery objectives
- ☑ Develop a recovery strategy
- ☑   1. Implement a backup storage strategy (e.g., offsite storage, electronic vaulting, tape rotation)
- ☑   2. Recovery site strategies
- ☑ Understand disaster recovery process
- ☑   1. Response
- ☑   2. Personnel
- ☑   3. Communications
- ☑   4. Assessment
- ☑   5. Restoration
- ☑ Provide training
- ☑ Test, update, assess and maintain the plan (e.g., version control, distribution)

Certified Information Systems Security Professional (CISSP®)

Candidate Information Bulletin

Effective Date: 1 January 2009

Cryptography

Overview

The Cryptography domain addresses the principles, means, and methods of disguising information to ensure its integrity, confidentiality, and authenticity.

The candidate will be expected to know basic concepts within cryptography; public and private key algorithms in terms of their applications and uses; algorithm construction, key distribution and management, and methods of attack; and the applications, construction and use of digital signatures to provide authenticity of electronic transactions, and non-repudiation of the parties involved.

Key Areas of Knowledge

☑ Understand the application and use of cryptography
☑   1. Data at rest (e.g., Hard Drive)
☑   2. Data in transit (e.g., "On the wire")
☑ Understand encryption concepts
☑   1. Foundational concepts
☑   2. Symmetric cryptography
☑   3. Asymmetric cryptography
☑   4. Hybrid cryptography
☑   5. Message digests
☑   6. Hashing
☑ Understand key management processes
☑   1. Creation/distribution
☑   2. Storage/destruction
☑   3. Recovery
☑   4. Key escrow
☑ Understand digital signatures
☑ Understand non-repudiation
☑ Understand methods of cryptanalytic attacks
☑   1. Chosen plain-text
☑   2. Social engineering for key discovery
☑   3. Brute Force
☑   4. Cipher-text only
☑   5. Known plaintext
☑   6. Frequency analysis
☑   7. Chosen cipher-text
☑   8. Implementation attacks

Certified Information Systems Security Professional (CISSP®)

Candidate Information Bulletin

Effective Date: 1 January 2009

- ☑ Employ cryptography in network security
- ☑ Use cryptography to maintain e-mail security
- ☑ Understand Public Key Infrastructure (PKI)
- ☑ Understand certificate related issues
- ☑ Understand information hiding alternatives (e.g., steganography, watermarking)

Certified Information Systems Security Professional (CISSP®)

Candidate Information Bulletin

Effective Date: 1 January 2009

Information Security Governance and Risk Management

Overview

Information Security Governance and Risk Management entails the identification of an organization's information assets and the development, documentation, and implementation of policies, standards, procedures and guidelines that ensure confidentiality, integrity, and availability. Management tools such as data classification, risk assessment, and risk analysis are used to identify the threats, classify assets, and to rate their vulnerabilities so that effective security controls can be implemented.

Risk management is the identification, measurement, control, and minimization of loss associated with uncertain events or risks. It includes overall security review, risk analysis; selection and evaluation of safeguards, cost benefit analysis, management decision, safeguard implementation, and effectiveness review.

The candidate will be expected to understand the planning, organization, and roles of individuals in identifying and securing an organization's information assets; the development and use of policies stating management's views and position on particular topics and the use of guidelines, standards, and procedures to support the policies; security awareness training to make employees aware of the importance of information security, its significance, and the specific security-related requirements relative to their position; the importance of confidentiality, proprietary and private information; employment agreements; employee hiring and termination practices; and risk management practices and tools to identify, rate, and reduce the risk to specific resources.

Certified Information Systems Security Professional (CISSP®)

Candidate Information Bulletin

Effective Date: 1 January 2009

Key Areas of Knowledge

- ☑ Understand and align security function to goals, mission and objectives of the organization
- ☑ Understand and apply security governance
- ☑   1. Organizational processes
- ☑   2. Define security roles and responsibilities
- ☑   3. Legislative and regulatory compliance
- ☑   4. Privacy requirements compliance
- ☑   5. Control frameworks
- ☑   6. Due care
- ☑   7. Due diligence
- ☑ Understand and apply concepts of confidentiality, integrity and availability
- ☑ Develop and implement security policy
- ☑   1. Security policies
- ☑   2. Standards/baselines
- ☑   3. Procedures
- ☑   4. Guidelines
- ☑   5. Documentation
- ☑ Define and implement information classification and ownership
- ☑ Ensure security in contractual agreements and procurement processes
- ☑ Understand and apply risk management concepts
- ☑   1. Identify threats and vulnerabilities
- ☑   2. Risk assessment/analysis
- ☑   3. Risk assignment/acceptance
- ☑   4. Countermeasure selection
- ☑ Evaluate personnel security
- ☑   1. Background checks and employment candidate screening
- ☑   2. Employment agreements and policies
- ☑   3. Employee termination processes
- ☑   4. Vendor, consultant and contractor controls
- ☑ Develop and manage security education, training and awareness
- ☑ Develop and implement information security strategies
- ☑ Support certification and accreditation efforts
- ☑ Assess the completeness and effectiveness of the security program
- ☑ Understand professional ethics
- ☑   1. (ISC)² code of professional ethics
- ☑   2. Support organization's code of ethics
- ☑ Manage the Security Function
- ☑   1. Budget
- ☑   2. Metrics
- ☑   3. Resources

Certified Information Systems Security Professional (CISSP®)
Candidate Information Bulletin
Effective Date: 1 January 2009

Legal, Regulations, Investigations, and Compliance

Overview

The Legal, Regulations, Investigations, and Compliance domain addresses computer crime laws and regulations; the investigative measures and techniques which can be used to determine if a crime has been committed, and methods to gather evidence.

Incident handling provides the ability to react quickly and efficiently to malicious technical threats or incidents.

The candidate will be expected to know the methods for determining whether a computer crime has been committed; the laws that would be applicable for the crime; laws prohibiting specific types of computer crime; methods to gather and preserve evidence of a computer crime, investigative methods and techniques; and ways to address compliance.

Key Areas of Knowledge

- ☑ Understand legal issues that pertain to information security internationally
- ☑   1. Computer crime
- ☑   2. Licensing and intellectual property (e.g., copyright, trademark)
- ☑   3. Import/Export
- ☑   4. Trans-border data flow
- ☑   5. Privacy
- ☑ Understand and support investigations
- ☑   1. Policy
- ☑   2. Incident handling and response
- ☑   3. Evidence collection and handling (e.g., chain of custody, interviewing)
- ☑   4. Reporting and documenting
- ☑ Understand forensic procedures
- ☑   1. Media analysis
- ☑   2. Network analysis
- ☑   3. Software analysis
- ☑ Understand compliance requirements and procedures
- ☑   1. Regulatory environment
- ☑   2. Audits
- ☑   3. Reporting

Certified Information Systems Security Professional (CISSP®)

Candidate Information Bulletin

Effective Date: 1 January 2009

Operations Security

Overview

Operations Security is used to identify the controls over hardware, media, and the operators with access privileges to any of these resources. Audit and monitoring is the mechanisms, tools and facilities that permit the identification of security events and subsequent actions to identify the key elements and report the pertinent information to the appropriate individual, group, or process.

The candidate will be expected to know the resources that must be protected, the privileges that must be restricted, the control mechanisms available, the potential for abuse of access, the appropriate controls, and the principles of good practice.

Key Areas of Knowledge

- ☑ Understand the following security concepts
- ☑ 1. Need-to-know/least privilege
- ☑ 2. Separation of duties and responsibilities
- ☑ 3. Monitor special privileges (e.g., operators, administrators)
- ☑ 4. Job rotation
- ☑ 5. Marking, handling, storing and destroying of sensitive information
- ☑ 6. Record retention
- ☑ Employ resource protection
- ☑ 1. Media management
- ☑ 2. Asset management
- ☑ 3. Personnel privacy and safety
- ☑ Manage incident response
- ☑ 1. Detection
- ☑ 2. Response
- ☑ 3. Reporting
- ☑ 4. Recovery
- ☑ 5. Remediation
- ☑ Prevent or respond to attacks (e.g., malicious code, zero-day exploit, denial of service)
- ☑ Implement and support patch and vulnerability management
- ☑ Understand configuration management concepts (e.g., versioning, baselining)
- ☑ Understand fault tolerance requirements

Certified Information Systems Security Professional (CISSP®)

Candidate Information Bulletin

Effective Date: 1 January 2009

Physical (Environmental) Security

Overview

The Physical (Environmental) Security domain addresses the threats, vulnerabilities, and countermeasures that can be utilized to physically protect an enterprise's resources and sensitive information. These resources include people, the facility in which they work, and the data, equipment, support systems, media, and supplies they utilize.

The candidate will be expected to know the elements involved in choosing a secure site, its design and configuration, and the methods for securing the facility against unauthorized access, theft of equipment and information, and the environmental and safety measures needed to protect people, the facility, and its resources.

Key Areas of Knowledge

- ☑ Participate in site and facility design considerations
- ☑ Support the implementation and operation of perimeter security (e.g., physical access control and monitoring, audit trails/access logs)
- ☑ Support the implementation and operation of internal security (e.g., escort requirements/visitor control, keys and locks)
- ☑ Support the implementation and operation of facilities security
- ☑ 1. Communications and server rooms
- ☑ 2. Restricted and work area security
- ☑ 3. Data center security
- ☑ 4. Utilities and HVAC considerations
- ☑ 5. Water issues (e.g., leakage, flooding)
- ☑ 6. Fire prevention, detection and suppression
- ☑ Support the protection and securing of equipment

Certified Information Systems Security Professional (CISSP®)

Candidate Information Bulletin

Effective Date: 1 January 2009

Security Architecture and Design

Overview

The Security Architecture and Design domain contains the concepts, principles, structures, and standards used to design, implement, monitor, and secure, operating systems, equipment, networks, applications, and those controls used to enforce various levels of confidentiality, integrity, and availability.

The candidate should understand security models in terms of confidentiality, integrity, information flow; system models in terms of the Common Criteria; technical platforms in terms of hardware, firmware, and software; and system security techniques in terms of preventative, detective, and corrective controls.

Key Areas of Knowledge

- ☑ Understand the fundamental concepts of security models (e.g., Confidentiality, Integrity, and Multi-level Models)
- ☑ Understand the components of information systems security evaluation models
- ☑   1. Product evaluation models (e.g., common criteria)
- ☑   2. Industry and international security implementation guidelines (e.g., PCI-DSS, ISO)
- ☑ Understand security capabilities of information systems (e.g., memory protection, virtualization, trusted platform module)
- ☑ Understand the vulnerabilities of security architectures
- ☑   1. System (e.g., covert channels, state attacks, emanations)
- ☑   2. Technology and process integration (e.g., single point of failure, service oriented architecture)
- ☑ Understand application and system vulnerabilities and threats
- ☑   1. Web-based (e.g., XML, SAML)
- ☑   2. Client-based (e.g., applets)
- ☑   3. Server-based (e.g., data flow control)
- ☑   4. Database security (e.g., inference, aggregation, data mining)
- ☑ Understand countermeasure principles (e.g., defense in depth)

Certified Information Systems Security Professional (CISSP®)

Candidate Information Bulletin

Effective Date: 1 January 2009

Telecommunications and Network Security

Overview

Telecommunications and Network Security domain encompasses the structures, transmission methods, transport formats, and security measures used to provide integrity, availability, authentication, and confidentiality for transmissions over private and public communications networks and media.

The candidate is expected to demonstrate an understanding of communications and network security as it relates to voice communications; data communications in terms of local area, wide area, and remote access; Internet/Intranet/Extranet in terms of Firewalls, Routers, and TCP/IP; and communications security management and techniques in terms of preventive, detective and corrective measures.

In today's global marketplace, the ability to communicate with others is a mandatory requirement. The data communications domain encompasses the network structure, transmission methods, transport formats and security measures used to maintain the integrity, availability, authentication and confidentiality of the transmitted information over both private and public communication networks.

The candidate is expected to demonstrate an understanding of communications and network security as it relates to data communications in local area and wide area networks; remote access; internet/intranet/extranet configurations, use of firewalls, network equipment and protocols (such as TCP/IP), VPNs, and techniques for preventing and detecting network based attacks.

Key Areas of Knowledge

- ☑ Establish secure data communications
- ☑ Understand secure network architecture and design
- ☑   1. OSI and TCP/IP models
- ☑   2. IP networking
- ☑ Secure network components
- ☑   1. Hardware (e.g., modems, switches, routers)
- ☑   2. Transmission media
- ☑   3. Filtering devices (e.g., firewalls, proxies)
- ☑   4. End-point security
- ☑ Establish secure communication channels
- ☑   1. Voice over IP (VoIP)
- ☑   2. Multimedia collaboration (e.g., remote meeting technology, instant messaging)
- ☑   3. Virtual Private Networks (VPN)
- ☑   4. Remote access
- ☑ Understand network attacks

Certified Information Systems Security Professional (CISSP®)

Candidate Information Bulletin

Effective Date: 1 January 2009

REFERENCES

(ISC)² does not intend that candidates purchase and read all of the books and articles listed in this reference list. Since most of the information tested in the examination pertains to a common body of knowledge, this additional information serves only as a supplement to one's understanding of basic knowledge. A reference list is not intended to be inclusive but is provided to allow flexibility. The candidate is encouraged to supplement his or her education and experience by reviewing other resources and finding information in areas which he or she may consider himself or herself not as skilled or experienced. (ISC)² does not endorse any particular text or author. Although the list may include more than one reference that covers a content area, one such reference may be enough. The candidate may also have resources available that are not on the list but which will adequately cover the content area. The list does not represent the only body of information to be used as study material.

Questions in the examination are also developed from information gained through practical experience. This reference list is not intended to be all-inclusive, but rather, a useful list of references used to support the test question development process. Use of the references does not guarantee successful completion of the test.

Below is the suggested reference list:

• (ISC)² Code Of Ethics	
• An Overview Of SSL V2	Adam Shostak
• Applied Cryptography	Schneier
• Black's Law Dictionary	Henry C. Black
• Building A Security Computer System	Morrie Gasser
• CCTV Surveillance-Video Practices And Technology	Herman Kruegle
• Cert Guide To System And Network Security Practices	Julia Allen
• Cisco TCP/IP	Lewis
• Commonsense Computer Security	Smith, Martin
• Computer & Communications Security	James A. Cooper
• Computer And Information Ethics	Wekert & Adeney
• Computer Audit, Control, And Security	Robert R. Moeller
• Computer Crime - A Crime Fighter's Handbook	Icove/Seger/Von Storch
• Computer Ethics And Society	M. David Erman
• Computer Networks: Protocols, Standards, And Interfaces	Black
• Computer Security	John M. Carroll
• Computer Security Basics	Russell & Gangemi
• Computer Security Handbook	Hoyt
• Computer Security Management	D.B. Parker
• Control And Security Of Information Systems	Fites, Philip E., Kratz, Martin P.J., Brebner, Alan F
• Counter Hack	Ed Skoudis
• Cryptography And Data Security	D. R. Denning
• Cryptography & Network Security	W. Stallings

Certified Information Systems Security Professional (CISSP®)

Candidate Information Bulletin

Effective Date: 1 January 2009

• Cryptography: A New Dimension In Data Security	Carl H. Meyer and Stephen M. Matyas
• Data Security & Controls	Edward R. Buck
• Data Security Management. Passwords, Userids And Security Codes	Steven J. Ross
• Database Security And Integrity	Fernandez , Summer and Wood
• Defending Your Digital Assets Against Hackers	Nichols
• Designing Network Security	Merike Kaeo
• Disaster Planning & Recovery	Alan Levitt
• Disaster Recovery Planning	Jon Toigo
• Effect Physical Security	Lawrence Fennelly
• E-Mail Security	B. Scheier
• Encyclopedia Of Computer Science And Engineering	A. Ralston and E. Reilly
• Fighting Computer Crime	Parker
• Fire Protection Handbook	National Fire Protection Association
• Fundamentals Of Criminal Investigations	Charles E. O'Hara.
• Hacker Proof	Lars Klander
• Hacking Exposed	Osborne
• Handbook Of Applied Cryptography	Alfred J. Menenzes, Paul C. Van Oorschot, Scott A Vanstone
• Handbook Of EDP Auditing.	Michael A. Murphy and Xenia Ley Parker
• Handbook Of Information Security Management	Krause-Tipton
• Handbook Of Information Security Management	Ruthberg/Tipton
• Handbook Of Personal Data Protection	W. Madsen
• Immediate Response	Schultz, P
• Implementing Internet Security	Cooper, Goggans, Halvey, Hughes, Morgan, Siyan, Stallings, Stephenson
• Incidence Response	Mandia
• Information Security Dictionary Of Concepts, Standards And Terms	William Caelli, Dennis Longly
• Information Systems Security: A Practitioner's Reference	Fites and Kratz
• Interconnections: Bridges And Routers	Radia Perlman
• Internet Cryptography	Smith
• Intrusion Detection	Escamilla
• ISP Liability Survival Guide	Timothy D. Casey
• Kahn On Codes: Secrets Of The New Cryptology	David Kahn.
• Management Strategies For Computer Security	William E. Perry
• Managing Information Security: A Program For The Electronic Information Age	James A. Schweitzer
• Mastering Network Security	Brenton
• Network Security	Fred Simmons
• Network Security: A Beginners Guide	Eric Maiwald.
• Official (ISC)² Guide to the CISSP Exam	Hanche, Berti, Hare
• OSI Reference Model	International Standards Organization.
• PC Security And Virus Protection Handbook	Pamela Kane
• PKI	Nash
• Practical Unix & Internet Security	Garfinkel/Spafford
• Pretty Good Privacy	Garfinkel
• Principles Of Security Management	Healy , Richard J. and Walsh, Dr. Timothy J.
• Risk Assessment And Management	Will Ozier
• Secure Computing - Threats And Safeguards	Rita Summers

•	Security Accuracy And Privacy In Computer System	Martin, James.
•	Security Architecture For The Internet Protocol (RFC2401)	Kent/Atkinson
•	Security Engineering	Anderson
•	Security ID Systems And Locks The Book Of Electronic Access Control	Joel Konicek & Karen Little
•	Security In Computing	Charles P. Pfleeger
•	Security Of Information And Data	Daler Torgeir
•	Survey Of Risk Assessment Methodologies	Peter S. Browne
•	Surviving Security	Andress
•	The NCSA Guide To PC And LAN Security	Stephen Cobb
•	The Point-To-Point Tunneling Protocol Technical Specification	Gurdeep Singh Pall, Kory Hanzeh, William Verthein, Jeff Taarud, Andrew Little
•	The Process Of Network Security	Wadlow
•	Tokens: A Comparison Of Password Generators	Hootman
•	Top-Down Network Design	Oppenheimer, Priscilla
•	Trade Knowledge	R. Sanovic & A. Terwilliger
•	Underground Guide To Computer Security	M. Alexander
•	Voice And Data Security	Archer, Core
•	Voice Network Fraud	Ray Horak
•	Web Publishing With HTML 4	Lemay
•	Web Security	Tiwana
•	Web Security & Commerce	Simson Garfinkel with Gene Spafford
•	Web Security Privacy And Commerce	Simson
•	Web Security Source Book	Rubin
•	Wireless Security	Merritt

Certified Information Systems Security Professional (CISSP®)

Candidate Information Bulletin

Effective Date: 1 January 2009

1. Which one of the following is the MOST important security consideration when selecting a new computer facility?

    (A)   Local law enforcement response times
    (B)   Adjacent to competitors' facilities
    (C)   Aircraft flight paths
    (D)   Utility infrastructure

    Answer - D

2. Which one of the following describes a SYN flood attack?

    (A)   Rapid transmission of Internet Relay Chat (IRC) messages
    (B)   Creating a high number of half-open connections
    (C)   Disabling the Domain Name Service (DNS) server
    (D)   Excessive list linking of users and files

    Answer - B

3. The typical function of Secure Sockets Layer (SSL) in securing Wireless Application Protocol (WAP) is to protect transmissions

    (A)   between the WAP gateway and the wireless device.
    (B)   between the web server and WAP gateway.
    (C)   from the web server to the wireless device.
    (D)   between the wireless device and the base station.

    Answer - B

Certified Information Systems Security Professional (CISSP®)

Candidate Information Bulletin

Effective Date: 1 January 2009

GENERAL EXAMINATION INFORMATION

1. <u>General Information</u>. The doors to all examination rooms will open at 8:00 a.m. Examination instructions will begin promptly at 8:30 a.m. All examinations will begin at approximately 9:00 a.m.

    The CISSP® exam will end at approximately 3:00 p.m. All other exams except the CSSLP will end at approximately 12:00 noon. The CSSLP exam will end at approximately 1:00 pm.

    Please note there will be no lunch break during the testing period of 9:00 a.m. through 3:00 p.m. However, you are permitted to bring a snack with you. You may, at your option, take a break and eat your snack at the back of the examination room. No additional time will be allotted for breaks.

2. <u>Examination Admittance</u>. Please arrive at 8:00 a.m. when the doors open. Please bring your admission letter to the examination. In order to be admitted, photo identification is also required. You will not be admitted without proper identification. The only acceptable forms of identification are a driver's license, government-issued identification card, or passport. No other written forms of identification will be accepted.

3. <u>Examination Security</u>. Failure to follow oral and written instructions will result in your application being voided and forfeiture of your application fee. Conduct that results in a violation of security or disrupts the administration of the examination could result in the confiscation of your test and dismissal from the examination. In addition, your examination will be considered void and will not be scored. Examples of misconduct include, but are not limited to, the following: writing on anything other than designated examination materials, writing after time is called, looking at another candidate's examination materials, talking with other candidates at any time during the examination period, failing to turn in all examination materials before leaving the testing room.

    You must not discuss or share reference materials or any other examination information with any candidate during the entire examination period. You are particularly cautioned not to do so after you have completed the exam and checked out of the test room, as other candidates in the area might be taking a break and still not have completed the examination. You may not attend the examination only to review or audit test materials. You may not copy any portion of the examination for any reason. No examination materials may leave the test room under any circumstances and all examination materials must be turned in and accounted for before leaving the testing room. No unauthorized persons will be admitted into the testing area.

Please be further advised that all examination content is strictly confidential. You may only communicate about the test, or questions on the test, using the appropriate comment forms provided by the examination staff at the test site. At no other time, before, during or after the examination, may you communicate orally, electronically or in writing with any person or entity about the content of the examination or individual examination questions.

4. Reference Material. Candidates writing on anything other than examination materials distributed by the proctors will be in violation of the security policies above. Reference materials are not allowed in the testing room. Candidates are asked to bring as few personal and other items as possible to the testing area.

    Hard copy language translation dictionaries are permitted for the examination, should you choose to bring one to assist you with language conversions. Electronic dictionaries will not be permitted under any circumstances. The Examination Supervisor will fully inspect your dictionary at check-in. Your dictionary may not contain any writing or extraneous materials of any kind. If the dictionary contains writing or other materials or papers, it will not be permitted in the examination room. Additionally, you are not permitted to write in your dictionary at any time during the examination, and it will be inspected a second time prior to dismissal from the examination. Finally, (ISC)² takes no responsibility for the content of such dictionaries or interpretations of the contents by a candidate.

5. Examination Protocol. While the site climate is controlled to the extent possible, be prepared for either warm or cool temperatures at the testing center. Cellular phones and beepers are prohibited in the testing area. The use of headphones inside the testing area is prohibited. Electrical outlets will not be available for any reason. Earplugs for sound suppression are allowed. No smoking or use of tobacco will be allowed inside the testing area. Food and drinks are only allowed in the snack area located at the rear of the examination room. You must vacate the testing area after you have completed the examination. If you require special assistance, you must contact (ISC)² Candidate Service (see address at the bottom of this document) at least one week in advance of the examination date and appropriate arrangements will be made. Due to limited parking facilities at some sites, please allow ample time to park and reach the testing area.

6. Admission Problems. A problem table for those candidates who did not receive an admission notice or need other assistance will be available 30 minutes prior to the opening of the doors.

7. <u>Examination Format and Scoring</u>.

- The CISSP® examination consists of 250 multiple choice questions with four (4) choices each.
- The CSSLP® examination consists of 175 multiple choice questions with four (4) choices each.
- The SSCP® examination contains 125 multiple choice questions with four (4) choices each.
- The ISSAP®, ISSEP®, and ISSMP® concentration examinations contain 125, 150, 125 multiple choice questions respectively with four (4) choices each.
- The Certified Authorization Professional (CAP®) examination contains 125 multiple choice questions with four (4) choices each.

There may be scenario-based items which may have more than one multiple choice question associated with it. These items will be specifically identified in the test booklet.

Each of these exams contains 25 questions which are included for research purposes only. The research questions are not identified; therefore, answer all questions to the best of your ability. Examination results will be based only on the scored questions on the examination. There are several versions of the examination. It is important that each candidate have an equal opportunity to pass the examination, no matter which version is administered. Expert certified information Security Architecture Professionals have provided input as to the difficulty level of all questions used in the examinations. That information is used to develop examination forms that have comparable difficulty levels. When there are differences in the examination difficulty, a mathematical procedure is used to make the scores equal. Because the number of questions required to pass the examination may be different for each version, the scores are converted onto a reporting scale to ensure a common standard. The passing grade required is a scale score of 700 out of a possible 1000 points on the grading scale.

8.   <u>Exam Results</u>. Examination results will normally be released, via email, within 4 to 6 weeks of the examination date. A comprehensive statistical and psychometric analysis of the score data is conducted prior to the release of scores. A minimum number of candidates must have taken the examination for the analysis to be conducted. Accordingly, depending upon the schedule of test dates for a given cycle, there may be occasions when scores are delayed beyond the 4-6 week time frame in order to complete this critical process. Results WILL NOT be released over the telephone. In order to receive your results, your primary email address must be current and any email address changes must be submitted to (ISC) ² Customer Support via email customersupport@isc2.org, or may be updated online in your candidate profile.

9.   <u>Exam Response Information</u>. Your answer sheet MUST be completed with your name and other information as required. The answer sheet must be used to record all answers to the multiple-choice questions. Upon completion, you are to wait for the proctor to collect your examination materials. Answers marked in the test booklet will not be counted or graded, and additional time will not be allowed in order to transfer answers to the answer sheet. All marks on the answer sheet must be made with a No. 2 pencil. You must blacken the appropriate circles completely and completely erase any incorrect marks. Only your responses marked on the answer sheet will be considered. An unanswered question will be scored as incorrect. Dress is "business casual" (neat...but certainly comfortable).

Certified Information Systems Security Professional (CISSP®)

Candidate Information Bulletin

Effective Date: 1 January 2009

Any questions should be directed to:

(ISC)² Candidate Services
33920 US Highway 19 North
Suite 205
Palm Harbor, FL 34684
Phone: 1.866.331.ISC2 (4722) in the United States
1.727.785.0189 all others
Fax: 1.727.683.0785

www.isc2.org/cissp

CISSP® CBK® REVIEW SEMINAR

(ISC)²

(ISC)²

AGENDA AND LOGISTICS

- Start time
- Breaks
- Mobile phones and pagers
- Fire escapes
- Instructor

What time do we start?

EMERGENCY PHONE # 911

ii

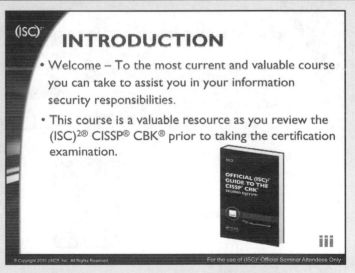

(ISC)²

INTRODUCTION

- Welcome – To the most current and valuable course you can take to assist you in your information security responsibilities.
- This course is a valuable resource as you review the (ISC)²® CISSP® CBK® prior to taking the certification examination.

OFFICIAL (ISC)²
GUIDE TO THE
CISSP® CBK®
SECOND EDITION

iii

WHAT IS (ISC)²®?

- Global not-for-profit organization
  - Based in Palm Harbor, FL
    - Offices in London; Tokyo; Hong Kong; Vienna, Va.
    - Worldwide affiliates
  - More than 70,000 certified professionals in 135 countries
  - (ISC)² sets the gold standard for information credentials
    - www.isc2.org

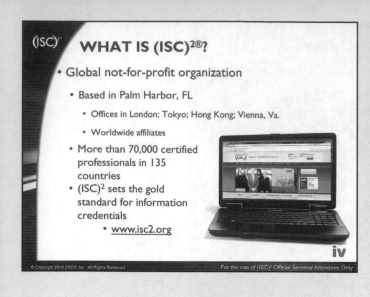

iv

BENEFITS OF (ISC)² MEMBERSHIP

- Member benefits
  - Continuing education
    - Security Leadership Series events
  - Discounts
    - Worldwide receptions, conferences, RSA, InfoSec, SecureAmerica
  - Face-to-face networking
  - Virtual networking
    - Career tools, InterSeC

v

BENEFITS OF (ISC)² MEMBERSHIP

- Industry awards
- Resources
  - InfoSecurity Professional Magazine
  - Information Security Perspective Journal: A Global Perspective
- Member-submitted security awareness materials
- Volunteer opportunities
  - www.staysafeonline.org

vi

CERTIFIED INFORMATION SYSTEM SECURITY PROFESSIONAL (CISSP®)

- Worldwide recognition of competence
- Practical understanding of information security issues and solutions
- ANSI accreditation based on the ISO/IEC 17024 standard
- Awareness of security challenges

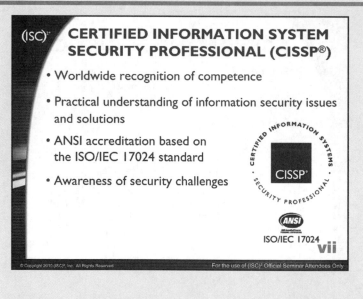

vii

(ISC)² — Introduction

ROLE OF THE CISSP®

- Develops and oversees the implementation of the organization's information security policies and procedures
- Provides advice on implementation of information security solutions and technologies
- Monitors compliance with regulatory bodies and employees, contractors, alliances, and other third parties

viii

THE CBK®

- The CISSP® CBK® is the taxonomy (collection) of all information security topics that a Certified Information System Security Professional should understand

- 10 domains are addressed in the CISSP® CBK®:

  - Access Control
  - Application Development Security
  - Business Continuity and Disaster Recovery Planning
  - Cryptography
  - Information Security Governance and Risk Management

  - Legal, Regulations, Investigations, and Compliance
  - Operations Security
  - Physical (Environmental) Security
  - Security Architecture and Design
  - Telecommunications and Network Security

ix

ASSOCIATE OF (ISC)²®

- The associate of (ISC)²® is designated for candidates who pass the CISSP® examination but are still building the necessary work experience

- It is the first step on your information security career path

- Receive all member benefits afforded to certified members

- Have two years from your exam date to acquire the work experience and complete the CISSP® certification process

x

SSCP CERTIFICATION STEPS

- Pass the CISSP® exam

- Provide a recent resume

- Complete the Examination Registration Form

- Submit a completed and executed Endorsement Form

xi

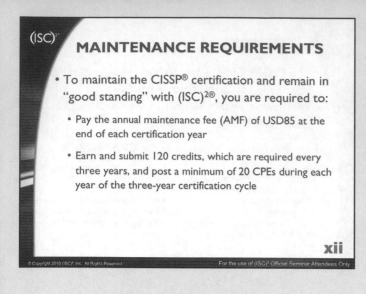

MAINTENANCE REQUIREMENTS

- To maintain the CISSP® certification and remain in "good standing" with (ISC)²®, you are required to:
  - Pay the annual maintenance fee (AMF) of USD85 at the end of each certification year
  - Earn and submit 120 credits, which are required every three years, and post a minimum of 20 CPEs during each year of the three-year certification cycle

xii

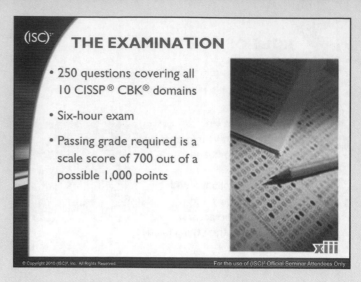

THE EXAMINATION

- 250 questions covering all 10 CISSP® CBK® domains
- Six-hour exam
- Passing grade required is a scale score of 700 out of a possible 1,000 points

xiii

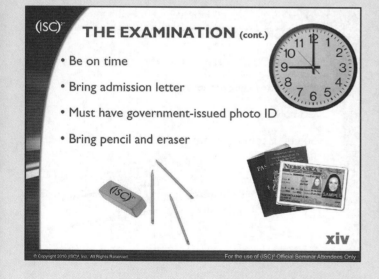

THE EXAMINATION (cont.)

- Be on time
- Bring admission letter
- Must have government-issued photo ID
- Bring pencil and eraser

xiv

SECURITY TRANSCENDS TECHNOLOGY

(ISC)²

xv

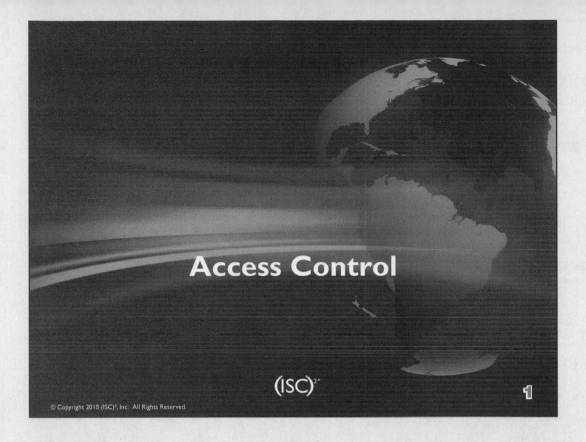

Access Control

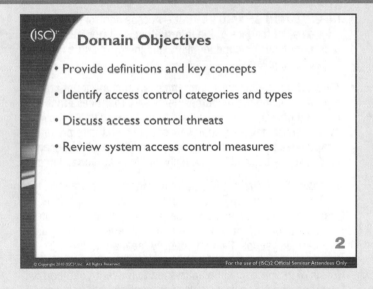

Domain Objectives

- Provide definitions and key concepts
- Identify access control categories and types
- Discuss access control threats
- Review system access control measures

- Access Control is the basic foundation of information security. A CISSP must thoroughly understand the definitions and key concepts of access control and must be able to consistently apply this knowledge when helping organization executives protect information resources.

- Access control is implemented differently depending on whether the area of implementation is physical, technical, or administrative. Access control categories include: preventive, detective, corrective, deterrent, recovery, directive, and compensating. These will often be used in combination.

- Organizations should focus their access control resources on the exposures and vulnerabilities likely to cause the most damage. A comprehensive threat analysis will identify the areas that will provide the greatest cost-benefit impact.

- The field of access control is constantly evolving. Organizations need to know what is available and what methods will best address the issues in their environment. They should also keep an eye on the horizon to prepare themselves for likely future threats or opportunities.

REFERENCE:

Information Security Management Handbook, Tipton & Krause, 5th edition, 2004 pg. 1965.

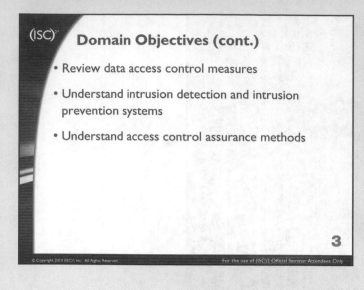

Domain Objectives (cont.)

- Review data access control measures

- Understand intrusion detection and intrusion prevention systems

- Understand access control assurance methods

3

- Data and system access control are not identical: A user may very well have access to a system without being able to access all of its data. Access to data or other areas often has to do with "need-to-know."

- Current intrusion detection and prevention systems are among the most powerful access control tools available. If used inappropriately, however, they can have a negative impact on the operation of access control measures.

- Access control assurance addresses the due diligence aspect of security. Implementing a control is part of due care, but due diligence involves regularly checking to ensure that the control is working as expected.

REFERENCE:

"Information Security Management Handbook," Tipton & Krause, 5th edition, 2004.

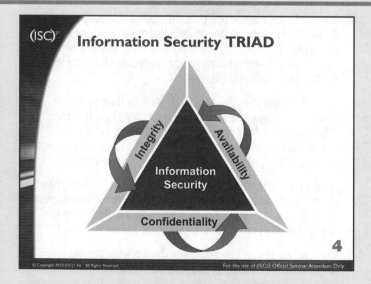

Information Security TRIAD

- **INFORMATION SECURITY TRIAD** – Access control has an impact on all of the legs of the Information Security TRIAD, with a primary focus on confidentiality and integrity and a lesser impact on availability.

- **AVAILABILITY** – Access control mechanisms must not prevent information, and the resources necessary to process that information, from being available to authorized users. However, access control mechanisms should be used to prevent unauthorized users from accessing a system and purposely or inadvertently causing it to be unavailable to authorized users.

- **INTEGRITY** – There are two parts to integrity in computer systems: data integrity and system integrity. Data integrity means that the data in the system accurately and completely represents the information intended, and reflects similar data in external systems. System integrity means that the system performs as intended, without exception. Because both forms of integrity must be addressed to prevent unauthorized changes, access control involves preventing both users and intruders from obtaining the kind of access that would enable them to make improper changes.

- **CONFIDENTIALITY** – Access control measures with respect to confidentiality focus primarily on preventing unauthorized access to sensitive or critical data and systems in order to prevent improper disclosure.

REFERENCE:

"Integrity in Automated Information Systems," National Computer Security Center Technical Report 79-91, Sept. 1991.

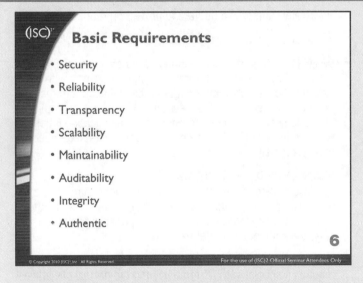

Domain Agenda

- **Definitions and Key Concepts**

- Access Control Categories and Types

- Access Control Threats

- Access to System

- Access to Data

- Intrusion Prevention & Detection Systems

- Access Control Assurance

5

Basic Requirements

- Security
- Reliability
- Transparency
- Scalability
- Maintainability
- Auditability
- Integrity
- Authentic

6

- **SECURITY** – Access control mechanisms must ensure that only authorized people or processes are able to access or modify sensitive data or programs, and then only in ways authorized by the organization. Access control mechanisms must also ensure that users have minimal opportunity to cause system unavailability.

- **RELIABILITY** – The assurance that the access control mechanisms function as expected, every time. For example, the failure of an access control system itself could cause a denial of service to the systems or data of the organization.

- **TRANSPARENCY** – Ideally, the operation of the access control mechanisms will have minimal impact on the ability of au-

thorized users to interface with the system and execute their job-oriented duties.

- **SCALABILITY** – Access control mechanisms should be able to handle a wide range of changing systems and user loads without compromising system performance.

- **MAINTAINABILITY** – Access control solutions must be maintainable to be effective. If the processes are too complicated or too time-consuming, administrators may not keep them up to date (e.g., conduct regular reviews of who should be allowed access to what).

- **AUDITABILITY** – Access control mechanisms should provide audit trails that will maintain records of system activity by a system, application process, and user. In conjunction with appropriate tools and procedures, audit trails can help accomplish several security-related objectives, including individual accountability, reconstruction of events, intrusion detection, and problem identification.

- **INTEGRITY** – Access control systems must be designed so as to protect subjects, objects, and permissions from unauthorized changes. The system should also maintain auditable records of when access control information has been accessed or changed.

- **AUTHENTIC** – Good access control mechanisms help ensure that data that is input is authentic.

REFERENCE:
NIST SP 800-14, http://csrc.nict.gov/publications/nictpubc/800-14/800-14.pdf

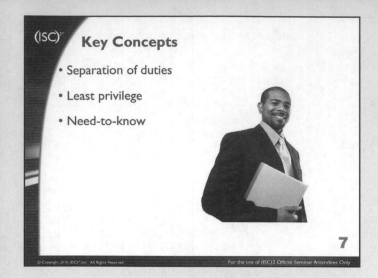

Key Concepts

- Separation of duties
- Least privilege
- Need-to-know

7

© Copyright 2010 (ISC)². Inc. All Rights Reserved.   For the use of (ISC)2 Official Seminar Attendees Only

- **SEPARATION OF DUTIES** – This most basic information security principle existed long before the advent of computers, but it is as important as ever. It is usually expressed in two parts:

  - No one person should have control over the complete processing of a transaction or series of transactions where that control would allow the person to manipulate the transaction(s) for personal gain. The transaction process is, therefore, broken down into individual steps that must be executed by different people.

  - Despite the enforcement of separation of duties, the two or more people needed to complete a transaction may col-

lude in order to commit fraud. Rotation of duties (moving employees in and out of jobs or job functions) may break up or reveal any such fraud. Collusion could only be re-established by bringing in a new participant. It is standard practice in some industries to require people in certain job functions to take two weeks of (mandatory) vacation. If fraud is taking place, the consequent anomalies are likely to be detected during this period.

- Separation of duties is a core element of the Clark-Wilson Integrity model.

- **LEAST PRIVILEGE** – The principle that people or processes should only be allowed access to the resources they absolutely need to accomplish their assigned work, and only for as long as necessary to complete that work.

- **NEED-TO-KNOW** – This principle is focused on access to sensitive or classified information. Not everyone who is cleared for higher levels of access to sensitive or classified systems actually needs all of the access available to him or her. Need-to-know restricts users from accessing information or systems not required to perform their jobs.

REFERENCE:

Fites, P. & Kratz, M. "Information Systems Security: A Practitioner's Reference," New York, Von Nostrand Reinhold, 1993.

IMAGE:

http://office.microsoft.com/en-us/clipart/

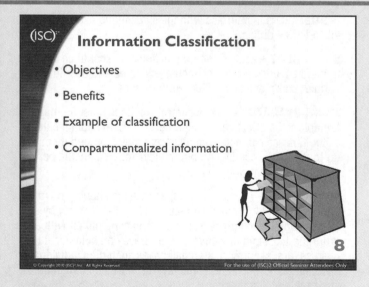

Information Classification

- Objectives
- Benefits
- Example of classification
- Compartmentalized information

8

© Copyright 2010 (ISC)². Inc. All Rights Reserved.   For the use of (ISC)2 Official Seminar Attendees Only

- **INFORMATION CLASSIFICATION** – IC is the proper assessment of the sensitivity and criticality of a given piece of information. Good IC ensures that information is neither improperly disclosed nor overprotected.

- **OBJECTIVES** –

  - To identify information-protection requirements based on organizational policy and the risk, or cost, of unauthorized disclosure, data/system corruption, or data value.

  - To standardize classification labeling throughout the organization. To ensure that every classification is provided the appropriate controls.

- To alert authorized holders to protection requirements.

- To comply with privacy laws, regulations, etc.

- **BENEFITS** – Data that is classified as sensitive or critical will be afforded a level of protection commensurate with its classification. Appropriate cost/benefits will accrue to the organization because increased controls will only be applied where they are most needed. Standard classification labeling will enable authorized holders to recognize what data needs to be protected.

- **EXAMPLE OF CLASSIFICATION** – The U.S. government employs a hierarchical range of classifications that include unclassified, confidential, secret, and top secret. The private sector may use classifications such as public, internal use only, and company confidential.

- **COMPARTMENTALIZED INFORMATION** – Is information that requires a special authorization beyond the normal classification system. This category is closely related to need-to-know.

REFERENCES:

"Information Security Management Handbook," Tipton & Krause, 5th Edition, 2004.

"Glossary of Infosec and Infosec Related Terms," Corey Schou PhD, Idaho State University, 1996.

"Information Security Policies, Procedures, and Standards," Thomas R. Peltier, ISBN 0849311373, CRC Press 2002, pg 115.

IMAGE:

http://office.microsoft.com/en-us/clipart/

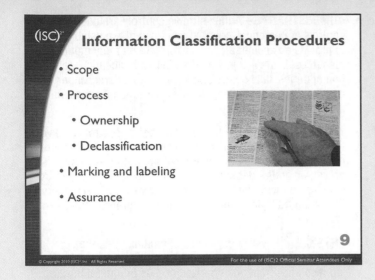

Information Classification Procedures

- Scope
- Process
  - Ownership
  - Declassification
- Marking and labeling
- Assurance

9

© Copyright 2010 (ISC)². Inc. All Rights Reserved.   For the use of (ISC)2 Official Seminar Attendees Only

- **SCOPE** – A risk and business impact analysis will evaluate all of the data handled by an organization and determine its value with respect to sensitivity and criticality. Points to consider in data valuation include: exclusive possession (trade secrets, etc.), usefulness, cost to create or recreate, legal or regulatory liability protection, convertibility/negotiability (electronic funds transfer, etc.), and operational impact if unavailable.

- **PROCESS** – The results of the risk and business impact analysis will help determine the minimum number of levels of classification necessary, as well as the appropriate policies and procedures for classification. Classification labels should be standardized and the appropriate level and method of access control determined. The goal is to achieve a consistent approach in the handling of classified information. This may require training the information owners or delegates, who are the ones responsible for assigning the initial classification. Classifiers must understand relevant regulations, customer

expectations, and business concerns. Owners are also responsible for a periodic review of classifications to ensure that they are still current, and for declassifying information that no longer requires special handling. (For example, government organizations often declare information automatically declassified after a certain number of years.)

- **MARKING AND LABELING** – All media containing sensitive and critical information must be marked in accordance with classification policy and procedures so that personnel are aware of what special handling measures to employ. Magnetic and optical media are normally labeled internally, electronically, and externally by easily read visual labels. Documents in hard copy forms are labeled externally on the cover and internally on the pages.

- **ASSURANCE** – Regular internal and external audits should review information-classification choices and adherence levels. Part of this review should focus on determining cases in which information is overclassified, which may in fact detract from the general intent and cost effectiveness of the access control methods employed. Information security personnel should regularly visit workstations and other areas where classified materials may be left unprotected and ensure that appropriate violation reports are made to supervisors and managers. Information security awareness programs should include training on classification and information handling in order to ensure that employees are aware of requirements. Employee performance evaluations should include a section having to do with handling classified information to bring employee attention to the importance of this process.

REFERENCES:

"Guideline for Information Valuation," ISSA, 1993.
http://www.praxiom.com/iso-17799-5.htm

IMAGE:

http://office.microsoft.com/en-us/clipart/

Domain Agenda

- Definitions and Key Concepts

- **Access Control Categories and Types**

- Access Control Threats

- Access to System

- Access to Data

- Intrusion Prevention & Detection Systems

- Access Control Assurance

10

© Copyright 2010 (ISC)², Inc. All Rights Reserved.   For the use of (ISC)2 Official Seminar Attendees Only

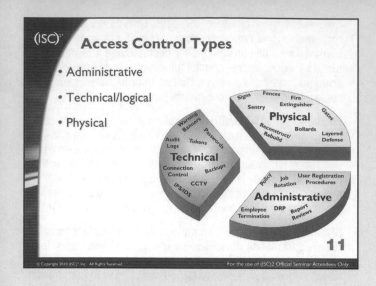

- **ADMINISTRATIVE** – Administrative controls are documented controls or personnel-oriented actions that are established to provide an acceptable level of protection for computing resources. Examples include training and education, separation of duties, dual control, policy and procedures, supervision, contingency and recovery plans, organizational ethics statements, etc.

- **TECHNICAL/LOGICAL** – Technical or logical controls involve the use of hardware or software mechanisms to protect computing resources and to ensure that unauthorized access is prevented and/or detected. Examples include access control software, antivirus/anti-spam/anti-spyware software, encryption, audit trails, logs, intrusion detection/prevention systems, etc.

- **PHYSICAL** – Physical controls are manual, structural, or environmental controls that protect facilities and computing resources from unauthorized access or natural threats. Examples include locks, doors, fences, guards, alarms, badges, mantraps, turnstiles, CCTV, motion detectors, sensors, earthquake-resistant server racks, etc.

REFERENCE:

"Handbook of Information Security Management," Krause and Tipton, Auerbach, 1998.

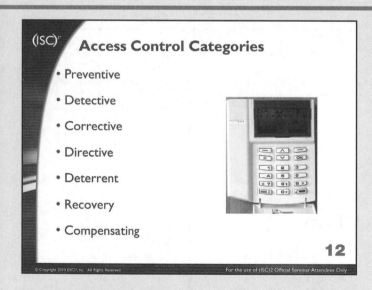

- **CORRECTIVE** – Corrective controls remedy the circumstances that enabled the unwanted activity, and/or return conditions to where they were prior to the unwanted activity.

- **DIRECTIVE** – Directive controls are those dictated by organizational and legal authorities.

- **DETERRENT** – Deterrent controls (often associated with directive controls) prescribe some sort of punishment, ranging from embarrassment to job termination or jail time for non-compliance. Their intent is to dissuade people from performing unwanted acts. Some technical controls – e.g., violation reports, web proxy filters, logon banners, etc. – also contain warnings.

- **RECOVERY** – Recovery controls restore lost computing resources or capabilities and help the organization to recover monetary losses caused by a security violation or incident.

- **COMPENSATING** – Compensating controls reinforce or replace normal controls that are unavailable for any reason. These are typically backup controls and usually involve higher levels of supervision and/or contingency plans.

- Note that these access control categories may be administrative, physical, or technical, or all of the above.

REFERENCES:

"Handbook of Information Security Management," Krause & Tipton, Auerbach, 1998.

Access Control Systems: Security, Identity Management and Trust Models: Messaoud, Benantar, Springer, Dec 2005.

- **PREVENTIVE** – Preventative controls block unwanted actions. Note, however, that their effectiveness is often directly related to whether employees see these controls as necessary or useful. Controls that seem overly stringent are likely to be bypassed. Again, training and awareness programs can be very helpful here.

- **DETECTIVE** – Detective controls identify, log, and alert management to unwanted actions or events, as or after they occur. These controls go hand in hand with preventive controls because they are triggered when the tolerance level for preventive controls has been reached. Common detective controls include audit trails, logs, intrusion detection mechanisms, checksums, and message integrity controls.

Access Control Examples

Controls	Administrative	Technical	Physical
Directive	Policy	Warning Banner	"Do Not Enter"
Deterrent	Demotion	Violation Report	"Beware of Dog"
Preventive	User Registration	Passwords, Tokens	Fences, Bollards
Detective	Report Reviews	Audit Logs, IDS	Sensors, CCTV
Corrective	Employee Termination	Connection Management	Fire Extinguisher
Recovery	DRP	Backups	Reconstruct, Rebuild
Compensating	Supervision Job Rotation	Keystroke Logging	Layered Defenses

13

- **ACCESS CONTROL EXAMPLES –** This table lists some examples of each main type and category of control. Note that many examples will fit into several places on the table. A deterrent has to be well advertised, effective, and monitored with consequences. An example is a web proxy filter which warns the user that access to unauthorized sites (e.g., social media) is monitored for appropriate use.

Domain Agenda

- Definitions and Key Concepts

- Access Control Categories and Types

- **Access Control Threats**

- Access to System

- Access to Data

- Intrusion Prevention & Detection Systems

- Access Control Assurance

14

DENIAL OF SERVICE – The act of reducing the availability of a system or its components below the level needed to support processing or communication, or any action or actions that prevent any part of a system from functioning as it is intended to, resulting in authorized users being denied use of the system.

PASSWORD CRACKERS – Password cracking programs are inexpensive, fast, effective, and simple to use. The most common include L0phtCrack, Crack, Brutis, and John the Ripper. Password crackers work either by sniffing traffic with a tool such as pwdump, or by downloading a copy of a password file. A dictionary attack will then compare the encrypted (hashed) words from a dictionary or other list of potential passwords with the values in the password file. When a match is found, the plaintext word (the password) is recorded for future use in obtaining system access.

A DICTIONARY ATTACK is used when the password to be cracked is believed to be based on a word that can be found in a list of common words. The dictionary used can be composed of generic words, such as an English language word list, or can be more refined, such as a list of commonly used and default passwords. Although faster than a brute force attack, dictionary attacks can be time consuming. They are also not guaranteed to work: A dictionary attack will not be able to crack a password not in the dictionary.

A BRUTE FORCE ATTACK uses massive resources rather than strategy or tactics. A distributed denial of service or an attack that tries all possible cryptographic keys are examples of brute force attacks. Brute force password attacks typically try every possible valid combination: For example, if a password is a minimum of 6 characters long, the attack will try aaaaaa, aaaaab, aaaaac, aaaaad, etc. To prevent (or slow down) a brute force attack, there is strength in numbers: The more characters a password contains, the longer the password can be and the greater the number of possible combinations. For example, a four-digit password composed of only digits 0-9 has only 10,000 possible passwords. If we were to allow the use of lowercase letters and digits, however, there would be 1.7 million possible combinations. An eight- to 12-character password, using the character set A-Z, a-z, and 0-9, generates 3,279,156,377 possible passwords. Brute force attacks are time consuming, but will always find a solution, given enough time and resources.

RAINBOW TABLES are lookup tables containing pre-hashed passwords used to speed up password cracking. Because a list of all possible hashed passwords would be very large, rainbow tables contain only as many as necessary to find a match in a hashed list. The rainbow table uses a math shortcut or reduction to speed the process. "The cracking time can be reduced by the square of the available memory, e.g., if you double the size of the tables, you can crack four times as fast." To help protect passwords against rainbow-table cracking, add a "salt," or random value, to the end of the password. This dramatically increases the possible number of password address values in the table and lengthens the search time, which makes cracking much more difficult. Nearly all modern operating systems do this.

KEYSTROKE LOGGERS – Are hardware or software tools designed to capture typing, typically login (identification and authentication) information. Controls include physical inspection, updating AV/SpyWare, and monitoring outgoing traffic.

SPOOFING/MASQUERADING – Spoofing is an active attack performed when one node on a network pretends to be another, trusted node. The apparent source of a packet or message will consequently be "spoofed" and look as if it comes from the trusted, rather than the rogue, node. Masquerading is an attempt to gain access to a system by posing as an authorized user and thus enjoying the authorized user's access privileges.

SNIFFERS – Packet sniffers are programs that read all traffic on a network and look for keywords, phrases, login IDs, and passwords, etc., in cleartext. Their original purpose was to monitor and analyze networks for performance and traffic. Several commercial packet-sniffing software examples include: SnifferPro, LANalyzer, snort, and Sniffit.

SHOULDER SURFING/SWIPING – Originally, the stealing of passwords by watching users sign on to systems at their workstations. Now also done at a distance using binoculars, cameras, or camcorders to observe or record phone numbers and authentication codes as well as passwords of users logging on to laptops. "Swiping" is when a Point of Sale (POS) Terminal or Automated Teller Machine (ATM) is modified to capture Personal Identification Numbers (PINs) as well as recording the card details.

DUMPSTER DIVING – Scavenging discarded information from an organization's trash containers (dumpsters) to obtain sensitive or other useful data. Discarded printouts often contain confidential information that can be used in extortion, social engineering, and system penetration activities. Paper and other media containing confidential information should be shredded rather than discarded.

EMANATIONS – Signals from devices that may be intercepted. Typical controls for emanations include shielding and grounding.

TOC/TOU – "Time of check" versus "time of use" is a race condition that takes advantage of changes in the state of the security of an object. Commonly a system only checks the access rights of a user at initial login. Users can then continue to use the system until the next time their authorization is checked – probably at their next login. If the users' permissions were removed subsequent to their login, they may well be able to continue using the system even though their rights were removed since they had logged in. This is an asynchronous attack based on the difference between when the access control system was checked and when a user used the controlled system.

REFERENCES:

"Computers At Risk," National Research Council, National Academy Press, 1991.

"Glossary of Infosec and Infosec Related Terms," Idaho State University, 1995.

"Computer Security Handbook," Fourth edition, Bosworth & Kabay, John Wiley & Sons, 2002.

"Handbook of Information Security Management," 4th Edition, Vol. 4, Tipton & Krause, Auerbach, 2003.

http://www.sei.cmu.edu/str/indexes/glossary/

NIST Special Publication 800-63: Electronic Authentication Guideline, http://csrc.nist.gov/publications/nistpubs/800-63/SP800-63V1_0_2.pdf

https://www.isc2.org/cgi-bin/content.cgi?page=738

http://cryptome.sabotage.org/nacsim-5000.htm

http://www.tscm.com/TSCM101tempest.html

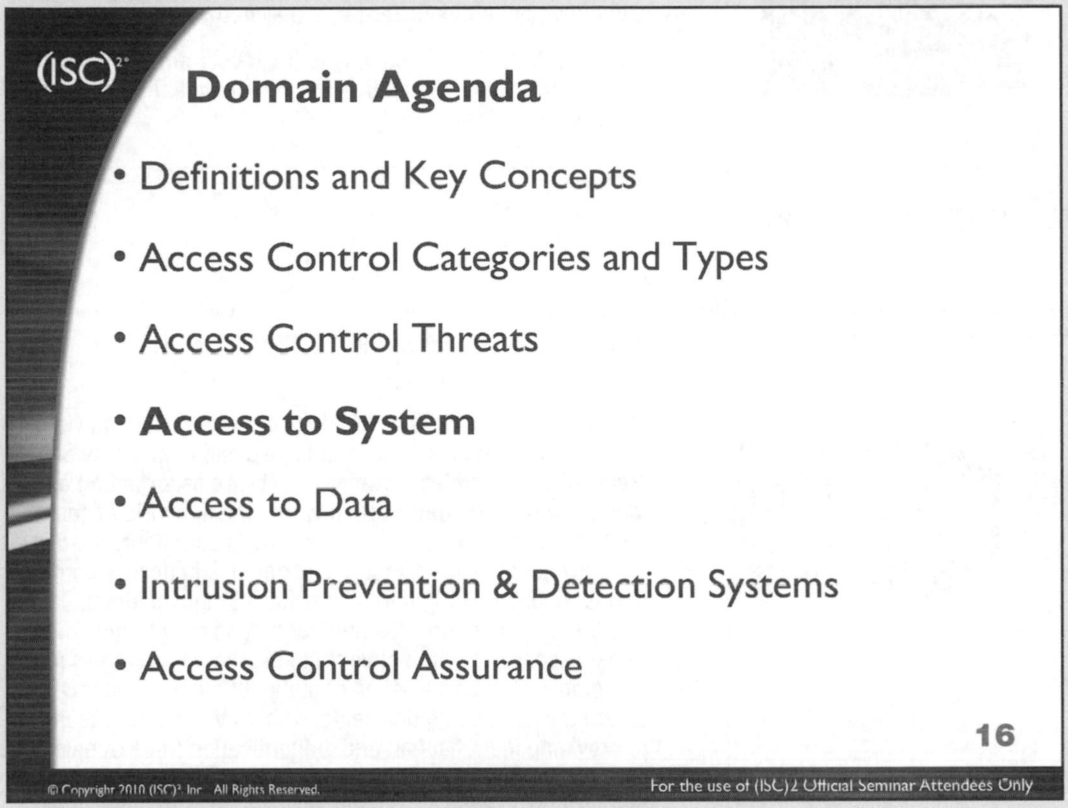
(ISC)²
Domain Agenda
• Definitions and Key Concepts
• Access Control Categories and Types
• Access Control Threats
• Access to System
• Access to Data
• Intrusion Prevention & Detection Systems
• Access Control Assurance
16
© Copyright 2010 (ISC)², Inc. All Rights Reserved.
For the use of (ISC)2 Official Seminar Attendees Only

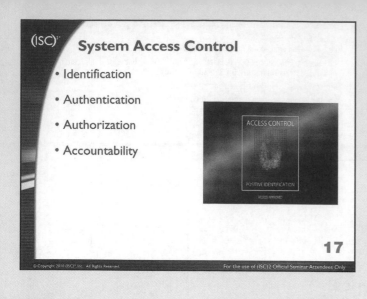

System Access Control

- Identification
- Authentication
- Authorization
- Accountability

17

- **IDENTIFICATION** – The process, generally employing unique, machine-readable names, that enables recognition of users or resources as valid accounts that were set up on the computer system.

- **AUTHENTICATION** – Verification, validation, or proof of the professed identification of a person or node.

- **AUTHORIZATION** – Specifies what a user is permitted to do (read, write, execute, delete, etc.) after being successfully identified and authenticated by the system.

- **ACCOUNTABILITY** – The ability to track user activity on a system. This requires positive, unique identification and an effective audit trail.

REFERENCES:

"Official Guide to the CISSP Exam," Glossary, Auerbach, 2004.
http://www.phptr.com/articles/article.asp?p=31546&rl=1

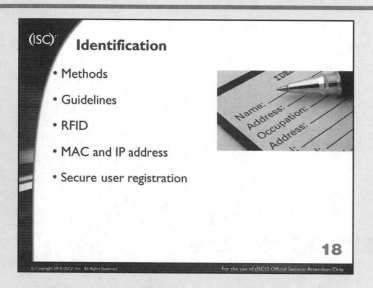

Identification

- Methods
- Guidelines
- RFID
- MAC and IP address
- Secure user registration

18

- **IDENTIFICATION** – The means by which a user provides a claimed identity to the system.

- **METHODS** – Most common identifications use a user name in the form of a UserID, Account Number, email address, or PIN (Personal Identification Number) for system access control, and badges for physical access control. Biometrics can be used for identification and/or authentication for system and physical access control.

- **GUIDELINES** – In order to maintain accountability, unless anonymity is an important factor (e.g., in some library systems), identifiers must be unique for each user. Identification data should be kept current and monitored. IDs of users who are absent or inactive for a prolonged period of time should be disabled. Standard naming conventions should be applied and should not relate to job functions. The process for issuing IDs should be documented and secure.

- **RFID** – Radio-frequency identification is a contactless technology for identification that uses transponders in the form of RFID tags attached to or embedded in either products, animals, or people. Data on the RFID tag is read by an RFID reader, which either pulls the complete data from the tag or uses a piece of information from the tag to retrieve additional details from a directory or database. The tag type and environ-

mental characteristics dictate the distance at which an RFID tag can be read by a reader.

- **MAC ADDRESSES AND IP ADDRESSES** – Are used individually or in conjunction in order to identify a system on a network. Many wired or wireless systems use these as a method of identification and authorization within the network. Access control based on MAC address filtering is commonly used in wireless networks as a first line of defense in access control. In this case, the MAC address provides first level identification and the user then provides another means of authentication to gain access. In wired environments, the MAC address is commonly used as a method of authentication in instances where the connecting device does not have another means of providing identification and authentication (for example, computer-driven machines, older handheld devices, printers and terminals, etc.). MAC addresses and IP addresses are both susceptible to spoofing attacks, where a third party may inject himself or herself into a network conversation and intercept traffic. While it's generally accepted as a good security practice to use MAC addresses as a means of identification, it is not good security practice to rely on it for authentication.

- **SECURE USER REGISTRATION** – A user interacts with a registration authority to become an authorized member of a security domain in two steps: 1) User Identification via a user identifier. The user may also establish various attributes during the registration function such as encryption keys, job title, phone number, email addresses, or role/authorization information. 2) User Validation. The strength or weakness of a security infrastructure will often depend upon the identification process. It is crucial that the registration authority establish appropriate procedures for the validation of a user's identity. Identity may be established through an in-person appearance (e.g., showing a driver's license in order to get an access control badge) or may be established entirely out-of-band, e.g., email. This transaction must be documented for later review. In the United States, procedures for this are outlined in Federal Information Processing Standard (FIPS) 201.

REFERENCES:

NIST Pub 800-14, "Generally Accepted Principles and Practices for Securing Information Technology Systems," 1996.
NIST Pub 800-57, http://csrc.nist.gov/publications/PubsSPs.html
http://csrc.nist.gov/groups/SNS/piv/npivp/index.html.

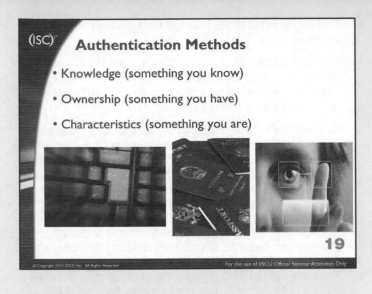

Authentication Methods

- Knowledge (something you know)
- Ownership (something you have)
- Characteristics (something you are)

19

- **AUTHENTICATION METHODS –** There are three primary authentication methods. Sensitive or critical information should be protected by employing at least two of them (two- or three-factor authentication).

- **KNOWLEDGE –** Something you know, such as a password, passphrase, or PIN.

- **OWNERSHIP –** For example, tokens and smart cards.

- **CHARACTERISTICS –** Biometrics are digitized representations of physical features (such as fingerprints) or physical actions (such as signatures).

REFERENCES:

NIST Pub. 800-14, "Generally Accepted Principles and Practices for Securing Information Technology Systems," 1996.

"Secrets and Lies," Schneier, John Wiley & Sons, 2000.

IMAGES:

http://office.microsoft.com/en-us/clipart/

http://www.infoworld.com/article/07/06/15/paypal-using-verisign-tokens_1.html

---

Authentication by Knowledge

- Password – p3nc!l
- Passphrase – t@lk@bou+th3w3@th3r
- Personal history – 1st pet, 1st address, 1st friend
- Graphical
- Guidelines

20

- **PERSONAL HISTORY –** Forgetting passwords happens. By collecting a great number of small details about a user at enrollment, system administrators and automated systems can challenge the user with three or more details not readily findable by another person at the user's workplace. In some systems, 20-30 data points are recorded and the challenge is a random subset drawn from these.

- **GRAPHICAL –** A graphical password is a type of password that uses a sequence of images, or sequence of points on an image, rather than a string of characters. A graphical password is easier to remember than a complex string of characters, offers a greater number of possible permutations than character-based password systems, and is resistant to "shoulder surfing."

- **GUIDELINES –** If passwords are used for authentication, the following conditions should be specified in the organization policy. Passwords should: have a minimum length of six characters, have special characters, not be found in online dictionaries, nor be related to the UserID. Passwords should be changed frequently and not reused. Users should be trained in the proper selection and protection of passwords, including not sharing them, avoiding easily guessed words, and not keeping them in unprotected places. Systems can be programmed to disable a UserID after a certain number of consecutive failed logon attempts. The user can be locked out for a few minutes, hours, or until the password is reset by a security officer. This prevents guessing attacks. On the other hand, the existence of lockouts can also enable an intruder to lock out several users by entering groups of incorrect passwords in a form of denial of service attack.

- **PASSWORD –** Static passwords are the oldest and most commonly used method of authentication for computer systems. They are also the weakest. In the current environment of high-powered computer systems, hackers can easily discover reusable passwords either through brute force or dictionary attacks. (Password shown: Pencil)

- **PASSPHRASE –** A series of words selected and easily remembered by a user. The user can manually convert the passphrase into a password, or the system can be programmed to do it automatically in accordance with an algorithm. Passphrases are stronger than passwords, but also take longer to input, particularly if the system converts it to a (virtual) password. The use of a combination of upper and lower case letters and numbers increases the strength of the password/passphrase. (Passphrase shown: Talk about the weather)

TOKENS – Credit card shaped devices or key fobs that generate dynamic (one-time) passwords and come in asynchronous (challenge-response) or synchronous (time- or event-based) versions. Tokens encrypt an input value with a secret key to display a one-time password. The secret key is assigned to each user's token during the token registration process. Some tokens are hand-held devices that resemble small calculators with a keyboard. They can be implemented in hardware or software. Note that some USB tokens use PKI technology and don't provide one-time passwords.

- **ONE-TIME PASSWORDS** – Typically change every minute or after every use. Because they are only used once, they are not subject to shoulder-surfing, replay attacks, or password sharing.

- **SMART CARDS** – Credit card shaped tokens that contain one or more microprocessor chips that accept, store, and send information through a reader and are used for authentication. They can be either contact or contactless. A significant benefit of smart cards is that the authentication process occurs at the reader, thereby avoiding the trusted-path (protecting logon information between the user and the authentication server) problem.

- **MEMORY CARDS** – Several varieties of magnetic stripe cards provide identification/authentication applications, usually oriented toward physical access control of restricted areas such as server rooms or parking areas.

- **RFID CARDS** – Radio-frequency ID cards identify products/items for shipping, tracking, and inventory control. The benefits are so great that several large wholesalers and distributors now insist that vendors supply RFID on individual or pallet products. RFID has also been tested (and in some cases is already in practice) for uses in other fields such as medicine, where it can identify patients and permanent surgical items. As of 2000, RFID technology has been used in passports (starting with Malaysia around 2000 and including the United States in 2006). Privacy and consumer-rights activists are against the use of RFID in passports, purchases, or medicine for fear of PII (personal identifiable information) being compromised. RFID is not suitable for use in credit cards.

- **RFID SECURITY** – Because RFID is a contactless technology, data transfer can be picked up by rogue readers. This vulnerability can lead to a variety of threats, including DoS, spoofing/masquerading, and compromising confidential data. Technologies such as encryption can be used in situations in which higher levels of security are necessary, but because the processing-power demands of encryption are high, this may not be economical (or even possible with some RFID tag types). Other more rudimentary attempts to protect data include shielding the tag data from RFID readers with anti-static bags, aluminum foil, or other coatings. The effectiveness of this type of shielding is highly debated, since the strength of the radio signal depends on the type of tag, antenna, environmental circumstances, and even the weather.

IMAGES:

Images with permission from, SmartCode Corp. http://www.smartcodecorp.com/products/

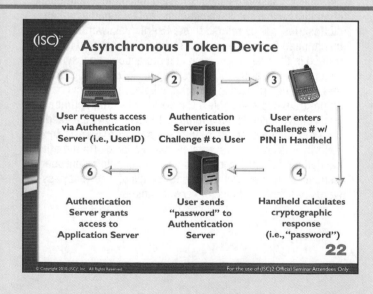

- **ASYNCHRONOUS TOKEN DEVICE** – Uses a numeric keyboard for challenge-response technology. Note that the correct answer to the challenge cannot be generated without the asynchronous token device and the correct PIN. The process is as follows:

  - **STEP 1:** The user initiates a logon request.

  - **STEP 2:** The authentication server provides a challenge (a random number that is the input value) that can only be answered by the user's token.

  - **STEP 3:** The user enters the challenge and PIN in the token.

  - **STEP 4:** The token generates the response (the password) to the challenge, which appears in the token's window.

  - **STEP 5:** The user provides the password to the authentication server.

  - **STEP 6:** Access is granted.

Synchronous Token

- Event-based synchronization
- Time-based synchronization

23

- **EVENT-BASED SYNCHRONIZATION –** Avoids the problem of time synchronization between the token and server by incrementing the counter with each use. The counter displays the input value the user needs to submit to the authentication server. The user presses a button in order to generate a one-time password which the user then enters at the workstation along with his or her PIN. If a password is created using the token but not used to logon, the counter in the server and the counter in the token become out of sync. Synchronous tokens can be implemented in proximity devices that enter the password automatically with the PIN. This is often used for continuous authentication where the user is only permitted access while within a defined range of the system. Once the user steps out of range, the unit will automatically lock down.

- **TIME-BASED SYNCHRONIZATION –** Requires that the clock in the token be within three or four minutes on either side of the clock in the authentication server. If the difference becomes too great, access will be refused until the clocks have been resynchronized. The token generates a new dynamic pass-word (usually every minute) that it displays in its window, and is entered with the user's PIN at the workstation to gain access. No token keyboard is required unless used to turn the token on.

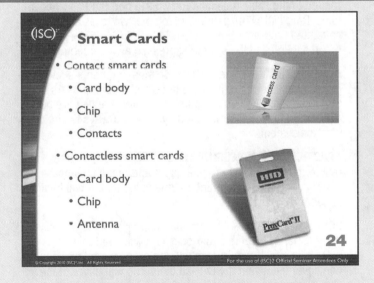

Smart Cards

- Contact smart cards
  - Card body
  - Chip
  - Contacts
- Contactless smart cards
  - Card body
  - Chip
  - Antenna

24

- **CONTACT SMART CARDS –** Provide power to the embedded microprocessors and power to communicate with readers. In order to establish communication, the card is inserted into the reader.

  - A significant advantage of contact smart cards is that the user authentication process takes place between the smart card and the reader at the user location. Since IDs and authentication data are not transmitted to a remote server thereby exposing sensitive information to sniffers or tappers, this avoids the trusted-path problem. Instead, the reader maintains a handshake with the authentication server and directly vouches for the authentication. A significant disadvantage, however, is users' propensity to leave the smart card in an unattended reader.

- **CONTACTLESS SMART CARDS –** Contain an embedded radio frequency transceiver and work in close proximity to the reader. Cards can have a range of a few inches to several feet, and current reports from security researchers indicate that attackers can "swipe" these cards using contactless attacks by just walking past the subject. Contactless cards should be protected in foil-lined card holders such as "Faraday Cages" in order to prevent unwanted data spillage.

REFERENCES:
"DoD Tructed Computer Evaluation Criteria," DoD Computer Security Center, 1983
http://www.wired.com/wired/archive/14.05/rfid.html

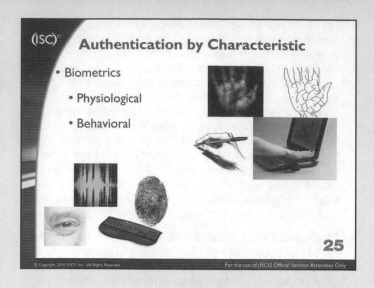

Authentication by Characteristic

- Biometrics
  - Physiological
  - Behavioral

25

- **BIOMETRICS** – Can be used for both identification and authentication. Biometrics consists of measuring various unique parts of a person's anatomy or physical activities and comparing those measurements against stored values. Biometrics can be broken into two different categories – static and dynamic. Static is what you are (i.e., your physiological characteristics) and dynamic is what you do (i.e., your behavioral characteristics).

  - **PHYSIOLOGICAL BIOMETRICS** – Measure features such as fingerprints, iris granularity, blood vessels on the retina, facial measurements, hand geometry, etc.

  - **BEHAVIORAL BIOMETRICS** – Measure dynamic characteristics such as voice inflections, keyboard strokes, signature motions, etc.

REFERENCES:

"Information Security Management Handbook," Tipton & Krause, 5th Edition, Auerbach, 2004.

NIST SP 800-76-1, Biometric Data Specification for Personal Identity Verification, January 2007. http://csrc.nist.gov/publications/nistpubs/800-76-1/SP800-76-1_012407.pdf

IMAGES:

Palm vein: http://212.227.105.104/imagepage.aspx?PI_ID=276 (Fujitsu Resource Library)

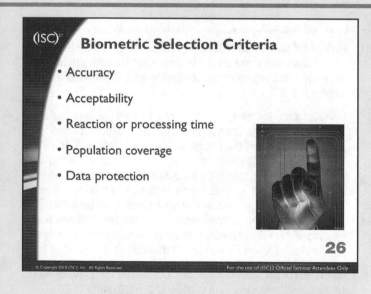

Biometric Selection Criteria

- Accuracy
- Acceptability
- Reaction or processing time
- Population coverage
- Data protection

26

- **ACCURACY** – The most critical characteristics are typically related to the False Rejection Rate (FRR) and the False Acceptance Rate (FAR). The point at which the two rates are equal is called the Crossover Error Rate (CER). The CER is the measure of the accuracy of the system expressed as a percentage.

- **ACCEPTABILITY** – Certain biometric measurements such as retinal scans are more invasive or objectionable to users than other methods such as signature dynamics. If users are not comfortable using the system, they may find ways to circumvent the system.

- **REACTION OR PROCESSING TIME** – The amount of time required for the system to read input and make the access control decision. IF the reaction time is too long it will begin to impact productivity.

- **POPULATION COVERAGE** – As the number of users increases, the number of readers and processors will need to increase to meet throughput requirements. Another note point on population coverage is that the chosen biometric will never fit the whole population. Voice recognition misses mutes. Fingerprints are a problem for amputees, etc.

- **DATA PROTECTION** – Data transmitted and stored must be encrypted, but data protection is more than encryption. The biggest problem with a biometric is that it is a very long complex static password. If I capture your fingerprint from another place (e.g., James Bond-style from a glass you picked up), can I replay the credential to get access to your laptop? Data protection here is more about authenticity. A missing exception criteria on this list is revocation – how do you revoke the credential when compromised?

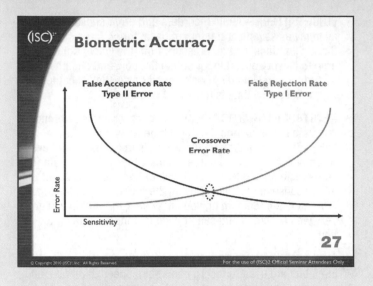

FALSE REJECTION RATE (FRR), TYPE I ERROR – Authentication fails when it should not. This happens when an authorized person is denied access.

FALSE ACCEPTANCE RATE (FAR), TYPE II ERROR – Authentication is successful when it should not be. This happens when an unauthorized person is granted access. This may happen because the biometric system cannot distinguish between the biometric signatures of different people. This is the far more serious of the two error conditions.

CROSSOVER ERROR RATE (CER) – As the sensitivity of the biometric system is adjusted, FAR & FRR values change inversely. The point at which the two values intersect is the Crossover Error Rate, which is the measure of system accuracy described as a percentage. In systems in which false accepts would be a serious security breach, security should be adjusted for greater sensitivity even though this will result in an increase in the number of false rejects.

REFERENCES:

"Secrets & Lies," Schneier, John Wiley & Sons, 2000.

"Computer Security Handbook," Bosworth & Kabay, 4th edition, John Wiley & Sons, 2002.

"Information Security Management Handbook," 4th edition, Vol. 3, Tipton & Krause, Auerbach, 2002.

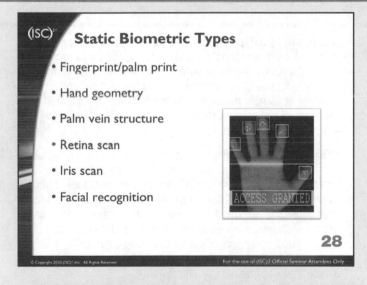

encrypted form in a database, on a token, or on a smart card.

RETINA SCAN – Analyzes the blood vessel pattern of the inside rear portion of the eyeball area (the retina) using a low level light source and a camera. Very accurate for identification and authentication, although susceptible to variations in a person's physical condition, such as those caused by diabetes, pregnancy, heart attacks, etc. These conditions would require a re-enrollment procedure. Not well accepted by users because of the feeling of intrusion, lack of sanitation, and potential privacy issues if medical information is compromised. Response time is faster for authentication than it is for identification, but averages four to seven seconds.

IRIS SCAN – Records unique patterns in the colored portion of the eye (the iris) caused by striations, pits, freckles, rifts, fibers, etc., using a small video recorder. Very accurate for identification and authentication and provides the capability for continuous monitoring to prevent session hijacking. Response time is one to two seconds and it is well accepted by users.

FACIAL RECOGNITION – Video cameras are used to measure certain facial features such as the distance between eyes, the shape of chin and jaw, the length and width of the nose, the shape of cheek bones and eye sockets, etc. Fourteen or so features are selected from 80 measurable features and are put into a facial database. Accurate for authentication because face angle can be controlled, but less accurate for identification in a moving crowd. Not well accepted as identification because of privacy implications. Well accepted otherwise and could provide continuous authentication.

REFERENCE:

http://www.fujitsu.com/emea/products/biometrics/details.html

FINGERPRINT/PALM PRINT – A fingerprint is the pattern of breaks and forks on the tip of a finger. A palm print is the physical structure of the palm. Both are considered to be highly accurate for authentication purposes. The system reaction time is five to seven seconds and user acceptability is generally good.

HAND GEOMETRY – Uses the length, width, thickness, and contour of the fingers. Highly accurate for authentication purposes. System response time is three to five seconds and user acceptability is good.

PALM VEIN STRUCTURE – The device detects the structure of the pattern of veins on the palm of the human hand via a near-infrared beam, causing veins to appear as a black pattern. This pattern is recorded by the sensor and is stored in

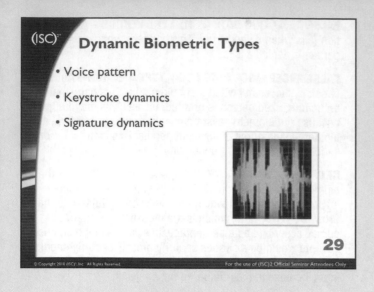

Dynamic Biometric Types

- Voice pattern
- Keystroke dynamics
- Signature dynamics

29

- **VOICE PATTERN** – Audio recorders and other sensors capture as many as seven parameters of nasal tones, larynx and throat vibrations, and air pressure from the voice. Not considered to be very accurate for authentication, and accuracy can be further diminished by background noise. Well accepted by users. Response time is from 10-14 seconds.

- **KEYSTROKE DYNAMICS** – Consists of recording a reference template by measuring the dwell time (how long a key is held down) and flight time (how long is taken between keys) when typing a selected phrase. Considered very accurate for authentication and lends itself well to two-factor authentication because of the ease of using the technology in the logon process itself. (Something you know plus something you do.) Very well accepted and can provide continuous authentication.

- **SIGNATURE DYNAMICS** – Sensors in the pen, stylus, or writing tablet are used to record pen stroke speed, direction, and pressure. Accurate for authentication and well accepted by users.

REFERENCES:

"Information Security Management Handbook," 5th Edition, Tipton & Krause, Auerbach, 2004.

"Information Security Management Handbook," 4th Edition, Volume 3, Tipton & Krause, Auerbach, 2000.

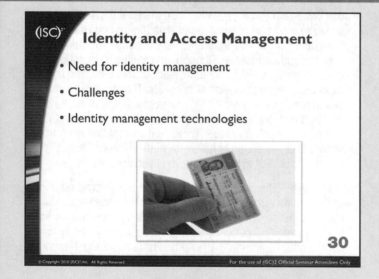

Identity and Access Management

- Need for identity management
- Challenges
- Identity management technologies

30

- **NEED FOR IDENTITY MANAGEMENT** – Identity management refers to a set of technologies used to manage information about the access rights of authorized users, including employees, contractors, customers, partners, and vendors. The process of identity management involves the management, authentication, authorization, provisioning, deprovisioning, and protection of identities.

- **CHALLENGES** – Modern enterprises run a complex array of heterogeneous systems and applications, including those used for network operations, directory services, application delivery, research and development, manufacturing, business management, etc. The diversity of these systems – each with its own administration software, people, and processes – and the fact that users typically access multiple systems, makes managing this data about users difficult at best, and an obstacle to doing business at worst.

- **IDENTITY MANAGEMENT TECHNOLOGIES** – Identity management systems are designed to centralize and streamline the management of user identity, authentication, and authorization data. This includes the use of directories as well as mechanisms to manage user profiles.

REFERENCES:

http://infosecuritymag.techtarget.com/2002/apr/cover_casestudy.shtml

What is Identity Management?, Rutrell Yasin, Information Security Magazine, April 2002.

http://www.infosecuritymag.com/2002/apr/cover_casestudy.shtml

IMAGE:

http://office.microsoft.com/en-us/clipart/

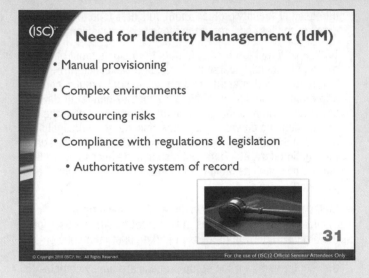

Need for Identity Management (IdM)

- Manual provisioning
- Complex environments
- Outsourcing risks
- Compliance with regulations & legislation
  - Authoritative system of record

31

puts information assets at greater risk.

- **COMPLIANCE WITH REGULATIONS & LEGISLATION** – It is difficult to evaluate compliance with regulatory and legislative requirements when user populations and their access to resources are not adequately identified. Large enterprise networks often have dozens of systems that each have their own user account life cycle issues, operations, and procedures. Frequently the access rights of users are not reviewed on a regular basis leading to many UserIDs that are not valid or are not reflective of current job responsibilities.

  - **AUTHORITATIVE SYSTEM OF RECORD** – The current regulatory environment is pushing businesses to implement an "Authoritative System of Record," or ASOR. The ASOR is the hierarchical parent system that tracks users, their accounts, and their authorization chains. The ASOR must contain the user's name, his or her accounts, the authorization history for each of those accounts, and a provision that will enable auditors to use the system.

REFERENCES:

Information Security Management Handbook, Tipton & Krause, 6th Edition, Auerbach, 2006.
"Making headway on ID management," Weinberg, Network World, 6/19/06

IMAGE:

http://office.microsoft.com/en-us/clipart/

- **MANUAL PROVISIONING** – Most organizations use a manual process to add or change user accounts. This process can be complex and time consuming.

- **COMPLEX ENVIRONMENTS** – Users who need to work with several different systems in multiple locations may have to maintain and use many different IDs and passwords, which results in user dissatisfaction.

- **OUTSOURCING RISKS** – Moving businesses offshore, and outsourcing daily operations or application development support

---

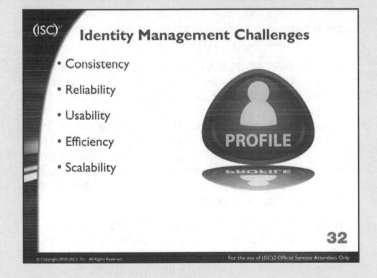

Identity Management Challenges

- Consistency
- Reliability
- Usability
- Efficiency
- Scalability

PROFILE

32

- **CONSISTENCY** – User profile data entered across different systems must be consistent. Data will include information such as names, login IDs, contact information, termination dates, etc. This situation will be further complicated if the different systems used have their own user-profile management capability.

- **RELIABILITY** – User profile data should be reliable – especially if it is used to control access to sensitive data or resources. That means that the process used to update user information on every system must produce data that is complete, timely, and accurate.

- **USABILITY** – Users who need to access multiple systems may be faced with multiple logon IDs, multiple passwords, and multiple sign-on screens. This complexity is burdensome to users and consequently leads to productivity and support costs.

- **EFFICIENCY** – Provisioning a user for access to multiple systems is a repetitive process. Using the mechanisms provided through an identity management system can decrease costs and improve productivity for both users and administrators.

- **SCALABILITY** – Organizations manage user profile data for a very wide spectrum of people and systems. An identity management system must scale to support the data volumes, systems, and peak transaction rates required by a changing environment.

REFERENCES:

"The identity management challenge," Oliver Rist, Paul Venezia, InfoWorld, 10/7/2005.
Federated Identify Management, Ajay Kumar, http://www.securitydocs.com/library/2782

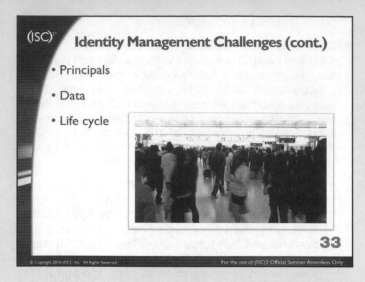

PRINCIPALS – Enterprises typically manage identity data for two kinds of principals: Insiders, including employees and contractors, and outsiders, including customers, partners, vendors, etc. Insiders typically spend their working hours involved with the enterprise. They are likely to access multiple internal systems and have relatively detailed identity profiles. There are often more outsiders than insiders to manage, although outsiders generally access only a few systems (i.e., CRM, e-Commerce, retirement benefits, etc.) and access these systems infrequently. Identity profiles about outsiders tend to be less detailed and less accurate than those kept for insiders.

DATA – Different kinds of data about principals must be managed, including personal, legal, and access control information. Personal information will include names, contact information, and demographic data such as gender or date of birth. Legal information will include information about the legal relationship between the enterprise and the principal such as Social Security number, compensation, contract, start date, termination date, etc. Data will also include access control information such as login credentials, including a login ID and password.

LIFE CYCLE – Provisioning includes three evolutions. 1) Initial setup: User profiles must be set up when a user joins the organization. The process of adding users depends on whether the user is an insider or an outsider. In either case, the requirements for the setup process are timely completion and entry of complete and accurate data. 2) Change and maintenance: Once set up, user accounts must be managed. This includes routine password changes, administrative actions such as name changes, adding and removing individual login accounts, and changing privileges on existing accounts, periodic review and certification of existing accounts and access levels. 3) Tear-down: When a user leaves an organization, his or her record should be appropriately flagged and access to systems disabled as reliably and quickly as possible.

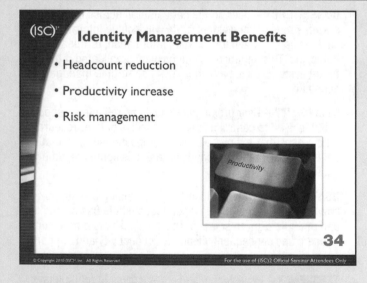

HEADCOUNT REDUCTION – Help desks and security administrators spend up to an estimated 35 percent of their time handling password resets and UserID problems. Utilizing the Identity Management (IdM) capability for self-service password management can eliminate much of this overhead. Self-service password management requires authentication by an alternate method before obtaining access to the reset process. This usually involves answering a random selection from a set of predetermined personal questions. Centralized management via identity management systems increases policy compliance and reduces costs by eliminating multiple local user-management systems.

PRODUCTIVITY INCREASE – Self-service password management is more efficient than calling the help desk or security administrator. Similarly, the use of single sign-on reduces the number of online identities that need to be administered, and business managers are then able to enjoy faster processing of user requests for account initiation, access requests, and other management issues. Coupling Role-Based Access Control (RBAC) with the IdM system provides increased efficiency because it greatly simplifies the access authorization by utilizing job functions as a guide.

RISK MANAGEMENT – The IdM workflow and reporting process provides tracking information for auditors, which enables compliance support. IdM typically provides better integrity of the identification process by the use of good (strong) passwords and multi-factor authentication methods as well as self-service passwords. Because the need to replicate user databases across multiple data-processing centers is avoided, central user databases also support Business Continuity Planning.

IMAGE:

http://office.microsoft.com/en-us/clipart/

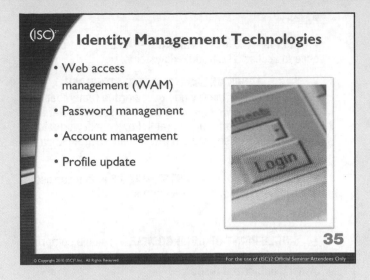

Identity Management Technologies

- Web access management (WAM)
- Password management
- Account management
- Profile update

35

systems and self-service resets.

- **ACCOUNT MANAGEMENT –** It is costly and difficult to manually provision for new systems access, adjustments as user responsibilities change, and termination of access in a timely manner. Account management systems automate the administration of user identities and can include the following features: a central facility for managing user access to multiple systems; a workflow system so users can submit requests for access changes (which are automatically routed for approvals and provisioning); automatic replication of data between multiple systems and directories; a facility for loading batch changes to user directories; and automatic creation, change, or removal of access to system resources based on policies and triggered by changes elsewhere.

- **PROFILE UPDATE –** User identity includes personal data such as name, telephone number, email address, home address, and date of birth, etc. Users are often able to change non-critical personal data. Changes should be easy to manage and be automatically reflected in systems such as the corporate directory or logon systems.

REFERENCES:

A Guide to Building Secure Web Applications by Open Web Application Security Project, http://www.cgisecurity.com/owasp/html/index.html

"Making headway on ID Management," Neil Weinberg, 06/ 19/ 2006, http://www.network-world.com/news/2006/061906-identity-management.html?page=1

"Defining Enterprise Identity Management," http://id-synch.com/docs/identity-management-defined.html

IMAGE:

http://office.microsoft.com/en-us/clipart/

- **WEB ACCESS MANAGEMENT (WAM) –** WAM mechanisms can administer user identity, authentication, and authorization concurrently for multiple web-based applications. WAMs handle the sign-on process for various web applications by using a plug-in on the front-end web server. Web accounts present authentication lockout choices, e.g., how many failed attempts should trigger an account lockout.

- **PASSWORD MANAGEMENT –** Users log onto most systems with a login ID and static password. Because reusable passwords are easy to compromise, organizations practicing due care require a password change interval ranging from 30 to 90 days. IdM requires password synchronization between

---

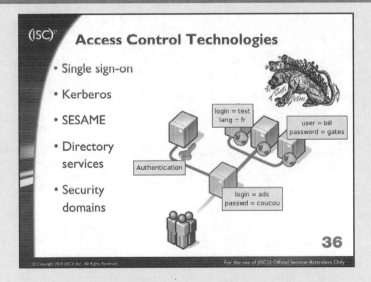

Access Control Technologies

- Single sign-on
- Kerberos
- SESAME
- Directory services
- Security domains

login = test
lang = fr

user = bill
password = gates

Authentication

login = ads
passwd = coucou

36

- **KERBEROS –** An SSO open-standards protocol for authentication in a single security domain. Kerberos is an authentication protocol that uses symmetric key encryption in three key pairs: Two authentication pairs are shared by the authenticator and a single principal and one session pair is shared between principals. The session-key pair is distributed in such a way that principals are required to trust the authenticator rather than each other.

- **SESAME –** The Secure European System for Applications in a Multi-Vendor Environment (SESAME) is a protocol developed by the European Union that addresses multiple or disparate security domains. Sesame is also an SSO.

REFERENCES:

Information Security Management Handbook, Tipton & Krause, 4th Edition, Auerbach, 2000.

Strategic Information Security, Wylder, Auerbach, 2004.

IMAGES:

http://vulture.open-source.fr/img/sso_forward.png

http://tabmok99.mortalkombatonline.com/kerberos.gif

- **SINGLE SIGN-ON (SSO) –** A centralized authentication database that administers access to multiple resources.

  - **LEGACY SINGLE SIGN-ON (SSO) –** Although many legacy systems do not support an external means to identify and authenticate their users, it is possible to store user credentials centrally, and automatically enter them where and when needed. This automation is typically done by scripting. The SSO system stores every user's password to every system. This causes concern with respect to availability: If the SSO system fails, denial of service results. If the SSO is compromised, controls over access to all systems may be lost.

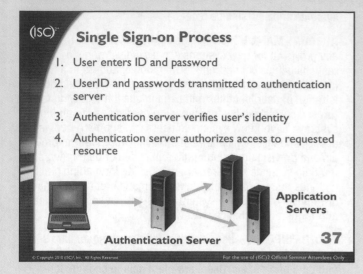

Single Sign-on Process

1. User enters ID and password
2. UserID and passwords transmitted to authentication server
3. Authentication server verifies user's identity
4. Authentication server authorizes access to requested resource

Application Servers

Authentication Server

37

- **SINGLE SIGN-ON (SSO) PROCESS** – Some users need access to several different computer systems or applications for their daily work. Instead of having to log on to each system separately, SSOs enable users to log on to the authentication server and still obtain access to all additional authorized networked systems without additional identification and authentication. SSO is also referred to as reduced sign-on, and is used in web-based environments in federated ID management systems.

- **PROS:**
  - **EFFICIENT LOGON PROCESS** – The user logs on only once to access all authorized systems.

  - **ENCOURAGES USERS TO CREATE STRONGER PASSWORDS** – With only one password to remember and control, users may be inclined to use passwords that are harder and more difficult to crack. Fewer passwords to manage should also result in fewer being written down in unsafe locations.

  - **CENTRALIZED ADMINISTRATION** – Ensures consistent application of policy and procedures.

- **CONS:**
  - **SINGLE POINT OF COMPROMISE** – A single compromised sign-in allows the intruder into all of the account owner's authorized resources.

  - **LEGACY INTEROPERABILITY** – It may be difficult to include unique computers or legacy systems in the single sign-on network.

  - **IMPLEMENTATION DIFFICULTIES** – Unusual types of systems may not interface well with SSO software.

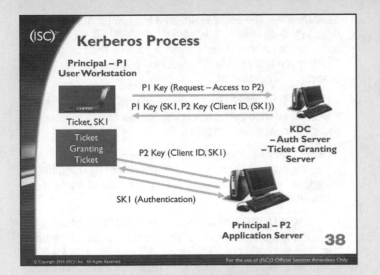

Kerberos Process

Principal – P1
User Workstation

P1 Key (Request – Access to P2)
P1 Key (SK1, P2 Key (Client ID, (SK1))

Ticket, SK1

Ticket Granting Ticket

P2 Key (Client ID, SK1)

SK1 (Authentication)

KDC
– Auth Server
– Ticket Granting Server

Principal – P2
Application Server

38

- **KERBEROS PROCESS** – All keys used to encrypt each step in the process are symmetric. Every user shares a unique, secret key based on his or her password with the Kerberos Key Distribution Center (KDC). Each available service (object) in the system also shares a unique key with the KDC.

  - To sign on, the user sends his or her ID and access request through the Kerberos client software on the workstation to the KDC. The authentication server of the KDC searches the KDC database to verify that the user is permitted access to the requested service, and sends an encrypted ticket to the user which includes the UserID, the session key, and the ticket for access to the requested service (object), encrypted with the key the object shares with the KDC.

  - The Kerberos client on the user workstation receives the ticket and requests the user's password. This is converted to the user's key and used to decrypt the user's part of the authentication-server reply. If the decryption succeeds, the user is authenticated and when ready, sends the ticket containing the ClientID and session key, encrypted with the key the object shares with the authentication server, to the application server with a request for service. Using the key it shares with the KDC, the application server decrypts the ticket. If the decryption is successful, because of its trust relationship with the KDC, the object now knows the identity of the user, has the session key, and can conduct encrypted communications sessions with the client.

  - Alternatively, if the client is going to need repeated services during the day, the client will request a Ticket Grant-

ing Ticket (TGT) from the authentication server that will enable it to deal directly with the Ticket Granting Server (TGS) to obtain a ticket without further interaction with the authentication server.

- **THE KEY DISTRIBUTION CENTER** – The KDC Server works as both an Authentication Server (AS) and a Ticket Granting Server (TGS).

  - The Authentication Server authenticates a principal via a pre-exchanged Secret Key based on the user's password that is shared with the KDC and stored in the KDC database. After receiving a request for service from the user, all further transmissions with the user's workstation are encrypted using this shared key. Authentication occurs when the Kerberos software on the user's workstation requests the password to create the shared key to decrypt the ticket from the Authentication Server. The ticket contains the session key necessary to communicate with the desired application server. This ensures that if the wrong password is supplied, the ticket can't be decrypted and the access attempt fails.

  - The Ticket Granting Server (TGS) provides a continuous means of obtaining additional tickets for the same or other applications after the initial authentication by the Authentication Server. Tickets have a lifetime of a day or less.

  - The security domain over which the KDC has control is called the Realm.

- **GUIDELINES** – Security depends on careful implementation and maintenance. Lifetimes for authentication credentials should be as short as feasible and should use time stamps to minimize the threat of replayed credentials. The KDC must be physically secured. Redundant authentication servers are strongly recommended. The KDC should be hardened and should not allow any non-Kerberos network activity.

- **LIMITATIONS** – Symmetric keys between realms can be a scalability issue. Another limitation is that many Kerberos implementations are built for single factor (password only) authentication, which may be inadequate for some situations. Kerberos based on smart card logon (PKI) is the (expensive) solution to this problem.

REFERENCE:

Kerberos: The Definitive Guide, Jason Garman, O'Reilly, 2003.

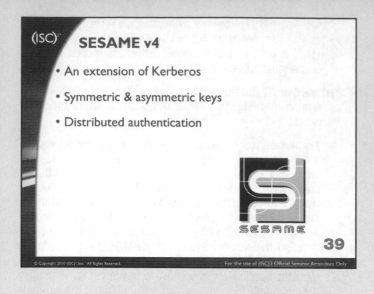

- **SESAME V4** – The Secure European System for Applications in a Multi-Vendor Environment (SESAME) is a European research and development project funded by the European Commission and developed to address some of the Kerberos processes' weaknesses.

- **EXTENSION OF KERBEROS** – It is essentially an extension of Kerberos, offering public key cryptography and role-based access control (RBAC) capabilities.

- **SYMMETRIC AND ASYMMETRIC KEYS** – It supports SSO and, unlike Kerberos, it improves key management by using both symmetric and asymmetric keys for protection of interchanged data.

- **DISTRIBUTED AUTHENTICATION** – The SESAME process is close to the Kerberos process. The client requests authentication from the Authentication Server (AS) using public-key data to establish identity, but instead of receiving a TGT from the TGS, the client receives a Privilege Attribute Certificate (PAC) from the Privilege Attribute Server (PAS).

REFERENCES:

http://srg.cs.uiuc.edu/Security/nephilim/Internal/SESAME.txt

https://www.cosic.esat.kuleuven.be/sesame/doc-txt/overview.txt

---

IMAGE:

https://www.cosic.esat.kuleuven.be/sesame/doc-txt/overview.txt

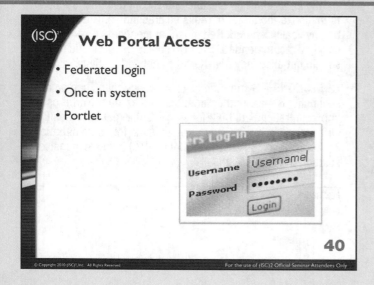

- **FEDERATED LOGIN** – Web portals present unique access control challenges for organizations. Frequently, what is wanted is a federated login capability whereby a user can log into the portal and then seamlessly access other systems using some sort of pass-through authentication.

- **ONCE IN SYSTEM** – Web portals offer a general risk to access controls from persons with access to the organization. With web portals, it is assumed that any person with an account is trustworthy, and many organizations do not configure strong authentication and authorization controls on the interior of their networks as a result. However, insiders can browse the network and access file shares or applications that have low security and may, therefore, access information to which they should not have access. Once in the system, insiders keep their account for unlimited time and may have unlimited access to resources.

- **PORTLET** – Information in other systems is often presented as a "portlet" – A small interactive application on the portal page. In order to secure this type of access, systems need to share a strong authentication system, such as a token-based authentication system. Users access the session in one domain (the portal) and their authenticated identity is passed to secondary domains (the individual applications). For example, a university may have a portal through which it allows its students to access the registration, email, and a courseware support application. Each of these three constituent systems must accept authentication from the portal and have a high trust mechanism to accept a user's credentials.

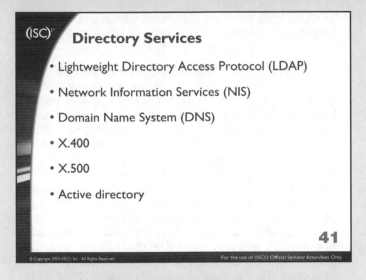

Directory Services

- Lightweight Directory Access Protocol (LDAP)
- Network Information Services (NIS)
- Domain Name System (DNS)
- X.400
- X.500
- Active directory

41

- **DIRECTORY SERVICES** – A directory service consists of applications that provide the means to hierarchically organize and manage information about network users and resources, and to retrieve the information by name association. It provides an interface to directory information for user account management and authorizations, and is a tool for organizing and locating needed information quickly. Examples are LDAP, NIS, and DNS.

- **LDAP** – Lightweight Directory Access Protocol – Specified in RFC 4511 – 4520, is a network-connected directory of organization resources. LDAP was initially used only as a directory of people on a network but today may include network resources such as authenticators, computers, and services. To attackers, however, this can be a reconnaissance treasure trove. As an access control technology, LDAP must be configured with correct authorization for querying, updating, and deleting. Protection principles that are applied to regular databases and resolution services must be applied here as well.

- **NIS** – Network Information Services – A peer-to-peer database of network services that has since been supplanted by LDAP because of its lack of authentication and scalability.

- **DNS** – Domain Name System – Is a directory service for resolution of Fully Qualified Domain Names (FQDN) to IP addresses (or the reverse). Originally used to make Internet resources easier to find but is now a resolution service for internal resources as well.

- **X.400** – X.400 is the messaging (notably email) standard specified by the ITU-T (International Telecommunications Union – Telecommunication Standardization Sector). It's an alternative to the more prevalent email protocol, Simple Mail Transfer Protocol (SMTP).

- **X.500** – X.500 Directory Service is a standard way to develop an electronic directory of people in an organization so that it can be part of a global directory available to anyone in the world with Internet access. Such a directory is sometimes called a global White Pages directory. The idea is to be able to look up people in a user-friendly way by name, department, or organization.

- **ACTIVE DIRECTORY** – An active directory (sometimes referred to as an AD) does a variety of functions, including provide information on objects, organize these objects for easy retrieval and access, allow access by end users and administrators, and allow the administrator to set up security for the directory.

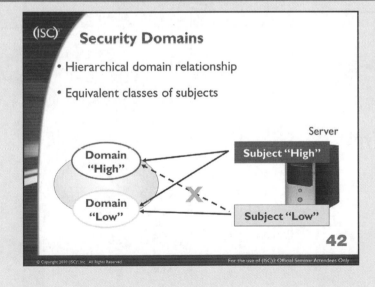

Security Domains

- Hierarchical domain relationship
- Equivalent classes of subjects

Server

Domain "High"

Domain "Low"

Subject "High"

Subject "Low"

42

- **SECURITY DOMAINS** – The set of objects that a subject in an information system is allowed to access. A security domain is based on trust between the elements of a domain that share a single security policy and single management. The security policy must specifically identify the set of objects that each user is authorized to access. In order to protect resources, each security domain encapsulates each resource into a distinct address space.

- **HIERARCHICAL DOMAIN RELATIONSHIP** – Following the Bell-LaPadula model, subjects are allowed to access objects at or lower than their access level. Domains of higher privilege are protected from domains of lower privilege. A server can contain more than one domain: For example, the diagram shows a server containing two separate security domains. Subjects are only authorized to access the appropriate domain level.

- **EQUIVALENT CLASSES OF SUBJECTS** – Each domain is encapsulated in a single subject with a separate address in order to achieve isolation from other domains. When objects are shared with other subjects, the objects are mapped to each subject's domain.

Access Control Languages

- Service Provisioning Markup Language (SPML)

- Security Assertion Markup Language (SAML)

- eXtensible Access Control Markup Language (XACML)

43

- **SERVICE PROVISIONING MARKUP LANGUAGE (SPML) –** "Provides an XML-based framework for managing the allocation of system resources within and between organizations. Encompassing the entire life-cycle management of resources, SPML defines the provisioning of digital services such as user accounts and access privileges on systems, networks, and applications, as well as non-digital or physical resources such as cell phones and credit cards."

- **SECURITY ASSERTION MARKUP LANGUAGE (SAML) –** v2 since 2002, "A provisioning system assumes 'the existence of a network service whose sole purpose is the execution and management of provisioning requests. A given Requesting Authority (client) sends the provisioning service a set of requests in the form of a well-formed SPML document. Based on a pre-defined service execution model, the provisioning service takes the operations specified within the SPML document and

executes provisioning actions against pre-defined service targets or resources'…." This markup language was the start of the DSML Directory Services Markup Language.

- **EXTENSIBLE ACCESS CONTROL MARKUP LANGUAGE (XACML) –** "Currently, there are many proprietary or application-specific access control policy languages. This means policies cannot be shared across different applications, and provides little incentive to develop good policy composition and auditing tools. Many of the existing languages do not support distributed policies, are not extensible, or are not expressive enough to meet new requirements. XACML enables the use of arbitrary attributes in policies, role-based access control, security labels, time/date-based policies, indexable policies, 'deny' policies, and dynamic policies – all without requiring changes to the applications that use XACML. Adoption of XACML across vendor and product platforms provides the opportunity for organizations to perform access and access policy audits directly across such systems." Note: Other access control privacy markup languages have been offered outside of the Oasis' projects. They are: Enterprise Privacy Authorization Language (EPAL) and Privacy Rights Markup Language (PRML).

- **OASIS –** The Organization for the Advancement of Structured Information Standards has put forth markup languages such as SPML, SAML, and XACML abstract the subject from the object.

REFERENCES:
http://www.oasis-open.org/news/oasis_news_11_19_03.php
http://www.oasis-open.org/committees/security/faq.php
http://www.oasis-open.org/committees/xacml/faq.php
http://www.synomos.com/html/EPML/

Domain Agenda

- Definitions and Key Concepts

- Access Control Categories and Types

- Access Control Threats

- Access to System

- **Access to Data**

- Intrusion Prevention & Detection Systems

- Access Control Assurance

44

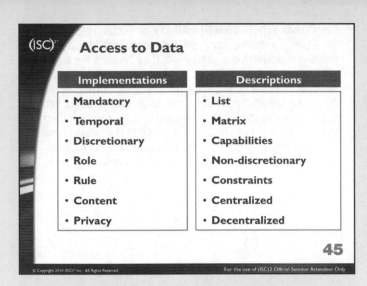

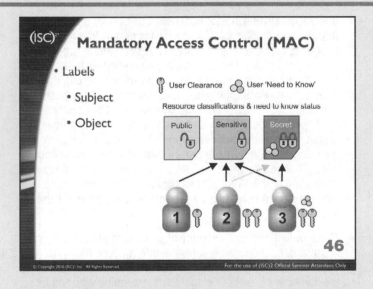

- **MANDATORY ACCESS CONTROL (MAC)** – As defined in the Orange Book (TCSEC), MAC is a "means of restricting access to objects based on the sensitivity (as represented by a label) of the information contained in the objects and the formal authorization (i.e., clearance) of subjects to access information of such sensitivity." MAC systems are more structured in their approach and more rigid in security in that they do not leave the decision making up to the resource owner. Instead, the system and the owner both participate in deciding whether to allow access.

- **LABELS** – The system compares the subject and object labels in accordance with the specifications from setup in order to make its decision as to whether to allow access. Because not all people with a privilege or clearance level for sensitive material need access to all sensitive information, the owner provides the "need-to-know" element.

REFERENCE:

"DoD Trusted Computer System Evaluation Criteria," DoD Computer Security Center, 1983.

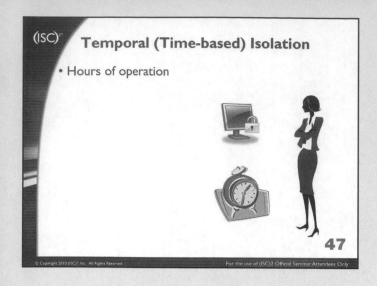

- **TEMPORAL (TIME-BASED) ISOLATION** – Often referred to as time-based access control, this technique provides a physical method of exercising a pseudo-MAC by labeling the classification, or sensitivity level, of an object and then setting up the system so as to process a particular sensitivity level only during a specific time range. Users with discretionary access to the available media are assumed to have appropriate privileges, or clearances. This is often used in combination with role-based access control, wherein users are only allowed to assume particular roles during specified times.

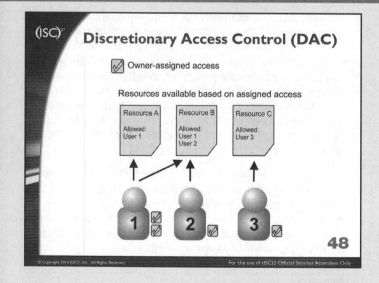

- **DISCRETIONARY ACCESS CONTROL (DAC)** – As defined in the Orange Book (TCSEC), DAC is "a means of restricting access to objects based on the identity of subjects and/or groups to which they belong. The controls are discretionary in the sense that a subject with a certain access permission is capable of passing that permission (perhaps indirectly) on to any other subject." Discretionary security control objectives are "security policies defined for systems that are used to process classified or other sensitive information and must include provisions for the enforcement of discretionary access control rules. That is, they must include a consistent set of rules for controlling and limiting access based on identified individuals who have been determined to have a need-to-know for the information."

- These definitions apply equally to public and private sector organizations processing sensitive information. They also apply to users or groups of users defined by roles. In practice, the owner or his or her delegate will determine who will be authorized access.

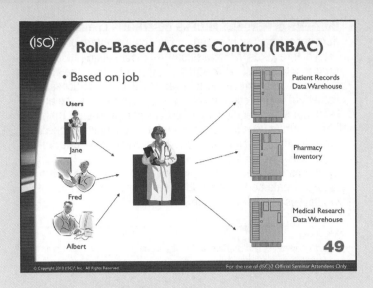

- **ROLE-BASED ACCESS CONTROL (RBAC)** – This graphic portrays a role-based access control environment. A role-based access control policy bases access control authorizations on the user's job functions. Determination of what roles have access to a file is at the owner's discretion. RBACs require "role engineering" to determine roles, authorizations, role hierarchies, and constraints. The real benefit of RBAC over other access control methods lies in its capability to represent the structure of the organization and force compliance with control policies throughout the enterprise.

REFERENCE:
http://csrc.nist.gov/rbac/

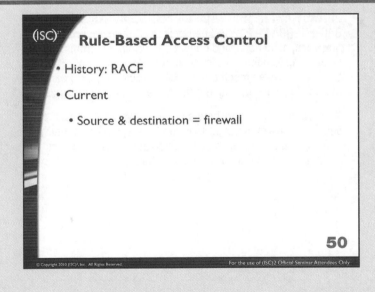

- **RULE-BASED ACCESS CONTROL** – In a rule-based system, access is based on a list of rules created or authorized by system owners that specify the privileges granted to users (i.e., read, write, execute, etc.). Because the object owner writes the rules, this is another example of DAC.

- **HISTORY** – Rule-based access control evolved out of the IBM system RACF.

- **CURRENT** – According to major firewall vendors, rule-based access control comes down to source and destination. Decisions are made by the system, which is programmed to enforce the security policy.

- NOTE: According to the National Institute of Standards and Technology, or NIST, there is no single, clear definition of rule-based access control.

REFERENCE:
http://csrc.nist.gov/rbac/

- **CONTENT-DEPENDENT ACCESS CONTROL** – Content dependent access control is based on the actual content of the data record. It requires the access control mechanism (the arbiter program) to actually look at the data in order to make access decisions. The result is better granularity because access is controlled at the record level in a file rather than at the file level, but it also requires more processing overhead. The arbiter program uses information in the object being accessed, (i.e., the content of a record) and the format of the question as the basis for authorization decisions. Example: Managers in an organization may have access to the payroll database to review data pertaining to their employees, but not to the employees of other managers.

REFERENCE:

"Content-dependent Protection," Martin, "Security, Accuracy, and Privacy in Computer Systems," Prentice-Hall, 1973.

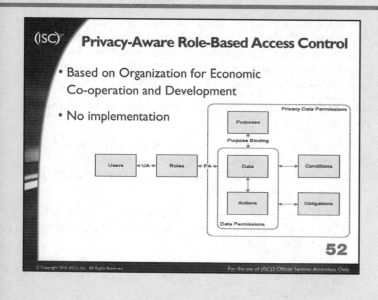

- **PRIVACY-AWARE, ROLE-BASED ACCESS CONTROL** – PARBAC or P-RBAC – PARBAC began in 2007. The importance of purposes, conditions, and obligations originates from Organization for Economic Co-operation and Development (OECD) Guidelines. These modifiers to RBAC require a great deal of mission logic, policy alignment, and technical knowledge.

- This graphic represents how a privacy-aware role-based access control system might function. Users, based on their role in the organization, will only be given access to resources that are required for them to accomplish their jobs.

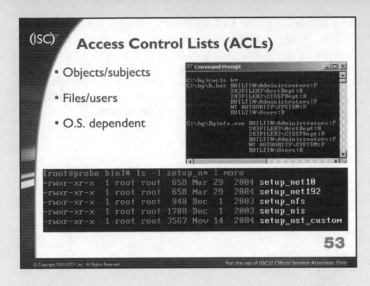

- **ACCESS CONTROL LISTS (ACLS)** – ACLs are the most common implementation of DAC. ACLs provide an easy method for specifying which users, or subjects, are allowed to access which object (i.e., files). This can be done graphically or at the command line.

- Each operating system vendor has its own way of representing ACLs. Classic UNIX systems have three subjects: owner, group, and world, with three permissions, which are read, write, execute. ACL support on Linux is available for the Ext2, Ext3, IBM JFS, ReiserFS, and SGI XFS file systems. Microsoft Systems have an unlimited number of subjects and 26 permissions.

- The graphic on the top of this slide shows what an access control list looks like in Windows while the graphic on the bottom of the slide shows a Unix access control list.

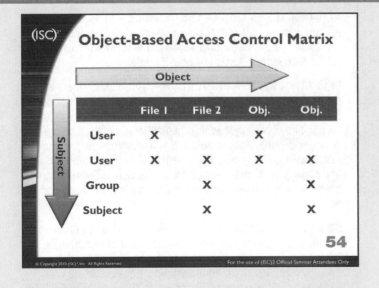

- **AN OBJECT-BASED ACCESS CONTROL MATRIX** – Is a collection of access control lists implemented by comparing the column of users or subjects with their rights of access to protected objects.

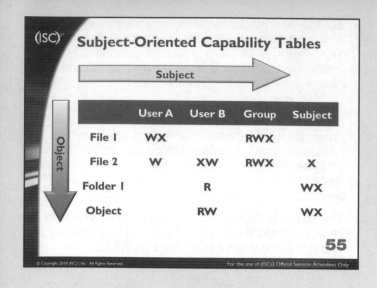

- **A SUBJECT-ORIENTED CAPABILITY TABLE** – Is a collection of access control lists implemented by comparing the column of objects with the rows of subjects. It is an inversion of an Object-Oriented Capability table and, like an Object-Oriented table, describes a system's object and subject interaction. A capability table will usually indicate the level of access provided to the user, i.e., read, write, or execute.

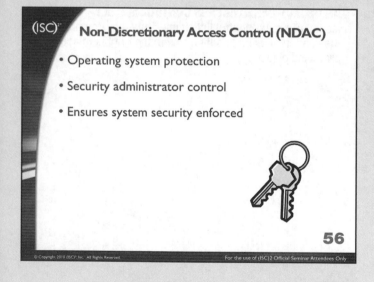

- **NON-DISCRETIONARY ACCESS CONTROL** – In non-discretionary access control, access rules are closely managed by the security administrator (usually the system administrator) rather than by the system or object owner.

- **OPERATING SYSTEM PROTECTION** – Non-discretionary access controls can be installed on many operating systems. Because a non-discretionary access control doesn't rely only on a user's compliance with organizational policy, it offers stronger security than is possible with discretionary access controls. Without NDAC, even if users try to implement and comply with well-defined file protection, a Trojan Horse program could change the protection to allow uncontrolled access.

- **SECURITY ADMINISTRATOR CONTROL** – Security administrators have sufficient control to ensure that sensitive or critical files are write-protected for integrity and readable only by authorized users for confidentiality. Because users can execute only those programs for which they are specifically authorized, the system is protected against the execution of untrustworthy programs.

- **ENSURE THAT SYSTEM SECURITY IS ENFORCED** – Non-discretionary access controls assist in ensuring that the system security mechanisms are enforced and tamperproof.

REFERENCE:

"Operating System Security: Adding to the Arsenal of Security Techniques," Ferraiolo & Mell, Computer Security Division, Information Technology Laboratory, NIST, 2006.

IMAGE:

http://office.microsoft.com/en-us/clipart/

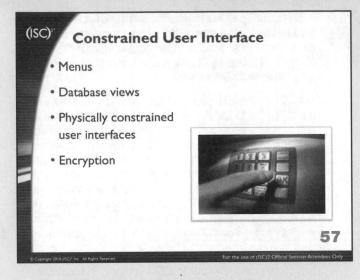

- **MENUS** – A widely used form of constrained user interface. When users log on, they are only presented with menu options that will lead them to approved parts of the system or processes. Users theoretically have no knowledge of the parts of the system for which they are not authorized.

- **DATABASE VIEWS** – Also called View-Based Access Control (VBAC). Database views are used when dealing with relational databases. They can be related to an established process used by the user, or created dynamically for each user upon logon to allow access to certain job-related parts of the database.

- **PHYSICALLY CONSTRAINED USER INTERFACES** – The user interface mechanism presents the user with a limited number of options, such as buttons to push at an ATM machine.

- **ENCRYPTION** – Constrains users by requiring a decryption key in order to access information stored on the system, or masks sensitive information so that the user cannot see it.

REFERENCES:

NIST SP 800 12, "An Introduction to Computer Security: The NIST Handbook," 1995.

"Writing Secure Code," Second Edition, Michael Howard and David LeBlanc, Microsoft Press, Dec 2002.

- **CONSTRAINED USER INTERFACE** – Users are only allowed access to specific functions, files, or other resources and are prevented from requesting access to unauthorized resources. As an example, some systems gray out icons that are not available for use in the current mode of operation. Constrained user interfaces can also be done through the use of:

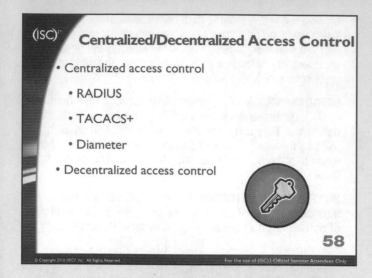

CENTRALIZED ACCESS CONTROL – One entity (individual, department, device) makes network access decisions. Owners decide which users can access specific objects and the administration supports these directives. Centralized authentication services are implemented through the use of authentication, authorization, and accounting (AAA) servers. Examples of AAA servers are RADIUS, TACACS+, and DIAMETER. The benefits of using AAA servers include:

- Decreased time to administer because all authentication is maintained on a single host.

- Reduction in configuration errors because of the use of similar formats for different access devices.

- Reduced need for administrator training because there is only one system to learn.

- Improved quality and speed of compliance auditing because all access requests are handled by one system.

- A reduction in help-desk calls because of the consistent user interface.

- The authentication process is separated from the communications process, enabling the consolidation of user authentication data on a centralized database.

RADIUS – The most popular AAA service uses two configuration files. The client configuration file has the client address and the shared secret for transaction authentication, and the user file has the user identification and authentication data and the connection and authorization information. To authenticate, the Network Access Server (NAS) decrypts the user's UDP access request, authenticates the source, validates the request against the user file, and responds by allowing or rejecting access, or requesting more information.

- **TACACS+** – An IETF standard that uses a single configuration file to control server operations, define users and attribute/value pairs, and control authentication and authorization procedures. An options section contains operation settings, the shared secret key, and the accounting file name. In order to authenticate, the client sends a service request with the header in cleartext and an encrypted body that contains UserID, password, and the shared key via TCP. The reply will contain a permit/deny and attribute/value pairs for connection configuration, as required.

- **DIAMETER** – Uses RADIUS as a base but is enhanced to overcome some inherent RADIUS limitations. Diameter consists of a base protocol and extensions. The base defines the message format, transport, error reporting, and the security used by all extensions. The extensions conduct specific types of authentication, authorization, or accounting transactions. DIAMETER also uses UDP but in a peer-to-peer rather than client/server mode. This allows servers to initiate requests and handle transmission errors locally, which reduces latency and improves performance. The user sends an authorization request through the NAS to the authentication server containing the request command, a session-ID, and the UserID and password, etc. The server validates the user's credentials and returns an answer packet containing attribute/value pairs for the service requested. The session-ID uniquely identifies the connection and resolves the RADIUS problem of duplicate connection identifiers in high-density installations.

- **DECENTRALIZED ACCESS CONTROL** – Access control decisions and administration are implemented locally, allowing the people closer to the resource security controls (such as department managers) to make access decisions. Note that this often results in confusion because it can lead to non-standardization and overlapping rights, which may cause gaps in the access control configuration.

REFERENCE:

"Centralized Authentication Services (RADIUS, TACACS, DIAMETER)," Stackpole, Data Security Management, Auerbach, 2000.

IMAGE:

http://office.microsoft.com/en-us/clipart/

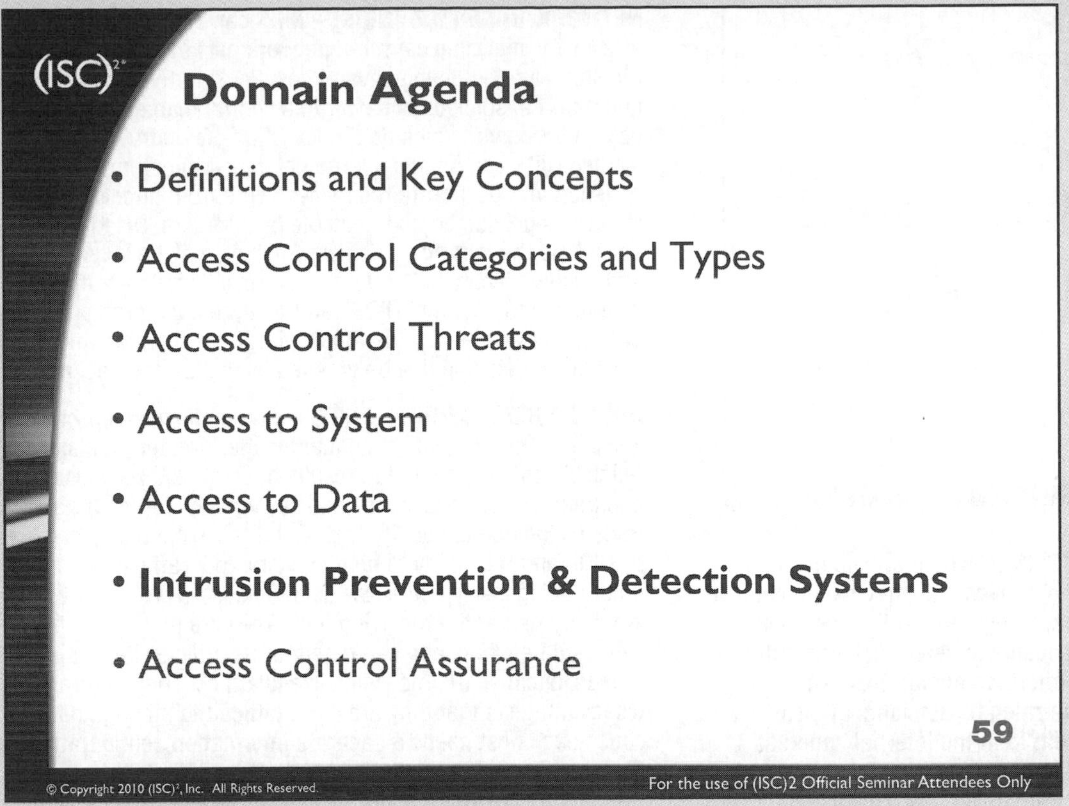
(ISC)²
Domain Agenda
• Definitions and Key Concepts
• Access Control Categories and Types
• Access Control Threats
• Access to System
• Access to Data
• Intrusion Prevention & Detection Systems
• Access Control Assurance
59
© Copyright 2010 (ISC)², Inc. All Rights Reserved.
For the use of (ISC)2 Official Seminar Attendees Only

- **Intrusion Detection Systems (IDS) and Intrusion Prevention Systems (IPS) require conscientious monitoring. The level and duration of monitoring will be dependent upon business goals. Use technically knowledgeable people to select, install, configure, operate, and maintain the system. Update the system frequently with expected profiles and new signatures of attacks.**

Intrusion Detection Systems

Network-Based	≈ Packet
Host-Based	≈ Permission
Application-Based	≈ Process

60

- **INTRUSION DETECTION SYSTEMS (IDS)** – Intrusion detection is the real-time monitoring of events as they happen in a computer system or network, using audit trail records and network traffic and analyzing events to detect potential intrusion attempts. Intrusions are efforts to compromise security mechanisms and can be perpetrated by outsiders or insiders. Outsiders attack the system from the Internet, whereas insiders are either authorized users trying to obtain higher privileges than authorized, or authorized users misusing authorizations. Intrusion Detection Systems (IDS) are software or hardware mechanisms that automate the process.

- IDS can only alert system management to perceived attacks rather than actually blocking or preventing them. The response can be passive and/or active. Active responses provide three types of automated actions: They obtain more information, terminate or interfere with the attacker's connection, or attack the intruder (which is not recommended). Passive responses include alarms, alerts, and reports.

- **IDS BENEFITS ARE:**

  - Providing an intruder deterrent control by increasing the risk of detection.

  - Detecting violations missed by other security mechanisms.

  - Handling probes, etc., used in preparation for attack by intruders.

  - Documenting ongoing threats to the enterprise.

  - Providing valuable evidence to support the investigation of successful attacks.

- **NETWORK-BASED IDS (NIDS)** – NIDS can detect potential attacks by analyzing captured network packets. One NIDS can monitor traffic affecting several hosts on a network segment and report suspicious behavior to a central management console. NIDS benefits include the fact that a few strategically-located NIDS can handle a large network without interfering with network traffic, are relatively secure from attack and, in stealth mode, can be undetectable by intruders. Disadvantages include the fact that software versions may be swamped and become incapable of detecting attacks in high-traffic environments, and that NIDS can't analyze encrypted packets. They are also often unable to tell whether a detected attack has succeeded, and can be crashed by malformed packets.

- **HOST-BASED IDS (HIDS)** – HIDS analyze information from a single computer and consequently offer greater precision, reliability and can show the results of an attack. HIDS use operating system audit trails and system logs for analysis. Benefits include the ability to detect attacks not discovered by NIDS and the ability to handle encrypted traffic captured before being encrypted at the sending host and/or after being decrypted at the receiving host. They are unaffected by switched networks and can detect other attacks, i.e., Trojan Horses, because of processing irregularities. Their central disadvantage is that they are more difficult to manage because each host needs a separate information configuration. Because they are on the actual host under attack, they can be disabled by the attacker or by denial of service attacks. Audit trails can generate large volumes of data requiring a great deal of storage resources. Finally, because HIDS are on the host, they cause performance degradation.

- **APPLICATION-BASED IDS (AIDS)** – Analyze what's going on in an application using the application's transaction log files. AIDS can detect when users are attempting to exceed their authorizations. AIDS are able to monitor the interaction of the user with the application and because they access the endpoints where the information is unencrypted, can also handle encryption situations. Disadvantages include the fact that application logs with less protection are more vulnerable and often can't detect Trojans or software tampering.

REFERENCES:

NIST SP 800-31, "Intrusion Detection Systems," 2000.

"Intrusion Detection Technology:…," Rosenthal, Data Security Management, Auerbach, 2002.

Information Security Management Handbook, 5th edition, Vol.2, Tipton & Krause, Auerbach, 2005.

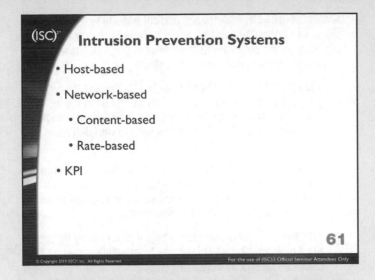

Intrusion Prevention Systems

- Host-based
- Network-based
  - Content-based
  - Rate-based
- KPI

61

- **INTRUSION PREVENTION SYSTEMS (IPS) –** Any hardware or software mechanism that has the ability to detect and stop attacks. An IPS differs from an IDS in that it can proactively block an attack and thus function as a policy-enforcing mechanism as well as an access control mechanism. An IPS is a proactive defense tool.

- **HOST-BASED IPS (HIPS) –** As with host-based IDS, a HIPS is installed on the system to be protected and intercepts requests to the system. A HIPS must be reliable, minimize performance impacts, and allow authorized operations.

- **NETWORK-BASED IPS (NIPS) –** Also called an in-line IPS, NIPS are in effect a combination of an IDS, a firewall (without the ability to proxy or NAT), and an IPS. A NIPS normally sits in-line on a segment and is transparent to the network infrastructure (i.e., has no IP address on the data plane). Upon detecting a dangerous packet or flow, it will send an alert, discard the packet, and mark the stream as bad. When the remaining packets arrive, they will also be discarded. Some solutions implement several action sets (i.e., rate limit, quarantine IP, permit/notify) that enable them to be integrated with other security-management solutions for automation purposes. NIPS have evolved over time to classify and enforce on layers 2–7. Because they are a potential single point of failure, however, they must implement high availability, high performance, and low latency characteristics so as not to impact network or application performance.

  - **CONTENT-BASED –** Depends on protocol analysis or signature matching in order to detect packets containing malicious content.

  - **RATE-BASED –** Is primarily focused on traffic flow irregularities. It monitors traffic for such things as apparent flood and scan attempts, etc. Interestingly, it looks for high-traffic volumes over a short time period and also keeps an eye out for stealth attacks, for instance low-rate connection floods combined with slow port scan attempts.

- **KPI –** Or Key Performance Indicators that can measure IDS for effectiveness. For example, an effective KPI for IDS can be defined as the number of false-positives identified by IDS over 30 days. Less than two means "Green," less than or equal to five means "Yellow," and greater than or equal to six means "Red." Note: If the status is continually Green for five or six months, it might mean that the IDS is tuned too high to be able to detect anything, or that the signature of the IDS may not be being periodically updated. It might also mean, however, that the IDS and other controls in the environment are adequate, and the process is working as it is supposed to be.

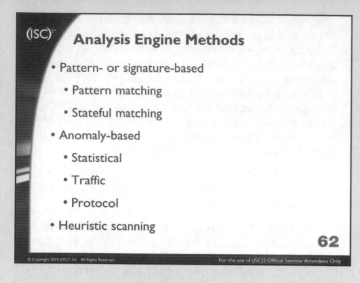

Analysis Engine Methods

- Pattern- or signature-based
  - Pattern matching
  - Stateful matching
- Anomaly-based
  - Statistical
  - Traffic
  - Protocol
- Heuristic scanning

62

- **PATTERN- OR SIGNATURE-BASED** – Identifies and matches current activity with stored patterns to detect a potential intrusion.

  - **PATTERN MATCHING** – A pattern-matching system scans packets to determine if specific byte sequences (known as "signatures") match the signature of known attacks. Often, the patterns are related to a certain service and port source or destination. Frequent updates of the signature files are required to maintain accuracy. Since it will report close matches, false positives may occur, particularly if the pattern is not unique, or lacks granularity.

  - **STATEFUL MATCHING** – Improves on simple pattern matching by looking for specific sequences appearing across several packets in a traffic stream rather than just in individual packets. Although more granular than pattern matching, it can still result in false positives.

- **ANOMALY-BASED** – Compares current activity with stored profiles of normal (expected) activity. These are only as accurate as the determination of what is normal. These are sometimes called profile-based systems.

  - **STATISTICAL** – Baselines of normal traffic and through-put activity are developed and deviations from these norms result in alerts in order to catch unknown attacks. Because of the challenge of precisely identifying normal activity, false positives occur often.

  - **TRAFFIC** – Identifies any unacceptable deviations from expected behavior based on traffic, and signals an alert. Traffic can also detect unknown services running on a network, unfamiliar attacks, and floods.

  - **PROTOCOL** – Protocol standards are provided by Requests For Comment (RFCs). Deviations from well-defined protocols identify signatureless attacks.

- **HEURISTIC SCANNING** – Heuristic scanning methods vary depending on the specific vendor technology utilized. Some allow emulation of the file's activities in a virtual sandbox, while others scan files more intensively, searching line by line for any offending sequences of code. Heuristics are designed to detect previously unknown virus threats, but as a result of consumer demand for an unobtrusive scanner, are not very successful at catching new ones. To minimize the risks of false positives, some vendors have cut back on the level of heuristics employed, or give users configurable options to lessen or increase heuristics as desired. As a result, traditional antivirus scanners (including those with heuristics) are only particularly adept at detecting and disinfecting known viruses.

REFERENCE:

Information Security Management Handbook, 5th edition, Tipton & Krause, Auerbach, 2004.

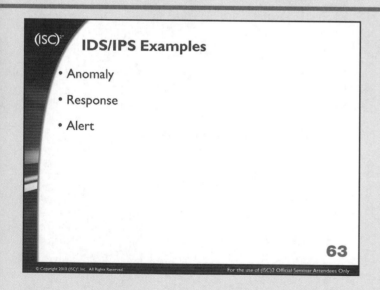

IDS/IPS Examples

- Anomaly
- Response
- Alert

63

- **ANOMALY EXAMPLES –**
  - Multiple failed logon attempts.
  - Users logging in at unusual times.
  - Unexplained changes to system clocks.
  - Unusual number of error messages.
  - Unexplained system shutdowns/restarts.

- **RESPONSE EXAMPLES –**
  - Dropping suspicious packets.
  - Denying access to suspicious users.
  - Reporting suspicions to other system hosts/firewalls.
  - Changing IDS configurations.

- **ALERT EXAMPLES –**
  - Instant messages.
  - Email messages.
  - Pager calls.
  - Audible alarms.

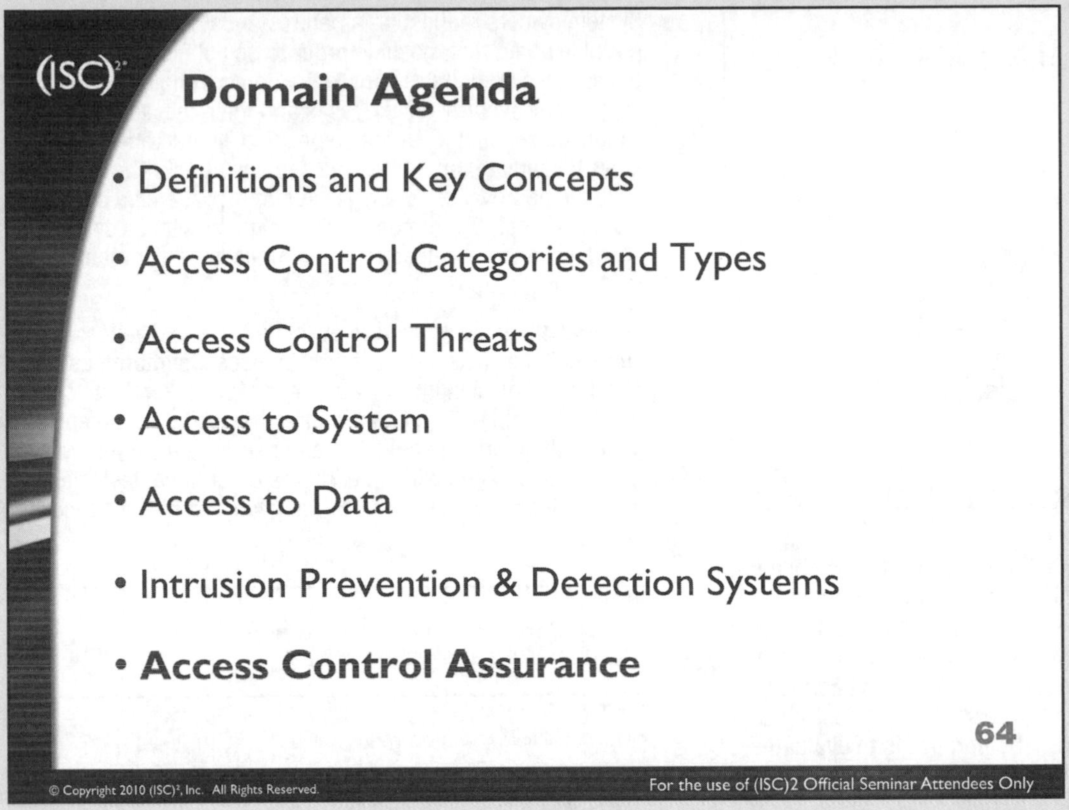

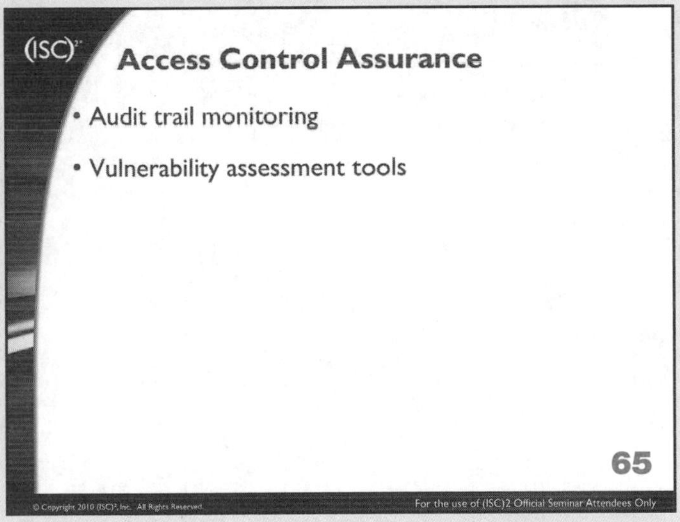

Domain Agenda

- Definitions and Key Concepts

- Access Control Categories and Types

- Access Control Threats

- Access to System

- Access to Data

- Intrusion Prevention & Detection Systems

- **Access Control Assurance**

64

Access Control Assurance

- Audit trail monitoring

- Vulnerability assessment tools

65

- **AUDIT TRAIL MONITORING** – An audit trail is a record of system activities. More specifically, an audit trail is a chronological record of system activities that makes possible a reconstruction, review, and examination of the sequence of activities that can then be used to indicate a possible intrusion, or to investigate an incident. Data generated by the system, network, application, or user activities are recorded. The records are then used to alert staff to activity that is suspicious and needs investigation, to provide details about intrusions, and to develop information for use in investigations or even in court.

- The configuration of an audit trail should include data about network connections, system-level events, application-level events, and user-level events (i.e., keystroke activity). Audit trails can create a great volume of data and audit logs may well exceed the administrative time and skills necessary to review and investigate events that seem suspicious. It may therefore be necessary to use some type of event filtering, or "clipping level," to properly determine how much of the log detail should be captured. Attackers often try to "scrub" logs to cover their tracks, therefore audit trails must be protected from any attempted changes (i.e., stored on read-only media). Audit trails can be used to detect changes to system configurations (either by attackers or by insiders, and either deliberately or by accident). For example, tripwire.

- **VULNERABILITY ASSESSMENT TOOLS** – These tools cover a wide spectrum of cost, complexity, etc., and must be tailored to the specific goals of the audit or security staff. All audits, however, should include the audit work papers which tie the staff work directly to the final report. Automated tools include: patch management programs, data audit programs to validate processing, file comparison programs to use in tracking changes, and computer-assisted audit techniques. The computer-assisted techniques include generalized and customized audit software, automated log review, application and system utility software, etc.

REFERENCES:

Computer Security Handbook, 4th edition, Bosworth & Kabay, John Wiley & Sons, 2002.

Glossary of INFOSEC & INFOSEC Related Terms, Vol. 1, Simplot Decision Center, Idaho State University, 1996.

NIST SP 800-92, Guide to Computer Security Log Management.

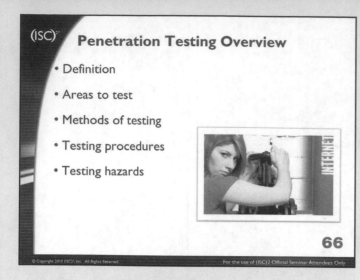

Penetration Testing Overview

- Definition
- Areas to test
- Methods of testing
- Testing procedures
- Testing hazards

66

- **PENETRATION TESTING OVERVIEW** – Pen tests (also called ethical hacking) consist of a formal set of steps and procedures similar to those tricks and techniques an intruder would be likely to use that are implemented to intentionally, at the invitation of the corporation requesting the penetration test, bypass a system's security controls and obtain unrestrained access to a system and its files. The purpose is to evaluate how well the enterprise can thwart an attack and how it might be compromised by a potential intruder.

- System owners requesting a pen test must be as specific as possible about their goals in order to be able to best evaluate the success of the test. Penetration testers should be able to explain any security weaknesses and their causes. The test should be conducted within a specified, limited time frame in order to emulate the reality of a genuine attack. The test must have the approval of enterprise senior management and, if it appears that further pen-testing might result in a system crash while the pen-testers are in process, senior management must reapprove the process.

- Penetration tests are used to evaluate the effectiveness of security countermeasures currently in place. Countermeasures may be technical, administrative, or physical. Pen tests can add to the credibility and, therefore, the position of an enterprise in the marketplace if management can show that they have exercised due diligence. On the other hand, tests can also alert top management that they have significant security weaknesses.

REFERENCES:

"Information Security Management Handbook," Tipton & Krause, 5th edition, 2004.

"PBX Vulnerability Analysis," NIST SP800-24.

IMAGE:

http://office.microsoft.com/en-us/clipart/

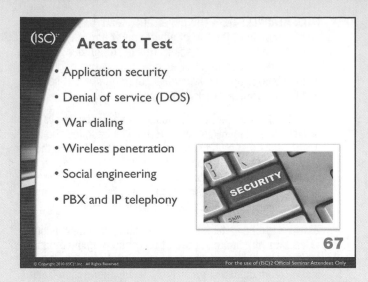

Areas to Test

- Application security
- Denial of service (DOS)
- War dialing
- Wireless penetration
- Social engineering
- PBX and IP telephony

67

- **APPLICATION SECURITY** – The objective of application-security testing is to evaluate the controls over applications and their corresponding process flows. Topics to be evaluated may include the application's resistance to buffer overflow, the usage of encryption, user authentication, integrity of the Internet user's session with the host application, and the use of cookies. Access to core business functionality introduced through web-based applications introduces new security vulnerabilities. Even with a firewall and other monitoring systems, security can be compromised when traffic must be allowed to pass through the firewall.

- **DENIAL OF SERVICE (DOS)** – The goal of DoS testing is to evaluate the system's susceptibility to attacks that might render it inoperable and cause it to "deny service," that is, to drop or deny legitimate access attempts. The importance of DoS vulnerabilities will depend on the relative importance of ongoing, continued availability of the information systems and related processing activities.

- **WAR DIALING** – War dialing is the technique of sequentially calling a range of telephone numbers in an attempt to identify modems, remote access devices, and maintenance connections of computers on a network. Users can inadvertently expose the organization to a significant vulnerability by connecting a modem to the organization's information systems. Once a modem or other access device has been identified, analysis and exploitation techniques are used to assess whether this connection can be used to penetrate the organization's network.

- **WIRELESS PENETRATION** – The introduction of wireless networks and other wireless devices such as keyboards, mice, and VGA projectors, whether through formal approved network configuration management or the inadvertent actions of well-meaning users, have introduced additional security exposures. In December 2007, researchers demonstrated the ability to capture and decrypt keystrokes from Microsoft's wireless keyboards as victims typed. Attackers continue to work on techniques to inject new keystrokes, thereby taking control of the computer.

- **SOCIAL ENGINEERING** – Often used in conjunction with blind and double-blind testing, social engineering is gaining critical or sensitive information through social interaction, typically with the organization's employees, suppliers, and contractors. Techniques may include posing as a representative of the IT department's help desk and asking users for their user account and password information, posing as an employee and gaining physical access to restricted areas, intercepting mail, or even dumpster diving to search for sensitive information on printed materials. Social engineering activities can test a less technical but equally important security component: the ability of the organization's people to contribute to or prevent unauthorized access to information and information systems.

- **PBX AND IP TELEPHONY** – It is important to find any holes in your PBX before the hackers do in order to avoid the costs of telephone fraud. This requires the evaluation of controls dealing with telephony technologies. An unsecured PBX can result in exposure to toll fraud, information theft, etc. Penetration tests should address system architecture, hardware, maintenance, software, and user features. For system architecture, tests should determine if administrative terminals can be switched to an unauthorized user, check for dual connections, and determine how functions are allocated. Under hardware, pen tests should check for susceptibility to tapping, evaluate information modification risks, and attempt to modify conferencing hardware. Under maintenance, tests should try to compromise remote access, eavesdrop using maintenance feature vulnerabilities or line testing capabilities, and abuse manufacturer's test features. With respect to software, tests should attempt to tamper with software loading and updates, evaluate features that might cause the system to crash, try to compromise passwords and physical security, and observe the functioning of alarms and audit trails. Under user features, tests should attempt to abuse the attendant console, try to reconfigure automatic call distribution, try to set up forwarding loops, attempt to compromise account codes/authorization codes and access codes, etc. Since computer-based telephony systems are susceptible to the same vulnerabilities as PBX systems, the same tests will apply.

REFERENCE:

Wireless: http://www.darkreading.com/document.asp?doc_id=140533

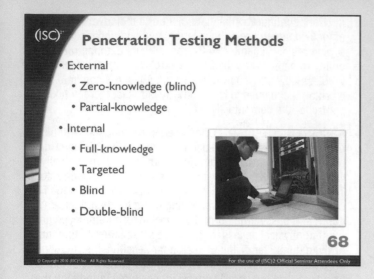

Penetration Testing Methods

- External
  - Zero-knowledge (blind)
  - Partial-knowledge
- Internal
  - Full-knowledge
  - Targeted
  - Blind
  - Double-blind

68

- **EXTERNAL** – External testing refers to attacks on the organization's network perimeter using procedures performed from the Internet or Extranet. The testing team should begin by targeting the company's externally visible servers or devices, such as the Domain Name Server (DNS), email server, web server, or firewall.

  - **ZERO-KNOWLEDGE (BLIND)** – The penetration team has no inside knowledge about the target and is expected to operate the same way as an outside hacker would. Sometimes this is called a "black box." The tester must obtain knowledge using tools, social engineering methods, and publicly available information.

  - **PARTIAL-KNOWLEDGE** – The team may have some inside information about the target.

- **INTERNAL** – Internal testing is performed from within the organization's technology environment. The focus is to understand what could happen if the network perimeter were successfully penetrated or what an authorized user could do to penetrate specific information resources within the organization's network.

- **FULL-KNOWLEDGE** – The penetration team has intimate knowledge about the target environment and is expected to act like an employee hacker. This is sometimes called a "white box" scenario. Pen-testing knowledge might include technology overviews, account numbers (UserIDs) and passwords, network diagrams, etc.

- **TARGETED** – The pen test is focused on a particular system or function and involves both internal IT personnel who are aware of the test being conducted, and the testers on the team. A targeted test typically takes less time and effort to complete than blind testing, but may not provide as complete a picture of an organization's security vulnerabilities and response capabilities as blind testing would.

- **BLIND** – In a blind-testing strategy, the testing team is provided with very limited information concerning the organization's information system's configuration. The penetration testing team must use publicly available information (such as company website, domain name registry, and Internet discussion board) to gather information about the target and conduct its penetration tests. Blind testing can provide information about the organization that may have been otherwise unknown, but it can also be more time consuming and expensive than other types of penetration testing (such as targeted testing) because of the effort required by the penetration testing team to research the target.

- **DOUBLE-BLIND** – Double-blind testing extends the blind-testing strategy in that with double-blind testing, the organization's IT and security staff are not informed beforehand and are "blind" to the planned testing activities. Double-blind testing can test the organization's security monitoring and incident identification, escalation, and response procedures. Double-blind penetration testing requires careful monitoring by the project sponsor to ensure that the testing procedures and the organization's incident response procedures can be terminated when the objectives of the test have been achieved.

IMAGE:
http://office.microsoft.com/en-us/clipart/

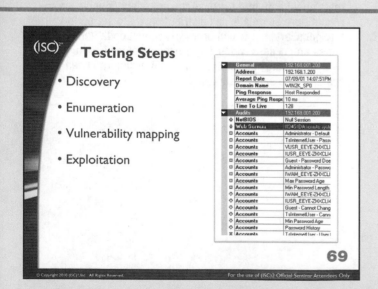

Testing Steps

- Discovery
- Enumeration
- Vulnerability mapping
- Exploitation

69

- **DISCOVERY** – The process of identifying and documenting information about the target. Mapping and surveillance techniques are used to find out as much about the target as possible.

- **ENUMERATION** – The use of intrusive methods to gain more

information. This could involve manually probing and scanning the target with commercial or freeware scanners to detect common flaws that lead to exposures and vulnerabilities.

- **VULNERABILITY MAPPING** – By now, the tester should have obtained enough information to map the environment profile for known vulnerabilities. Based on the information discovered, the tester can decide which type of attack to try and whether to choose known attacks or exploits or new attacks, taking into consideration the possible countermeasures that might be encountered and the methods of overcoming such countermeasures.

- **EXPLOITATION** – Taking advantage of identified vulnerabilities to gain user privileges and escalating them into privileged access. Timing is important here because the greatest danger of discovery to the tester is during the actual attack.

REFERENCE:
"Information Security Management Handbook," Tipton & Krause, 5th edition, 2004.

IMAGE:
http://www.amtsoft.com/retina/images/ret_scan.gif

- **PRODUCTION INTERRUPTION** – The pen test should be carefully designed to protect the enterprise from inadvertent downtime and potential loss of business during a successful penetration. It may not be practical to allow the tester to have access to production systems except during periods of minimal traffic.

  - **APPLICATION ABORT** – Some of the tools used to mount an attack may cause an application to abort. Therefore, the tester must remain alert during the progress of the test to ensure that this does not happen, and to receive permission to continue if this is threatened. An example might be the use of buffer overflow to obtain control of an application.

  - **SYSTEM CRASH** – If a system crash is imminent during a pen test, the tester must stop and advise the system operations staff so that if a crash actually occurs, the system staff knows what caused it and can take appropriate actions to recover.

- **DOCUMENTATION** – The penetration testing team's final report should include the initial goals of the test, the general methodology employed, the information discovered during the test, an overall summary of the security in comparison with a known case, a comparison of the initial goals with the final result, and recommendations for the improvement of the target's security posture.

  - **IDENTIFIED VULNERABILITIES** – The report will contain very sensitive information about the status of security in

the enterprise, so access should be restricted to those with a need-to-know. Test results will help identify vulnerabilities and gaps in security measures.

- **COUNTERMEASURE EFFECTIVENESS** – Both the capabilities of the IDS/IPS intrusion response and how well the organization's IT and security staff responded to the pen test should be described, particularly if the test was a double-blind. If the organization's IT and security staff were not notified, were they aware of the penetration testing because they caught the penetration team in the act, or did they become aware because systems started to "randomly" crash and/or lock up?

- **RECOMMENDATIONS** – Will include suggested additional countermeasures. If social engineering was a factor, recommendations will address this specifically.

- **KPI** –

- Penetration tests can be measured for effectiveness. The effective Key Performance Indicators (KPI) for a penetration test can be measured by the length of time systems penetrated go undetected. If the number of systems penetrated without being detected over the course of 30 days is less than two, this would register as "Green." If the number of systems penetrated is less than or equal to four, we would register this as "Yellow," and if the number penetrated is greater than or equal to five, we would label this "Red." Note that the Green, Yellow, or Red indication numbers may vary depending on your environment. Note as well that a continuous registering of Green over three to four months may indicate that the penetration test process may require additional knowledge/tools/newer signatures to make it more effective, e.g., a newer version of metaspl0it or latest signature for the tool, etc.

- Vulnerability mapping can also be measured with KPI. Vulnerabilities are mapped against industry standards such as CVE (Common Vulnerabilities and Exposure; www.cve.mitre.org). Vulnerability mapping that measures tool effectiveness can be represented as the total number of vulnerabilities less the number of vulnerabilities mapped with known CVE number/total number of vulnerability * 100 over 30 days. For example: Less than 10 percent means Green. Greater than 10 percent and less than 20 percent means Yellow. Greater than 20 percent means Red.

Domain Summary

- Definitions and Key Concepts

- Access Control Categories and Types

- Access Control Threats

- System Access

- Data Access

- Intrusion Detection and Prevention Systems

- Access Control Assurance

71

Security Transcends Technology

(ISC)²

72

Review Questions

ACCESS CONTROL

1. Access control is implemented by several categories and types. The three types are administrative, technical, and

   A. preventive.
   B. deterrent.
   C. physical.
   D. discretionary.

2. Which one of the following provides access control assurance?

   A. Incident response handling
   B. Penetration testing
   C. The reference monitor
   D. Vulnerability mapping/scanning

3. The two parts of integrity are the system and the

   A. data.
   B. process.
   C. information.
   D. transaction.

4. Separation of duties forces collusion to commit fraud. Collusion can BEST be broken up by which one of the following?

   A. Supervision
   B. Need to know
   C. Rotation of duties
   D. Awareness training

5. The main benefit of an information classification program is

   A. to meet military security requirements.
   B. to give data the appropriate level of protection.
   C. to save the company money.
   D. to meet regulatory requirements.

6. How does centralized identity and access management (IAM) support compliance with regulations?

   A. It improves security governance by taking scattered identity data and centralizing it, so it can be more easily reviewed for appropriateness.
   B. It reduces the time spent on manually managing accounts.
   C. It is required by Sarbanes-Oxley (SOX), section 404, which lists specific internal controls including IAM.
   D. It prevents unauthorized access to company resources using a centralized control application.

7. What is an authoritative system of records (ASOR)?

   A. A hierarchical end system that contains users, accounts, and authorizations for that system.
   B. An active directory (AD), where all users are created and managed.
   C. A hierarchical parent system that tracks users, accounts, and authorization chains.
   D. A lightweight directory access protocol (LDAP) directory, where all users are created and managed.

8. What is an advantage of legacy single sign-on (SSO)?

   A. It provides a single system where all authentication information is stored.
   B. It allows integration of old, non-interoperable systems into the SSO process.
   C. It provides a single technology allowing all systems to authenticate the users once using the same technology.
   D. It allows users to authenticate once – no matter how many different systems they wish to access.

9. Which one of the following measures is used to control the emanations from electronic equipment?

   A. Kerberos
   B. Remote Authentication Dial-In User Server/Service (RADIUS)
   C. Internet Protocol Security (IPSec)
   D. TEMPEST

10. Which one of the following is an alternative authentication system used in single sign-on?

    A. Secure European System for Applications in a Multi-vendor Environment (SESAME)
    B. DIAMETER
    C. TEMPEST
    D. SOCKS

11. In mandatory access control (MAC), the need-to-know element is defined for each asset by the

    A. operating system.
    B. information owner.
    C. security administrator.
    D. system administrator.

12. In content dependent access control, the key element that determines the effective access authorization is the

    A. arbiter program.
    B. system administrator.
    C. data owner.
    D. security administrator.

13. A compensating control is

    A. a control used by the executive compensation committee to align salaries to assigned duties.
    B. an alternate control used when another control fails.
    C. a control that compensates for the weaknesses built into automated risk management programs.
    D. a control that compensates for vulnerabilities such as buffer overflows and logic bombs that may be present in commercial software.

14. How can an attacker cause an intrusion prevention system (IPS) to become an attack tool?

    A. By directly attacking the IPS and embedding it with a RAT (remote access trojan).
    B. By switching it into detection mode, as opposed to prevention mode.
    C. By implementing a buffer-overflow attack against it.
    D. By generating a false attack causing the IPS to block legitimate traffic.

15. How can attackers exploit password security guidelines to their advantage?

    A. By intentionally performing failed authentication for many users causing them to lock out of the system.
    B. By using brute force password cracking tools to expose weak passwords.
    C. They cannot. Implementing password security guidelines ensures passwords cannot be exploited.
    D. By being able to assume what type of passwords will be used, thus making password guessing a lot easier.

16. Why are passphrases considered more secure than passwords?

    A. Passphrases use more complex characters than passwords.
    B. Passphrases are made of a series of passwords, making them harder to apply a brute force attack.
    C. Passphrases are used to protect access to encryption keys, which are far more secure than passwords.
    D. Passphrases are made up of easy to remember sentences, thus allowing users to remember them better than they can remember meaningless passwords.

17. What is a major disadvantage of token-based authentication versus password-based authentication?

    A. It is easier to compromise a system if it is protected by passwords than if it is protected by token authentication.
    B. Tokens require more administrative overhead.
    C. Tokens cannot be replaced as easily as passwords.
    D. Passwords are simpler to use than tokens.

18. What is a major advantage of smart cards versus memory cards?

    A. Smart cards use stronger encryption to protect the information on them than the encryption used by memory cards.
    B. Memory cards are sensitive to electro-magnetic interference (EMI), which can erase the card content.
    C. Smart cards are less secure than memory cards.
    D. Authentication of the user occurs on the smart card, as opposed to over the network with a memory card.

19. On a biometric authentication system, which of these statements is true?

    A. A system with a higher Type-II error rate is less permissive.
    B. A system with a higher Type-I error rate is less permissive.
    C. A system with a higher Type-II error rate is more secure.
    D. A system with a higher Type-II error rate is less secure.

20. What does the hierarchical domain relationship mean?

    A. Objects can be accessed by subjects that are at or lower than the objects' access level.
    B. Subjects are allowed to access objects at or lower than their access level.
    C. Hierarchical directories support a data structure that is hierarchical.
    D. Hierarchies between objects contained in hierarchical directories are maintained in the directory.

Application Development Security

(ISC)²

Domain Agenda

- **Overview of Applications Security**

- System Life Cycle Security

- Applications Security Issues

- Database Security

2

- This is the agenda for this domain. The course starts with examining the concept of system life cycle security and how to understand the system life cycle methodology and how to integrate security into the phases of the life cycle.

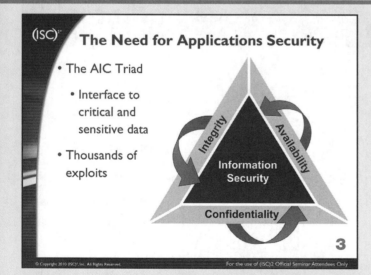

The Need for Applications Security

- The AIC Triad
  - Interface to critical and sensitive data
  - Thousands of exploits

3

- **THE NEED FOR APPLICATIONS SECURITY –** It would be difficult to determine which domain is most important to overall information security today. Certainly policies are crucial, access control is integral, telecommunications is pivotal, but perhaps applications are the most vulnerable. Applications are THE interface to the systems and data of the organization – the place where data is exposed, modified, deleted, and corrupted. Applications are the point of contact between users and data; whether those users are highly trained or computer-challenged, and whether they are trusted employees or global customers.

- **THE AIC TRIAD –** The AIC Triad is an important reference in this domain. It highlights the importance of system and data availability – the need to ensure the right data is accessible in a timely manner. A poorly written application can logjam an entire network and lead to endless frustration and increased costs to the organization in credibility, sales, and customers.

- Applications, by their very nature, are designed to change data, initiate transactions, and compile information. This is where the controls need to be identified, designed, and implemented to ensure that all changes are accurate, authorized, and recorded correctly. Controls have to be built into the application to prevent contamination of data and databases.

- Since an application is the window into the organization, it reveals data to the applicant and must be a primary line of defense. It must ensure that each user can only view the correct data and not uncover information for the wrong person.

- **THOUSANDS OF EXPLOITS –** It would be impossible to count all the exploits that have already been done through vulnerable applications and malicious attacks. Most attacks today focus on web applications because they tend to be insecure, open to the public, not well protected from attack, and easily accessible – most firewalls, for example, allow application-destined traffic through without rigorous review.

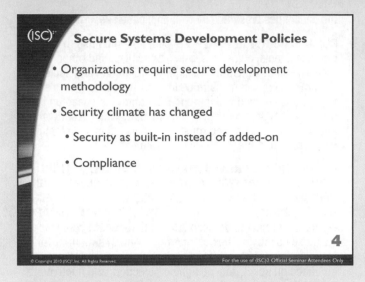

Secure Systems Development Policies

- Organizations require secure development methodology

- Security climate has changed

  - Security as built-in instead of added-on

  - Compliance

4

- **DEVELOPMENT STANDARDS AND POLICIES** – Worldwide initiatives are beginning to provide publicly-available guidelines for securely developing software, embedding security features within software products, and deploying into a secure customer environment.

- **ORGANIZATIONAL REQUIREMENTS** – Many corporations are beginning to require and provide guidelines for developing secure applications. This includes setting up a suitable software development environment and structuring their development processes to address security concerns and business functionality.

- **SECURITY CLIMATE** – Persuading vendors to build security into their software is not easy, since most vendors are primarily focused on the functionality of their products and on increasing their return on investment, rather than security. This is because software customers have not been demanding security features in their products. The security climate has now changed: According to Jeanie Larson, program manager of the Incident Management Division at the US Department of Energy, while the absolute number of cyber security attacks is declining, the focus is shifting toward targeted attacks where one compromised workstation can do more damage than could any number of infections.

- **SECURITY AS BUILT-IN** – Addressing security effectively can only be achieved through an approach that builds security concepts and controls into the design, build, and implementation of the system. A legacy system may not have been built with adequate controls by today's standards, so the cost and effectiveness of the security that is added on later is usually impacted negatively.

- **COMPLIANCE** – Many regulations and compliance requirements demand that systems track and control the access permissions of users and other entities carefully. This requires logs to be set up at critical control points to provide audit trails.

REFERENCE:

"The Changing Landscape of Cyber Threats" (June 4, 2008) Speaking at the Government Forum of Incident Response and Security Teams, http://www.federalnewsradio.com/?nid=169&sid=1415201

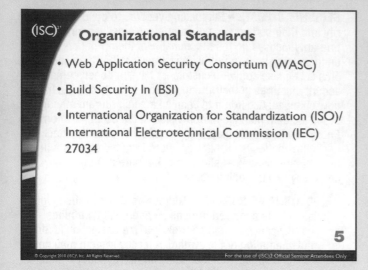

Organizational Standards

- Web Application Security Consortium (WASC)
- Build Security In (BSI)
- International Organization for Standardization (ISO)/ International Electrotechnical Commission (IEC) 27034

5

- **STANDARDS** – These organizations provide information for software vendors and the public that is intended to create secure environments for software development, to aid in developing internal code standards, to incorporate security features in software products, and to deploy into secure environments.

- **THE WEB APPLICATION SECURITY CONSORTIUM (WASC)** – The WASC is an international group of experts, industry practitioners, and organizational representatives who produce open source and widely agreed upon best-practice security standards for the World Wide Web. The WASC facilitates the exchange of ideas and organizes a number of industry projects. It also releases technical information, and contributes articles, security guidelines, and other useful documentation to the industry. Businesses, educational institutions, governments, application developers, security professionals, and software vendors all over the world utilize these materials to assist with the challenges presented by web application security.

- **BUILD SECURITY IN (BSI)** – BSI contains and links to best practices, tools, guidelines, rules, principles, and other resources that software developers, architects, and security practitioners can use to build security into software at every phase of its development. BSI content is based on the principle that software security is fundamentally a software engineering problem and must be addressed in a systematic way throughout the software development life cycle.

- **INTERNATIONAL ORGANIZATION FOR STANDARDIZATION (ISO) / INTERNATIONAL ELECTROTECHNICAL COMMISSION (IEC) 27034: INFORMATION TECHNOLOGY SECURITY TECHNIQUES, GUIDELINES FOR APPLICATION SECURITY (DRAFT)** – This is a project to develop information-security guidance for those specifying, designing/programming, procuring, or implementing application systems. The standard will provide guidance on specifying, designing/selecting, and implementing information-security controls through a set of processes integrated into an organization's systems development life cycles. The standard will be "systems development life cycle (SDLC)-method agnostic"; in other words it will not mandate particular development methods, approaches, or stages, but will be written in a general manner to be applicable to all. In this way, it will complement other systems-development standards without conflicting with them. Due to the breadth of this topic, the standard will be a multi-part, detailed standard. ISO/IEC 27034 Part 1 is currently at the working draft stage. The remaining parts are under development.

REFERENCES:

https://buildsecurityin.us-cert.gov/daisy/bsi/home.html

http://www.sse-cmm.org/model/model.asp

http://www.webappsec.org/

http://www.iso27001security.com/html/27034.html

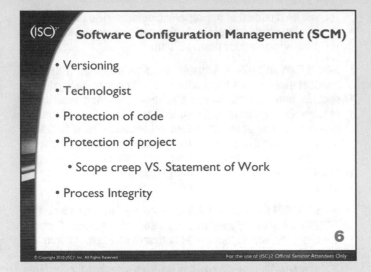

- **SOFTWARE CONFIGURATION MANAGEMENT (SCM)** – SCM is the process of controlling software by managing the versions of all components and the relations between them. A configuration control board (CCB) reviews and approves all changes to system software. Members of the SCM include software developers, test engineers, quality engineers, systems engineers, CM engineers, and specialty engineers (e.g., security and safety engineers). The goal of SCM is to limit the ability of unauthorized individuals to access and make unauthorized modifications and potentially malicious **CHANGES TO CODE**. CCBs provide direction for what is to be included in the next software-build release. This topic is covered in more detail in the Operations domain.

- **PROTECTION OF PROJECT** – Controlling the scope of a project begins on day one with a corresponding project plan/agreement or **STATEMENT OF WORK (SOW)**. The statement of work lists all the tasks to be completed as a part of the project. The SOW often is the agreed-upon list of objectives and deliverables that makes up a contract between the business units and the developers. When development is outsourced, this is often a critically important part of the contract and changes to the SOW are often expensive and will impact delivery dates. **SCOPE CREEP** is "a condition in which the scope of a project continues to increase, typically in an uncontrolled fashion, throughout the development process." The real problem with scope creep is that as the scope of a project increases, the elements that are included in the increased scope are typically not properly designed or engineered to satisfy the security requirements of the original project. This results in a greater likelihood of security defects.

- **PROCESS INTEGRITY** embodies the development of a consistent process and policy throughout the software development life cycle. With today's emphasis on data-breach prevention, process integrity now includes creating a culture of improved security along with team training for identifying security vulnerabilities early in the SDLC. The motto is: "Detecting and correcting security vulnerabilities early in the application development life cycle, prior to deployment and operations, results in significant risk and cost reduction."

- Because software vendors have not traditionally put emphasis on security during the SDLC, they have unwittingly produced insecure applications that have led to inadvertent disclosure of sensitive corporate information or of private or regulated information that has led to fines, lower stock prices, and damage to companies' reputations. Companies are now having to ensure that their applications are secure or risk "having to explain to consumers and regulators how code defects allowed attackers to steal people's sensitive and perhaps regulated information."

REFERENCES:

"Application Security Dev STIG v2r0.1," October 19, 2007.

Feiman, Joseph and Neil McDonald, *Building Secure Application Solutions*, Gartner Research, June 2006.

Wiegers, Karl, *Software Requirements*, 2nd edition, Microsoft Press, Redmond, WA, 2003.

System Development Controls

- Project Management
  - Complexity of Systems and Projects
- Secure by Design
  - Controls Built In to Software
- Secure by Default

7

- **PROJECT MANAGEMENT CONTROLS –** Systems and Software Development Projects rarely meet the expectations of the business and seldom fully integrate the required security principles. Organizations must follow good project-management controls, including a systems-development methodology (such as a SDLC) that involves both the business and the security department throughout the lifespan of the project. Good project-management controls include change-management controls to prevent uncontrolled changes and scope creep.

  - **COMPLEXITY OF SYSTEMS AND PROJECTS –** The complexity of business processes and systems today makes security more difficult than ever. Many applications are built to interface with numerous back-end systems or data sources, often through some form of middleware. The integration of data and systems makes the protection of data all the more difficult and increases the risk that data will be modified or improperly disclosed. The complexity of systems and projects also makes complying with privacy regulations more difficult.

- **SECURE BY DESIGN –** A system must be designed with the mindset that it needs to be secure. This requires the systems, security, and business analysts to begin gathering security requirements as early as possible in the SDLC. Just as the accurate gathering of business requirements is critical to developing a system that meets the expectations and requirements of the business, so also the "discovery" and documentation of the security needs is crucial to the delivery of a secure system.

  - **CONTROLS BUILT IN TO SOFTWARE –** Software can be either a security weakness or a security strength. Properly designed and implemented software can help enforce the accuracy of changes to data, ensure that data is not shared with unauthorized people, ensure that the systems function correctly through transaction balancing and reports, and track all access to data.

- **SECURE BY DEFAULT –** Most organizations today realize the need to be "security-conscious." To one level or another, they mandate the level of security that they wish to maintain in the organization. As seen in the Information Security Governance and Risk Management (ISGRM) domain, this sets policies, standards, and baselines for the organization to follow. One important consideration is in the delivery of systems to users. Should a system have its security features enabled by default (delivery of the product to the users in a "locked-down" mode) or should the system be delivered in a easy-to-operate state that requires the user to enable the security features they choose to engage? This is a decision that must be made depending on several factors such as: the criticality of the system and data, the operational environment, and the proficiency of the users.

Secure Development Excuses

- You cannot build security around an application, you have to build it in
  - "We need security? Then we'll use SSL"
  - "We need strong authentication? PKI will solve all our problems"
  - "We use a secret/military-grade encryption"
  - "We had a hacking contest and no one broke it"
  - "We have an excellent firewall"
  - "We'll add it later; let's have the features first"

8

- **SECURE DEVELOPMENT EXCUSES –** The above are common assertions. Traditionally, developers worked on systems that were used only in corporate environments in which hacking was not considered a real threat. The complexity (and sometimes the unfriendliness) of the applications added to the barriers to entry. With the explosion of the Internet, however, came an explosion of software vulnerabilities. Attacks have become a profitable business. As Peteanu writes, "One of the best weapons you can have in your arsenal is clean code. Others include software configurations that are secure by default – so resilient that even vulnerable code can't be attacked successfully – and security products that block or recover from attacks."

- **SECURE DEVELOPMENT –** Secure software development requires the applications themselves to be secure, not just rely on a secure transport protocol such as SSL or a strong firewall. The use of PKI will only help if the access control permissions in the system support the security needs. PKI will not prevent an authorized user from making errors or possibly making fraudulent changes. Penetration testing is also an important security control but it will not provide assurance that all the security weaknesses in the logic or implementation have been identified.

REFERENCES:

Peteanu, Razvan; "Best Practices for Secure Development"; v4.01, Oct, 2001: www.arcert.gov.ar/webs/textos/best_prac_for_sec_dev4.pdf

Howard, Michael, Steve Lipner; *Security Development Life cycle: SDL: A Process for Developing Demonstrably More Secure Software;* Microsoft Publishing; 2006.

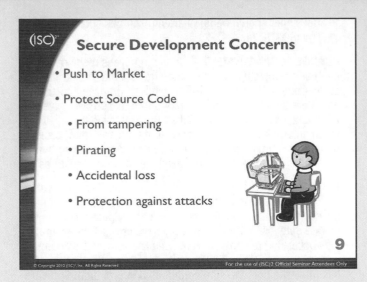

Secure Development Concerns

- Push to Market
- Protect Source Code
  - From tampering
  - Pirating
  - Accidental loss
  - Protection against attacks

9

© Copyright 2010 (ISC)², Inc. All Rights Reserved.   For the use of (ISC)2 Official Seminar Attendees Only

- **SECURE DEVELOPMENT –** Software protection requirements extend from the creation of the code, through to code storage, retrieval, shipment, and installation.

- **PUSH TO MARKET –** The pressure to deliver a product quickly is often the largest factor affecting security – there is simply no time and no budget for security – the drive to keep up with competitors, exploit new technologies, and lead the market means that security is often neglected and not included in the design of the system.

- **PROTECTION OF SOURCE CODE –** The organization must protect source code libraries from unauthorized access or the ability of a malicious person to implant a virus or unauthorized code into the source code.

  - **FROM TAMPERING/PIRATING –** A Secure Development Environment focuses on protecting against source-code tampering or pirating, and ensuring that, especially in distributed coding environments, there are controls in place that allow access only to those authorized to develop, modify, add, compile, and debug source code. This includes

the use of encryption when transporting source code.

- The fact is that software is often most vulnerable at the development stage where developer tools are readily available to modify code. As Sennett writes: "The controls exerted at the development state are very important for security: as far as the threat to the operational system is concerned it is arguable that the greatest vulnerability occurs while it is under development. If the software can be attacked at this stage, particularly if it can be attacked after the completion of the evaluator's work, the fact of evaluation counts for nothing." [1]

- **ACCIDENTAL LOSS –** Source code often represents considerable value as the Intellectual Property of an organization. Its loss or compromise, whether through error or theft, may lead to extraordinary costs and system outages. Many organizations have found that source code can be lost or deleted through poor library management resulting in the inability to maintain or repair problems that arise later.

- **PROTECTION AGAINST ATTACKS –** Of development itself, Barnum writes: "Given the greater risks that software faces compared to physical objects, it is essential that software be built with security in mind. To do this, the developers must have a solid understanding of the attacker's perspective to anticipate and thwart expected types of attacks. This is especially true when the assets protected by the software are just as valuable as physical assets protected in bank vaults. Just as bank vaults are built considering all known high-risk attacks that they may face, software should be built considering all applicable known types of attack." [2]

REFERENCES:

(1) Sennett, C.T., "Development Environment for Secure Software"; November, 1987. http://stinet.dtic.mil/oai/oai?verb=getRecord&metadataPrefix=html&identifier=ADA191889

(2) Barnum, Sean, Amit Sethi; Cigital, Inc; "Introduction to Attack Patterns"; 2006-11-07; https://buildsecurityin.us-cert.gov/daisy/bsi/articles/knowledge/attack/585-BSI.html

Secure Development - Physical

- Controlled access areas
  - Development versus Operations
- Project security

10

© Copyright 2010 (ISC)², Inc. All Rights Reserved.   For the use of (ISC)2 Official Seminar Attendees Only

- **SECURE DEVELOPMENT - PHYSICAL –** Development and project work should only take place in a secure, controlled environment. Access should be limited to project and development personnel only, and, ideally, developers should not have access to production and operational areas. A leak of project data may compromise the business strategy of the organization and a developer who obtains access to production may be able to install unauthorized code.

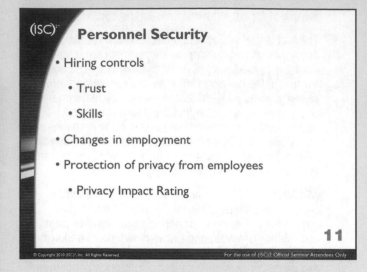

Personnel Security

- Hiring controls
  - Trust
  - Skills
- Changes in employment
- Protection of privacy from employees
  - Privacy Impact Rating

11

- **HIRING CONTROLS –** When designing a secure process from the ground up, make sure that each person brought into the organization has undergone a background check. In highly-sensitive areas, implement a full security-clearance process in order to increase the odds against hiring a coder who could subvert the design process, leak data to competitors, or install backdoors into the system.

  - **TRUST –** The application developer knows more about systems operations than anyone else and several attacks have come from developers who knew how to exploit the system for their own purposes. The organization must also protect itself so that the source code they have paid an employee or an outsourced company to develop is not stolen or copied.

  - **SKILLS –** A quick search of Internet blogs reveals the lack of skill of many programmers today. They share confidential corporate data and process flows in an untrusted community as they seek advice on how to address coding problems. Good hiring practices ensure that any developer has the required skill to perform the duties and also knows where to find assistance if required. Due diligence today would also ensure that any developer hired knows security fundamentals and threats. For example any web

developer should be familiar with sources such as the OWASP TOP Ten.

- **CHANGE IN EMPLOYMENT –** When employees move on to another organization, the exit interview should remind them of their obligation not to divulge business-process information. Care should be taken to ensure that all software given to an employee is recovered when the employee leaves, and when an employee moves around in the organization, access permissions must be corrected to remove access to software libraries or programs that the developer no longer requires.

- **PRIVACY IMPACT RATING –** A Privacy Impact Rating is part of the risk assessment performed in the software development life cycle. This assessment helps to identify possible leaks of private data, or violation of privacy laws or regulations, that may occur due to software functionality. Software is an important piece in the overall Information Security structure, as it is often the doorway into confidential information. Software must be designed to enforce least privilege and need to know, which means that data is protected from improper access – even by employees. The Privacy Impact Rating looks at the data that would be accessible by this system/program and identifies sensitive data that must be adequately protected. This would result in the DESIGN of the system incorporating data security controls. Perhaps this will result in credit card data being encrypted or displayed as asterisks even to employees, or view-based controls that prevent a user from seeing segments of a database that are not appropriate. Performing this type of analysis is critical in order to avoid significant costs from possible violations after delivery of the software. Different privacy practices are required depending on the nature of the user data and the uses for which such data is collected. For example, user data transferred between business partners requires different levels of notice and consent depending on the category of data collected.

REFERENCES:

Microsoft, "Privacy Guidelines for Developing Software Products and Services"; V. 2.1a, April 19, 2007. http://www.microsoft.com/downloads/details.aspx?FamilyId=C48CF80F-6E87-48F5-83EC-A18D1AD2FC1F&displaylang=en

TRUSTe is an independent trust authority. See http://www.truste.org.

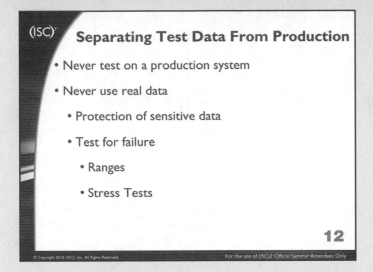

Separating Test Data From Production

- Never test on a production system
- Never use real data
  - Protection of sensitive data
  - Test for failure
    - Ranges
    - Stress Tests

12

- **NEVER USE REAL DATA** – Using data that is real or close to being real has proven to be invaluable when testing software, but it may involve serious security considerations that are often overlooked. When using real data for testing, make sure to follow all regulations for any data that fall under privacy or other governing regulations. Ensure that simulated data is not mixed with real data.

  - **TEST FOR FAILURE** – The purpose of testing is only partially to see if the system works correctly. It is also important to test error routines and the resilience of the system to failure.

    - **RANGES** – Test using both acceptable and unacceptable data values – checking the size of fields, the ability to truncate data that is too large and prevent buffer overflows, and the input of alphabetic characters or negative numbers into a numerical field.

    - **STRESS TESTS** – The system must also be tested to ensure that it can handle the number of transactions or users that may be using the system at once. This is often called stress testing.

- **NEVER TEST ON A PRODUCTION SYSTEM** – Never test on a live production system. This is the ideal – but we do know that some systems can only undergo their final tests in production. Testing in production can lead to data corruption, partial or total loss of data from user mishaps or exploited vulnerabilities, and can cause significant disruptions to daily business. Furthermore, if the system processes confidential data, the testing process may result in violations of privacy – granting developers access to sensitive information. Traditionally, developers are not careful with test data and reports, and developers will leave copies of test data or reports lying around in an insecure manner or discarded without being shredded.

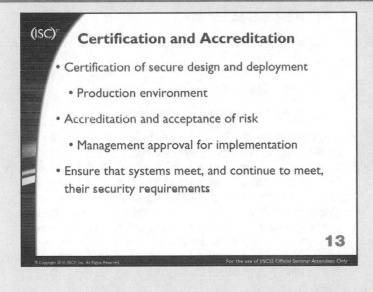

Certification and Accreditation

- Certification of secure design and deployment
  - Production environment
- Accreditation and acceptance of risk
  - Management approval for implementation
- Ensure that systems meet, and continue to meet, their security requirements

13

- **CERTIFICATION OF SECURE DESIGN AND DEPLOYMENT** – This is an important process to ensure that applications are designed and delivered in a manner which does not put the organization at undue risk. Certification is done during the design and development process with an aim to ensuring that the risks were identified, and cost-effective controls were designed and implemented in a way which effectively mitigated the risks.

  - **PRODUCTION ENVIRONMENT** – Unlike a product evaluation process under the Common Criteria, certification is done according to the real production environment. The goal is to ensure that the system will be secure in the real world – so certification is a review of the system and its environmental factors as well. These factors include user training, product support and security of the environment, power and network stability, and documentation.

- **ACCREDITATION AND ACCEPTANCE OF RISK** – Accreditation of the system is the formal approval by Senior Management that a system or application is authorized for implementation. It is the formal acceptance by management of the identified risks of operating the system. Accreditation is granted based on the reports from the certifier and the project team.

- **MEET SECURITY REQUIREMENTS** – Certification and accreditation is an ongoing process that watches for any changes to a system or its environment that could affect its security posture. A major change would initiate a new certification and accreditation process.

Domain Agenda

- Overview of Applications Security

- **System Life Cycle Security**

- Applications Security Issues

- Database Security

14

System and Project Management

- Project Management-Based Methodology

  - Systems Security Engineering-Compatibility Maturity Model Integration (SSE-CMMI)

- SLC vs. SDLC

  - System Life Cycle

  - System Development Life Cycle

15

(1) Initial (chaotic, immature)

(2) Managed (disciplined, capable)

(3) Defined (documented, consistent)

(4) Quantitatively Managed (predictable) and

(5) Optimizing (constant improvement)

- **SLC VERSUS SDLC** – The difference between "system life cycle" and "system development life cycle" is that the former is concerned not only with the development phases but with the post-development operation and maintenance phases as well. The traditional system's development life cycle only includes the development phases of a project and ends shortly after implementation. In today's literature, however, because most programs are under continuous review and improvement, we see the term SDLC being used during the entire life of a system or application thereby replacing the term SLC.

- During the 1960s, the development and maintenance of software made up almost 75% of the cost of an overall systems project. Because of the expenses associated with the software, industry research turned to the discipline of software engineering. Software engineering stated that software products had to be planned, designed, constructed, and released according to engineering principles.

- Note that of the various security guidelines discussed in security management and security architecture, Information Technology Infrastructure Library (ITIL) has the most extensive material on application and system development.

- **PROJECT MANAGEMENT** – Why are we talking about system life cycles under the aegis of application security? System development is a complex task, particularly with complicated modern information systems. The best way to ensure security is to make certain that no mistakes are made during the development stage. It is, therefore, vitally important to manage the system and project life cycle, particularly the development stage.

  - **SSE-CMMI** – This focus has become formalized in the **CAPABILITY MATURITY MODEL INTEGRATION,** which predicts the success of an organization with respect to five levels of management maturity. The levels are:

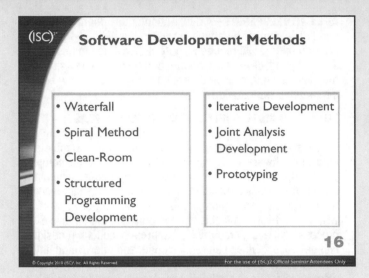

- **SOFTWARE DEVELOPMENT METHODS** – There are a number of software development methods. The following list provides a brief overview of some of them. When applying, mixing, or matching any of these methods, be sure to consider whether they adequately address stakeholder's appetite for risk.

- **WATERFALL** – The traditional waterfall life cycle method dates back to the early 1970s and is probably the oldest known method for developing software systems. Each phase contains a list of activities that must be performed before the next phase begins.

- **SPIRAL METHOD** – A distinguishing feature of the spiral method is that each phase adds a risk assessment review. Schedules and estimated costs to complete are revised each time the risk assessment is performed. The decision as to whether to continue or to cancel the project is made based on the results of each of these risk assessments.

- **CLEAN-ROOM** – Zero Defect approach – Developed in the 1990s as an engineering process for the development of high-quality software, this is named after the process of cleaning electronic wafers in a wafer fabrication plant. In software application development, it is a method of controlling defects in the software by writing code correctly the first time rather than trying to find the problems once they are there. Essentially, clean-room software development focuses on "defect prevention" rather than "defect removal." Reduced development time is achieved through an incremental development strategy and in not having to rework the code. This method spends more time in the design phase rather than in the testing, etc., phases.

- **STRUCTURED PROGRAMMING DEVELOPMENT** – Is a method that programmers use to design and develop programs that enforce considerable influence on the quality of the finished products in terms of coherence, comprehensibility, freedom from faults, and security. It is one of the most widely-known programming development models. The methodology promotes discipline, allows introspection, and provides controlled flexibility. It requires that processes be defined, development be modular, and each phase subject to reviews and approvals. It also allows for security to be added in a formalized, structured approach.

- **ITERATIVE DEVELOPMENT** – This model allows for successive refinements of requirements, design, and coding. The scope of the project may be exceeded if clients change requirements. In addition, changes in requirements, design, and specifications make it difficult to ensure that security controls are adequate in the new product.

- **JOINT ANALYSIS DEVELOPMENT (JAD)** – A management process based on having key players communicate at critical phases of the project, which helps developers work effectively with users. The focus is on having the people who actually perform the job (those who have the best understanding of the job) work together with those who are designing a solution. JAD-facilitation techniques bring together a team of users, expert systems developers, and technical experts throughout the development life cycle.

- **PROTOTYPING** – The objective is to build a simplified version (prototype) of the application, release it for review, and use the feedback from the users (clients) to build a second, better version. This is repeated until clients are satisfied with the product. It is a four-step process: Initial concept, Design and implement initial prototype, Refine prototype until acceptable, Complete and release final version.

REFERENCES:

http://www.business-esolutions.com/islm.htm

Software Development Methods (cont.)

- Modified Prototype Model
- Exploratory Model
- Rapid Application Development
- Agile Development

- Computer Aided Software Engineering
- Component-Based Development
- Reuse Model
- Extreme Programming

17

- **MODIFIED PROTOTYPE MODEL (MPM)** – Allows for the basic functionality of a desired system or component to be formally deployed very quickly. This relies on the concept that most functionality is provided by 20% of the software code, so breaking the system into small sections that will provide basic function, and then building the systems as a series of small functional sections, will speed up the development process.

- **EXPLORATORY MODEL** – A set of requirements is built with what is currently available or known – but with the acknowledgement that some of the requirements are not yet known or understood and will require "exploration" as the system begins to take shape. Assumptions are made as to how the system might work and further insights and suggestions are combined to create a usable system. This is often done when developing a system with new technology or a reengineered business process.

- **RAPID APPLICATION DEVELOPMENT (RAD)** – RAD is a form of rapid prototyping that requires strict time limits on each phase and relies on tools that enable quick development. This may be a disadvantage if decisions are made so rapidly that it leads to poor design.

- **AGILE DEVELOPMENT** – A description of development with short development iterations to reduce risk. Like extreme programming, agile requires highly skilled small teams that are designing, developing, and testing their work in small functional components and through continuous review ensuring that it is working correctly.

- **COMPUTER AIDED SOFTWARE ENGINEERING (CASE)** – The technique of using computers to help with the systematic analysis, design, development, implementation, and maintenance of software. CASE is most often used on large, complex projects that involve multiple software components and many people. It provides a mechanism for planners, designers, code writers, testers, and managers to share a common view of where a software project is at each phase of the life cycle process. By having an organized approach, code and design can be reused, which can reduce costs and improve quality. The CASE approach requires building and maintaining software tools and training the developers who will use them.

- **COMPONENT-BASED DEVELOPMENT** – The process of using standardized, building-block components that can be used to assemble (rather than develop) an application. The components are encapsulated sets of standardized data and standardized methods of processing data that together offer economic and scheduling benefits to the development process.

- **REUSE MODEL** – An application built from existing components.

- **EXTREME PROGRAMMING (XP)** – XP follows a specific structure designed to simplify and expedite the process of developing new software. XP teams design software for specific functionalities without adding any functionalities not specifically requested that might slow down the process, and keep the development course simple through systematic and regular testing and design improvements.

REFERENCES:

http://www.business-esolutions.com/islm.htm

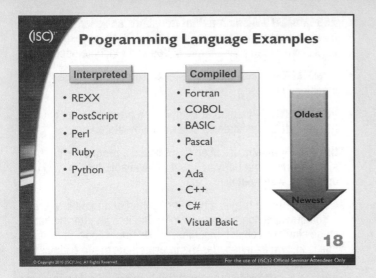

Programming Language Examples

Interpreted	Compiled
• REXX	• Fortran
• PostScript	• COBOL
• Perl	• BASIC
• Ruby	• Pascal
• Python	• C
	• Ada
	• C++
	• C#
	• Visual Basic

Oldest → Newest

18

- **PROGRAMMING LANGUAGES** – The choice of programming language has security implications. Categorization of programming languages can be done many ways, including the distinction between interpreted and compiled languages. The following is a list of some programming languages divided into interpreted and compiled, as well as the aspects that make each of them interesting.

- **INTERPRETED LANGUAGES** –

  - **REXX (RESTRUCTURED EXTENDED EXECUTOR)** – A scripting language designed to be easy to read and learn.

  - **POSTSCRIPT** – A page-description language for desktop publishing and laser printers developed by Adobe. It solved the crude dot matrix versus plotter printing problem.

  - **PERL** – A scripting language originally developed for text manipulation. Its major strength is the programmer-supported community, "Comprehensive Perl Archive Network" (CPAN). CPAN is the largest freely-available code library.

  - **RUBY** – Most scripting languages are optimized for speed on the computer, but Ruby is optimized for user experience.

  - **PYTHON** – According to the author of Python, Guido van Rossum: "Python is an interpreted, interactive, object-oriented programming language. It incorporates modules, exceptions, dynamic typing, and very high-level dynamic data types and classes. Python combines remarkable power with very clear syntax. It has interfaces to many system calls and libraries, as well as to various window systems, and is extensible in C or C++. It is also usable as an extension language for applications that need a programmable interface. Finally, Python is portable: it runs on many UNIX variants, on the Mac, and on PCs under MS-DOS, Windows, Windows NT, and OS/2."

- **COMPILED LANGUAGES** – A more human-readable language (source code) is translated to more optimized machine language (machine code). (Note that it can be argued that almost any language can be compiled.)

  - **COBOL, FORTRAN (COMMON BUSINESS-ORIENTED LANGUAGE AND FORMULA TRANSLATION)** – COBOL and Fortran are among the original high-level programming languages. The "goto" construct in Fortran is derided for contributing to unstructured "spaghetti" code.

  - **BASIC (BEGINNER'S ALL-PURPOSE SYMBOLIC INSTRUCTION CODE)** – As its name implies, BASIC was designed to enable non-technical people to write programs.

  - **PASCAL** – A small, reliable, and efficient programming language designed to teach systematic programming practices, named after the mathematician Blaise Pascal. The Pascal language enabled programmers to define their own datatypes.

  - **C** – Devised in 1972 by Dennis Ritchie as a system-implementation language for the UNIX operating system. The use of "strcpy" in C leads to a tendency to buffer-overflow conditions.

  - **ADA** – Originally designed for embedded and real-time systems, which require a high degree of dependability. Ambiguities will typically cause Ada's compiler to reject the code.

  - **C++** – An enhancement to "C with Classes" that adds virtual functions, operator overloading, multiple inheritance, templates, and exception handling.

  - **C#** – Takes an opposite view of programming, focusing architecture first and syntax second. Most compiled languages are written without consideration for the underlying architecture. C# focuses on the underlying Common Language Infrastructure (CLI) specification. C# can be used on multiple computer platforms.

  - **VISUAL BASIC** – The goal of a visual programming language is to make programming easier by borrowing from the object-orientation language and displaying it in a graphical or visual manner.

REFERENCES:

http://www.pascal-central.com/ppl/index.html

http://cpan.org/

http://www.artima.com/intv/ruby4.html

http://www.python.org/doc/faq/general/#why-was-python-created-in-the-first-place

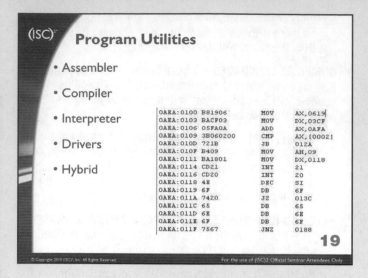

- **ASSEMBLER** – A program that translates an assembly-language program into machine language. Close correspondence between assembly mnemonic codes and machine opcodes.

- **COMPILER** – Translates a high-level (source) language into machine language.

- **INTERPRETER** – Instead of compiling a program all at once, the interpreter translates it statement-by-statement.

- **DRIVERS** – Drivers are used to interface a program with the system. The correct drivers must be available for the type of operating system in use.

- **HYBRID** – There is also a hybrid of compilation and interpretation in which source code is compiled into an intermediate stage similar to object, machine, or assembly code. In Java, this is known as bytecode. The intermediate stage code is then interpreted as necessary. The intent of the two-step process is to provide for compatibility between systems, since machine code is platform specific. The interpreter (the Java Virtual Machine in Java) is particular to each platform but can handle the intermediate code produced on any platform.

- Java is not the only language to use this type of system. It was implemented as long ago as the UCSD-p system for Pascal.

REFERENCES:

http://ugweb.cs.ualberta.ca/resources/java/faq/compile.html

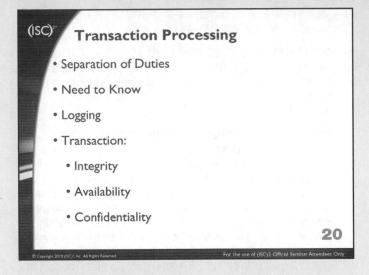

Transaction Processing

- Separation of Duties
- Need to Know
- Logging
- Transaction:
  - Integrity
  - Availability
  - Confidentiality

20

- **TRANSACTION PROCESSING** – A transaction occurs when the application takes an input, processes it, and produces an output of some kind. Transaction analysis includes examining the path the input data takes throughout the application and the resulting output based on the processed input. Attackers often use input streams to attack applications.

- **SEPARATION OF DUTIES AND NEED TO KNOW** – An information system must support the security principles of separation of duties and need to know. Sensitive transactions must be designed so that an internal or external person cannot change data maliciously or execute an operation that should require dual control or the approval of another party. The application must also enforce need to know and not disclose data to unauthorized persons.

- **LOGGING** – Any changes to data should be logged with a record of who made the change as well as the time, date, and details of the change. This is important in order to verify changes or to investigate suspicious activity. Any request to access sensitive data must also be recorded to validate compliance with privacy regulations or organizational policy.

- **TRANSACTION INTEGRITY** – Assures that the information/data have not been altered inappropriately by either an authorized user or an attacker at any stage during the transaction. It also verifies that the software code is operating per the requirements for the transaction processing. Integrity controls include:

  - **EDIT CHECKS** – Ensuring input data is within acceptable ranges or meets criteria.

  - **BALANCING** – Ensuring the transactions completed properly by matching input with output.

  - **DATA/INPUT VALIDATION** – Confirmation that action requested by the user was intentional (the "Are You Sure?" box).

  - **ERROR HANDLING/INFORMATION LEAKAGE** – Ensuring that errors are handled correctly and that errors do not provide an attacker with information on the operation of the system.

  - **LOGGING/AUDITING** – All access to sensitive data or changes to data should be logged to the user or process that initiated the request.

- **CRYPTOGRAPHY** – Data at rest and data in transit – ensure that sensitive data is encrypted so that it cannot be read by unauthorized users.

- **SECURE CODE ENVIRONMENT** – Ensure copies of source and object code are preserved and protected and that unauthorized changes cannot be made to production systems.

- **SESSION MANAGEMENT** – Login/logout – problems of unauthorized access can arise when a user leaves a session open or closes a browser without logging out first.

- **TRANSACTION AVAILABILITY** – Availability for transaction processing around the clock and around the world is a serious challenge. Efficient processing is making good use of resources; unnecessarily large queries that would affect system performance should be limited by design. Critical systems should be designed with redundancy and failover.

- **RECOVERY OF POSTED TRANSACTIONS** – In the event that the system provides online transaction processing, records must be kept to provide the recovery of lost data in the event of system failure. In the case of database changes solution such as remote journaling should be considered; other options may include electronic vaulting; these are all covered in both Business Continuity Planning and the Operations Security domains.

- **SYSTEM AND APPLICATION SOFTWARE BACKUPS** – Providing backups of operating system and application software ensures that programs are available in the event of an outage or system crash. Purchased source code (or extra copies) should be kept in escrow. (Redundancy controls in relation to backups and hardware redundancy are covered more fully in the Operations Security and Telecommunications and Network Security Domains.)

- **TRANSACTION CONFIDENTIALITY** – The very purpose of most applications is to provide a level of access to data. This may include read access, or the ability to modify the data. The application must, therefore, provide the necessary security measures. Practices include:

  - Ensuring no sensitive data is transmitted in the clear, internally or externally.

  - Ensuring that the application is implementing "known good" cryptographic algorithms.

  - Ensuring that there are authorization mechanisms in place.

  - Ensuring that the application has clearly defined the user types and the rights of said users.

  - Ensuring there is a "least privilege" stance in operation.

  - Ensuring that the authorization mechanisms work properly, fail securely, and cannot be circumvented.

  - Ensuring that authorization is checked on every request.

  - Ensuring that development/debug back-doors are not present in production code.

REFERENCES:

http://www.owasp.org/index.php/Transaction_Analysis

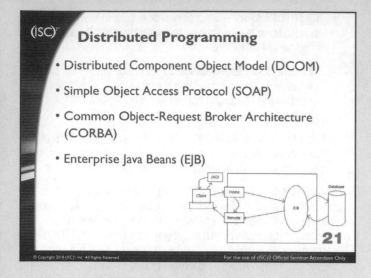

Distributed Programming

- Distributed Component Object Model (DCOM)
- Simple Object Access Protocol (SOAP)
- Common Object-Request Broker Architecture (CORBA)
- Enterprise Java Beans (EJB)

21

- **DISTRIBUTED PROGRAMMING** – Distributed programming requires abstract communication between hosts. Distributed computing entails programs located on different computers cooperating in the same application. Applications are divided into components, each of which are able to operate in a different location/platform. The four major protocols in use today are DCOM, SOAP, CORBA, and EJB.

- **DISTRIBUTED COMPONENT OBJECT MODEL (DCOM)** – DCOM is a Microsoft-only protocol. It is also enabled by default on all versions of Windows. DCOM was the extension of COM – and allowed application objects to work together despite being located on different computers. [1] DCOM is the means by which the "Blaster worm" was able to spread.

- **SIMPLE OBJECT ACCESS PROTOCOL (SOAP)** – SOAP is a replacement for DCOM. SOAP Version 1.2 provides the definition of the XML-based information that can be used for exchanging structured and typed information between peers in a decentralized, distributed environment.

- **COMMON OBJECT-REQUEST BROKER ARCHITECTURE (CORBA)** – CORBA is a platform neutral and open set of standards. CORBA allows applications to communicate with one another regardless of where they are stored. It is based upon the Object Request Broker (ORB) concept. The Object Request Broker (ORB) establishes a client/server relationship between objects. Using an ORB, a client can transparently locate and activate a method on a server object either on the same machine or across a network. Note that since CORBA manages service requests to objects, it, and Object Request Brokers in general, are examples of the reference monitor concept from security architecture applied to distributed systems.

- **ENTERPRISE JAVA BEANS (EJB)** – EJB is a server-side Java component that abstracts both the web server and the database. It serves web applications via a browser and places the security requirements on the server side.

REFERENCES:

[1] DCOM http://msdn.microsoft.com/en-us/library/ms809340.aspx

SOAP: http://www.w3.org/TR/2007/REC-soap12-part0-20070427/

http://java.sun.com/javaee/5/docs/tutorial/doc/bnbls.html

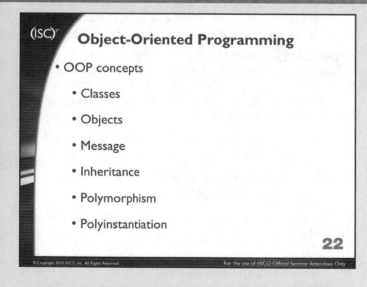

Object-Oriented Programming

- OOP concepts
  - Classes
  - Objects
  - Message
  - Inheritance
  - Polymorphism
  - Polyinstantiation

22

- **OBJECT-ORIENTED PROGRAMMING (OOP)** – Code reuse reduces development time and thus reduces programming costs. C++ is an example of an OOP language – it combines the traditional C programming language with object capabilities. When building traditional programs, the programmers must write every line of code from scratch. With OOP, programmers can reuse prewritten blocks of code (objects). The advantage of OOP is that an object can be used repeatedly in different applications and by different programmers.

- Various aspects of OOP can assist with security; for example, data and functions can be hidden from the outside world. Functions may also be hidden from developers, however, and care must, therefore, be used when relying on security protection in OOP.

- Objects are encapsulated, possibly providing some security.

- Objects have methods (code with interfaces) and attributes (data) encapsulated together.

- **CLASSES** – Templates for objects.

- **OBJECTS** – Instances of the classes.

- **MESSAGE** – Objects request services by sending messages to other objects.

- **INHERITANCE** – An object that is called by another object or program derives its data and functionality from the calling object.

- **POLYMORPHISM** – Different objects may respond to the same command in different ways. An object that is derived from a class for which security has been defined may for example inherit its security characteristics or functions. Note, however, that the functions may not be fully secure in the new object.

- **POLYINSTANTIATION** – Creating a new version of an object by changing its attributes. May be used in support of security by removing data, or may be a risk due to removal of security features. Polyinstantiation is also the technique used to prevent inference violations. Essentially, it allows different versions of the same information to exist at different classification levels. Users at a lower classification level will not be aware of data that exists at a higher classification level.

Domain Agenda

- Overview of Applications Security

- System Life Cycle Security

- **Applications Security Issues**

- Database Security

23

- This section is broken into two pieces. The first section looks at the flaws and other security issues in an application caused by poor design, poor coding, or user misuse. The second section looks at applications security issues related to intentional attacks and malware.

Applications Security Issues

- Building security in

- Adding defense-in-depth

- Cryptographic protection of data

- Secure architecture

24

- **APPLICATIONS SECURITY ISSUES** – Attacks on applications, particularly web applications, are on the rise. Focus is now shifting toward building security into software applications and adding to the defense-in-depth approach. As Hoare writes: "[T]here are two ways of constructing a software design: One way is to make it so simple that there are obviously no deficiencies and the other way is to make it so complicated that there are no obvious deficiencies." As software applications become more complex, there is a tendency to assess the security through observation and experimentation rather than by examining its construction. Software consumers, particularly in corporations and defense, are now using tools and services to assure that software applications have been reviewed for known types of security weaknesses.

- Organizations such as the U.S. Department of Homeland Security have added Internet resources for software developers with recommended coding practices for secure application development: https://buildsecurityin.us-cert.gov/daisy/bsi/home.html

- **CRYPTOGRAPHIC PROTECTION OF DATA** – Web applications rarely use cryptographic functions properly to protect data and credentials. Sensitive data may be stored unencrypted and in an insecure area. Attackers can use poorly protected data to conduct identity theft and other crimes such as credit card fraud.

- **SECURE ARCHITECTURE** – Applications must be placed correctly into the network and systems architecture. Many flaws are created by improper design – putting sensitive files on web servers or unmanaged calls from the application to the internal resources.

REFERENCES:

https://buildsecurityin.us-cert.gov/daisy/bsi/articles/knowledge/assurance/973-BSI.html (C.A.R. Hoare, 1980 Turing Award Lecture).

Lipson, Howard, Chuck Weinstock, "Evidence of Assurance: Laying the Foundation for a Credible Security Case," May 23, 2008; https://buildsecurityin.us-cert.gov/daisy/bsi/articles/knowledge/assurance/973-BSI.html

Jackson, Joab, Government Computer News, "The New Weakest Links," June 9, 2008; http://www.gcn.com/cgi-bin/udt/im.display.printable?client.id=gcn&story.id=46418

Martin, Robert A., Sean Barnum, Steve Christey, "Being Explicit About Security Weaknesses," Crosstalk, March, 2007. www.stsc.hill.af.mil/crosstalk/2007/03/0703Martin.html

Application Security Principles

- Validate all input and output
- Fail Secure (closed)
- Make it simple
- Defense in Depth
- Only as secure as your weakest link

25

- **VALIDATE ALL INPUT AND OUTPUT** – All input and output should be validated. Only allow data input that can be verified as valid, and only allow output of data to authorized personnel.

- **FAIL SECURE (CLOSED)** – Should an application fail, it should fail in such a way that it is secure rather than failing and leaving everything open. An example is a web application: Should the user attempt anything disallowed, the program should fail the transaction and not provide access to the system.

- **MAKE IT SIMPLE** – If a security system is too complex, it will either not be used or users will find ways to circumvent it in some way. An example is a rigorous password check where users have to write passwords down because they are too complex.

- **DEFENSE IN DEPTH** – The system should be designed so that if one component fails to catch a security event, or is bypassed, a second layer of defense will protect the system and data.

- **ONLY AS SECURE AS THE WEAKEST LINK** – Attackers will try to find any weak point and attempt to exploit it. Any weak point in the system may lead to an exploit of the entire system/application.

Secure Coding Issues

- Buffer overflow
- SQL injection
- Cross-site scripting (XSS)
- Dangling pointer
- Invalid hyperlink
- Secure (encrypted) web application traffic risks
- JavaScript attacks against sandbox

26

- **BUFFER OVERFLOW** – A weakness of both poor coding practices and programming language vulnerabilities (typically C or C++). The buffer overflow is one of the oldest and most common program vulnerabilities and has existed almost since interactive computing began.

  - Buffers represent the memory containers for programs executed by computers.

  - Programs In execution define the size of buffers they will use. The amount of data that the program will send to the buffer is unknown until the time of execution.

  - Overflow is the process of putting more than is expected into a container (buffer), which spills over (is written) into the adjoining memory areas or buffer space.

  - When data overflows one buffer it flows into the memory allocated for another program or system area.

  - This may cause improper modification of data or improper processing, and, in a worst case, the malware may begin to execute and launch malicious code.

  - When an input to a program is more than expected, the program should reject the data (truncate it).

  - A buffer overflow can be done either by a user as an accidental input of too much data into a program field or an intentional act by a hacker to cause system failure or compromise.

    - Stopping buffer overflows:

      - Technically: This is an easy problem to fix. In most cases it just requires the programmer to check all incoming data to ensure it is of an acceptable size and value. Check all bounds on array and pointer references for all executing code. Ensure that all incoming code is checked including input from other systems or processes.

      - When our computing environment is adversarial, attackers will look for these flaws and use them as an opportunity to execute their code, thus taking control of our computing resources.

- **SQL INJECTION** – Inserting a series of SQL statements into a "query" by manipulating data input into an application. This

may allow the attacker to obtain data from databases that would not be available through the application. This may be prevented by performing edit checks on all input.

- **CROSS-SITE SCRIPTING (XSS)** – "XSS flaws occur whenever an application takes user-supplied data and sends it to a web browser without first validating or encoding that content. XSS allows attackers to execute script in the victim's browser that can hijack user sessions, deface websites, possibly introduce worms, etc." (From OWASP (Open Web Application Security Project) top 10)[4]

- **DANGLING POINTER** – An error in software code that points to an object that has been deleted. The pointer may still address a valid memory location and cause that area to be corrupted. This may result in a program bug that is difficult to find, or it may cause a program to crash. They can now be exploited in languages known for not de-allocating memory.

- **INVALID HYPERLINK** – Typical exploits from invalid hyperlinks are "Forced Browsing," where a user can guess a link and gain access to hidden or special URLs.

- **SECURE (ENCRYPTED) WEB APPLICATION TRAFFIC RISKS** – Encryption is often thought of as a perfect protection, however, if the data between the client and the server are encrypted, an IDS cannot see the traffic. If an adversary can take control of the encrypted session (such as in a man-in-the-middle attack), the secure web application can be used against the organization since the firewall and IDS will be blind to the encrypted data and not able to provide protection.

- **JAVASCRIPT ATTACKS** – Revealing the network address translation (NAT) ID and allowing an attacker to "peruse network addresses located inside the local network."[1] When a user visits any web page that has either been infected with malware or designed to distribute malware, the malware infects and takes control of the browser running on the user's PC. The browser is then instructed to "hand over" the network information. [2]

  - **HISTORY STEALING** – JavaScript running in the user's browser reveals the web-surfing history, allowing the attacker to create "look-alike spoofed sites containing malware or infecting the sites the user is visiting." [3]

  - **PERFORM INTRANET PORT SCANS** – JavaScript can force the browser to "make certain types of requests to the internal IP addresses" even If the browser's JavaScript has been disabled." [5]

- **JAVASCRIPTS RUN IN A "SANDBOX"** that allows them to perform web-related actions. A sandbox is a controlled area with resources for guest programs to run. The problem occurs when JavaScripts allow access to parts of a Java plug-in outside the sandbox and then allows access to a Java applet. What was contained is now out of the sandbox.

REFERENCES:

(1) Greenemeier, Larry, InformationWeek, http://www.informationweek.com/news/internet/showArticle.jhtml?articleID=201300295

(2) Black Hat USA 2007 Conference – Las Vegas, Grossman and Hansen, SecTheory.

(3) Greenemeier, Larry, InformationWeek, http://www.informationweek.com/news/internet/showArticle.jhtml?articleID=201300295

(4) http://owasp.org

(5) www.informationweek.com/news/internet/showArticle.jhtml?articleID=201300295

- Various users may find and fix bugs.

- Attackers may find vulnerabilities.

- Disclosure (full/partial) is related.

- **VENDOR PROPRIETARY SOFTWARE** – Many applications are written in a proprietary language or else the source code is not available to the purchaser of the license to use the software. This protects the Intellectual Property of the vendor and also ensures that the customer will have to go to the vendor for most modifications to the software. From a security perspective, this can be both good and bad; the risk of a vulnerability being found in the software may be lower since the source code is not available to hackers, but the ability to test the software may also be limited. A backdoor put in by the vendor may be difficult to detect. Another risk is related to the vendor not being able to provide ongoing support for the product. In the case of vendor bankruptcy or the vendor deciding to discontinue that product, the customer who bought the license may not be able to obtain support for that system. This may be addressed through escrow agreements.

- **ESCROW** – Escrow is the practice of keeping a valuable item in trust with a third party. This may be a good practice in the arena of source code protection. The vendor of proprietary software and the customer who purchases the license make an agreement that a copy of the up-to-date source code will always be kept by a trusted third party. In the event that the customer can prove that the vendor has failed to support his or her product according to the terms of the agreement, the customer can apply to the escrow agent (the trusted third party) for a copy of the source code that he or she can then use for maintenance purposes.

- **IFRAMES** – Normal frames subdivide a browser window into sections, whereas iFrames (inline Frames, or "floating frames") allow a developer to load a new document into an existing document. The new document may integrate seamlessly into the existing document, or it may be distinct if a border is set around it. A hidden iFrame is used to import external data into an existing page by setting the height and width of the iFrame to zero. Most of the risks associated with iFrames are related to printing (the embedded data may not print properly), copyright issues, and compatibility.

- **RACE CONDITION** – A race condition is a false assumption about the current state of a program or a variable in a program that allows integrity to be reduced. When two or more processes use the same resource, each process can falsely depend on the state of that resource being constant. But each process can affect the resource. For example: The glass is full of water and under an opaque box; whoever gets thirsty first drinks; the other assumes the glass to be full, and reaches for an empty glass. In this case perhaps two processes access the same file but the first one to use it deletes it once it has completed, causing the other process to fail.

- A particular type of race condition for file access is a Time of Check/Time of Use (TOC/TOU); where control information is changed between the time that the system security functions check the contents of the variables and when the variables are actually used.

- **APPLICATION PROGRAMMING INTERFACE (API)** – Is a contract between a caller and a call-ee. The caller can be a computer program that sends a request to an operating system, library, or service. This call is made through a defined application interface. An API is usually compiled when an application is built. Typical API problems are introduced during development and include providing excess permission and poor error handling. Poor error handling can occur when the error provides too much information to possible attackers, and also when error handling produces more problems, or does not handle them at all. Examples include:

  - **CATCH NULLPOINTEREXCEPTION** – Catching NullPointerException should not be used as an alternative to programmatic checks to prevent de-referencing a null pointer.

  - **EMPTY CATCH BLOCK:** Ignoring exceptions and other error conditions may allow an attacker to cause unexpected behavior unnoticed.

  - **OVERLY-BROAD CATCH BLOCK:** Catching overly-broad exceptions promotes complex error handling code that is more likely to contain security vulnerabilities.

  - **OVERLY-BROAD THROWS DECLARATION:** Throwing overly broad exceptions promotes complex error-handling code that is more likely to contain security vulnerabilities.

- **THERE ARE TWO TYPES OF PUBLISHING POLICIES FOR APIS:**

  - **FREELY AVAILABLE** – Such as those for Microsoft Windows and Apple. These allow anyone to write software on their platforms.

  - **CONTROLLED** – Allow only licensed entities to write software to their platforms and thereby control what software can interface with their product.

- **OPEN SOURCE** – Open source software is often misunderstood as "free" software. With open source software, the source code is available to the user or purchaser, whereas with most software, only the executable or object code is available. The security implications are debated, but most analysts feel that the fact that large numbers of users are able to examine open source code results in systems with fewer unanticipated vulnerabilities. Phases of open source code development/release:

  - Vendor makes source code available for examination, modification, extension.

REFERENCES:

ISO/IEC JTC 1 N 8557, 2007-04-05 V3 provides guidelines for API standardization.

Tsipenyuk, Katrina, Brian Chess, Gary McGraw; "Seven Pernicious Kingdoms: A Taxonomy of Software Security Errors"; www.fortify.com/docs/Fortify_TaxonomyofSoftwareSecurityErrors.pdf

http://www.cs.tut.fi/~jkorpela/html/iframe.html

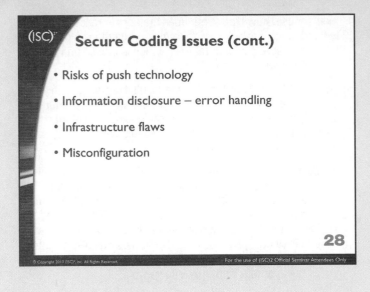

Secure Coding Issues (cont.)

- Risks of push technology
- Information disclosure – error handling
- Infrastructure flaws
- Misconfiguration

28

- **RISKS OF PUSH TECHNOLOGY –** Push technology allows information such as weather, sports scores, and product updates to be pushed out to users and remote machines without the user having to request the information or initiate an update. This technology provides a communications enhancement that also can present a risk to users if they become associated with a malicious website, find themselves subscribed to a site that they did not request, or become victims of an infected download.

- **INFORMATION DISCLOSURE – ERROR HANDLING –** An application developer often writes error routines that provide the information needed to troubleshoot a problem. Unfortunately this may lead to the disclosure of too much information to the user. A malicious user may then use that information to re-engineer an attack to execute successfully.

- **INFRASTRUCTURE FLAWS –** These are core protocol flaws, such as lack of authentication in IP or DNS. These may lead to poisoning of the DNS tables or allow attackers to hide their identity through spoofing their IP addresses.

- **MISCONFIGURATION –** A zero or low security posture due to a setup error by administrator. Leaving ports open or services enabled that are not required are common misconfiguration errors.

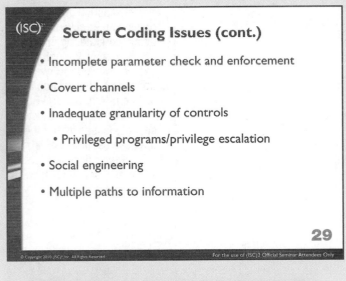

Secure Coding Issues (cont.)

- Incomplete parameter check and enforcement
- Covert channels
- Inadequate granularity of controls
    - Privileged programs/privilege escalation
- Social engineering
- Multiple paths to information

29

- **INCOMPLETE PARAMETER CHECK AND ENFORCEMENT –** Failure to check the inputs to ensure they do not contain: malformed data, incorrect type, or improper length. This is a special case of malformed input.

- **COVERT CHANNELS –** Means of surreptitiously transferring information from a higher classification compartment to a lower classification. Discussed further in both Access Control and Security Architecture and Design domains. There are two types:

    - **STORAGE CHANNELS –** Communicate by modifying a stored object.

- **TIMING CHANNELS –** Transmit information by affecting the relative timing of events.

- **INADEQUATE GRANULARITY OF CONTROLS –** A common fault in applications is that the application was not designed to differentiate between users of different levels – for example, in a multi-level user environment where the application does not adequately check the permission levels of the user at the time of execution, and may inappropriately display data to a low level user that was only intended to be available for a higher level user. This is due to the failure of the access control process of the application to be granular enough.

    - **PRIVILEGED PROGRAMS/ESCALATION –** Programs which operate at a higher permission level than necessary may pose a risk if they become infected with a Trojan.

- **SOCIAL ENGINEERING –** This is always a threat that must be addressed with separation of duties and training. Since the users of the application have access to data that others cannot see, they may be subject to influence from other people wanting them to disclose data improperly.

- **MULTIPLE PATHS TO INFORMATION –** Multiple paths to information occurs when objects and applications allow several paths (methods) to obtain the same result, such as access a program or data through icons, menus, or shortcut keys. It is important to ensure that all of these roads enforce the same level of security.

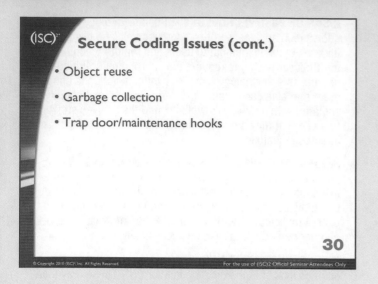

Secure Coding Issues (cont.)

- Object reuse
- Garbage collection
- Trap door/maintenance hooks

30

- **OBJECT REUSE** – An object previously used for another application or information storage may contain sensitive residual data. Note that objects may be physical (drive storage) or logical (memory or variable assignments).

- **GARBAGE COLLECTION** – De-allocation of storage following program execution. Garbage collection may be both good and bad. Programs written in C must have specific functions for garbage collection and memory de-allocation. If this is not done, the program may run out of memory. Programs written in Java have efficient garbage collection and more efficient

memory use. However, sometimes memory is reassigned without being cleared, and, therefore, precautions must be taken to ensure confidential information is erased immediately after use.

- **TRAP DOOR** – A Trap Door is a mechanism embedded in a program that allows the normal security access procedures to be bypassed. Another term for trap door is "maintenance hook." A maintenance hook typically deals with the O/S, while trap door is used for applications.

  - **MAINTENANCE HOOKS (BACKDOOR)** – Software developers often code "backdoors," or "maintenance hooks" in their code to enable them to re-enter the system and perform certain tests or administrative functions. The backdoor is sometimes left in a fully developed system either by design or accident. Backdoors can also be introduced into software by poor programming practices such as the infamous buffer overflow error.

  - **A MAINTENANCE HOOK** – Is a hidden software or hardware mechanism intentionally placed in a system by a vendor that can be triggered to circumvent system protection mechanisms – usually for administrative or license verification purposes. The function will generally provide unusually high or even full access to the system either without an account or from a normally restricted account and is activated in some innocent-appearing manner (for example, as a key sequence at a terminal).

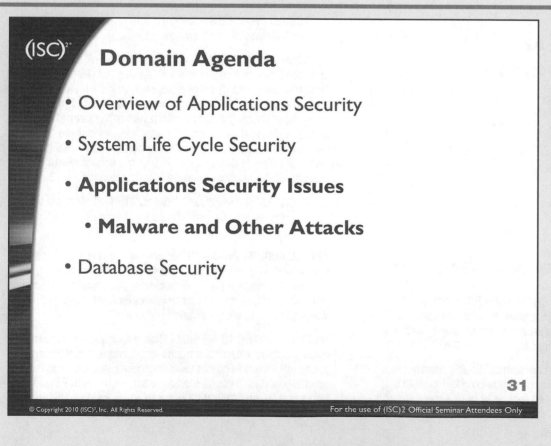

Domain Agenda

- Overview of Applications Security

- System Life Cycle Security

- **Applications Security Issues**

  - **Malware and Other Attacks**

- Database Security

31

- This section of the course deals with attacks that are launched either against an application or through the use of malicious software (malware). This section is different from the previous section of application security issues in that the previous section was related to coding or design errors whilst this section is focused on intentional attacks.

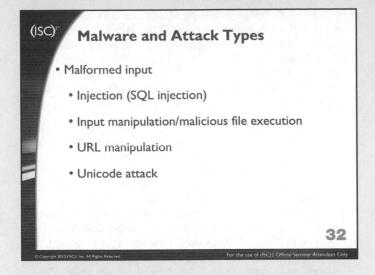

Malware and Attack Types

- Malformed input
  - Injection (SQL injection)
  - Input manipulation/malicious file execution
  - URL manipulation
  - Unicode attack

32

© Copyright 2010 (ISC)², Inc. All Rights Reserved.   For the use of (ISC)2 Official Seminar Attendees Only

- **MALWARE AND ATTACK TYPES** – Both OWASP (Open Web Application Security Project, www.owasp.org) and OSVDB (Open Source Vulnerability Database, www.osvdb.org) have the same malware and attack categorizations.

- **MALFORMED INPUT** – Malformed Input Attacks (more generally known in security literature as malformed data) involve various means of getting illicit commands or packets through defensive measures. For example, denial of service packets that would normally be rejected by a firewall can be fragmented to the point that the firewall no longer recognizes the individual fragments as malicious. Commands (such as "dir") can be sent to a web server in Unicode ("%c0%af"), which the server will properly interpret and act upon, but which a content filter may not recognize as commands. An attack using malformed input frequently involves commands or code

that are somehow crafted to appear to be merely data, hence the name malformed data.

- **THERE ARE MANY TYPES OF MALFORMED INPUT** – From Unicode based attacks to buffer overflows or the submission of incompatible data (alphabetic characters in a numeric field). Some of them are described below. Most malformed input attacks are easily addressed through input validation and better error management.

  - **INJECTION FLAWS** – These occur when user-supplied data is sent to an interpreter as part of a command, query, or data. SQL Injection is a good example of this: Attackers can access or modify data in a database, or execute commands on a server and access sensitive data.

  - **INPUT MANIPULATION / MALICIOUS FILE EXECUTION** – Code is vulnerable to remote file inclusion that allows attackers to include hostile code and data.

  - **URL MANIPULATION** – Used both for administrative and adversarial purposes. Administrators use this to redirect a user from a simple URL to a complex URL. This makes it easier for the end user to access a site, however, an adversary can use URL manipulation to redirect users to an unintended site.

  - **UNICODE ATTACK** – Unicode representations of control information may be passed by a firewall, but "correctly" (negatively) interpreted by the server.

REFERENCES:

http://www.owasp.org/index.php/Top_10_2007

http://www.webappsec.org/projects/threat/classes/ssi_injection.shtml

http://osvdb.org/search/advsearch

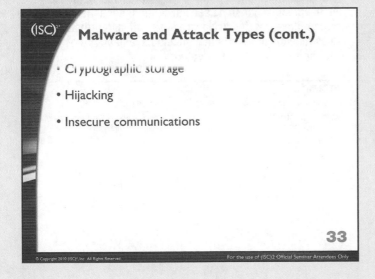

Malware and Attack Types (cont.)

- Cryptographic storage
- Hijacking
- Insecure communications

33

© Copyright 2010 (ISC)², Inc. All Rights Reserved.   For the use of (ISC)2 Official Seminar Attendees Only

- **CRYPTOGRAPHIC OR CRYPTOGRAPHIC STORAGE** – Several organizations have become victims of employees or malicious outsiders encrypting corporate data and "holding it hostage," only agreeing to disclose the key to unlock the data when their financial demands are met.

- **HIJACKING** – A post-session setup and typically post-authentication attack wherein the adversary assumes someone else's valid credentials. A CSRF (Cross Site Request Forgery) attack forces a logged-on victim's browser to send a pre-authenticated request to a vulnerable web application, which then forces the victim's browser to perform a hostile action to the benefit of the attacker.

- **INSECURE COMMUNICATIONS** – Applications frequently fail to encrypt network traffic when appropriate. When sensitive information is sent unencrypted over insecure channels, attackers will be able to read it. "Information Disclosure," or "Information Leakage and Improper Error Handling Applications," can unintentionally leak information about their configuration, internal workings, or violate privacy through a variety of application problems thereby allowing attackers to gain detailed system information.

- **DENIAL OF SERVICE (DOS)** – Consuming the resources on the system and thus limiting the resources for the use of others. This is an attack against availability. DoS does not generally involve erasure or destruction of data or resources. These attacks do not need to be complex: For example, invalid searches on websites can cause a denial of service.

  - **DISTRIBUTED DENIAL OF SERVICE (DDOS)** – A Distributed Denial of Service is executed by using several machines to simultaneously attack a victim system. Usually these are compromised machines that have been infected with a zombie program and are a part of a botnet of infected machines under the control of the bot master or bot herder. The use of many machines at once amplifies the attack and can cause network outage or unavailability of the target system. The structure of a DDoS attack requires a master computer to control the attack, a target of the attack, and a number of computers in the middle that the master computer uses to generate the attack. These computers in between the master and the target are variously called agents or clients, but are usually referred to as running "zombie" programs.

- **BOTNETS** – Most major viruses since the summer of 2003 have been designed to create large botnets (typically 10,000+ compromised machines, but sometimes groups of more than 250,000). Increasingly used as a resource to rent out for DDoS attacks and, therefore, extortion. An organization under threat of attack from such a botnet would be nearly helpless to defend itself and subject to the loss of business as a result of the attack – and may choose to pay the attacker rather than fight the problem. As one example, a DDOS attack against the IP range for the country of Estonia succeeded in choking off all Internet access for that country for an extended period of time in September 2007. Spam botnets are also used to feed out new versions of viruses or phishing attacks.

- **FAST FLUX BOTNETS** – Fast flux botnets enable a spammer to bypass the block lists of anti-spam organizations (which block the IP that spam is seen to come from as soon as a pattern of spamming activity is detected) because the IP that the spam is coming from can be changed every minute as the various compromised machines are used in sequence for a few hundred emails at a time. This is done through DNS manipulation and a feature of the STORM Worm. This technique is being used by phishers to host their fake sites on different IPs every minute to make it very difficult to take them down. Thus, whitelisting and blacklisting are ineffective against spam from botnets. Term and Bayesian filtering, however, generally, are effective controls.

- **DATA HIDING IN DIGITAL WARRENS** – A local computer has many places for an adversary to hide information from normal view. As many as 11 have been identified by H. Berghel, D. Hoelzer, and M. Sthultz. One classic digital warren is Slack Space – the unused portion of the hard disk between the end of the file and the end of the file cluster.

- **ALTERNATE DATA STREAMS** – A relatively unknown compatibility feature of NTFS, Alternate Data Streams (ADS) provides hackers with a method of hiding rootkits or hacker tools on a breached system and allows them to be executed without being detected by the systems administrator.

- **NON-TECHNICAL ATTACKS** – Non-technical threats may be related to social engineering (covered previously), the viewing of screens containing sensitive data (hence the need for screen filters), or the disclosure of sensitive information on sales receipts or reports that should have been protected or had the sensitive data encrypted.

REFERENCES:

http://www.sans.org/reading_room/whitepapers/securecode/386.php

source: H. Berghel, D. Hoelzer, and M. Sthultz, Data hiding tactics for Windows and Unix file systems; www.berghel.net/publications/data_hiding/data_hiding.php

Building Secure Software, ISBN 0-201-72152-x

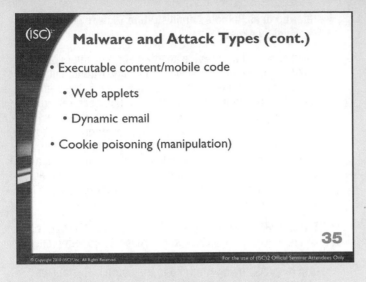

Malware and Attack Types (cont.)

- Executable content/mobile code
  - Web applets
  - Dynamic email
- Cookie poisoning (manipulation)

35

- The concept of mobile code has been called many names: mobile agents, mobile code, downloadable code, executable content, active capsules, remote code, etc. All these deal with the local execution of remotely sourced code.

- Agent software is generally differentiated from other forms of mobile code by additional autonomy of the program, and should, therefore, be subject to additional controls.

- "Dynamic" email is particularly dangerous. Unless a specific need is demonstrated, it may be best to have policies restricting the functions available within email and mail user agent (MUA) software.

- In regard to the Web, note that Java applets are usually subject to a sandbox (discussed later), whereas JavaScript has no such protection.

- **COOKIE POISONING** – Cookies are small pieces of text stored on a user's computer by a browser from a web server. Most often these are used to record session information, shopping cart details, and user preferences. However they can also be manipulated or changed by the user. For example, in the case where the cookie contains total value of goods in the shopping cart, the ability of the user to change this value may result in the order being processed for a price of the user's choosing.

- **EXECUTABLE CONTENT/MOBILE CODE** – Code that is downloaded to the user's machine and executed. Running programs on a computer may give the program unexpected access to resources on the machine.

  - **WEB APPLETS** – Small programs written in Java, scripting languages, or ActiveX controls.

  - **DYNAMIC EMAIL** – Active scripts or links included in email messages.

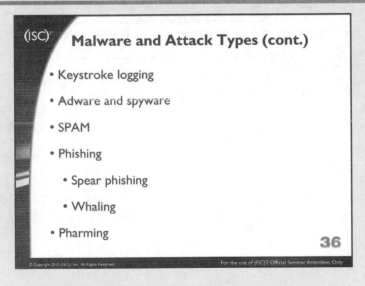

Malware and Attack Types (cont.)

- Keystroke logging
- Adware and spyware
- SPAM
- Phishing
  - Spear phishing
  - Whaling
- Pharming

36

- **KEYSTROKE LOGGING** – A software or hardware tool for capturing data entry.

- **ADWARE AND SPYWARE** – Intended as marketing, not malice. Installed with other software as a separate function or program. Generates unwanted or irrelevant advertising, or reports on user activities, possibly including other installed programs. There is a lot of controversy over a number of technologies generally described as adware or spyware. Most people would agree that the marketing functions are not specifically malicious, but what one person sees as "aggressive selling" another will see as an intrusion or invasion of privacy.

- **SPAM** – Unwanted email solicitation.

- **PHISHING** – Attempts to trick a user into divulging personal information for the purposes of fraud or identity theft. It often takes the form of counterfeit messages or websites mimick-

ing banks or other institutions. Phishing is a major problem and is increasing in scope and sophistication. Phishers may redirect input from legitimate sites or use DNS poisoning to redirect users who attempt to contact (for example) a bank's legitimate website. Some phishing messages even carry warnings about security risks and phishing messages.

- **SPEAR PHISHING** – Whereas most phishing attacks are broadcast attacks spread indiscriminately over a large population in the hopes of catching a few true targets into the "net" of the attack, spear phishing is a targeted phishing attack directed at a specific individual. One example is sending a phishing attack that contains personal data about the victim to make the attack seem more realistic.

- **WHALING** – Whaling is a type of spear phishing targeted specifically at executives of an organization. It attempts to deceive the executives into clicking on a link in an email that purports to be an unpaid invoice or a complaint about the organization and draws them to a malicious website that captures keystrokes or gathers other sensitive data.

- **PHARMING** – A pharming attack takes the victim to an unintended website. This may be through DNS poisoning or a compromise of the victim's machine. While the victim believes that he or she is going to one location, the manipulation of the DNS entry or bypassing of the DNS lookup through a compromise of the local machine causes the victim to end up at a site that most probably mimics the true destination site.

REFERENCES:

H. Berghel, D. Hoelzer, and M. Sthultz, Data hiding tactics for Windows and UNIX file systems; www.berghel.net/publications/data_hiding/data_hiding.php

Building Secure Software, ISBN 0-201-72152-x

`http://www.networkworld.com/news/2007/111407-whaling.html

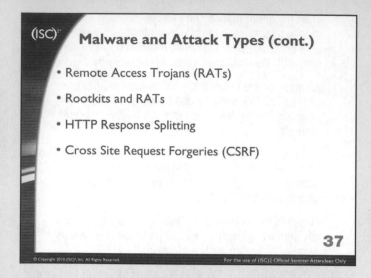

Malware and Attack Types (cont.)

- Remote Access Trojans (RATs)
- Rootkits and RATs
- HTTP Response Splitting
- Cross Site Request Forgeries (CSRF)

37

- **REMOTE ACCESS TROJANS (RAT)** – Inappropriate over-the-network control of a host. Several malware attacks (sub-seven, etc.) were able to remotely take control of a victim machine.

- **ROOTKITS AND RATS** – Rootkits allow an attacker to gain administrator level access to a compromised machine. The attacker usually installs the rootkit once gaining access, and this allows the perpetrator continued access in the future. Rootkits are accurately called backdoors and may be used as keystroke loggers. Most rootkits disguise themselves very well and may be nearly impossible to detect or remove without reconfiguring the entire machine. Sony became notorious for installing rootkits on machines as a part of its Digital Rights Management process.

  - **RAT (REMOTE ACCESS TROJAN)** – The authors of Remote Access Trojans (RATs) would generally like these to be

referred to as Remote Administration Tools to convey a sense of legitimacy.

- RATs and zombies provide an interesting example of an error in the use of technical terminology. Traditionally, the program run on the naïve user's computer, or the computer that is running such a program, has been referred to as a client, particularly when it is part of a botnet. Technically, however, the RAT or zombie agent program is providing a service at the request of the malicious controller. Therefore, properly the controller would be the client, and the controlled user computer (and the software running on it) would be the server. However, this correct usage is almost never followed.

- **HTTP RESPONSE SPLITTING** – HTTP Response Splitting is a technique used by an attacker for cross site scripting and other similar attacks. The attacker places a carriage feed into the http response being returned to the source. This allows the attacker to then submit his or her own code to the server which sees the carriage feed as the signal that the header is finished and accepts the text that follows (in this case the text supplied by the attacker) as the body of the message.

- **CROSS SITE REQUEST FORGERIES (CSRF, OR ONE-CLICK ATTACKS)** – The CSRF attack exploits a user who is logged in to a secure server and tricks that user into executing an unintended command. It takes advantage of the session management vulnerabilities in many web browsers and servers that will accept any submission from the authenticated user without requiring reauthentication or confirmation. This can be used to cause the user to make purchases, change account information, or take other action on behalf of the attacker.

REFERENCES:

http://searchmidmarketsecurity.techtarget.com/sDefinition/0,,sid198_gci547279,00.html

http://www.owasp.org/index.php/Cross-Site_Request_Forgery_(CSRF)

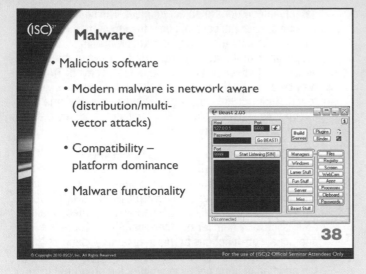

- **MALICIOUS SOFTWARE (MALWARE)** – Software or programs intentionally designed to penetrate a system, break security policies, or carry malicious or damaging payloads. Programming bugs or errors are not generally considered to be malware. Examples of malicious software include backdoors, data diddlers, DDoS (Distributed Denial of Service) programs, hoax warnings, logic bombs, pranks, RATs (Remote Access Trojan), trojans, spyware, viruses, worms, zombies, etc.

  - It is sometimes hard to make a hard and fast distinction between malware and bugs. For example, if a programmer left a buffer overflow in a system and it created a loophole that can be used as a backdoor or a maintenance hook, did he do it deliberately?

  - It should be noted that malware is not just a collection of utilities for an attacker. Once launched, malware can continue an attack without reference to the author or user, and in some cases will expand the attack to other systems. There is a qualitative difference between malware and the attack tools, kits, or scripts, that have to be under an attacker's control, and which are not considered to fall within the definition of malware.

- **NETWORK AWARE** – Modern malware is network aware. In the modern computing environment, nearly everything, including mainframes, which were previously isolated, is attached to everything else. Whereas older trojans were subject to a limited distribution by fooling users on bulletin board systems, and early generation viruses required disk exchange via sneakernet and infection of shareware or possible pirating of software to spread, current versions of malware leverage network functionality and flaws to spread across networks.

  - **MULTI-VECTOR ATTACKS** – Modern malware can be distributed through emailing of executable content in attachments, compromise of active content on web pages, and even direct attacks on server software. Many newer attacks can take multiple forms

- Attack payloads can attempt to compromise objects accessible via the net, can deny service by exhausting resources, can corrupt publicly available data on websites, or spread plausible but misleading information.

- **COMPATIBILITY - PLATFORM DOMINANCE** – It has long been known that the number of variants of viruses or other forms of malware is directly connected to the number of instances of a given platform. The success of a given piece of malware is also related to the relative proportion of a given platform in the overall computing environment (attacks are generally mounted at least semi-randomly: attacks on incompatible targets are wasted and, conversely, attacks on compatible targets are successful and may help to escalate an attack).

  - The modern computing environment is one of extreme consistency (regardless of the complaints of network administrators). The Intel platform has extreme dominance in hardware, and Microsoft has a near monopoly on the desktop. In addition, compatible application software (and the addition of functional programming capabilities in those applications) can mean that malware from one hardware and operating system environment can work perfectly well in another.

- **MALWARE FUNCTIONALITY** – The functionality added to application macro and script languages has given them the capability to either directly address computer hardware and resources, or to easily call upon utilities or processes which have such access. This means that objects previously considered to be data and, therefore, immune to malicious programming, must now be checked for malicious functions or payloads.

  - In addition, these languages are very simple to learn and use, and the various instances of malware carry their own source code, in plaintext and sometimes commented, making it simple for individuals wanting to learn how to craft an attack to gather templates and examples of how to do so, without even knowing how the technology actually works. This expands the ability of authors of such software enormously. Some examples of programs or utilities that make the development of malware easier for the low-level cracker include:

    - MS Office macros

    - MS Windows Script Host (.vbs)

    - "Active" Web content

    - HTML, VBScript, Jscript++, etc.

    - Macro and script viruses, etc., can carry source code.

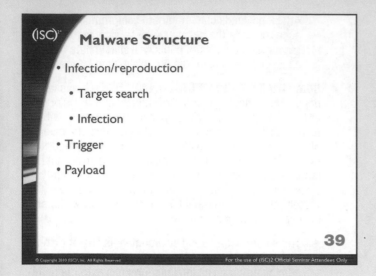

detect, an appropriate object to infect. The search may be active, as in the case of some file infectors that take directory listings to find appropriate programs of appropriate sizes, or it may be passive, in the case of macro viruses that infect every document as it is saved. There may be some additional decisions taken once an object is found. Some viruses may try to actually slow the rate of infection to avoid detection. Most will check to see if the object has already been infected.

- **INFECTION** – The next action will be the infection itself. This may entail the writing of a new section of code to the boot sector, the addition of code to a program file, the addition of macro code to the Microsoft Word NORMAL.DOT file, the sending of a file attachment to harvested email addresses, or a number of other operations. There are additional sub-functions at this step as well, such as the movement of the original boot sector to a new location, or the addition of jump codes in an infected program file to point to the virus code. There may also be changes to system files, to try and ensure that the virus will be run every time the computer is turned on. This can be considered the insertion portion of the virus.

- **TRIGGER** – The second major component of a virus is the virus trigger. The virus may look for a certain number of infections, a certain date and/or time, a certain piece of text, or simply blow up the first time it is used. As noted, a virus does not actually have to have either a trigger or a payload.

- **PAYLOAD** – The payload of a virus can be pretty much anything, from a simple one time message, to a complicated display, to reformatting of the hard disk. However, the bigger the payload, the more likely it is that the virus will get noticed.

- **MALWARE STRUCTURE** – Malicious software is typically built containing several basic components, although not all may be present in each specific program. Insertion (or infection) means to become resident in the target system. Avoidance, otherwise known as stealth, is the method used to evade detection. Eradication is the means by which malware removes traces of itself following a trigger. Propagation or replication is considered the province of viruses and worms only, and is what makes a program a virus.

- **INFECTION/REPRODUCTION** – The first and only necessary part of a structure is the infection mechanism. This is the code that allows a virus to reproduce, and thus to be a virus. The infection mechanism itself has a number of parts to it.

- **TARGET SEARCH** – The first function is to search for, or

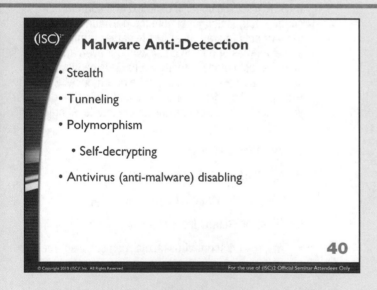

and return only information suitable to the uninfected object. This type of stealth was present in one of the earliest MS-DOS viruses, Brain (if you gave commands, on an infected system, to display the contents of the boot sector, you would see the original boot sector, and not the infected one).

- **POLYMORPHISM** – Polymorphism (literally "many forms") refers to a number of techniques which attempt to change the code string on each generation of a virus. These range from using modules that can be rearranged to encrypting the virus code itself, leaving only a stub of code that can decrypt the body of the virus program when invoked. Polymorphism is sometimes also known as **SELF-ENCRYPTION** or self-garbling, but these terms are imprecise and not recommended. Examples are the Whale virus and Tremor. Many polymorphic viruses use standard "mutation engines," such as MtE. These pieces of code actually aid detection because they have a known signature.

- **ANTIVIRUS (ANTI-MALWARE) DISABLING** – A number of viruses also demonstrate some form of active detection avoidance, which may range from disabling of on-access scanners in memory to deletion of antivirus and other security software from the disk (Zonealarm is a favorite target).

- **STEALTH** – The term "stealth" is used inconsistently even within the virus research community. One common use is as a reference to all forms of anti-detection technology.

- **TUNNELING** – A more specific usage refers to an activity also known as tunneling, which (in opposition to the usage in VPNs) describes that act of tracing interrupt links and system calls in order to intercept calls to read the disk or perform other measures that could be used to determine that an infection exists. A virus using this form of stealth would intercept a call to display information about the file (such as its size)

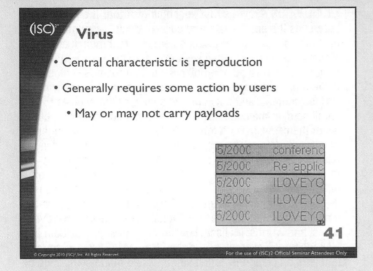

- **CENTRAL CHARACTERISTIC IS REPRODUCTION** – A virus is defined by its ability to reproduce and spread. A virus is not just anything that goes wrong with a computer, and virus is not simply another name for malware. Trojan horse programs and logic bombs do not reproduce themselves.

- **GENERALLY REQUIRES SOME ACTION BY USERS** – A virus usually requires some action from the user to trigger the infection. This may include launching an executable, opening an attachment or installing a program.

  - A worm, which is sometimes seen as a specialized type of virus, is sometimes distinguished from a virus, since a virus generally requires an action on the part of the user to trigger or aid reproduction and spread (there will be

more on this distinction in the slide on worms). The action on the part of the user is generally a common function, and the user generally does not realize the danger of the action, or the fact that he or she is assisting the virus.

- **MAY OR MAY NOT CARRY PAYLOADS** – The only requirement for a program to be defined as a virus is that it reproduces. There is no requirement that the virus carries a payload, although many do. In many cases (in most cases of "successful" viruses), the payload is limited to some kind of message. A deliberately damaging payload, such as erasure of the disk or system files, usually restricts the ability of the virus to spread, since the virus uses the resources of the host system. In some cases, a virus may carry a logic bomb or time bomb which triggers a damaging payload at some date or under some delayed condition.

- Because a virus spreads and uses the resources of the host, it provides a kind of power to software that parallel processors provide for hardware. Therefore, some have theorized that viral programs could be used for beneficial purposes, similar to the experiments in distributed processing that are testing the limits of cryptographic strength (various types of network management functions, and updating of system software, are seen as candidates). However, the fact that viruses change systems and applications is seen as problematic in its own right. Many viruses which carry no overtly damaging payload still create problems for systems. The difficulties of controlling viral programs have been addressed in theory, but the solutions are also known to have faults and loopholes.

REFERENCES:

http://all.net/books/virus/index.html

- **VIRUS TYPES** – Are generally distinguished by the way they spread or the target they attack. These terms do not necessarily indicate a strict division. A file infector may also be a system infector. A script virus that infects other script files may be considered to be a file infector, although this type of activity, while theoretically possible, is unusual in practice. There are also difficulties in drawing a hard distinction between macro and script viruses.

- **FILE INFECTOR** – Infects program (object) files. System infectors that infect operating system program files (such as COMMAND.COM in DOS) are also file infectors. File infectors can attach to the front of the object file (pre-penders), attach to the back of the file and create a jump at the front of the file to the virus code (appenders), or overwrite the file or portions of it (overwriters). A classic is Jerusalem. A bug in early versions caused it to add itself over and over again to files, making the increase in file length detectable.

- **BOOT SECTOR INFECTOR (BSI)** – Infects the master boot record, system boot record, or other boot records and blocks on physical disks (the structure of these blocks varies, but the first physical sector on a disk generally has some special significance in most operating systems, and usually is read and executed at some point in the boot process). BSIs usually copy the existing boot sector to another unused sector, and then copy themselves into the physical first sector, ending with a call to the original programming. Examples are Brain, Stoned, and Michelangelo.

- **SYSTEM INFECTOR** – A somewhat vague term. Some use the term to indicate viruses that infect operating system files, or boot sectors, such that the virus is called at boot time, and have or may have pre-emptive control over some functions of the operating system (the Lehigh virus infected only COMMAND.COM on MS-DOS machines). In other usage, a system infector modifies other system structures, such as the linking pointers in directory tables or the MS Windows system Registry, in order to be called first when programs are invoked on the host computer. An example of directory table linking is the DIR virus family. Many email viruses target the Registry: Magistr can be very difficult to get rid of.

- **EMAIL VIRUS** – A virus that specifically, rather than accidentally, uses the email system to spread. While virus infected files may be accidentally sent as email attachments, email viruses are aware of email system functions. They generally target a specific type of email system (Microsoft's Outlook is the most commonly used), harvest email addresses from various sources, and may append copies of themselves to all email sent, or may generate email messages containing copies of themselves as attachments. Some email viruses may monitor all network traffic, and follow up legitimate messages with messages that they generate. Most email viruses are technically considered to be worms, since they often do not infect other program files on the target computer, but this is not a hard and fast distinction. There are known examples of email viruses that are file infectors, macro viruses, script viruses, and worms. Melissa, Loveletter, Hybris, and SirCam are all widespread examples, and the CHRISTMAS exec is an example of an older one. Email viruses have made something of a change to the epidemiology of viruses. Traditionally, viruses took many months to spread, but stayed around for many years in the computing environment. Many email viruses have become "fast burners" that can spread around the world, infecting hundreds of thousands or even millions of machines within hours. However, once characteristic indicators of these viruses become known, they die off almost immediately.

- **MULTIPARTITE** – Originally this term was used to indicate a virus that was able to infect both boot sectors and program files. Current usage tends to mean a virus that can infect more than one type of object, or to infect or reproduce in more than one way. Examples are Telefonica, One Half, and Junkie. Traditional multipartites are not very successful.

- **MACRO VIRUS** – A virus that uses macro programming of an application such as a word processor (most known macro viruses use Visual Basic for Applications in Microsoft Word: some are able to cross between applications and function in, for example, a Powerpoint presentation and a Word document, but this ability is rare). Macro viruses infect data files and tend to remain resident in the application itself by infecting a configuration template, such as MS Word's NORMAL.DOT. Although macro viruses infect data files, they are not generally considered to be file infectors: A distinction is generally made between program and data files. Macro viruses can operate across hardware or operating system platforms as long as the required application platform is present (for example, many MS Word macro viruses can operate on both the Windows and Mac versions of Word). Examples are Concept and CAP. Melissa is also a macro virus, in addition to being an email virus: it mailed itself around as an infected document.

- **SCRIPT VIRUS** – Script viruses are generally differentiated from macro viruses in that script viruses are usually standalone files that can be executed by an interpreter, such as Microsoft's Windows Script Host (.vbs files). A script virus file can be seen as a data file in that it is generally a simple text file, but it usually does not contain other data, and generally has some indicator (such as the .vbs extension) that it is executable. Loveletter is a script virus.

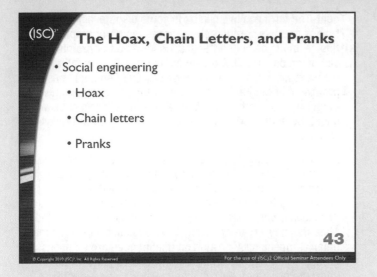

The Hoax, Chain Letters, and Pranks

- Social engineering

  - Hoax

  - Chain letters

  - Pranks

43

- **HOAX/CHAIN LETTERS** – Hoax warnings have an odd double relation to viruses. First off, hoaxes are usually warnings about "new" viruses: new viruses which do not, of course, exist. Second, hoaxes generally carry a directive to the user to forward the warning to all addresses available to that user. Thus, these descendants of chain letters form a kind of self-perpetuating spam. Hoaxes use an odd kind of social engineering, relying on people's naturally gregarious nature and desire to communicate and on a sense of urgency and importance, using the desire that people have to be the first to provide important new information.

- **CHAIN LETTERS** – Chain letters are a form of spam, propagated by well-meaning users in many cases. They can be used to convince people to take inappropriate action, such as sending emails all over the world and leading to the harvesting of email addresses.

- **PRANKS** – Intended as humor, not malice, could still cause problems ("Joke" screen could cover important alert message). Pranks are very much a part of the computer culture. So much so that you can now buy commercially produced joke packages that allow you to perform "Stupid Mac (or PC, or Windows) Tricks." There are innumerable pranks available as shareware. Some make the computer appear to insult the user; some use sound effects or voices; some use special visual effects. A fairly common thread running through most pranks is that the computer is, in some way, nonfunctional. Many pretend to have detected some kind of fault in the computer (and some pretend to rectify such faults, of course making things worse). One entry in the virus field is PARASCAN, the paranoid scanner. It pretends to find large numbers of infected files, although it doesn't actually check for any infections. Generally speaking, pranks that create some kind of announcement are not viral, and viruses that generate a screen or audio display are rare. The distinction between jokes and trojans is harder to make, but pranks are intended for amusement. Joke programs may, of course, result in a denial of service if people find the prank message frightening. One specific type of joke is the "easter egg," a function hidden in a program, and generally accessible only by some hidden sequence of commands. These may be seen as harmless, but note that they do consume resources, even if only disk space, and also make the task of ensuring program integrity much more difficult.

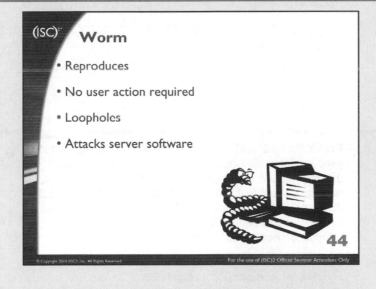

Worm

- Reproduces

- No user action required

- Loopholes

- Attacks server software

44

- **REPRODUCES** – A worm reproduces and spreads, like a virus and unlike other forms of malware. Originally, the distinction was made that worms used networks and communications links to spread, and that a worm, unlike a virus, did not directly attach to an executable file. The origin of the term "worm program" matched that of modern distributed processing experiments: a program with "segments" working on different computers, all communicating over a network (Shoch and Hupp, 1982).

- **NO USER ACTION REQUIRED** – A worm may spread rapidly without requiring any action by the user.

- **LOOPHOLES** – A worm will usually directly probe network-attached computers to exploit a specific weakness or loophole. Generally, worms look for a specific piece of server or utility software that will respond to network queries or activity. Examples of worms are the Internet/Morris Worm of 1988, and more recently Code Red and a number of Linux worms, such as Lion.

- **ATTACKS SERVER SOFTWARE** – This is because many who write worms know that the servers are turned on all the time. This allows the worm to spread at a faster rate. Blaster is possibly one of the most successful worms, due to the fact that the function it used (DCOM) is available on all versions of Windows, desktop as well as server.

REFERENCES:

http://virusall.com/worms.shtml

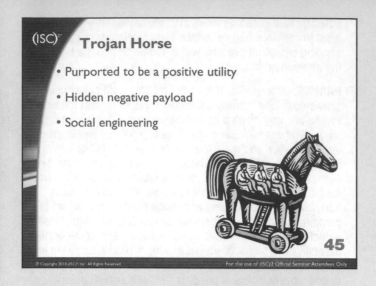

Trojan Horse

- Purported to be a positive utility
- Hidden negative payload
- Social engineering

45

- **TROJAN HORSE –** Trojans, or trojan horse programs, are the largest class of malware. However, the term is subject to much confusion, particularly in relation to computer viruses.

- **PURPORTED TO BE A POSITIVE UTILITY –** A trojan is a program that pretends to do one thing while performing another, unwanted action.

- **HIDDEN NEGATIVE PAYLOAD –** The extent of the "pretense" may vary greatly. Many of the early PC trojans relied merely on the filename and a description on a bulletin board. "Login" trojans, popular among university student mainframe users, mimicked the screen display and the prompts of the normal login program and could, in fact, pass the username and password along to the valid login program at the same time as they stole the user data. Some trojans may contain actual code that does what it is supposed to be doing while performing additional nasty acts that it does not tell you about.

- **SOCIAL ENGINEERING –** A major component of trojan design is the social engineering component. Trojan programs are advertised (in some sense) as having some positive compo-

nent. The term positive can be in some dispute, since many trojans promise pornography or access to pornography, and this seems to be quite effective. However, other promises can be made as well. A recent email virus, in generating its messages, carried a list of a huge variety of subject lines, promising pornography, humor, virus information, an antivirus program, and information about abuse of the recipient's account. Sometimes the message is simply vague and relies on curiosity.

- An additional confusion with viruses involves trojan horse programs that may be spread by email. In years past, a trojan program had to be posted on an electronic bulletin board system or a file archive site. Because of the static posting, a malicious program would soon be identified and eliminated. More recently, trojan programs have been distributed by mass email campaigns, by posting on Usenet newsgroup discussion groups, or through automated distribution agents (bots) on Internet Relay Chat (IRC) channels. Since source identification in these communications channels can be easily hidden, trojan programs can be redistributed in a number of disguises, and specific identification of a malicious program has become much more difficult.

- Some data security writers consider that a virus is simply a specific example of the class of trojan horse programs. There is some validity to this usage, since a virus is an unknown quantity that is hidden and transmitted along with a legitimate disk or program, and any program can be turned into a trojan by infecting it with a virus. However, the term virus more properly refers to the added, infectious code rather than the virus/target combination. Therefore, the term trojan refers to a deliberately misleading or modified program that does not reproduce itself.

REFERENCES:

http://www.frame4.com/content/pubs/comp_trojans.txt

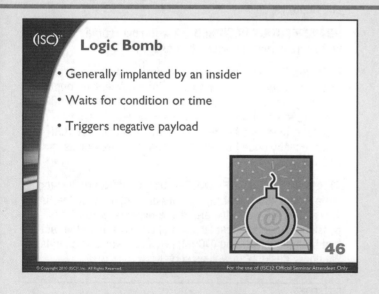

Logic Bomb

- Generally implanted by an insider
- Waits for condition or time
- Triggers negative payload

46

- **GENERALLY IMPLANTED BY AN INSIDER –** A logic bomb is generally implanted in, or coded as, part of an application under development or maintenance. Unlike a RAT or trojan, it is difficult to implant a logic bomb after the fact, unless it is during program maintenance. A trojan or a virus may contain a logic bomb as part of the payload. A logic bomb involves no reproduction, no social engineering.

- **WAITS FOR CONDITION OR TIME –** This is sometimes a date or event, such as deleting a certain file.

- **TRIGGERS NEGATIVE PAYLOAD –** The payload can be almost anything that can be inserted into the system.

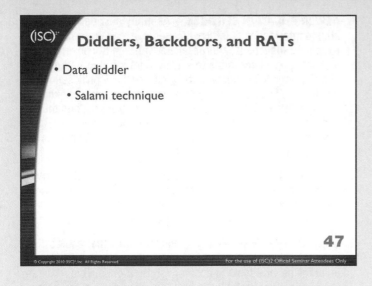

Diddlers, Backdoors, and RATs

- Data diddler
  - Salami technique

47

- **DATA DIDDLER** – Payload in a Trojan or virus that deliberately corrupts data, generally by small increments over time. Because of incremental changes, it is difficult to determine which data is corrupted. Because modification happens over time, backups may also be corrupted. The data diddler is a particularly invidious type of malware. Also, while it was relatively rare in the early days of malicious software, experts have recently seen a rise in the number of instances of this payload.

  - **SALAMI TECHNIQUE** – One example of a data diddler is the salami attack. The analogy is shaving a thin slice of meat that may not be noticed by the owner from a large salami. One notorious salami attack was accomplished by writing a program that accumulated the extra fractions of a cent (smallest level of U.S. currency) that were calculated during bank interest computations and previously just discarded through a rounding-down process. This attack placed those fractions of a cent into a separate bank account where it quickly grew to a large sum of money.

Protection From Malicious Code

- Policies
- Tools
- Monitoring
  - Operation
    - Egress scanning
  - Integrity checkers

48

Make the effectiveness of the system a prime consideration. Do not place undue emphasis on ease of use or pretty system interfaces that mask a lack of basic operational effectiveness.

- **MONITORING** – Automated scanning is a good first line of defense, but is much less effective than manual scanning. Manual scanning should be done regularly as a backup.

  - **OPERATION** – Regularly check that your anti-malware systems are, in fact, operating. Many users like to rely on disinfection to deal with malware: It seems a quick and easy solution. Note, however, that disinfection is not always effective, and, in many cases, is not possible. The preferred and safer method of dealing with malware is to delete all malware found, and replace infected items from a safe backup source. Activity monitoring and auditing is particularly important on communications systems. Monitoring of open ports and outgoing email may not prevent you from becoming infected, but it will often point out that you are infected or have a RAT or zombie installed.

    - **EGRESS SCANNING** – Note the importance of egress scanning. Certain types of traffic or volumes of outbound traffic may indicate the presence of malware, even if regular scanning software does not detect it on individual machines.

  - **INTEGRITY CHECKERS** – An integrity checker will only work if the data is correct to begin with! The integrity checker compares current file sizes and executables with stored values. When a new executable tries to run, or a file has changed size inexplicably, the integrity checker will notify the user and possibly quarantine the suspicious activity.

- **POLICIES** – Effective and workable policies are one of the best protections against malware of all kinds. Most malware is permitted entry, or even aided, by users running software from questionable sources. Make specific checks of your operating system, server, and protective software. Keeping patched and updated is an important part of malware protection. Patch management is, itself, an important matter and will be discussed in the Operations Security domain.

- **TOOLS** – There are numerous commercial and open source anti-malware tools available today. The important issues are to keep the signature files up to date and ensure that scans of incoming traffic and the system are done. When reviewing anti-malware systems, remember what the basic purpose is.

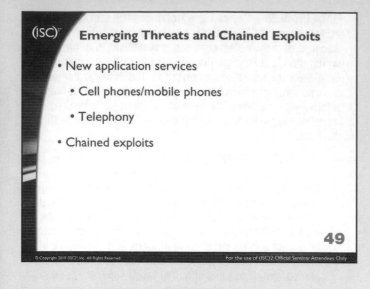

Emerging Threats and Chained Exploits

- New application services
  - Cell phones/mobile phones
  - Telephony
- Chained exploits

49

- **NEW APPLICATION SERVICES –** As many new devices are able to interface with internal systems, access internal data, execute transactions, and/or take advantage of convergence technologies, new threats to systems are starting to emerge. The systems developer, architect, and security professional will have to ensure that these devices do not open backdoors into systems or data, that any changes or transactions they perform meet with the integrity and confidentiality rules, and that there is enough bandwidth and capacitance to support multiple new connections.

  - **DATA PRIVACY –** Access to data over these devices may not be secure according to current or future data privacy regulations. Also data stored on these devices may be vulnerable to compromise if the device is lost or stolen.

- **CHAINED EXPLOITS –** Many attacks are now the result of a combination of attacks merged together. Attackers may leverage several tools to accomplish their ends. This requires the applications architect to be even more diligent to ensure that the application is robust enough and resilient enough to withstand a multi-faceted attack.

Domain Agenda

- Overview of Applications Security

- System Life Cycle Security

- Applications Security Issues

- **Database Security**

50

For the use of (ISC)2 Official Seminar Attendees Only

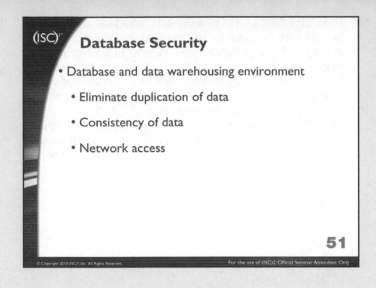

- **DATABASE AND DATA WAREHOUSING ENVIRONMENT –** Databases form a major part of today's field of information processing. Confidentiality of certain types of data and the ready availability of certain databases are frequent concerns, but in the normal course of events, integrity of the data is probably of greatest concern to those involved with database management and administration. The combining of data from many databases into one larger database (a data warehouse) for the purposes of research, trend, and pattern identification, and customer service is a new area of risk. The use of a data warehouse may lead to privacy concerns.

- Databases provide exceptional benefits to an organization through providing consistency of data. Since all the data can be stored in one place that is accessible through a network to anyone with access to the database, this saves the duplicate storage of data in multiple locations and thereby greater consistency or accuracy of data.

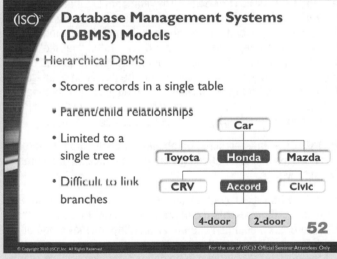

a process called normalization. A hierarchical database is a single tree of data where the data is structured in tiers or levels of information – each tier being a more detailed level of the data represented by the higher level.

- **PARENT/CHILD RELATIONSHIPS –** The data is structured so that the data under a higher level would be known as the child, whereas the higher level data represents the parent. A child may only have one parent, but a parent may have many children.

- **LIMITED TO A SINGLE TREE –** Each database is a self-contained unit and is separate from any other database. When data must be retrieved from several databases, this requires precise coding and addressing to access the intended data.

- **DIFFICULT TO LINK BRANCHES –** Since each branch is related to the tree through the parent, and is not linked to any other branch, it requires the program to move up through the branch to the common parent before data from several branches can be combined.

- A directory tree is an example of a hierarchical system. Accessing data in a hierarchical system requires mapping out the route to the data piece-by-piece through each layer of the data (or by looping through the parent-child relationships) rather than directly via joins and indices in an RDBMS model.

- **HIERARCHICAL DBMS –** The hierarchical model is the oldest of the database models and is derived from the Information Management Systems of the 1950s and 1960s. It allowed data to be stored in a manner that grouped all related data, but it was cumbersome to link some data fields together. The reason for the limitation on linking was due to the fact that data was often stored in sequential devices such as tape and searching for an additional link might have meant re-reading the entire file. Even today, there are hierarchical legacy systems that are still being operated by banks, insurance companies, government agencies, and hospitals.

  - **STORES RECORDS IN A SINGLE TABLE –** Relational databases tend to separate data into several tables using

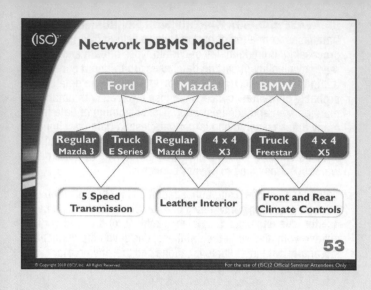

- **NETWORK DBMS** – The network data model introduced in 1971 is an extended form of the hierarchical database structure. "Network DBMS" does not refer to the fact that the database is stored on the network, but rather to the method by which data is linked to other data. The network model represents its data in the form of a network of records and "sets" (groups of related records) that are related to each other, forming a network of links. Compared with the hierarchical model on the previous slide, this allowed faster linking of data elements but is not commonly used today in favor of Relational Databases.

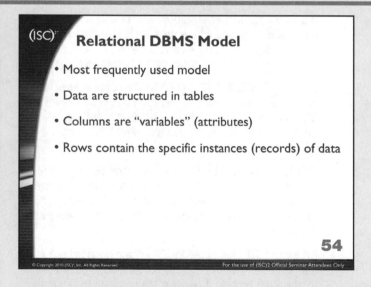

- **MOST FREQUENTLY USED** – The relational database is so frequently used that many people think it is the only database model. In addition, because of its traditionally tabular form, some people believe that any structured "flat file" is a relational database. In fact, proper relational databases have a formal definition which assists with the provision of integrity of the data. Part of the formal definitions used in relational databases come from the Clark/Wilson integrity model discussed in the Security Architecture and Design domain.

- **TABLES** – In a relational database model, the data is stored in two-dimensional relations (or tables) that consist of columns and rows.

- **COLUMNS** – Each column is a descriptor of the database record – it represents the characteristics or attributes of the record. Each column is defined according to what range of data would be allowed to be stored in the column. Just as in a spreadsheet, a column can be defined, for example, as a "currency" (with an indicator for a dollar or euro, decimal places, and way to depict negative values) or "date" and the acceptable date format.

- **ROWS** – Each row in the table is a record, such as a customer record, employee record, etc.

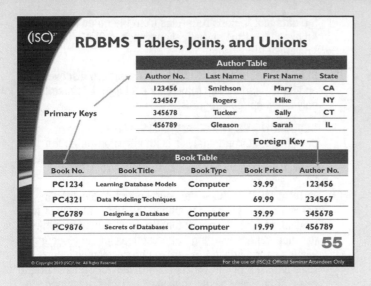

55

- **JOINS & UNIONS** – In order to connect several tables together, the user of the database will link two tables by some value. The querying of multiple tables for a result is a join. A

Union places the further requirement on a join to have matching data types and attributes.

- **PERFORMING JOINS** – The usual way to perform joins is comparing a **PRIMARY KEY** and a **FOREIGN KEY**.

  - **PRIMARY KEY** – A Primary Key uniquely identifies each row and assists with indexing the table by the DBMS. The rules of Entity Integrity require the primary key to be a unique and "not null" value.

  - **FOREIGN KEY** – When the primary key value is in another table, where it is not the primary key, this is referred to as a "foreign key." The rules of Referential Integrity require any foreign key to be a legitimate value in the table where the primary key resides.

- In this example: The Author Table has a unique attribute of author number (primary key). The Books Table has the author number as an attribute (foreign key). A database query could be constructed to join the tables together to list the author of each book.

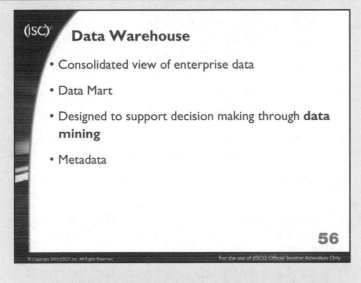

56

- **CONSOLIDATED VIEW OF ENTERPRISE DATA** – Originally, the distinguishing characteristic of a data warehouse was that a regular database was used in daily operations and contained operational data and a data warehouse was a database used for analytical purposes. A data warehouse combines all of the data from various databases into one large data container. Recently, some enterprises have been attempting to build their operational databases on data warehouse concepts.

- **DATA MART** – A database or collection of databases designed to help managers make strategic decisions about their business. Whereas a data warehouse combines databases across an entire enterprise, data marts are usually smaller and focus on a particular subject or department. Some data marts, called dependent data marts, are subsets of larger data warehouses.

- **DESIGNED TO SUPPORT DECISION MAKING THROUGH DATA MINING** – A well-designed and implemented data warehouse can be used to:

  - Understand business trends and make better forecasting decisions.

  - Bring better products to market in a timelier manner.

  - Analyze daily sales information and make quick decisions that can significantly affect a company's performance.

- Data warehousing can be a key differentiator in many different industries. At present, some of the most popular data warehouse applications include:

  - Sales and marketing analysis across all industries.

  - Inventory turn and product tracking in manufacturing.

  - Category management, vendor analysis, and marketing program effectiveness analysis in retail.

  - Profitable lane or driver risk analysis in transportation.

  - Profitability analysis or risk assessment in banking.

  - Claims analysis or fraud detection in insurance.

- **DATA MINING** – Data mining is the searching of the data in a data warehouse to extract valuable information from the data in the warehouse. Proper data mining will reveal trends, patterns, or unique characteristics from the data that can be used for further benefit. For example a medical data warehouse may contain data that can be used to learn patterns about disease, a commercial data warehouse may yield data about buying trends and customer preferences.

- **METADATA** – Metadata is the term used to describe the knowledge gleaned from data mining. It is, quite simply, data about the data in the data warehouse. Metadata is the gold that can be gathered from looking at the data that, if used properly, may assist an organization in reaching its objectives through better marketing, faster research, etc.

REFERENCES:

http://www.dwinfocenter.org/

Knowledge Discovery in Databases (KDD)

- Methods of identifying patterns in data
- KDD and AI techniques
  - Probabilistic models
  - Statistical approach
  - Classification approach
  - Deviation and trend analysis
  - Neural networks
  - Expert system approach
  - Hybrid approach

57

- **METHODS OF IDENTIFYING PATTERNS IN DATA** – The knowledge-discovery process takes the data from data mining and accurately transforms it into useful and understandable information. This information is usually not retrievable through standard retrieval techniques but can be uncovered through the use of artificial intelligence (AI) techniques.

- **SOME KDD METHODS THAT USE ARTIFICIAL INTELLIGENCE (AI) TECHNIQUES -**

  - **PROBABILISTIC MODELS** – Useful for applications involving uncertainty, such as those used in planning and control systems.

  - **STATISTICAL APPROACH** – Used to generalize patterns in the data and to construct rules from the noted patterns. An example of the statistical approach is OLAP (On-Line Analytical Processing).

- **CLASSIFICATION APPROACH** – Uses pattern discovery and data cleaning and may reduce a large database to only a few specific records.

- **DEVIATION AND TREND ANALYSIS** – An example of deviation and trend analysis is an intrusion-detection system that filters a large volume of data so that only the pertinent data is analyzed.

- **NEURAL NETWORKS** – The neural network is helpful in detecting the associations among the input patterns or relationships. Note, however, that the system may be subject to "superstitious learning." Superstitious learning occurs when a neural network is misled into developing incorrect rules or assumptions. Since a neural network tries to create rules for behavior based on past experience, sustained abnormal activity may actually "teach" the system to develop incorrect rules. Organized data nodes are arranged in layers, and links between the nodes have specific weighting classifications based on repeated use of links.

- **EXPERT SYSTEM APPROACH** – Uses a knowledge base (rule base) and an algorithm based on the operation of a human expert. In the expert system approach, the knowledge base could be the human experience that is available in an organization. Since the system reacts to a set of rules, if the rules are faulty, the response will also be faulty.

- **HYBRID APPROACH** – Combines two or more of the techniques covered above.

Database Security Issues

- Inference
- Aggregation
- Unauthorized access
- Improper modification of data
- Unauthorized data mining

- Query attacks
- Bypass attacks
- Interception of data
- Web security

58

- **DATABASE SECURITY ISSUES** – Database security is a specialized field. Some security issues are extremely resistant to amelioration, such as:

  - **INFERENCE** – The ability of user with limited (unauthorized) access to deduce (infer) information from observing authorized information.

  - **AGGREGATION** – The ability to combine data classified at a lower level in order to learn something classified at a higher level. A particular type of aggregation attack is the small/multiple query attack, where the user is permitted to access small amounts of data and then is able to subvert the system controls that did not let them see data classified at a higher level by collating the data.

- **UNAUTHORIZED ACCESS** – Access to data not approved by the information owner.

- **IMPROPER MODIFICATION OF DATA** – Changing data at an unauthorized time or in an unauthorized manner.

- **UNAUTHORIZED DATA MINING** – Data mining is the analysis of data in a database or data warehouse that reveals hidden values in the data. This can be used by unauthorized persons to gather data that they should not have had access to leading to an inference or aggregation attack.

- **QUERY ATTACKS** – By asking or querying the database in a round-about manner, rather than simply and directly, queries that would otherwise be restricted via access control are permitted.

- **BYPASS ATTACKS** – Bypass attacks take advantage of multiple paths to the information. The application may be secured by access controls, but if the data file is stored on the disk in clear text, the information may be accessible via system utilities.

- **INTERCEPTION OF DATA** – Capturing the data when it is moving between databases or applications.

- **WEB SECURITY** – Organizations frequently suffer from security breaches related to the poor configuration of their networks and databases. Placing a database containing sensitive information where it might be accessed directly through a web server has resulted in many serious incidents.

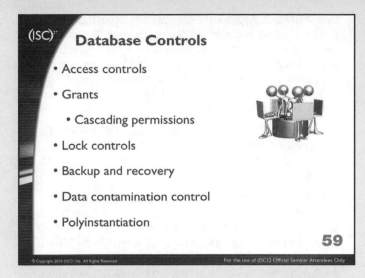

Database Controls

- Access controls
- Grants
  - Cascading permissions
- Lock controls
- Backup and recovery
- Data contamination control
- Polyinstantiation

59

- **ACCESS CONTROLS –** Access controls for databases range from simple password protection to complex user/role structure. The focus is to provide security mechanisms that prevent unauthorized outsiders and insiders from attempting to exceed their authority. Security recommendations now state that individual database user accounts be created for each individual accessing the database to allow for accountability and logging.

- **GRANTS –** Grants security is a form of access control wherein each user is given access to specific data objects using various privilege types. "Object privileges" assign the right to perform a particular operation on a specific object. "System privileges" cover many areas of access with a broad brush with grants such as "select any table." "Role security" allows the user to gather related grants into a collection. Since the role is a predefined collection of privileges grouped together, privileges are easier to assign to users, since granting them access to a role gives them access to all the privileges associated with that role.

  - **CASCADING PERMISSIONS –** Occur as an individual grants access to others. If the "grantor's" permissions are removed, the permissions of everyone below him or her in the access cascade will also be removed.

- **LOCK CONTROLS –** Used to control read and write access to specific rows of data in relational systems, or objects in object-oriented systems. Locks ensure that only one user at a time can alter data. Better programming, logic, and testing reduce deadlocking problems. When databases must be shared, as in OLTP systems, simple access control is not sufficient and dynamic lock controls that change with the state of the system or record must be used instead. These allow multiple people to view a given record, but allow only the first, for example, to make a change or update. At times the controls must be more complex and adaptable (e.g., allowing multiple updates, but only within the "window" of, for example, stock available).

- **BACKUP AND RECOVERY –** Data retention policy, BCP, and business rules will define what level of data loss is acceptable. Internal database backup, checkpoints, and journals will limit loss due to system failure. External backups will limit loss due to corruption and hardware failure.

- **DATA CONTAMINATION CONTROL –** Protecting data from improper modification can be accomplished through the enforcement of access controls, edit checks in the front-end application, or through the efforts of the DBMS to prohibit a change that should not be permitted by the database structure or schema.

- **POLYINSTANTIATION –** A control used to protect multi-level databases from inference and aggregation by allowing for two values to exist for a single field that correspond to two different user clearances.

REFERENCES:

Burleson, Donald, Control access with Oracle grant security, http://www.build-erau.com.au/architect/database/soa/Control-access-with-Oracle-grant-security/0,339024547,320276631,00.htm

Chapple, Mike; Access Controls in SQL: Your Guide to Databases; http://databases.about.com/od/security/a/accesscontrols.htm

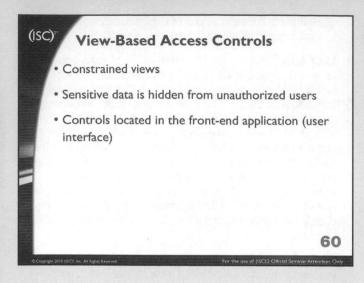

View-Based Access Controls

- Constrained views
- Sensitive data is hidden from unauthorized users
- Controls located in the front-end application (user interface)

60

© Copyright 2010 (ISC)², Inc. All Rights Reserved.   For the use of (ISC)2 Official Seminar Attendees Only

- **CONSTRAINED VIEWS** – An example of a "constrained user interface" is discussed in the Access Controls Domain. In the database world, "views" are defined as something that will filter the data available to users according to their access permissions and "need-to-know." A "view" is really a logical subset of the data – that portion of the data in the database that is available to the user.

- **SENSITIVE DATA IS HIDDEN FROM UNAUTHORIZED USERS** – Views are "windows" into the contents of the database. In other words, they allow you to create ways to look at data contained within a database.

- **CONTROLS LOCATED IN THE FRONT-END APPLICATION (USER INTERFACE)** – In most cases, the application that calls to the database management system will call a pre-set or predefined view. Since the query engine usually has free rein over the database, controls must be in place so that a user cannot bypass the front-end and directly access and manipulate the data.

Transaction Controls

- Content-based access control
- Commit statement
- Three-phase commit
- Database rollback
- Journals/logs
- Error controls

61

© Copyright 2010 (ISC)², Inc. All Rights Reserved.   For the use of (ISC)2 Official Seminar Attendees Only

- **CONTENT-BASED ACCESS CONTROLS** – These allow users to specify access control policy based on object features. They automatically apply policy to new objects created, allow users to share content on the Internet, and maintain privacy and safety. Content-based access control systems are based on analyzing the data itself and determining whether the user can (or should) have access to that data. A web-filtering program is an example of a content-based access control system. It may, for example, analyze the text for suspicious words or language that the user is not allowed to view based on policy. These systems are substance based rather than table- or field-based access-control implementations. Content-based access control is more granular than the access provided by a traditional reference monitor and is provided through software code that examines the data and makes an access decision. This process is known as an "arbiter" program.

- **COMMIT STATEMENT** – This writes any and all changes that have occurred to the data during the current transaction to the database, releases any locks that have been placed on data, and destroys any result sets that have been returned from a query. When managing changes to a database, individual transactions (a logical operation) can be executed together as a group or individually. When a transaction changes data, it is done in isolation from other transactions, and when it's done, the data is "committed" – which means that the change is now

available to other transactions. For a group of transactions to be handled together as a unit, they must be contained within a logical transaction (indicated by a "begin" statement, the individual statements, an "end" statement, and then a "commit." Note that an "end" can imply a "commit" or vice versa, depending on the database). The session has a view of the database isolated from other sessions during a transaction that may be a single statement affecting every row in a table, or a group of several statements affecting a few rows of a few tables. When the session commits its changes, they are visible to other sessions. The database needs to manage the degree of "locking" during access to data which is part of another uncommitted transaction. Note as well that there are a variety of levels of "lock isolation" that a database is able to implement.

- **THE THREE-PHASE COMMIT PROTOCOL (3PC)** – A distributed algorithm that allows all nodes in a distributed system to agree to commit a transaction. This is also known as a non-blocking protocol. "Two-phase commit" is a blocking protocol – vulnerability. The 3PC places an upper bound on the amount of time required before a transaction commits or aborts, thus ensuring that a resource lock will timeout. A three phase commit is provided when the client requests permission to make a change to a database, the database approving the change but not making the change until the client returns a reply indicating the transaction completed correctly.

- **DATABASE ROLLBACK** – Cleanly returning to a previous state. If some part (but not a whole) of a transaction is submitted to the database, the rollback mechanism will point to the last whole transaction (the last commit point).

- **JOURNALS/LOGS** – A transaction-by-transaction listing of what has occurred in the database. These logs are critical to the rollback process.

- **ERROR CONTROLS** – Typically about user input error, these check input data to ensure it follows the database rules (as per the schema) prior to making the change to the database. Some errors would be caused by violations of entity or relational integrity. Errors may also be caused by errors in SQL code or select statements.

REFERENCES:
http://ei.cs.vt.edu/~cs5204/sp99/distributedDBMS/sreenu/3pc.html

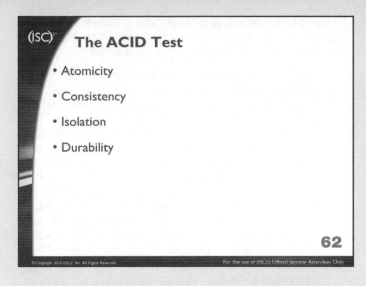

The ACID Test

- Atomicity
- Consistency
- Isolation
- Durability

62

- **ATOMICITY** – All the parts of a transaction's execution that are either all committed or all rolled back. Essentially, all changes take effect, or none do.

- **CONSISTENCY** – The point at which the database is transformed from one valid state to another valid state, remaining compliant with the rules of the database.

- **ISOLATION** – Guarantees that the results of a transaction are invisible to other transactions until the transaction is complete.

- **DURABILITY** – Ensures that the results of the completed transaction can survive future system and media failures.

Database Interface Languages/Methods

- Structured Query Language (SQL)
- Open Database Connectivity (ODBC)
- Extensible Markup Language (XML)
- Object Linking and Embedding (OLE)
- Active X Data Object (ADO)
- Dynamic data

63

- **DATABASE INTERFACE LANGUAGES** – Rather than having specific libraries written for each programming language that might need to access a database, interface languages provide standard "calls" that can be used from within any programming system and for a variety of database management systems. This eases the complexity of programming with databases and also provides a measure of interchangeability if the database engine must be altered, or the user application is to be applied to a different database.

- **STRUCTURED QUERY LANGUAGE (SQL)** – SQL, the ANSI standard, is the root language for interaction with data, including interaction with the database design, or schema. SQL has been extended by vendors to include PL/SQL and T-SQL among others. The current Standard (SQL:2003) includes extensions for increased functionality, such as Call-Level Interface, Management of External Data, Object Language Bindings, Information and Definition Schemas, Routines and Types for the Java Programming Language, and XML-Related Specifications.

- **OPEN DATABASE CONNECTIVITY (ODBC)** – ODBC is an application programming interface that allows a variety of programming languages to connect to databases. ODBC acts as an interpreter. This has been traditionally implemented as a closed-source DLL (dynamic-link library) in the Microsoft operating systems. An alternative open source connector is iODBC (Independent ODBC) which is designed to be language, platform, and database independent.

  - A DLL is an executable file that contains a function that can be called from multiple programs.

- **EXTENSIBLE MARKUP LANGUAGE (XML)** – XML defines the nature or characteristics of the data and what each piece of data means or represents. It is used in conjunction with other languages, such as HTML. A number of XML-derived languages have security implications for web applications.

- **OBJECT LINKING AND EMBEDDING** – Allows linking and embedding data from one (Microsoft) application to others. For example, this would allow a Word document to "host" embedded data from other applications such as PowerPoint, flash animations, and pie charts.

- **ACTIVE X DATA OBJECT** – Part of Microsoft's COM architecture, ADO allows a developer to access many different data sources and formats through an Application Program Interface (API).

- **DYNAMIC DATA** – Dynamic data allows the developer to write programs that will interface easily with underlying databases using LINQ to SQL. This framework allows the validation of data input and management of create, read, update, and delete (CRUD) permissions.

REFERENCES:
http://docs.openlinksw.com/mt/iodbc.html.
http://msdn.microsoft.com/en-us/library/1ez7dh12.aspx
http://www.asp.net/dynamicdata/

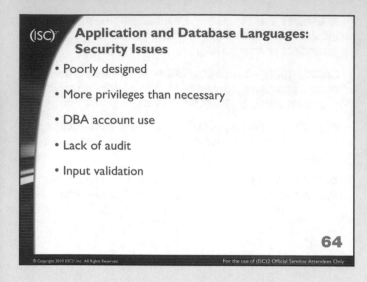

- Applications introduce some of the most common database attack avenues.

- **POORLY-DESIGNED APPLICATIONS** – Poorly-designed applications that are available to the Internet provide a pathway for an unlimited number of malicious users to access sensitive data.

- **MORE PRIVILEGES THAN NECESSARY** – An application that accesses the database with any more privileges than those required to manipulate the data in any way other than that intended subjects the data to unauthorized exposure. Databases and applications that do not audit access to elevated privileges or sensitive data leave no trail that exposure has occurred.

- **DBA ACCOUNT USE** – When an application uses elevated priv-

ileges to the database (it is not unusual to find an application that uses a DBA account that owns all application-database objects to operate), the entire database is at risk.

- It is, therefore, important to review all applications to discover how the most stringent security can be applied. Make sure to review the authentication method that the application uses to connect to the database. The authentication used must meet all the requirements for that method; that is, passwords must meet complexity, expiration, and history requirements, be encrypted when stored and transmitted, and credentials must be stored in a secure, restricted location. Review database accounts used by the application to access the database and determine whether the minimum privileges required have been granted. Applications may often unnecessarily require elevated privileges. Any stated requirement for elevated privileges should be verified. Determine and set application protections to prevent the return or display of unauthorized database information, such as product and version, table names, or other database object information when queried or when errors occur.

- **LACK OF AUDIT** – All changes to a database should be recorded and a journal retained that records both the change made and the originator of the change.

- **INPUT VALIDATION** – Where input validation does not occur, the database process can be compromised, and this can lead to attack on the host system (i.e., XSS and SQL Injection).

REFERENCES:
Database Security Technical Implementation Guide V8 R1; 19 September 2007; Department of Defense Information Systems Agency; http://iase.disa.mil/stigs/index.html

---

Domain Summary

- Overview of Applications Security

- System Life Cycle Security

- Applications Security Issues

- Database Security

- Here are the topics you have covered in this domain. At this point, you should understand this material and be able to apply it.

Security Transcends Technology
(ISC)²
© Copyright 2010 (ISC)², Inc. All Rights Reserved.
66

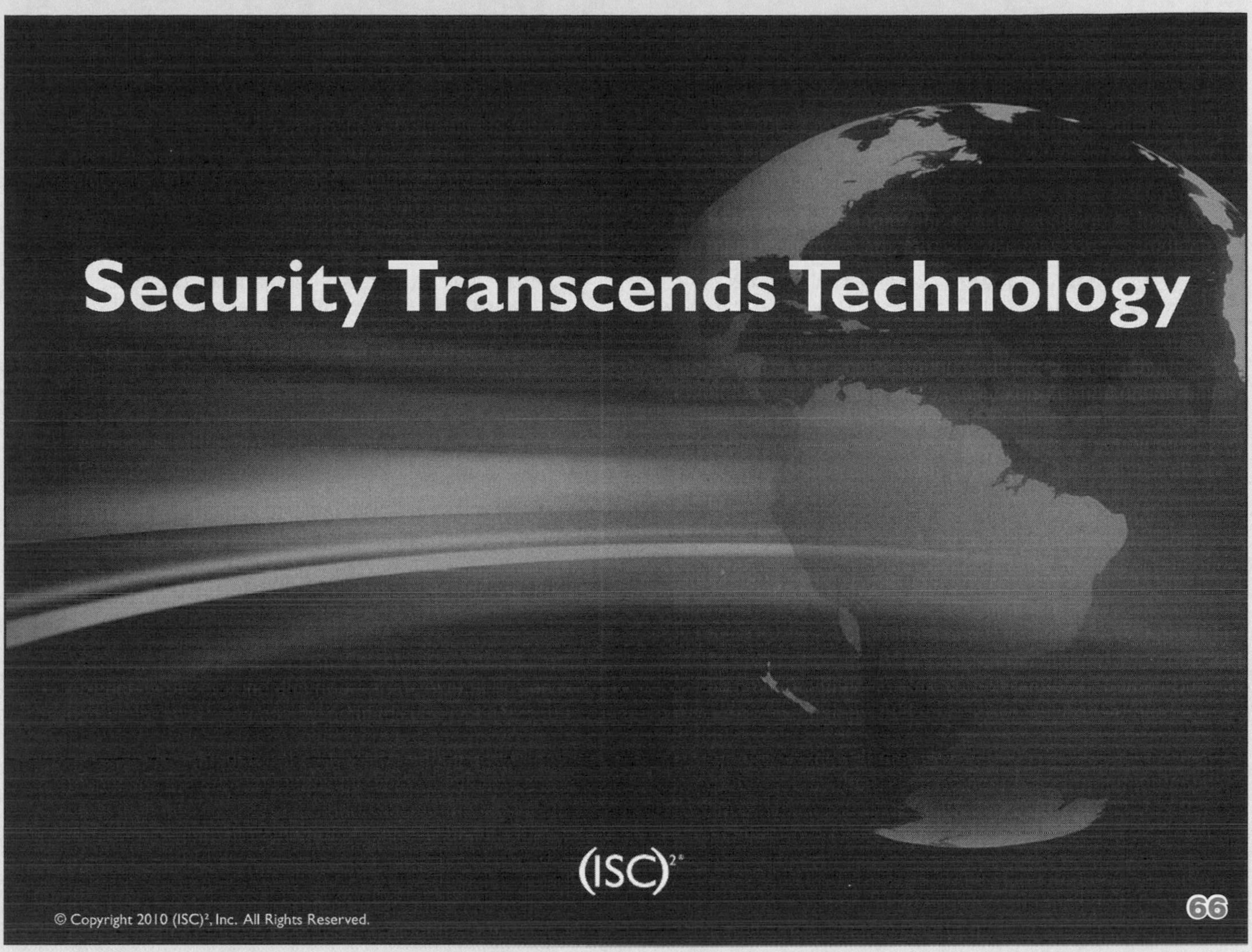

Review Questions

APPLICATION DEVELOPMENT SECURITY

1. Which software development method focuses on preventing defects by emphasizing writing the code correctly the first time?

   A. The spiral model
   B. The waterfall model
   C. The clean-room model
   D. The prototyping model

2. What does "separation of duties" mean in software development guidelines for transaction processing?

   A. There should be two different people writing each transaction to ensure it is secure.
   B. Sensitive transactions must be designed to require a minimum of dual control or the approval of another party.
   C. Sensitive transactions must be designed so that an internal or external person cannot change data.
   D. The software developer cannot be the same person as the one approving the software for release to production.

3. How can a buffer overflow vulnerability be prevented?

   A. By using blacklists that contain all characters that can be potentially harmful and not allowing those into the function.
   B. By installing patches to fix buffer overflow vulnerabilities.
   C. By programming with C++ instead of C because C++ is not vulnerable to buffer overflows, unlike C.
   D. By using strongly typed programming languages, implementing bounds and input checking, and using safe functions.

4. How can the use of escaping prevent Structured Query Language (SQL) injections?

   A. By allowing the application to "escape" – stop running, if an attack occurs, thus preventing the attack from succeeding.
   B. By "translating" all input from the user to the specific character schemes supported by the database management system (DBMS), so it will interpret all user input as merely text.
   C. By only allowing parameterized queries to run on the system, and blocking other queries from running.
   D. By not allowing the input to include the "ESC" command, which can cause the attacker to take over the application and the database management system (DBMS).

5. How is an interpreted language application different from a compiled language application?

   A. Interpreted languages do not require the entire source code to be compiled to machine code before the application can run.
   B. Interpreted applications are limited to a specific platform; compiled applications can run on any platform.
   C. Compiled applications are limited to a specific platform; interpreted applications can run on any platform.
   D. Interpreted applications execute faster than compiled applications.

6. Which of the following statements is true?

   A. Common object request broker architecture (CORBA) provides the definition of the extensible markup language (XML)-based information that can be used for exchanging structured and typed information between peers in a decentralized, distributed environment.
   B. Distributed component object model (DCOM) is a Microsoft-only protocol and runs over remote procedures call (RPC).
   C. Simple object access protocol (SOAP) requires ActiveX to run as the underlying framework.
   D. RPC provides comprehensive security capabilities protecting DCOM implementation over it from attacks and misuse.

7. Why is it important to build security into the application as opposed to just adding it later?

   A. It is not – both approaches are equally appropriate.
   B. It conforms to the concept of "secure by obscurity," which provides security by obscuring it within the application itself.
   C. Building security into the application provides more layers of security and can be harder to circumvent.
   D. Building security into the application can reduce development time, allowing the application to be released to production sooner.

8. **What is a common issue to consider regarding cryptographic protection of data?**

   A. Using cryptographic data protection controls needs to also include appropriate key creation, storage, and management.

   B. It requires getting licenses for the cryptographic algorithms.

   C. Using cryptographic data protection controls requires expensive hardware security modules (HSM) to store the keys securely.

   D. Smart cards are required to store the keys securely.

9. **What is the goal of software configuration management (SCM) as it applies to application security?**

   A. SCM controls software by managing the versions of all components and the relations between them.

   B. SCM ensures that software configuration is up-to-date, accurate, and that only authorized software versions are used.

   C. SCM is part of configuration management, in general, and it integrates with and relies on change management.

   D. SCM aims to prevent unauthorized individuals from accessing and making unauthorized modifications and potentially malicious changes to code.

10. **How can a statement of work (SOW) protect against software development project risks?**

    A. A SOW includes a risk analysis which helps identify the potential risk elements the project may be exposed to.

    B. A SOW includes a qualitative risk analysis which helps identify the potential risk elements the project may be exposed to.

    C. A SOW lists agreed-upon objectives and deliverables, which could prevent scope creep.

    D. A SOW defines the business terms of the project engagement, including fees, staff, and legal terms of the engagement.

11. **What are the reasons testing systems with live data or testing in a production environment is not recommended?**

    A. If the system processes confidential data, the testing process may result in violations of privacy.

    B. The testing process might not provide realistic results, since the live data cannot be sanitized.

    C. Based on the concept of "need to know," the developers are not authorized to view live data.

    D. Testing with live data violates privacy regulatory requirements.

12. **What is the purpose of the Capability Maturity Model Integration for Development (CMMI-DEV)?**

    A. CMMI-DEV measures the maturity and capability levels of the organization's development processes.

    B. CMMI-DEV measures the maturity and capability levels of system integration in the organization.

    C. CMMI-DEV helps organizations improve their development and maintenance processes for both products and services.

    D. CMMI-DEV is a process improvement maturity model for the development of products and services.

13. **Which of the following is one of the key values of extreme programming?**

    A. Courage – to tell the truth about progress and estimates, and to fear nothing because no one works alone.

    B. Pair programming – all production code is written by two programmers working together on a single computer.

    C. Honesty – to tell the truth, the whole truth, and nothing but the truth, about the development process.

    D. Transparency – acceptance tests are run often and the scores are published.

14. **What is the PRIMARY security issue with application backdoors?**

    A. They are a form of malicious code that can allow an attacker to gain improper access to the system.

    B. Backdoors are planted in code by malicious programmers to allow them to circumvent the system's access controls.

    C. Backdoors are legitimate development tools that should be removed from the system before release to production to avoid their abuse by unauthorized users or intruders.

    D. Backdoors can lead to denial of service if a hacker attacks the backdoor vulnerability.

15. **After being closed for the weekend, Acme Corporation finds on Monday morning that all of its servers are running slowly. The CPU utilizations are showing 100 percent utilization. Network traffic is also exceptionally high. At the close of business on Friday, all systems were behaving normal. Closer examination is likely to reveal which of the following infestations?**

    A. Data diddler

    B. Distributed denial of service (DDoS)

    C. Virus

    D. Worm

16. The primary key is used to uniquely identify records in a database. By adding additional variables to the primary key, two items with the same identifier can be differentiated. This is often used to prevent inference attacks. Which of the following is best described by this scenario?

    A. Polymorphism
    B. Polyalphabetic
    C. Polyinstantiation
    D. Polyvariabolic

17. A database that uses pre-defined groupings of data that can only be accessed based upon a user's authorization level, uses which of the following access control models or concepts?

    A. Role-based access control
    B. Database view control
    C. Mandatory access control
    D. Non-discretionary access control

18. Which of the following database attacks describes an attack where the perpetrator uses information gained through authorized activity to reach conclusions relating to unauthorized data?

    A. Unauthorized access attack
    B. Bypass attack
    C. SQL attack
    D. Inference attack

19. One of the most significant differences between the software development life cycle (SDLC) and the system life cycle (SLC) is that the SDLC does not include which of the following phases?

    A. Post-development operation and maintenance
    B. Startup/requirements
    C. Development/construction
    D. Operational testing

20. A corporation has created a new application for tracking customer information as well as its product database. Of the following individuals, who should be given full access and control over this application?

    A. The application owner
    B. No one
    C. Security administrator
    D. Application developer

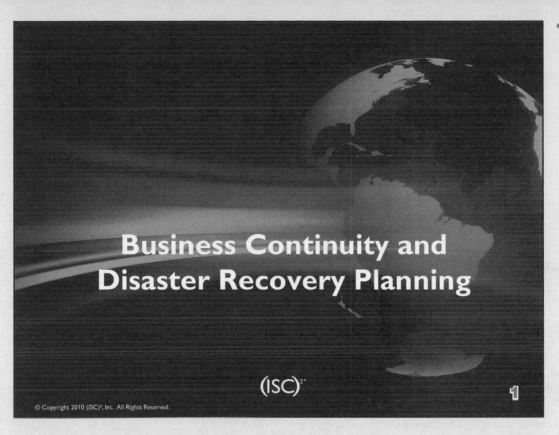

Business Continuity and Disaster Recovery Planning

(ISC)²

1

From the CISSP® CBK®: "The Business Continuity Planning (BCP) and Disaster Recovery Planning (DRP) domain addresses the preparatory activities, processes, and practices required to ensure the preservation of the business in the face of major disruptions to normal business operations. BCP and DRP involve the identification, selection, implementation, testing, and updating of processes and specific actions necessary to prudently protect critical business processes from the effects of major system and network disruptions and to ensure the timely restoration of business operations if significant disruptions occur."

(ISC)²

Domain Agenda

- **Business Continuity Management (BCM) Project Planning**

- Understanding the Organization

- Recovery Strategy Selection

- Creating the Plan(s)

- Developing and Implementing Response

- Testing, Update, and Maintenance of the Plan

2

This is the agenda of topics to be covered in this domain.

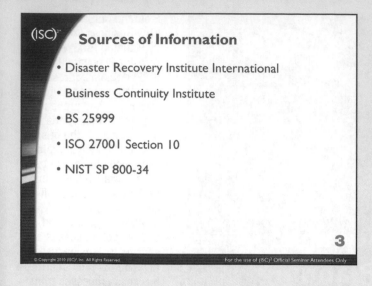

- In 2003, the leaders in Business Continuity joined together to create The Professional Practices for the Business Continuity Planner. "This body of knowledge is accepted by both DRI International and by the Business Continuity Institute (BCI) based in the United Kingdom." This document's information is mirrored in many other documents. For example: BS 25999-1, ISO 27001-section 10, and NIST Special Publication 800-34, Contingency Planning Guide for Information Technology (IT) Systems.

- The BCI Good Practices Guideline (GPG), Version 2009.2, of 15 March 2009, is an extension/improvement to the previous professional practices document. This domain closely maps to the format and terminology of the BCI GPG document.

- One other source bears special mention for deep details: www.disasterrecoverybooks.com is a website dedicated to disaster recovery books and software.

REFERENCES:

http://www.thebci.org/gpgdownloadpage.htm

http://www.drj.com/GAP/

http://www.disasterrecoverybooks.com/data/index.htm

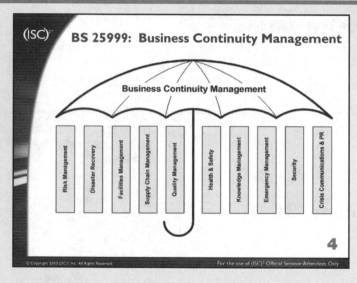

- **BUSINESS CONTINUITY MANAGEMENT –** This field is now commonly referred to as business continuity management. As such it includes all the disciplines related to business continuity, disaster recovery, and incident management, and works closely with many other areas as seen on this slide. Even though the umbrella illustration may seem to indicate that all these areas are a subset of BCM, that is not the case, rather, BCM integrates with all of these areas to a greater or lesser extent.

- **BS 25999** is BSI's (British Standards Institution, www. bsigroup.com) standard in the field of business continuity management (BCM). This standard replaces PAS 56, a Publicly Available Specification, published in 2003 on the same subject. This is an important document in that it outlines a strong business continuity management program that has become the template for many organizations and is a key component of the Good Practice Guidelines advocated by the Business Continuity Institute (www.thebci.org), one of the world's leading organizations in the field of business continuity management.

- **STRUCTURE –** BS 25999 is a business continuity management (BCM) standard in two parts.

  - The first, "BS 25999-1:2006 Business Continuity Management. Code of Practice," takes the form of general guidance and seeks to establish processes, principles, and terminology for business continuity management.

  - The second, "BS 25999-2:2007 Specification for Business Continuity Management," specifies requirements for implementing, operating, and improving a documented business continuity management system (BCMS), describing only requirements that can be objectively and independently audited.

  - A useful means of understanding the difference between the two is Part 1 is a guidance document and uses the term "should," Part 2 is an independently verifiable specification that uses the word "shall." Certification (independent verification) to this standard is available from two accredited certification bodies, LRQA and BSI (LRQA was accredited on 13 June 2008 and BSI was accredited on 5 August 2008), and is a multi-stage process usually involving a number of initial assessment visits. The assessor will then make a recommendation that the organization receive certification or not. After initial certification a number of surveillance visits are made to ensure that the organization is still in compliance.

- **CONTENTS –** The contents of the code of practice (BS 25999-1) are as follows:

  - **SECTION 1 –** Scope and applicability. This section defines the scope of the standard, making clear that it describes generic best practice that should be tailored to the organization implementing it.

  - **SECTION 2 –** Terms and definitions. This section describes the terminology and definitions used within the body of the standard.

- **SECTION 3** – Overview of business continuity management. A short overview is the subject of the standard. It is not meant to be a beginner's guide but describes the overall processes, its relationship with risk management, and reasons for an organization to implement it, along with the benefits.

- **SECTION 4** – The business continuity management policy. Central to the implementation of business continuity is having a clear, unambiguous, and appropriately resourced policy.

- **SECTION 5** – BCM program management. Program management is at the heart of the whole BCM process and the standard defines an approach.

- **SECTION 6** – Understanding the organization. In order to apply appropriate business continuity strategies and tactics, the organization has to be fully understood, including its critical activities, resources, duties, obligations, threats, risks, and overall risk appetite.

- **SECTION 7** – Determining BCM strategies. Once the organization is understood, the appropriate overall business continuity strategies can be defined.

- **SECTION 8** – Developing and implementing a BCM response. The tactical means by which business continuity is delivered. These include incident management structures, incident management, and business continuity plans.

- **SECTION 9** – Exercise, maintenance, audit, and self-assessment of the BCM culture. Without testing the BCM response, an organization cannot be certain that it will meet its requirements. Exercise, maintenance, and review processes will enable the business continuity capability to continue to meet the organization's goals.

- **SECTION 10** – Embedding BCM into the organization's culture. Business continuity should not exist in a vacuum but become part of the way that the organization is managed.

- The contents of the specification (BS 25999-2) are as follows:

  - **SECTION 1** – Scope. Defines the scope of the standard, and the requirements for implementing and operating a documented business continuity management system.

- **SECTION 2** – Terms and definitions. This section describes the terminology and definitions used within the body of the standard.

- **SECTION 3** – Planning the business continuity management system (PLAN). Part 2 of the standard is predicated on the well-established Plan-Do-Check-Act model of continuous improvement. The first step is to plan the BCMS, establishing and embedding it within the organization.

- **SECTION 4** – Implementing and operating the BCMS (DO). Actually implement one's plans. This section encompasses four sections of Part 1, that is, understand the organization, determine BC strategy, develop and implement a BCM response, and finally exercise/maintenance/review.

- **SECTION 5** – Monitoring and reviewing the BCMS (CHECK). To ensure that the BCMS is continually monitored, the Check stage covers internal audit and management review of the BCMS.

- **SECTION 6** – Maintaining and improving the BCMS (ACT). To ensure that the BCMS is both maintained and improved on an ongoing basis, this section looks at preventative and corrective action.

- **TIMELINES** – The first part of BS 25999 (BS 25999-1:2006) was published by the British Standards Institution in December 2006. The second part of BS 25999 (BS 25999-2:2007) was published in November 2007.

- **DEVELOPMENT** – As always, if the standard becomes effective enough it will be taken over by ISO much as ISO:9001 became an international standard.

- There are a number of similar worldwide standards:

  - **NORTH AMERICA** – Published by the National Fire Protection Association NFPA 1600: Standard on Disaster/Emergency Management and Business Continuity Programs.

  - **WORLDWIDE** – Published by the International Organization for Standardization (ISO), ISO/PAS 22399:2009 Guideline for incident preparedness and operational continuity management.

  - **AUSTRALIA** – Published by Standards Australia HB 292-2006: A practitioner's guide to business continuity management HB 293-2006: Executive guide to business continuity management information assurance.

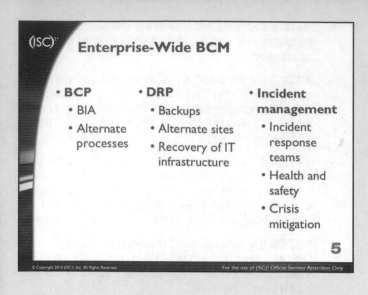

- Enterprise-wide BCM consists of several components. Each of these components will be examined in more detail throughout this domain.

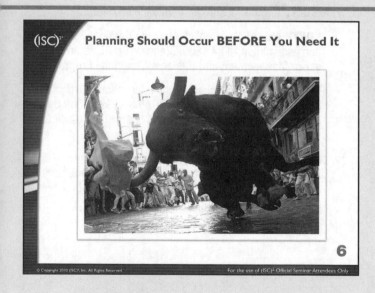

- **PLANNING SHOULD OCCUR BEFORE YOU NEED IT –** The freelance photographer who took this picture probably wished he or she had a business continuity plan (BCP) in place prior to this moment. The core principle of business continuity planning is to be prepared BEFORE disaster strikes. A good BCM project will avert disasters, minimize the impact of ones that do occur, and enable the organization to continue to deliver critical products and services despite an interruption.

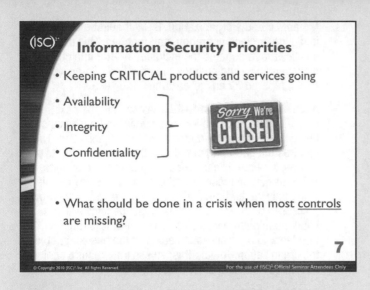

Information Security Priorities

- Keeping CRITICAL products and services going
- Availability
- Integrity
- Confidentiality

Sorry We're CLOSED

- What should be done in a crisis when most <u>controls</u> are missing?

7

- **INFORMATION SECURITY PRIORITIES** – The goal of business continuity is to keep **CRITICAL OPERATIONS** going. Obviously this means that availability is a key concern in this domain. However, it is during a crisis that **MANY OF THE NORMAL CONTROLS AND SAFEGUARDS ARE LACKING**, so it is imperative to be even more diligent to preserve integrity and confidentiality during a crisis than it is during normal operations. Security of the facility is especially challenging in the event of fire or a similar facility-related incident; providing adequate protection of sensitive data or papers may be quite difficult.

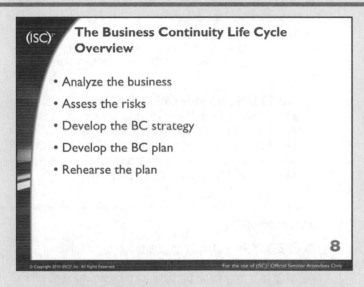

The Business Continuity Life Cycle Overview

- Analyze the business
- Assess the risks
- Develop the BC strategy
- Develop the BC plan
- Rehearse the plan

8

departments and will also help identify if any parts of the organization already have plans or procedures in place to deal with an unplanned event.

- **ASSESS THE RISKS** – There are two aspects to every risk to your organization:
  - How likely is the risk to happen?
  - What effect will it have on your organization?
  - Business continuity management will provide a framework for assessing the impact of each risk. Many organizations define (quantify) their risk levels in terms of cost.

- **DEVELOP THE BC STRATEGY** – Whatever type of organization you are, you will probably choose one of the following strategies:
  - Accept the risks – change nothing.
  - Accept the risks, but make a mutual arrangement with another business or a business continuity partner to ensure that you have help after an incident.
  - Attempt to reduce the risks.
  - Attempt to reduce the risks and make arrangements for help after an incident.
  - Reduce all risks to the point where you should not need outside help.
  - Your attitude to risk will be partly based on the costs of delivering effective business continuity. When working these out, remember to include both money and people's time.

- **OVERVIEW OF THE BCM LIFE CYCLE** – There are five steps that should be followed when developing a business continuity management plan:
  - **1.** Analyze your business.
  - **2.** Assess the risks.
  - **3.** Develop your strategy.
  - **4.** Develop your plan.
  - **5.** Rehearse the plan.
  - Due to the rapidly changing nature of business conditions, the process is not static but cyclical.
  - Once you have worked through and completed Step 5, it is necessary to go back to Step 1 and review the whole process again to ensure that any external or internal changes have not made elements of the plan redundant.

- **ANALYZE YOUR BUSINESS** – This is the first stage of the business continuity management life cycle as it is necessary to understand at the outset exactly where your business is vulnerable. You will need the fullest possible understanding of the important processes inside your organization and between you and your customers and suppliers.
  - This stage of the process will also help to gain the involvement and understanding of other people and

- **DEVELOP THE BC PLAN** – Once your strategy has been decided upon, the plan can be put in place. Business continuity management plans will look different for different organizations.

- A good plan will be simple without being simplistic. You will never be able to plan in detail for every possible event. Remember that people need to be able to react quickly in an emergency: Stopping to read lots of detail may make that more difficult.

- **REHEARSE YOUR PLAN** – The BCM plan is a living document and sometimes you only discover any weaknesses in it when you put it into action. Rehearsal helps you confirm that your plan will be connected and robust if you ever need it. Rehearsals are also good ways to train staff to have business continuity responsibilities.

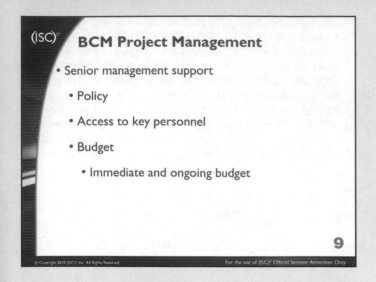

BCM Project Management

- Senior management support
  - Policy
  - Access to key personnel
  - Budget
    - Immediate and ongoing budget

9

- **BCM PROJECT MANAGEMENT** – BCM is like any other project – it requires support from senior management, governance, budget, and direction in order to succeed.

- **SENIOR MANAGEMENT SUPPORT** – Is the organization undertaking the BCM project just to satisfy an audit, or is it a serious attempt to be prepared for disaster? Senior management must support the project in a visible manner such as providing a formal announcement or kick-off to launch the project, a charter to provide the authority to gather information, and adequate budget.

  - **POLICY** – Business continuity is a culture that must be integrated into the organization. BCM should be embedded into every project, operation, and function. This requires a policy that mandates the inclusion of BCP into change management – and outlines the intention of management to be prepared for any interruption or disaster.

- **ACCESS TO KEY PERSONNEL** – As seen in the next section of this domain, the key to a successful business continuity plan is to really understand the organization. That requires the gathering of data on the organization, its processes, dependencies, critical services, and functions, etc. This information must be gathered from the key people who really understand and know the organization – how processes work and what their dependencies are and what the minimum levels of service are. This requires the BCP team to have access to some of the busiest people in the organization. To gain this access may require senior managers to facilitate the meetings.

- **BUDGET** – BCM costs money – and depending on the size and complexity of the organization, it may cost a lot of money. It costs money for software, office space, staff, and emergency supplies, but most of all it costs every department time to gather and provide the necessary documentation.

  - **IMMEDIATE AND ONGOING BUDGET** – BCM must be started with a view toward a long-term, sustainable program – one that is kept up to date and current with changes in the business. On an annual basis, a budget must be allocated for testing, alternate site agreements, and maintenance of the program.

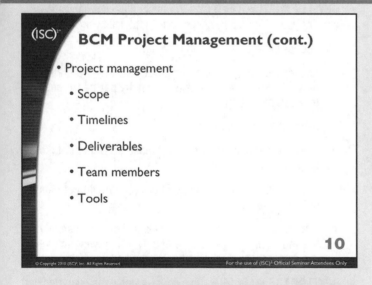

BCM Project Management (cont.)

- Project management
  - Scope
  - Timelines
  - Deliverables
  - Team members
  - Tools

10

- **BCM PROJECT MANAGEMENT** – BCM projects often fail due to lack of program management and unwise use of resources. Some of the key factors in all program management include addressing the factors listed on this slide.

  - **SCOPE** – BCM may be focused on one department, one product or service, one region or one line of business. It is important to commence the project with a clear definition of the scope of the project and which areas are to be addressed in the work effort.

  - **TIMELINES** – A BCM effort must not just run in an uncontrolled manner. Like any other project, it requires careful management, oversight, defined deliverables, milestones, and deadline dates. All tasks should be set with deadlines and review cycles.

- **DELIVERABLES** – In the end, the project must deliver an approved, reliable plan that is designed as much as possible to prevent and prepare for a crisis, manage an incident, and return the business back to normal operations as quickly and efficiently as possible. The deliverables will include addressing all critical business functions and the continuity resource requirements that are needed to sustain that business.

- **TEAM MEMBERS** – The key to a successful BCM project will be having access to the right people, and through those people, the right information! A BCM effort is based on understanding the organization. This requires people who know the business and how the various parts of the business interact and depend on one another. Access to the right people may be one of the most obvious examples of having obtained senior management support.

- **TOOLS** – There are many tools that can assist the business continuity planner in gathering and sorting information and creating a documented plan. Choosing a tool that fits the scale and price constraints of the project is important as it will greatly assist in managing, delivering, and maintaining a successful project.

- **AWARENESS, DATA, IMPLEMENTATION** – Initiating a BCP program involves coordinating a number of activities:

  - Awareness-raising events that maintain enthusiasm for undertaking a BCP program.

  - Data collection activities that will identify the choice of continuity options used to support the organization's objectives.

  - Implementing measures to mitigate the impact of an incident should it occur as the program is being developed.

- **STAFF AND BUDGET** – An initial staff and budget must be established before the BCP effort begins. Without people and money, there is no way to accomplish such a labor-intensive process.

- **RESULT MUST BE A LONG-TERM, SUSTAINABLE PROGRAM** – The end product from the BCP effort must be a long-term, sustainable program that meets the needs of the organization. It should be specific enough to be meaningful yet general enough to accommodate minor changes without needing to be totally reworked.

  - The initiation process should be constructed from activities described throughout this domain. These might include:

    - Awareness-raising activities.

    - Data collection and continuity option selection.

    - Measures to mitigate specific perceived threats.

    - Identifying and implementing low cost "quick wins."

  - A project-management method to monitor progress should be selected. Allow sufficient time to support each activity with appropriate awareness and skills training. This is a methodical, long-term integration into the organization: Doing something for the sake of making it look as if the project is getting somewhere is detrimental to the BCP.

- **REVIEW PROGRESS MONTHLY** – The organization should have a satisfactory state of readiness by the end of a successful initiation of a BCP program – often demonstrated by a desktop exercise of the incident-management procedures. Monthly progress reviews should be held to ensure that milestones are being met and cost projections are accurate. If the project is either over cost or behind schedule, the BC manager/planner must adjust the plan to correct the situation.

Documentation

- Review current BCP, if available

- Documentation may not equal capability

- Staff must be trained to use any necessary software

- Types of BCM documents

- Review/update as directed by policy

12

- **REVIEW CURRENT BCP IF AVAILABLE –** An important part of the process is to manage all BCP documentation. This needs to be carried out in a manner that is consistent, easy to understand, and provides both operational and audit/review support. The level and type of documentation should be appropriate to the type and size of the organization. Organizations that are certified against other management standards such as ISO 9000 or ISO 27001 will need to review how BCP documentation fits within the requirement of those standards. The BCP documentation has three purposes: to manage the program effectively, to prove the effective management of the program during an audit, and to have current and effective documentation available during a disruption for incident management and critical business resumption.

- **DOCUMENTATION MAY NOT REFLECT CAPABILITY –** Although it is important to maintain BCP documentation, its presence is not proof of an organization's capability to respond to an incident.

- **STAFF TRAINING –** Staff must be adequately trained to operate any software used in the BCP. Those responsible for maintaining plans should be able to update their documentation, since this promotes ownership and reduces the clerical overhead of central BCP administration. Software might include word processing, spreadsheets, databases, and specialized software. Note that the maintenance of BCP documentation should be integrated into the organization's change-management procedures.

- **TYPES OF BCM DOCUMENTS –** A current set of BCM documentation may include:

  - BCP policy, including scope and principles

  - Business impact analysis

  - Risk and threat assessment

  - BCP strategies, including papers supporting the choice of the strategies adopted

  - Response plans

  - Test schedule and reports

  - Awareness and training program

  - Service level agreements with customers and suppliers

  - Contracts for third party recovery services such as workspace and salvage

- **REVIEW/UPDATE AS DIRECTED BY POLICY –** The review cycle for each document should be identified in the sections that relate to its creation and use. The documentation and controls should be reviewed by internal or external audit on a timescale defined by the auditors.

Domain Agenda

- BCM Project Planning

- **Understanding the Organization**

- Recovery Strategy Selection

- Creating the Plan(s)

- Developing and Implementing Response

- Testing, Update, and Maintenance of the Plan

13

- **THE NEXT PHASE OF A BUSINESS CONTINUITY PROJECT IS PERHAPS THE MOST IMPORTANT PHASE –** It is quite aptly entitled "Understanding the Organization." Understanding the organization is the key to creating BCP and DRP plans that will prepare the organization for any type of crisis, as well as enable recovery in the shortest time possible.

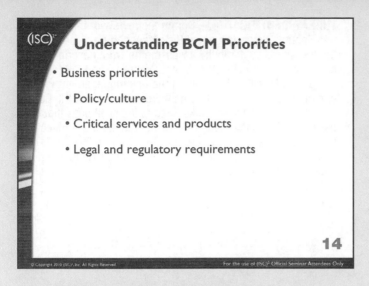

- **BUSINESS PRIORITIES** – To understand the BCM priorities, the organization must understand itself. What business is it really in? What are the most critical services it provides and what are the critical timelines that make some activities more critical than others?

  - **POLICY/CULTURE** – BCM is a demonstration of the organization's commitment to succeed and continue operations despite an interruption. The BCM effort must be aligned with the culture and priorities of the organization and reflect corporate values. A BCM project that does not align correctly with the culture of the organization is destined to failure. The BCM effort should start with a clear mandate from senior management backing the effort and often written in a charter letter that affirms the right of the BCM team to meet with all business units and document business processes.

- **CRITICAL SERVICES AND PRODUCTS** – An organization has many components, ranging from operations to finance, and from human resources to communications. While every component is important for normal operations, some areas are much more time-critical than others. The outage of these time-critical areas would have a much larger impact on the organization than the loss of a less time-critical operation. One of the primary tasks of the BCM is to identify what are the time-critical products or services the organization provides – these are the ones that must be addressed first in the continuity plan, since they are the areas that would engender the greatest impact in the shortest timeframe.

- **LEGAL AND REGULATORY REQUIREMENTS** – Many organizations are subject to regulations and legislative requirements for service delivery, privacy, incident reporting, etc. The BCM project must consider all applicable regulations in developing BCP and DRP documents.

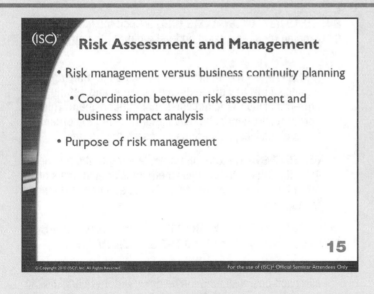

- **RISK MANAGEMENT** – Risk assessment and management is a separate discipline but closely related to BCM. Risk considers all threats, vulnerabilities, and asset value in calculating impact (consequence) and acceptable risk levels. The work done by risk management is valuable to the business continuity plan to ensure that all risks have been addressed, and the work of the business continuity effort makes sure that all outstanding residual risks have been addressed.

  - **COORDINATION BETWEEN RISK AND BUSINESS CONTINUITY** – Whereas risk management is concerned with events that are highly likely or have the highest impact, business continuity is usually focused on events that would be catastrophic in nature (extreme levels of impact – leading up to complete organizational failure) but are rare in likelihood.

- **PURPOSE OF RISK MANAGEMENT** – Risk management, as seen in the "Information Security Governance and Risk Management" domain, looks at and assesses all risks and ensures that risks are addressed through countermeasures, safeguards, and other controls. Risk management is to ensure that all risks are mitigated to an acceptable level and, for the most part, looks at risk from the perspective of identifying and mitigating adverse events that would have the highest likelihood and/or the highest impact on the organization.

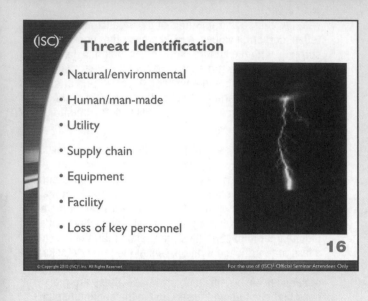

Threat Identification

- Natural/environmental
- Human/man-made
- Utility
- Supply chain
- Equipment
- Facility
- Loss of key personnel

16

- **THREAT IDENTIFICATION** – During the review of the "Information Security Governance and Risk Management" domain, the threat and vulnerability assessments were described in some detail and need not be repeated here. The BCM team will primarily review the work of the risk management team to ensure that all risks and threats were addressed. If the BCM team believes that some risks remain, they will pass that data back to Risk Management for review. The important objective for the BCM team is to ensure that there are no "hidden" risks that have not been uncovered, but that could lead to a serious business interruption.

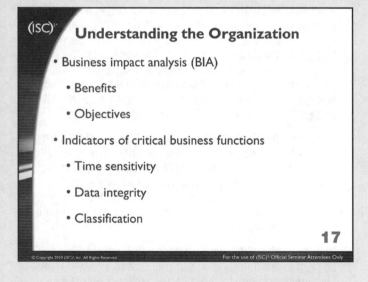

Understanding the Organization

- Business impact analysis (BIA)
  - Benefits
  - Objectives
- Indicators of critical business functions
  - Time sensitivity
  - Data integrity
  - Classification

17

- **BUSINESS IMPACT ANALYSIS (BIA)** – Good business continuity planning requires a good understanding of the organization.

  - **BENEFITS** – The benefits of a BIA include identifying the organization's key products and services and defining the time-criticality of the activities that support them. This part of the BCP must be fully integrated into the organization's objectives, obligations, and statutory duties.

  - **OBJECTIVES** – A thorough understanding of the business will often highlight business inefficiencies and focus on priorities that would not otherwise be apparent to senior management.

- **INDICATORS OF CRITICAL BUSINESS FUNCTIONS ARE ESSENTIAL TO UNDERSTANDING THE ORGANIZATION:**

  - **TIME SENSITIVITY** – How many minutes, hours, or days can each business function be down before unacceptable impacts accumulate? This value represents the maximum tolerable downtime (MTD). An MTD that has been adjusted downward to allow for unforeseen issues is called the recovery time objective (RTO). It sets functional requirements for recovery strategy.

  - **DATA INTEGRITY** – During a disaster, recovery relies on the integrity of the data backup stored offsite. The recovery point objective (RPO) measures the tolerance for data loss.

  - **CLASSIFICATION** – The data's classification level will direct how carefully backups and recovery site operations need to be protected.

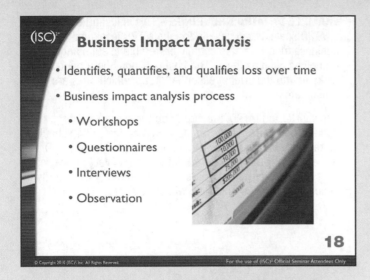

Business Impact Analysis

- Identifies, quantifies, and qualifies loss over time
- Business impact analysis process
  - Workshops
  - Questionnaires
  - Interviews
  - Observation

18

- **IDENTIFIES, QUANTIFIES, AND QUALIFIES LOSS** – The business impact analysis (BIA) is the foundation on which the entire BCP process is built. It identifies, quantifies, and qualifies the business impacts of a loss, interruption, or disruption of business processes on an organization and provides the data from which appropriate continuity strategies can be

determined. A BIA can be used to identify the timescale and the extent of the impact of a disruption at several levels in an organization.

- **BUSINESS IMPACT ANALYSIS PROCESS:**
  - Identify discrete business activities and the owners of these processes.
  - Identify suitable staff from whom the information can be sought about the business processes.
  - Identify impacts that might result in damage to the organization's reputation, assets, or financial position.
  - Quantify the timescale within which the interruption of each business activity becomes unacceptable to the organization.
  - **WORKSHOPS, QUESTIONNAIRES, INTERVIEWS, OBSERVATION** – Data collection methods, tools, and techniques used to gather the information needed to carry out the business impact analysis include: workshops, questionnaires (whether paper and/or automated software), interviews (structured and unstructured), and observation of business processes.

Business Impact Analysis (cont.)

- Business justifications for budget
- MTD/MTPD
- RPO
- Document dependencies
  - Third party dependencies and liabilities
  - Service level agreements

19

- **BUSINESS JUSTIFICATIONS FOR BUDGET** – The budget for disaster planning and restoration, and the chosen recovery strategy to be assigned to each business process, will depend on the outcome of the business impact analysis.

- **MAXIMUM TOLERABLE DOWNTIME (MTD) OR MAXIMUM TOLERABLE PERIOD OF DISRUPTION (MTPD)** – The period of time after which an organization's viability will be irrevocably threatened if delivery of a particular product or service cannot be resumed. It is often convenient to link activities with similar recovery requirements in order to form a timeline of activities. This drives the selection of the recovery strategy and timeframes.

- **RECOVERY POINT OBJECTIVE (RPO)** – RPO is about data loss. It is the point (level/currency) to which information must be restored following a disruption. The organization must know

how much data it can afford to lose without incurring an unacceptable level of damage. If the loss of a few minutes' worth of data would cause massive financial or reputational loss, then a backup strategy must be developed that will prevent that loss. This would require a more expensive option such as data mirroring, in contrast with an organization that could choose a daily tape backup strategy, since it could potentially lose hours or a day's worth of data without catastrophic consequences.

- **DOCUMENT DEPENDENCIES** – It is important to document all the dependencies and interactions between systems and departments. While preparing the BIA it is possible to look at the requirements from the perspective of the system and its functions, or to approach the analysis from the perspective of a product, service, or department. The core requirement is to determine what the relationships are between the systems, operations, and data flow. And what will need to be addressed when preparing the eventual business continuity plans.

  - **THIRD PARTY DEPENDENCIES AND LIABILITIES** – The agreements in place with third parties that could result in either upstream or downstream liabilities must be taken into account. Sending or receiving incorrect data may result in major damage to systems and operations.

  - **SERVICE LEVEL AGREEMENTS (SLA)** – Organizations often rely on service level agreements to ensure that they receive and provide a required standard of service. These can relate to acceptable outage times, committed repair times, maintenance windows, and operational and performance standards. To fail to meet the SLA requirements will often result in financial penalties or loss of contract. The SLAs must be documented to ensure that the recovery strategy meets the agreed-on standards.

Example of MTPD Groupings

Item	Required recovery time following a disaster
Non-Essential	30 Days
Normal	7 Days
Important	72 Hours
Urgent	24 Hours
Critical/Essential	Minutes to Hours

20

- **EXAMPLE OF MTPD GROUPINGS –** This is just an example of a MTPD scale. When calculating the MTPD levels for various business functions, it is usually preferable to set standard groupings such as these. The business units determine which tasks fit into the critical/essential group, which ones are urgent, etc.

- The shorter the MTPD, the higher on the recovery list the function will be. For example, those with a critical listing should be restored before those with an urgent listing. The MTPD will eventually assist in determining the recovery strategies. That is, a shorter period of recovery will identify the priority in which the business functions will be restored.

Incident Readiness & Response

- Planners become leaders
- Be prepared
- Triage
- Incident management
- Success = return to operations
- Application of lessons learned

21

- 3a. Manage response through appropriate prepared plans, or,
- 3b. Escalate to incident management team.
- 4. Communicate what has happened to senior management.

- **INCIDENT MANAGEMENT –** There are many incident management methods. The following is a generic one:

  - Contain – Is there anything that can be done immediately to prevent the problem from getting worse?
  - Look at the plan – Is there a pre-planned response that fits this incident?
  - Follow the documented procedure.
  - Predict the likely outcome and predict a "worst case" outcome.
  - Escalate the response to the required level within the organization.
  - Implement the response strategy.
  - Evaluate the progress of the response against the likely outcome.
  - Review the effectiveness of the response.

- **SUCCESS = RETURN TO OPERATIONS –** The outcome of a successful response is a controlled return of the organization to business as usual.

- **APPLICATION OF LESSONS LEARNED –** As soon as possible after the interruption, the organization's response should be evaluated and any necessary changes should be made to procedures, personnel, or contracts.

- **PLANNERS BECOME LEADERS –** Although business continuity planning is primarily a planning activity, it is inevitable that the BCP team will be expected to provide a lead role during incident response.

- **BE PREPARED –** BCP professionals should maintain a state of readiness so that if an incident occurs, incident management will take over smoothly. The BCP team will have the best, most detailed knowledge of the overall strategies and actions that will need to be immediately invoked. It will need to support line management with assessment and invocation activities until the incident management team is fully operational. It is often assumed that those who have developed the plan are the best individuals to respond to an incident, but the personality characteristics required of planners and leaders are often contradictory. Any difficulties in this area should be exposed by a realistic set of plan exercises.

- **TRIAGE –** The triage process is:

  - 1. Receive notification of problem.
  - 2. Assess situation.

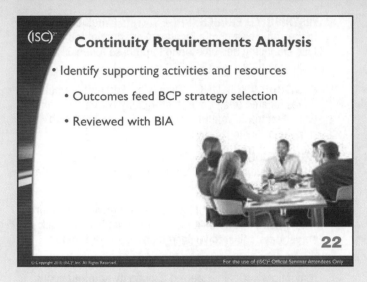

Continuity Requirements Analysis

- Identify supporting activities and resources
- Outcomes feed BCP strategy selection
- Reviewed with BIA

22

© Copyright 2010 (ISC)², Inc. All Rights Reserved.   For the use of (ISC)² Official Seminar Attendees Only

to be at levels higher than normally used in order to cope with backlogs. For example, in a call center, additional staff may be needed to cope with the extra calls following an interruption, and supporting IT systems may need to have a higher capacity to cope with this additional number of users.

- **IDENTIFICATION OF NECESSARY RESOURCES –** Quantify the resources (e.g., people, technology, telephony) required to maintain the business functions at an acceptable level and within the maximum tolerable period of disruption. This identification process should take into account any extra activity that will be generated by the interruption and the need to clear backlogs.

- **OUTCOMES FEED BCP STRATEGY SELECTION –** The outcomes from a continuity requirements analysis are:

  - An understanding of the resources required after a resumption to provide agreed-upon service levels.

  - An understanding of the interdependencies between internal activities and on external suppliers.

  - This information feeds directly into the business continuity recovery strategy stage. The resource requirements will provide the data to evaluate alternative recovery solutions for adequacy of size and performance.

- **REVIEWED WITH BIA –** The continuity requirements analysis should be performed at the same time as the BIA.

- **SUPPORTING ACTIVITIES –** The continuity requirements analysis phase collects information on the resources and activities required to resume and continue the business activities at the level required. This step is usually undertaken at the same time as the BIA information is being gathered. This provides the information from which an appropriate recovery strategy can be determined or recommended. Resource requirements can be dependent on both internal and external sources. It is often assumed that the resources required after a disruption will be smaller than those necessary for normal operations – at least for a period of time. In some cases, however, the resources in the early stages of recovery may need

Domain Agenda

- BCM Project Planning

- Understanding the Organization

- **Recovery Strategy Selection**

- Creating the Plan(s)

- Developing and Implementing Response

- Testing, Update, and Maintenance of the Plan

23

© Copyright 2010 (ISC)², Inc. All Rights Reserved.   For the use of (ISC)² Official Seminar Attendees Only

- This section of the domain covers selecting your recovery strategy.

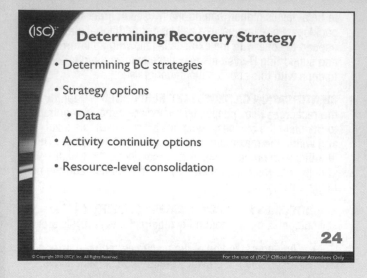

Determining Recovery Strategy

- Determining BC strategies
- Strategy options
  - Data
- Activity continuity options
- Resource-level consolidation

24

- **DETERMINING BUSINESS CONTINUITY STRATEGY –** A key element of good business continuity management. Business continuity strategy seeks to build on the detailed analysis drawn from the "understanding the organization" stage in order to choose appropriate continuity strategies that meet the objectives defined in the BIA. The business continuity strategy must support the organization's objectives, obligations, and statutory duties in a cost-effective manner.

- **STRATEGY OPTIONS –** Information was collected about the critical functions' data, RPOs, and RTOs during the BIA. Back-up approaches and strategies provide the data with which IT systems can restore from a crash or unanticipated destruction of records. The main data backup strategies are as follows:

  - **REPLICATION –** Disk replication or recovery images optimize recovery. Data is written to two disks and provides high availability.

- **DISTRIBUTED PROCESSING –** Servers (whether located in the same or multiple locations) are configured with load balancing and clustering to process requests and exchange data.

- **ELECTRONIC VAULTING –** Data is backed up to remote drives located offsite over high-quality communication links. Electronic vaulting may be supplemented with remote journaling.

- **REMOTE JOURNALING –** Transactions or journal files are periodically transmitted to the remote drives located offsite.

- **MEDIA ARCHIVES –** Media are backed up and transported to an offsite location. There are three methods to back up server data: full archive, incremental, and differential.

- **STORAGE AREA NETWORK –** High-performance local or remote networks that permit backup by heterogeneous computers.

- **ACTIVITY CONTINUITY OPTIONS –** The activity continuity options include "hot," "warm," "mobile," "cold," etc. (We will discuss these in detail later on in this course.)

- **RESOURCE-LEVEL CONSOLIDATION –** The occurrence of a disaster may permit the consolidation of systems or personnel. In instances where equipment may need to be replaced or an activity must be moved to an alternate location, one consideration is the consolidation of systems and workgroups to realize economies of scale or achieve reduction of duplicate operations. Caution must be taken, however, to ensure that the consolidation does not further interrupt business recovery.

Determining Recovery Strategy (cont.)

- High-level strategies

- RTO < MTPD

- Separation distance

- Cost/benefit analysis

- Address specific business types

  - Different business functions have different recovery solutions

25

- **HIGH-LEVEL STRATEGIES** – This section looks at the various high-level strategies available to protect product and service delivery. Before the appropriate strategy can be selected, a current BIA must be in place. The purpose of this step is to ensure that the overall continuity strategy appropriately supports the delivery of the organization's products and services.

- **RECOVERY TIME OBJECTIVE (RTO)** – An organization may want to set an RTO that allows time for unforeseen difficulties during the recovery. Note that the faster the recovery requirement, the greater the cost of the solution is likely to be – which means that setting the RTO is a business decision.

- **RTO < MTPD** – Decide on a recovery time objective (RTO) for the product or service. (This will be shorter than the MTPD.) The RTO will take the level of confidence in the accuracy of the MTPD into account.

- **SEPARATION DISTANCE** – What is offsite? How far away

should a recovery site be located? Since incidents may damage a large geographic area, it is important to consider the potential types of incidents when selecting a recovery location. An organization that is prepared for earthquake or hurricane will need to select a recovery site farther away from that of an organization that is preparing for fire. The recovery site must be reachable by staff and have the resources necessary to recover within the desired time frame. This may require storing data and records at the recovery location.

- **COST-BENEFIT ANALYSIS** – The determination of the best recovery strategy is often dependent on cost, availability of choices, business priorities, and appetite for risk. The business continuity management team should recommend a solution that strikes a balance between cost, time, and impact to determine the solution that provides the best overall benefit to the organization.

- **ADDRESS SPECIFIC BUSINESS TYPES** – Issues with specific business services:

  - **CALL CENTER** – Call centers handling incoming calls will usually have MTPD measured in hours rather than days. The usual solution involves having two or more geographically dispersed centers which load-share the calls.

  - **E-COMMERCE** – Strategy choice will depend on how important the entire organization believes these services are.

  - **MANUFACTURING** – Manufacturing at more than one site increases resilience.

  - **SUBCONTRACTING** – There are usually various processes which can be duplicated by other manufacturers.

  - **WAREHOUSING STOCK** – Offsite stock can provide a time window during which supply can be maintained while a disruption is resolved.

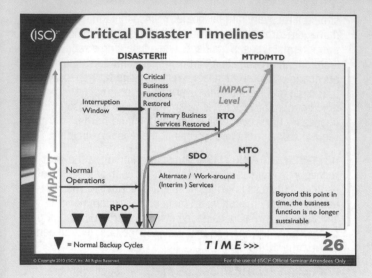

Critical Disaster Timelines

- **CRITICAL DISASTER TIMELINES –** This diagram is an example of a recovery effort. The first area on the left represents normal operations, including regular backups. The leftmost vertical line represents the occurrence of a disaster. This begins a period of disruption known as the interruption window. Service is not available during this time period. The second line from the left represents the establishment of minimal service levels – perhaps a manual workaround or other process that provides at least partial service. The length of the interruption window is the time between the disaster and the establishment of minimal service. This level of service should be available by the SDO – service delivery objective.

- **ONCE THE CRITICAL BUSINESS SERVICES ARE PROPERLY ESTABLISHED, THE INTERIM SERVICES ARE TURNED DOWN. THIS SHOULD BE ACCOMPLISHED BY THE RTO –** Recovery time objective. Depending on the severity of the disaster, the organization may operate in this condition for an extended period of time. It is important that the RTO is less than the MTPD. If service is not restored prior to the point in time declared to be the MTPD, the business is not likely to recover.

  - The next major step is the restoration of the business to normal and the closure of the incident.

- **LOSS OF DATA –** Since the last data backup taken was a time period prior to the disaster, the data that changed between the time of the backup and the time of the disaster is lost. This is an indication of the RPO – recovery point objective which the organization had set. It represents the most current level of data that can be recovered following a disaster.

- **KEY DEFINITIONS:**

  - **MAXIMUM TOLERABLE PERIOD OF DISRUPTION/MAXIMUM TOLERABLE DOWNTIME (MTPD/MTD) –** The maximum period of significant loss or disruption of primary (critical) services that can be sustained before PERMANENT, unrecoverable conditions are encountered.

  - **RECOVERY POINT OBJECTIVE (RPO)**

    - Based on acceptable data loss.

    - Indicates latest point in time in which it is acceptable to recover the data.

  - **RECOVERY TIME OBJECTIVE (RTO)**

    - Based on acceptable downtime.

    - Indicates the desired point in time at which the business operations will resume after a disaster.

  - **ADDITIONAL PARAMETERS IMPORTANT IN DEFINING RECOVERY STRATEGIES:**

    - Interruption window:

      - Time between point of failure and restoration of critical services.

    - Service delivery objective (SDO):

      - Interim level of alternate services until normal services are restored.

    - Maximum tolerable period of disruption/maximum tolerable downtime:

      - The period of time after which an organization's viability will be irrevocably threatened if delivery of a particular product or service cannot be resumed.

- **RECOVERY ALTERNATIVES** – A BC coordinator considers each alternative's ability to support critical business functions, its operational readiness compared with RTO, and cost. Specifications for workspace, security requirements, IT, and telecommunications are examined. There are generally three approaches for recovery: One is a dedicated site operated by the organization, such as a multiple processing center. The second approach is a commercially leased facility, such as a hot site, or the improvement of an existing location such as a warm site or cold site. The third approach is an agreement with an internal or external facility. (Addressed on the next slide.)

- Remember that commercial providers offer services to numerous organizations. Make sure to find out important issues such as how priority status is determined after a disaster that affects many customers; what the costs are for test time, declaration fee, and maximum recovery days are; and whether the specifications for workspace, security requirements, IT, and telecommunications are suitable for critical business functions. Ask as well whether there are suitable accommodations for staff rest, showering, and catering, etc.

- **A MULTIPLE PROCESSING CENTER OR MIRRORED SITE** supports 100 percent availability. It is always ready and is under the organization's control. It is the highest cost because it requires fully redundant or duplicate operations and synchronized data and is continuously operated by the organization.

- **MOBILE SITES OR TRAILERS** may be leased or owned by the organization. These are self-contained, portable data centers with power generators. Note that there will be a time delay while the trailer is driven to the recovery location, set up and configured, and data loaded.

- A **HOT SITE** features fully provisioned IT and offices. Data must be retrieved and loaded before operations are resumed. Some commercial hot sites allow data backups to be stored nearby for a fee.

- A **WARM SITE** has some common IT, communications, power, and HVAC. IT equipment (such as servers and communications) must be procured and transferred to the site, and the data must be retrieved and loaded.

- A **COLD SITE** is an empty data center with heating ventilation and air conditioning (HVAC) and power. It is the least expensive option, but it requires substantial time to ramp up. All equipment and telecommunications must be procured, delivered, and configured. In a lengthy interruption, some organizations begin recovery in a hot site and transition over to a warm site or cold site as time goes on and the sites can be set up.

Processing Agreements

Agreement	Description	Considerations
Reciprocal or Mutual Aid	Two or more organizations agree to recover critical operations for each other.	Technology upgrades/ obsolescence or business growth. Security and access by partner users.
Contingency	Alternate arrangements if primary provider is interrupted, i.e., voice or data communications.	Providers may share paths or lease from each other. Question them.
Service Bureau	Agreement with application service provider to process critical business functions.	Evaluate their loading, geography and ask about backup mode.
Remote Working Arrangements	Ability to telecommute or work from home.	Sensitive data controls, unauthorized equipment.

28

- **PROCESSING AGREEMENTS** – Another approach to recovery alternatives is to identify organizations with equivalent IT configurations and backup technologies, such as another company, contingent carrier, or a service bureau. A formal support agreement in the event of an interruption is established between these organizations. Draft agreements should be carefully reviewed by IT, security, and legal departments.

    - **RECIPROCAL OR MUTUAL AID** – The organization may enter into a reciprocal agreement, also known as mutual aid or consortium agreement, with a company that has similar technology. A consortium agreement is where a number of companies agree to support the other members. Careful consideration must be given before committing to this approach. For example, can each organization continue its primary business while supporting the agreement partner? Can the equipment and infrastructure support both organizations? Testing to confirm technical and extra-load

processing compatibility is strongly encouraged. Another concern is the sensitivity of the information and any regulations that might surround that information, as it may be accessible by the agreement partner's administrators or users. Be careful as well that one partner does not upgrade or retire technology rendering processing incompatible.

- **CONTINGENCY** – An organization may contract for contingency carriers (such as backup communications) or contingent suppliers (diesel fuel, raw materials) should their primary supplier experience an interruption. Considerations are maintenance fee and activation time. Another concern is that carriers (especially communications carriers) may share the same cable or routing paths. It is prudent to question them.

- **SERVICE BUREAU** – A service bureau example is an application service provider that has extra capacity (such as a call center to handle incoming calls). Organizations may contract for contingent use of this capacity. (Note that there are similar concerns to the ones having to do with the reciprocal agreement.) Consider whether the vendor might increase its business and consume its extra capacity, or whether it might modify its hardware or configurations.

- **REMOTE WORKING ARRANGEMENTS** – The fear of a pandemic and the need to create flexible working arrangements for employees has led organizations to consider alternate working arrangements such as working from a remote office, or working from home. The considerations related to this option are the transmission and storage of sensitive data in an insecure, unmanaged environment, the use of rogue or unauthorized equipment to connect to the network, the bandwidth and capacity for external connections, and the requirements for safety and insurance at a remote location.

- In this section, you'll learn how to create your plan.

Domain Agenda

- BCM Project Planning

- Understanding the Organization

- Recovery Strategy Selection

- **Creating the Plan(s)**

- Developing and Implementing Response

- Testing, Update, and Maintenance of the Plan

29

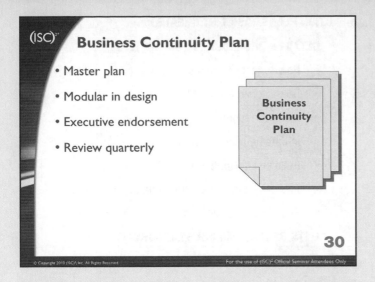

Business Continuity Plan

- Master plan
- Modular in design
- Executive endorsement
- Review quarterly

Business
Continuity
Plan

30

process with which to enable the organization to resume all of its business processes within their various RTOs. The mere existence of a business continuity plan does not demonstrate a BCP competence or capability, but the presence of a current plan that has been produced by the organization does suggest an effective capability. The plan should be action oriented and should, therefore, be easy to reference quickly – for example, it should not include documentation that will not be required during an incident. The BC plan will always contain assumptions about the maximum scale of the incident. If these are exceeded, the matter should be escalated to the incident management team to resolve.

- **MODULAR IN DESIGN –** A business continuity plan should be modular in design so that separate sections can be supplied to teams on a need-to-know basis. Ensure that all regularly changing information (such as contact details) is kept in appendices at the back of the plan. (It is easier to amend an appendix than an entire document.) The text of the document should reference job titles rather than individual names. Whatever the planning solution, there must be a clearly defined and documented control and change-management process for the production, update, and distribution of the business continuity plan.

- **EXECUTIVE ENDORSEMENT –** A business continuity plan should be approved by an executive such as the company president, CEO, etc.

- **REVIEW QUARTERLY –** Some information within a business continuity plan (e.g., contact details) will require monthly or quarterly review. Other information should be formally reviewed annually and tested through exercising.

- **MASTER PLAN –** The business continuity plan pulls together the response of the entire organization to a disruptive incident by facilitating the resumption of critical business activities. Those using the plan should be able to analyze information from the response teams concerning the impact of the incident, select and deploy appropriate strategies from those available in the plan, direct the resumption of business units according to agreed-upon priorities, and pass progress information to the incident management team. It is rarely possible to write an effective business continuity plan unless the key elements of the resumption strategy are in place or are well advanced in their planning. The purpose of a business continuity plan is to provide a documented framework and

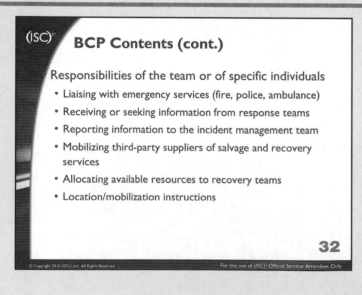

Business Continuity Plan Contents

- When team will be activated
- Means by which the team will be activated
- Places to meet
- Action plans/task list created
- Reporting

31

© Copyright 2010 (ISC)², Inc. All Rights Reserved.   For the use of (ISC)² Official Seminar Attendees Only

- **WHEN TEAM WILL BE ACTIVATED** – The circumstances under which the team will be activated should be documented, and the persons able to initiate the call-out (declare the disaster) decided. Due to the nature of incidents, the circumstances should allow some flexibility and encourage action where there is doubt, since it is easier to stand down an activated team than activate them after the incident has gone out of control.

- **MEANS BY WHICH THE TEAM WILL BE ACTIVATED** – The means by which the team will be activated should be documented so that decisions can be made in the shortest possible time.

- **PLACES TO MEET** – The team should agree in advance to a number of possible meeting places in the event of an incident. Meeting places should favor those/the area with the resources required to deal with the incident. On invocation, the first notified should identify both the most suitable meeting place and a fallback location based on the available information about the incident.

- **ACTION PLANS/TASK LIST CREATED:**
  - **DETAILED PROCEDURES FOR THE TEAM:**
    - How to respond to invocation.
    - How decisions are to be made.
    - Mobilize resources.
    - Initiate activity recovery.
    - Receive information from other teams.
    - Report status to incident management team.
    - Resource requirements.
  - **LISTS OF THE AVAILABLE RESOURCES:**
    - Personnel.
    - Facilities and supplies.
    - Technology, communications, and data.
    - Security.
    - Transportation and logistics.
    - Emergency cash and payments.
    - Resource requirements for resumption of each activity.
    - Customer information.
    - Contact details.
    - Legal documents such as contracts and insurance policies.
    - Service level agreements forms.
    - Checklists.

- **REPORTING** – Management of the crisis relies on regular reports and updates from the various recovery teams. Reporting schedules and formats should be set up in the plan.

BCP Contents (cont.)

Responsibilities of the team or of specific individuals

- Liaising with emergency services (fire, police, ambulance)
- Receiving or seeking information from response teams
- Reporting information to the incident management team
- Mobilizing third-party suppliers of salvage and recovery services
- Allocating available resources to recovery teams
- Location/mobilization instructions

32

© Copyright 2010 (ISC)², Inc. All Rights Reserved.   For the use of (ISC)² Official Seminar Attendees Only

- This slide provides a list of specific team or individual responsibilities that must be addressed and assigned. A second and third person should be assigned for each in case the primary person is on vacation, out sick, etc.

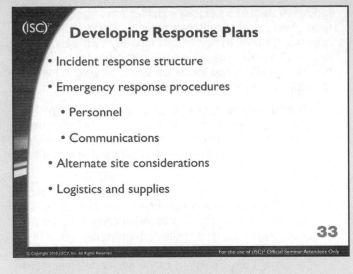

Developing Response Plans

- Incident response structure
- Emergency response procedures
  - Personnel
  - Communications
- Alternate site considerations
- Logistics and supplies

33

- **INCIDENT RESPONSE STRUCTURE** – A BCP response includes the development of appropriate, detailed action plans to ensure continuity of activities, and effective incident management that will answer the question: "What do we do now?" The documented elements in this step may include:
  - Emergency response procedures.
  - Personnel notification.
  - Backup and offsite storage.
  - Communications technologies.
  - Alternate site considerations.
  - Logistics and supplies.

- **EMERGENCY RESPONSE PROCEDURES:**
  - Event reporting.
  - Life, health, and safety.
  - Damage assessment plan.
  - Triage and escalation.

- Disaster declaration.
- Notification.
- Communication.

- **PERSONNEL NOTIFICATION INCLUDES:**
  - Executive succession planning.
  - Executive crisis management roles.
  - Bc coordinator and teams.
  - Notification lists.
  - Public relations.

- **COMMUNICATIONS INCLUDE:**
  - Emergency systems.
  - Business systems communications and networks.

- **ALTERNATE SITE CONSIDERATIONS INCLUDE:**
  - Utilities.
  - Communications.
  - Environmental protections.
  - Workspace protection.

- **LOGISTICS AND SUPPLIES INCLUDE:**
  - Personnel and materials transportation.
  - Personnel support and welfare.
  - Remote worker environment activation.
  - Emergency funds access.
  - Protection against fraud and looting.
  - Safety and legal issues.
  - Escalated management authority.

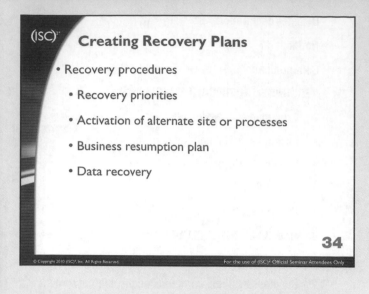

Creating Recovery Plans

- Recovery procedures
  - Recovery priorities
  - Activation of alternate site or processes
  - Business resumption plan
  - Data recovery

34

- **CREATING RECOVERY PLANS** – The recovery plans are the heart of the business continuity program. The plans are the actions, resources, personnel, and recovery strategies, all put into a logical order. The plans outline the steps for recovery, the responsibilities, and the techniques to be used in the resumption of business processes or services.

  - **PRIORITIES** – Many tasks must be done in the correct order, and many systems are more critical to the recovery than others. The priorities must be addressed and leadership provided to enable smooth recovery of the most time-critical systems.

  - **ACTIVATION** – The declaration of a disaster and the decision to resume operations at an alternate site require the staff to be deployed to the location to bring it into service. Depending on the type of site (hot, warm, cold, etc.), the amount of work required, and the time required to activate the site will vary. The plans may allow for different recovery sites depending on the scale of the disaster.

  - **BUSINESS RESUMPTION PLAN** – Once the alternate site is ready, or the alternate processes prepared, business can resume. This will include the deployment of personnel, and the availability of supporting data and communications.

  - **DATA RECOVERY** – The recovery of data will include the recovery of data from a backup location, the loading of the data on the systems, the recovery of work in progress at the time of the disaster, and enabling the method to be used for new data entry – which may, for an initial time period, mean the use of a paper-based or manual process.

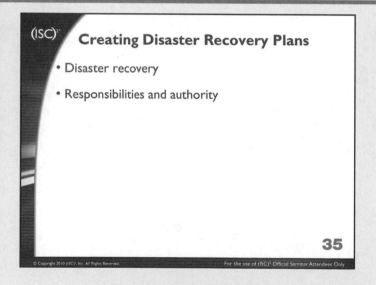

Creating Disaster Recovery Plans

- Disaster recovery
- Responsibilities and authority

35

- **DISASTER RECOVERY** – Disaster recovery refers to the restoration of IT processing capability and infrastructure and is, therefore, a key component of business continuity management. While the business may run in an alternate format on manual procedures for a short while, it needs the core IT infrastructure to be rebuilt as quickly as practical. Plans need to be written to address the build-out and configuration of the facility and equipment, restoration of data, rewiring of communications networks, and reinstatement of support systems.

- **RESPONSIBILITIES AND AUTHORITY** – As with all plans, the disaster recovery plan should outline what tasks need to be done, what order they are to be done in, who is responsible for each task, and who manages and controls the work effort.

- Since this may be happening at the same time as incident management and business continuity support, this should be managed by a separate team comprised of technical experts and system engineers who can rebuild the failed systems and restore processing capability.

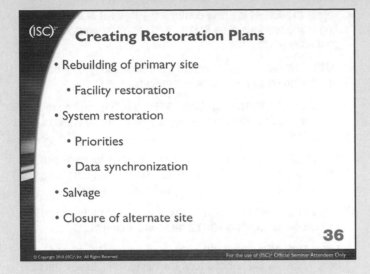

Creating Restoration Plans

- Rebuilding of primary site
  - Facility restoration
- System restoration
  - Priorities
  - Data synchronization
- Salvage
- Closure of alternate site

36

- **RESTORATION** – One of the main differences between planning and implementation is the final act of restoration. A key indicator after the plan is put into action is the ability to restore to a primary location. The primary facility must be stabilized and secured and after a more detailed damage assessment is conducted, a decision must be made as to whether to return. Assuming the site is recoverable, the plan must include restoration.

  - **SEPARATE FUNCTION AND TEAM** – The salvage and restoration team is separate from the BC team. The BC team deploys to the alternate location in order to bring up the critical systems prior to their RTO. The DR team remains at the original location in order to restore it to its original condition as soon as possible.

- **FACILITY RESTORATION** – Once the salvage operations have been completed in an area, restoration – restoring full operational capability at the original location – may begin.

- **SYSTEM RESTORATION** – "System restoration" means fully restoring all systems to their original locations and regaining full operational capability.

  - **PRIORITIES** – The priorities for system restoration and moving back to the primary site are the opposite of the priorities during the initial business continuity effort. In order to prove that the migration plan and restored systems and networks are stable and working correctly, the least important systems and processes are moved back first.

  - **DATA SYNCHRONIZATION** – A critical activity during the restoration effort is the synchronization of the data. This includes updating the data with changes made since the last backups, the re-entry of manual or interim processing, and starting new backup schedules.

- **SALVAGE** – The salvage team will ensure that the building is safe before work starts up again. Wiring, cabling, and other network and telephone equipment may need to be replaced/installed depending on the impact of incident. Remember that a lack of visible physical damage doesn't mean there is no internal damage. Each piece must be fully tested prior to it being considered salvageable.

- **CLOSURE OF ALTERNATE SITE** – The restoration team is often responsible for the clean up of the alternate site. This includes the recovery of equipment and supplies at the alternate site, and the clean up and restoration of supplies and data stored at the alternate location.

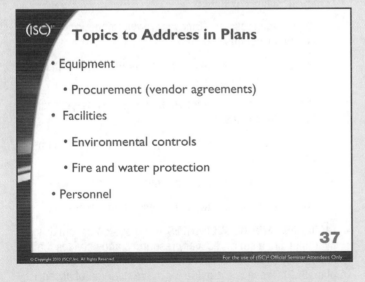

Topics to Address in Plans

- Equipment
  - Procurement (vendor agreements)
- Facilities
  - Environmental controls
  - Fire and water protection
- Personnel

37

- **TOPICS TO ADDRESS IN PLANS** – A plan must be comprehensive and complete. Many plans have overlooked areas such as logistics – the movement of equipment and people, the transfer of data from a backup site to the recovery location, and the provisioning of support for people required to work at the alternate location – water, food, accommodations, etc.

- This is just a partial list of items to include in a complete, reliable plan.

- **EQUIPMENT** – The plan should include a detailed list of equipment that is required as well as any equipment that must be moved from the original location.

  - **PROCUREMENT** – The plan should contain a copy of the vendor agreements and contracts that have been negotiated to provide equipment from vendors.

- **FACILITIES** – The plan should include a list of the required facilities, their location, and detailed information about these sites.

  - **ENVIRONMENTAL CONTROLS** – This is a list of all the required controls that must be at each location.

  - **FIRE AND WATER PROTECTION** – This includes the plan to provide protection from threats like fire and water, including floods.

- **PERSONNEL** – One of the most difficult resources to replace is skilled and trusted personnel. The plan should include how the facilities will be operated if a significant number of key personnel are killed or are not available during the crisis.

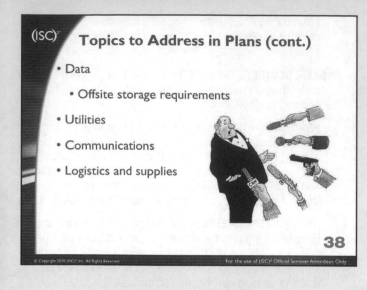

Topics to Address in Plans (cont.)

- Data
  - Offsite storage requirements
- Utilities
- Communications
- Logistics and supplies

38

- Topics to address in plans continued – This list is a continuation of the previous slide that lists items often overlooked in continuity plans

- **DATA** – The plan should contain a list of which type of data is required to be stored at offsite locations.

  - **OFFSITE STORAGE REQUIREMENTS** – This section of the plan includes the storage requirements for all types of data.

- **UTILITIES** – What are the utility requirements for each site? These requirements must be documented in the plan in case a site must be relocated or an alternate site selected.

- **COMMUNICATIONS** – As with the utilities, the communication requirements must also be documented in the plan.

- **LOGISTICS AND SUPPLIES** – This part of the plan must be very inclusive and not overlook the necessities to operate at each location, including personnel support items and personal hygiene items to support the staff during the crisis.

Resource-Level Consolidation

- Consolidation plan
- Availability of solutions
- Consolidate, approve, and implement
- Outcomes and deliverables

39

- **AVAILABILITY OF SOLUTIONS** – It is possible that the contracted recovery services required by the business processes do not exist in the vicinity. Some organizations have decided to provide their own recovery facilities and offer to share them (commercially) with other companies faced by the same dilemma.

- **CONSOLIDATE, APPROVE, IMPLEMENT** – This process includes the following stages:

  - Aggregating resource recovery requirements from the continuity options section.

  - Evaluating the costs and benefits for each option that can satisfy RTOs and scale.

  - Providing executive management with a strategic evaluation of the options.

  - Ensuring that executive management agrees to the options chosen.

  - Creating an implementation project and action plans.

  - Implementing an on-going process to ensure review.

- **OUTCOMES AND DELIVERABLES** – The outcomes and deliverables are a set of recovery resources and services that can be deployed under the control of the business continuity plan (BCP). These will provide for the restoration of acceptable functionality for business activities and for information recovery, both within their respective RTO and RPO.

- **CONSOLIDATION PLAN** – Having selected appropriate tactics for resumption of each business activity, the BCP team will be required to consolidate the resource requirements, determine how to source them, and document their inclusion in the plan. The parameters for resources for each activity will be derived from the RTOs, and the numbers or scale determined from the continuity requirements analysis. The purpose of this step is to coordinate and provide a predetermined level of resources to enable the implementation of the continuity options selected for each activity. This consolidation is necessary if resources are to be purchased (as a better price is likely to be achieved with a single order).

Domain Agenda

- BCM Project Planning

- Understanding the Organization

- Recovery Strategy Selection

- Creating the Plan(s)

- **Developing and Implementing Response**

- Testing, Update, and Maintenance of the Plan

40

- Developing and implementing the plans for incident management and response are critical to the successful recovery of the organization and protection of assets, individuals, and mission.

Incident Response Management

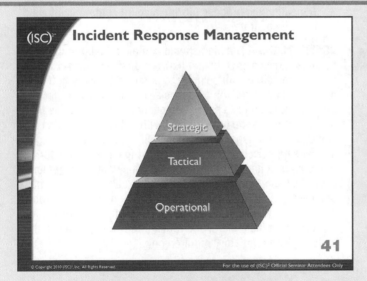

41

- One model of incident response, borrowed from the UK Emergency Services, shows three tiers of incident response. These are often referred to as Gold, Silver, and Bronze, or Strategic, Tactical, and Operational. When applied to an organization's response structure, the responsibilities are as follows:

- **STRATEGIC LEVEL: INCIDENT MANAGEMENT PLAN (IMP)** – The IMP defines how the strategic issues of a crisis affecting the organization would be addressed and managed by the chief executive/senior managers. This may be the point at which the incident is not entirely within the scope of the business continuity plan. Examples may include crises that do not result from interruptions (such as a hostile takeover or media exposure) and those where the impact is over a wider area than what was allowed for in the BCP strategy, such as in

a national emergency. The media response to any incident is usually managed through an IMP, though some organizations manage the media under a BCP.

- The incident management plan is sometimes called a crisis management plan, but reporting in the media that you have invoked your crisis management team may lead people to think you feel you have a CRISIS on your hands. The term "incident" has less negative connotation and so is preferred.

- **TACTICAL LEVEL: BUSINESS CONTINUITY PLAN (BCP)** – The BCP addresses business disruption, interruption, or loss, from the initial response to the point at which normal business operations are resumed. The BCPs will be based upon agreed upon business continuity strategies and will provide procedures and processes for both the business continuity and resource recovery teams. In particular, the plans allocate roles and their associated accountability, responsibility, and authority. The plans must also detail the relationships and the principles for dealing with a number of external players in the response (such as recovery service suppliers and emergency services, etc.).

- If the event falls outside the scope of the assumptions upon which the business continuity plan was based, the situation should be escalated to those responsible for implementing the incident management plan (IMP).

- **OPERATIONAL LEVEL: ACTIVITY RESUMPTION PLANS** – For an operational department, the plans provide resumption of normal business functions. For departments, such as Facilities and IT that are managing infrastructure, the plans will provide a logical and technical structure for restoring services or provisioning alternative facilities.

- **CRISIS MANAGEMENT –** The term "incident management team" (or IMT) may be applied to what others would call a "crisis management" or "response" team. It is important that an organization chooses language that fits into its culture and structure. Where a BC response is required, there is almost always a need to involve the IMT if only to make them aware of the situation in case it escalates.

- **RAPID RESPONSE IS CRITICAL –** Case studies of major incidents suggest that effective and rapid management of a crisis is the most significant factor in protecting an organization's brand from financial and reputation damage. For organizations with no plans in place, the incident management plan (IMP) may be the first element to develop and will provide a limited amount of protection while other plans are developed. The purpose of an IMP is to provide a documented framework to enable an organization to manage any crisis event regardless of cause.

  - **TRIAGE –** Triage is the initial gathering and assessment of the information related to the incident. The responder must determine whether the incident is real or a false positive. It is important to have alarms and other monitoring systems to alert the incident response team of a possible incident.

  - **NOTIFICATION –** Notification is the initial alerting of team members to a possible incident. This may also include evacuation of personnel.

    - **HEALTH AND SAFETY –** The highest priority in any crisis is the health and safety of personnel. The plans must include evacuation plans, assembly points, protective clothing, and emergency treatment.

- **ESCALATION –** Once the presence of an incident has been confirmed and it is not just a false positive, the incident response teams need to be notified and the team members assembled.

  - **EXECUTIVE SUCCESSION –** In the event that a manager or other important person in the BCM team is not available, the succession plan must be implemented. All team members should be informed of the change in personnel and responsibilities.

- **STEPS TO DEVELOP AN INCIDENT MANAGEMENT PLAN –** Steps in developing an incident management plan include:

  - Appointing an owner.

  - Defining the scope and objectives.

  - Developing and approving an incident management plan development process and program.

  - Agreeing on the responsibilities of the incident management team.

  - Deciding on the structure, format, components, and content of the plan.

  - Determining the strategies, such as alternative locations, on which the plan is based.

  - Gathering information to populate the plan.

  - Nominating individuals and deputies.

  - Agreeing upon and validating the plan.

  - Repeating the process for the incident communications plan (if separate).

- **ACTION PLANS –** The plan should contain initial prompts for action, such as a stakeholder list. The business impact analysis may contain useful pointers to potential impacts that will need to be managed. As all crises are different, the incident management plan is a set of components and resources that may be useful to the team tasked with activating the plan. The incident management plan should be modular in design so that single sections can be supplied to individuals and/or teams on a need-to-know basis. An incident management plan must support the role of the organization's incident management team during a crisis event and demonstrate preparation for effective incident management to the media, markets, customers, stakeholders, and regulators in compliance with statutory and regulatory requirements.

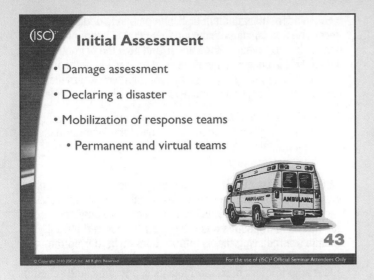

- **INITIAL ASSESSMENT** – All precautions were taken to avoid an incident, the risk assessment was done thoroughly, the controls were designed to prevent failure or incident, and the awareness programs ensured that everyone was being careful to prevent errors; regardless, incidents will happen. Some are accidental, some intentional; some are people related while others are caused by equipment or utility failure or natural disaster. Regardless of the cause, the first step in incident management is to detect the presence of a problem and then ensure health and safety. Once that is done, the next steps are to contain or control the incident and stop it from spreading further.

- **DAMAGE ASSESSMENT** – Depending on the nature and cause of the incident, the methods of containment and repair are very different. This requires the incident management team to determine the cause of the incident and the extent of the damage. The damage may be related to finances, facilities, reputation, health, production, or delivery of services, to name a few. The assessment of damage will also trigger the decision of whether or not to declare a disaster (based on the anticipated time required to return to normal) and move operations to an alternate site, or commence the recovery operations and activate appropriate response teams.

- **DECLARING A DISASTER** – For many organizations, the declaration of a disaster is a significant event that may require notification to shareholders, community leaders, and other affected parties. The declaration of a disaster represents the decision to relocate operations to an alternate location. This mobilizes the business continuity and disaster recovery teams and begins the process of resuming operations according to the schedules and plans that were set up. The declaration of a disaster should be the responsibility of a senior manager, based on the information provided by the damage assessment team.

- **MOBILIZATION OF RESPONSE TEAMS** – The type or nature of the incident will determine the appropriate response. Some incidents may require a highly technical team to sort through logs, while other incidents may require forensic accountants to review financial systems. It is critical to have the contact details for the team members so that they can be reached when needed.

  - **PERMANENT AND VIRTUAL TEAMS** – most organizations will have a small permanent team that is mobilized in nearly every incident. This team will provide core coordination and management functions, while other virtual team members are called as needed to provide crucial support. These virtual team members will be chosen based on their specialized skills. The virtual team may include health and safety personnel, communications and public relations, representatives from the business units, and external experts, to name a few.

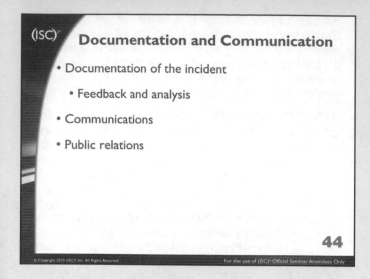

Documentation and Communication

- Documentation of the incident
  - Feedback and analysis
- Communications
- Public relations

44

In an incident management plan, one person is dedicated to recording and documenting everything that is happening during the crisis: who, what, where, when, and how the actions were taken. This is an invaluable document for reviewing the incident later and discovering opportunities for improvement of incident management, processes, and personnel.

- **FEEDBACK AND ANALYSIS** – This document is mostly used during the feedback stage once the incident has been contained and there is opportunity to review the crisis in more detail.

- **COMMUNICATIONS** – When reviewing incidents that organizations have faced, one of the most common problems they faced during the crisis was ineffective communications. From an internal perspective it is often hard to ensure the right people are receiving timely information – whether up the team structure to support strategic decision making; or down the team structure to support logistics, priorities, and scheduling. Traditional methods of communication may not be available, since personnel may be scattered in different locations and phone systems may not work. This can lead to confusion, rumours, and loss of credibility for the organization. Current technologies should be considered for enhancing communications, including extranet, mobile phones, and Short Message Service (SMS) capabilities.

- **PUBLIC RELATIONS** – The public relations department has the delicate task of dealing with the media, outside agencies, possibly family members, and influencing public opinion. It should be trained in how to handle crisis communications and have prepared scripts that ensure that complete and correct information is provided in a timely manner.

- **DOCUMENTATION AND COMMUNICATION** – Perhaps the areas of documentation and communication are often thought of as secondary matters and not as critical as the technical and management side of incident planning. However, poorly communicated incidents and lack of supporting reports or evidence have caused many incidents that may have been handled effectively in most ways, to cause the failure of the organization or the inability to learn or correctly determine the root cause of the incident.

- **DOCUMENTATION OF THE INCIDENT** – From the moment an alert is first received that may indicate an incident, logs should be maintained that record the details of the alert, what was done, and begin tracking the response efforts to the problem.

Domain Agenda

- BCM Project Planning

- Understanding the Organization

- Recovery Strategy Selection

- Creating the Plan(s)

- Developing and Implementing Response

- **Testing, Update, and Maintenance of the Plan**

45

- A plan cannot be trusted unless it has been tested and maintained. This next section will examine testing techniques and the triggers for maintaining the plans, and communicating and training the staff in their roles in BCM.

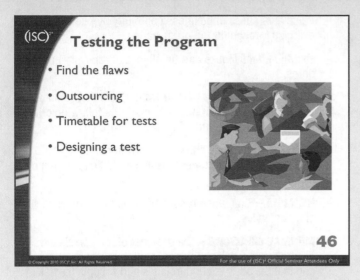

Testing the Program

- Find the flaws
- Outsourcing
- Timetable for tests
- Designing a test

46

- **FIND THE FLAWS** – To be successful, a testing program must begin simply and escalate gradually to ensure efficient use of resources. The core objective of a test is to ensure that flaws in the plan are discovered so that they can be corrected. Testing also trains personnel in their role in an incident and ensures that each person is competent to fulfill that role.

- **OUTSOURCING** – The responsibility for service delivery remains with the original organization, even if it has outsourced a service. As such, the organization should test to make sure that the outsourcing company is able to deliver on its obligations. Similarly, suppliers of products or services whose failure would cause significant disruption to the organization should be asked to demonstrate their recovery capability. Testing of outsourced activities should be a contractual requirement arranged via service level agreements (SLAs).

- **TIMETABLE FOR TESTS** – The BCP policy should outline the timetable and responsibilities for the test program. The purpose of the test program is to ensure that all plan information is verified and that all plans are rehearsed.

- **DESIGNING A TEST:**

  - Draw up a list of all recovery processes.

  - Decide on a suitable type of test activity for each process.

  - Draw up a list of all personnel or groups involved in each process.

  - Devise a timetable of test activities that ensures that all relevant personnel are included in the test activity.

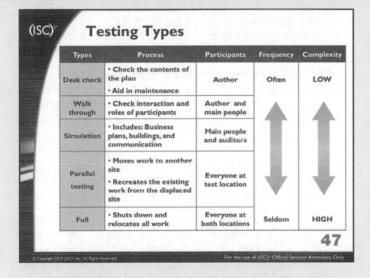

Testing Types

Types	Process	Participants	Frequency	Complexity
Desk check	• Check the contents of the plan • Aid in maintenance	Author	Often	LOW
Walk through	• Check interaction and roles of participants	Author and main people		
Simulation	• Includes: Business plans, buildings, and communication	Main people and auditors		
Parallel testing	• Moves work to another site • Recreates the existing work from the displaced site	Everyone at test location		
Full	• Shuts down and relocates all work	Everyone at both locations	Seldom	HIGH

47

- **TYPES OF TESTS** – Tests performed depend on the requirements to exercise the plan and the level of assurance required to ensure that the plan will work properly in a crisis situation. Observers of the tests may include administrators, umpires, auditors, and subject matter experts (SMEs). Administrators take notes of success, missing elements, and deficiencies. Umpires test against test metrics. Auditors confirm that organization objectives are met. SMEs observe to provide recommendations. Participants should be restricted to using only the material available from the offsite storage or alternate storage facility.

- **CHECKLIST OR DESK CHECK** – Exercises are uncomplicated and low cost. Participants review plan contents and check information such as phone numbers, equipment, and locations.

- **STRUCTURED WALK-THROUGH (OR TABLE-TOP OR CLASS-ROOM EXERCISE)** – Also uncomplicated and low cost. Team members meet and discuss each plan element and procedure across several meetings. They step through the plans and

have some role interaction, but all is done within the confines of the conference room. They assess effectiveness and limitations. Deficiencies or areas for improvement are noted for the test report and post-test review.

- **SIMULATIONS (ALSO KNOWN AS FUNCTIONAL TESTS, OR WAR GAMES)** – Cost and complexity are increased, as simulations require planning and coordination. Simulations typically include a pretend disaster and all teams exercise their training and judgment and simulate their actions. Team communications should also be simulated to emulate realism; for example, personnel role-play the offsite storage and recovery site rehearsal activities or may contact them with no advance notice. A fire drill is an example of a common simulation exercise in that it tests the evacuation plan, and the role of the fire wardens to ensure proper clearance of the facility.

- **PARALLEL TESTING** – Is higher cost and more complex, as it takes advantage of test time at the actual recovery site. Note that parallel testing does not impact operations. Commercial contracts include a minimum of one test week per year. This may be more difficult to arrange with a mutual aid agreement. The benefit of parallel testing is that recovery site processing results can be compared with the primary site's processing. Another benefit is that recovery procedures may be more fully tested and personnel more fully trained. A parallel test is basically an operations test to show that critical systems can be run at the alternate site.

- **FULL INTERRUPTION** – The highest cost and most complex. Primary operations are shut down and continuity relies solely on recovery procedure accuracy, completeness, and personnel ability. Full interruption should only be considered after successful parallel testing and only conducted under steering committee authorization. Full interruption testing is not usually recommended for large organizations because of the possibility of creating an actual outage that might precipitate an actual disaster.

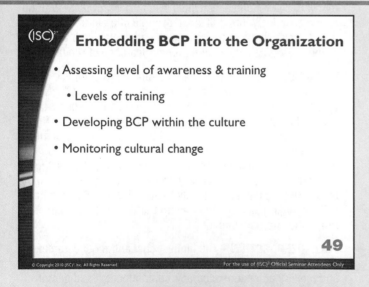

Testing BCP Arrangements

- Test, rehearsal, exercise
- Combining individual tests to ensure complete coverage
- Stringency, realism, and minimal exposure
  - Risks of testing
- Scope and documentation of a test
- Outcomes

48

- **TEST, REHEARSAL, EXERCISE** – "Testing" is a generic phrase used to describe the testing of business continuity plans, rehearsing team members and staff, and testing of technology and procedures.

- **COMBINING INDIVIDUAL TESTS TO ENSURE COMPLETE COVERAGE** – Each individual test activity should form part of an overall test program and may need to be scheduled with supporting training activities. By doing several smaller tests, the opportunity for test success is raised and the complexity of the tests may be reduced. The purpose of testing is to:

  - Evaluate the organization's BCP competence.
  - Identify missing information or areas for improvement.
  - Highlight assumptions which need to be questioned.
  - Provide information and instill confidence in test participants.
  - Develop teamwork.

- Raise awareness of business continuity by publicizing the exercise throughout the organization.
- Test the effectiveness and timeliness of recovery procedures.

- **STRINGENCY, REALISM, AND MINIMAL EXPOSURE** – In order for any test to be useful, it needs to meet the following criteria: stringency, realism, and minimal exposure.

  - **STRINGENCY** – Tests should be carried out using the same procedures and methods as would be used in a real event.

  - **REALISM** – Simulation proves the viability of plans in such circumstances.

  - **MINIMAL EXPOSURE** – The designer of the test should ensure that the risk and impact of disruption are minimized and that the business understands and accepts the risk.

  - **RISKS OF TESTING** – There is always the risk that a test may actually harm the business by causing a real outage, and there is the risk that a ongoing test may hide a real crisis that is developing at the same time.

- **SCOPE AND DOCUMENTATION OF A TEST** – Each test must have a defined scope and test objectives. This allows the management of the test the ability to ensure that no parts of the plan were overlooked, and measurement or determination of whether the test was successful in that it met its initial objectives. The test team will conduct the test and record the results, assess and report the results, and address any issues raised.

- **OUTCOMES** – The outcomes of the BCP testing process include validation that the business continuity and recovery strategies are effective and that team members and staff are familiar with their roles, accountability, responsibilities, and authority in response to an incident.

Embedding BCP into the Organization

- Assessing level of awareness & training
  - Levels of training
- Developing BCP within the culture
- Monitoring cultural change

49

- **ASSESSING LEVEL OF AWARENESS & TRAINING** – To be successful, BCP must become a part of normal business management. Opportunities exist to introduce and enhance an organization's BCP culture at all points in the BCP process. Systems and processes must be developed and maintained with the attitude to build recovery systems and preparation for incidents right into the process itself. People should be trained

to know how to detect a problem and what to do if something does go wrong.

- **LEVELS OF TRAINING** – Depending on a person's role in the organization and responsibilities during a crisis, he or she must be adequately trained. While all personnel need basic training (evacuation plans, how to respond to an alert), some people will need more advanced training and skills development.

- **DEVELOPING BCP WITHIN THE CULTURE** – The leadership of the organization must ensure that the BCP is fully integrated throughout the organization. This is accomplished through routine evaluation of the plan, rehearsals, and good organizational procedures. The CISSP is not usually the leader of the BCP effort, but your involvement is critical to the effectiveness of the plan and preserving information security controls even during a disaster.

- **MONITORING CULTURAL CHANGE** – A key indicator of the successful embedding of BCP into an organization is successful feedback. Feedback can be obtained in several ways, including via questionnaires, direct questioning of staff members, and through informal questions. Whenever a change to the plan is made, it must be approved, tested, and training must be adjusted to ensure that everyone understands the change.

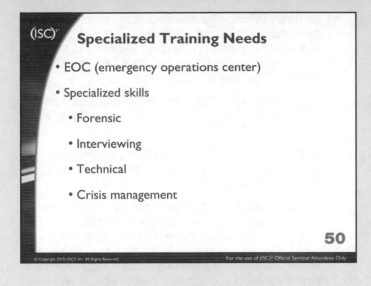

Specialized Training Needs

- EOC (emergency operations center)

- Specialized skills

  - Forensic

  - Interviewing

  - Technical

  - Crisis management

50

- **SPECIALIZED TRAINING NEEDS –** The members of the incident management team, business continuity team, and disaster recovery team, as well as the other specialized groups such as representatives from finance, communications, and human resources, need training that will prepare them for the roles they must play in a crisis.

- **EMERGENCY OPERATIONS CENTER –** The EOC is the central management point for a crisis. The staff assigned to it must be able to handle the stress and decision-making responsibilities associated with a disaster. They require training in organizational skills, crisis management, and communications.

- **SPECIALIZED SKILLS –** The teams will often call on specialists (virtual team members) to assist the organization through the crisis. These personnel must also have the required skills to perform their roles effectively and professionally. Some of the specialized skills that may be required are listed here.

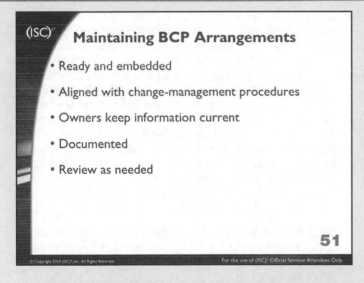

Maintaining BCP Arrangements

- Ready and embedded

- Aligned with change-management procedures

- Owners keep information current

- Documented

- Review as needed

51

- **READY AND EMBEDDED –** The BCP maintenance program ensures that the organization remains ready to handle incidents despite the constant changes that all organizations experience. To be effective, the BCP maintenance program should be embedded within the organization's normal and change-management processes rather than being a separate structure that can be forgotten. Most of the issues that show up in tests and exercises are the result of internal changes within the organization – staff, locations, or technology. The purpose of the business continuity and incident management maintenance process is to ensure that the organization's BCP capability remains effective

despite changes to internal business processes and external influences. Effective change management is a prerequisite for maintaining the BCP program.

- **ALIGNED WITH (TRIGGERED BY) CHANGE-MANAGEMENT PROCEDURES –** The review may be triggered by the change-management process highlighting the proposed change, by post-test "learning points" action plans, or via an audit report. Assess whether changes and amendments create a new training, awareness, and/or communication need and whether the changes will affect, and necessitate changes to, the current plan. Distribute updated, amended, changed BCP policy, strategies, solutions, processes, and plans to key stakeholders under the formal change (version) control process.

- **OWNERS KEEP INFORMATION CURRENT –** Each plan owner is responsible for updating the team's BC plans and dynamic data such as staff out-of-hours contact numbers, team tasks, notification and supplier contact details, contingency-box contents, etc.

- **DOCUMENTED –** The outcomes from the BC maintenance process include a documented BC monitoring and maintenance program, a maintenance report, and a clearly defined and documented BCP maintenance report action plan agreed and "signed-off" by an appropriate senior manager.

- **REVIEW AS NEEDED –** The frequency of a BCP maintenance program review will be dependent upon the nature, scale, and pace of business change.

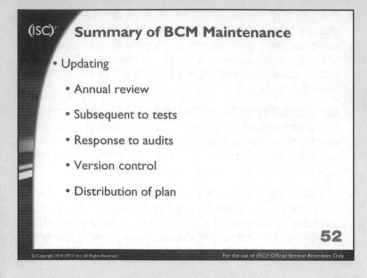

- **SUMMARY OF BCM MAINTENANCE –** As seen in the previous slides, it is important to keep the BCP plans up to date. Some of the key issues around plan maintenance are addressed here.

- **UPDATING –** The plans require updating as the organization changes and staff move around. The BCM coordinator is responsible to ensure that the plan is reviewed by all local managers on an annual basis to ensure that their staff, systems, information, and technical needs are shown correctly.

- **ANNUAL REVIEW –** The BCM coordinator should have a key performance indicator objective to ensure that the reviews of the plans are completed annually and that the training and awareness programs have kept up with the changes in staff and roles in the plan.

- **SUBSEQUENT TO TESTS –** The deficiencies noted during tests must be addressed and resolved as quickly as practical.

- **RESPONSE TO AUDITS –** Any audit recommendations should be considered and resolved according to their priority, materiality, and resource availability.

- **VERSION CONTROL –** BCM plans are confidential documents but they must be available when needed. They must also be stored in a format that can easily be accessed during a test or a crisis, and care must be taken to ensure that all staff are working from the same version. Version control is an important function of BCM. All changes to the plan should be logged and distributed in an approved manner.

- **DISTRIBUTION OF PLANS –** Organizations will often number their paper copies of plans to track each copy. Sometimes abbreviated versions are given to individuals who may have a specific task during the crisis but do not require access to the entire plan. Copies are also stored electronically and may be accessed through an extranet, mobile phone, or other medium as appropriate.

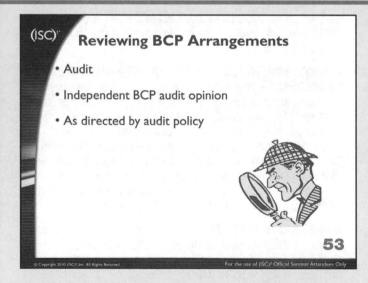

- **AUDIT –** An audit function provides remedial recommendations as a result of performing an impartial review against defined standards and policies. Auditing is designed to verify that processes have been followed correctly, not that the solutions adopted are necessarily correct. The audit should be conducted against a BCP policy and appropriate standards identified by it. The purpose of a BCP audit is to scrutinize an organization's existing BCP competence and capability, verify them against predefined standards and criteria, and deliver a structured audit opinion report. This approach assumes that if the process is correct and properly applied, the outcome should provide an effective and fit-for-purpose BCP competence and capability. The BCP audit (as with BC planning, implementation, and maintenance) focuses on a complex process and requires interaction with a wide range of managerial and operational roles from both a business and technical perspective. The methods used for audit should be determined by those undertaking the audit.

- **INDEPENDENT BCP AUDIT OPINION –** The outcomes should be an independent BCP audit opinion report and a remedial action plan (or plans) that are agreed to and approved by senior management.

- **AS DIRECTED BY AUDIT POLICY –** The policy concerning the frequency of audit should be clearly defined and documented within the organization's audit policy and standards.

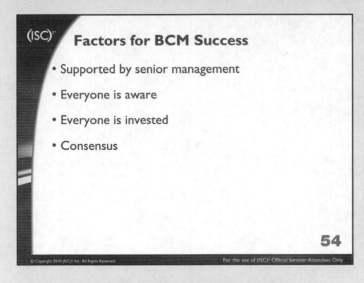

Factors for BCM Success

- Supported by senior management
- Everyone is aware
- Everyone is invested
- Consensus

54

awareness effort, consultation in itself helps raise awareness and may help prepare the way for commitment to new working practices.

- **EVERYONE IS INVESTED** – Focus on the business priorities of the organization. Relating the campaign message to corporate and individual WIIFM ("What's In It For Me?") factors helps provide justification for the BCP and the working practices that support it. Tailor the awareness campaign and its messages to target audiences. These audiences will be both internal (for example, BCP practitioners and general staff) and external (for example, key stakeholders and third parties that are dependent on, or may adversely affect, the organization's own business continuity planning effort). External awareness is particularly important where BCP operates in an outsourced environment.

- **CONSENSUS** – Organizational culture is manifested in shared values, operating norms, styles, and patterns of behavior. It is frequently described as "the way we do things around here" or "what you have to do to get on." Experience has shown that behavioral change initiatives fail to attract lasting commitment unless attitudes and beliefs are also engaged. One specific belief – "It will never happen to me"– is a particular barrier to BCP. In order to really change behaviors, it is necessary to influence attitudes. In order to influence attitudes, it is necessary to develop and establish beliefs. Thus, achieving cultural change can be a subtle and lengthy process.

- **SUPPORTED BY SENIOR MANAGEMENT** – Visible and continued support by senior management. This must include adequate budget to support the continuity plans as well as awareness campaign over time. It is also important to gain commitment from managers and operational staff who are required to implement business continuity planning.

- **EVERYONE IS AWARE** – Consultation with everyone involved in developing the BCP. As well as providing focus for the

---

Domain Summary

- BCM Project Planning

- Understanding the Organization

- Recovery Strategy Selection

- Creating the Plan(s)

- Developing and Implementing Response

- Testing, Update, and Maintenance of the Plan

55

- These are the topics areas covered in this domain. It is critically important for the CISSP candidate to be familiar with the stages of business continuity management and the IT-related issues in each stage.

Security Transcends Technology
(ISC)²®
© Copyright 2010 (ISC)², Inc. All Rights Reserved.
56

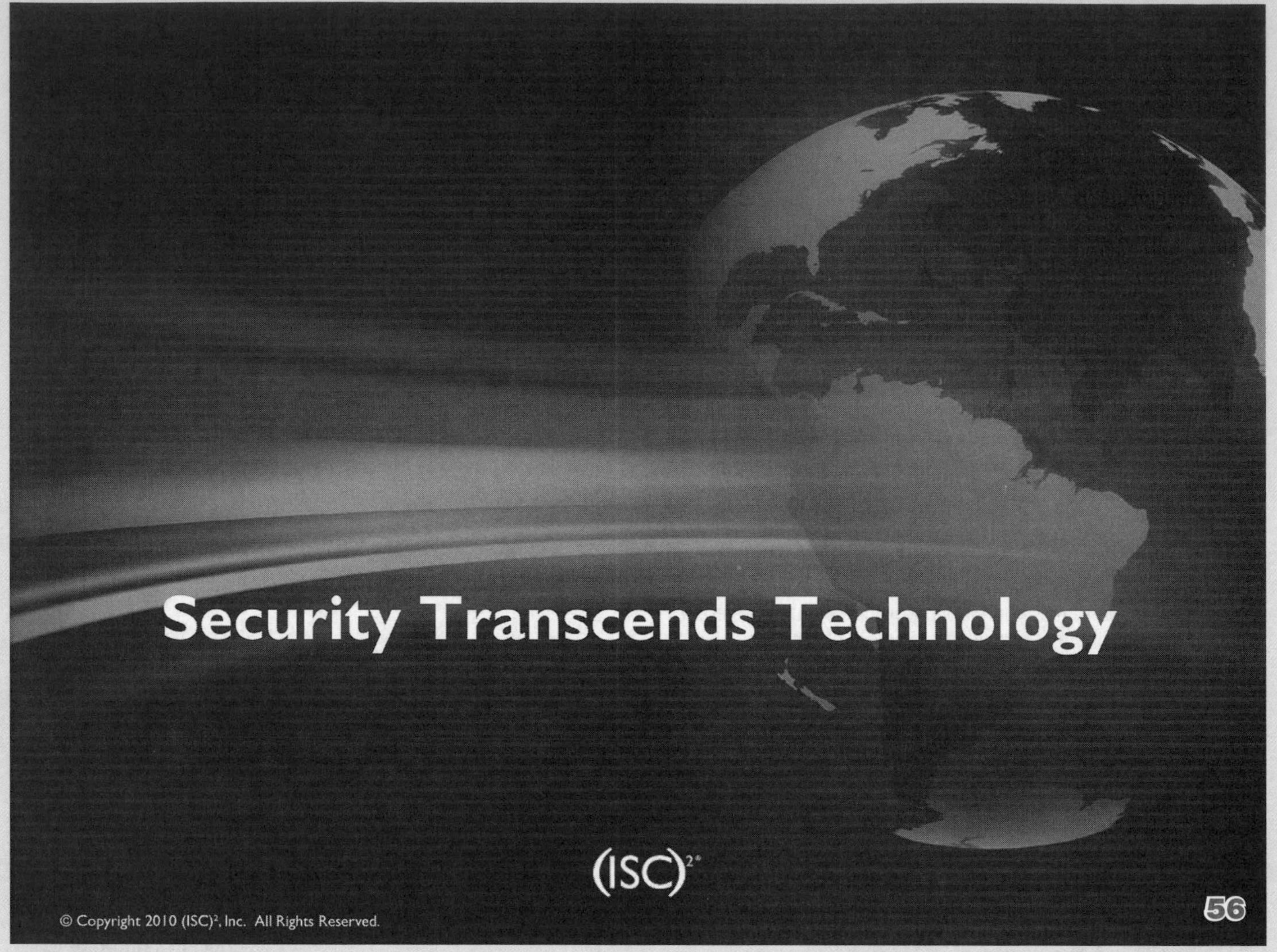

Review Questions

BUSINESS CONTINUITY AND DISASTER RECOVERY PLANNING

1. Which of the following contains references to expected business continuity planning (BCP) practices that organizations must implement?

   A. ISO 17799:2008, section 1
   B. ISO 27005:2008, section 8
   C. ISO 27002:2005, section 10
   D. ISO 27001:2005, annex A

2. What process identifies the business continuity requirements for the organization's assets?

   A. Risk analysis
   B. Business impact analysis
   C. Threat analysis
   D. Asset classification

3. A contingency plan should be written to

   A. address all possible risk scenarios.
   B. address all likely risk scenarios.
   C. remediate all vulnerabilities.
   D. recover all operations.

4. Which of the following components make up enterprise-wide business continuity management?

   A. Business continuity planning (BCP), disaster recovery planning (DRP), and incident management
   B. Business resiliency planning (BRP), disaster preparedness and reconstitution planning (DPRP), and incident management
   C. Business impact analysis (BIA), contingency planning, and incident management
   D. Capacity planning, risk analysis, inventory management, and business continuity planning (BCP)

5. BS 25999 is based on which well-established continuous improvement model?

   A. Six-sigma
   B. Plan-do-check-act (PDCA)
   C. Total quality management (TQM)
   D. SEI capability and maturity model integration (CMMI)

6. What is the main goal of business continuity?

   A. To ensure the confidentiality, integrity, and availability of business assets.
   B. To ensure the business is able to continue operations throughout different incidents.
   C. To ensure the business maintains sensitive assets at their required protection level.
   D. To ensure the business is able to continue operations throughout different disasters.

7. What are the five (5) steps that should be followed when developing a business continuity plan?

   A. Conduct a business impact analysis, assess the risks, develop a strategy, develop a plan, and rehearse the plan.
   B. Conduct a business impact analysis, assess the risks, develop a strategy, develop a plan, and establish training requirements.
   C. Analyze the business, assess the risks, develop a strategy, develop a plan, and rehearse the plan.
   D. Analyze the business, assess the risks, develop a strategy, develop a plan, and establish training requirements.

8. Of the choices below, which best describes the reasons for business continuity management (BCM) project failure?

   A. Timelines not being adhered to and unwise use of resources.
   B. Timelines not being adhered to and incorrect staff assigned to assist in the project.
   C. Lack of program management and unwise use of resources.
   D. Lack of program management and incorrect staff assigned to assist in the project.

9. Which of the following is not typically a part of business continuity management documentation?

   A. Business impact analysis
   B. Risk and threat assessment
   C. Response plans
   D. Certification and accreditation plan (CAP)

10. What is the difference between risk management and business continuity planning (BCP)?

    A. BCP is concerned with events that are highly likely or have the highest impact, while risk management is usually focused on events that would be catastrophic in nature but are rare in likelihood.
    B. Risk management is concerned with events that are highly likely or have the highest impact, while BCP is usually focused on events that would be catastrophic in nature but are rare in likelihood.
    C. BCP is concerned with events that, on rare occasions, may impact business, while risk management is always focused on monetary loss.
    D. BCP is usually focused on events that would be catastrophic in nature but are rare in likelihood, while risk management is always focused on monetary loss.

11. Which of the following is a correct statement concerning the maximum tolerable downtime (MTD)?

A. A MTD that has been adjusted upward to allow for unforeseen issues is called the recovery time objective (RTO).

B. A MTD that has been adjusted downward to allow for planned outages is called the recovery time objective (RTO).

C. A MTD that has been adjusted upward to allow for planned outages is called the recovery time objective (RTO).

D. A MTD that has been adjusted downward to allow for unforeseen issues is called the recovery time objective (RTO).

12. Which of the following is used to identify the timescale and the extent of the impact of a disruption at several levels in an organization?

A. A business impact analysis (BIA)

B. Recovery time objective (RTO)

C. Maximum tolerable downtime (MTD)

D. Mean time between failure (MTBF)

13. Contractual terms used to ensure adequate service, often relating to acceptable outage times, committed repair times, maintenance windows, and operational and performance standards, are generally referred to as

A. systems status and operational usage agreements (SSOUA).

B. operational effectiveness and utilization agreements (OEUA).

C. master services and operations agreement (MSOA).

D. service level agreements (SLA).

14. During a recovery effort, the length of the interruption window is best described by the time

A. it takes to contact the backup center and the establishment of minimal service.

B. between the disaster and the establishment of minimal service.

C. it takes to contact the backup center and restore to fully operational status.

D. between the disaster and restoration to fully operational status.

15. After completing your business continuity plan, your Business Continuity Team concludes that your company must have a fully redundant IT infrastructure which provides 100 percent availability. Which recovery alternative is best suited for your organization?

A. Mobile site/trailer

B. Hot site

C. Fail-Safe site

D. Multiple processing/mirrored site

16. Which type of processing agreement would be most applicable when planning for a pandemic?

A. Service bureau

B. Mutual aid

C. Contingency

D. Remote working arrangements

17. Which type of testing requires processing and operations executed at the recovery site, but does not involve the primary site?

A. Walk-through test

B. Parallel testing

C. Simulation testing

D. Full testing

18. What is a major risk involved with the maintenance and availability of the business continuity plan documentation?

A. It can be used to facilitate attacks against the organization.

B. It can be very expensive to maintain and manage.

C. It contains intellectual property (IP) information, which must be copyright protected.

D. It must be changed every time change management approves a change to organization systems.

19. When should a full interruption test be conducted?

A. At least annually

B. On significant change

C. After successful parallel test

D. Only with senior executive authorization

20. An evacuation drill is scheduled. The day of the event, an employee reports to work with a leg cast. As a business continuity (BC) coordinator, what action should you take?

A. Direct the employee to follow evacuation procedures.

B. Direct the employee to stay at his or her desk.

C. Direct the employee to take the elevator prior to the test and wait at the assembly point.

D. Direct the employee to stay at his or her desk, and direct the supervisor to report that the employee reported to the assembly area.

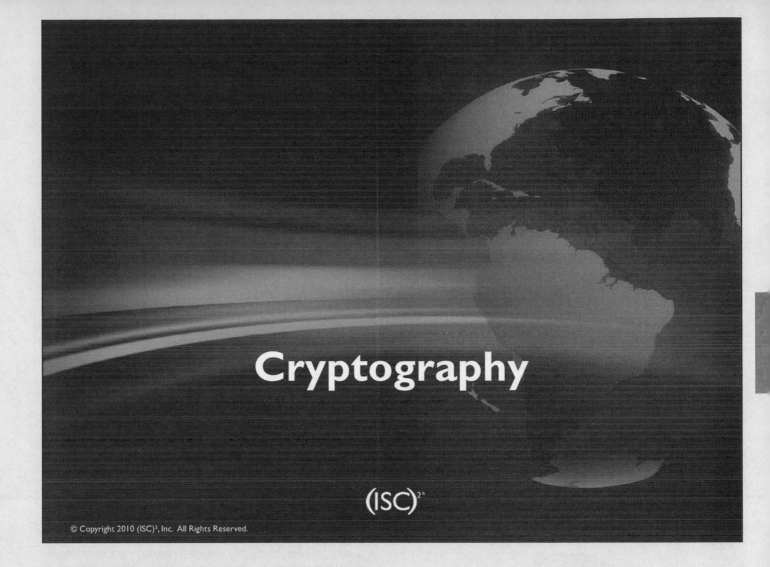

Cryptography

(ISC)²

Domain Agenda

- **Definitions**
- History
- Uses
- Cryptographic Methods
- Encryption Systems
- Algorithms
- Cryptanalysis and Attacks
- Implementations

2

Concepts and Definitions

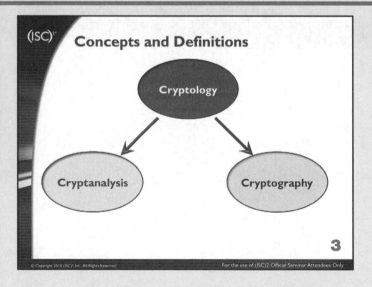

- **CRYPTOLOGY** – The study of cryptography and cryptanalysis.

- **CRYPTANALYSIS** – The practice of defeating the protective properties of cryptography. Reading protected information, altering messages or integrity values, and violating authentication schemes are all forms of cryptanalysis. The practice of testing cryptographic algorithms to determine their strength or resistance to compromise is also a form of cryptanalysis.

- **CRYPTOGRAPHY** – The word cryptography is based on the Greek words "kryptos" (hidden) and "graphia" (writing). It is a mathematical manipulation of information that prevents the information from being disclosed or altered.

3

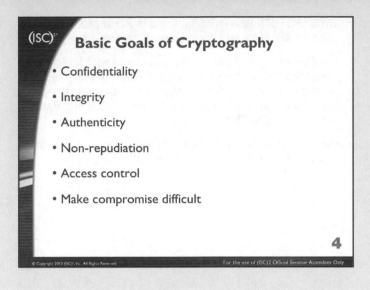

Basic Goals of Cryptography

- Confidentiality
- Integrity
- Authenticity
- Non-repudiation
- Access control
- Make compromise difficult

- **ENSURE CONFIDENTIALITY OF SENSITIVE INFORMATION –** Cryptography ensures the confidentiality of sensitive information by preventing unauthorized persons from being able to understand or, in some cases, even detect the presence of a message.

- **ENSURE INTEGRITY OF INFORMATION –** By detecting whether a message has been tampered with or corrupted.

- **VERIFY THE AUTHENTICITY OF COMMUNICATIONS –** In terms of ensuring that the message has been sent to the correct person and in the correct order, including prevention of replay attacks. This is accomplished by many implementations of cryptography, including IPSec and SSL.

- **SUPPORT NON-REPUDIATION –** By sender and/or receiver. Simply put, the sender cannot deny that he or she sent the message. This is achieved using digital signatures and other techniques to validate the identity of the sender and receiver.

- **PROVIDE FOUNDATION FOR SECURE ACCESS CONTROL –** Encrypted passwords and token-based access control devices provide access control protection for systems and applications.

- **MAKE COMPROMISE TOO EXPENSIVE OR TIME-CONSUMING –** All cryptographic protection is ultimately breakable. The purpose of cryptographic protection is to make the attack either too expensive or too time-consuming to be worth the effort.

REFERENCE:
http://searchsecurity.techtarget.com/tip/0,289483,sid14_gci936670,00.html

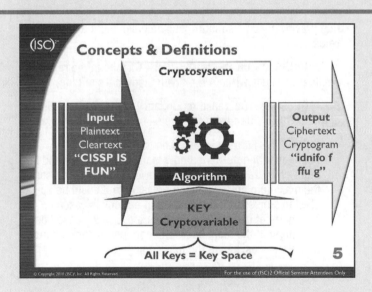

Concepts & Definitions

- **CRYPTOSYSTEM –** The device or process used to perform encryption and decryption operations.

- **PLAINTEXT/CLEARTEXT –** This is the natural or human-readable form of a message.

- **CIPHERTEXT/CRYPTOGRAM –** This is the enciphered, encrypted, or scrambled form of a message.

- **CRYPTOGRAPHIC ALGORITHM –** The mathematical function that determines the cryptographic operations.

- **CRYPTOVARIABLE (KEY) –** The (often secret) value used in the transformation of the message in a cryptographic operation that controls the operation of the algorithm in a unique, predictable manner.

- **KEY SPACE –** The total number of keys available to the user of a cryptosystem.

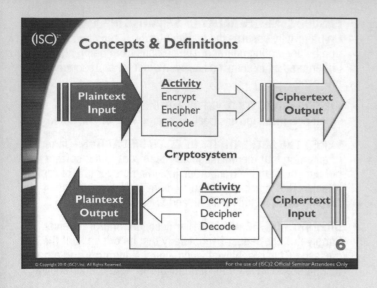

- **ENCRYPT/ENCIPHER** – Scrambling a plaintext message by using an algorithm, usually in conjunction with a key.

- **ENCODE** – Encoding a message is similar to enciphering or encrypting the message except that it does not use a key. This is often done so that the message can be transmitted through a different system. An example is Base 64, which encodes message attachments.

- **DECIPHER/DECRYPT/DECODE** – Descrambling an encrypted message and converting it into plaintext.

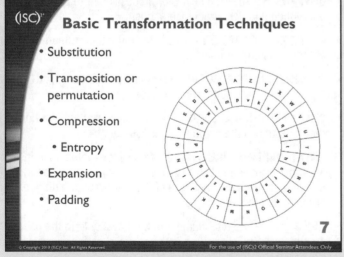

that provide specific substitutions between input and output values.

- **TRANSPOSITION OR PERMUTATION** – Change in the relative position of values without replacing them (bit-shuffling).

- **COMPRESSION** – Decrease redundancy before plaintext is encrypted. This is often used to save on bandwidth and storage.

  - **ENTROPY** – Entropy is based on the work of Claude Shannon that determined how many binary bits would be required to transmit one character of text. This represents the maximum amount of compression that could be applied to a message. The amount of entropy is based on the total number of variables represented (usually based on the length of the alphabet – the more characters the more random values, hence the less compression).

- **EXPANSION –**

  - Expanding the plaintext by duplicating values found in the plaintext.

  - Typically used to increase the size of plaintext to match the size of keys or subkeys.

- **PADDING** – Adding additional material to the plaintext message before it is encrypted to assist with encryption, address weaknesses in an algorithm when particular messages are encrypted, and foil traffic analysis.

- These are some of the techniques that have been used to provide diffusion and confusion. Confusion has been accomplished through complex substitution schemes, typically using "substitution boxes" or S-Boxes (lookup tables that manage the substitution) that can be either static or dynamic (built from the key). Initialization Vectors are also used to provide greater confusion. Diffusion has been accomplished using many of the other means, most notably permutation (transposition) and key mixing.

- **SUBSTITUTION** – Is replacement of one value for another. Substitution boxes (S-boxes): Static or dynamic lookup tables

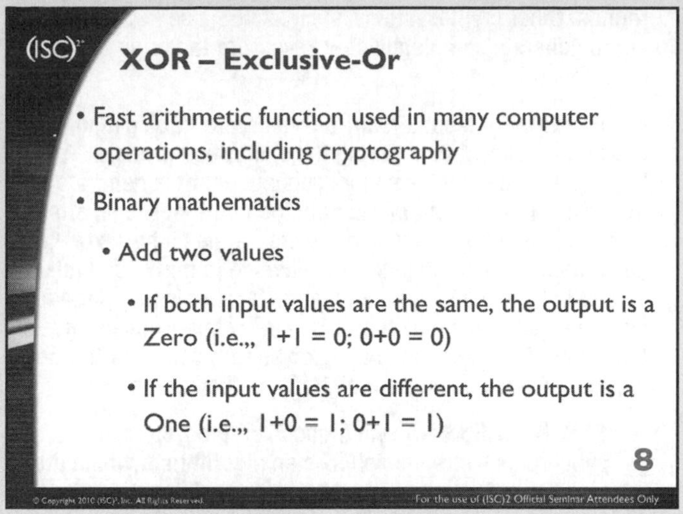

XOR – Exclusive-Or

- Fast arithmetic function used in many computer operations, including cryptography

- Binary mathematics

  - Add two values

    - If both input values are the same, the output is a Zero (i.e., 1+1 = 0; 0+0 = 0)

    - If the input values are different, the output is a One (i.e., 1+0 = 1; 0+1 = 1)

8

- **EXCLUSIVE-OR (XOR) –** Is a basic transformation technique and another name for binary addition: An XOR operation results in 0 if the two values being combined are the same; and 1 if they are different. XOR is used in many stream and block ciphers for substitution operations. This same operation is used in calculating simple parity for RAID.

For example, add the bytes:

$$11110001$$
$$\underline{01010101}$$

The output is 10100100

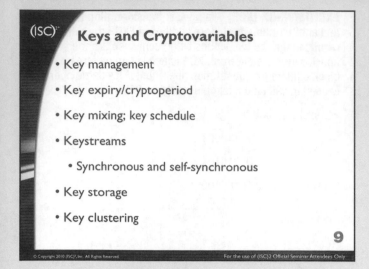

- **KEYS AND CRYPTOVARIABLES –** For the users of a crypto-system, the keys are the most visible and important part of the implementation. Just as for an automobile, users do not need to understand how an engine works in order to use the vehicle, all they require to use the vehicle is the correct key. The same can be said for cryptography: The user does not need to see or even understand the workings of the algorithm, all the user requires is the correct key. The key is the secret value that the user uses to operate the cryptosystem. Just like the key to an automobile, the best way to protect someone from stealing an asset that should be protected is to protect the key that operates the system.

- **KEY MANAGEMENT –** Refers to the principles and practices of protecting keys throughout their lifecycle, from the time we first choose a key throughout the use, storage, and finally expiry of the key.

- **KEY EXPIRY/CRYPTOPERIOD –** All keys should be changed on a regular basis. Each time a key is used, it becomes a little more susceptible to compromise. Just as a password should be changed on a regular basis, so also the key should be replaced. The length of time a key should be used is relative to the type of algorithm and the level of protection required.

- **KEY MIXING/KEY SCHEDULE –** Most modern algorithms use a key scheduler to make the breaking of the cryptosystem more difficult. For example, the user of DES inputs a key with a nominal length of 56 bits (the actual length is 64 bits but eight bits are used for parity and not a part of the actual key), and each time DES does a round of substitution and transposition, it uses 48 bits of the key. For each round (DES does 16 rounds), DES generates a new 48 bit key out of the original 56 bits input by the user. Each bit is therefore used in 14 of the rounds. Other cryptosystems, such as AES, use key schedulers to generate completely new keys from the original key for each round.

- **KEYSTREAMS –** Most stream-based cryptographic algorithms use a keystream during the encryption process. The keystream is a pseudo-random sequence that is generated from the input key and mixed with the input message, often using a simple XOR calculation to create the ciphertext. The keystream must be statistically unbiased (a fairly even mix of 1s and 0s), have a long period before it repeats (the period), and be unpredictable (it should be nearly impossible to guess the value of the next digit in the keystream based on the value of the previous one or more digits in the keystream).

  - **SYNCHRONOUS –** A synchronous cryptosystem, or synchronous stream cipher, is an algorithm in which the keystream is generated based on the original key, bit-by-bit, in sync with the arrival of the plaintext. The keystream is generated and merged (XOR'd) with the plaintext as the plaintext is received.

  - **SELF-SYNCHRONOUS –** A self-synchronous cryptosystem, or non-synchronous stream cipher, is an algorithm in which the keystream is generated based upon previously generated ciphertext and the cryptovariable, or key. Since the keystream can only be computed after the calculation of the previous ciphertext, the output of the keystream is asynchronous with the arrival of the plaintext.

- **KEY STORAGE –** Perhaps the most risky part of any implementation of cryptography is the secure storage of the key. The key must be protected from the adversary, both in transit and in storage. Later in the domain we will look at some methods of protecting keys through the use of hardware and software solutions.

- **KEY CLUSTERING –** Ideally, every time a different key is used in a cryptosystem the output of the encryption should be different even if the plaintext is the same. Key clustering is the term used to represent a weakness that would exist in a cryptosystem if two different keys would generate the same ciphertext from the same plaintext. This would mean that either key could also be used to decrypt the ciphertext. The more keys that could be used to generate the same result, the easier it would be to attack the cryptosystem. Cryptographic algorithms are tested to ensure that they are not vulnerable to key clustering.

REFERENCES:
http://www.its.bldrdoc.gov/fs-1037/dir-035/_5239.htm
Cryptography: Theory and Practice, Douglas R. Stinson, 2nd Edition. Chapman & Hall, 2002.

Initialization Vector (IV)

- Encrypting similar messages will create patterns of ciphertext, even when using different keys. Predictability is an enemy of cryptography.

- An IV is a random value added to the plaintext message before encrypting so that each ciphertext will be substantially different.

- The recipient will also need the IV to decrypt the message.

10

- **INITIALIZATION VECTOR (IV)** – The IV is a random value that is XOR'd with the plaintext message before encryption. It will ensure that even if a similar message is encrypted many times, there will be less chance of detecting a pattern in the ciphertext outputs. The IV will be sent along with the encrypted message to the recipient. The recipient will need to extract the IV from the message (using XOR) to recover the true plaintext and understand the message. According to the standards, the IV does not need to be encrypted, since it is only a junk or random value, but some systems will encrypt it before transmission.

Work Factor

- Effort (time and resources) needed to break cryptographic protection

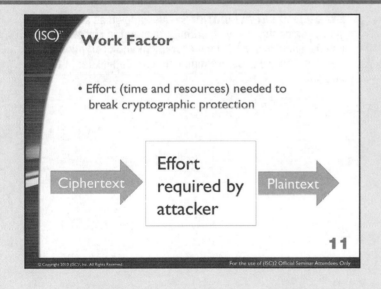

11

- **WORK FACTOR** – An estimate of the effort/time needed to overcome a protective measure by an attacker with specified expertise and resources. It is commonly used as a way to measure the amount of resources that would be required to brute-force a given algorithm or cryptosystem. The above example shows an attacker breaking ciphertext, but the work factor is not limited to this attack. It refers to the effort required by the attacker to attack many other things as well, such as hash functions, keys, digital signatures, etc.

- A crypto system is said to be "broken" when there is a way to decrease the work factor to a reasonable level. All cryptosystems will be crackable eventually; the objective is to use a system that is computationally infeasible to crack.

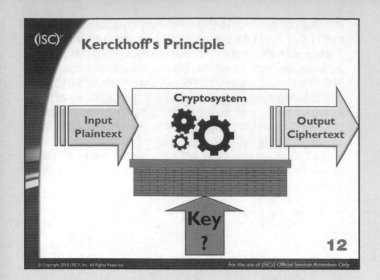

knowledge of the method and operation of the cryptographic algorithm, the strength of the cryptosystem is dependent on the secrecy of the key. The core aspect of cryptographic security, therefore, centers around protection of the keys. The difficulty (or work factor) for the cryptanalyst is the effort required to determine the correct key. For that reason, key length is the primary method used for determining the relative strength of cryptosystems.

- **KERCKHOFF'S PRINCIPLE** – States that the strength of a cryptosystem is based on the secrecy of the key and not on the secrecy of the algorithm. Proposed by Auguste Kerckhoff in 1883. This is the basic premise from which determining the strength of all modern cryptographic algorithms is calculated. Kerckhoff's Principle assumes that even if the adversary attempting to break the cryptographic algorithm has complete

- **BRITTLENESS** – Systems that fail badly are brittle, and systems that fail well are resilient. A resilient system is dynamic; it might be designed to fail only partially, or degrade gracefully; it might adjust to changing circumstances. In general, automated systems – which do one thing very well, but only one thing – are brittle.

- **"SECURITY BY OBSCURITY"** – Security Through Obscurity (STO) is the belief that a system of any sort can be secure so long as nobody outside of its implementation group is allowed to find out anything about its internal mechanisms. Hiding account passwords in binary files or scripts with the presumption that "nobody will ever find it" is a prime case of STO. This is very dangerous to security.

REFERENCE:
http://www.schneier.com/crypto-gram-0205.html

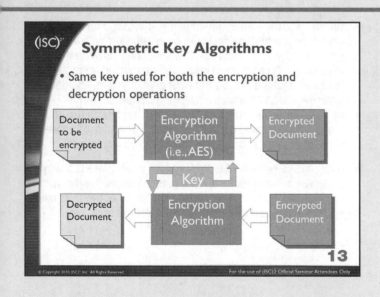

- **SYMMETRIC KEY ALGORITHMS** – Also known as secret key, same key, or single key algorithms, symmetric key algorithms use the same key in both the encryption and decryption process. These will be examined in more detail later in this domain.

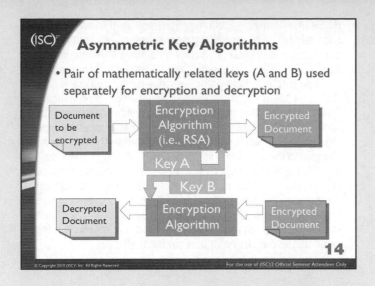

Asymmetric Key Algorithms

- Pair of mathematically related keys (A and B) used separately for encryption and decryption

Document to be encrypted → Encryption Algorithm (i.e., RSA) → Encrypted Document

Key A

Key B

Decrypted Document ← Encryption Algorithm ← Encrypted Document

14

- **ASYMMETRIC KEY ALGORITHMS –** Also known as public key algorithms, asymmetric algorithms use a pair of mathematically related keys (one known as the public key, which can be shared with everyone; and one known as the private key, which must be kept secret). The core principle to asymmetric cryptography is that the keys always work in a pair – if one half of the key pair is used in the encryption process, then the other half of that pair is the one that MUST be used to decrypt the message. These will be examined in more detail later in this domain.

Certificates

- A certificate proves who owns a public key

- Issued by a Certificate Authority (CA)

- Registration Authority

15

- **CERTIFICATE –** A digitally signed, special block of data that contains a public key and the identifying information for the entity, or principal, that owns the associated private key. Certificates are typically formatted in ASN.1 (Abstract Syntax Notation 1), commonly in a format referred to as X.509. Certificates can be self-signed (that is the public key is signed using its own associated private key) or they may be signed by a Certificate Authority.

- **CERTIFICATE AUTHORITY (CA) –** A CA is a trusted entity or third party that issues and signs public key certificates, thereby attesting to the validity of the public keys. CAs also manage the certificate lifecycle, including Certificate Application, Certification (authentication of the applicant), Issuance, and Revocation.

- **REGISTRATION AUTHORITY (RA) –** The RA is the primary organization that verifies a Certificate Applicant's information and identity. The RA works hand-in-hand with the CA to verify the applicant's information before the CA issues the certificate. The RA handles verification, enrollment, registration, issuing and reissuing credentials; and credential updates, additions, and revocation as the local agent on behalf of the CA.

REFERENCE:
http://www.ietf.org/rfc/rfc2459.txt

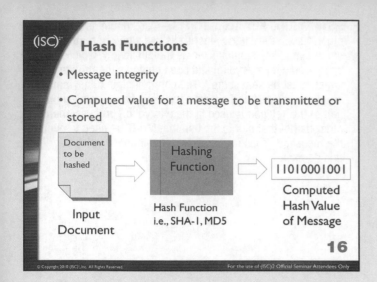

- **HASH FUNCTIONS** – Hash functions are used to ensure message integrity. For example, when a message is sent over a communications channel, it may be altered either accidentally or intentionally while in transit. The purpose of a hash function is to calculate a unique value for the message so that any changes to the original message would be noticed. Prior to transmitting the message, the sender calculates the hash value of the message using a commonly available hash algorithm. The resulting hash value is sent to the recipient along with the message. In some cases, the hash value (or digest as it is often called) will be cryptographically protected. The recipient computes a hash of the received message using the same algorithm as the sender. If the hash of the received message is the same as the one sent by the originator, there is some level of assurance that the message received is the same as the one sent and has not been altered.

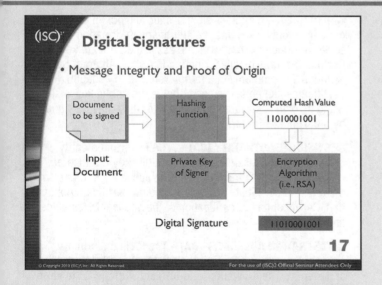

- **DIGITAL SIGNATURES** – A Digital Signature provides two primary benefits: it proves that the message has not been altered (Message Integrity) and it proves who sent the message (Proof of Origin and non-repudiation). The Digital Signature is created by encrypting a hash of the message with the private asymmetric key of the sender. This creates a signed hash that can only be unlocked using the public asymmetric key of the sender. As long as you have confidence that only the sender has access to his or her private key, and that you truly have the sender's correct public key, you know that the message must have come from that sender.

- The reason to sign a hash of the message instead of signing the message itself is that asymmetric cryptographic algorithms tend to be very slow and computationally intensive to use, so the operation of signing the short hash of the message instead of the message itself saves a lot of time and cost.

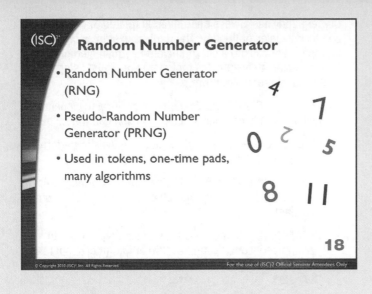

Random Number Generator

- Random Number Generator (RNG)
- Pseudo-Random Number Generator (PRNG)
- Used in tokens, one-time pads, many algorithms

18

- **RANDOM NUMBER GENERATORS –** RNGs are a key to cryptographic implementations. The problem is that computers are very poor at random number generation. A computer quickly falls into a pattern and selects numbers of a predictable value that can be guessed or computed by an attacker. One of the most famous examples of this was the attack on Netscape 95 when the random number generator was based on time of day and was easily broken. This has also been exploited in TCP sequence number attacks.

- Many cryptographic implementations require truly random values to be used to be strong enough to resist attack. Products like SSL and hybrid cryptosystems that select a secret key each time they are used need to select truly random numbers and not just the same ones as before.

- **PSEUDO-RANDOM NUMBER GENERATORS –** PRNGs are used in keystream applications that generate a seemingly random set of values to XOR with the plaintext. It appears to be random but it is not truly random. The sequence of keystream values is based on the value of the key. This is necessary since the same keystream sequence must be generated at the receiving end to decrypt the ciphertext.

Domain Agenda

- Definitions

- **History**

- Uses

- Cryptographic Methods

- Encryption Systems

- Algorithms

- Cryptanalysis and Attacks

- Implementations

19

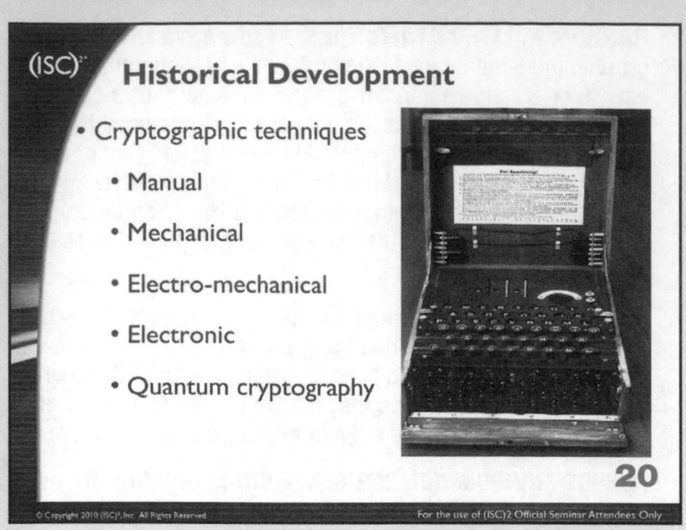

Historical Development

- Cryptographic techniques
  - Manual
  - Mechanical
  - Electro-mechanical
  - Electronic
  - Quantum cryptography

20

- Cryptography has always been directly related to the media and technologies of the day. The earliest examples of cryptography date back to a set of ancient Egyptian hieroglyphics from approximately 2000 BC that were encrypted using a simple substitution algorithm.

  - **MANUAL** – Cryptographic methods performed by hand using a variety of tools (still used on some one-time pads).

  - **MECHANICAL** – The use of mechanical tools to perform encryption and decryption (the cipherdisk).

  - **ELECTRO-MECHANICAL** – The use of electro-mechanical devices to perform cryptographic operations (the Enigma machine).

  - **ELECTRONIC** – Computer-based technologies used to perform very complex and secure cryptographic operations (software and hardware based algorithms – AES, RSA, etc.).

  - **QUANTUM CRYPTOGRAPHY** – Using single-photon light emissions to provide secure key negotiation.

REFERENCE:

The Codebreakers: The Comprehensive History of Secret Communication from Ancient Times to the Internet, David Kahn, Scribner, 1996.

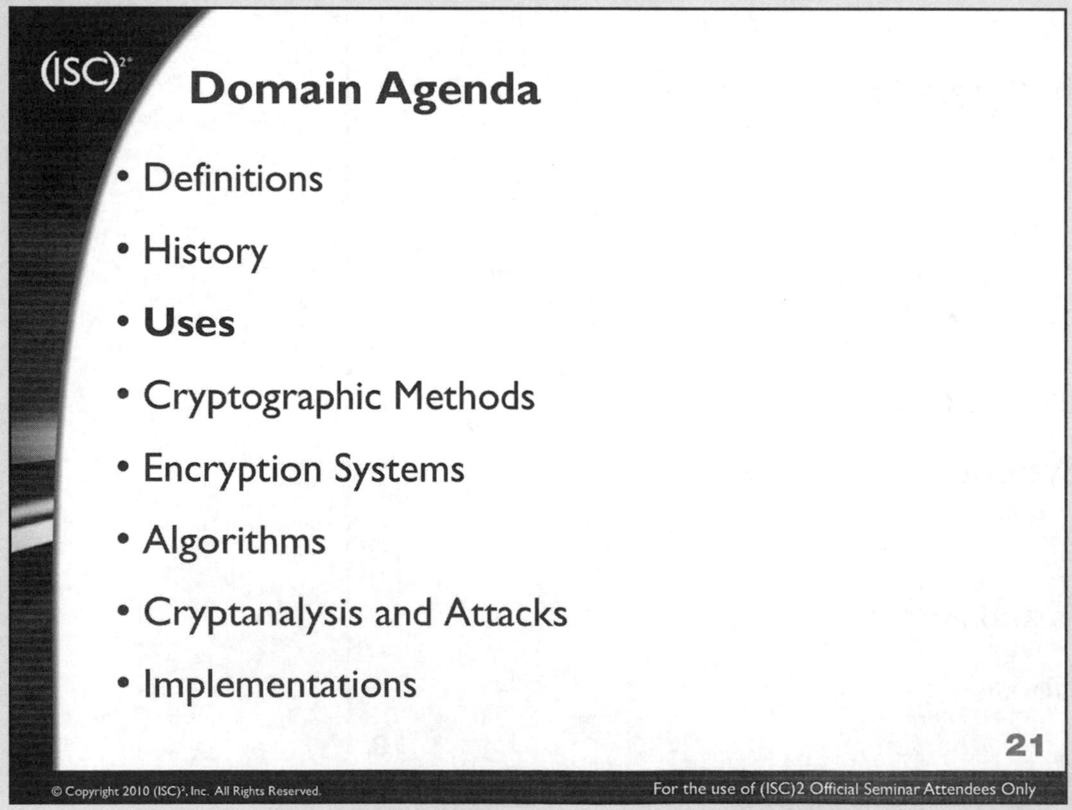

Domain Agenda

- Definitions

- History

- **Uses**

- Cryptographic Methods

- Encryption Systems

- Algorithms

- Cryptanalysis and Attacks

- Implementations

21

Uses of Cryptography

- Protecting information
  - Transit
    - Email, VPNs, e-commerce, VOIP, etc.
  - Storage
    - Disk encryption
  - System access
    - Passwords, remote login

22

- **USES OF CRYPTOGRAPHY** – For many years, cryptography was the exclusive property of the military and was even protected by laws governing the use of munitions (weapons of war). However, cryptography has many uses in today's society. Cryptography provides many benefits that can be used by nearly everyone to protect information – whether that information must be protected in transit or storage.

- **TRANSIT** – Information moves around the world at an unprecedented rate but, while in transit, it is subject to accidental or intentional compromise – unauthorized changes to the data, or being read by unauthorized persons. Cryptography provides for the confidential transmission of data and, furthermore, ensures that the data has not been altered while in transit.

- **STORAGE** – Data at rest, or in storage, must be protected from unauthorized changes or access. Encrypting sensitive information (such as credit card data) can protect it from unauthorized access; and cryptographic access controls can ensure that only people with a "need to know" can gain entrance to protected systems.

  - **DISK ENCRYPTION** – The weakest part of any cryptographic implementation is usually the user. Users can fail to abide by policy and fail to encrypt the data, or they may fail to protect the passwords used to gain authorized access. The simplest way to ensure that data stored on a disk or USB stick is encrypted is to remove the user from the operation; encrypt automatically so that all the data stored on the media is encrypted even if the user does not enable the encryption. Another alternative is to encrypt data in the application – for example, to encrypt credit card numbers automatically so that they are stored in the database, or shown on reports, in an encrypted format.

- **SYSTEM ACCESS** – Most system access today is controlled by cryptographic functions – whether through passwords, pre-shared keys (wireless), or remote access tokens. This prevents unauthorized access to a system unless the user has the correct key or secret value. Full-disk and file-based encryption should be combined to best prevent data leaks. Full disk encryption is beneficial, as current partial disk encryption techniques can be bypassed by the end-user who saves files in unencrypted folders or the security configuration is weak (for example, the encryption key is stored in system files).

Domain Agenda

- Definitions

- History

- Uses

- **Cryptographic Methods**

- Encryption Systems

- Algorithms

- Cryptanalysis and Attacks

- Implementations

23

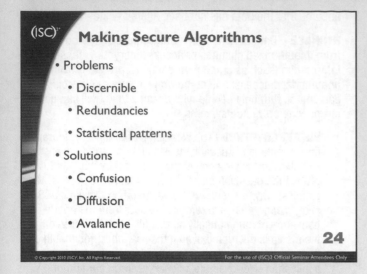

- **MAKING SECURE CRYPTOGRAPHIC ALGORITHMS –** Claude Shannon was one of the fathers of modern information theory. In his 1949 paper "Communication Theory of Secrecy Systems," he explained that the biggest problems with making a truly secure secrecy system lay with the redundancy of natural language typical to the plaintext and the fact that (apart from ideal OTP, or one time pad, schemes) the keys being used are smaller than the plaintext and may be reused.

- **PROBLEMS –** Simple cryptosystems are not very secure.

  - **DISCERNIBLE –** Knowing the language that was used in the plaintext, statistical analysis allows the cryptanalyst to attempt "frequency analysis" attacks against the system, using common patterns in language, until the analyst finds the right plaintext. The goal of a secure cryptographic algorithm then, should be to make it extremely difficult for the cryptanalyst to get to the single, correct answer, by providing as many equally probable options as possible. The assumption is that the "enemy cryptanalyst" knows which cryptographic algorithm is being used, and that the attacker's task lies solely with identifying the most probable plaintext from a given ciphertext, without knowing which key was chosen.

  - **REDUNDANCIES –** Redundancies tend to make the cryptanalyst's job easier. It may be thought of as the tendency for plaintext to provide more information than is strictly necessary to communicate one's message. For example, the "u" after "q" in the English language is essentially redundant. These redundancies allow the cryptanalyst to test available keys to find out which ones are the most probable since they would allow the cryptanalyst to quickly test the keys to see if they generate improbable plaintext. For example, if a potential key being used to crack a ciphertext message results in an English plaintext message that has a "q" followed by any character other than "u," it is not a probable key.

  - **STATISTICAL PATTERNS –** Statistical Patterns in the plaintext can be revealed in the ciphertext if the algorithm does not obscure them. For example, a simple substitution algorithm can be defeated through frequency analysis of the ciphertext letters as compared to their frequency of use in the original language. In the English language, the letter "e" is the most common. Other patterns occur in the frequency of short words, such as "the," "and," or "that," and in endings of words such as "tion."

- **SOLUTIONS –**

  - **CONFUSION –** Is the principle of hiding patterns in the plaintext by substitution. This makes it more difficult for the cryptanalyst to directly relate ciphertext sequences with plaintext words. A perfect cryptosystem would allow a character in ciphertext to decrypt as any possible plaintext character.

  - **DIFFUSION –** Is the property of transposing the input plaintext throughout the ciphertext so that a character in the ciphertext would not line up directly in the same position in the plaintext.

  - **AVALANCHE –** Is achieved when the plaintext bits affect the entire ciphertext so that even a change of one bit in the plaintext would change half of the entire cipher text. In the case of quality block ciphers, such a small change in either the key or the plaintext should cause a drastic change in the ciphertext. If a block cipher or cryptographic hash function does not exhibit the avalanche effect to a significant degree, then it has poor randomization, and thus a cryptanalyst can make predictions about the input, being given only the output.

REFERENCES:

Shannon, Claude "Communication Theory of Secrecy Systems," Bell System Technical Journal, vol.28(4), page 656–715, 1949

csrc.nist.gov/archive/aes/round1/conf2/papers/massey.pdf

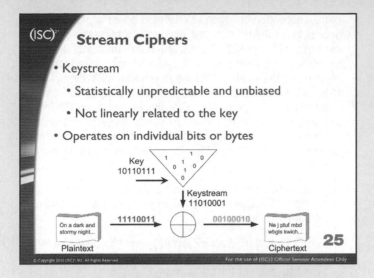

- **STREAM CIPHERS** – A keystream (sequence of bits used as a key) is generated and combined with the plaintext using a bitwise Exclusive-OR (XOR). This keystream can be generated independently of the plaintext (synchronous stream cipher) or it can be dependent on the data and its encryption (self-synchronizing stream cipher). Note that stream ciphers are usually much faster than any block cipher and that unlike block ciphers, they tend to result in different ciphertexts even when the same key is used. This is because stream ciphers are most commonly implemented in specialty optimized hardware using IVs.

- **KEYSTREAM** – Encryption is accomplished by XORing the plaintext with a keystream of pseudo-randomly generated numbers. The cryptosystem generates the keystream in a pseudo-random sequence through the properties of a random number generator (RNG) or pseudo-random number generator (PRNG).

  - **STATISTICALLY UNPREDICTABLE AND UNBIASED** – The keystream must be unpredictable having approximately as many 1s as 0s and the same possibility for the next value in the keystream to be either 1 or a 0.

  - **NOT LINEARLY RELATED TO THE KEY** – The keystream generated by the keystream generator should not be related to the key. Knowledge of either the key or the keystream should not provide information about the other value.

- **OPERATES ON INDIVIDUAL BITS OR BYTES** – The keystream operates on individual bits of plaintext or on individual characters by XORing (bit comparison).

  - **ADVANTAGES –**

    - Emulates a one-time pad.

    - In a traditional stream-based cipher, there is no size difference between plaintext and ciphertext. More modern examples provide compression during the encryption operation, which saves as much as 30 percent of the bandwidth or storage for the encrypted message.

    - Because it has minimal memory requirements, it is very suitable for hardware implementation and serial communications.

  - **DISADVANTAGES -**

    - Can be difficult to implement correctly.

    - Generally weaker than a block-mode cipher.

    - Difficult to generate a truly random unbiased keystream. Recent cracks of a stream-based cipher were made possible because the keystream being generated was found to have a value of "1," 60 percent of the time.

REFERENCE:
http://security.ece.orst.edu/koc/ece575/rsalabs/tr-701.pdf

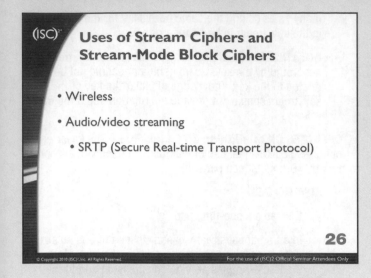

Uses of Stream Ciphers and Stream-Mode Block Ciphers

- Wireless
- Audio/video streaming
  - SRTP (Secure Real-time Transport Protocol)

26

- **STREAM-CIPHER USES –** Block ciphers (e.g., AES in CBC mode) are used more often than stream ciphers, but stream ciphers provide faster encrypt and decrypt speeds, simpler hardware implementation, improved robustness in error-prone environments, and are better able to scale up with increases in bandwidth demands. These features make stream ciphers more suitable for certain scenarios, such as heterogeneous (mixed wired and wireless) environments, and for real-time applications (e.g., voice over IP and multimedia).

- **WIRELESS –** The 802.11 standard describes the communication that occurs in wireless local area networks (LANs). Wired Equivalent Privacy (WEP) and Wi-Fi Protected Access (WPA) use RC4 to protect wireless communication from eavesdrop-

ping. A secondary function of WEP is to prevent unauthorized access to a wireless network, although this function is not an explicit goal in the 802.11 standard. A stream cipher operates by expanding a short key into an infinite, pseudo-random keystream and the sender XORs the keystream with the plaintext to produce ciphertext. The recipient has a copy of the same key and uses it to generate an identical keystream. XORing the keystream with the ciphertext yields the original plaintext. This mode of operation makes stream ciphers vulnerable to several attacks. WEP is widely considered a misuse of stream ciphers.

- Bluetooth also uses a stream cipher, in this case its custom "E0" cipher, which is proving to be weaker than originally thought.

- Wi-Fi Protected Access 2 (WPA2) uses AES (block cipher) in CTR mode (a stream mode) to generate the keystream used to encrypt the transmission.

- **AUDIO/VIDEO STREAMING –** VoIP phones may encrypt audio streams via SRTP (Secure Real-time Transport Protocol). SRTP is a security profile for RTP that adds confidentiality, message authentication, and replay protection. SRTP is ideal for protecting VoIP traffic because it can be used in conjunction with header compression and has no effect on IP Quality of Service. SRTP achieves high throughput and low packet expansion by using AES in CTR mode as fast stream-mode implementation of a block cipher for encryption, an implicit index for synchronization, and universal hash functions for message authentication. SRTP is a suitable choice for the most general scenarios as well as the most demanding ones.

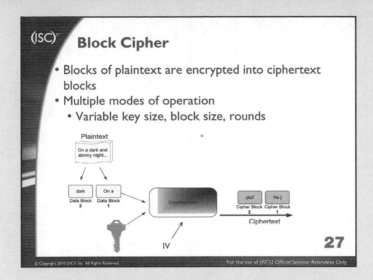

Block Cipher

- Blocks of plaintext are encrypted into ciphertext blocks
- Multiple modes of operation
  - Variable key size, block size, rounds

27

modes of operation have been invented for block ciphers. The most common mode of operation, Cipher Block Chaining (CBC), uses an IV. The IV is mixed (using XOR) with the input data to make the plaintext different each time the encryption operation is performed, thereby making the ciphertext different as well. There are other modes of operation that use IVs for the same purpose (albeit in a different manner).

- **STRENGTH OF BLOCK CIPHERS** – Block ciphers are mathematical algorithms typically made up of a series of simple mathematical functions, such as XOR, addition, and substitution. Modern block ciphers are stronger than their historical counterparts because of differing key lengths, block sizes, and number of rounds:

  - **KEY LENGTH** – Modern block ciphers mix larger keys (128 bits or more) with the data. Since there are many possible keys (2^128 possibilities), finding the one key that produces a specific ciphertext is very time consuming. According to Shannon Coding Theory, this key mixing process produces confusion of the input bits.

  - **BLOCK SIZE** – Modern block ciphers break messages into fairly large size chunks (128 bits). This increases the number of possible ciphertexts that a particular plaintext input is able to produce, making a search very expensive in terms of memory space. The increase in the number of ciphertext that a particular plaintext input is able to produce allows for a larger number of permutations, and increases bit diffusion, according to Shannon Coding Theory.

  - **ROUNDS** – A "round" is a series of mathematical operations that must be performed in sequence on an algorithm. Modern block ciphers use 10 or more rounds to encrypt a single block of plaintext into ciphertext. This repetition increases the mixing of the inputs to the algorithm (i.e., plaintext and key), which diffuses plaintext bits through a complex series of simple functions. This produces an avalanche effect, where one bit from the plaintext affects many bits in the resulting ciphertext.

- **FIXED-SIZED BLOCKS** – Unlike streaming ciphers, block ciphers operate on plaintext that has been chopped up into fixed-sized blocks. The typical block value will be a multiple of 8 bits (ASCII) or 16 bits (Unicode). Larger blocks are considered to be more secure.

- **MULTIPLE MODES OF OPERATION** – Block mode ciphers provide more operational flexibility than a stream mode cipher. Depending on the requirements, the modes of operation, key length, block size, and number of rounds of computation can be varied. Many block mode ciphers can also detect changes to a message.

- **INITIALIZATION VECTOR** – In some modes of operation, the use of an Initialization Vector (IV) will add additional complexity to the enciphering operation. Because block ciphers are mathematical algorithms, the same inputs produce the same outputs (e.g., encrypting Message "1" with Key "A" will give the same results every time unless some randomization is provided through the use of an Initialization Vector). Block ciphers in their simplest mode (called Electronic Code Book [ECB] mode) will produce the same ciphertext given the same key and same plaintext. This consistency obviously makes cryptanalysis easier. Because of this condition, different

REFERENCE:

http://www.cs.colorado.edu/~jrblack/class/csci7000/f03/papers/tweak-crypto02.pdf

---

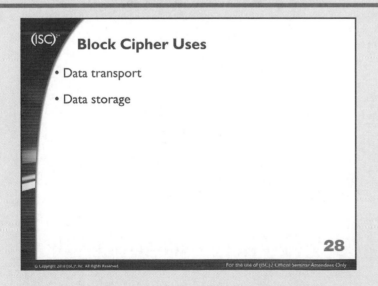

Block Cipher Uses

- Data transport

- Data storage

28

- **DATA TRANSPORT** – All modern web browsers come with Secure Sockets Layer (SSL) and Transport Layer Security (TLS). Both of these protocols provide Cipher Suites that include AES (Advanced Encryption Standard) and Triple DES (Data Encryption Standard). IPSec-based VPNs also use block ciphers to encrypt the communication between endpoints.

- **DATA STORAGE** – Although stream ciphers have traditionally been used for disk encryption because of their speed, block ciphers (such as AES in Counter Mode) are used in modern secure disk-storage solutions because of their greater ability to frustrate cryptanalysis. Encryption of similar files under a steam cipher opens possibilities for cryptanalysis after XORing these files together, as is done in WEP attacks. AES is not subject to these attacks, and Counter Mode provides protection for similar files (using an Initialization Vector). With modern computer speeds well into the gigahertz range and multi-core processors commonplace, the processing power necessary for AES for storage protection is easily available. TrueCrypt, the free, open source secure disk storage solution, is an example of this use.

Domain Agenda

- Definitions
- History
- Uses
- Cryptographic Methods
- **Encryption Systems**
- Algorithms
- Cryptanalysis and Attacks
- Implementations

29

Basic Cryptosystems

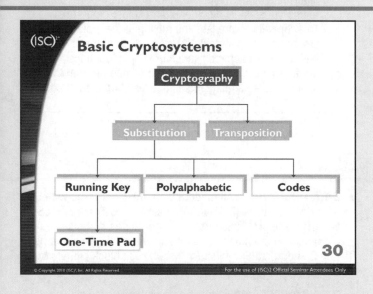

- **BASIC CRYPTOSYSTEMS –** Most traditional cryptosystems operate through the use of substitution or transposition of the plaintext data in order to create the ciphertext.

- **SUBSTITUTION –** Substitution is the action of replacing one letter or value for another. Each of the methods of substitution shown on the slide will be described in more detail later in the course.

- **TRANSPOSITION –** Changing the order of the input data so that the letters appear in a different order in the output ciphertext. This is also called permutation.

30

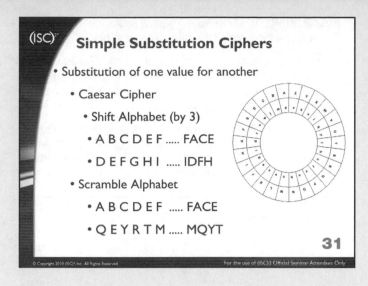

Simple Substitution Ciphers

- Substitution of one value for another
  - Caesar Cipher
    - Shift Alphabet (by 3)
      - A B C D E F ..... FACE
      - D E F G H I ..... IDFH
  - Scramble Alphabet
    - A B C D E F ..... FACE
    - Q E Y R T M ..... MQYT

31

- **SIMPLE SUBSTITUTION CIPHERS** – Disguise a message by substituting or replacing one letter or value for another. In Shift Alphabet, the ciphertext is obtained by shifting the alphabet by three positions. For example, the plaintext word "face" would read as "IDFH." In Scramble Alphabet, the ciphertext is obtained by using a completely scrambled alphabet to rewrite the message.

- **EXAMPLE OF SIMPLE SUBSTITUTION CIPHER** – Caesar Cipher, named after Julius Caesar. This was the cipher that he used to communicate with his military leaders. The substitution can be performed by aligning two alphabets, both of which are in order, except that one is rotated by a number of positions.

- **WEAKNESSES OF SIMPLE SUBSTITUTION CIPHERS** – These algorithms are subject to "frequency analysis." Because the characteristics of the language are known – in English, for example, the fact that the most commonly used letters in order of frequency are e, t, a, i, o, n, s, h, r, d, l, u – frequency analysis can be used to break the code.

REFERENCES:
http://secretcodebreaker.com/caesar.html
http://www.simonsingh.net/The_Black_Chamber/caesar.html

IMAGE:
http://www.blueangel.demon.co.uk/alberti.html

Simple Transposition/Permutation

- Columnar – rearranging the message in a table
  - Plaintext "This is an example of transposition"
  - Cipher "tsaoni hamfst inptpi selroo ixeasn"
- Key: grid shape & reading direction
- Example: the Spartan Scytale

T	H	I	S	I
S	A	N	E	X
A	M	P	L	E
O	F	T	R	A
N	S	P	O	S
I	T	I	O	N

32

- **SIMPLE TRANSPOSITION/PERMUTATION CIPHERS** – Disguise a message by rearranging the letters (or bits) in the message. The terms transposition and permutation are synonymous in this context.

- **COLUMNAR TRANSPOSITION** –

  - **GENERATING CIPHERTEXT FROM PLAINTEXT** – In this example, the plaintext is placed into a table of five columns in size. The ciphertext is then obtained by "reading" the table vertically.

  - **MULTIPLE WAYS TO PRODUCE CIPHERTEXT** – A transposition cipher algorithm can work in a variety of ways; even in the example given, "reading" the table could be done in a different order or sequence.

- **EXAMPLE** – Scytale Rod (Sparta, 400 BC). Scytale is a simple transposition cipher system that employs a rod of a certain thickness around which was wrapped a long, thin strip of parchment or leather. The plaintext would then be written horizontally down the rod, adding extra characters to pad up the strip. The parchment would then be unwrapped and sent to its destination. The receiver would need to possess a rod of the same diameter to decipher the message.

REFERENCES:
http://nem.passagen.se/tan01/transpo.html
Thomas Kelly, "The Myth of the Skytale," Cryptologia, July 1998, pp. 244–260.

Polyalphabetic Ciphers

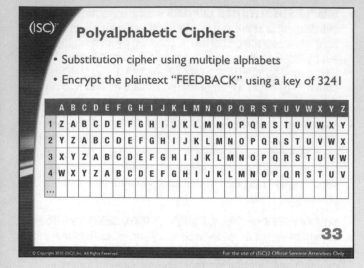

- Substitution cipher using multiple alphabets
- Encrypt the plaintext "FEEDBACK" using a key of 3241

	A	B	C	D	E	F	G	H	I	J	K	L	M	N	O	P	Q	R	S	T	U	V	W	X	Y	Z
1	Z	A	B	C	D	E	F	G	H	I	J	K	L	M	N	O	P	Q	R	S	T	U	V	W	X	Y
2	Y	Z	A	B	C	D	E	F	G	H	I	J	K	L	M	N	O	P	Q	R	S	T	U	V	W	X
3	X	Y	Z	A	B	C	D	E	F	G	H	I	J	K	L	M	N	O	P	Q	R	S	T	U	V	W
4	W	X	Y	Z	A	B	C	D	E	F	G	H	I	J	K	L	M	N	O	P	Q	R	S	T	U	V
...

33

- **POLYALPHABETIC CIPHERS** – A simple substitution cipher that uses multiple alphabets rather than just one.

  - Using the example on this slide, the word "FEEDBACK" would encrypt as: _____ (find the answer on the next slide). Note that polyalphabetic ciphers are resistant to frequency analysis.

- **VIGENÈRE CIPHER** – Named after Blaise de Vigenère, who published a more difficult version of this type of polyalphabetic cipher in 1586. The Vigenère cipher is a polyalphabetic cipher that uses a keyword rather than a number as the key.

REFERENCE:

http://www.simonsingh.net/The_Black_Chamber/vigenere_cracking.html

Running Key Ciphers

- Use the value of plaintext letters and a values of key based on a shared book

Value of Message 'THIS ...'	T	H	I	S		S
	19	7	8	18
+ Value of Key 'on periodic ...'	O	N	P	E
	14	13	15	4
= Value of Ciphertext	33	20	23	22
	-26			
	7	20	23	22
Ciphertext	H	U	X	W

A	B	C	D	E	F	G	H	I	J	K	L	M	N	O	P	Q	R	S	T	U	V	W	X	Y	Z
0	1	2	3	4	5	6	7	8	9	10	11	12	13	14	15	16	17	18	19	20	21	22	23	24	25

34

- **RUNNING KEY CIPHERS** – This form of encryption is done by using the numerical value of letters in the plaintext and is coded and decoded by using a copy of the text in a book as the key. Sender and recipient determine the key by agreeing on a point in the book (e.g., a page number) from which to start the encryption. The key would then "run" as long as the plaintext, and the value of each letter of the key would be "added" to the value of each letter of the plaintext. If the total of the two letters is greater than 25, 26 would be subtracted from the result. The combined value of the letters would be the value of the ciphertext letter.

- The answer to the encryption challenge on the previous slide is "CCACYYYJ."

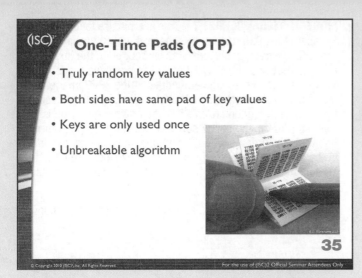

One-Time Pads (OTP)

- Truly random key values
- Both sides have same pad of key values
- Keys are only used once
- Unbreakable algorithm

35

© Copyright 2010 (ISC)², Inc. All Rights Reserved.   For the use of (ISC)2 Official Seminar Attendees Only

- **ONE-TIME PADS (OTP) –** OTPs are also known as Vernam ciphers, after G. S. Vernam, who first described this sort of scheme in 1917. The important concepts here are that the keys are the same size (length) as the plaintext message and that the keys must be randomly generated for this scheme to be truly effective. It is the requirement for randomness that makes OTPs particularly challenging to generate, since the best that we can typically achieve when generating such pads using computer processors are pseudo-random values.

- **RANDOM KEYS –** If OTPs are not random or are reused, they can be resolved to simpler running-key ciphers.

- **ORIGINATOR AND RECEIVER HAVE SAME PAD OF KEY VALUES –** Each party must have the same pad of truly random key values. The values of the pad are then combined with the values of the message to create the cipher text – similar to the approach used in the running key cipher example.

- **EACH KEY IS USED ONLY ONCE AND THEN DISCARDED –** The pad must only be used once.

- **ONLY UNBREAKABLE ALGORITHM –** This is the only algorithm that is provably unbreakable by exhaustive search (brute force) provided that:

  - Pad generation is truly random.
  - No keys are reused.
  - All pads are securely destroyed after use.

- **VENONA PROJECT –** Is probably the best example of mis-use of one-time pads. KGB Codebooks were reused and this enabled the United States to decipher encrypted messages (www.nsa.gov).

IMAGE:

Image used with permission of Rijmenants, Dirk. Cipher Machines & Cryptology: http://users.telenet.be/d.rijmenants

---

Steganography

- Art of hiding information
- Plaintext hidden/disguised
- Prevents a third party from knowing that a secret message exists
- Traditionally accomplished in a number of ways:
  - Physical techniques
  - Null ciphers

36

© Copyright 2010 (ISC)², Inc. All Rights Reserved.   For the use of (ISC)2 Official Seminar Attendees Only

- **STEGANOGRAPHY –** Unlike encryption, which uses an algorithm and a seed value to scramble or encode a message to make it unreadable, steganography makes the communication invisible. Steganography simply takes one piece of information and hides it within another. For example, to "steal" the LSB (least significant bit) of each byte on a picture image and use it to contain the message data will affect the color only slightly, and "bury" the message in an unnoticeable manner. Only through a direct, visual comparison of the original and the processed image can the analyst detect the possible use of steganography. Because the suspect system typically only stores the processed image, the analyst will have nothing to use for a comparison and consequently will have no way to tell whether the image in question contains hidden data.

- **ART OF HIDING INFORMATION –**

  - Value of plaintext hidden/disguised by device or algorithm.

- Can be hidden in image or in a datafile.

- **PLAINTEXT HIDDEN/DISGUISED –** The message is NOT en-crypted but hidden inside another message (covertext).

- **PREVENTS A THIRD PARTY FROM KNOWING THAT A SECRET MESSAGE EXISTS –** The goal is to prevent a third party from detecting that a secret message exists.

- **TRADITIONALLY ACCOMPLISHED IN A NUMBER OF WAYS –**

  - **PHYSICAL TECHNIQUES –** Invisible inks, microdots, etc. Microdots are highly-reduced photographic images. These were used by spies in WWII to carry a secret message in a microdot used as a period or other punctuation in a letter.

  - **NULL CIPHERS –** Characters of plaintext are combined with non-cipher characters (nulls) to hide the plaintext. Null ciphers do NOT scramble or encipher the message, but do make it more difficult to detect the existence of an actual message. While this is not strictly a cryptographic technique, it is used by some cryptographic algorithms to either disguise patterns in natural language that may make encrypted messages easier to crack, or to pad plaintext blocks before operating on them.

  - Example: Divide message and hide in another message.

    - Message: "Buy gold now."
    - Have the message appear as every sixth word in a sentence.
    - Sentence "I have been trying to BUY you a nice gift like GOLD or an antique but prices NOW are really high."

REFERENCE:

http://www.securityfocus.com/infocus/1684

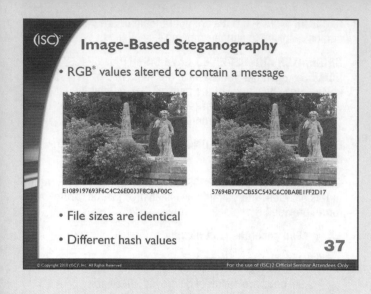

MODERN STEGANOGRAPHY – This is a picture taken at Eynsham Hall, Oxfordshire, UK, one of the (ISC)2 training sites in 2006. The secret message was embedded in the image using a freeware tool called Jpegx. The message reads "This file has a hidden message embedded in the JPEG image." The MD5 hashes (underneath each photo) were calculated using the MD5 hash function from RSA. The original message is extracted from the file by the software which reads the information that was created when the original message was hidden in the picture. Once the original message is extracted, the file is recreated and saved on the drive where it can be accessed as any other file.

* RGB Values – Red, Green, and Blue (color) intensity values

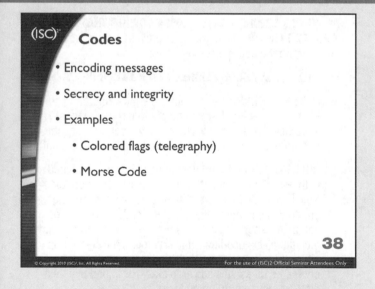

CODES – An example of the need for codes: A group of navy ships is operating under conditions of radio silence to avoid detection by the enemy. Maneuvering signals and comments are communicated by flag signals. A separate flag is used for each letter. To send a paragraph of information would be a real workout for the signalmen, so codes are used to minimize the effort and time involved. For instance, the letters BZ are the signal that the addressee performed well or did a good job.

ENCODING MESSAGES – A phrase is converted to a simple value. For example, the phrase "All is quiet, no incidents to report" may be converted to a much simpler code of AOK-N. This saves the sender and receiver time in producing and recording the message. This was especially important in the days of the telegraph where the cost of sending each letter was high.

SECRECY AND INTEGRITY – Encoding a message also provides some message protection because the attacker would not know the meanings of the phrases. The sender and receiver may also use a codebook to easily encode and decode common phrases or even monetary amounts so that they would not be understood by anyone not possessing the codebook. Examples of this would be when a message was sent using Morse Code or flags on naval ships. Sending phrases in a shortened form would save a lot of effort and time.

REFERENCE:
ISBN 0684831309

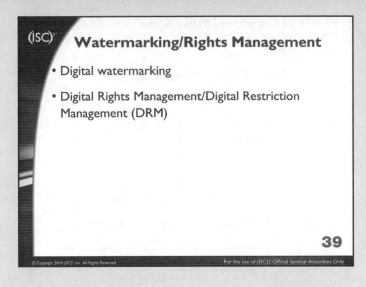

Watermarking/Rights Management

- Digital watermarking
- Digital Rights Management/Digital Restriction Management (DRM)

39

- **DIGITAL WATERMARKING** – Similar to physical watermarks created during the paper manufacturing process, digital watermarks are visible or invisible markings embedded within a digital file to indicate copyright or other handling instructions, or to embed a fingerprint to detect unauthorized copying and distribution of images. Visible watermarks can be easily detected and are NOT considered steganographic in nature. The first mention of the term "digital watermark" can be found in a seminal paper by Andrew Tirkel and Charles Osborne (Tirkel, Rankin, Van Schyndel, Ho, Mee, Osborne. "Electronic Water Mark." DICTA 93, p.666-673).

- **DIGITAL RIGHTS MANAGEMENT/DIGITAL RESTRICTION MANAGEMENT (DRM)** – DRM technologies make use of steganography and other techniques to extend digital watermarking in order to place strict usage conditions on the display and reproduction of digital media. These techniques are combined with emerging hardware and software to strictly enforce the policies embedded in the DRM-protected digital media.

Domain Agenda

- Definitions
- History
- Uses
- Cryptographic Methods
- Encryption Systems
- **Algorithms**
- Cryptanalysis and Attacks
- Implementations

40

Slide 41

Modes of Symmetric Block Ciphers

- Block Modes
  - Electronic Code Book (ECB)
  - Cipher Block Chaining (CBC)
- Stream Modes
  - Cipher Feed Back (CFB)
  - Output Feed Back (OFB)
  - Counter (CTR)
  - Counter with CBC-MAC (CCMP)

41

© Copyright 2010 (ISC)², Inc. All Rights Reserved.   For the use of (ISC)2 Official Seminar Attendees Only

- **MODES OF SYMMETRIC BLOCK CIPHERS –** A number of different operational modes have been developed that enable block ciphers to:

  - Encrypt short or long messages securely.

  - Allow a block cipher to act more like a stream cipher.

  - Take advantage of multiprocessing to perform multiple operations at the same time.

  - Contain the effects of errors in operation.

  - Perform computationally-intensive operations before plaintext is received by the cryptosystem.

- The following slides will discuss all of these modes.

REFERENCE:
http://csrc.nist.gov/groups/ST/toolkit/BCM/index.html

Slide 42

Electronic Code Book (ECB)

- Each block of plaintext is encrypted independently using the same key

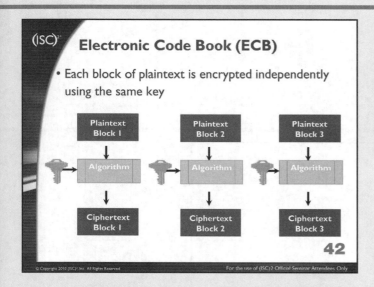

42

© Copyright 2010 (ISC)², Inc. All Rights Reserved.   For the use of (ISC)2 Official Seminar Attendees Only

- **ELECTRONIC CODE BOOK (ECB) –** ECB has the following characteristics:

  - **ADVANTAGES -**

    - **EACH OPERATION CAN BE RUN IN PARALLEL –** Provided that the computing platform can provide multitasking or multiprocessing, it is possible to run all plaintext blocks through the system in parallel. This saves processing time.

    - **ERRORS ARE CONTAINED WITHIN THE OPERATION –** If an error occurs during encryption, the error is contained within that operation and does not affect any of the others. This may help some systems that use ECB deal with errors more effectively.

  - **DISADVANTAGES -**

    - **ONLY SUITABLE FOR SHORT MESSAGES –** Identical plaintext blocks will always result in the same ciphertext blocks when encrypted using the same key. This consistency would make it relatively simple to break a long message that was encrypted using ECB mode.

  - **CAN ONLY OPERATE ON FULL-SIZED BLOCKS –** ECB does not offer the ability to operate on smaller block sizes.

  - **VERY LITTLE CAN BE ACCOMPLISHED AHEAD OF TIME –** Unlike other modes which offer some pre-processing ability, ECB can't perform any operations before it receives the plaintext.

  - **EACH OPERATION CAN BE TREATED AS A SEPARATELY ATTACKABLE PROBLEM –** Since the encryption operation on each block is discrete (a separate activity) and all operations use the same key, a cryptanalyst can treat each operation as a separate problem to solve – with the same answer. This is another reason ECB is not suitable for long messages – the longer the message, the easier it is to crack.

- In practice, ECB is used for messages that are one block in size. For example, ECB may be used to encrypt the IV used in CBC, CFB, or OFB modes, or for the countervalue for CTR mode before these values are exchanged. (It will typically use a separate key for this purpose.) See the following slides for descriptions of each of these modes.

- **ECB USE –** The weakness of ECB means that its use is not recommended and considered against best practice according to Ferguson and Schneier in "Practical Cryptography."

REFERENCE:
http://www.rsa.com/rsalabs/node.asp?id=2170

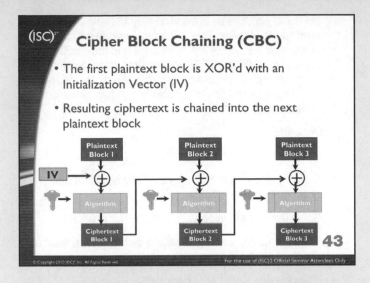

Cipher Block Chaining (CBC)

- The first plaintext block is XOR'd with an Initialization Vector (IV)
- Resulting ciphertext is chained into the next plaintext block

43

- **CIPHER BLOCK CHAINING (CBC)** – CBC is a frequently-used mode for bulk data encryption as well as for many network protocols that use cryptography (e.g., SSH). The process is as follows:

  - The first block of plaintext is XOR'd with an Initialization Vector and the result is then encrypted to get the first block of ciphertext.

  - The ciphertext result of the previous operation is used in place of the IV to be chained into the next plaintext block.

- **INITIALIZATION VECTOR (IV)** – The IV is typically a pseudo-randomly-generated value that is exactly the same size as the block with which it is XOR'd. The IV is used to ensure that the CBC is not subject to the same problem encountered by ECB's repetition of the same ciphertext block when the same key is used to operate on an identical plaintext block. A different IV must be generated for every message, making every resulting ciphertext different, even when the same key is being used. This helps protect both the plaintext and the key.

- **ADVANTAGES** –

  - Suitable for long messages with many blocks.

- **DISADVANTAGES** –

  - Can only operate on full-sized blocks.

  - Each operation must be run in serial.

  - Very little can be accomplished by the system before plaintext blocks are available.

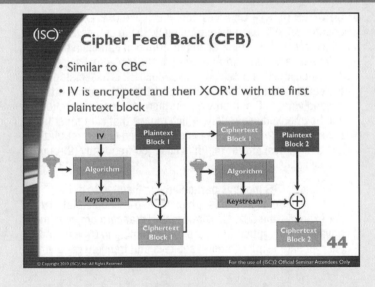

Cipher Feed Back (CFB)

- Similar to CBC
- IV is encrypted and then XOR'd with the first plaintext block

44

- **CIPHER FEED BACK (CFB)** – CFP is very similar to CBC except that in CFB, IV is encrypted and its result is XOR'd with the first plaintext block. The ciphertext result of the previous operation is used in place of the IV for the next plaintext block.

- CFB is infrequently used because except for the fact that it is a stream mode and can encrypt the IV before seeing any plaintext blocks, there is very little to recommend this mode over Cipher Block Chaining (CBC).

- **ADVANTAGES** –

  - Because it is stream mode, it can operate on smaller blocks.

  - Auditable for long messages with many blocks.

- **DISADVANTAGES** –

  - Each operation must be run in serial.

  - Very little can be accomplished by the system before plaintext blocks are available.

REFERENCE:
http://www.pvv.ntnu.no/~asgaut/crypto/thesis/node16.html

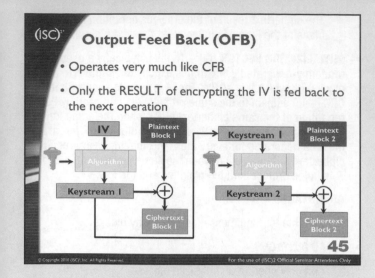

Output Feed Back (OFB)

- Operates very much like CFB
- Only the RESULT of encrypting the IV is fed back to the next operation

45

ing the serial operations, there is no way to communicate the error to the receiver. This will tend to create cascading errors through the rest of the operations and the result will be impossible to decrypt. OFB is, therefore, not typically used in communication protocols or bulk data encryption for data storage unless there are careful checks put into place to detect and mitigate errors.

- **ADVANTAGES -**
  - Stream mode can operate on smaller blocks.
  - Suitable for long messages with many blocks (although errors may cause problems).
  - Some (but not all) operations may be run in parallel.
  - A great deal can be accomplished by the system before plaintext blocks are available.
  - Transmission errors are contained.

- **DISADVANTAGES -**
  - Errors during encryption can cascade through the series of operations that follow the error.
  - Not fully parallelizable. This is why CTR is preferable to OFB in the modern era of multi-CPU and multi-core machines.

REFERENCE:
http://www.rsa.com/rsalabs/node.asp?id=2173

- **OUTPUT FEED BACK (OFB) –** Operates very much like CFB. Although the differences between CFB and OFB are subtle, they have a profound effect on its advantages and disadvantages. OFB is able to perform many operations in parallel (XOR operations against plaintext blocks), although it has to continue to generate the "stream" in serial. Keep in mind, however, that provided the cryptosystem has someplace to store the results, all the serial operations can be performed before any plaintext is available.

- The big advantage AND disadvantage to OFB lies in the effect of errors. If an error occurs during a XOR operation against plaintext, the error can be contained, but if it occurs dur-

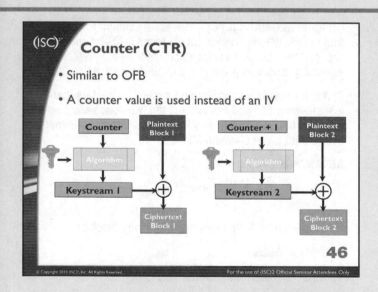

Counter (CTR)

- Similar to OFB
- A counter value is used instead of an IV

46

- **COUNTER (CTR) –** Operates very much like OFB except that a counter value is used instead of an IV. Using counters allows all aspects of this mode to be performed in parallel while still being able to perform a great deal of pre-processing before plaintext is received. The added risk is associated with the counter itself. If the counter repeats itself, it offers little beyond what ECB can provide. Furthermore, each operation can be attacked separately, which means that care must be taken to ensure that the key is not revealed (e.g., through the use of subkeys) and/or that it is changed frequently (through re-keying).

- In practice, CTR mode is particularly well suited to data-communications protocols run on limited-resource platforms. For example, the 802.11i Wireless LAN standard employs the Advanced Encryption Standard (AES) running in CTR mode to encrypt data using changing subkeys and frequent re-keying.

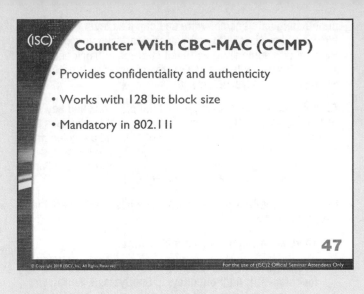

Counter With CBC-MAC (CCMP)

- Provides confidentiality and authenticity

- Works with 128 bit block size

- Mandatory in 802.11i

47

- **COUNTER WITH CBC - MAC (CCM)** – According to NIST SP 800-38C, "CCM may be used to provide assurance of the confidentiality and the authenticity of computer data by combining the techniques of the Counter (CTR) mode and the Cipher Block Chaining-Message Authentication Code (CBC-MAC) algorithm."

- CCM is based on an approved symmetric key-block cipher algorithm the block size of which is a 128 bit (AES) algorithm. CCM cannot be used with the 3DES Algorithm which has a block size of 64 bits.

- CCM is intended for use when all of the data is available in storage before CCM is applied. It is not designed to support partial processing or stream processing.

REFERENCE:

http://csrc.nist.gov/publications/nistpubs/800-38C/SP800-38C_updated-July20_2007.pdf

---

DES – Data Encryption Standard

- DES
  - 56 bit key
  - 16 Rounds of transposition and substitution
  - Fixed 64 bit block size
- Double DES (DDES)
  - Meet-in-the-Middle attack
- Triple DES (TDES)
  - DES-EEE3; EEE2; EDE3; EDE2

48

- **DES** – DES was the standard symmetric algorithm to be used for Sensitive but Unclassified (SBU) data transmission by all departments in the US federal government. It was chosen by NIST and NSA (National Security Agency) based on the Feistel cipher known as Lucifer.

  - **56 BIT KEY** – DES used a 56 bit key with 8 bits of parity (so 64 bits in total length but an effective key size of 56 bits).

  - **16 ROUNDS OF TRANSPOSITION AND SUBSTITUTION** – DES performed 16 rounds of transposition and substitution to the input in the creation of the ciphertext. At the receiving end, those 16 rounds would also be performed to decrypt the message.

  - **FIXED 64 BIT BLOCK SIZE** – DES had a fixed 64 bit block size – each input and output block would be 64 bits in length.

- DES was replaced first by Double DES (DDES) and then by Triple DES (TDES) as it was proven to be increasingly easy to break DES by brute force attacks.

- **DOUBLE DES (DDES)** – DDES uses two 56-bit keys. The message is encrypted by one key and re-encrypted by the second. DDES was thought to provide an effective key strength of a 112-bit cipher but was successfully attacked by the "meet-in-the-middle" analytic attack. (This is a mathematical trick that assumes that in the case of a multi-part operation, it is simplest to work forward from the beginning and work backward from the end to find where they meet.)

- **TRIPLE DES (TDES)** – TDES was published by IBM in 1978 as an extension to DES. In TDES, the input data is encrypted three times. The strength of Triple DES depends on the mode of operation chosen, and the number of keys being used. While the effective key size of Triple DES is 168-bits (3x56 bits), its effective security is less, since Triple DES is also subject to the Meet-in-the-Middle attack. Due to weaknesses against some known and chosen plaintext attacks, 3TDES implementation is considered to have an effective strength of 112 bits while a 2TDES (two-key Triple DES) implementation is considered to have an effective strength of around 80 bits. In general, EDE (Encrypt-Decrypt-Encrypt) modes are considered stronger than EEE mode. In EDE mode, the plaintext is encrypted with one key, decrypted with another key (which will not produce plaintext since it is the wrong key), and then re-encrypted with either the first or third key (depending on whether two-key or three-key TDES was chosen). The EEE mode operates as three consecutive encryption operations, using two or three keys.

  - Attacks on 2TDES have been proposed by Merkle and Hellman and Van Oorschot and Wiener, but the resource and time requirements of these attacks make them impractical even on today's computing platforms.

  - The key storage requirements for three-key 3DES is 192 bits (3 x 64), the true key length is 168 bits (3 x 56), but the effective strength is just 112 bits. It also requires three times more computing power than does DES. This can be a significant penalty.

  - DES has now been replaced by AES.

REFERENCE:

http://csrc.nist.gov/publications/fips/fips46-3/fips46-3.pdf

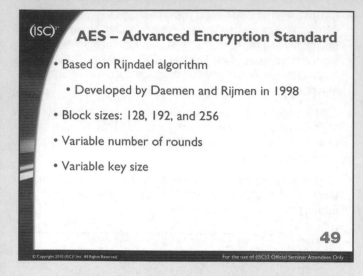

AES – Advanced Encryption Standard

- Based on Rijndael algorithm
  - Developed by Daemen and Rijmen in 1998
- Block sizes: 128, 192, and 256
- Variable number of rounds
- Variable key size

49

- **AES (RIJNDAEL)** – Rijndael was developed in 1998 by two Belgian cryptographers, Joan Daemen and Vincent Rijmen and was named the winner of the AES (Advanced Encryption Standard) competition in 2000. The flexibility of Rijndael is one of its biggest strengths: It can be implemented very effectively in both hardware and software and can also leverage different block and key sizes, although the standardized version of Rijndael was somewhat restricted in terms of block and key sizes. AES was published as Federal Information Processing Standard (FIPS) PUB 197 in 2001.

- **BLOCK SIZES** – Rijndael supports multiple block and key sizes between 128 and 256 bits, although the AES only uses the 128-bit block size. And a block size of 128 and a key length of 128, 192, and 256 are approved for use. Rijndael operates on a fixed array (table) of bytes typically called the "state." For AES, the state is a 4 byte x 4 byte table.

- **VARIABLE NUMBER OF ROUNDS** – The basic AES operation works as follows:

  - There are a variable number of rounds.

  - To encrypt, each round (except the last round) consists of four stages: 1. AddRoundKey; 2. SubBytes; 3. ShiftRows; 4. MixColumns. The final round replaces the MixColumns stage with a final AddRoundKey operation.

REFERENCE:
http://csrc.nist.gov/publications/fips/fips197/fips-197.pdf

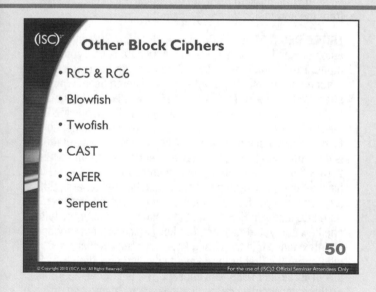

Other Block Ciphers

- RC5 & RC6
- Blowfish
- Twofish
- CAST
- SAFER
- Serpent

50

- **RC5** – Designed by Ron Rivest in 1994, it followed in the footsteps of an earlier algorithm, RC2, in providing a great number of variations: It supports block sizes of 32, 64, and 128 bits, key sizes up to 2040 bits, and can allow for up to 255 rounds. The original recommended settings were 64-bit blocks, 12 rounds and 128-bit keys (often written as RC5-64/12/16, the last number being the key size in bytes). Eighteen or more rounds are now recommended granting that a differential cryptanalysis attack was used successfully against a 12-round RC5 in 1998. Messages based on smaller 56-bit and 64-bit key sizes have also been broken by Distributed.net (the same people who helped crack DES) as part of RSA Security's cracking challenges. RC5 is patented by RSA.

- **RC6** – Also designed by Ron Rivest and fundamentally similar to RC5. It was a finalist for AES but lost to Rijndael. Also patented by RSA.

- **BLOWFISH** – Designed by Bruce Schneier in 1993. Blowfish is a Feistal cipher with 64-bit blocks and a variable key size between 32 and 448 bits. It is considered one of the fastest block-cipher algorithms available, but it does require more memory than many others making it less suitable for constrained devices. It was never patented: Schneier chose specifically to put Blowfish into the public domain.

- **TWOFISH** – Designed by a large team that included Schneier, Twofish is related to Blowfish but uses a larger 128-bit block size and key sizes up to 256 bits. It is comparable to Rijndael in speed although it is a little slower when using 128-bit keys.

- **CAST** – CAST is a Feistel-based method of encryption patented by Entrust but available for commercial and non-commercial use without a license. CAST-128 uses a 64-bit block size and a 128-bit key size. CAST-256 was a candidate for AES and uses a 128-bit block size and a 128- to 256-bit key size.

- **SAFER** – A family of block ciphers designed by James Massey, who co-created IDEA. There are a number of variants available that differ in block and key sizes, although they all share the same simple structure.

- **SERPENT** – A block cipher designed by Ross Anderson, Eli Biham, and Lars Knudson as a candidate for AES. (It came in second in the competition.) Like most other AES candidates, it uses a 128-bit block size with 128-bit, 192-bit, and 256-bit keys. Serpent can take advantage of parallel processing and also has a relatively conservative approach: Following Biham's cryptanalysis work, the designers were concerned that while a fewer number of rounds might be sufficient, a larger number of rounds (32) would be better.

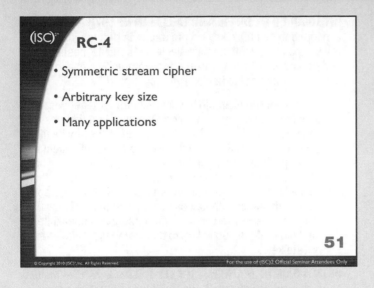

- **RC-4** – RC-4 was created by Ron Rivest of RSA Security in 1987. It is a symmetric stream cipher with an arbitrary key size and is one of the most common stream-based ciphers used today, including in applications such as: TLS (Transport Layer Security), WEP (Wired Equivalent Privacy), WPA (Wi-Fi Protected Access), TKIP (Temporal Key Integrity Protocol), Microsoft XBox, Oracle SQL, Microsoft PPTP, Microsoft Office, and Adobe Acrobat. Unfortunately, it is often implemented incorrectly (as in WEP and PPTPv1), and, even when implemented correctly is still subject to modification attacks. This is also due in part to its lack of diffusion. This is part of the reason it is not accepted by NIST.

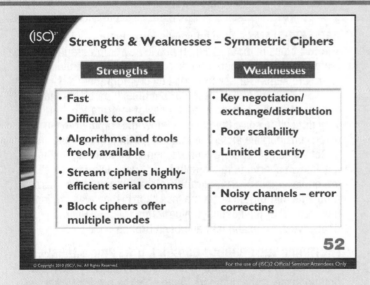

- **STRENGTHS OF SYMMETRIC-KEY CRYPTOGRAPHY –**

  - Very fast. Large amounts of data can be encrypted in very little time.

  - Providing sufficiently large keys, very difficult to break.

  - Algorithms and tools used for symmetric encryption are freely available.

  - Stream ciphers ensure highly-efficient, serial communications.

  - Block ciphers offer multiple modes suitable for many common applications and common software/hardware implementations.

- **WEAKNESSES OF SYMMETRIC-KEY CRYPTOGRAPHY –**

  - **KEY NEGOTIATION/EXCHANGE/DISTRIBUTION –** Because the symmetric key cannot be sent through the same channel as the encrypted data, another form of key negotiation or distribution must be used. These include key negotiation using the Diffie-Hellman Key Agreement Protocol, Key Exchange using RSA or ECC (Elliptic Curve Cryptography), or sending the key in an alternate channel such as via courier, or telephone. This is known as "out-of-band messaging."

  - **POOR SCALABILITY –** Each user requires a different key to communicate confidentially with each other user. With a purely symmetric key algorithm where the keys are retained for future use, the number of keys required are: n(n-1)/2, where n is equal to the number of users. For example, 10 users would require 45 keys: 10(10-1)/2=45.

  - **LIMITED SECURITY –** Symmetric algorithms provide limited security in that they are primarily good for confidentiality and some integrity, but do not provide for proof of origin, access control, or non-repudiation.

  - **NOISY CHANNELS AND ERROR CORRECTING –** A message being sent over an insecure channel may be subject to noise, data loss, or interference. If the message were encrypted with a symmetric algorithm that uses chaining during the encryption process, then any loss or change to the encrypted message could make the entire rest of the message unintelligible. Therefore, most algorithms have error correcting features or the ability to re-synchronize the message in the event that it is altered. Error correction is commonly done using Message Integrity Controls, which will be discussed shortly.

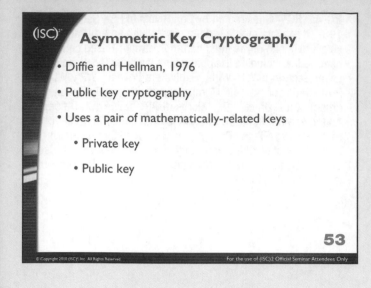

- Diffie and Hellman, 1976
- Public key cryptography
- Uses a pair of mathematically-related keys
  - Private key
  - Public key

53

- **INTRODUCED BY DIFFIE AND HELLMAN IN 1976** – The basic concept behind public key cryptography is that two halves of the key pair will combine for a value of 1. This is most easily understood when the one value (for example 7) is the inverse of the other half of the key pair (for example 1/7).

  - If the following example is used: A cryptographer wants to encrypt a message value of 49; encrypting the message (i.e., message = 49) with one half of the key would give the result of 343, and decrypting the result would be accomplished by multiplying the other half of the key pair (1/7) against the ciphertext. To make it more difficult than a simple inverse, modular arithmetic is used. The person who holds the private key can easily compute the value of the public key. However, it is computationally infeasible for the holder of the public key to determine the value of the private key.

- **USES A PAIR OF MATHEMATICALLY-RELATED KEYS** – Instead of using a single key to both encrypt and decrypt messages, asymmetric key cryptosystems use a pair of mathematically-related asymmetric keys known as a key pair.

  - **PRIVATE KEY** – Kept secret.

  - **PUBLIC KEY** – Freely distributed.

  - When you encrypt with one, you can ONLY decrypt with the other.

REFERENCE:
http://www.maths.mq.edu.au/~steffen/old/PCry/report/node8.html

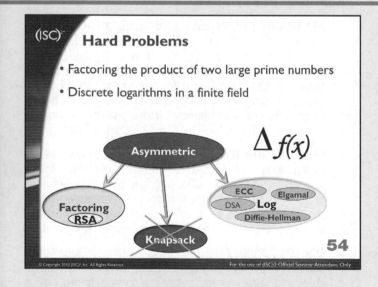

- Factoring the product of two large prime numbers
- Discrete logarithms in a finite field

54

- **HARD PROBLEMS** – Also known as intractable problems. The two types of math in use in public key cryptography are factoring prime numbers and discrete logarithms. The ideal "hard problems" for asymmetric key cryptographic algorithms are so-called "one-way trapdoor functions": problems that are easy to solve given certain pieces of information, but very difficult to solve if you don't know the trapdoor (even given considerable expertise and computing resources). The effectiveness of hard problems depends on there not being any known shortcuts to the solution. "Knapsack functions" are one example of cryptographic algorithms based on hard problems that turned out to be less "hard" than was originally believed. All of the knapsack algorithms (Merkle-Hellman and Chor-Rivest, for example) have been broken.

- **FACTORING THE PRODUCT OF TWO LARGE PRIME NUMBERS** – Multiplying two large prime numbers is relatively easy, but finding those prime numbers when only the product is known is hard.

- **DISCRETE LOGARITHMS IN A FINITE FIELD** – Logarithms are relatively easy, but finding a discrete logarithm when a number of equally-possible options are available, is hard.

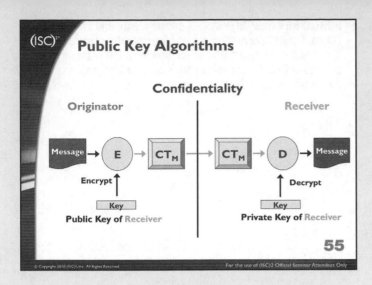

- **PUBLIC KEY ALGORITHMS** – Public Key Algorithms ensure confidentiality. Encrypting a message with the receiver's public key provides confidential transmission of the message because the only key that can open the message is the corresponding private key of the recipient.

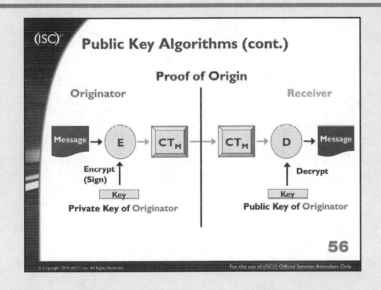

- **PUBLIC KEY ALGORITHMS (CONT.)** – Public Key Algorithms also ensure proof of origin. When a message is encrypted (signed) with the sender's private key, the recipient can verify the source of the message because the message can only be opened with the sender's public key.

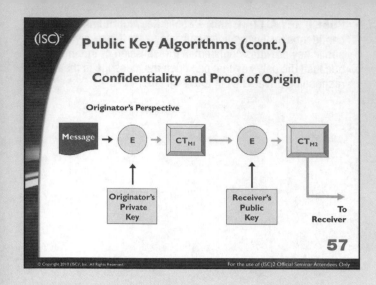

- **PUBLIC KEY ALGORITHMS –** Confidentiality and Proof of Origin. Double encrypting a message with the private key of the sender and then with the public key of the receiver will provide both confidentiality and proof of origin. The operations will normally be done in this order.

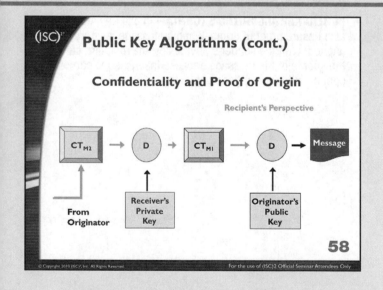

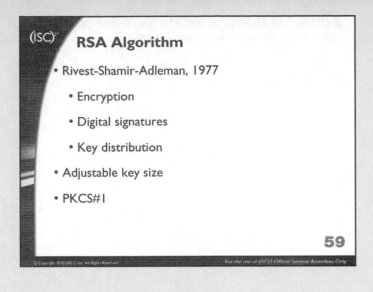

- **RSA** – Patented in 1977. RSA is a highly flexible set of encryption protocols used for encryption, digital signatures, and key distribution. As key size increases, computing cost increases.

- **PKCS#1–** Is the implementation of the RSA algorithm. It is currently in version 2.1.

- How the RSA algorithm works:
  - Find two prime numbers, and call them p and q.
  - Multiply them and call the result n.
  - Choose a public value less than n relatively prime with (p-1) and (q-1), and call it e.
  - Find d such that e * d = 1 mod (p-1)*(q-1).
  - Make n and e PUBLIC, and keep d, p, and q SECRET.
  - To encrypt message m, ciphertext c = me mod n.
  - To decrypt, m = cd mod n.

REFERENCE:
http://www.di-mgt.com.au/rsa_alg.html

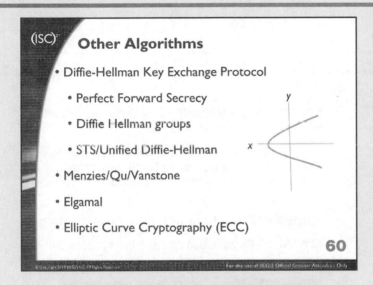

Exchange) and S/MIME (Secure Multipurpose Internet Mail Extension) since a longer key is much stronger than a short key.

- **UNIFIED DIFFIE HELLMAN** – One weakness with D-H was the Man-in-the-Middle attack where a person could impersonate the two end parties and intercept their communications. This led to the development of the Station to Station (STS) key agreement protocol by Diffie, Van Oorscht, and Weiner in 1992. This used public key certificates to authenticate the end parties. This is known as Unified Diffie-Hellmann.

- **MENZIES/QU/VANSTONE** – MQV is another asymmetric algorithm based on the Diffie-Hellman theorem and can use either finite fields or elliptic curve groups for authenticated key agreement.

- **ELGAMAL** – First described by Taher El Gamal in 1984. Its main advantage lies in the fact that it has not been patented and can, therefore, be freely used. Its big disadvantage is that the ciphertext created using Elgamal is twice the size of the original plaintext. In addition, Elgamal is known to be extremely "malleable" and may allow an attacker to make changes to the plaintext using changes in the ciphertext. Elgamal is often confused with the Elgamal digital signature scheme which came out that same year. The Elgamal signature scheme is rarely used.

- **ELLIPTIC CURVE CRYPTOGRAPHY (ECC)** – Uses an algebraic system defined on points of an elliptic curve to provide public-key algorithms. It can be used for key negotiation, data encryption, and digital signatures. It is very fast and efficient and has small key sizes. ECC smaller key sizes offer roughly the equivalent strength to larger RSA keys (such as 1024-bit RSA = 160-bit ECC). It is very suitable for resource-constrained applications.

- **DIFFIE-HELLMAN KEY EXCHANGE PROTOCOL** – The first public-key cryptosystem (1976). It allows two entities to negotiate a session key that can be used to exchange secret information, without ever revealing their private keys. The patent expired in 1997.

  - **PERFECT FORWARD SECRECY** – Often called forward secrecy, PFS is the principle used in D-H that even if two private keys are used in negotiating a secret value (shared secret) as in Diffie-Hellman, and one of those private keys is later compromised, it will not be possible to determine either the secret key or the other private key from the knowledge of the compromised private key.

  - **DIFFIE-HELLMAN GROUPS** – D-H groups determine the length of the base prime numbers that will be used in calculating the key pairs. This is important to ensure a strong implementation of D-H for TLS, IKE (Internet Key

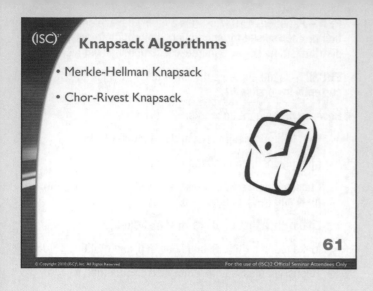

- **BOTH OF THE KNAPSACK ENCRYPTION SCHEMES HAVE BEEN BROKEN** – Merkle-Hellman Knapsack was developed in 1978 and was based on subset sum problems in combinatorics. Chor-Rivest Knapsack was developed in 1984 and revised in 1988.

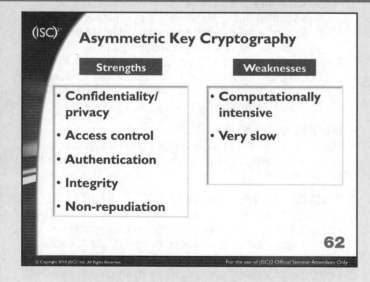

- **STRENGTHS -**
  - **CONFIDENTIALITY/PRIVACY** – Data cannot be decrypted without the associated private key.
  - **ACCESS CONTROL** – Only the holder of the private key can open a confidential message. This is in contrast to a symmetric algorithm where several people may share a secret key.
  - **AUTHENTICATION** – The identity of sender is confirmed.
  - **INTEGRITY** – Confirmation that data has not been tampered with.
  - **NON-REPUDIATION** – Sender cannot deny sending.
- **WEAKNESSES -**
  - Computationally Intensive.
  - 1,000 or more times slower than symmetric key cryptography.

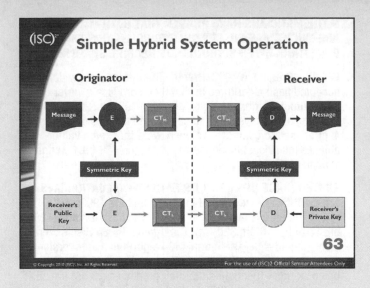

- **SIMPLE HYBRID SYSTEM OPERATION** – Takes advantage of the strengths of different cryptographic techniques. This graphic shows a simple hybrid cryptographic operation. The speed and confidentiality benefits of symmetric encryption are used in the encryption of the message, whereas the excellent key distribution properties of asymmetric encryption are used to securely transmit the session key (symmetric) that was used to encrypt the message, to the receiver.

  - Symmetric Key Cryptography is good for bulk data encryption.

  - Asymmetric Key Cryptography is good for key exchange and digital signatures.

  - Message Integrity Controls are good for detecting changes (not shown in this diagram– see next slide).

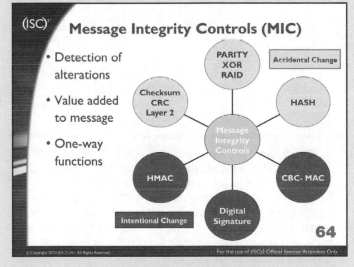

- **MESSAGE INTEGRITY CONTROLS (MIC)** – MICs detect alterations (whether intentional or accidental) to a message during transmission. A MIC is a special value that is calculated based on the message contents and added to the message to be sent. This value can be used by the recipient to check for any errors or changes to the message by recalculating the MIC from the received message and ensuring that it has the same value as the MIC sent by the originator.

- In addition to traditional MIC values, such as parity bits and checksums, a special branch of cryptography has been developed using one-way functions to compute a MIC that can be used for message integrity purposes.

- **ACCIDENTAL CHANGE** – The top three choices in the diagram

show the three basic integrity controls (Checksum, Parity, Hash Function) that can detect accidental errors in the received transmission (i.e., a bit flipped in a network transmission). None of these will deter a determined attacker who can not only alter the message, but alter the integrity controls to match.

- **INTENTIONAL CHANGE** – To protect against an intentional integrity attack, we need to use one of the three bottom choices: HMAC, Digital Signatures, or CBC-MAC. We can encrypt a hash of the message with the private key of an asymmetric key pair (which generates a digital signature); we can generate a hash of a message that has been concatenated with a secret key, which is an example of HMAC (see RFC 2104 or FIPS 198); or we can use a special function called a CBC-MAC, which uses DES-CBC to calculate a hash value.

- An example of CBC-MAC is the ANSI X9.9 DES-MAC function, which computes a DES CBC function over the entire message using a secret key and generates a 64-bit output value. The AES is used in the same way, as is done in WPA2 implementations, for example. (Note that the ANSI X9.9 DES-MAC function is used by the financial community and is also documented as NIST document FIPS-113.)

- The HMAC (RFC 2104) uses a standard hash function (such as MD5 or SHA-1) and hashes the message with a secret key, but without a secret key algorithm such as DES. HMACs run much faster than CBC-MAC functions, are believed to be just as secure, and support the interchangeable use of different standard hash functions as necessary. As such, they are increasingly replacing MAC functions for integrity controls, as with SSL and IPSec.

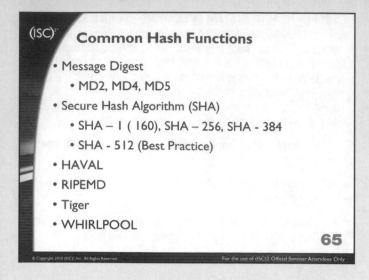

Common Hash Functions

- Message Digest
  - MD2, MD4, MD5
- Secure Hash Algorithm (SHA)
  - SHA – 1 (160), SHA – 256, SHA - 384
  - SHA - 512 (Best Practice)
- HAVAL
- RIPEMD
- Tiger
- WHIRLPOOL

65

- **COMMON HASH FUNCTIONS** – Message Digest, Secure Hash Algorithm, HAVAL, RIPEMD, Tiger, and WHIRLPOOL.

- **MESSAGE DIGEST** – MD2/4/5 are all considered too weak for digital signatures due to weaknesses demonstrated in pre-image collision resistance.

- **SECURE HASH ALGORITHM (SHA) -**

  - SHA-1 (1994): Fixed-length, 160-bit hash value.

  - New versions of SHA offer greater key space and are more suitable for larger messages:

    - SHA-256: Suitable for the same kinds of messages as SHA-1 but is less likely to have a collision with other documents.

    - SHA-384 and SHA-512: Designed for much larger messages.

  - (Note that the number indicates the size of the resulting hash.)

- MATHEMATICIANS HAVE PROVEN THAT BOTH MD AND SHA ARE MUCH MORE SUSCEPTIBLE TO COLLISIONS THAN WAS ONCE THOUGHT. FIPS STANDARDS REQUIRE SHA-512.

- **HAVAL** – Created in 1992. HAVAL differs from most widely-accepted hash algorithms in that it can produce a variety of hash output lengths (128 bits, 160 bits, 192 bits, 224 bits, and 256 bits) and allows users to specify the number of rounds (3, 4, or 5) used to generate the hash. Note that some vulnerabilities (collisions) have been found in the 128-bit, 3-round version of HAVAL.

- **RIPEMD (RACE INTEGRITY PRIMITIVES EVALUATION MESSAGE DIGEST)** – Developed in Belgium in the 1990s. Like HAVAL, RIPEMD is available in a variety of hash lengths (128-bit, 160-bit, 256-bit, 320-bit). The original RIPEMD sets were fashioned after the traditional MD4 algorithm. Later versions of RIPEMD (such as RIPEMD-160) are generally recognized as being stronger functions than their predecessors but are still not as widely used as SHA.

- **TIGER** – Created in 1996 and designed for speed on 64-bit machines. Tiger and Tiger 2 outputs are represented as 48-bit hexadecimal hashes. The Tiger algorithm uses 24 rounds and incorporates intricate functions of rotations, S-Box lookups, operation mixing with XOR, and addition/subtraction. The full 24-round function currently has no known/published weaknesses or collisions.

- **WHIRLPOOL** – Adopted by the ISO and IEC standards' bodies after its development in 2000 for the NESSIA (New European Schemes for Signatures, Integrity, and Encryption) project. It has since undergone two revisions that have strengthened the algorithm. The WHIRLPOOL function returns a 128-bit hexadecimal hash.

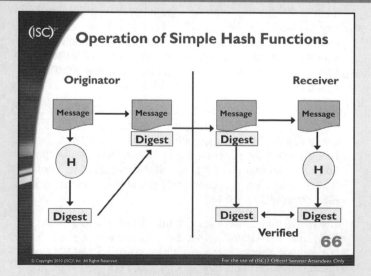

Operation of Simple Hash Functions

Originator   Receiver

Verified

66

- **SIMPLE HASH FUNCTIONS** – A hash function is used to determine whether a message has been altered or changed (i.e., in transit or storage). The process is as follows: The sender hashes the message with a one-way hashing function. The sender sends both the message and the hash (also referred to as the digest) to the recipient. The recipient then uses the same one-way hashing function to hash the received message and compares the two hash values. If the values are the same, the recipient has some assurance that message has not been changed. (Note, however, that integrity is not guaranteed. Since the hash was not cryptographically protected as it traversed an insecure network, it was possible for an attacker to change both the message and the hash.)

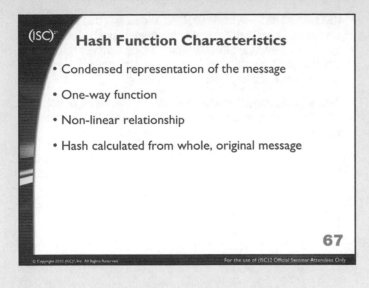

Hash Function Characteristics

- Condensed representation of the message
- One-way function
- Non-linear relationship
- Hash calculated from whole, original message

67

- **HASH FUNCTION CHARACTERISTICS** – Good hash functions have a number of important features:

- **PRODUCE A "CONDENSED REPRESENTATION" OF THE ORIGINAL MESSAGE** – The hash that is created from a message is specific to that message and can be used to detect any changes to the message. A good hash will resist birthday attacks; it should be mathematically infeasible to find another message with the same hash.

- **SHOULD BE A ONE-WAY FUNCTION** – A hash function is relatively simple to calculate from the original message but is computationally infeasible to derive the original message from its hash.

- **NON-LINEAR RELATIONSHIP BETWEEN HASHES** – The combined hash values of two independent messages would not be equal to the hash value of the combined message.

- **SHOULD DERIVE THE HASH USING THE WHOLE, ORIGINAL MESSAGE** – The hash must be calculated on the entire message so that any changes in the original message would have a noticeable impact on the output hash.

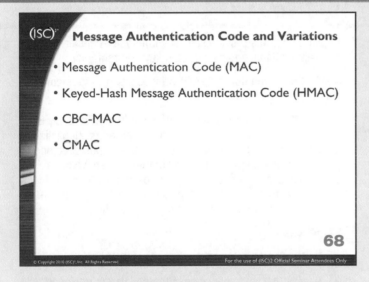

Message Authentication Code and Variations

- Message Authentication Code (MAC)
- Keyed-Hash Message Authentication Code (HMAC)
- CBC-MAC
- CMAC

68

of the key. (The key must be kept secret, analogous to a key used for bulk data encryption. This is unlike a digital signature in which the public key does not need to be secret, just authentic.) As long as the recipient has the correct key, they can regenerate a hash from the message they receive that should create the same hash as was sent by the sender.

- **CBC-MAC** – Generates a hash value by encrypting a message with a symmetric key and an IV of zero. All except the last block of the encrypted message is discarded and the last block is used as the MAC value. In the case of DES, this would be a 64-bit value, whereas in the case of AES it would be a 128-bit value. Since encryption in CBC mode chains the cipher text into subsequent cryptographic operations, any alteration of the message would affect the value of the last block, hence the use of the last block for a MAC. The disadvantage of CBC-MAC is that it is significantly slower than an HMAC.

- **CMAC** – The core of the CMAC algorithm is a variation of Cipher Block Chaining MAC algorithm (CBC-MAC). According to NIST SP 800-38B, "The basic (CBC-MAC) has security deficiencies…." These weaknesses make CBC-MAC only suitable for fixed-length messages. CMAC can be considered a mode of operation of AES and some other block ciphers. CMAC is also known as OMAC & XMAC. CMAC provides stronger assurance of data integrity than a checksum or an error detecting code. CMAC is designed to detect both accidental and intentional, unauthorized modifications of the data.

- It is important to note that the key used in an HMAC or CBC-MAC or CMAC construction must not be the same key used to perform bulk data encryption of the same piece of data (e.q., with AES CBC mode). This is one of the appeals of the CCM mode – it safely creates a key schedule for CTR mode for encryption and for CBC-MAC for integrity using different subkeys.

- **MESSAGE AUTHENTICATION CODE (MAC)** – Used to authenticate a message by using a secret key as an input with which to produce a tag. The tag can be verified by users (who also possess the secret key), thereby proving both the authenticity and the integrity of the message. MAC is different from MIC (Message Integrity Check) in that the MIC does not use a secret key and can, therefore, only verify integrity. MAC can detect unauthorized modification of the message, whereas MIC cannot.

- Note that using the term "MAC" by itself is discouraged because the term means different things to different people. Instead, use the specific term, such as hash, or keyed hash, CDC-MAC, or checksum.

- **KEYED-HASH MESSAGE AUTHENTICATION CODE (HMAC)** – Uses cryptographic hash functions in conjunction with a key. The key is concatenated with the message and then the combined message and key are hashed. The strength of HMAC is dependent upon the hash function used and the protection

REFERENCE:

RFC 2104, "HMAC: Keyed-Hashing for Message Authentication," M. Bellare, R. Canetti, and H. Krawczyk.

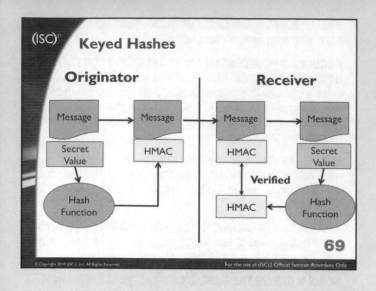

- **KEYED HASHES** – A basic hash on a message can be intercepted and changed. We use cryptographic hash algorithms to achieve message authentication, which involves mixing a HASH algorithm with a pre-shared key. The adversary would need to know the key to create a collision.

- This is implemented in IPSec for integrity checking of both ESP (Encapsulating Security Payload) & AH (Authentication Header).

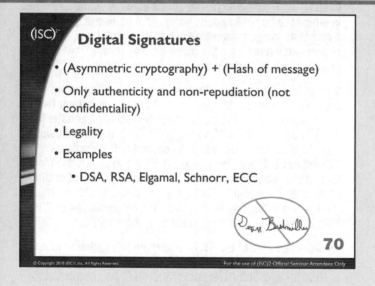

- Digital Signatures provide sender authenticity-checking and non-repudiation using asymmetric key cryptography.

- NOTE: Digital signatures do NOT provide any message confidentiality protections!

- **LEGALITY** – If the encryption is intact and the private key is held by the rightful owner, it must be accepted by all parties in the transaction. The American Bar Association has developed guidelines for accepting digital signatures that have been adopted in some US states and other participating countries. A digital signature is not accepted globally for transactions and specifically not for high-dollar, high-risk situations.

- **EXAMPLES -**

  - Digital Signature Algorithm/Standard (DSA/DSS)

  - Uses SHA-1 and special asymmetric system designed for DSA (512 to 1024 key space).

  - RSA – Combined with hash function, such as MD5 or SHA.

  - Elgamal Signature Scheme

  - Schnorr Groups

  - ECC

REFERENCE:
http://www.abanet.org/scitech/ec/isc/dsgfree.html

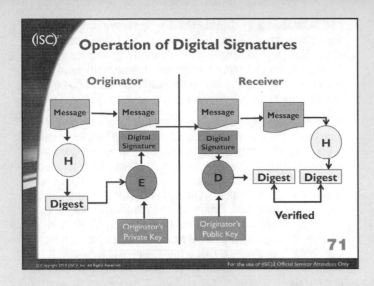

Operation of Digital Signatures — slide 71

- **OPERATION OF DIGITAL SIGNATURES –** The Digital Signature is a cryptographically protected hash of the message. It is created by hashing the message with a hashing algorithm (such as MD-5 or SHA-512), and then encrypting the hash (digest) of the message with the private key of the originator. The hash will prove message integrity, and the signing of the hash with a private key will provide proof of origin, since the signature could only be decrypted using the originator's public key.

- **LIMITATIONS –** The problem is knowing that the receiver has the real public key of the originator, not the public key of an imposter or man-in-the-middle. This is accomplished through the use of certificates.

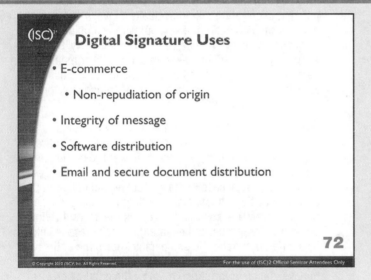

Digital Signature Uses — slide 72

- E-commerce
  - Non-repudiation of origin
- Integrity of message
- Software distribution
- Email and secure document distribution

- **E-COMMERCE:**

  - **NON-REPUDIATION OF ORIGIN –** By signing a message with a private key, the originator has offered his or her guarantee that the message has come from him or her. This guarantee can only be verified, however, when the receiver knows that he or she has the public key for the correct person. For this, a certificate is used, issued by a trusted third party. Unless the process is automated, most recipients do not take the time to verify that the certificate is valid.

  - **INTEGRITY OF MESSAGE –** The originator encrypts the hash with his or her private key. This protects the hash from modification by an attacker and proves that the message received is the same as the one hashed by the originator.

  - **SOFTWARE DISTRIBUTION –** Digital signatures are used for software distribution to provide integrity and non-repudiation

of source. A software vendor would apply for a certificate via a registration authority (RA). After the software has been though the RA's accreditation process, the software would be signed. Customers are able to verify the signature when they install the software.

- The following is directly from NIST:

  - The DSA is used in the distribution of software. A digital signature is applied to software after it has been validated and approved for distribution. Before the software is installed or run on a computer, the signature could be verified to be sure no unauthorized changes (such as the addition of a virus) have been made. The digital signature is verified to ensure the integrity of the software. Code signing digital certificates can be purchased for use in conjunction with Microsoft's Authenticode technology; this enables you to digitally sign 32-bit or 64-bit .exe (PE files), .cab, .dll, and .ocx files.

  - A digital signature certificate is an encrypted electronic document that contains information that verifies a company's identity, encoded in a highly secure format. A server is used to send digital signature certificates and electronic countersignatures to authenticate an identity. Internet browser software retrieves the digital signature certificate and electronic countersignature containing verification of the identity.

  - It is intended to provide identification, authentication, and non-repudiation via the use of digital signature technology as a means for individuals and business entities to be authenticated when accessing, retrieving, and submitting information with the government.

REFERENCE:
http://csrc.nist.gov/publications/nistbul/csl94-11.txt

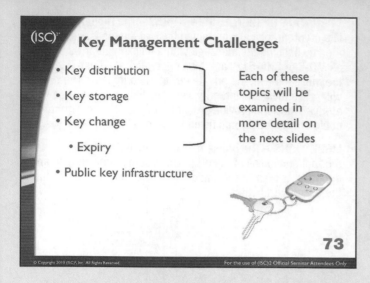

Key Management Challenges

- Key distribution
- Key storage
- Key change
  - Expiry
- Public key infrastructure

Each of these topics will be examined in more detail on the next slides

73

- **KEY MANAGEMENT** – Perhaps the greatest challenge associated with a secure cryptographic implementation is the management of the keys. Keys must be kept secret, yet they must be available when required. Even old keys must be retained to decrypt old backup files or data.

- **KEY MANAGEMENT CHALLENGES** – Some symmetric algorithms (e.g., DES) have some weak keys, while other algorithms (e.g., AES) have no such known weakness. Proper checks must be performed to ensure that no weak keys are accepted as part of the key-generation process, based upon the algorithm with which the key will be used.

- **EXPIRY** – The use of a cryptographic key for a long period of time increases the risk that an adversary will be successful in cryptanalytic attacks. Attacks on cryptographic algorithms are based upon the number of ciphertexts available for study. The greater the number of ciphertexts, the better chance an adversary has to break a cryptosystem. Expiry ensures that a key is never overused. Expiry may be based upon the amount of traffic, the amount of traffic over time, or purely time-in-use. Key Management processes ensure that a key is never used past its expiry, and that a replacement is available to seamlessly take over protection of data following the expiration period.

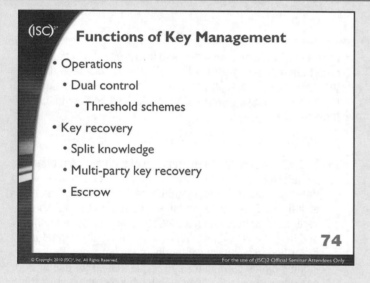

Functions of Key Management

- Operations
- Dual control
  - Threshold schemes
- Key recovery
- Split knowledge
- Multi-party key recovery
- Escrow

74

- **OPERATIONS –**

  - **DUAL CONTROL** – Protecting a sensitive process or operation by requiring the active participation of two or more separate entities (persons). Dual control ensures that no one person can misuse a key to perform an action that is not allowed, for example, signing a certificate with bogus identification information.

    - **THRESHOLD SCHEMES** – When more than one party is required to complete a transaction, a threshold scheme may be used. Threshold schemes require more than one person from a group to authorize a task, for example, but any two or more people from that group can successfully complete the task. An example of this is signing authority on a check. The company may require at least two signatures on a check, and there are five people who are authorized to sign checks. Any two people from the group of five would be able to provide those signatures.

- **KEY RECOVERY –**

  - **SPLIT KNOWLEDGE** – Two or more parties have independent information that individually conveys no useable information about the key, but when combined in a special manner or device, reconstructs the key. Split knowledge protects the key from accidental or malicious compromise, as it requires that no one individual has full knowledge of the key, and that more than one individual is required to reconstruct the key.

  - **MULTI-PARTY KEY RECOVERY** – One way to protect a secret is to ensure that no one person knows the entire secret. For example, a company may want to protect its private key but struggles with the fear that perhaps if only one person had access to the secret key, the holder of that secret could be untrustworthy, leading to a compromise of that secret. One solution is to break the secret key into three or more pieces, and ensure that each piece is held by a different person. No one person knows the entire secret and it would require several people to work together to have enough information to know the entire secret formula. Properties of dual control should be maintained in MPR. Two basic mechanisms are used in MPR: modular addition and threshold schemes.

  - **KEY ESCROW** – A process, mechanism, or entity that can recover a lost or destroyed cryptographic key. Key escrow systems are typically made up of three components: a user component that handles the generation and use of cryptographic keys, an escrow component that saves the keys, and a recovery component that provides the restoration services. The most widely known key escrow system is the US government's Escrowed Encryption Standard (EES) associated with the Clipper Chip and the Skipjack cryptographic algorithm.

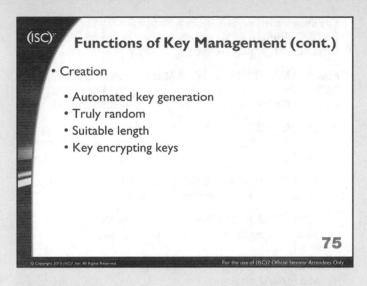

75

Functions of Key Management (cont.)

- Creation
  - Automated key generation
  - Truly random
  - Suitable length
  - Key encrypting keys

- **CREATION –**

  - **AUTOMATED KEY GENERATION –** Automated key generation prevents user bias from entering into the generation process, protects against accidental reuse of key material, and provides quick key production.

- **TRULY RANDOM –** Key generation should always produce random keys. However, there are many instances where pseudo-random number generators are not really producing random bits. Truly random data is required for strong cryptographic keys and can only be produced by physical forces (e.g., radioactive decay, noisy diodes, etc.). Carl Ellison notes: "True-random sources can be considered unconditionally unguessable, even by an adversary with infinite computing resources, while pseudo-random sources are good only against computationally limited adversaries."

- **SUITABLE LENGTH –** Key Generation must generate enough bits for a complete key. Generating 64 random bits, and concatenating them together to get 128 bits, provides only 64 bits of randomness.

- **KEY ENCRYPTING KEYS –** Generation of Key Encrypting Keys (KEKs) (i.e., keys that are used to encrypt other keys) is no different than generating any other kind of key. Care must be taken, however, to ensure that the data used to generate the KEK is not related in any way to the data used to generate the keys the KEK is being used to protect.

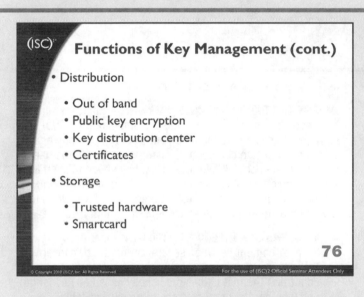

Functions of Key Management (cont.)

- Distribution
  - Out of band
  - Public key encryption
  - Key distribution center
  - Certificates

- Storage
  - Trusted hardware
  - Smartcard

- **KEY DISTRIBUTION –** Getting newly-generated keys to the parties who need to use them for secure communication. There are a number of solutions to this problem:

  - **OUT OF BAND –** Using an "out-of-band" communication channel, which means using some other communication medium to exchange the keys (e.g., personally meet the other party and physically exchange keys, use FedEx to mail the keys, etc.). Out-of-band distribution does not guarantee secure delivery, but it increases its likelihood.

  - **PUBLIC KEY ENCRYPTION –** Public Key Encryption is the most common modern solution to the key distribution problem. There are two general methods for this process:

    - **SECRET KEY CONSTRUCTION –** Using Diffie-Hellman, Elgamal, or similar public key techniques, engage in an online protocol to exchange values that generate or construct a new secret key, which eavesdroppers will not be able to construct. Make sure to take precautions against man-in-the-middle attacks in these protocols.

    - **SECRET KEY DELIVERY –** Using RSA encryption, Elga-

mal, or similar public key techniques, one party encrypts a chosen secret key with the receiving party's public key, guaranteeing that only the intended receiving party, which has the corresponding private key, can decrypt and recover the chosen secret key. There are protocols (e.g., SSL) that allow both parties to contribute key material with which to generate the secret key.

  - **KEY DISTRIBUTION CENTERS (KDC) –** KDCs are centralized repositories that hold long-term secrets about every user, and distribute transaction keys to allow users to share for short-term communication. KDCs are used in the Kerberos key management scheme.

  - **CERTIFICATES –** Used to distribute public keys to communicating partners. The Certificate includes a digital signature to prevent modifications to the key or accompanying identifying information.

- **STORAGE –** Secure storage of cryptographic keys requires secure hardware to protect either the keys themselves, or the key encrypting key (KEK) that decrypts the keys and allows them to be used.

  - **TRUSTED HARDWARE –** Hardware that has been evaluated according to a particular set of certification criteria, typically according to FIPS 140-2 or the Common Criteria.

  - **SMARTCARDS –** Credit card-sized plastic cards with an embedded chip that can be inserted into a reader or placed near a wireless reader to activate. Smartcards are self-contained computing devices that have their own CPU, memory, and non-volatile storage. Many smartcards today include dedicated cryptographic hardware engines that are resistant to power attacks and can perform key generation, encryption, decryption, and public key operations in milliseconds. ISO 7816, EMV (Europay, Mastercard, VISA), and PC/SC standards define the interfaces, frameworks, and services with which most smartcards comply. These standards allow strong authentication for generation and use of cryptographic keys and services.

Public Key Infrastructure (PKI)

- Binds people/entities to their public keys
  - Prevent Man-in-the-Middle attack
- Public keys are published and are certified by digital signatures

77

- **PUBLIC KEY INFRASTRUCTURE** – PKI is the platform to enable the secure transport of documents, e-commerce, and email over an insecure network, through the implementation of Public (Asymmetric) Key Cryptography in an organization. This also requires management of the infrastructure to issue certificates through a trusted party and verification of user's public keys.

- **PUBLIC KEY INFRASTRUCTURE BINDS A PEOPLE/ENTITIES TO THEIR PUBLIC KEYS** – Ensures that the public key is associated with a "proven" person or entity.

- **PUBLIC KEYS ARE PUBLISHED AND CERTIFIED BY DIGITAL SIGNATURES** – Certificates are issued by the Certificate Authority (CA) and protected by the CA's digital signature.

  - **CROSS-CERTIFICATION** – CAs cross-certify each other – i.e., recognize each other's certificates – which allows entities associated with different CAs to trust each other.

  - **CERTIFICATE REVOCATION LISTS (CRLS)** – Identify certificates that have been canceled or revoked.

  - **X.509 STANDARD** – Specifies the standard layout for public key certificates and certificate revocation lists.

REFERENCE:
http://www.ietf.org/rfc/rfc2459.txt

Strong Cryptographic PKI Solutions

- Use evaluated solutions
- High work factor
- Publicly-evaluated cryptographic algorithms
- Training
- Import and export of cryptography
  - Wassenaar Agreement
- Law enforcement issues

78

- **SELECTION OF STRONG CRYPTOGRAPHIC SOLUTIONS FOR PKI** – Use nationally/internationally standardized solutions by using products tested by either the Common Criteria or FIPS 140-2 standard.

- **CHOOSE SOLUTIONS WITH A SUFFICIENTLY HIGH WORK FACTOR** – A work factor long enough to dissuade an attacker.

- **USE PUBLICLY-EVALUATED CRYPTOGRAPHIC ALGORITHMS AND CRYPTOSYSTEMS** – It is difficult to create a strong cryptographic algorithm. Having a product that has undergone close and public scrutiny will result in more confidence in the cryptographic operations than a product that has not undergone such analysis and testing.

- **ENSURE THAT USERS ARE PROPERLY TRAINED** – Users must be clear on how to use the system. The number one failure in all technical solutions, cryptographic or otherwise, is the end user's lack of knowledge or execution.

- **IMPORT AND EXPORT OF CRYPTOGRAPHY** – Many countries have had strict laws regarding the use and export of cryptography. This is due to the recognition of cryptography as a valuable weapon in conflict and a dangerous tool in the hands of criminal elements. While these laws have been relaxed in some jurisdictions, it is still a challenge for a multinational company to ensure that it does not break local laws when it moves data equipment into and out of the country.

  - **WASSENAAR AGREEMENT** – The Wassenaar Agreement is an agreement between several countries that governs the movement of cryptographic algorithms between those countries. The restrictions are usually based on key length and whether the product is commercially available.

- **LAW ENFORCEMENT ISSUES** – Commonly available commercial and open source encryption can hinder law enforcement in executing investigations. Commonly available cryptographic software packages, such as PGP, GPG, and TrueCrypt, do not require key escrow or the deployment of a key available to law enforcement either directly or leveraged through a third party. The idea of providing encryption keys to law enforcement entities is in conflict with the ideas underlying the use of encryption in commerce, as well as the increasing number of regulatory requirements, such as HIPAA and PCI, that require managed data to be encrypted. Concerns over key management and the conflict between the goals of commerce and law enforcement were largely responsible for the rejection of the Clipper Chip in 1993 due to its Key Escrow properties.

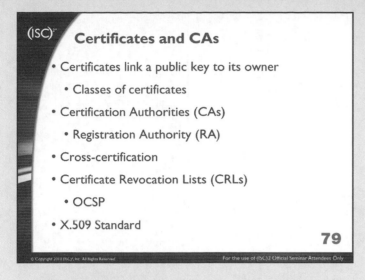

Certificates and CAs

- Certificates link a public key to its owner
  - Classes of certificates
- Certification Authorities (CAs)
  - Registration Authority (RA)
- Cross-certification
- Certificate Revocation Lists (CRLs)
  - OCSP
- X.509 Standard

79

- **CERTIFICATES** – Certificates link or bind a public key to its owner. This ensures that the senders know they are encrypting a message, or validating a signature, with the correct key belonging to the correct person.

  - **CLASSES OF CERTIFICATES** – There are various classes of certificates available. Each class represents the amount of trust that the recipient can have in the validity of the certificate and the authenticity of the owner of the public key provided. A Class One certificate is often free and has a fairly loose linkage between the public key and an email address, for example. A Class Three certificate is used on commercial business transactions and other trusted applications and requires a stringent process of authentication (and much higher price) to ensure that the certificate is only created for the correct person and with the correct key.

- **CERTIFICATE AUTHORITIES** – CAs act as a trusted third party to validate the owners of public keys, and issue a certificate that attests to the validity of the public key and how much trust we may have in that validity. Some CAs offer a fee-based service, while others are free and available to anyone who wants to register for a certificate.

  - **REGISTRATION AUTHORITIES** – RAs operate as the representatives of the CAs and accept the applications for certificates on behalf of the CAs.

- **CROSS-CERTIFICATION** – CAs cross-certify each other – i.e., recognize each other's certificates – which allows entities associated with different CAs to trust each other.

- **CERTIFICATE REVOCATION LISTS (CRLS)** – Identify certificates that have been canceled or revoked. If a person believes that his or her private key associated with the public key on a certificate has been compromised, he or she will advise the CA to revoke the certificate and put it on a CRL. Another time that a certificate is placed on a CRL is when the holder of the certificate no longer requires the certificate (such as the employee left the company). The certificate should be revoked so that it cannot be used improperly.

  - **ONLINE CERTIFICATE STATUS PROTOCOL (OCSP)** – When a person is entering into a trusted relationship with another entity, such as with online banking, he or she should always check whether the certificate he or she has is still valid. This can be done manually or automatically online by using a protocol such as OCSP.

- **X.509 STANDARD** – Specifies the standard layout for the fields on public key certificates and certificate revocation lists.

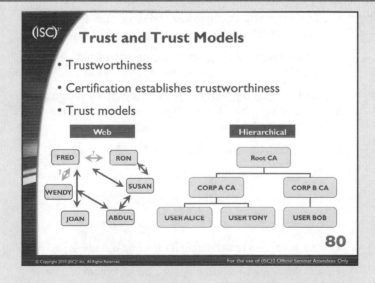

Trust and Trust Models

- Trustworthiness
- Certification establishes trustworthiness
- Trust models

80

- **TRUST AND TRUST MODELS** – Although asymmetric key cryptography simplified the problems of key management and key distribution, it still has problems with trust, including:

  - How can I be certain that people are who they say they are?

  - If someone vouches for someone else, how do I know that I can trust that person?

- **CERTIFICATION ESTABLISHES THE TRUSTWORTHINESS OF PUBLIC KEYS** – By linking a public key to a person or organization. There are two main trust models:

  - **WEB OF TRUST** – In which the entities trust enough people in common to make it unreasonable for everyone to be subverted. Each person can authenticate other users.

  - **HIERARCHICAL TRUST** – Each entity puts its trust in a parent organization, checking at higher and higher levels until there is a common organization, then working back down the levels to the destination entity.

Domain Agenda

- Definitions
- History
- Uses
- Cryptographic Methods
- Encryption Systems
- Algorithms
- **Cryptanalysis and Attacks**
- Implementations

81

Cryptanalysis

- Art and science of breaking codes
- Attack vectors
  - Key
  - Algorithm
  - Implementation
  - Data (ciphertext or plaintext)
  - People – social engineering
- Assumptions

82

- **CRYPTANALYSIS IS THE ART AND SCIENCE OF BREAKING CODES, INCLUDING:**

  - Cracking the code to obtain plaintext out of ciphertext.

  - Finding out the cryptographic keys themselves.

  - Investigating and correcting flaws in cryptographic algorithms and cryptosystems.

  - Defeating the protective measures of the cryptosystem, i.e., message integrity, authentication of messages, and access control.

- **ATTACK VECTORS –** In order to protect the keys from being discovered through cryptanalysis:

  - The algorithm must be functionally complex.

  - The relationship between key and keystream should not be easy to determine.

  - The keystream generation should be statistically unpredictable.

- In order to protect against frequency analysis, the keystream should be non-, or infrequently, repeating and contain the same number of 1s as 0s (statistically unbiased).

- **ASSUMPTIONS WITH RESPECT TO ATTACKS -**

  - The algorithm (method) is known.

  - Your adversary has all of your encrypted text.

  - Plaintext and/or the keys may not be known.

  - Your adversary is searching for the key you are using.

  - Attacks may be mounted against the algorithm or a particular implementation (cryptosystem).

  - Some cryptanalytic techniques are common to many cryptographic solutions while others are specific to particular types of cryptographic algorithms or cryptosystems.

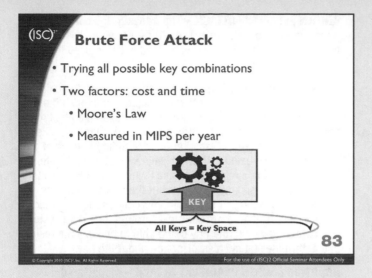

Brute Force Attack

- Trying all possible key combinations
- Two factors: cost and time
  - Moore's Law
  - Measured in MIPS per year

All Keys = Key Space

83

- **A BRUTE FORCE ATTACK INVOLVES -**

  - Trying all possible keys until finding the one that results in the correct cleartext.

  - **PROCESSING –** A brute force attack can involve significant costs in terms of the amount of processing required to try quadrillions (in the case of DES) or more keys looking for the right one.

  - **TIME –** This will depend on how many computers can be assigned to the task in parallel.

- **REMEMBER THAT -**

  - All cryptographic algorithms can eventually be broken using brute force attacks, although it is not always the most practical choice. The one-time pad is the only exception.

  - Some algorithms (particularly key derivation methods) operate deliberately slowly to make a brute force attack even more difficult. For example, when it became clear that the MD4 hash function was particularly susceptible to brute force, Ron Rivest slowed its operation for MD4's replacement, MD5.

- **TWO FACTORS: COST AND TIME -**

  - **MOORE'S LAW –** (Gordon Moore, Intel founder).

    - Processing speed doubles every 18 months for the same price.

    - Advances in technology and computing performance will always make brute force an increasingly practical attack on keys of a fixed length.

  - Note, however: In 2007, Dual core Intel computers gave six times the speed of previous computers in one year. Quad core computers give even more speed. Quantum computing is predicted to give us many orders of magnitude more computing power than we have today in far less than the time suspected.

  - **ATTACKS ARE MEASURED IN MIPS PER YEAR –** Number of instructions a million-instruction-per-second (MIPS) computer can execute in one year.

Brute Force

Bits	Number of keys	Brute Force Attack Time
56	7.2×10^{16}	20 hours
80	1.2×10^{24}	54,800 years
128	3.4×10^{38}	1.5×10^{19} years
256	1.15×10^{77}	5.2×10^{5} years

$$\Delta f(x)$$

84

- **BRUTE FORCE –** The table gives the times required for a brute force attack on various key lengths using what people call "Deep Crack" technology. Deep Crack technology was developed in 1998 by the EFF (Electronic Frontier Foundation). Deep Crack was capable of trying a million DES keys per microsecond against a readable ASCII string challenge phrase – also known as the RSA DES Challenge. Even at this prodigious rate, it takes about 20 hours to try all possible keys. This machine cost about $250,000 to design and build, and in theory it makes DES worthless. Today, however, we can have the same computing power of Deep Crack in a much smaller format called Copacobana. Copacobana uses off-the-shelf hardware and computer chips.

- Obviously, as the key length grows beyond 100 or so, the number of keys quickly becomes astronomical. Note that if the brute force approach is possible, there is no real defense against it. The only hope of forestalling successful cracking is to have so many possible keys that it is not feasible to try them all in a reasonable amount of time. To put the information on the chart into perspective: The Big Bang happened nearly 15 billion years ago – on the order of 15×10^9 years.

- The new AES standard, Rijndael, supports 128- and 256-bit keys. Even taking into account the staggering advances in computing power and cryptanalysis, 256-bit keys should be pretty safe for the next decade or so. It does appear, however, that quantum cryptanalysis may provide the ultimate brute force attack. Because of the peculiar ways that quantum computing operates, it would be theoretically possible to search an entire set of possible keys instantly (using quantum factorization).

  - How long would it take to crack DES with a pentium4 @ 3Ghz = 545 years?

  - $10,000 U.S. will break DES in 8.7 days using Copacobana. Using Copacobana and $250,000 today, it would take less than one second. Real-time cracking of DES is possible.

  - Today $1,000,000 spent building Copacobana makes ECC 112 bit feasible to brute force crack in less than a year.

REFERENCE:
http://www.copacobana.org/paper/CHES2006_copacobana_slides.pdf

IMAGES:
http://www.copacobana.org/paper/CHES2006_copacobana_slides.pdf
http://www.cryptography.com/resources/whitepapers/DES-photos.html

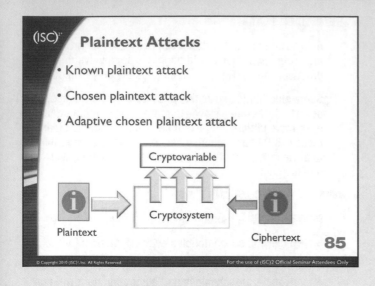

Plaintext Attacks

- Known plaintext attack
- Chosen plaintext attack
- Adaptive chosen plaintext attack

- **KNOWN PLAINTEXT ATTACK –** The attacker has both the plaintext and the ciphertext. The attacker uses analysis to try to determine the key or cryptovariable being used in the encryption process.

- **CHOSEN PLAINTEXT ATTACK –** Sometimes called "batch" or "indifferent" chosen plaintext attacks to distinguish them from adaptive chosen plaintext attacks. Chosen plaintext attacks are particularly relevant in the case of asymmetric key cryptography where the attacker has the ability to encrypt any desired plaintext using a known public key. Chosen plaintext attacks can also be relevant in cases where the key is embedded in tamper-resistant hardware but the attacker still has access to the system to force it to encrypt desired plaintext. The attacker is able to run plaintext through the cryptosystem and obtain the result, thereby being able to analyze the results and determine statistical information about the key.

- **ADAPTIVE CHOSEN PLAINTEXT ATTACK –** Modifying the chosen plaintext based on the results of previously chosen plaintext. The attacker has use of the encryption device for more than one message. Patterns may emerge if the attacker puts similar texts into the device.

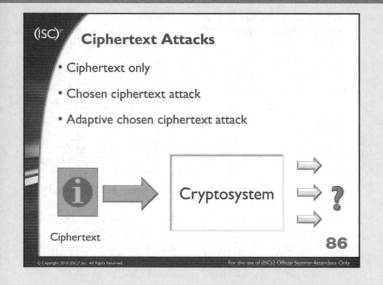

Ciphertext Attacks

- Ciphertext only
- Chosen ciphertext attack
- Adaptive chosen ciphertext attack

- **CIPHERTEXT-ONLY ATTACK –** In a ciphertext-only attack, we assume that the attacker has samples of the encrypted text but may not know the algorithm, key, or the system. This is the most difficult attack, since the cryptanalyst has the least amount of information to work with.

- **CHOSEN CIPHERTEXT ATTACK –** The attacker has access to ciphertext and the system that was used to generate it. The attacker can run pieces of ciphertext through the cryptosystem and obtain the plaintext. This would then lead to a Known Plaintext Attack, or a Differential or Linear Cryptanalysis attack.

- **ADAPTIVE CHOSEN CIPHERTEXT ATTACK –** The attacker has access to the cryptosystem and can not only run pieces of ciphertxt through the system as in the Chosen Ciphertext Attack, but now they can also modify the ciphertext to see what the effect of the modification is on the resulting plaintext.

- **STREAM –** Stream ciphers are essentially substitution ciphers and, as such, are subject to frequency analysis. If the keystream is not sufficiently random, the stream cipher will be crackable. RC4, the most common stream cipher, was implemented within 802.11 Wired Equivalent Privacy. This keystream and initialization vector repeat fairly frequently, providing clues to the key that was used to generate it.

  - **FREQUENCY ANALYSIS AND OTHER STATISTICAL ATTACKS –** In these attacks, the attacker has the advantage of knowing the characteristics of the plaintext language. Knowing the frequency of certain letters or predictable patterns (such as "qu") makes the job of the cryptanalyst much easier.

  - Statistical attacks are especially effective when the keystream is not truly random and contains a biased number of 1s compared to 0s, or vice versa.

- **IV OR KEYSTREAM ANALYSIS –** Examining large numbers of generated IVs or keystreams to determine whether there are weaknesses, repetitions, statistical biases (more 1s than 0s), or whether it is possible to predict portions of the keystream.

  - Requires no plaintext or ciphertext. Needs only access to the keystream and IV-generation components.

  - Typically an attack against the implementation of an algorithm rather than upon the algorithm itself.

- **BLOCK –**

  - **LINEAR CRYPTANALYSIS –** Uses large amounts of plaintext and the corresponding ciphertext to find information about the key. Similarities between a series of plaintexts and their corresponding ciphertexts provide some data about the block size, key length, and function of the algorithm.

  - **DIFFERENTIAL CRYPTANALYSIS –** Two or more similar plaintexts are encrypted using the same key and compared. The cryptanalyst can determine some statistical data about the key being used.

  - **LINEAR-DIFFERENTIAL CRYPTANALYSIS –** Combination of the previous two.

  - **ALGEBRAIC ATTACKS –** Examines the algorithm itself to find predictability, limitations, or the effect of a set of keys that may be subject to grouping (where two operations by two keys might equal a single operation by another key).

  - **FREQUENCY ANALYSIS –** Using the statistics of the language to break a ciphertext.

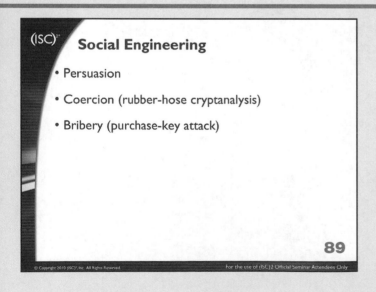

Attacks Against Hash Functions

- Dictionary Attacks
  - Based on known lists of common words
- Birthday Attacks
  - Attack the hash value
  - Attack the initialization vector
- Rainbow Table Attacks
  - Hash reductions
  - Salts

88

- **ATTACKS AGAINST HASH FUNCTIONS** – Dictionary Attacks, Birthday Attacks, and Rainbow Table Attacks -

- **DICTIONARY ATTACKS -**

  - A dictionary attack is used against password files or hashed values. It hashes common words or password combinations to obtain a collision on a password hash.

- **BIRTHDAY ATTACKS -**

  - Used to find weaknesses based on the Birthday Paradox. The Birthday Paradox states that there is a 50 percent chance that two out of a group of 23 people will have the same birth date. Increase the group to 60 people and the chances are more than 99 percent. The birthday paradox is relevant to cryptanalysis in that it describes the amount of effort that must be made to determine when two randomly-chosen or generated values will be the same. (These are called collisions.) Weaker hash functions will result in many such collisions. Hash functions may collide when two pieces of text result in the same digest value. The likelihood of such collisions will increase if there are weaknesses in the hash function, or if digests are generated against overly-large texts.

- While birthday attacks are most often associated with hash functions, they are also common to other cryptographic functions, notably the key scheduling used in symmetric key ciphers, IV generation, and even discrete logarithm calculations. For example, attacks on Wired Equivalent Privacy (WEP) took advantage of the fact that an IV used with a static RC4 key was only 24 bits (providing 17 million potential combinations), but because of the birthday paradox, collisions in the value of the IV occurred approximately every 4096 packets. This provided the cryptanalyst with combinations of plaintext and ciphertext that were encrypted using the same key and the same IV.

- **RAINBOW TABLE ATTACKS** – Rainbow tables are used to find original plaintext for a particular hash (e.g., a password). They are a more advanced version of simple reverse-hash lookup tables and don't require much time or memory. Rainbow tables are generated to be unique to the hash function used (MD5, LM, NTLM), the length of the password, and the characters allowed (alphabetical, numerical, special characters). The chains in rainbow tables are combinations of one-way hashes and reductions. You start with a hash and follow its series of hashes and reductions through the rainbow chains until you emerge with a final (original) plaintext.

  - **HASHES AND REDUCTIONS** – A hash function maps plaintexts to hashes and the reduction function maps hashes to plaintexts (though, often, not the original plaintext but some other plaintext).

  - **COMBATING RAINBOW TABLES WITH SALTS** – Salts are often used to throw off rainbow chains by injecting an initial value into the plaintext, or concatenating it with the original plaintext.

Social Engineering

- Persuasion

- Coercion (rubber-hose cryptanalysis)

- Bribery (purchase-key attack)

89

- Most technical attacks are not needed due to the weakest link, people.

- **SOCIAL ENGINEERING CRYPTANALYTICAL ATTACKS** – Rely on the manipulation of people to circumvent the security processes. Whether through persuasion, intimidation, or theft, social engineering is one of the easiest cryptanalytical attacks to perform.

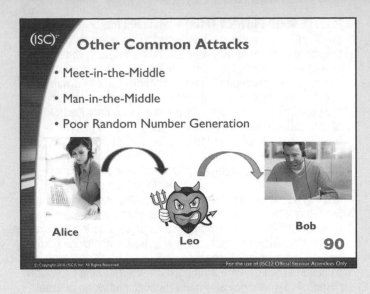

- **MEET-IN-THE-MIDDLE ATTACKS** – A mathematical analysis that attacks a problem from both ends and attempts to find the solution by working toward the center of the operation from both sides.

- **MAN-IN-THE-MIDDLE ATTACKS** – As shown in the diagram, the attacker intercepts and modifies the data being transmitted. This is especially dangerous in the key exchange or key negotiation process where the end users may think they have each others' public key, where in fact they have the public key of the attacker.

  - When Alice wants to talk to Bob, Henry is listening.

  - To Alice, Henry pretends to be Bob.

  - To Bob, Henry pretends to be Alice.

- **POOR RANDOM NUMBER GENERATION** – The weakness with the Netscape '95 implementation was its difficulty in choosing a good random number generator. Ideally, the creation of random numbers will result in the same number of random values as there are possible plaintexts.

Domain Agenda

- Definitions

- History

- Uses

- Cryptographic Methods

- Encryption Systems

- Algorithms

- Cryptanalysis and Attacks

- **Implementations**

91

Common Secure Email Protocols

- Privacy Enhanced Mail (PEM)

- Pretty Good Privacy (PGP)

- Secure Multipurpose Internet Mail Extensions (S/MIME)

92

- **COMMON SECURE EMAIL PROTOCOLS** – There have been a number of standards developed for email security over the years. Since standard email offers no security or privacy protection, there have been a number of efforts intended to address the deficiencies. Most have focused on providing message integrity and encryption services, but some have also addressed key management and non-repudiation:

- **PRIVACY ENHANCED MAIL (PEM)** – PEM was developed as a standard by the Internet Research Task Force (IRTF) and the Internet Engineering Task Force (IETF). It provided a series of enhancements for standard 7-bit messages for message authentication and cryptography. Before other PKI standards were widely available, it described a basic PKI Infrastructure to support sender authentication using routines taken from the RSA asymmetric key cryptosystem. Later, it was also improved to include X.509 certificate support. It used the Data Encryption Standard (DES) running in Cipher-Block-Chaining (CBC) mode for message confidentiality, although it could also use Electronic Code Book (ECB) or Triple DES-EDE2 for key management purposes. For message integrity, it used either MD2 or MD5 hash algorithms. It has largely been superseded by other protocols, largely because it is not compatible for mail formatted using Multipurpose Internet Mail Extensions (MIME).

- **PRETTY GOOD PRIVACY (PGP)** – While not intended solely for email, PGP has commonly been used to provide message confidentiality and integrity. Like PEM, it is a hybrid cryptosystem that uses both symmetric and asymmetric key cryptography. Messages are encrypted using a randomly chosen symmetric session key and a copy of the session key encrypted using the recipient's public key (thus ensuring that only the holder of the related private key can decrypt it). PGP is extremely flexible with the use of cryptographic algorithms – it has, for example, been able to use RSA, Diffie-Hellman, and Elgamal for asymmetric key cryptography. It can also provide message integrity through the use of a standard hash function and digital signatures (typically through the use of the Digital Signature Standard or DSS). It has the ability to work with standard X.509 public key certificates as well as its own proprietary certificate format, and has been known to work with both a CA-based trust model as well as its traditional web of trust. With the advent of Multipurpose Internet Mail Extensions (MIME), PGP has since also been redeveloped as an alternative extension to S/MIME or MOSS (MIME Object Security Services) as PGP/MIME.

- **SECURE MULTIPURPOSE INTERNET MAIL EXTENSIONS (S/MIME)** – Originally developed by RSA, S/MIME was heavily backed by most early Internet developers, which may explain some of its success and why it has become the de facto standard for email privacy and authentication services. Building from PEM and MOSS, it is based on Public Key Cryptography Standards (PKCS) and focuses strictly on a hierarchical trust model based on Certification Authorities, although self-signed certificates can be supported. Most commercial implementations use RSA for asymmetric key cryptography, Triple DES for symmetric key, and SHA-1 for hashing. Some will also support other algorithms (for example, Diffie-Hellman for asymmetric and DSS for signature services). Many implementations are available as plug-ins to common email client software.

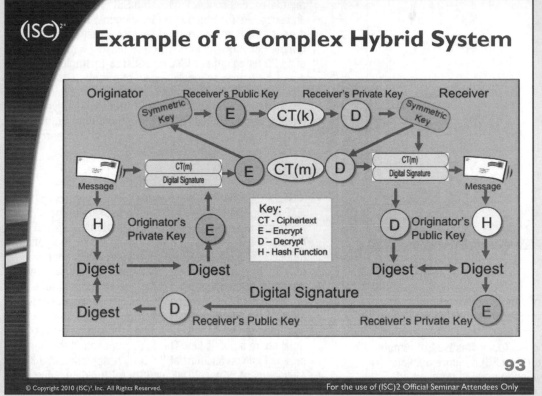

Example of a Complex Hybrid System

Key:
CT - Ciphertext
E – Encrypt
D – Decrypt
H - Hash Function

93

- Hash the message to be sent creating a hash or digest, using a hashing algorithm (SHA-512? MD5?). The hash is useful for message integrity.

- Sign the hash with the private key of the originator. This creates a digital signature. Since this can only be opened with the public key of the originator, the recipient will know whom the message came from.

- Append the digital signature to the message and send it to the recipient.

- NOTE: In real life, we would have hashed the encrypted message instead of the plaintext message, but we wanted to show the operations in a logical flow. The reason for hashing the encrypted message is that it is more resistant to attack.

- **EXAMPLE OF A COMPLEX HYBRID SYSTEM –** This is an example of almost everything covered in this domain. In it we attempt to send a confidential email to the recipient while also providing message integrity, proof of origin, and proof of delivery. This is a simple example of what is done in products such as PGP.

- **THE STEPS TO ACCOMPLISH THIS TASK ARE:**

  - Choose a symmetric key algorithm (AES? DES?) and choose a secret key.

  - Encrypt the message with the chosen symmetric key algorithm and the secret key.

  - Encrypt the symmetric (secret) key with the receiver's public key (a message – in this case the symmetric key – encrypted with a public key can only be opened with the corresponding private key), so the symmetric key will be sent confidentially to the receiver. Send the encrypted symmetric key to the recipient.

    - NOTE: We chose to use RSA or ECC for the public key algorithm. With Diffie-Hellman, we would have negotiated the secret key instead of choosing it ourselves and encrypting it.

- The recipient will decrypt the message that contains the encrypted symmetric key using his or her private key, and then use that symmetric key to decrypt the message.

- The recipient will decrypt (validate) the signature using the originator's public key (he or she will have received that key in a certificate sent to him or her by the originator. The certificate will validate that the recipient truly has the public key of the originator). The certificate would be issued by a Certificate Authority (CA) and be digitally signed by the CA so that the recipient knows it has not been altered.

- Decrypting the digital signature will present the hash value to the recipient that the originator had created and signed.

- The recipient could hash the received message and create his or her own digest of the message. This will be compared with the digest sent from the originator to ensure that the message was not changed en route.

- **PROOF OF DELIVERY –** To provide proof of delivery, the recipient will sign a digest of the message as well and send it back to the originator. That way the originator knows that the correct message was received and the recipient would not be able to change the message at a later date.

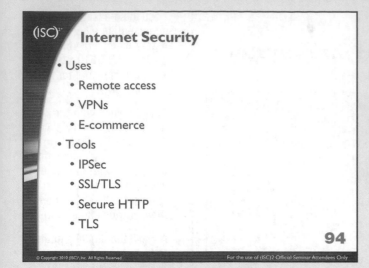

USES -

REMOTE ACCESS – Remote Access environments allow users or endpoints to connect to a central Infrastructure remotely, usually via web browser. (This is an attractive feature of SSL-VPN solutions.) Today, this type of remote access is most often secured by SSL (Secure Sockets Layer), which uses encryption to provide both integrity and confidentiality of the connection. In this configuration, the remote access client and the host to which it connects intend to leverage PKI Infrastructure with asymmetric key exchange to securely initiate the connection. Remote access "tunnels" are provisioned as needed and dissolved after the session has ended. Previous remote access solutions used VPN-type tunnels and required more management and a pre-configured agent on the endpoint.

VPNS (VIRTUAL PRIVATE NETWORKS) – Allow organizations to securely extend a network beyond the confines of its physically-connected infrastructure. Traditionally, VPNs have been more "static" in nature and are provisioned as permanent or semi-permanent links, much like a typical physical infrastructure. The static configurations leveraged IPSec technology for creating secure tunnels between two or more locations. In recent years, SSL and TLS technologies have also been tweaked and used in VPN implementations to offer a more dynamic VPN experience for remote access VPNs. VPN topologies can be point-to-point, hub-and-spoke or any combination of the two.

E-COMMERCE – Has a variety of meanings and components, including use of e-commerce for secure online purchases as well as secure Internet-based connectivity between partners, suppliers, and vendors. Online purchases through a web browser will typically use HTTPS, a version of HTTP traffic secured with TLS over port 443. These transactions are created and secured similarly to remote-access connections using SSL/TLS. When vendors and suppliers (or trading partners) connect "behind the scenes" to share information through a (usually static) remote network, the infrastructure may look more like that of a VPN using either IPSec or SSL/TLS technology for security. E-commerce receives a lot of attention in security planning and implementations, since financial and usually other PII (personal identifiable information) is traversing a generally unsecured network. Data integrity, confidentiality, and authentication are key in any e-commerce transaction.

TOOLS -

IPSEC – IP Security, a set of protocols developed by the IETF to support secure exchange of packets at the IP layer. IPSec has been deployed widely to implement Virtual Private Networks (VPNs). IPSec supports two encryption modes: Transport and Tunnel. Transport mode encrypts only the data portion (payload) of each packet but leaves the header untouched. The more secure Tunnel mode encrypts both the header and the payload. On the receiving side, an IPSec-compliant device decrypts each packet. For IPSec to work, the sending and receiving devices must share a public key. This is accomplished through a protocol known as Internet Security Association and Key Management Protocol/Oakley (ISAKMP/Oakley), which allows the receiver to obtain a public key and authenticate the sender using digital certificates.

SSL/TLS – Secure Sockets Layer, a protocol developed by Netscape for transmitting private documents via the Internet. SSL uses a cryptographic system that uses two keys to encrypt data – a public key known to everyone and a private or secret key known only to the recipient of the message. All modern web browsers support SSL, and many websites use the protocol to obtain confidential user information, such as credit card numbers. By convention, URLs that require an SSL connection start with https instead of http (see above).

SECURE HTTP (S-HTTP) – Another protocol for transmitting data securely over the World Wide Web. Whereas SSL creates a secure connection between a client and a server over which any amount of data can be sent securely, S-HTTP is designed to transmit individual messages securely.

TLS – Transport Layer Security, a protocol that guarantees privacy and data integrity between client/server applications communicating over the Internet. TLS is application protocol-independent. Higher-level protocols can layer on top of the TLS protocol transparently. Based on Netscape's SSL 3.0, TLS supersedes and is an extension of SSL. TLS and SSL are not interoperable.

Domain Summary

- The CISSP candidate should be familiar with:

- Types of cryptographic algorithms

- Principles of cryptography

- Cryptanalysis

- Uses of cryptography

95

Security Transcends Technology

(ISC)²

96

Review Questions

CRYPTOGRAPHY

1. In which type of cryptanalytic attack is a cryptosystem's work factor MOST relevant?

   A. Differential cryptanalysis

   B. Chosen plaintext attacks

   C. Linear-differential cryptanalysis

   D. Brute force attacks

2. RC4 and RC5

   A. are related symmetric key cryptographic algorithms, although RC5 was designed to accommodate larger key sizes.

   B. both employ repeated substitution and permutation transformations on each plaintext block.

   C. are unrelated symmetric key cryptographic algorithms, although they were created by the same individual.

   D. address the need for message integrity controls that resist intentional changes.

3. Which of the following is the most common attack against message digests used to determine the original plaintext?

   A. Ciphertext only attack

   B. Dictionary attack

   C. Known plaintext attack

   D. Linear cryptanalysis attack

4. If a cryptographic algorithm is found to be highly susceptible to chosen ciphertext attacks, it may allow the attacker to

   A. take advantage of the algorithm's malleability.

   B. use differential power analysis to determine how many rounds are being used during the encryption sequence.

   C. encrypt any desired plaintext to achieve a desired ciphertext.

   D. simplify exhaustive search through all possible keys supported by the algorithm.

5. The process of hiding information in photos, music, and videos in such a way as to make the alteration invisible to casual observers is called

   A. steganography.

   B. Optimal Asymmetric Encryption Padding (OAEP).

   C. a null cipher.

   D. expansion.

6. Which of the following is typically used to help two parties agree on a session key without exchanging secret information?

   A. Initialization vectors (IVs)

   B. Exclusive-or (XOR) operations

   C. Rivest-Shamir-Adleman (RSA)

   D. Diffie-Hellman

7. Keyed hashes and digital signatures differ in what way?

   A. Keyed hashes employ symmetric keys alone while digital signatures employ symmetric keys and hash functions.

   B. Keyed hashes combine a hash function with a shared symmetric key while digital signatures combine a hash function with an asymmetric key.

   C. Keyed hashes provide for message integrity while digital signatures provide for message confidentiality.

   D. Keyed hashes are intended to detect accidental changes while digital signatures are intended to detect intentional changes.

8. What is the MOST significant advantage that the Advanced Encryption Standard (AES) offers over the Data Encryption Standard (DES)?

   A. Larger key space due to larger key sizes.

   B. More efficient operation when used in general-purpose computing devices.

   C. Smaller key sizes with greater strength per bit than DES.

   D. More block cipher modes are supported.

9. For what application would Electronic Code Book (ECB) mode be MOST acceptable?

   A. Encryption of Wi-Fi communications.

   B. Applications where high security is required.

   C. Encrypting small executable files.

   D. Encrypting large graphic image files.

10. What is the BEST way to verify that a digital signature is valid?

    A. Verify the digital signature through a manual comparison of the hash value.

    B. Obtain the public key from the partner and verify the digital signature.

    C. Obtain a public key certificate from a trusted certification authority, and verify the digital signature using that key.

    D. Use a hash algorithm to determine if the message has been altered.

11. Hash collisions are

    A. failures of a given cryptographic hash function to complete successfully.
    B. repetitions within a message digest that indicate weaknesses in the hash algorithm.
    C. matching message digests found during the verification of a digital signature.
    D. two different input messages that result in the same message digest value.

12. What would likely be the FIRST step in the establishment of an encrypted session using hybrid encryption systems, such as secure socket layer (SSL) or Internet protocol security (IPSEC)?

    A. Key negotiation and exchange of symmetric keys.
    B. Exchange of public keys.
    C. Determination of a suitable hash function.
    D. Out-of-band communications to negotiate which cryptographic algorithms and settings will be used.

13. When used In cryptographic applications, certification

    A. provides the ability to verify the authenticity of public keys.
    B. ensures that a secure process is being used to generate and store keys.
    C. refers to the process used to verify the integrity and authenticity of received messages.
    D. provides evidence that security controls were implemented as designed.

14. When should a certification authority place a certificate on a certifioate rcvocation list (CRL)?

    A. The certificate has not been used for an extended period of time.
    B. The session key has been compromised.
    C. The certificate has expired.
    D. The private key of the certificate owner has been compromised.

15. Application developers working for a civilian company want their application to be able to encrypt sensitive data when it is stored on user laptops. What would be the BEST option to address their needs?

    A. Develop a set of secure algorithms for the application based upon the latest industry standards.
    B. Provide an evaluated hardware cryptosystem that can be used to encrypt bulk data efficiently.
    C. Use an industry-standard software-based cryptosystem that can be accessed through a series of documented application programming interfaces (APIs).
    D. Recommend that all users be authenticated using unique digital certificates.

QUESTIONS 16-18 apply to the following scenario:

You are a security architect working for a large bank, and have been asked to evaluate a variety of cryptographic algorithms that are being considered as candidates for a proprietary electronic funds transfer (EFT) application.

Your bank has three funds transfer offices, one each in New York, London, and Tokyo. Several funds transfer agents work in each office and can send funds to any of the other offices. Each transaction must be identified as authentic and the agent who sent it must be verifiable. The quantity of data per transaction is small.

Please answer the following three questions.

16. What is the best way to identify the agent who initiated a particular transaction?

    A. Have the agent encrypt the message with his or her private key.
    B. Have the agent encrypt the hash with his or her private key.
    C. Have the agent encrypt the message with his or her symmetric key.
    D. Have the agent encrypt the hash with his or her public key.

17. You need to provide confidentiality. To do this you will

    A. recommend using a one-way hash as the cryptographic algorithm to provide the necessary confidentiality.
    B. recommend that all transactions be digitally signed before they are transmitted over an unsafe network.
    C. sign the transfer order with the sender's private key.
    D. encrypt the transfer order with the recipient's public key.

18. You are already digitally signing and encrypting each message. You need to be sure that each message is received. Your BEST course of action is to

    A. instruct the receiver to digitally sign and return the message.
    B. instruct the receiver to digitally sign and return the message hash.
    C. implement an automatic receipt of message function in the application.
    D. have your in-house certification authority digitally countersign each message and its timestamp.

19. What is a major legal issue related to encryption?

   A. Some countries have legal restrictions on export and import of encryption material or maximum key lengths.

   B. Using encryption requires paying license royalties to the developers of encryption tools.

   C. Encryption algorithms are protected by copyright, and cannot be used without explicit license.

   D. Encryption systems that use the SKIPJACK algorithm are illegal for use within the United States.

20. What is a major legal problem related to encryption?

   A. Attackers can hide malicious information and tools by encrypting them on our systems.

   B. Digital signatures might not be accepted as an appropriate alternative to hand-written signatures.

   C. Encrypted information can contain legally sensitive information.

   D. Digital signatures are not a legally admissible alternative to hand-written signatures.

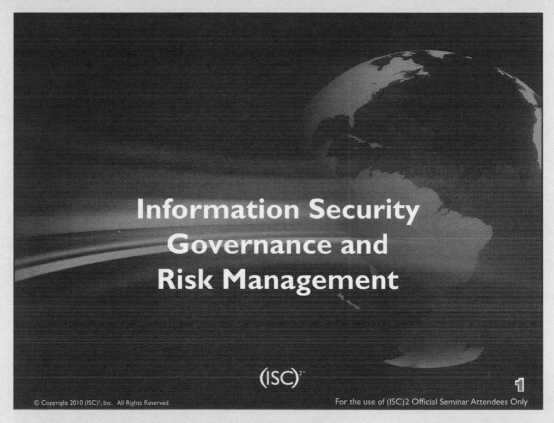

Information Security Governance and Risk Management

(ISC)²

- **FROM THE CISSP® CBK®, THE DEFINITION OF THIS DOMAIN** – Information Security Governance and Risk Management entails the identification of an organization's information assets and the development, documentation, and implementation of policies, standards, procedures, and guidelines that ensure confidentiality, integrity, and availability. Management tools such as risk assessment and risk analysis are used to identify the threats, classify assets, and rate their vulnerabilities so that effective security controls can be implemented.

- Risk management is the identification, measurement, control, and minimization of loss associated with uncertain events or risks. It includes overall security review, risk analysis, selection and evaluation of safeguards, cost benefit analysis, management decision, safeguard implementation, and effectiveness review.

- The CISSP candidate is expected to understand the core components of an information security management system (ISMS), including:

- Planning, organizing, budgeting, and implementing a program to provide systems and data availability, integrity, and confidentiality.

- Developing, implementing, and monitoring compliance with security policies, and their supporting baselines, guidelines, standards, and procedures.

- Defining appropriate roles and responsibilities throughout the organization, from executive management to third parties.

- Identifying a robust risk management program which encompasses practices and processes to assess and address risk.

- Deploying security awareness training.

Domain Agenda

- Information Security Management System (ISMS)
  - **Business Drivers**
  - Governance
    - Roles and Responsibilities
    - Security Planning
    - Security Administration
- Risk Management
- Ethics

2

Information Security Environment

3

- Organizations must contend with a complex web of laws, regulations, requirements, technology, competitors, and partners while pursuing their business objectives. These outside forces can change frequently and interact with each other, often in unpredictable ways. Senior management must also take many inside forces into account, including morale, labor relations, productivity, cost, and cash flow. Within this environment of multiple, turbulent forces, management must develop an effective security program. The primary objective of the security program, as with any security-related endeavor, is appropriate risk management. Risk management tries to ensure that each risk an organization is exposed to is identified and appropriately avoided, mitigated, transferred, or accepted. Proper handling of a risk is based on its potential to have a negative impact on the organization's assets.

- In valuing assets, it is important to remember that assets such as reputation, customer confidence, and employee morale are difficult to quantify.

- A successful security program will work within the culture (or cultures) of an organization.

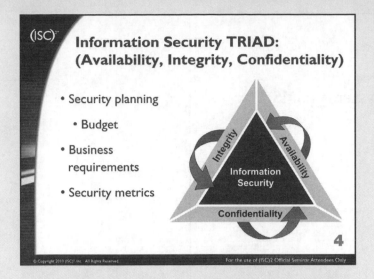

**Information Security TRIAD:
(Availability, Integrity, Confidentiality)**

- Security planning
  - Budget
- Business requirements
- Security metrics

Integrity · Availability · Confidentiality · Information Security

4

AIC TRIAD. The TRIAD is the foundation of what we are trying to accomplish through security policies, standards, procedures, baselines, and guidelines.

- **AVAILABILITY** – Availability has to do with providing access to the information system and data when required by the business. The levels of availability required will be different for every organization and even between departments in the same organization. Some departments may require continuous availability where an outage of seconds would be a crisis, whereas other areas may be content with a basic level of availability (normal business hours, for example) where system failure would be an inconvenience rather than having a critical impact on operations. A complete information security program must understand and address these differences.

- **INTEGRITY** – There are two central concerns with respect to integrity: ensuring that data and processes are protected from improper modification and ensuring that the operations of the information system are reliable and performing as expected – i.e., that the organization can have confidence in the quality of the data and processing.

- **CONFIDENTIALITY** – Protecting information from improper disclosure. The release of sensitive or private data (whether trade secrets, intellectual property, or data related to private individuals) can damage the success or the reputation of an organization.

- **SECURITY PLANNING** – It is rare to find an organization that puts a strong emphasis on security. Security does not automatically appear on the organization's list of priorities when compared with other objectives, such as profitability, competition, or efficiency. Security requires an adequate annual budget that must be justified and spent wisely. The CISSP must understand how to set up a security plan, budget, objectives, and metrics. A well-executed program will help ensure that management sees the value of security.

- **BUSINESS REQUIREMENTS** – The AIC triad provides a way to explain the intangible aspects of security in a manner that can be understood by management. Security must be viewed in relation to the requirements of the business – how much availability does the organization need? What are the confidentiality requirements? The security needs are mandated by the mission and objectives of the organization and it is those requirements that must be met in the security plan.

- **INFORMATION SECURITY AIC TRIAD** – The overarching goals of information security (IS) efforts are addressed through the

- **SECURITY METRICS** – The AIC triad provides goals for which a set of metrics can be developed to measure the success of the security program. For example, how much downtime did the network suffer from? Was that a serious factor for the business? That is a measurement of availability. When the CISSP measures the current state or level of availability against what the business expects (and is willing to pay for!) then there is a solid way to demonstrate the value of a security program and the improvement year over year in meeting the business requirements.

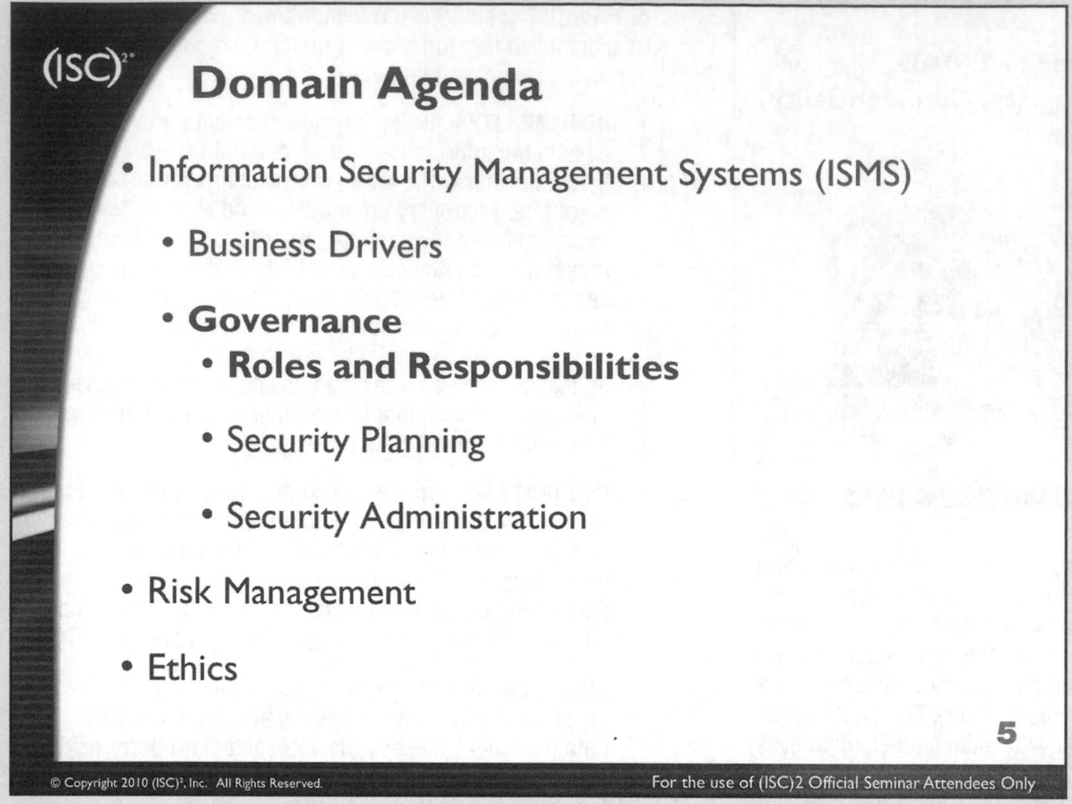

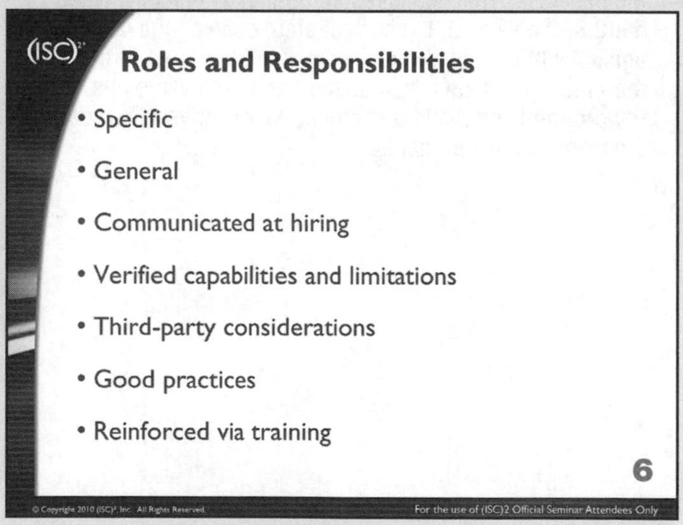

Domain Agenda

- Information Security Management Systems (ISMS)

  - Business Drivers

  - **Governance**
    - **Roles and Responsibilities**

    - Security Planning

    - Security Administration

- Risk Management

- Ethics

5

Roles and Responsibilities

- Specific
- General
- Communicated at hiring
- Verified capabilities and limitations
- Third-party considerations
- Good practices
- Reinforced via training

6

- **ROLES AND RESPONSIBILITIES** – Specific security functions must be assigned to designated security professionals as their primary duty, but security is not a function of a single person, group, or team. All employees must be aware of their roles and responsibilities with respect to creating a secure environment.

- **SPECIFIC** – In addition to delegating certain responsibilities for security to specific individuals, in many cases, specific rules defining acceptable or unacceptable behavior should be put in place.

- **GENERAL** – General rules should be used to cover the majority of personnel and situations so that everyone in the organization understands that they have personal responsibility for maintaining security.

- **COMMUNICATED AT HIRING** – The responsibility of each user to follow security procedures must be communicated at the time of hiring and followed up annually in order to continuously educate all employees in the security culture of the organization.

- **VERIFIED CAPABILITIES AND LIMITATIONS** – Access to resources should be assigned based on job function and need to know. An organization might, for example, decide that developers should not be allowed to enter the operations area.

- **THIRD-PARTY CONSIDERATIONS** – Ensure that the security requirements are made known to all vendors, and temporary or contract staff working on the systems or premises.

- **GOOD PRACTICES** – Security needs to be simple, relevant, understandable, and communicated. Putting policies in place (such as those for passwords) will help users comply with the organization's security goals.

- **REINFORCED VIA TRAINING** – All employees should be given annual security awareness training.

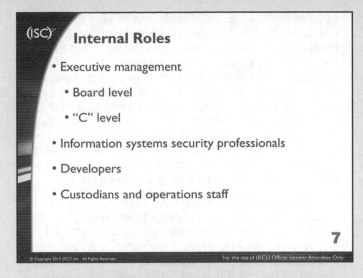

Internal Roles

- Executive management
  - Board level
  - "C" level
- Information systems security professionals
- Developers
- Custodians and operations staff

7

and strategic direction. This requires them to set the tone and culture for the organization through tools such as policy, reporting, audit, and public relations.

- **EXECUTIVE MANAGEMENT** – Publish and endorse security policies establishing goals, objectives, and overall responsibility for asset protection. Senior management sets the tone for the information security program and bears ultimate responsibility for any security breaches and the results of the organization's chosen risk mitigation strategies.

  - **BOARD LEVEL** – The members of the board of directors are becoming liable for breaches and damages suffered by the organization they oversee. They must play a larger role in ensuring that assets are protected and that the organization is compliant with legislation. This requires regular reporting and monitoring of systems and follow-up with audit recommendations.

  - **"C" LEVEL** – The chief officers of the organization (CEO, CFO, CIO, etc.) are responsible for day-to-day operations and management. As such they control budget, priorities,

- **INFORMATION SYSTEMS SECURITY PROFESSIONALS** – Information security professionals are responsible for the design, implementation, management, and review of the organization's security policies, standards, baselines, procedures, and guidelines.

- **DEVELOPERS** – Systems designers, developers, implementers, and other associated project staff must understand the elements of security architecture and design. This is explored in more detail in the Architecture and Applications domains.

- **CUSTODIANS** – As their name suggests, custodians are those who have care or custody of information assets. Custodians are responsible for ensuring the security of the information entrusted to them by the information owners. These individuals are often pressured to maintain system performance and availability. Operations staff must understand the importance of following procedures and policy and which integrates adequate security controls.

  - Their role is to maintain systems performance and availability based on business requirements. Custodians must be aware of the risks to information, particularly the risks posed by social engineering.

  - **OPERATIONS STAFF** – Operations plays a key role ensuring that policies and procedures are implemented and adhered to as defined. They are often charged with ongoing patch maintenance. The operations staff is in a unique position of seeing incidents as they unfold. Keen staff with adequate tools and proper alerting procedures can potentially cut off an attack before it damages key systems or data.

• **SECURITY STAFF –** The security function is often split between IT/network security and physical security, but organizations implement security staff under a variety of models. Some organizations have an individual department just for security, others distribute security responsibilities to a range of employees throughout the organization, and yet others implement both of these models to varying degrees. Security staff is responsible for developing and implementing the security plan. Implementation often requires the deployment of equipment, procedures, policies, and other measures necessary for the organization to realize and maintain a secure posture. Security staff are often responsible for full management of the installed security equipment with the exception of actual monitoring, which falls to the 24/7 operations staff. As such, they must ensure that the equipment is adequately sized, configured, and maintained (including patch management) and that alert/alarm functions work as planned.

• **DATA AND SYSTEM OWNERS –** Individual data and system owners play a key role in the security program and are responsible for performing essential information security tasks. Data owners perform tasks such as information classification, setting user access conditions, and deciding on business continuity priorities. System owners decide on user access permissions, system change control, backup, and disaster recovery.

• **USERS –** Are responsible for using resources appropriately, in compliance with procedures, while preserving the availability, integrity, and confidentiality of assets. Responsibilities also include end user applications (e.g., spreadsheets, SharePoint) where the end user fully controls access security.

• **LEGAL, COMPLIANCE, AND PRIVACY OFFICER –** While this has always been an important role within an organization, the position of legal, compliance, and privacy officer has become increasingly important in recent years. This role is far reaching and has significant implications if poorly executed. The officer must keep up with all current requirements (governmental, legal, industry, corporate) and work with other organizations to ensure that compliance is built into the organization's policy and implemented as an integral part of the whole. A poorly-executed policy often leads to loss of corporate or personal confidential data. The loss of either can place a significant financial burden on the organization.

• **INTERNAL AUDITORS –** Internal auditors often police the ongoing operation of an organization to ensure that it meets all regulatory requirements. Their role is to ensure compliance and minimize impact of any noncompliance by discovering it (or other issues) prior to external audits or data breaches. Internal auditors can often make recommendations that would otherwise not be readily acknowledged. They work closely with the legal, compliance, and privacy officer and are often the liaison with external auditors.

• **PHYSICAL SECURITY –** Physical security is critical to the successful implementation of a security plan. As in logical network or systems security, a multi-layered approach with various controls and locks guarding access to important components is best. This also extends to remote facilities or equipment (such as a wiring closet located on upper floors). Two factor (or more) authentication is becoming common for access to highly secure facilities.

  • **CONVERGENCE WITH IS SECURITY –** As the cost of implementing various approaches continues to plummet and the range and availability of tools and methods grow, the line between one kind of security tool and another continues to blur. This can be seen most clearly in the merging of high-tech physical security methods with information systems. Is an IP camera monitoring a space a concern of the physical security staff? Or is it IS security? How about a retinal or fingerprint scan? A temperature or infrared monitoring system?

  • We are going to continue to witness a great deal of convergence of physical and IS security both because of advances in technology and because physical and IS security are going to rely increasingly heavily on each other.

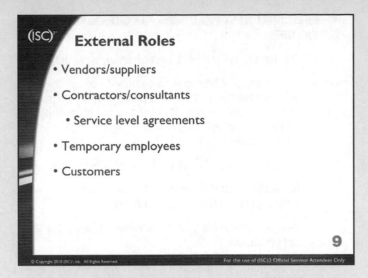

External Roles

- Vendors/suppliers
- Contractors/consultants
  - Service level agreements
- Temporary employees
- Customers

9

- **THIRD-PARTY CONSIDERATIONS** – All of these groups create different but equally challenging situations for computer, network, and information security efforts. Establish procedures that address these groups on a group-by-group basis to ensure that EVERYONE with access to systems, information, assets, network, etc., complies with the same (or more) stringent security as do full-time employees.

- **VENDORS/SUPPLIERS** – Will often need access to systems for maintenance or upgrades. They must adhere to the local security policies.

- **CONTRACTORS** – May work at the facility and seem to be "just like any other employee." As is the case with vendors, however, your organization may have little control over their companies' practices.

  - **SERVICE LEVEL AGREEMENTS (SLAS)** – Prior to providing access to an outsider, care must be taken to ensure that the outsider has proper clearance and awareness of policies and procedures. The contractor should be bound by SLAs that mandate how work must be done and procedures and timelines that must be followed.

- **TEMPORARY EMPLOYEES** – Have no vested interest in or loyalty to the organization and, therefore, pose increased risks.

- **CUSTOMERS** – Are demanding more and more online services. This increases security challenges as the organization strives to balance accessibility of data with privacy concerns; and integrity of process with customer-driven applications.

- Best practice with respect to contractors, vendors/suppliers, or temporary employees: Grant temporary IDs or access as appropriate and ensure that both are removed at the completion of the project.

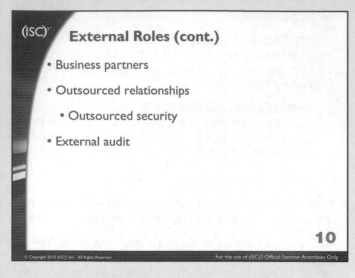

External Roles (cont.)

- Business partners
- Outsourced relationships
  - Outsourced security
- External audit

10

- **BUSINESS PARTNERS** – The information age has spurred an increasingly global, interconnected, and competitive business climate. This has led to an increase in partnerships, along with an increase in associated complications and consequences. For example, organizations must be aware that existing or former business partners may become allied with a competitor. When today's business partner becomes tomorrow's competitor, the company may well be able to leverage knowledge gained from the former partnership to its advantage. It is, therefore, more important than ever that potential consequences and mitigation measures be considered before forming a business partnership. As today's networks make it possible to establish partnerships around the world and work collaboratively on projects among groups that may never meet each other, the requirement for security also increases.

- **OUTSOURCED RELATIONSHIPS** – Also increasingly common. Outsourcing offers benefits that include access to expertise and experience, economies of scale, increased efficiency, and real-time service, all of which can allow an organization to focus on its core business objectives. Drawbacks include the risk that the provider will not in fact be able to provide the services required. Outsourced providers may also not be able to respond to needed changes, such as those brought on by the growth of the organization. Organizations must be cautious, meticulous, and resolute when establishing and documenting requirements in their service level agreements and contracts. An awareness and understanding of related legal and regulatory issues (e.g., privacy laws) are also essential. Organizations must ensure that the outsourcing contracts address the protection of information that is entrusted to the vendors. The organization should monitor the providers to ensure that problems are identified and promptly addressed. Organizations must also recognize that ultimate accountability can never be outsourced.

- **ADDITIONAL BEST PRACTICES FOR OUTSOURCING INCLUDE:**
  - Conducting an onsite inspection and interview.
  - Reviewing qualifications. In addition to company-provided information, look for information from resources, including publications, the Internet, and organizations that provide a reporting and monitoring function (e.g., Better Business Bureau in the United States).
  - Reviewing policies and documented procedures.
  - Reviewing financial statements, internal and external audit reports, and third-party reviews.
  - Reviewing references and interviewing former/existing customers.
  - Reviewing the organization's business continuity plan (BCP).
  - Executing a non-disclosure agreement (NDA).

- **OUTSOURCED SECURITY** – If properly planned, executed, and monitored, information security can be successfully outsourced. Key considerations include:
  - Ensuring that the organization is not subject to legal restrictions regarding outsourcing security.
  - Carefully establishing requirements for outsourced security services.
  - Understanding how the services will be provided.
  - Ensuring that services provided are those desired (e.g., prevention as well as detection).
  - Ensuring that outsourced security services include both contract and security expertise.

- **EXTERNAL AUDIT** – External audit provides a valuable role in ensuring compliance with standards and an objective review of business processes. In many jurisdictions, external auditing is a legal requirement. Auditors will usually measure an organization against best practices and internationally recognized standards and report on gaps or issues of noncompliance.

REFERENCES:

http://www.cert.org/archive/pdf/omss.pdf
http://www.ffiec.gov/ffiecinfobase/booklets/information_security/03_info_sec_strategy.htm
http://www.scmagazineuk.com/MSSPs-Find-the-perfect-partner/article/105520/

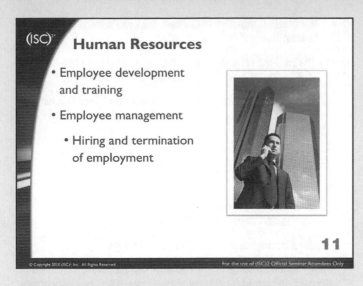

Human Resources

- Employee development and training
- Employee management
  - Hiring and termination of employment

11

- **EMPLOYEE DEVELOPMENT AND TRAINING –** "Employee development" includes the functions of employee training and education. Lack of skilled staff is a major factor for many organizations seeking to establish security departments and programs. Employee development through training and experience may be a key to establishing a competent and diligent workforce.

- **EMPLOYEE MANAGEMENT –** Employee management includes the oversight, administration, supervision, and leadership provided to staff. Obviously this is an important issue for security staff in a rapidly changing regulatory environment that demands proof of compliance, adherence to policy, and protection of intellectual property.

  - **HIRING AND TERMINATION OF EMPLOYMENT –** To protect management and the company, all personnel actions should be processed through the HR department using established procedures. In order to avoid possible security concerns, ideally, no local manager should be allowed to hire or fire employees, contractors, and temps without the oversight of HR to control the process. This prevents the hiring or termination of employees in violation of labor laws and prevents the employment or release of an employee without proper notification to system administrators. Procedures should include defining an approved, standard checklist that will cover matters such as keys, ID cards, passwords, equipment loaned out to an employee (laptops, cell phones, pagers), etc. The human resources department may also be liable if there are violations of labor laws or contractual agreements, therefore they should be involved in all matters dealing with employee hiring, development, discipline, and termination.

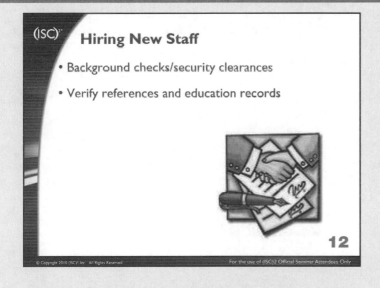

Hiring New Staff

- Background checks/security clearances
- Verify references and education records

12

- **BACKGROUND CHECKS/SECURITY CLEARANCES –** It is a good practice to look into the background of a potential employee as much as possible so as to prevent hiring the wrong person into a trusted role. Note, however, that there are legal concerns when it comes to background checks. It is important to respect the rights of individuals and the laws of the country in which people are hired.

- **VERIFY REFERENCES AND EDUCATION RECORDS –** Laws supersede any company policy and an individual's rights must be protected. However, it is important that efforts be made to verify the information provided by prospective employees, including following up with references, verifying educational records, etc.

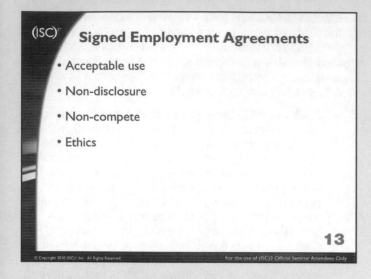

Signed Employment Agreements

- Acceptable use
- Non-disclosure
- Non-compete
- Ethics

13

- **SIGNED EMPLOYMENT AGREEMENTS** – Make signing of non-disclosure agreements, non-compete agreements, and organizational policy agreements part of the hiring process.

- **ACCEPTABLE USE** – An acceptable use policy (AUP) outlines expectations and requirements relating to proper use of IT resources. An AUP is an essential component of an employment agreement and should also be tied to training. A signed AUP provides documented proof that employees are aware of their responsibilities with respect to using company IT resources. Issues addressed in an acceptable use policy include:

  - Aligning the use of corporate IT resources with corporate policy and ethical values.

  - Establishing that employees are responsible and accountable for all actions that they take while using IT resources.

  - Required security practices.

  - Proper use of the Internet.

  - Proper use of email.

  - User telecommuter agreement.

  - Notification that use of IT resources is, or may be, subject to monitoring.

  - Restrictions relating to intellectual property rights and the prohibition of illegal copying of licensed software.

  - Restrictions regarding the downloading of files (including images, audio, and video) unless there is an explicit business-related need.

  - Restrictions relating to the use of computers for entertainment e.g., online shopping or playing games during working hours.

  - Protection of computer software and hardware from viruses and computer hackers.

  - Identification and authentication of users.

- **NON-DISCLOSURE (NDA)** – The goal of protecting sensitive information should be clearly stated during the hiring process and reinforced through reminders and audits to ensure the protection of confidential or sensitive information.

- **NON-COMPETE** – Because employees will learn sensitive information about the organization, its processes, and its customers, employees should be prohibited from starting a business in the same market for a fixed period of time. If non-compete contracts are in place, the likelihood of employees competing is lower, but not eliminated.

- **ETHICS** – A code of ethics is a statement tied to company policy. This statement is signed by the employee as a condition of employment and establishes standards and expectations regarding ethical behavior and adherence to legal requirements and best practices. While an AUP serves to protect company resources, a code of ethics serves to protect and promote the reputation of the company.

REFERENCES:
http://www.workforce-connection.org/technology/acceptable_use_policies.htm
http://www.oecd.org/dataoecd/54/22/37019249.pdf
www.hklaw.com/content/whitepapers/Infopack.pdf

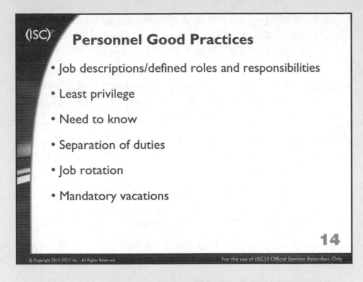

Personnel Good Practices

- Job descriptions/defined roles and responsibilities
- Least privilege
- Need to know
- Separation of duties
- Job rotation
- Mandatory vacations

14

- **JOB DESCRIPTIONS/DEFINED ROLES AND RESPONSIBILITIES –** Clearly defined job descriptions and defined roles and responsibilities help ensure that each person knows what his or her responsibilities are. Job descriptions, roles, and responsibilities are derived from the governance tools of policies, baselines, guidelines, and standards.

- **LEAST PRIVILEGE –** Means giving users only the level of permissions needed to do their job.

- **NEED TO KNOW –** Is closely related to compartmentalization. The fewer people who have permission to access particular data, the less chance there is of someone inappropriately revealing or corrupting the information.

- **SEPARATION OF DUTIES –** Breaking a job into a series of smaller tasks, each of which must be executed by a different person. This helps prevent errors or fraud, since the work of one employee must be "checked" by another and no one person has complete control over a sensitive process. This disallows one individual from performing all tasks required in a transaction.

- **JOB ROTATION –** The movement of employees through various job functions. Job rotation can help with cross-training and with ensuring succession planning. It can also sometimes break up collusion or expose an employee who is not following procedures and perhaps introducing a risk to the organization by taking shortcuts.

- **MANDATORY VACATIONS –** Mandatory vacations are a routine practice in some industry sectors as a forced leave without access to organization resources for the express purpose of detecting fraud or collusion.

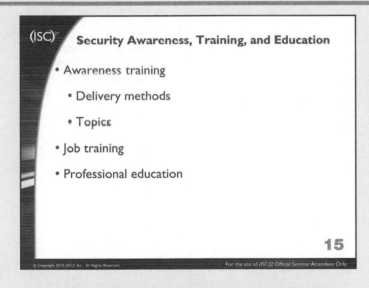

Security Awareness, Training, and Education

- Awareness training
  - Delivery methods
  - Topics
- Job training
- Professional education

15

- **SECURITY AWARENESS, TRAINING, AND EDUCATION –** Three different concepts all of which apply to the development of staff. Awareness programs should start from the first day of employment and address policy, social engineering, and security requirements. Training and education are often expensive, but staff must have adequate skills to maintain a security posture and to maintain equipment and manage projects and other key business operations. Such programs are often delivered just as needed in order to use training budgets effectively.

- **AWARENESS TRAINING –** Provides employees with a reminder of their security responsibilities.

- **DELIVERY METHODS –** The objective is to motivate personnel to comply with requirements. The campaign must be creative, with a variety of delivery methods (posters, facilitated sessions, CBT) and the depth and type of topics should change frequently and target audiences appropriately. It must be interesting to the audience. Reward employees who follow practices to protect the physical area and equipment, select strong passwords, and report security violations.

- **TOPICS –** The awareness sessions should address the threat and risk environment, the policies of the organization, and best practices in security.

- **JOB TRAINING –** Provides the skills employees need to perform the security functions associated with their jobs. Training time and money is always limited and IT professionals are typically particularly interested in remaining professionally current in their ever-changing field. Training must, therefore, focus on the skills that employees need for their current position unless management has specifically chosen to train them for another position. Make sure that training programs are not directed at staff who will merely use them as an avenue to a better paying job elsewhere. Training should focus on security-related job skills, specifically address the security requirements of the organization, increase the ability to hold employees accountable for their actions, and provide specialized or technical training as needed for specific personnel.

- **PROFESSIONAL EDUCATION –** Provides decision-making and security management skills important for a successful organizational security program.

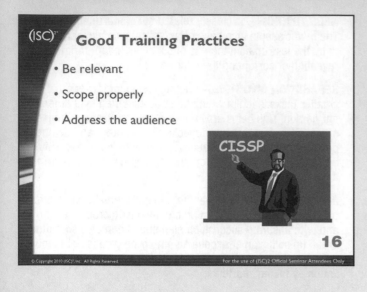

Good Training Practices

- Be relevant
- Scope properly
- Address the audience

16

For the use of (ISC)2 Official Seminar Attendees Only

- **BE RELEVANT** – This can be accomplished by focusing on the relevant and important topics of the day and ensure the content of the program is aligned with the responsibilities of the audience.

- **SCOPE PROPERLY** – Scope the training to fit the subject matter. As many technical experts have found, it is very easy to lose your audience by providing too much data.

- **ADDRESS THE AUDIENCE** – Each group has different interests and the material you present will be filtered through their personal bias. Some examples are:

  - **MANAGEMENT** – Cost savings (note that a risk analysis will yield this type of information), the need to protect information, and the need for efficient and effective security.

  - **DATA OWNER AND CUSTODIAN** – Easily followed instructions. Outline their responsibilities and obligations.

  - **OPERATIONS PERSONNEL** – Non-intrusive security.

  - **USER** – Productivity, easy compliance, understanding requirements.

  - **SUPPORT PERSONNEL** – Their role, cost-effective compliance.

Domain Agenda

- Information Security Management Systems (ISMS)
  - Business Drivers
  - **Governance**
    - Roles and Responsibilities
    - **Security Planning**
    - Security Administration
  - Risk Management
  - Ethics

17

For the use of (ISC)2 Official Seminar Attendees Only

- Security only happens by means of a plan and procedures; an unmanaged security program is not effective or efficient.

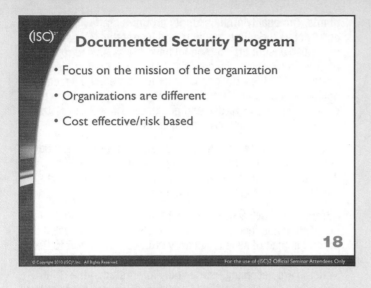

- **FOCUS ON THE MISSION OF THE ORGANIZATION** – Demonstrate how information security can help achieve company's objectives.

- **ORGANIZATIONS ARE DIFFERENT** – Different organizations will have different security requirements; for example, information security requirements differ greatly between government, military, and commercial ventures. Each has a different set of priorities based on its overall mission. Company culture may limit or dictate what is an acceptable security level or behavior. Security solutions must be developed with due consideration for the business's mission and environment.

- **COST EFFECTIVE/RISK BASED** – Determining the value of information systems and assets, as well as cost-benefit analysis, will justify adopting and implementing appropriate security controls and risk-mitigation efforts.

zation's functional plans fit into this category. This would include larger initiatives such as a network redesign, installation of new equipment and controls, and tracking of incidents over a period of months.

- **OPERATIONAL LEVEL PLANNING** – Focuses on "fighting fires" at the keyboard level. This is planning for the near-term that directly affects the ability of the organization to accomplish its objectives. This is concerned with detecting, responding, and recovering from incidents effectively and ensuring compliance and monitoring of systems operations.

- **SEAMLESS TRANSITION BETWEEN LEVELS** – Actions must transition seamlessly between the different levels. The CISSP should be able to see a clear pattern from daily tasks to the ultimate goal of long-term security strategy. The efforts and programs being performed in the short or mid-term should ideally align with the more distant objectives.

- **NOTE** – Some organizations (especially the US DoD) reverse the definitions of operational and tactical planning, using the expression "operational" to describe a strategy that is set out over the next months or quarter and "tactical" to define daily or weekly strategies. The order of these is not important – but the concept of security planning and having metrics, goals, and management at all levels is very important.

REFERENCE:

http://www.dtic.mil/doctrine/jrm/jplan.doc

- **LEVELS OF SECURITY PLANNING** – Plans and actions from all three levels must work together. This requires detailed planning. Information security management consists of a series of plans with short-, medium-, and long-term goals. A security program must have a measurable way of showing progress and maturity.

  - **STRATEGIC PLANNING** – Focuses on the high-level, long-range requirements of the company's long-term plan. Examples of this include the company's overarching security policy and the alignment of the security program with the direction of the organization.

  - **TACTICAL PLANNING** – A more mid-term focus on events that will affect the entire organization. Many of an organi-

Security Program Management

- Staffing
- Reporting

20

ments. The quality of the security program staff will depend on effective recruiting, training, and leadership. Management must also ensure that personnel have the skills and resources required to do their jobs and that personnel are provided with up-to-date job descriptions in order to help ensure accountability. Desired traits of new staff may include the ability to provide required expertise and guidance and work in a stressful, demanding, teamwork environment.

- **REPORTING** – Establishing clearly defined reporting relationships is a central part of security planning and should be documented in policy. Reporting relationships should ensure the appropriate separation of duties.

- A trend that saw security oversight migrating away from IT's jurisdiction has recently reversed. A 2007 survey revealed that more than half of all lead security officers now report to IT. This can be explained, at least in part, by the fact that security systems are becoming increasingly integrated in the IT infrastructures, thereby binding IT and security oversight together. Companies must establish a reporting structure that best suits their unique environment.

- **STAFFING** – A successful information security management program requires an adequate number of effective, well-trained security staff. The number of employees needed will depend on the organization's size and its security require-

---

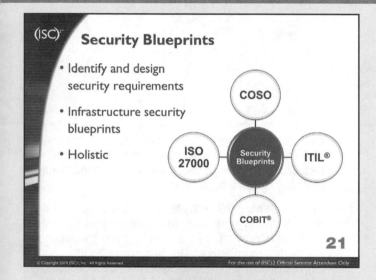

Security Blueprints

- Identify and design security requirements
- Infrastructure security blueprints
- Holistic

COSO
ISO 27000
Security Blueprints
ITIL®
COBIT®

21

- **IDENTIFY AND DESIGN SECURITY REQUIREMENTS** – Provide a structure within which requirements and solutions can be arranged. Security frameworks are used to ensure that security is considered holistically after careful consideration of a wide range of threats, vulnerabilities, and organizational requirements. Architects normally use these blueprints and frameworks when designing an overall layered security solution. A security specialist may tailor security best practices to form a comprehensive security structure, including policy, procedures, and technical architecture. Each component should directly reflect a policy decision. The plans should be mutually supportive. All areas should be considered, even though they may not need to be addressed in the final security plan. An effective security architecture will always be able to "connect the dots" between the business decisions of the organization, how these are reflected in the principles, policies, and standards of the organization, how they have been turned into requirements, and how the requirements map to the blueprints.

- **INFRASTRUCTURE SECURITY BLUEPRINTS** – Infrastructure security blueprints reflect:

  - The security requirements of a specific company/infrastructure.
  - Specific business priorities and decisions.
  - Regulatory requirements.
  - All aspects of security across the entire infrastructure.
  - The security policy approved by senior management.

- **HOLISTIC** – Here is a definition of "holistic security architecture" from the CIO website "The ABCs of Security," by Scott Berinato and Sarah Scalet:

  "Holistic security means making security part of everything and not making it its own thing. It means security isn't added to the enterprise; it's woven into the fabric of the application. Here's an example. The non-holistic thinker sees a virus threat and immediately starts spending money on virus-blocking software. The holistic security guru will set a policy around e-mail usage; subscribe to news services that warn of new threats; re-evaluate the network architecture; host best practices seminars for users; and use virus blocking software and, probably, firewalls." (www.cio.com)

COBIT® is a registered trademark of ISACA (www.isaca.org).

ITIL® is a registered trademark of the Office of Government Commerce in the United Kingdom and other countries.

ISO 27000 – Is the series of standards specifically reserved for information security.

COSO – Committee of Sponsoring Organizations of the Treadway Commission (www.coso.org).

Each of these security blueprints is covered in the Security Architecture domain.

ISO/IEC 27000 Series = ISMS Blueprints

- 27000:2009 – Overview and vocabulary
- 27001:2005 – Attainable certification
- 27002:2005/Cor1:2007 – Code of practice
- 27003:2010 – ISMS implementation guidance
- 27004:2009 – Information security measurement
- 27005:2008 – Information security – risk management
- 27006:2007 – Certification vendor process
- 27799:2008 – Information security for health care organizations

22

- **THE 27000 SERIES BY THE INTERNATIONAL ORGANIZATION FOR STANDARDIZATION AND THE INTERNATIONAL ELECTROTECHNICAL COMMISSION (ISO/IEC)** – Are a group of documents that discuss blueprints for information security management systems (ISMS).

- **27000:2009** – Overview and vocabulary.

- **27001:2005** – "Information Security Management Systems Requirements Specification" – The core document which "specifies the requirements for establishing, implementing, operating, monitoring, reviewing, maintaining and improving a documented Information Security Management System within the context of the organization's overall business risks. It specifies requirements for the implementation of security controls customized to the needs of individual organizations or parts thereof."

- **27002:2005/COR1:2007** – Code of practice derived from ISO 17799 and BS-7799.

- **27003:2010** – ISMS implementation guidance.

- **27004:2009** – Information security measurement.

- **27005:2008** – A standard for information security risk management.

- **27006:2007** – Specifies requirements and provides guidance for bodies providing audit and certification of an information security management system (ISMS), in addition to the requirements contained within ISO/IEC 17021 and ISO/IEC 27001. It is primarily intended to support the accreditation of certification bodies providing ISMS certification.

- **27799:2008** – A guide for information security for health sector organizations.

REFERENCE:

http://www.iso.org

IT Security Requirements

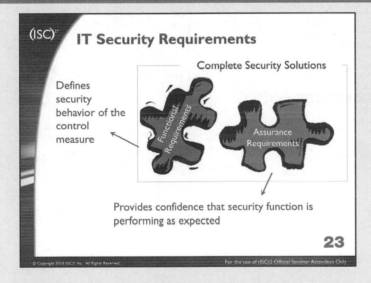

Complete Security Solutions

Defines security behavior of the control measure

Functional Requirements

Assurance Requirements

Provides confidence that security function is performing as expected

23

- **SECURITY SOLUTIONS** – All security solutions should be designed with two focus areas: the functional requirements of the solution and the assurance requirements that the functional solution is working correctly. For example, a complete "firewall solution" would be having the firewall handling traffic and denying or permitting access correctly – the functional requirement – and, the "logging and monitoring" aspect addressing the assurance requirements of the firewall solution by ensuring that the firewall is working properly and providing the expected level of protection in relation to the risks that the firewall was intended to control.

  - **FUNCTIONAL REQUIREMENTS** – Functional requirements are the things most often thought about when considering security controls. They should be layered and meet a specific security requirement. They should not depend on another control. They should fail safe, i.e., in the event of a failure they maintain the security of the systems. This is the due care function.

  - **ASSURANCE REQUIREMENTS** – Assurance mechanisms confirm that security solutions are selected appropriately, performing as intended, and having the desired effect. For example, IDS, audit logs, BCP tests and audits. Some criteria used to evaluate the operation of security solutions are: internal/external audit reports, periodic review by management, security reviews (internal), checklists, supervision, third-party reviews, and penetration tests. This is the due diligence function.

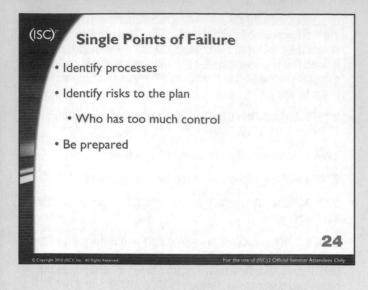

- **SINGLE POINTS OF SYSTEMS FAILURE** – In security planning, the CISSP must be able to identify any point in the security fabric that has a significant risk but inadequate layered defenses, e.g., if the authentication server in Kerberos for single sign on is down and prohibits users from accessing the system.

- **IDENTIFY PROCESSES** – Security planning must begin with defining the scope of the area of responsibility and then identifying all processes and dependencies within that scope.

- **IDENTIFY RISKS TO THE PLAN** – Draw from experience and from case studies to understand where the potential failures are.

  - **WHO HAS TOO MUCH CONTROL** – Always watch for too much authority being placed with one individual. Examples might include one person having too much authority, a lack of cross training, no fallback for a broken control, or an inadequate check and balance system in place.

- **BE PREPARED** – Senior management may be reluctant to address single points of failure at first due to costs, disruptions to the business, and an inertia to change, therefore, the security professional should be prepared to deliver a solid business plan outlining the risks of single points of failure, the recommended solutions, and the cost/benefit analysis that is required to "sell" the security strategy to management.

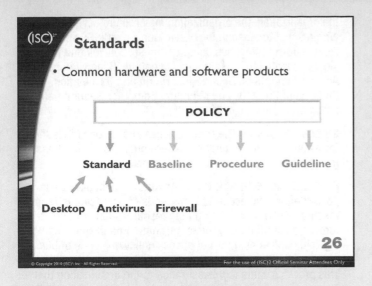

- Policy is the authoritative official statement of what the security goals of the organization are. Supporting elements to policy must be concrete enough for individuals to execute at their level of management and literal enough to implement at the lowest levels of the organization.

- **MANAGEMENT'S GOALS AND OBJECTIVES IN WRITING** – If it is not written down, it will not get done. The organizational policy mandates the security needs within the company.

  - The overarching security policy should be kept "high-level," straightforward, and short.

    - If It Is too complex, It may not be read or understood.

    - If it is too generic, it may be meaningless and irrelevant.

- The length and content of this critical document is as unique as the company itself and must be created with that in mind. It is good to introduce an appendix outlining the "terms of reference."

- Policy is an authoritative document that must be endorsed by senior management and, as such, will be referenced frequently if written properly. Policies are of no value if not read, available, current, and enforced.

- Policies must be posted in a location that is available to every employee for review. They must be current and reflect new laws and regulations.

- All employees must be kept aware of the policies through an annual review. A record of this review with each employee should be maintained.

- **DOCUMENTS COMPLIANCE** – Policy documents how the company is complying with laws, regulations, and standards of due care.

- **CREATES SECURITY CULTURE** – Policy establishes the internal environment for the security program. Explains what assets and principles the organization considers valuable.

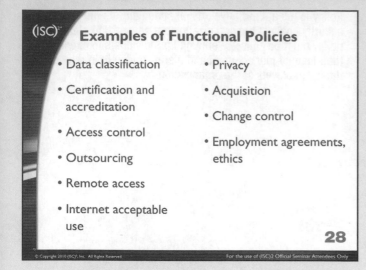

FUNCTIONAL POLICIES – The high-level security policy of the organization is usually short and quite general. It is not specific enough to deal with individual concerns such as technology, incident management, or data classification. Therefore, the high-level policy is usually supported by a series of functional policies that deal with specific issues. The following are some examples of functional policies:

DATA CLASSIFICATION – Data classification policies are very dependent on scope, laws, information type, and organization type.

CERTIFICATION AND ACCREDITATION – Certification and accreditation policy is a requirement used by many governments and military organizations as a means to ensure that security is designed into systems and then implemented correctly. The certification ensures that all security controls are implemented as designed, work correctly, and produce the intended result.

ACCESS CONTROL – Access control policies define what methods of access are acceptable. Depending on the size of the organization in question, the access control policy may actually be composed of several policies such as remote access policy, acceptable use policy, telephony access policy, network access policy, server access policy, etc.

OUTSOURCING – Outsourcing IT services potentially presents a number of risks to an organization. Depending on the specific requirements, size, and individual characteristics of

the organization, the organization may require several policies with respect to outsourcing. Kevin Beaver, a CISSP specializing in outsourcing, has documented six policies that he considers essential to outsourcing: Acceptable Usage, Information Access, Information Destruction, Hiring and Termination, Removal of Property, and Minimum Computer Requirements (www.principlelogic.com).

REMOTE ACCESS – The remote access policy describes the terms and conditions under which remote access solutions may be used to access the organization's network.

INTERNET ACCEPTABLE USE – An Internet acceptable use policy defines the acceptable methods of accessing Internet resources when using computing resources and infrastructure. As a precautionary measure, some organizations now explicitly define the Internet access policy in a code of business conduct that the employee is required to read and sign. This provides some legal assurance to the organization that the employee is aware of and understands the policy and the implications of noncompliance.

PRIVACY – Privacy policies vary from country to country and sometimes from state to state. The security professional must know the requirements of privacy regulations regarding the protection, dissemination, and destruction of personally identifiable information (PII).

ACQUISITION – Acquisition policy typically addresses potential vendor influence over purchasing agents and may, for example, limit what "gifts" decision makers are allowed to receive.

CHANGE CONTROL – Change control policy (discussed in the application domain) protects production systems from unauthorized changes. Change control policy will address configurations, hardware and software functionality, project scope, and baselines.

EMPLOYMENT AGREEMENTS, ETHICS – A code of ethics is a statement tied to company policy. This statement is signed by the employee as a condition of employment. It establishes standards and expectations regarding ethical behavior, adherence to legal requirements, and best practices. While an acceptable use policy serves to protect company resources, a code of ethics policy serves to provide guidance for behavior and protects and promotes the reputation of the company.

REFERENCE:

www.principlelogic.com

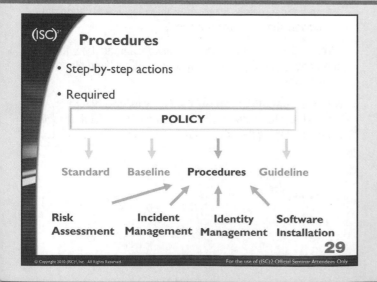

PROCEDURES – Ensure that policy is enforced by mandating how a task will be completed. This provides a consistent and traceable method of ensuring that any activity that may have security implications is done in an approved manner. Procedures are statements of step-by-step actions to be performed to accomplish a security requirement, process, or objective. They are one of the most powerful tools available in the security arsenal.

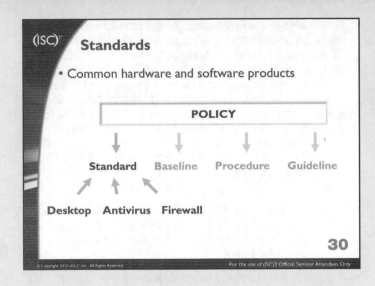

- **STANDARDS** – Are the standardized hardware or software solutions selected to address security risks and applied throughout the enterprise. An example might be using a specific antivirus product or password generation token throughout the organization. This often reduces cost of ownership by allowing large, blank purchase agreements with vendors. Standardized training further reduces costs. Standards are essential because they allow for a basis for common practices across an organization rather than having each individual department operating in its own separate (and in some cases noncompliant) environment. It also helps reduce the seams that can develop between sections, departments, and subordinate organizations. Note, however, that if vulnerability is exploited by a threat agent, the entire organization will be at risk. Security designers must take this into account and build in appropriate controls when designing the network.

- Standards can also be guidelines created by government, industry, or other organizations that have been formally adopted by the organization. For example, an international standard such as ISO/IEC 27002 may be adopted by an organization as the template for its security program.

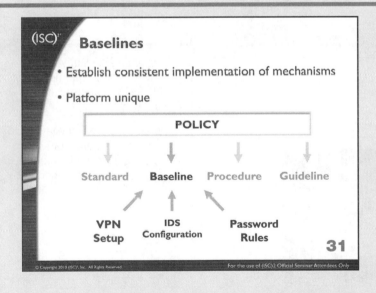

- **BASELINES** – Are the benchmarks used to ensure that a minimum level of security is provided across multiple implementations of the systems, networks, and products used by the organization. Baselines are descriptions of how to implement security mechanisms such as the configuration of a device or tool to ensure a consistent level of security throughout the organization. Different systems (platforms) have different methods of handling security issues. Baselines inform user groups how to set up security for each platform so that the desired level of security is consistently achieved.

- **PLATFORM UNIQUE** – Baselines are often specific to the vendor product being used and due to the characteristics of the vendor product the baseline configuration may be unique to that product.

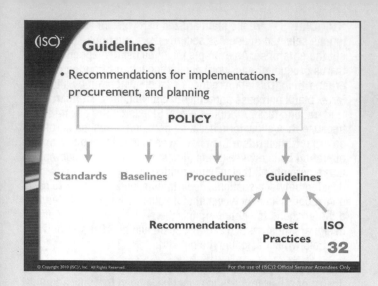

- **GUIDELINES** – Unlike standards, which mandate company policy, guidelines are simply recommendations. They may be white papers, best practices, or formats for the security program used by an organization. Guidelines are often used to help provide structure to a security program and to outline recommendations for procurement and deployment of acceptable products and systems. Make sure that the careless use of words doesn't unintentionally transform a guideline into a company standard. For example, an overarching statement in a security policy signed by the CEO stating that "this company will follow the recommendations of the ISO 17799 guideline" makes the ISO 17799 "guideline" mandatory.

- The course will look at the TCSEC, ITSEC, and common criteria guidelines in the Security Architecture domain. These guidelines provide a standard method of evaluating the security functionality of a product.

- Security Technical Implementation Guides are an example of a guideline used in the U.S. military and can be found at: http://iase.disa.mil/stigs/stig/index.html. The use of such guidelines allows the organization to follow already tested procedures and learn from best practices.

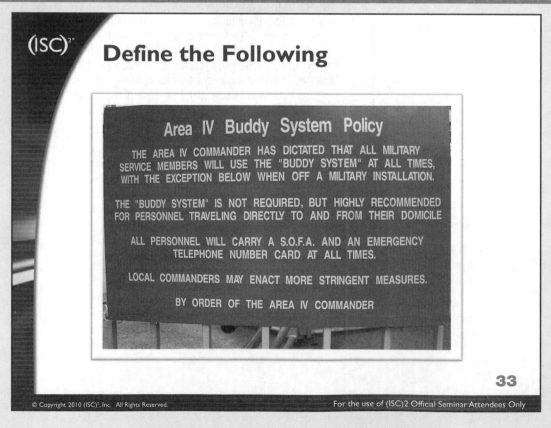

- According to what you have learned, what does the following represent and why?

- What does this tell you about implementations of information security management in the real world?

threats and vulnerabilities.

Domain Agenda

- Information Security Management Systems (ISMS)
  - Business Drivers
  - Governance
    - Roles and Responsibilities
    - Security Planning
    - Security Administration
- **Risk Management**
- Ethics

34

- **RISK MANAGEMENT** is a process for efficiently allocating limited resources to mitigate risks associated with business processes and the assets deployed to support them.
  - **RISK ANALYSIS** is the central part of this process and focuses on the identification of assets and their associated

- **RISK ASSESSMENT** goes one step further and evaluates and prioritizes the identified risks. Risk management includes risk analysis and assessment as an initial step. The risk assessment report provides a basis for determining how best to manage the identified risks. For each identified risk, a decision is made as to whether to avoid, accept, transfer, or mitigate the probability and/or impact of the risk.

- **RISK MITIGATION** is the process of addressing the risks presented in the risk assessment report. Depending on the severity of the risk, there may be several options to choose from when addressing risk.

- **EVALUATION AND ONGOING MONITORING** is the realization that risk changes over time and the organization needs to repeat the risk assessment on a regular basis to identify new risks and to verify whether risk mitigation controls are working effectively.

Risk Management Overview

- Identifying and reducing total risks
- Choosing mitigation strategies
- Setting residual risk at an acceptable level
- Integrating risk management processes into the organization

35

- **RISK MANAGEMENT OVERVIEW** – Risk management is the effort applied to manage exposure before a threat takes advantage of a vulnerability. It is a proactive activity designed to prevent possible breaches or incidents through the identification of possible threats, the selection of appropriate risk-control countermeasures or safeguards, and the continuous monitoring of the risk environment.

- **RISK IDENTIFICATION** – Risk management (and specifically through its sub-areas of risk assessment and evaluation and assurance) identifies potential problems before they occur so that risk-handling activities may be planned and invoked as needed across the life of the product, project, or organization.

- **CHOOSING A STRATEGY/ACCEPTABLE RISK** – Mitigation strategy is a management decision, not a technical one. It will be based upon all business factors. Once the mitigation strategy has been chosen, management is stating that whatever risk is left (the "residual risk") is acceptable to the organization.

- **ONGOING PROCESS** – Risk management is a continuous process that must be woven into the business processes of an organization. Since the risk environment is constantly changing with technology, new threats, and new business initiatives, diligence is needed to ensure that changes to the level of risk to an organization are identified promptly.

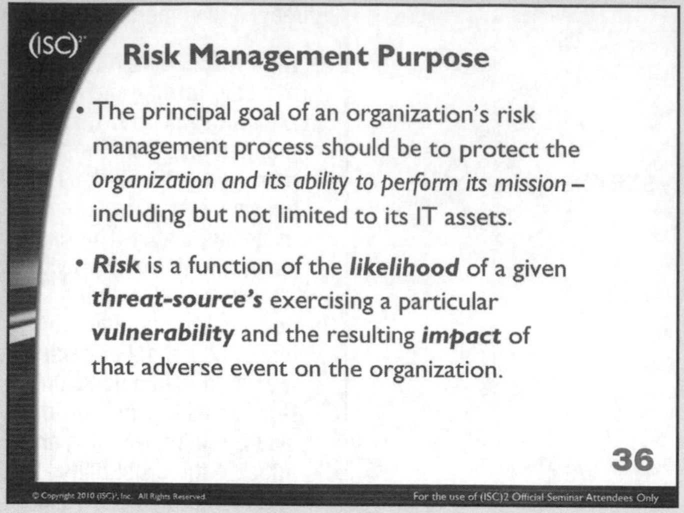

Risk Management Purpose

* The principal goal of an organization's risk management process should be to protect the *organization and its ability to perform its mission* – including but not limited to its IT assets.

* *Risk* is a function of the *likelihood* of a given *threat-source's* exercising a particular *vulnerability* and the resulting *impact* of that adverse event on the organization.

36

* **DEFINITION OF RISK FROM NIST SP 800-30 –** (1) The probability that a particular threat-source will exercise (accidentally trigger or intentionally exploit) a particular information system vulnerability and (2) the resulting impact if this should occur.

* www.csrc.nist.gov

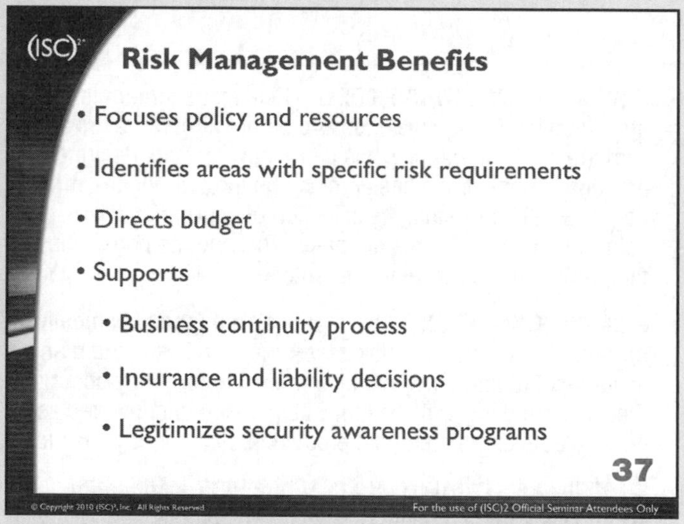

Risk Management Benefits

* Focuses policy and resources

* Identifies areas with specific risk requirements

* Directs budget

* Supports

  * Business continuity process

  * Insurance and liability decisions

  * Legitimizes security awareness programs

37

* **FOCUSES POLICY AND RESOURCES –** Risk analysis ensures that the resources and policy of an organization are directed appropriately. Functional experts from each area should be part of the risk analysis process to help determine asset value and dependencies and to assess the potential impact of risks on the organization.

* **IDENTIFIES AREAS WITH SPECIFIC RISK REQUIREMENTS –** There are areas of the company that operate under specific legal regulations. The financial and health care sectors have specific regulatory requirements. You will need to determine whether you are dealing with any such legal obligations before beginning a risk analysis.

* **DIRECTS BUDGET –** With limited personnel, money, and tools, risk analysis ensures that the resources of the organization are targeted at the areas of greatest risk and at making sure that there are no gaps in the security process.

* **SUPPORTS –** A risk analysis effort also supports many other associated activities such as the business continuity planning project and business impact analysis. It also provides information for corporate insurance premium calculations and lends legitimacy to security awareness programs.

Risk Management Definitions

- Asset
- Threat-source/ agent
- Threat
- Exposure
- Vulnerability
- Likelihood

- Attack
- Controls
- Countermeasures
- Safeguards
- Total risk
- Residual risk

38

- **RISK MANAGEMENT DEFINITIONS –** The organization must work from a common set of terms when conducting risk analysis. Understanding and using terminology correctly is particularly important when presenting risk-analysis efforts to senior management to ensure clear understanding of the risk program. These definitions are drawn from NIST SP 800-30.

- **ASSET –** Something that is of value to the organization in accomplishing its goals and objectives.

- **THREAT-SOURCE OR THREAT AGENT –** Any circumstance or event with the potential to cause harm to an IT system. Threat-sources can be natural (earthquakes, floods), environmental (chemicals, pollution, long-term power failure) or human. Human threats are those that are either enabled by or caused by human beings, such as unintentional acts (inadvertent data entry) or deliberate actions (network-based attacks, malicious software upload, unauthorized access to confiden-

tial information).

- **THREAT –** Any potential danger to information or an information system.

- **EXPOSURE –** An opportunity for a threat to cause loss, or the amount of loss suffered as a result of an attack.

- **VULNERABILITY –** A flaw or weakness in system security procedures, design, implementation, or internal controls that might be exercised (whether accidentally or intentionally) and cause a security breach or a violation of the system's security policy.

- **LIKELIHOOD –** The probability that a potential vulnerability be exercised within the construct of the associated threat environment.

- **ATTACK/EXPLOITATION –** An action intending to cause harm. An effort by a threat agent to launch a threat by exploiting a vulnerability in an information system.

- **CONTROLS –** Administrative, technical, or physical measures and actions taken to try and protect systems. They include countermeasures and safeguards.

- **COUNTERMEASURES –** Controls applied after the fact; reactive in nature.

- **SAFEGUARDS –** Controls applied before the fact; proactive in nature.

- **TOTAL RISK –** Includes the factors of threats, vulnerabilities, and current value of the asset.

- **RESIDUAL RISK –** The amount of risk remaining after countermeasures and safeguards are applied.

REFERENCE:
HTTP://csrc.nist.gov/publications/nistpubs/800-30/sp800-30.pdf

---

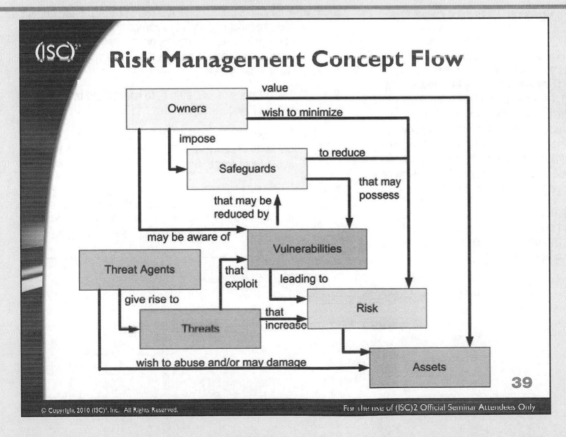

Risk Management Concept Flow

39

- This is a valuable outline of the concepts of risk management as described in the common criteria.

REFERENCE:
http://www.commoncriteriaportal.org/ public/files/CCPART1V3.1R1.pdf

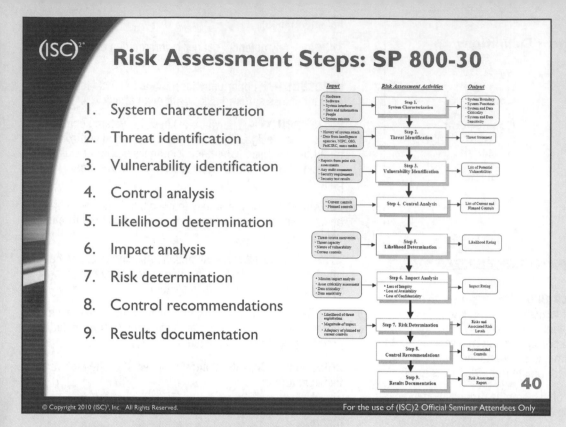

Risk Assessment Steps: SP 800-30

1. System characterization
2. Threat identification
3. Vulnerability identification
4. Control analysis
5. Likelihood determination
6. Impact analysis
7. Risk determination
8. Control recommendations
9. Results documentation

- According to NIST SP 800-30, there are nine steps to the risk assessment process. The output of the ninth step gives management the options for mitigation. The cycle is started again by evaluation. A good risk analysis should provide data to explain the company's risk environment to management in terms they understand. The process of risk analysis should remain focused on the objectives set on "what does this mean to the company?" and "what is the value of this to the company?"

- **A BRIEF DESCRIPTION OF EACH STEP DIRECTLY FROM THE NIST PUBLICATION:**

  STEP 1. In assessing risks for an IT system, the first step is to define the scope of the effort. In this step, the boundaries of the IT system are identified, along with the resources and the information that constitute the system. Characterizing an IT system establishes the scope of the risk assessment effort, delineates the operational authorization (or accreditation) boundaries, and provides information (e.g., hardware, software, system connectivity, and responsible division or support personnel) essential to defining the risk.

  STEP 2. The goal of this step is to identify the potential threat-sources and compile a threat statement listing potential threat-sources that are applicable to the IT system being evaluated.

  STEP 3. The goal of this step is to develop a list of system vulnerabilities (flaws or weaknesses) that could be exploited by the potential threat-sources.

STEP 4. The goal of this step is to analyze the controls that have been implemented, or are planned for implementation, by the organization to minimize or eliminate the likelihood (or probability) of a threat's exercising a system vulnerability.

STEP 5. The likelihood that a potential vulnerability could be exercised by a given threat-source can be described as high, medium, or low.

STEP 6. A business impact analysis (BIA) prioritizes the impact levels associated with the compromise of an organization's information assets based on a qualitative or quantitative assessment of the sensitivity and criticality of those assets.

STEP 7. The purpose of this step is to assess the level of risk to the IT system.

STEP 8. The goal of the recommended controls is to reduce the level of risk to the IT system and its data to an acceptable level.

STEP 9. A risk assessment report is a management report that helps senior management, the mission owners, make decisions on policy, procedure, budget, and system operational and management changes.

REFERENCE:

HTTP://csrc.nist.gov/publications/nistpubs/800-30/sp800-30.pdf

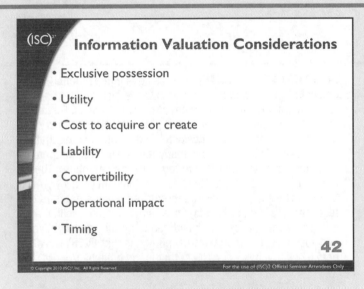

Risk Assessment - Asset Valuation

- Tangible assets
  - Hardware, software, facilities, documentation, customer lists, and intellectual property
- Intangible assets
  - Personnel, reputation/brand, and morale

41

- **RISK ASSESSMENT – ASSET VALUATION -** Assigning values to assets during risk assessment provides a basis for prioritizing, evaluating, and treating risks. Asset values may be expressed in monetary (quantitative) or relative (qualitative; e.g., high-medium-low) terms. Assets and their related values can be classified as follows:

- **TANGIBLE ASSETS –** Replacement cost of IT facilities, property, hardware, software, documentation, supplies, and IT staff.

- **INTANGIBLE ASSETS –**
  - Value of goodwill/reputation/brand.
  - Replacement cost of data.
  - Inherent value of data.
  - Classification of the information stored, processed, or transmitted by the asset.
  - Contextual value.
    - Mission Relationship – Value of the system to the mission of the organization.
    - Age – As information gets older the risk profile also changes.
- Security categories describe the acceptable values for potential impact in various levels such as low, moderate, high, or not applicable.

REFERENCES:
www.ogclo.gov.hk/eng/prodev/download/g51_pub.pdf
www.cse-cst.gc.ca/documents/publications/gov-pubs/itsg/mg3.pdf
http://iac.dtic.mil/iatac/download/Vol11_No1.pdf
http://csrc.nist.gov/publications/fips/fips199/FIPS-PUB-199-final.pdf

Information Valuation Considerations

- Exclusive possession
- Utility
- Cost to acquire or create
- Liability
- Convertibility
- Operational impact
- Timing

42

- **INFORMATION VALUATION AND CONSIDERATIONS –** Risk is usually based on the value of an asset. One of the most valuable assets to organizations today is information. The value of the information to the organization is crucial to the determination of acceptable risk. There are many different characteristics of information that determine its value. The primary value-related attributes of information are listed below. These attributes provide a framework for assessing the overall value of information.

- **EXCLUSIVE POSSESSION –** The value of information may be tied to the extent to which it is exclusively held. This attribute relates to loss of confidentiality of information. A trade secret may provide great value to an organization. However, if the information falls into the hands of an adversary or becomes public, that value may be lost. Note that the value of information is often dependent on its value to an adversary or competitor.

- **UTILITY –** Utility relates to the integrity and relevance of information. To have value, information must be undamaged and relevant to the organization. For example, customer data that has become lost, corrupted, or outdated has lost its usefulness and value. Also, information of great value to one part of the organization may have negative value – in the form of maintenance and liability costs – to other parts of the organization that are required to store, process, and update the information.

- **COST TO ACQUIRE OR CREATE –** A relatively straightforward, conservative method of determining information value.

- **LIABILITY –** An organization has an obligation to protect the information entrusted to it. The value of information for this category is based on the potential cost to an organization if the availability, integrity, and/or confidentiality of the information are compromised.

- **CONVERTIBILITY –** Convertibility relates to information that either represents value intrinsically (for example, electronic funds transfer, inventory lists) or has intrinsic value (for example, intellectual property). Such information has value because it can be converted into cash, profit, or some other tangible asset.

- **OPERATIONAL IMPACT –** Information may also be valued based on the impact to the organization if the availability, integrity and/or confidentiality of the information are compromised.

- **TIMING –** Some information is more valuable at some "times" than others. For example, financial information is more valuable at year end, or just prior to the release of earnings statements, than it is at other times.

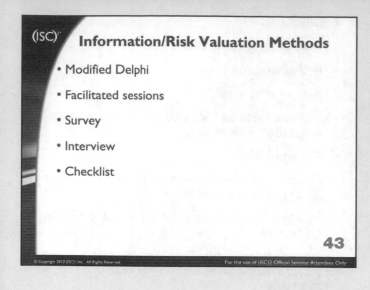

Information/Risk Valuation Methods

- Modified Delphi
- Facilitated sessions
- Survey
- Interview
- Checklist

43

- **MODIFIED DELPHI** – A structured communication process that facilitates effective group decision making when addressing a complex problem. It is a proven method for enabling a group of experts to reach a consensus and is characterized by anonymity, iteration, statistical filtering of output, and informed input. The Modified Delphi technique provides more informed initial input to the process as a means of accelerating convergence to a consensus. The Modified Delphi technique has been described as the most useful, efficient, and credible method for valuing intangible information assets.

- **FACILITATED SESSIONS** – Are less structured than the Modified Delphi technique. Open-ended questions and other techniques are used to stimulate discussion and efficiently gather information. Both technical and non-technical business managers and support staff pool their experience and expertise in order to arrive at a consensus.

- **SURVEY** – Survey and analysis of information gathered from stakeholders using directed questionnaires is used to establish information value.

- **INTERVIEW** – Stakeholders provide input via interviews, allowing for efficient collection of information.

- **CHECKLIST** – A checklist can provide an efficient and structured method for gathering information. As with the survey and interview methods, however, there is little or no exchange of information and opinions.

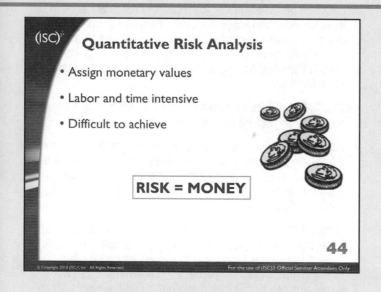

Quantitative Risk Analysis

- Assign monetary values
- Labor and time intensive
- Difficult to achieve

RISK = MONEY

44

- **QUANTITATIVE RISK ANALYSIS** – Assigns independent, objective, numeric monetary values to the elements of risk assessment and the assessment of potential losses. Quantitative risk analysis is very labor and time intensive. It is very difficult (and some say, impossible) to do a purely quantitative risk analysis. This is because many items, such as company reputation, are hard to value in terms of cash numbers. These items lend themselves better to qualitative analysis. When all elements (asset value, impact, threat frequency, safeguard effectiveness, safeguard costs, uncertainty, and probability) are quantified, the process is considered to be fully quantitative. The easy way to remember this method is that EVERYTHING gets a dollar value – or at least that is the objective.

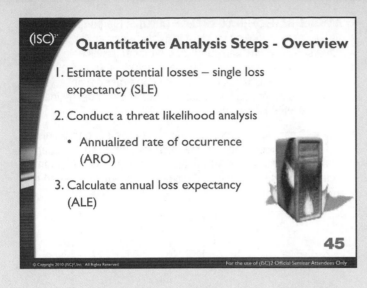

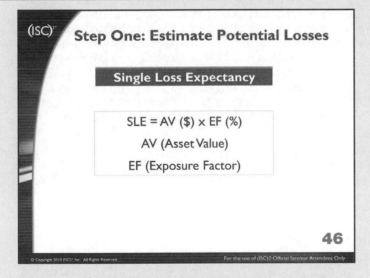

- What this means: Calculate the asset value as a function of how often it will be successfully attacked in a given period of time (annually). We will go over this process in detail on the next few slides.

- The impact on productivity, lost time, customer satisfaction, and confidence.

- The financial or criminal penalties for which the organization would be liable in the case of mishandled data.

- Who has the information? The value of information for adversaries may be far greater than the perceived value of the data to the original organization.

- An organization may also realize additional revenue through the sale of customer data.

- Value of intellectual property – loss of trade secrets, marketing plans.

- Convertibility/negotiability – Identity details, credit card numbers, and transaction details may have value to the thief.

- **THE EXPOSURE FACTOR (EF)** is expressed as a percentage of the asset value. If loss can be limited to one type, you can determine the impact on the asset by percentage of the asset value lost. Types of losses to consider: physical destruction/ theft of assets, loss of data, theft of information, indirect theft of assets, and delayed processing. If the loss type is unknown, the exposure factor is set at 100 percent.

REFERENCE:
ISBN-13: 978-0-7506-7113-2 Roper, Carl. p15

- **A SINGLE LOSS EXPECTANCY (SLE)** is the estimate of the amount of damage that an asset will suffer due to a single incident. Asset categories include people, facilities, equipment, materials, information, activities, and operations. The asset should be valued at replacement cost, not at the accounting amortized value.

- **THE VALUE OF INFORMATION AND INFORMATION SYSTEMS IS DEPENDENT ON FACTORS SUCH AS:**

  - The cost of recovering or rebuilding lost data or processing power.

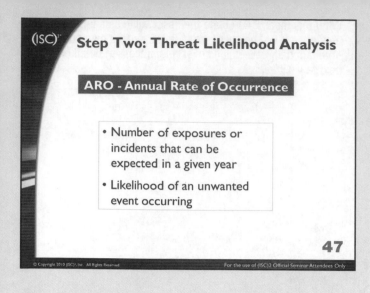

Step Two: Threat Likelihood Analysis

ARO - Annual Rate of Occurrence

- Number of exposures or incidents that can be expected in a given year
- Likelihood of an unwanted event occurring

47

- **ANNUAL RATE OF OCCURRENCE (ARO)** is the number of times per year that an incident is likely to occur. Knowing the adversaries' intent, capability, and motivation will help determine the ARO. Categories of threats include: internal, environmental, criminal, military, competitor, and random observer. All categories of threats times the number of expected incidents per year must be calculated.

- The ARO can be difficult to predict. It is based in part on historical data, but changes in the environment will often affect future predictions. The ARO is often expressed as a fraction when an incident is only likely to occur once over a period of years.

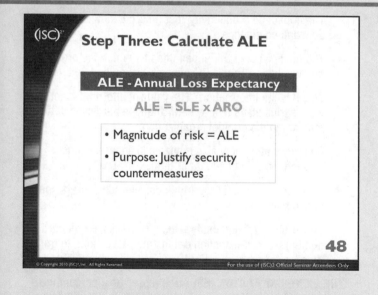

Step Three: Calculate ALE

ALE - Annual Loss Expectancy

$$ALE = SLE \times ARO$$

- Magnitude of risk = ALE
- Purpose: Justify security countermeasures

48

- **THE ANNUAL LOSS EXPECTANCY (ALE)** provides an estimate of the yearly financial impact to the organization from a particular risk. This number helps determine how much money the organization is justified in spending on countermeasures in order to reduce the likelihood or impact of an incident. There should be a direct correlation between the amount of money spent on security and the amount of benefit (cost benefit analysis) realized through the reduction in risk.

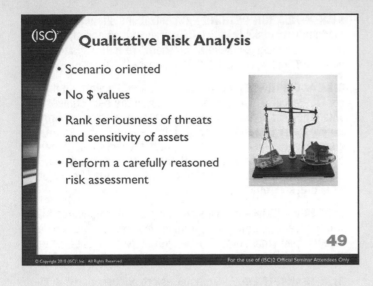

Qualitative Risk Analysis

- Scenario oriented
- No $ values
- Rank seriousness of threats and sensitivity of assets
- Perform a carefully reasoned risk assessment

49

- **QUALITATIVE RISK ANALYSIS** – Instead of applying monetary value as with quantitative risk analysis, qualitative risk analysis evaluates the impact or effect of threats on the business process or the goals of the organization.

- **SCENARIO ORIENTED** – Qualitative risk analysis is scenario oriented and is done for every department in the organization. Input comes from the department itself, but is often derived from many other sources as well. Every threat to every department's business function is described in a threat scenario and the expected impact from each of these threats is graded on a scale indicating the severity of the threat (e.g., high, medium, or low) to the department's business functions. The likelihood of an event occurring is also ranked. Make sure to take the effectiveness of existing controls against threats into account. The cumulative, weighted ranking of the unmitigated risks across all departments describes the severity of the total risk to the organization.

- **PERFORM A CAREFULLY REASONED RISK ASSESSMENT** – A qualitative risk analysis is a carefully reasoned process and requires a good deal of judgment. The most difficult part of this process is formulating the questions so that respondents are able to give accurate data. The advantage of a qualitative risk assessment is that it frequently results in a better understanding of the business processes by the system owners and business units, as well as improved communications between the parties working on the risk-analysis efforts.

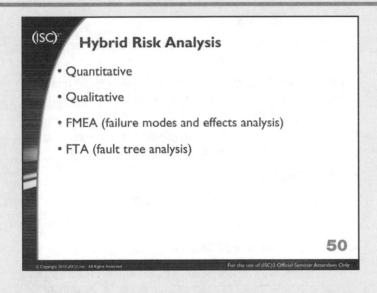

Hybrid Risk Analysis

- Quantitative
- Qualitative
- FMEA (failure modes and effects analysis)
- FTA (fault tree analysis)

50

- **QUANTITATIVE/QUALITATIVE** – A purely quantitative risk assessment is generally thought to be impossible and a purely qualitative process does not provide defined statistical or financial data. Hybrid risk analysis combines the two processes and uses a quantitative valuation for tangible assets and a qualitative assessment for intangible assets. Assets that cannot be readily assigned a dollar value are methodically prioritized instead.

- **FMEA (FAILURE MODES AND EFFECTS ANALYSIS)** – Is a risk assessment effort originally concerned with manufacturing defects and it focuses on the upstream and downstream impact of a failure. It defines a risk in immediate, near-term and long-term impact.

- **FTA (FAULT TREE ANALYSIS)** – Is an analytical technique for system safety. It is used to consider all possible threats and then "trim" down to the most relevant risks.

- Both FMEA & FTA would be used as inputs to a quantitative or qualitative analysis.

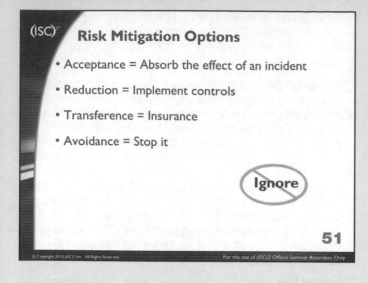

Risk Mitigation Options

- Acceptance = Absorb the effect of an incident
- Reduction = Implement controls
- Transference = Insurance
- Avoidance = Stop it

Ignore

51

- **RISK MITIGATION OPTIONS –** Organizations should be able to identify the risks to which they are exposed and should act in order to moderate these risks. There are four ways to deal with risk: Accept, reduce, transfer, or avoid.

- **RISK ACCEPTANCE –** Accepting the risk and absorbing the cost if it occurs. Risk acceptance is often the best choice when the cost to mitigate the threat is very high or the impact is very low. When risk acceptance is the choice, it is an important requirement for an appropriate level of management to sign off as acknowledgement of the risk and to indicate concurrence. If risk is accepted at a point in time, it must be re-addressed routinely.

- **RISK REDUCTION –** Involves selecting countermeasures that will reduce exposure or loss if the event occurs. This is where CISSPs spend most of their time with respect to risk management.

- **RISK TRANSFERENCE –** Transfer risk to another party. Businesses often transfer risk to an insurance company by buying insurance.

- **RISK AVOIDANCE –** Decide to suspend the activity, either temporarily or permanently.

- **RISK IGNORANCE –** Although an attractive option to many organizations, this is not an acceptable risk mitigation strategy!

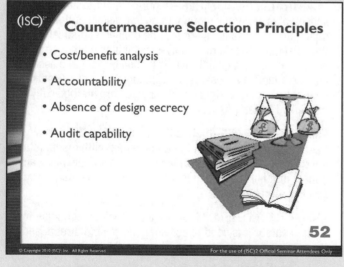

Countermeasure Selection Principles

- Cost/benefit analysis
- Accountability
- Absence of design secrecy
- Audit capability

52

- **COUNTERMEASURE SELECTION PRINCIPLES –** Consider the total cost of a control measure, which is much more than just the initial purchase price. The total cost of a safeguard will include:

  - Selection.
  - Acquisition (materials and mechanisms).
  - Construction and placement.
  - Environment modification.
  - Nontrivial operating cost.

  - Maintenance, testing.
  - Potential side effects (vulnerabilities that are inherent to the safeguard added).

- **COST/BENEFIT ANALYSIS –** Remember not to spend more to protect an asset than the asset is worth! The cost must be justified by the potential loss.

  - Countermeasures should be implemented according to the value the organization expects to derive from them.

- **ACCOUNTABILITY –**

  - At least one person for every safeguard.
  - Include accountability in performance reviews.

- **ABSENCE OF DESIGN SECRECY –**

  - Changeability of safeguards (i.e., the ability to change out the countermeasure at some time in the future without having extraordinary costs for rework), interoperability with other safeguards, confidence in the design (common criteria evaluation).

- **AUDIT CAPABILITY –**

  - Safeguards must be testable.
  - Include auditors in design and implementation.

Countermeasure Selection (cont.)

- Vendor trustworthiness

- Independence of control and subject

- Universal application

- Compartmentalization

- Defense in depth

- Isolation, economy, and least common mechanism

- **VENDOR TRUSTWORTHINESS** – Review past performance.

- **INDEPENDENCE OF CONTROL AND SUBJECT (SEPARATION OF DUTIES)** – Make sure that the person maintaining the countermeasure (the controller) is in a separate population group from the persons or activity (the subject) being controlled by the countermeasure.

- **UNIVERSAL APPLICATION** –

  - Imposes safeguards uniformly.

  - Minimizes exceptions.

- **COMPARTMENTALIZATION** – A safeguard's role is relative to its environment and relationship to other safeguards. In case a safeguard fails, this principle localizes the impact by restricting the extent of the breach to a defined area.

- **DEFENSE IN DEPTH** – Defense in depth establishes serial hurdles, or layers of security. When employed properly, this allows the organization to detect that something is happening and take positive action prior to a threat adversely affecting its assets. Make sure, however, that safeguards are not layered such that if one of them fails, it defeats the others. Each safeguard should be as simple as practicably possible in order to reduce the possibility of configuration errors.

- **ISOLATION, ECONOMY, AND LEAST COMMON MECHANISM** –

  - Isolate every safeguard from every other safeguard so that a failure of one device does not affect multiple systems or affect redundancy provisions.

  - Minimize dependence on common mechanisms (common power supply, common network connections, etc.).

  - Simple designs are more reliable and more cost effective.

Countermeasure Selection (cont.)

- Acceptance and tolerance by personnel

- Minimum human intervention

- Sustainability

- Reaction and recovery

- Override and fail-safe defaults

- Residuals and reset

- **ACCEPTANCE AND TOLERANCE BY PERSONNEL** – Countermeasures that are not acceptable to personnel (and management) are soon bypassed or defeated. An example of this is the implementation of some biometrics that is seen as a health risk or unnecessarily intrusive. Take care not to implement controls that pose unreasonable constraints on performance, productivity, or normal behavior.

- **MINIMUM HUMAN INTERVENTION** – Reduces the possibility of errors and "exceptions" by reducing the reliance on administrative staff to maintain the control.

- **SUSTAINABILITY** – An effective control must be implemented along with cost-effective maintenance and upgrade procedures. Every control must also be clearly designated as the responsibility of an individual or job role.

- **REACTION AND RECOVERY** – The ability of the countermeasure to detect and react to an incident and capture the relevant information related to the incident. The countermeasure must do the following when activated:

  - Avoid asset destruction and stop further damage.

  - Prevent disclosure of sensitive information through a covert channel.

  - Maintain confidence in system security.

  - Capture information related to the attack and attacker.

- **OVERRIDE AND FAIL-SAFE DEFAULTS** – In the event of a suspected incident, the countermeasure should default to "no access" or preserve the system in a secure state. In order to prevent a denial of service, however, there should be a way to disable or override the control.

- **RESIDUALS AND RESET** – During the recovery period from an incident, the countermeasure must be protected from further attacks while being reset. It must return to a secure condition and protect logs from destruction.

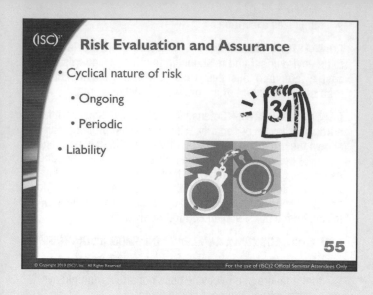

Risk Evaluation and Assurance

- Cyclical nature of risk
  - Ongoing
  - Periodic
- Liability

55

- **CYCLICAL NATURE OF RISK –** U.S. and EU regulatory bodies have mandated risk management as a business process. Risk management is ongoing and cyclical in nature. The frequency with which it should be re-evaluated is based upon the speed of change in each industry or organization.

  - **ONGOING –** A common method of ensuring that risks are identified and mitigated rapidly is through continuous auditing and risk monitoring. This places some responsibility on the local manager to monitor risk and compliance and ensure that any abnormalities are identified as quickly as possible.

  - **PERIODIC –** Risk must be re-examined on a scheduled, periodic basis. Otherwise it can be too easy to miss emerging threats or a control that is not working effectively.

- **LIABILITY –** Management has the responsibility of remaining informed about risk management activities and to make the final decisions. If they fail to do so, they are potentially in violation of regulatory or industry standards. This is one of the reasons that internal auditors should report directly to senior executives rather than through the normal chain of command.

REFERENCE:

http://csrc.nist.gov/publications/drafts/800-39/SP800-39-spd-sz.pdf

---

Domain Agenda

- **Information Security Management Systems (ISMS)**
  - **Business Drivers**
  - **Governance**
    - **Roles and Responsibilities**
    - **Security Planning**
    - **Security Administration**
  - **Risk Management**
  - **Ethics**

56

- You will be required to sign the (ISC)² code of ethics before you can take the exam and become a CISSP. It's essential that you understand it and can apply it to real-world situations. The objectives of this section:

  - Understand the ethical responsibilities of user groups within the organization.

  - Understand the (ISC)² codes of ethics for CISSPs and how to abide by them.

  - Understand the ethical guidelines for proper usage of the Internet.

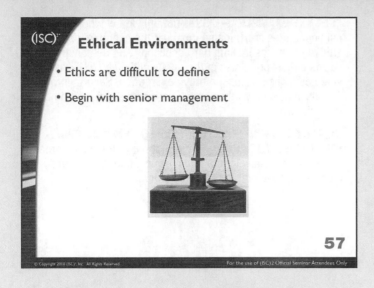

Ethical Environments

- Ethics are difficult to define
- Begin with senior management

57

- **ETHICAL ENVIRONMENTS** – The first concept of ethical behavior is to "do no harm."

  - The ethics of an organization must be clearly defined and communicated to all employees. Every person has a different set of ethical beliefs, which means that the organization must define its overall culture of ethical behavior and describe its own ethical position so that employees can make appropriate decisions. Ethics should be covered as part of regular awareness training and as a condition of employment.

- **GUIDELINES FOR THE ESTABLISHMENT OF ETHICS** – The organization's ethical positions and practices must be communicated to employees:

  - Corporate ethics, including the ethical use of computer assets.

  - Ethics included in functional policies (privacy, email, acceptable use, etc.).

  - Active monitoring of network activities combined with responsible investigation of incidents and enforcement.

  - Handbooks and guides.

  - Training.

  - Reviews.

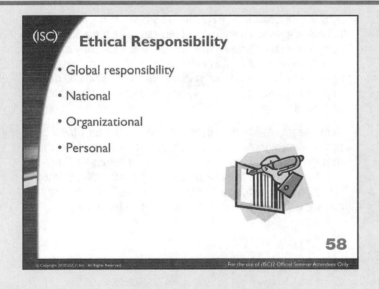

Ethical Responsibility

- Global responsibility
- National
- Organizational
- Personal

58

- **GLOBAL RESPONSIBILITY** – Many people are aware of their responsibility to behave ethically toward global issues – hunger, poverty, abuse, narcotics, and the environment.

- **NATIONAL** – The responsibility a person feels for his or her country also mandates acceptable behavior and legitimizes actions. Many people feel it is better to promote the interests of their country above that of other regions or individuals.

- **ORGANIZATIONAL** – Each organization sets its own standards for employee behavior and interaction with competitors, customers, and suppliers. Employees are bound by those even if that may not be exactly the same as their personal ethics.

- **PERSONAL** – The dilemma comes when the ethical demands on one group conflict with the demands of another. Then the person must make a decision as to which set of ethics is preeminent. It is not uncommon that the ethics of an organization may be very different – either more strict – or more lax, than those of the employee. This is a difficult position for the employee to be in.

Ethical Responsibilities of all CISSPs

- "Set the example"

- Encourage adoption of ethical guidelines and standards

- Inform users about ethical responsibilities through security awareness training

59

- **"SET THE EXAMPLE"** – CISSPs not only know where the ethical boundaries are, but also must set the example for others. This often means making hard decisions and demonstrating strong ethical principles in their daily activities. (ISC)² has provided ethical guidelines to provide direction. Security professionals should adopt these guidelines and encourage others to do the same.

- **CISSPs CAN ENCOURAGE ADOPTION OF ETHICAL GUIDELINES AND STANDARDS** – Through the creation of statements of ethics, especially in relation to ethical use of Internet access, email, and other computer systems.

Basis and Origin of Ethics

- Religion
- Law
- National interest
- Individual rights
- Common good/interest
- Enlightened self-interest
- Professional ethics/practices
- Standards of good practice
- Tradition/culture

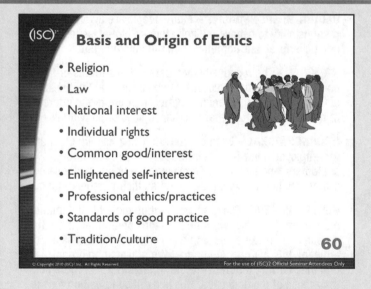

60

- **BASIS AND ORIGIN OF ETHICS** – There are many factors that influence a person's ethical beliefs – such as those listed here. It is easy to understand why there are so many different beliefs about what is "good ethical behavior." Not everyone sees ethics in the same way. This is why organizations need to provide ethical boundaries and interpretations for their employees.

- Some people define their ethics by law or religion, others by personal gain or advantage. Many people are bound by ethics through a social group or association they belong to. Since people enter a company with so many possible ethical interpretations, the company needs to define "its" ethical position and values, in order to provide guidance to its employees.

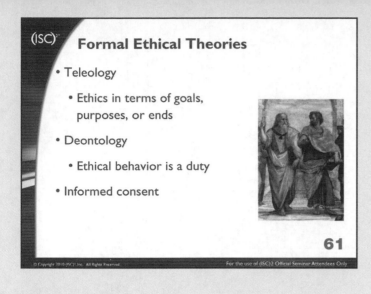

- **FORMAL ETHICAL THEORIES** – There are formal ethical theories beyond mere tradition or law. Most of these theories fall into one of two categories.

- **TELEOLOGY** – Teleological theories and approaches are based on outcomes. They try to provide the greatest good for the greatest number of individuals.

  - Utilitarianism, the most good for the most people.

- **DEONTOLOGY** – Deontological theories subscribe to the belief that each person has pre-existing requirements to do good. It is their duty to do so.

  - Many religions are deontological in their teachings.

- **INFORMED CONSENT** – Ethics may also be based on a conscious decision by the person involved to participate in a hazardous activity. This applies to experimental surgery, testing of a new pharmaceutical drug, or working in a hazardous environment. Informed consent requires the person involved to understand the possible implications and effects of his or her actions and be competent and able to make a decision.

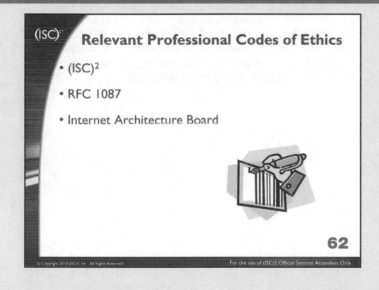

- **RELEVANT PROFESSIONAL CODES OF ETHICS** – There are several codes of ethics that apply to this discussion. However, we will focus on the (ISC)2 code of ethics over the next few slides. We will also note the published statements from the Internet Architecture Board (IAB) explaining what it considers ethical and appropriate behavior.

(ISC)² Code of Ethics Preamble

- "Safety of the commonwealth, duty to our principals, and to each other requires that we adhere, and be seen to adhere, to the highest ethical standards of behavior."

- "Therefore, strict adherence to this code is a condition of certification."

63

(ISC)² Code of Ethics Canons

- "Protect society, the commonwealth, and the infrastructure."

- "Act honorably, honestly, justly, responsibly, and legally."

- "Provide diligent and competent service to principals."

- "Advance and protect the profession."

64

- **(ISC)² CODE OF ETHICS CANONS –** These canons are listed in order of importance. It will not always be possible to apply all of the canons because there are situations in which they may conflict, such as where our responsibility to society may override our responsibility to our principals.

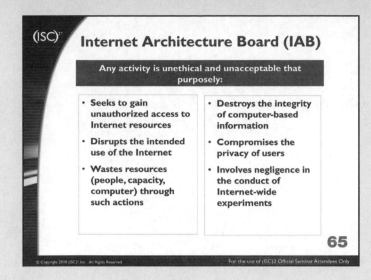

Internet Architecture Board (IAB)

Any activity is unethical and unacceptable that purposely:

- Seeks to gain unauthorized access to Internet resources
- Disrupts the intended use of the Internet
- Wastes resources (people, capacity, computer) through such actions

- Destroys the integrity of computer-based information
- Compromises the privacy of users
- Involves negligence in the conduct of Internet-wide experiments

65

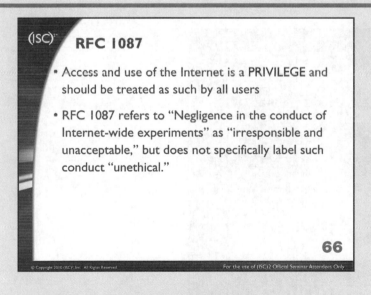

RFC 1087

- Access and use of the Internet is a PRIVILEGE and should be treated as such by all users

- RFC 1087 refers to "Negligence in the conduct of Internet-wide experiments" as "irresponsible and unacceptable," but does not specifically label such conduct "unethical."

66

REFERENCE:
ftp://ftp.rfc-editor.org/in-notes/rfc1087.txt

Domain Summary

- Information Security Management (ISMS)
  - Business Drivers
  - Governance
    - Roles and Responsibilities
    - Security Planning
    - Security Administration
- Risk Management
- Ethics

67

Security Transcends Technology

(ISC)²·

68

Review Questions

INFORMATION SECURITY, GOVERNANCE, AND RISK MANAGEMENT

1. **Which of the following is a standard rather than a policy?**
   - A. Data classification
   - B. Access control
   - C. Privacy
   - D. Ethernet

2. **Which of the following would include information security best practices?**
   - A. ISO 25999
   - B. "Taking candy from a baby"
   - C. ISO 27002
   - D. Understanding that ethics are situational

3. **Which of the following is correct?**
   - A. ALE = ARO x EF
   - B. ARO = EF x SLE
   - C. ALE = SLE x ARO
   - D. SRO = ALE x SLE

4. **IT systems are normally operated by**
   - A. auditors.
   - B. custodians.
   - C. CISSPs.
   - D. management.

5. **From a security perspective, mandatory vacations**
   - A. make it easier to detect fraud.
   - B. keep employees fresh.
   - C. make it easier to find out who can be replaced.
   - D. comply with the least privilege principle.

6. **Security awareness**
   - A. is the same as professional education.
   - B. includes background checks and verifying education.
   - C. makes it easy to find out who is a security risk.
   - D. begins the first day of employment.

7. **Which one of the following is a primary step in qualitative risk analysis?**
   - A. Develop scenarios
   - B. Conduct a threat analysis
   - C. Determine annual loss expectancy
   - D. Estimate potential losses

8. **Guidelines are**
   - A. recommendations.
   - B. the same as standards.
   - C. mandatory.
   - D. part of high-level policy statements.

9. **It is possible to**
   - A. totally eliminate risk.
   - B. do a totally qualitative risk assessment.
   - C. do a totally quantitative risk assessment.
   - D. have ARO equal a negative number when doing a qualitative risk assessment.

10. **When establishing the value of information, the least important factor is what?**
    - A. Trade secrets
    - B. Operational impact
    - C. Value of the information to others
    - D. Quantity of information

11. **Which of the following is the FIRST (ISC)² canon?**
    - A. Advance and protect the profession.
    - B. Protect society, the commonwealth, and the infrastructure.
    - C. Provide competent service to principals.
    - D. Act honorably, honestly, justly, responsibly, and legally.

12. **Risk management principles include all the following except**
    - A. avoidance.
    - B. ignorance.
    - C. acceptance.
    - D. mitigation.

13. **Assurance mechanisms provide us with**
    - A. confidence in the appropriateness of controls.
    - B. the SLE during risk assessment.
    - C. a measure of the likelihood of security breaches.
    - D. the standards to be followed to be compliant with policy.

14. **When selecting countermeasures,**

   A. we should always select the most expensive because they provide better security.
   B. cost must exceed or equal the benefit obtained.
   C. cost of the countermeasure should be less than the value of the asset.
   D. technical countermeasures are better than operational ones.

15. **Which is least likely to be the basis for personal ethics?**

   A. Mandated actions
   B. Law/justice/sense of fairness
   C. Religious beliefs
   D. Professional code of ethics

16. **The right amount of security is**

   A. the more secure, the better.
   B. based on the analysis of the users.
   C. determined by the level of acceptable risk.
   D. impossible to achieve.

17. **Information classification is the responsibility of**

   A. executive management.
   B. information owner.
   C. data custodians.
   D. IT system owner.

18. **IT Governance is made up of which of these components:**

   I. Roles and Responsibilities
   II. Security Planning
   III. Security Administration
   IV. Risk Assessment

   A. I, II, III
   B. I, II, IV
   C. I, III, IV
   D. II, III, IV

19. **Which of the following is the definition of risk acceptance?**

   A. Not mitigating the risk and absorbing the cost when and if it occurs.
   B. Passing risk to another party.
   C. Discontinuing the activity due to the identified risk.
   D. Providing countermeasures to reduce the risk and strengthen the security posture.

20. **Qualitative risk assessments are scenario-based and are measured by**

   A. percentages.
   B. calculation of ARO.
   C. high/medium/low.
   D. dollar values.

Legal, Regulations, Investigations, and Compliance

1

Domain Objectives

- The student will obtain a basic working knowledge of:

  - Computer crime

  - International legal issues

  - Incident response

  - Forensic investigation

  - Compliance

2

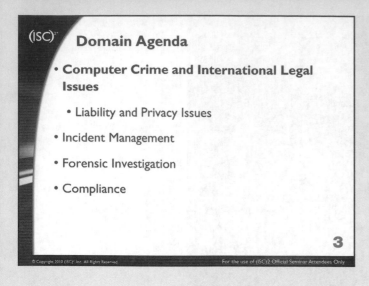

This slide presents the agenda for this domain. We will start by talking about computer crime and international legal issues.

COMMON LAW – May roughly be considered "judge-made law." Common law is a system of law derived from judicial decisions, rather than statutes or ordinances passed by the legislative branch of government. Common law emerged from the imposition of a universal legal system by a centralized power in 11th-century England.

CIVIL LAW – Disputes are settled by reference to written legal codes, derived typically from legislation. Civil law is highly systematized and structured and relies on declarations of broad, general principles, often ignoring the details. Civil law is the most widespread legal system. The Roman legal system introduced this emphasis on written legal codes.

RELIGIOUS LAW – An example of religious law is Muslim law, which is practiced by a significant portion of the world's population. Law is considered to be decreed by a Supreme Being. Lawmakers and law scholars do not create laws, they attempt to discover the truth of law.

CUSTOMARY LAW – Customary law consists of the written and unwritten rules which have developed from the customs and traditions of communities.

MIXED LAW – A combination of legal systems. For example, common law and civil law.

- NOTE: Maritime law is not addressed in this discussion,

although it is an excellent example of the harmonization of international law.

CRIMINAL LAW – Criminal law falls under the umbrella of common law, and tends to be the legal system most people have seen on TV, movies, etc.

- DEALS WITH BEHAVIOR OR CONDUCT – Common law deals with addressing the behaviors or conduct that are seen as harmful to the general public and/or society in general.

- TYPICALLY THE PUNISHMENT METED OUT BY THE CRIMINAL COURTS INVOLVES SOME LOSS OF PERSONAL FREEDOM FOR THE GUILTY PARTY – Incarceration, punishment, including monetary punishments in the way of fines, or restitution to the court or victim are not uncommon.

PRINCIPLES OF A TORT –

- DUTY – The defendant must owe a legal duty to the victim. A duty is a legally enforceable obligation to conform to a particular standard of conduct. Except in malpractice and strict liability cases, the duty is set by what a "reasonable man of ordinary prudence" would have done. There is a general duty to prevent foreseeable injury to a victim.

- BREACH OF THE DUTY – The defendant breached that duty.

- CAUSATION – The breach was the cause of an injury to the victim. The causation does not need to be direct: Defendant's act (or failure to act) could begin a continuous sequence of events that ended in plaintiff's injury, a so-called "proximate cause."

- DAMAGES (INJURY) – There must be an injury. In most cases, there must be a physical or financial injury to the victim, but sometimes emotional distress, embarrassment, or dignitary harms are adequate for recovery.

  - As a recent example, the loss of personal information from stolen laptops raises the fear of identity theft. If a person were to sue the company then the first three elements are made, but unless someone is actually harmed, the court will dismiss (grant summary judgment should a case even be brought).

- **CATEGORIES OF A TORT –**

  - **INTENTIONAL TORTS –** Assault, battery, false imprisonment, intentional infliction of emotional distress.

  - **WRONGS AGAINST A PERSON –** Automobile accident, slip and fall, dog bite.

  - **WRONGS AGAINST PROPERTY –** Nuisance against nearby landowner.

  - **DIGNITARY WRONGS –**

    - Invasion of privacy: intrusion on seclusion, unreasonable publicity given to private life, publicity placing person in false light.

    - Civil rights violations.

  - **ECONOMIC WRONGS –** Patent infringement, copyright infringement, "unfair competition," trademark infringement.

  - **NEGLIGENCE –** Wrongful death.

  - **NUISANCE –** Trespassing.

    - **STRICT LIABILITY –** Defect in either manufacturing or design of product, failure to warn of risks.

- **ADMINISTRATIVE LAW –** Also known in some countries as regulatory law.

  - **LAW CREATED BY ADMINISTRATIVE AGENCIES BY WAY OF RULES, REGULATIONS, ORDERS, AND DECISIONS –** Administrative law encompasses the laws and legal principles defining the powers, procedures, processes, and acts of administrative agencies. Administrative authority entails the power for rulemaking, adjudication, or enforcement of a specific regulatory agenda based on the course of agency's operation.

  - **AREAS COVERED BY ADMINISTRATIVE LAW –** Considered a branch of public law, administrative law deals with diverse areas such as international trade, manufacturing, environment, taxation, broadcasting, immigration, and transport.

REFERENCES:

http://www.bartleby.com

The Columbia Encyclopedia, Sixth Edition 2001-05

http://www.law.cornell.edu/wex/index.php/Administrative_law

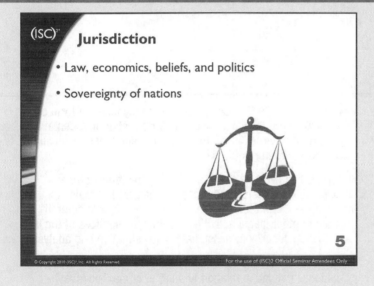

- **JURISDICTION –** Law enforcement organizations can, and do, work together to pursue and prosecute criminals despite jurisdictional or, possibly, international boundaries. However, when there are conflicts in economics, beliefs, or politics, such organizations may work against each other and compete for evidence or jurisdictional rights to enforce the law.

- **SOVEREIGNTY –** Laws, of course, are different from country to country and cannot always be enforced across international boundaries. In order to stop criminals from taking advantage of this legal loophole, nations are making efforts to harmonize their laws with other nations in order to promote uniform enforcement and cooperation where possible.

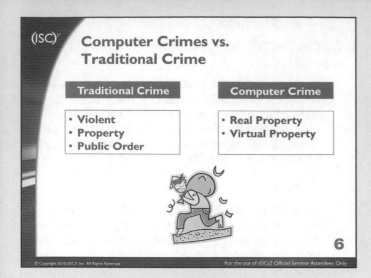

TRADITIONAL CRIME – Traditional crime is typically categorized into three areas: violent crime, property crime, and public crime.

- Violent crime: A crime where the offender uses, or threatens to use, violence against the victim.

- Property crime: Burglary, theft, larceny, arson, vandalism.

- Public order crime: Siegel (2004) defines both public order crime and victimless crime as "crime which involves acts

that interfere with the operations of society and the ability of people to function efficiently."

- **TWO SEPARATE WORLDS OF CRIME ARE NOW OVERLAPPING:**

  - The traditional world of crime is now increasingly using computers in order to facilitate crime (e.g., identity theft, child pornography and exploitation, fraud, banking scams, and drug trafficking).

  - The second world involves computer crimes such as hacking, denial of service attacks, virus replication, and network intrusions. As yet, law enforcement is generally unprepared to deal with this second world.

- **COMPUTER CRIME** – Computer crime takes many forms. It is an expanding criminal activity and new methods are being devised every day. This puts ever-increasing demands on law enforcement agencies to keep up with technological advances, the vulnerabilities introduced by the advances, and the criminals who exploit them. A distinction that is important here is that computer crime is harder to detect, increasingly sophisticated, and can involve tangible as well as intangible assets (e.g., intellectual property).

REFERENCES:
http://www.fdle.state.fl.us/fc3/
http://www.apsu.edu/oconnort/3010/3010lect07.htm

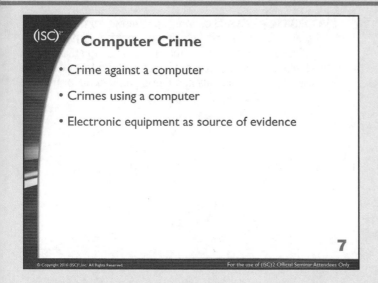

- **COMPUTER CRIME** – Computer crime may take the form of an attack directly against a computer or network. A denial of service or virus, for example, is an attack that specifically targets computer equipment.

- **CRIMES USING A COMPUTER** – Many traditional crimes now use computers. While these crimes are not really a "computer" crime per se, the use of a computer to commit fraud or other illegal activities requires the services of the information security professional for investigation and analysis.

- **SOURCE OF EVIDENCE** – The computer is often a source of evidence needed in relation to another crime. The investigation of mobile phones, cameras, and laptops can all be sources of evidence. In fact, most network devices can be sources of evidence.

- All of these are an important part of forensics today.

REFERENCES:
http://www.usdoj.gov/criminal/cybercrime/cc.html
http://www.rbs2.com/ccrime.htm

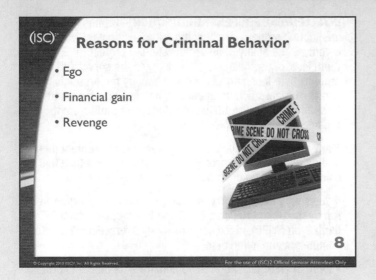

Reasons for Criminal Behavior

- Ego
- Financial gain
- Revenge

8

- **REASONS FOR CRIMINAL BEHAVIOR –** There are many reasons that a person decides to commit a known crime. In many cases the justification process criminals go through in their minds actually leads to them believing that their actions are justified. Former employees may believe that the company "owes" them something and any actions that they do are right.

- **EGO –** Many criminals are motivated by a need to prove themselves. They use the risk and challenge to demonstrate their skill to their friends or co-conspirators.

- **FINANCIAL GAIN –** Financial gain is perhaps the most common reason for crime. The criminal steals money, intellectual property, or other valuables for his or her benefit or the benefit of another party.

- **REVENGE –** Revenge is often undertaken as a way to "get back at" a company or individual that has "wronged" the perpetrator. This may be an activist who does not approve of the company's ethics or business model, it may be politically motivated, or even a disgruntled customer who is unhappy with a service or product received.

- **COUNTERMEASURES –** The security specialist needs to take steps to prevent, detect and react to criminal behavior. Depending on the type of motivation for the crime, the best prevention may be a deterrent, reducing the opportunity for crime, or increasing the difficulty level.

REFERENCE:
http://www.crime-research.org/

International Cooperation

- Initiatives related to international cooperation in dealing with computer crime

- The Council of Europe (CoE) Cybercrime Convention

2000

COUNCIL CONSEIL
OF EUROPE DE L'EUROPE

9

- **INTERNATIONAL COOPERATION –** Law enforcement is working together through organizations such as federal police forces, Interpol, and other agencies to address the problems of computer-based crime. Some of the key initiatives are investigating child pornography, money laundering, terrorism, and botnets.

- **INITIATIVES RELATED TO INTERNATIONAL COOPERATION IN DEALING WITH COMPUTER CRIME –** Computer crime is international in scope and, therefore, requires an international solution rather than a domestic approach based on archaic concepts of borders and jurisdictions.

- International responses to computer crime have met with mixed results. The Council of Europe (CoE) Cybercrime Convention is a prime example of a multilateral attempt to draft an international response to criminal behaviors targeted at technology and the Internet. One of the Cybercrime Convention's stated objectives is to assist international enforcement efforts by creating a framework for domestication and cooperation between ratifying states regarding issues related to establishing jurisdiction as well as extradition of the accused.

- **EXTRADITION IS ONLY AVAILABLE, HOWEVER:**

  - By treaty.

  - Generally, when there has been a crime under both jurisdictions (for example, France can't extradite the eBay CEO because of auctions of Nazi memorabilia – a crime in France, but protected speech in the United States).

  - When parties have ensured that law enforcement officials have the authority to investigate and prosecute cybercrime, as well as assist international cooperation in the fight against computer-related crime.

REFERENCE:
http://conventions.coe.int/Treaty/EN/Treaties/HTML/185.htm

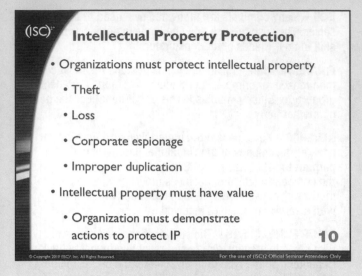

Intellectual Property Protection

- Organizations must protect intellectual property
  - Theft
  - Loss
  - Corporate espionage
  - Improper duplication
- Intellectual property must have value
  - Organization must demonstrate actions to protect IP

10

- **INTELLECTUAL PROPERTY PROTECTION** – Crimes against intellectual property are becoming increasingly relevant and common. The ability of an organization to protect its IP from theft, loss, or espionage is often a key to the survival of the organization. If one firm is allowed to copy the products of another organization unhindered, that copying may result in loss of market, competitive advantage, and profit from the organization it was copied from.

- Many organizations today aggressively seek to protect their IP and do not hesitate to prosecute any organization they feel is using their IP in an unauthorized manner.

- IP laws vary from country to country but the main organization run by the United Nations, the World Intellectual Property Organization (WIPO), is the common body overseeing IP-related complaints and enforcement.

- Failure of an organization to demonstrate its desire to protect its IP may result in the loss of the IP.

REFERENCES:
www.wipo.int
www.irawinkler.com – author of the book 'The Spies Among Us'

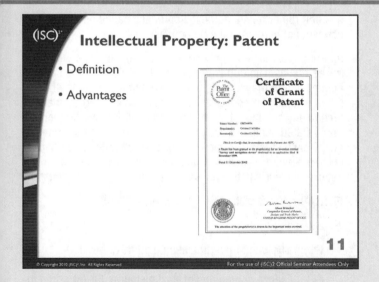

Intellectual Property: Patent

- Definition
- Advantages

Certificate of Grant of Patent

11

- **PATENTS** – Patents protect novel, useful, and non-obvious inventions. The World Intellectual Property Organization (WIPO), an agency of the United Nations, looks after the filing and processing of international patent applications. WIPO rules do not override national patent rules (e.g., time periods) unless the sovereign nation has agreed by treaty to accept WIPO.

- **ADVANTAGES:**

  - Patents are the strongest form of intellectual property protection.

  - The patent owner has a legally enforceable right to prevent others from using the patented invention for a specific period of time (usually 20 years).

  - Once a patent is granted, it is published in the public domain in order to stimulate other innovations.

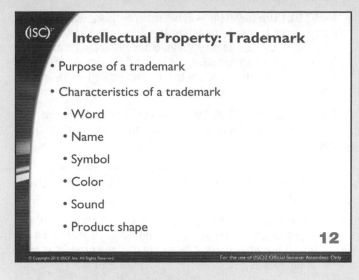

PURPOSE OF A TRADEMARK –

- Protects the "good will" that merchants or vendors invest in the recognition of their products.

- Gives the owner of the markings exclusive rights over the item for which the trademark was granted.

CHARACTERISTICS OF A TRADEMARK –

- A trademark can be any:

  - Word.

  - Name.

  - Symbol.

  - Color.

  - Sound.

  - Product shape.

  - Device.

- It is possible that the trademark could be a combination of these used to identify goods and distinguish them from those made or sold by others.

- NOTE: You cannot trademark a number or common word. This is why Intel invented the word Pentium (as Standard Oil did with Exxon, 20 years ago). Unique colors can be trademarked, thus "Novell Red" and "UPS Brown." Identifiable packaging (such as an M&M bag) is called "Trade Dress."

- Trademarks are registered with a government registrar.

- The World Intellectual Property Organization (WIPO) oversees international trademark law efforts, including international registration.

- International harmonization of trademark laws began in 1883 with the Paris Convention that prompted the Madrid Agreement of 1891.

REFERENCE:
http://www.uspto.gov/web/offices/pac/doc/general/index.html#ptsc

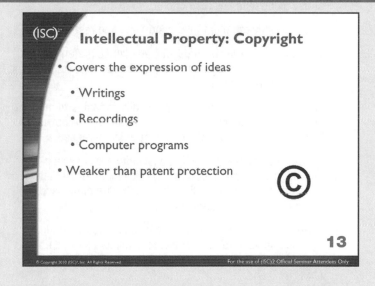

- **COPYRIGHT COVERS THE EXPRESSION OF IDEAS –** Rather than the ideas themselves.

  - It protects artistic property such as writings and recordings, and protects computer programs from direct copying of the source code or software logic.

- **WEAKER THAN PATENT PROTECTION –** Copyright protection is weaker than patent protection, but the duration of the period of protection is considerably longer: e.g., 75 years under United States copyright laws.

  - NOTE: U.S. law was recently amended and some copyrights have been extended, depending on the date of issue, whether the holder is living or dead, or whether the holder is a corporation. Time periods vary by holder; for example, individuals are given a copyright of their own lifetime plus 50 years.

- The international Berne Convention provides a minimal amount of protection for citizens of member countries. Not all countries are members, however!

- NOTE: In most countries, once the work or property is completed or is in a tangible form, copyright protection is automatically assumed.

REFERENCE:
http://fairuse.stanford.edu/

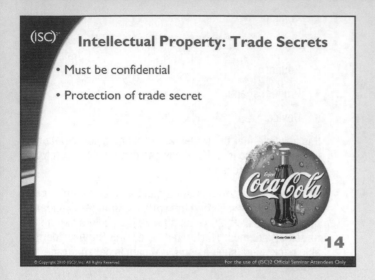

Intellectual Property: Trade Secrets

- Must be confidential
- Protection of trade secret

14

- **INTELLECTUAL PROPERTY: TRADE SECRETS –** Intellectual property refers to proprietary business or technical information, processes, designs, practices, etc., that are confidential and critical to the business.

- **MUST BE CONFIDENTIAL –** In order to be categorized as a trade secret, the trade secret must not be common knowledge and it must provide some economic benefit to the company. It may provide a competitive advantage, for example, or at the very least allow the company to compete equally in the marketplace. A good example is Coca Cola's beverages formulae.

- **PROTECTION OF TRADE SECRET –** The organization must demonstrate that it has taken reasonable steps to protect its trade secrets.

  - Trade secrets are often at the heart of industrial and economic espionage cases and are the proverbial crown jewels of some companies.

  - NOTE: There is no expiration date for trade secrets. They expire only if the trade secret is no longer secret or if it no longer has an economic benefit (e.g., if the product is out of production).

REFERENCE:
http://www.ipwatchdog.com/tradesecret.html

Intellectual Property: Software Licensing

- Categories of software licensing:
  - Freeware
  - Shareware
  - Commercial
  - Academic
- Master agreements and end user licensing agreements (EULAs)

15

- **CATEGORIES OF SOFTWARE LICENSING:**

  - **FREEWARE –** Is software which can be used, copied, studied, modified, and redistributed without restriction.

  - **SHAREWARE –** Is a marketing method for commercial software, whereby a trial version is distributed in advance and without payment, as is common for proprietary software. Shareware software is typically obtained free of charge, either by downloading from the Internet or on magazine cover-disks. A user is able to try out the program, and thus shareware has also been known as "try before you buy," demoware, trialware, and by many other names.

  - **COMMERCIAL –** Is computer software sold for commercial purposes, or that serves commercial purposes.

- **ACADEMIC –** Is a software license available for restricted use by teachers, students, or other approved purposes.

- **MASTER AGREEMENTS AND END USER LICENSING AGREEMENTS (EULAS) –** EULAs are the most prevalent method of specifying usage rights.

  - Master agreements set out the general overall conditions of use along with any restrictions.

  - EULAs specify more granular conditions and restrictions.

  - Various third parties have developed license metering software to ensure and enforce compliance with software licensing agreements.

  - With high-speed Internet access readily available to most employees, the ability – if not the temptation – to download and use pirated software has greatly increased.

  - Prevalence and frequency of illegal software is exceedingly high, 36 percent worldwide. This would mean that for every two dollars worth of legal software purchased, one dollar's worth of software was pirated.

  - These numbers are often used to calculate losses under the assumption that everyone who is using a pirated copy would have bought it had the pirate copy not been available.

  - Though not all countries recognize the forms of intellectual property protection previously discussed, the work of several international organizations and industrialized countries seems to be somewhat successful in curbing the official sanctioning of intellectual property rights violations (i.e., software piracy).

Encryption Import and Export Law

- Strong encryption restrictions
- No enemy states
- Controls on dual-use goods
- Wassenaar Arrangement

Wassenaar Arrangement
on Export Controls for Conventional Arms and Dual-Use Goods and Technologies

16

- **ENCRYPTION IMPORT AND EXPORT LAW –** Previously, United States export law prohibited the exportation of encryption software that was capable of using a key larger than 40 bits.

- **STRONG ENCRYPTION RESTRICTIONS –** This was considered "strong" encryption. This law also prohibited the exportation of software with drop-in or plug-in encryption capabilities because it could be easily modified. United States companies can now export any encryption software to individuals, commercial firms, or other non-government end users in any country.

- **NO ENEMY STATES –** Many countries have had laws regarding the import of cryptographic tools. These laws frequently required the importer of equipment containing strong cryptography to provide the government or law enforcement with a copy of their private keys. The regulations do not change restrictions on exports to countries that are classified as state supporters of terrorism, including Cuba, Iran, Iraq, Libya, North Korea, Sudan, and Syria.

- **CONTROLS ON DUAL-USE GOODS –** Cryptography has long been considered a munition, or a weapon of war. Therefore many countries restricted its use as they would other military weapons. Since cryptography can be used both for commercial purposes, as well as military purposes, it can be considered a dual-use product and is protected as a military weapon even if it is intended to be used in a commercial environment.

- **WASSENAAR ARRANGEMENT –** Thirty-nine countries are parties to the Wassenaar Arrangement which specifies all controlled dual-use goods, including encryption products and products that use encryption.

REFERENCES:

http://www.bis.doc.gov/encryption/

http://www.cisco.com/web/about/doing_business/legal/global_export_trade/general_export

http://www.wassenaar.org/index.html

Domain Agenda

- Computer Crime and International Legal Issues
  - **Liability and Privacy Issues**
- Incident Management
- Forensic Investigation
- Compliance

17

- The next section of the course will look more specifically at legal issues related to:
  - Liability.
  - Negligence.
  - Protection of privacy and personally identifiable information (PII).

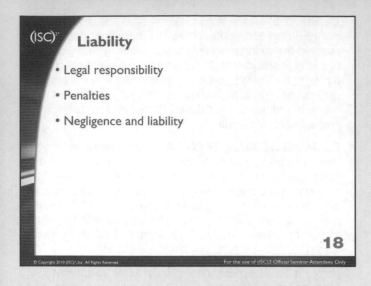

Liability

- Legal responsibility
- Penalties
- Negligence and liability

18

- **LIABILITY** – In the western world's increasingly litigious culture, concepts such as liability, due care, and reasonableness become particularly important.

- **LEGAL RESPONSIBILITY** – When organizations are weighing the costs versus benefits of certain actions, inactions, and exposure to lawsuits, then demonstrating reasonable corporate behavior, security controls, and overall due diligence becomes very important. The organization, and the individuals who make up the organization, are responsible for protecting others from unreasonable harm.

  - For example, negligence can be claimed if the organization does not provide adequate safety gear or training.

- **PENALTIES** – Penalties for negligent actions can range from compensation for the aggrieved party, to criminal penalties for violation of law.

- **NEGLIGENCE AND LIABILITY** – Negligence is an important factor in determining liability.

  - NOTE: However, concepts such as negligence are ethereal, and will in fact be determined by the courts or other quasi-legal body.

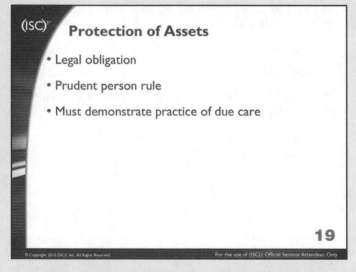

Protection of Assets

- Legal obligation
- Prudent person rule
- Must demonstrate practice of due care

19

- Cash.

- Personnel.

- Customers.

- The local community.

- Management must be able to demonstrate how it has worked to execute those responsibilities through:

  - Due care.

  - Monitoring.

  - Policy.

  - Physical protection.

  - Due diligence.

- **PRUDENT PERSON RULE** – The general test for appropriate and responsible protection of assets is often referred to as the "prudent person rule." It considers what actions a careful person would take to protect the assets of the organization from harm or unnecessary risk.

- **MUST DEMONSTRATE DUE CARE** – The obligation is on the trusted person to show attention to providing adequate protection. The aggrieved or injured party often has an advantage in proving that the level of care was not adequate, since the party can demonstrate that he or she has suffered some level of harm.

- **LEGAL OBLIGATION** – Fiduciary responsibility addresses the responsibility of a trusted person to carefully and prudently protect the assets or interests of others who trust or depend on that person.

  - An employer has a responsibility to protect employees.

  - Parent to protect children.

  - Vendor to protect clients, etc.

  - Recognition of this responsibility is demonstrated through careful and planned approaches to safeguarding assets. The organization has a responsibility to protect the assets it has:

REFERENCE:
http://www.investopedia.com/articles/08/fiduciary-responsiblity.asp

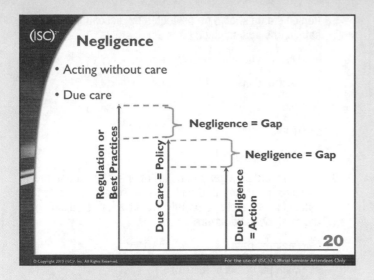

ACTING WITHOUT CARE – Negligence can be defined as acting without care, or failing to act as a reasonable and prudent person would under similar circumstances. Part of an adequate security program is to determine:

- The gap between best practice and the organization's current security posture (due care).

- The gap between the intent of policy and other controls.

- The effectiveness of the controls (due diligence).

DUE CARE

- Due care is the requirement that officers and other executives with fiduciary responsibilities meet certain requirements to protect the company's assets.

- "Due care" and "due diligence" are terms that have found their way into discussions of corporate governance.

- These requirements include the safety and protection of technology and information systems that fall under the term "corporate assets."

- **DUE DILIGENCE** – "Due diligence" is an ethereal concept that is often judged against a continually moving benchmark, or the degree of prudence that might be properly

expected from a reasonable person in the circumstances. While due care is often seen to be the steps taken prior to an incident to provide adequate protection and controls, due diligence is often seen as the need to follow up and ensure that the controls and protection implemented as due care are then working correctly.

- **REQUIRES A COMMITMENT TO ONGOING RISK ANALYSIS AND RISK MANAGEMENT PROCESSES**

  - The dynamic nature of information security requires a commitment to ongoing risk analysis and risk management processes, a good understanding of generally accepted business and information security practices within the applicable industry, as well as international standards and those dictated by legislation and/or regulations.

  - The increase in government scrutiny of information system practices has resulted in many companies allocating their security budgets to this process in order to be compliant with the various current, and pending, regulatory requirements.

  - Some estimates indicate that information security budgets will rise from the current average of approximately 5 percent of the overall IT budget to as much as 15 percent in direct response to requirements for regulatory compliance.

- **DUE CARE VS. DUE DILIGENCE** –

  - **DUE CARE** – Setting policy: Avoid actions that would create an unsafe or hostile work environment.

  - **DUE DILIGENCE** – Enforcing policy: Take actions such as monitoring firewalls and training to enforce the intent of policy.

  - Simply stated, due care is saying and doing what you will do, while due diligence is ensuring that your actions are working.

  - Due care can be equated to doing the right thing and due diligence to ensuring that due care actions are effective.

REFERENCES:

Due Care: http://dictionary.law.com/default2.asp?typed=due+care&type=1
Diligence: http://dictionary.law.com/default2.asp?selected=515&bold=Diligencellduell

---

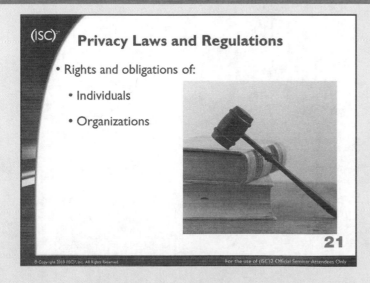

RIGHTS AND OBLIGATIONS – Privacy laws address the rights

and obligations of individuals and organizations.

- **INDIVIDUALS** – The threat of identity theft and breach of personal security has led many individuals to take steps to prevent the loss or misuse of their personal data.

- **ORGANIZATIONS** – Privacy is one of the primary areas where business – in virtually every industry – is forced to deal with regulations and regulatory compliance. An organization requires information in order to accomplish its mission, but the organization must be familiar with the regulations and the expectations of customers regarding:

  - Collection.

  - Sharing.

  - Storage.

  - Processing of personal information.

- The actual enactment of regulations or laws dealing with privacy depends on the jurisdiction.

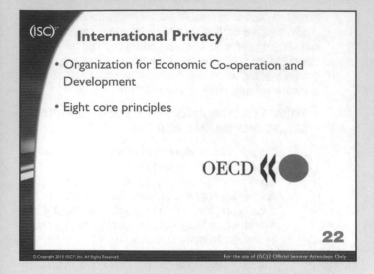

- **PRIVACY AND THE ORGANIZATION FOR ECONOMIC CO-OP-ERATION AND DEVELOPMENT (OECD) –** The OECD is a group of 30 member countries sharing a commitment to democratic government and the market economy. It has eight core principles pertaining to the protection of privacy and personal information.

- **EIGHT CORE PRINCIPLES -**

  1. There should be limits to the collection of personal data and any such data should be obtained by lawful and fair means and, where appropriate, with the knowledge or consent of the data subject.

  2. Personal data should be relevant to the purposes for which they are to be used and, to the extent necessary for those purposes, should be accurate, complete and kept up to date.

  3. The purposes for which personal data are collected should be specified no later than at the time of data collection. The subsequent use of personal data must be limited to the fulfillment of those purposes for which it was collected or such others as are not incompatible with those purposes and as are specified on each occasion of change of purpose.

  4. Personal data should not be disclosed, made available, or otherwise used for purposes other than those specified above except:

     - With the consent of the data subject.

     - By the authority of law.

  5. Personal data should be protected by reasonable security safeguards against such risks as:

     - Loss or unauthorized access.

     - Destruction.

     - Use.

     - Modification.

     - Disclosure of data.

  6. There should be a general policy of openness about developments, practices, and policies with respect to personal data. Means should be readily available for establishing the existence and nature of:

     - Personal data.

     - Main purposes of their use.

     - Identity and usual residence of the data controller.

  7. An individual should have the right:

     - To obtain from a data controller, or otherwise, confirmation of whether or not the data controller has data relating to him or her.

     - To have communicated to him or her any data relating to him or her:

       - Within a reasonable time.

       - At a charge, if any, that is not excessive.

       - In a reasonable manner.

       - In a form that is readily intelligible to him or her.

       - To be given reasons if a request made is denied, and to be able to challenge such denial.

     - To challenge data relating to him or her and, if the challenge is successful, to have the data erased, rectified, completed, or amended.

  8. A data controller should be accountable for complying with measures that give effect to the principles stated above.

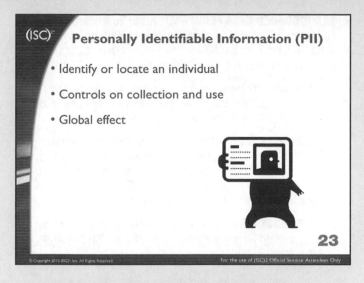

- Fax number.
- Email address.
- Financial profiles.
- Social security number.
- Credit card information.
- NOTE: PII does not include information that is collected anonymously or demographic information not connected to an identified individual.

- **CONTROLS ON COLLECTION AND USE** – Many countries have passed national legislation addressing the policy concerns resulting from personal information collection and use.

- **GLOBAL EFFECT** – Differences in these national laws cause some confusion when a company is moving information across national borders. Strong privacy protections for citizens of one country may be undermined if a citizen of that country:

  - Purchases a product from another country.
  - Travels to another country.
  - Communicates by email outside the country.

REFERENCES:
http://www.p3pwriter.com/LRN_000.asp
http://www.accessmylibrary.com/coms2/summary_0286-23465925_ITM

- **PERSONALLY IDENTIFIABLE INFORMATION (PII)** – Refers to information that identifies or can be used to identify, contact, or locate the person to whom the information pertains.

- **IDENTIFY OR LOCATE AN INDIVIDUAL** – This information may include linking it with information identified from other sources, including, but not limited to:

  - Name.
  - Address.
  - Telephone number.

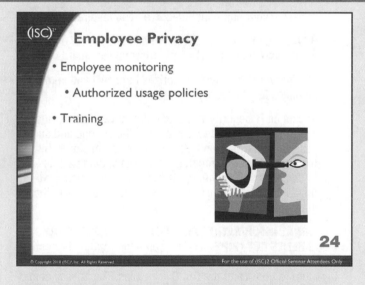

- **AUTHORIZED USAGE POLICIES** – There are usually exceptions to REP that allow monitoring of Internet usage, email, and telephone (e.g., VoIP), including:

  - Court orders.
  - Corporations' right to protect their interests.
  - Waivers of REP – employees signing usage policies, etc., waiving their expectation of privacy. Waivers are probably the most popular exception used today.
  - Make sure you have the legal right to waive your REP. (For example, you and your spouse use the laptop your boss gave you to use. You may have no REP, but does your spouse? Did your waiver apply to him/her?) Make sure your employees have a legal right to waive their REPs. For example, does the spouse of an employee using the employer's laptop have a REP?
  - Different countries will answer this question differently.

- **TRAINING** – Training ensures employees know and follow company policy and, in the event of litigation, training will limit the company's exposure.

REFERENCE:
http://www.gcn.com/online/vol1_no1/42852-1.html

- **EMPLOYEE PRIVACY** – Organizations and businesses have varying approaches to handling employee privacy issues. These approaches are often related to local labor laws and the level of risk for the business.

- **EMPLOYEE MONITORING**

  - Laws regulating a business's right to monitor employees are different between countries.
  - Businesses do not have carte blanche in monitoring their employees. The concept of a reasonable expectation of privacy (REP) is usually of central importance here.

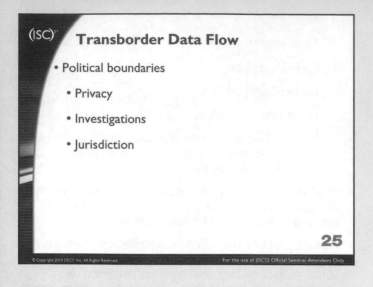

Transborder Data Flow

- Political boundaries
  - Privacy
  - Investigations
  - Jurisdiction

25

- **TRANSBORDER DATA FLOW** – When the flow of electronic data crosses political boundaries between countries or states, legal conflicts may arise over the ownership of the information and over who is entitled to use it.

  - **PRIVACY** – This has been a growing concern due to privacy laws and the increasing amount of data that is permitted to cross political boundaries.

  - **INVESTIGATIONS** – This is a concern when an organization operates in several countries with differing privacy laws, or when an organization outsources a function to a company operating in another jurisdiction that requires the transmission of data to another country.

  - **JURISDICTION** – The nature of networks also impacts jurisdiction for investigation and information gathering by law enforcement.

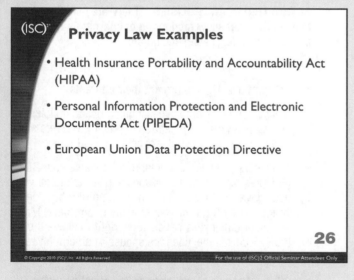

Privacy Law Examples

- Health Insurance Portability and Accountability Act (HIPAA)

- Personal Information Protection and Electronic Documents Act (PIPEDA)

- European Union Data Protection Directive

26

to having your name included in a hospital directory.

- HIPAA requires staff training, the appointment of a privacy officer, and the establishment of formal safeguards.

- The HIPAA Privacy Rule authorizes both civil and criminal penalties for violations.

- Impact on IT, security, and audit: Whenever patient data is stored or transmitted, a record of the change and an associated permission linked to a document signed by the patient must be recorded. Patients should be able to decipher the potential path of their information, and most importantly, must legally be granted access to that information.

- **PERSONAL INFORMATION PROTECTION AND ELECTRONIC DOCUMENTS ACT (PIPEDA)** – Personal Information Protection and Electronic Documents Act (PIPEDA) from Canada is similar in nature to HIPAA and the OECD principles. The privacy commissioner of Canada oversees compliance with the Privacy Act and the Personal Information Protection and Electronic Documents Act (PIPEDA), Canada's private sector privacy law.

- **EUROPEAN UNION DATA PROTECTION DIRECTIVE** – European Union Data Protection Directive, Article 28, deals specifically with IT professionals and audit. In each EU state, an independent agency monitors and enforces the legislation.

REFERENCES:
http://www.privacyrights.org/fs/fs8a-hipaa.htm – HIPAA
http://www.privcom.gc.ca/aboutUs/index_e.asp
http://www.bis.org/publ/bcbs107.htm

- **PRIVACY LAW EXAMPLES** – This is a list of some of the better-known privacy laws.

- **THE HEALTH INSURANCE PORTABILITY AND ACCOUNTABILITY ACT (HIPAA)** – The Health Insurance Portability and Accountability Act (HIPAA) was passed by Congress in 1996 to set a national standard for electronic transfers of health data. At the same time, Congress saw the need to address growing public concern about privacy and security of personal health data.

  - Before HIPAA, your right to privacy with respect to health information varied depending on what state you lived in, and access to your own medical records was not guaranteed by federal law. You now have a choice when it comes

Domain Agenda

- Computer Crime and International Legal Issues

  - Liability and Privacy Issues

- **Incident Management**

- Forensic Investigation

- Compliance

27

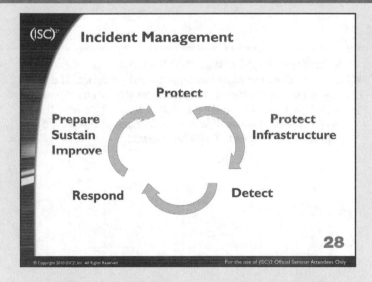

Incident Management

28

- **INCIDENT MANAGEMENT** – Is about proactively preparing for, and reactively responding to, an incident.

- **INCIDENT** – Any event that has the potential to negatively impact the business or its assets

- Proactive measures include steps to prepare/sustain/improve response capability and to protect the infrastructure when an incident does occur. The reactive process is called **INCIDENT RESPONSE (IR)** and includes the steps to detect events, triage, and respond. All of these components must be determined by organizational policy. The next slides will examine each step in more detail.

- **INCIDENT RESPONSE IS THE PRACTICE OF:**

  - Detecting a problem.

  - Determining cause.

  - Minimizing damage.

  - Resolving the problem.

  - NOTE: Each step in the response process should be recorded for future reference.

- Incident response has become one of the primary functions of today's information security department. The increased importance is due to ever increasing attacks against networks. The three main elements of incident response are:

  1. **DETECTION,** which involves logging and alerting internal or external events that may lead to an incident.

  2. **TRIAGE,** which consists of detection, classification, prioritization, and notification. The goal in triage is to understand the situation.

  3. **RESPONSE,** which is about executing the pre-planned procedures and capabilities based upon the situation.

- Incident response and computer or network forensics are different disciplines. Both are investigative in nature, but forensics assumes that the evidence will have to be admissible in a court of law and, therefore, handles evidence with this standard in mind.

- The most complete open source documents on the topic of incident response on the web are Handbook for Computer Security Incident Response Teams (CSIRTs) from CMU/SEI and NIST Special Publication 800-61 Computer Security Incident Handling Guide.

REFERENCES:

Definition taken from Incident Response and Computer Forensics, 2nd Edition
Prosise, Mandia & Pepe (2004)

http://www.cybercrime.gov/ccmanual/appxb.html

http://www.cert.org/archive/pdf/csirt-handbook.pdf

http://csrc.nist.gov/publications/nistpubs/800-61/sp800-61.pdf

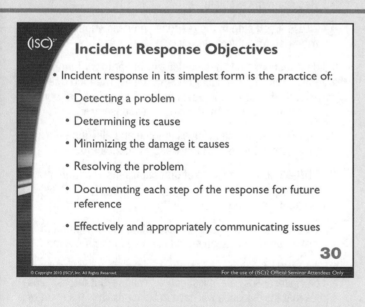

Incident Response: Overview

- **Response capability**
  - Policy and guidelines
  - Response
- **Incident response phases**
  - Triage
  - Containment
  - Investigation
  - Analysis and treatment
  - Recovery
- **Debriefing**
  - Metrics
  - Public disclosure

29

- **INCIDENT RESPONSE: OVERVIEW** – The next section will deal with each of these three main aspects of an organization's incident response (IR) program:

  - Response capability.

  - Incident response phases.

  - Debriefing.

- Incident response, or more precisely, incident handling, has become one of the primary functions of today's information security department and thus those professionals working in this capacity.

- This increased importance is a direct result of the fact that attacks against networks and information systems appear to be increasing annually.

- While statistics related to the exact increase in the volume of attacks and the corresponding economic cost are impossible to calculate given the lack of universal reporting, the gross trends indicate significant increases in the last few years. Not only are the volume of attacks increasing but the types of attacks undergo almost continuous modifications.

- Today we see spam, phishing scams, worms, spyware, distributed denial of service attacks (DDoS), and other imaginative, yet malicious attacks and mutations inundating our personal computers, networks, and corporate systems on a daily basis.

- Care must be taken not to confuse IR with computer or network forensics. They are not synonymous. While they are both investigative in nature, computer forensics has a higher standard of proof than IR.

- With computer forensics, the assumption is that the evidence must be admissible in a court of law and thus evidence is handled with that standard in mind.

REFERENCES:

Definition from: Prosise, Mandia, and Pepe, Incident Response and Computer Forensics Second Edition. 2004, New York: McGraw-Hill/Osborne.

Incident Response Objectives

- Incident response in its simplest form is the practice of:

  - Detecting a problem

  - Determining its cause

  - Minimizing the damage it causes

  - Resolving the problem

  - Documenting each step of the response for future reference

  - Effectively and appropriately communicating issues

30

- **INCIDENT RESPONSE OBJECTIVES** – This outlines the primary objectives of an incident response program. The incident response process developed by an organization should include a process to deal with each of these objectives. It is very important to have clearly identified and pre-approved rehearse procedures that will be followed.

Response Capability

- The foundation for incident response (IR) includes:
  - Policy
  - Authority
  - Procedures
  - Approved
  - Management of evidence

31

overseen by, the legal department. That makes the investigation and result privileged attorney work-product (in the United States and many other common law jurisdictions, of course).

- The policy must be clear, concise, and provide a mandate for the incident response/handling team.

- **APPROVED –**

  - When an event becomes an incident, it is essential that an approved, methodical approach be followed.

  - A methodical approach allows for the proper documentation and collection of information that may be of importance to the latter stages/phases of the response.

  - If you get to the phase of discovery (let alone testimony) in a case that goes to trial, you will be asked if you followed standard procedure, and if you are sure you did not leave out any steps (or if you did, why?). Having and following a checklist will help maintain admissibility.

- **MANAGEMENT OF EVIDENCE –** Being prepared to respond to an incident means having the necessary equipment required to seize and document evidence. This may include a "crash box" containing key items needed to respond to the incident such as:

  - Cables.

  - Hard drives.

  - Write protect cables, etc.

- **THE FOUNDATION FOR INCIDENT RESPONSE (IR):**

  - **POLICY –** As always the first step begins with the POLICY!

  - **AUTHORITY –** Policy should state who has the authority to initiate the response to an incident.

    - Incident response should be optional, leaving the organization the right to determine whether or not to investigate an incident. (If policy requires that all incidents must be investigated, and yet it is found that some incidents are not investigated, then employees can rightly consider that the "real" policy is not to investigate.)

  - **PROCEDURES –**

    - Corporate incidents should be managed by, or

Incident Response – External Parties

- Escalation process
- Interaction with third-party entities

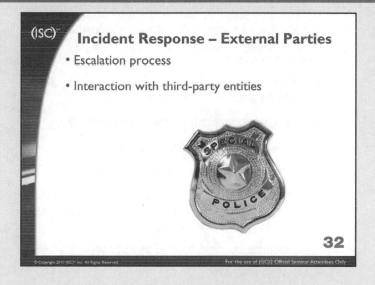

32

- **INCIDENT RESPONSE POLICY –** Provides direction for employees for:

- **ESCALATION PROCESS –** Employees should be trained and have approved procedures that include when an incident or crime must be reported to higher management, outside agencies, or law enforcement.

- **INTERACTION WITH THIRD-PARTY ENTITIES –** Such as the media, government, and law enforcement authorities. This is a complex issue, involving:

  - Jurisdiction (which country, or in the United States, which state or federal agency has control).

  - Status of the crime (already committed, in progress, or planned).

  - Nature of the evidence (circumstantial, conclusive).

  - Nature of the crime (in many jurisdictions a crime, such as child abuse, must be reported).

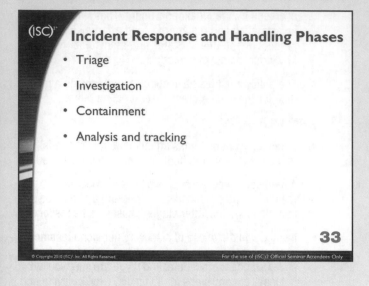

- **INCIDENT RESPONSE AND HANDLING PHASES** – We will spend the next few slides discussing each of these phases in more detail.

  - Incident response is a very dynamic process, with very fuzzy lines between the various phases.

  - Phases are often conducted in parallel and each has some natural dependencies on the other. Often the output of one phase or stage in the handling of an incident produces input for a subsequent phase.

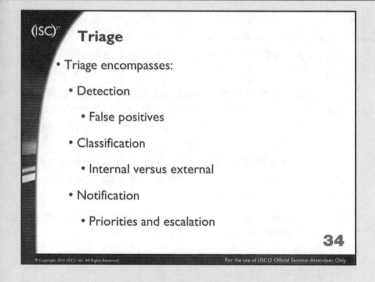

- **TRIAGE** – The consensus of the various models is that the first step in incident handling is some type of triage process.

  - **DETECTION** – Before any incident can be managed, it is necessary to be aware of the ongoing problem. This may be through monitoring, an alarm, or, perhaps, a call from a customer or user.

  - **CLASSIFICATION** – Classification of the incident begins immediately once the incident is detected.

    - Is the event externally or internally triggered?

    - Is the event on one system or many?

    - What is the root cause versus the symptoms?

  - **NOTIFICATION** – Notification includes the escalation process of documenting and following the approved escalation process to alert (notify):

    - Senior management or other departments.

    - Business partners.

    - Law enforcement that an incident has occurred.

- **NOTE: PRIORITIZATION IS ONE OF THE MOST IMPORTANT ASPECTS HERE** – Higher priorities get taken care of first!

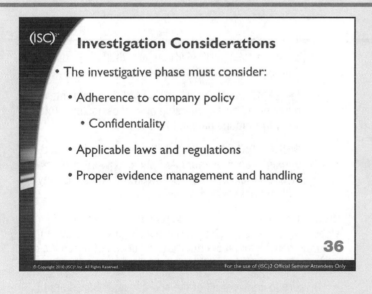

Investigation Phase Objectives

- Desired outcomes of this phase are:
  - Reduce the impact
  - Identify the cause
  - Get back up and running in the shortest possible time
  - Prevent the incident from re-occurring

35

- **INVESTIGATION PHASE OBJECTIVES** – The desired outcomes of this phase are listed on the slide.

- The investigative phase is often where computer forensics and proper evidence management are crucial. We will discuss this in more detail in the computer forensics section.

Investigation Considerations

- The investigative phase must consider:
  - Adherence to company policy
    - Confidentiality
  - Applicable laws and regulations
  - Proper evidence management and handling

36

- **ADHERENCE TO COMPANY POLICY** – An investigation must start with the review of company policy and ensure that all applicable laws and regulations are addressed.

  - **CONFIDENTIALITY** – Confidentiality of the investigation must be protected as much as possible. To leak an investigation may result in the loss of evidence, claims of bias against certain individuals, and increased liability. No details of the investigation can be revealed except after careful consideration and precautions.

- **APPLICABLE LAWS AND REGULATIONS** – Potential evidence must be handled correctly in accordance with rules of evidence or it runs the risk of being inadmissible in the event of civil or criminal litigation, or even as grounds for terminating someone's employment.

- **PROPER EVIDENCE MANAGEMENT AND HANDLING** – Once evidence becomes inadmissible, that status cannot be cured. Therefore, always assume that the intent is to go forward with a civil or criminal complaint.

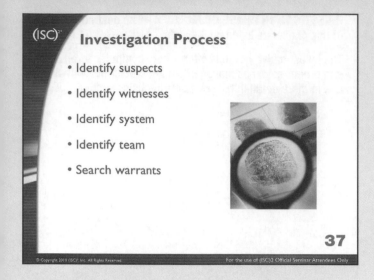

**INVESTIGATION PROCESS – ** Incident management primarily focuses on activities of a digital nature. Investigations widen the scope to include all wrong-doing. The investigative process can be described as follows (in no specific order):

- **IDENTIFY SUSPECTS** – The potential threats (suspects) will depend on the type of organization.

- **IDENTIFY WITNESSES** – The goal is to obtain the facts of the case without alerting the suspects. The people with the information/evidence can range from the non-technical office worker to forensic experts.

- **IDENTIFY SYSTEM** – Know the scope of the crime scene and the possible locations of evidence.

- **IDENTIFY TEAM** – The team must be qualified to deal with all the facets of the investigation including:

  - Legal.

  - Technical.

  - Security issues.

- **SEARCH WARRANTS** – If the evidence is not completely within the company's property, law enforcement will need to be involved. Obtaining a warrant and protecting the secrecy of the investigation may be of great importance. If evidence is required by law enforcement, however, it is important to follow the conditions of the warrant precisely.

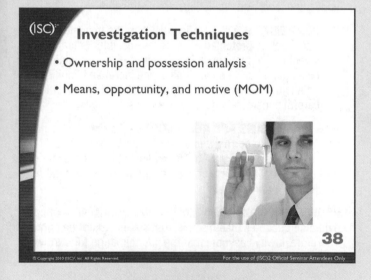

OWNERSHIP AND POSSESSION ANALYSIS – Is used to identify the individual or individuals who:

- Created.

- Modified.

- Accessed a file or any of the relevant data. Evidence of knowledgeable possession may be based on analysis of one or more of the following factors:

  - **TIME FRAME ANALYSIS:** Placing the subject at the computer at a particular date and time may help determine ownership and possession.

  - **APPLICATION AND FILE ANALYSIS:** The contents of a file may indicate ownership or possession by containing information specific to a user.

  - **HIDDEN DATA ANALYSIS:** If the passwords needed to gain access to encrypted and password-protected files are recovered, the passwords themselves may indicate possession or ownership.

- Results obtained from any single one of these investigative steps may not be enough to allow investigators to draw an accurate conclusion. It is important to consider the results as a whole. As a final step in the investigation process:

- Be sure to consider all of the sources and assessments involved in the analysis process.

- Review the incident in its entirety to identify a suspect.

- Reach a conclusion.

MEANS, OPPORTUNITY, AND MOTIVES (MOM) – Identifying people with:

- Means (ability).

- Opportunity (chance).

- Motive (reason) can be very helpful in identifying the suspects in a crime.

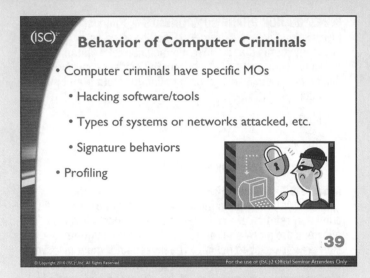

Behavior of Computer Criminals

- Computer criminals have specific MOs
  - Hacking software/tools
  - Types of systems or networks attacked, etc.
  - Signature behaviors
- Profiling

39

- Other signature behaviors such as:
  - Programming syntax.
  - Email messages.
  - Bragging notices, etc.
- **SIGNATURE BEHAVIORS** – Can be used to:
- Provide insight into the thought processes of the attackers.
- Identify the attacker, the attacker's skill level (or at least the tools used).
- Link other criminal behaviors together, thereby assisting law enforcement in piecing together other offenses by the same individual.
- Assist in the interview and interrogation process.
- Provide strategies for use in disciplinary hearings or at trial when the accused will be the most defensive.
- **PROFILING** – The art/science of profiling has gained popularity with the public in the last few years. Criminals often fit a certain profile. For example, a fraud is most likely to be committed by a person between 40 and 55, whereas attacks such as a denial of service tend to be more common among younger people. Those who are interested in getting more in-depth knowledge of this area should look at the work of Canter and Investigative Psychology, as well as Paul Britton and Douglas & Hazelwood (former FBI profilers).

- **COMPUTER CRIMINALS HAVE SPECIFIC MOs** – Research has shown that the motivation and profile of computer criminals is very similar to that of more traditional criminals. Just like traditional criminals, computer criminals have specific behaviors, or "modus operandi" (MOs), that characterize their actions. Signature behaviors can be used to conduct psychological crime-scene analysis, or "profiling," for both digital and physical crime scenes. Identifying the MO often leads to the identification of possible suspects.

- **MOS MAY INCLUDE:**
  - Hacking software/tools.
  - Types of systems or networks attacked, etc.

Interviewing vs. Interrogation

- Open-ended questioning
  - General gathering
  - Cooperation
  - Seek truth

- Closed-ended questioning
  - Specific aim
  - Hostile
  - Dangerous

40

- **INTERVIEWING VERSUS INTERROGATION** – Both interviewing and interrogation seek to collect data related to an investigation.

- **INTERVIEWING**
  - Interviewing is both an art and a science and should only be conducted by professionals who have had proper train-

ing, and, even then, only after consultation with appropriate legal counsel.

- As InfoSec professionals, we may be asked to provide input or observe an interview in case any technical information needs clarification, etc.

- Witnesses are sources of information who may be either willing or unwilling participants in the investigative process. The purpose of interviewing is information gathering with the objective of seeking/determining the truth.

- Suspects are the individuals who investigators believe may be associated with the criminal activity.

- **INTERROGATION** – Interrogation is an adversarial technique where the suspect is put under real or perceived stress (often through being accused of complicity in the crime) in order to compel him or her to confess or divulge specific information. The suspect's goal is to either establish his or her innocence or to deceive the investigator.

  - Interrogation should only be done by trained professionals in controlled situations. An interviewer or interrogator should never work alone.

REFERENCE:
http://www.forwardedge2.com/pdf/bestPractices.pdf

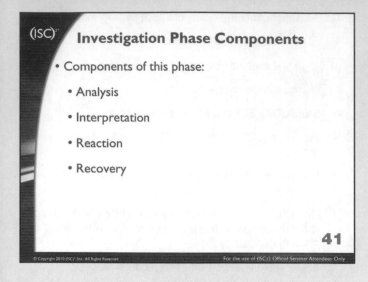

Investigation Phase Components

- Components of this phase:
  - Analysis
  - Interpretation
  - Reaction
  - Recovery

41

- **INVESTIGATION PHASE COMPONENTS –** Handling the investigation can be extremely difficult and complex. There are many routes that the investigation can take and many possible conclusions reached from the evidence gathered. The challenge for the investigator is to find the truth from among the fiction and discover:
  - Motives.
  - Suspects.
  - Nature of the evidence.

- **ANALYSIS AND INTERPRETATION –** To determine the true reasons and nature of the crime may take a lot of careful sifting and interpretation of the evidence and personnel involved. The missteps are many and the traps of reaching a wrong conclusion are very easy to fall into. The investigator must discover the real cause and extent of the situation and correctly identify the parties who perpetrated the offense. A clever criminal may be very deceptive and mislead the investigator, and the evidence may not be easy to find.

- **REACTION AND RECOVERY –** The steps of reaction and recovery are covered in the next few slides.

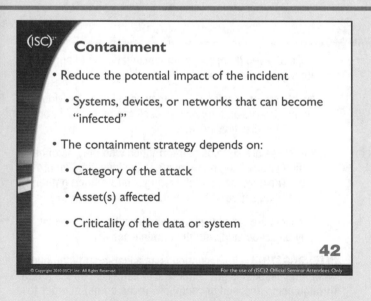

Containment

- Reduce the potential impact of the incident
  - Systems, devices, or networks that can become "infected"
- The containment strategy depends on:
  - Category of the attack
  - Asset(s) affected
  - Criticality of the data or system

42

- **CONTAINMENT –** Containment is stopping the spread of the incident and limiting its impact on other:
  - Systems.
  - Departments.
  - Personnel.

- **REDUCE THE POTENTIAL IMPACT OF THE INCIDENT –** Containment is similar to quarantining a patient until the exact nature of the disease or pathogen is determined (i.e., a virus outbreak).
  - A proper containment strategy actually buys time for a proper investigation and determination of a root cause.

- **THE CONTAINMENT STRATEGY DEPENDS ON:**
  - **THE CATEGORY OF THE ATTACK –** Internal versus external
  - **THE ASSETS AFFECTED –** Routers, files, networks, etc.
  - Criticality of the data or systems affected to the mission of the organization. What would be the impact if the system/data were not available for a time period?

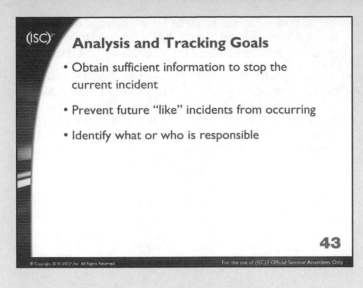

Analysis and Tracking Goals

- Obtain sufficient information to stop the current incident
- Prevent future "like" incidents from occurring
- Identify what or who is responsible

43

- **ANALYSIS AND TRACKING GOALS** – Remember these are ultimate goals – obtainable in an ideal world, but they may not be possible/attainable in all cases.

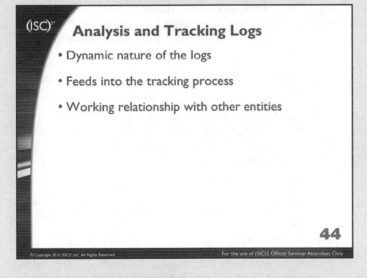

Analysis and Tracking Logs

- Dynamic nature of the logs
- Feeds into the tracking process
- Working relationship with other entities

44

- **LOG FILE RETENTION:**
  - There is legislation pending in the US Congress (2006) that would require longer retention of log files.
  - Other industrialized countries are unlikely to follow suit (this opinion is based on the differing attitudes toward privacy in the United States vs. the rest of the industrialized world, and discussed earlier in this domain).

- **FEEDS INTO THE TRACKING PROCESS:**
  - Analysis feeds into the tracking process in order to weed out false leads or intentionally spoofed sources.
  - Tracking often takes place in parallel with the analysis and examination.

- **WORKING RELATIONSHIP WITH OTHER ENTITIES** – A good working relationship with other entities such as:
  - Internet service providers.
  - Other response teams.
  - Law enforcement.

- NOTE: This concept is an important element in the incident response process.

- **DYNAMIC NATURE OF THE LOGS:**
  - One of the biggest enemies to the tracking process is the dynamic nature of many of the logs, both internal and external.
  - Log files do not last forever:
    - In fact, most ISPs purge or overwrite their logs in a fairly short time frame (i.e., 72 hrs).
    - The clock begins ticking when the incident occurs, not when it is reported or detected. Several hours may have elapsed between the actual attack and the notification.

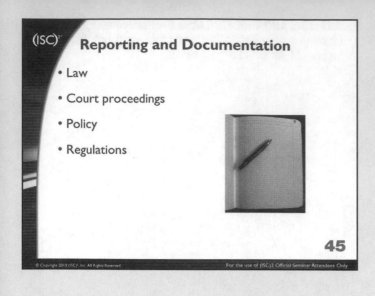

- **REPORTING** – The final outcome of reporting and documentation should ensure that enough data is provided to the right people so as to best address the incident and limit recurrence.

- If your organization is involved in court proceedings or wishes to seek reparations, the documentation must be sufficient to win the case. Your organization's policy will direct the detail level and process for reporting. If your organization is bound by other regulatory bodies, then policy will have to be adjusted according to those rules.

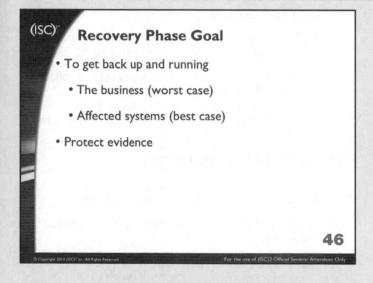

- **RECOVERY PHASE GOAL** – The recovery phase is concerned with resuming business operations and supporting the systems and processes that are critical for the business to meet its mission.

- **TO GET BACK UP AND RUNNING** – In this phase, time is crucial.

  - **THE BUSINESS** – In a worst case situation, the recovery may require the rebuilding of the entire business operations – we will look at this in more detail in the business continuity domain.

  - **AFFECTED SYSTEMS** – In a less severe case, this may require the rebuilding and recovery of affected systems, temporary workarounds, or use of alternate processes.

- **PROTECT EVIDENCE**

  - Care must be taken not to rush into this phase. Once information, data, or evidence is contaminated it cannot be decontaminated – this will be reiterated in the computer forensics section.

  - The investigator must be careful not to overlook other attacks that may be happening on the systems, such as when an attack on one component "masks" another more serious attack.

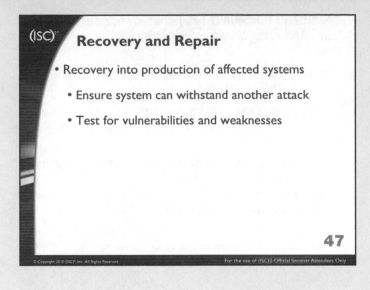

- **RECOVERY AND REPAIR** – This phase is concerned with getting all affected systems and operations back to normal.

- **RECOVERY INTO PRODUCTION OF AFFECTED SYSTEMS** – Once the root cause analysis has provided sufficient information regarding the extent of the damage and nature of the incident, the recovery process should begin.

  - **ENSURE SYSTEM CAN WITHSTAND ANOTHER ATTACK** – The exact strategy and techniques used to recover depend on the type of incident and the characteristics of the "patient."

    - There is no sense putting a system back in production if it is just going to be immediately attacked and destroyed or taken over by the same attack that affected it in the first place.

  - **TEST FOR VULNERABILITIES AND WEAKNESSES** – The system must be tested and hardened against attacks; especially the kind(s) of attacks that were directed against it originally.

- Information security professionals should have a tool box of tools that simulate real world attacks that they can run against their systems before the systems are placed back into production.

- Currently, once a system/network has been successfully attacked, the word gets out to the underground community and it becomes like a wounded swimmer in shark infested waters – subsequent attacks are extremely likely.

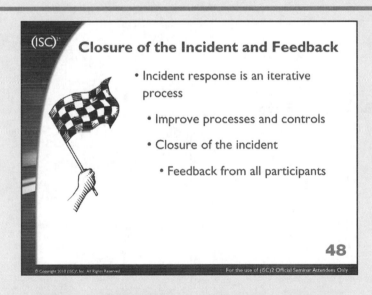

- Detected earlier.

- Resolved faster.

- **CLOSURE TO THE INCIDENT** – What exactly constitutes incident closure is dependent upon a number of variables:

  - Nature or category of the incident.

  - Desired outcome by the organization (i.e., business resumption, prosecution, system restoration).

  - Success of the team in determining the root cause and source of the incident.

  - End of financial accounting related to the incident cost.

- **FEEDBACK FROM ALL PARTICIPANTS** – It is important to gather information from everyone involved in the incident to ensure that the best improvements can be made. Each person or department involved may have a different perspective and the combined experiences will allow the development of better procedures in the future.

  - **USE OUTPUT TO ADAPT OR MODIFY POLICY AND GUIDELINES** – A side benefit to the formalism of the debriefing/feedback is the ability to start collecting meaningful data that can be used to develop/track performance metrics for the response team.

- **CLOSURE OF THE INCIDENT** – In order to learn as much as possible from the incident, with a mind to ensure that the next incident is either avoided or handled even more effectively, it is important to have a final review and formal feedback session about the incident. The purpose of this is to gather as much information as possible that can assist in improving processes and controls and improve the entire incident handling procedure.

- **INCIDENT RESPONSE IS AN ITERATIVE PROCESS** – We must be prepared for future incidents and each incident may help us to learn and improve so that future incidents are:

  - Less damaging.

Communication about the Incident

- Public disclosure
- Authorized personnel only

49

- **COMMUNICATION ABOUT THE INCIDENT** – Consider the long-term effect of any actions when dealing with the public or the press.

- **PUBLIC DISCLOSURE** – There are two possible outcomes from a public disclosure of an incident:

  - **COMPOUND THE NEGATIVE IMPACT** – If not handled well, public disclosure may result in a very negative impact on the organization.

  - **PROVIDE AN OPPORTUNITY TO REGAIN PUBLIC TRUST** – If disclosure is properly handled, and if the organization is perceived as being open and forthright, public disclosure may create confidence in the organization.

  - NOTE: In some countries/jurisdictions, legislation requires the disclosure of suspected or successful security breaches, particularly of personally identifiable information.

- **AUTHORIZED PERSONNEL ONLY** – Communication about the incident should be handled by authorized personnel only.

  - Only trained public relations, human resources, and otherwise properly trained/authorized individuals should handle the communications and external notifications.

  - Denial and "no comment" are not an effective public relations strategy in today's information culture!

Domain Agenda

- Computer Crime and International Legal Issues

  - Liability and Privacy Issues

- Incident Management

- **Forensic Investigation**

- Compliance

50

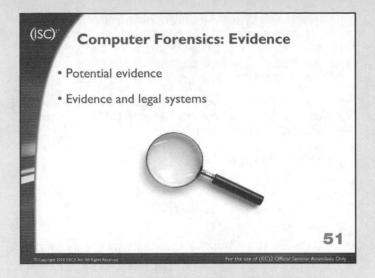

Computer Forensics: Evidence

- Potential evidence
- Evidence and legal systems

51

- **COMPUTER FORENSICS** – Computer forensics is really a marriage between the law and computer science; information technology and engineering. It includes evidence or potential evidence that may be in digital or electronic form and in storage or on the wire. Computer forensics is only about 25 years old; in contrast, latent fingerprint analysis goes back to the 1800s.

  - Computer forensics is the examination of evidence related to a crime. It is generally broken into three categories:

    - Investigation of media (hard drives, flash memory, cameras).
    - Investigation of network traffic (denial of service).
    - Investigation of software (malicious code).

- **POTENTIAL EVIDENCE** – Historically, computer forensics was differentiated from network and code analysis, but today this entire area is known as "digital evidence," as this more accurately captures the nature of the field. The Digital Forensic Science Research Workshop (DFRWS) defines digital forensic science as:

  - "The use of scientifically derived and proven methods toward the preservation, collection, validation, identification, analysis, interpretation, documentation and presentation of digital evidence derived from digital sources for the purpose of facilitating or furthering the reconstruction of events found to be criminal, or helping to anticipate unauthorized actions shown to be disruptive to planned operations."

- **EVIDENCE AND LEGAL SYSTEMS** – Computer forensics is generally applied according to the standards of evidence admissible in a court of law, but there are times a forensics investigation is done merely to sort out what happened. Since each jurisdiction may have different rules of evidence, the examiner must follow the local requirements regarding evidence handling. Certainly a good rule is to handle all investigations to a court-standard of evidence handling, since it is usually impossible to tell if the investigation will eventually end up as a serious court matter.

Computer Forensics: Evidence

- Identification of evidence
- Collecting of evidence
  - Use appropriate collection techniques
  - Reduce contamination
  - Protect the scene
  - Maintain the chain of custody and authentication

52

- **IDENTIFICATION OF EVIDENCE** – The identification process refers to the process of discovering the location of all data that may assist in investigating the situation and may later have to disclose in a legal proceeding. It is not necessarily "criminal" in nature.

- **COLLECTING OF EVIDENCE** – In the past, identification was fairly trivial – you seized the "thing" that the monitor was sitting on. In most cases, the "thing" had a keyboard and mouse attached to it as well. Today, identifying containers or potential containers of digital evidence is very difficult. Small scale digital devices (i.e., cell phones, cameras, PDAs, thumb drives, USB watches, GPS devices, iPods, Xbox, TiVos, etc.) can all store data, may be networkable, and are, therefore, potential sources of digital evidence.

  - **USE APPROPRIATE COLLECTION TECHNIQUES** – Adhere to principles appropriate to a criminal investigation. Use sound, repeatable, collection techniques that allow for the demonstration of the accuracy and integrity of evidence, or copies of evidence. The generally accepted method today is to use some kind of "hardware write-blocking device" between the suspect's hard drive and the forensic

examination system. This allows an examiner or first responder to conduct a field preview on the hard drive and then make forensic bit stream copies for later archiving and analysis. A forensic bit stream image captures every sector on the drive from zero until the last sector.

- Backups (or merely copying) do not capture the unallocated or residual data on a drive (i.e., deleted files). Examples of imaging software are:

- FTK Imager.

- DD.

- EnCase.

- Safeback.

- NOTE: These are good for Windows/Linux, but not effective to analyze cell phones, Palm, BlackBerry, etc., though there are some specialized tools available for these as well.

- **REDUCE CONTAMINATION** – A critical component of evidence gathering is to keep contamination and the destruction of the scene to a minimum.

- **PROTECT THE SCENE** – Protect the "crime scene" from unauthorized individuals: Once a scene has been contaminated, there is no "undo" or "redo" button to push. The damage is done! Only those individuals with knowledge of basic crime scene analysis should, therefore, be allowed to deal with the scene. If the scene does become contaminated, it is vital that proper documentation is done. While contaminating a crime scene does not necessarily negate the derived evidence, it does make it harder for the investigator, since all kinds of avenues for attack and questions by the opposition/suspect are now available.

- **MAINTAIN THE CHAIN OF CUSTODY AND AUTHENTICATION** – Right from the beginning, record and document all activity related to the evidence. The chain of custody is important to demonstrate the evidence has been handled properly and is not subject to unauthorized alteration.

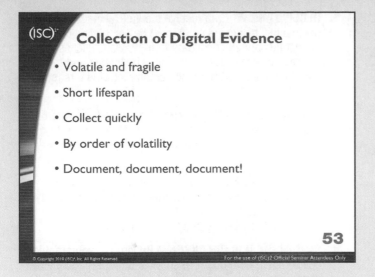

Collection of Digital Evidence

- Volatile and fragile
- Short lifespan
- Collect quickly
- By order of volatility
- Document, document, document!

53

horse programs or hostile scripts that might run and destroy evidence. With this process, however, whatever data was in RAM would be lost.

- **COLLECT QUICKLY** – Today's system can hold 16 Gbs of RAM and upward. A great deal of potential evidence could, therefore, be lost if the system were rebooted. The new trend is to try and capture the RAM and/or conduct a live analysis. The difficulty is that doing so can result in changing the crime scene; a running system can undergo various state changes and other operations. Furthermore, an attempt to collect data in RAM actually changes the RAM.

- **BY ORDER OF VOLATILITY** – Some creative legal defense strategies have claimed that the malicious software that caused the criminal activity ran only in RAM, and that once the system was powered off, all traces of this software were erased as well. As unlikely as this sounds, there have been worms/viruses released that have been resident only in RAM that have disappeared when the system is restarted (i.e., SQL Slammer worm). The challenge will remain between the investigator and the criminal to gather evidence in a manner that is trustworthy and free from accusations that the evidence was changed in some way during the investigative process.

- **DOCUMENT** – The most important part of evidence handling is to document all activities and actions taken with regard to the evidence.

REFERENCE:
www.helix.com for a live forensics CD/ISO and good discussions

- **VOLATILE AND FRAGILE** – Digital evidence is volatile, "fragile," and may have a short lifespan. It must, therefore, be collected quickly and in order of volatility (the most volatile first). An example of the volatile or fragile nature is RAM (cache memory, primary/random access memory, swap space).

- **SHORT LIFESPAN** – Data in RAM is lost when the electrical current is stopped. The traditional approach to incident response was to shut the system down, usually by pulling the plug from the back of the system (in case there was a UPS) or pulling the battery in the case of a laptop. Controlled shutdowns (CRTL + ALT + DELETE) were avoided in case of Trojan

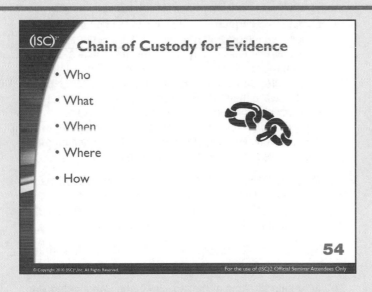

Chain of Custody for Evidence

- Who
- What
- When
- Where
- How

54

tion, or its return to the owner, or permanent archiving. Treating evidence properly requires following a formal, well-documented process. **ANY BREAK IN THIS CHAIN CAN CAST DOUBT ON THE INTEGRITY OF THE EVIDENCE** and on the professionalism of those directly involved in either the investigation or the collection and handling of the evidence.

- Documentation tracks:
  - Who
  - What
  - When
  - Where
  - How . . . etc.
  - and forms part of a standard operating procedure that is used in all cases.

- One of the ways that the "when" element of the chain of custody will be addressed will be via a time stamp showing when the evidence was collected and in what order. For this reason it is important to record the time on any system or network that is the source of evidence.

- **CHAIN OF CUSTODY** – At the heart of dealing effectively with any evidence, including digital/electronic evidence, is the **CHAIN OF CUSTODY FOR ACCURACY/INTEGRITY.**

- The chain of custody refers to evidence handling, and follows evidence through its life cycle from identification to destruc-

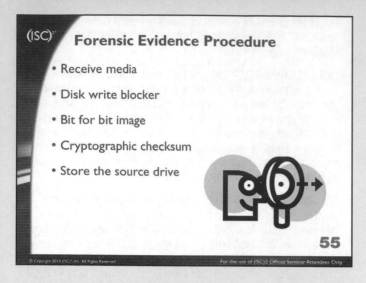

Forensic Evidence Procedure

- Receive media
- Disk write blocker
- Bit for bit image
- Cryptographic checksum
- Store the source drive

55

- **FORENSIC EVIDENCE PROCEDURES –** The forensic analyst should always follow a well-defined process when examining digital media for evidence, regardless of the software used. Evidence laws can vary by jurisdiction and that is why collection procedures must be worked out in advance of an incident so any response can be swift. That process is to:

1. **RECEIVE MEDIA –** The receive media (the media that the original will be copied onto) must be completely clean and not contain any residual data from previous use. As soon as the evidence is received it must be logged and the date/time and identity of the person receiving it must be recorded.

2. **DISK WRITE BLOCKER –** Attach the media to a system, using some sort of device that prevents the media from being changed. (An example is a disk write blocker for a hard drive.)

3. **BIT FOR BIT IMAGE –** Make a bit for bit image copy of the entire source drive onto a sanitized target drive. Usually two copies are made in order to have a control copy in the event that the working copy is damaged.

4. **CRYPTOGRAPHIC CHECKSUM –** Record a cryptographic checksum of both drives to show that the target copy is the same as the source.

5. **STORE THE SOURCE DRIVE –** Remove and store the source drive – only analyze the target drive.

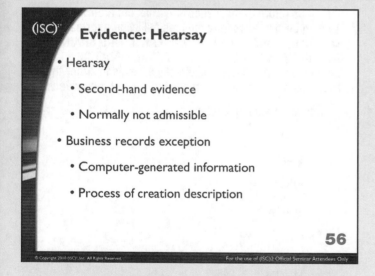

Evidence: Hearsay

- Hearsay
  - Second-hand evidence
  - Normally not admissible
- Business records exception
  - Computer-generated information
  - Process of creation description

56

- **HEARSAY –** Hearsay is evidence that is based on what the witness was told rather than on his or her personal knowledge and is not normally admissible in court.

  - **THE CLASSIC DEFINITION OF HEARSAY IS –** A statement made to a witness where the witness cannot personally attest to its accuracy.

  - This is a United States legal concept but has counterparts in some other nations.

- Computer-generated information can fall into this category because the presenter of the evidence is merely telling what a tool or device "says" (the results or logs of an IDS, for example) and, without adequate protection, computerized records can be manipulated, changed, destroyed, or in other ways made invalid in terms of a court. In most cases, computer-generated records, or the results of analysis tools, will only be accepted if the presenter can demonstrate clear knowledge of how the system creates the records and how the tools are used.

- **BUSINESS RECORDS EXCEPTIONS –** There are exceptions to the hearsay rule for computer-generated information. Computer-generated information may be allowed when it can be proven that business documents were created:

  - By a person with knowledge who can attest to how the records/information were created.

  - At or near the time of the incident being investigated, and vouched for by persons with knowledge of their creation and use.

  - In the course of regularly conducted business rather than generated just for the investigation.

  - As a regular practice of that business.

  - NOTE: They must be entered into evidence in court by testimony of the custodian or other qualified witness.

Evidence Analysis and Reporting

- Scientific methods for analysis
  - Characteristics of the evidence
  - Comparison of evidence
  - Event reconstruction
- Presentation of findings
  - Interpretation and analysis
  - Format appropriate for the intended audience

57

- **USING THE SCIENTIFIC METHODS FOR ANALYSIS**
  - Determine the characteristics of both primary and secondary evidence, including:
    - Source.
    - Reliability.
    - Permanence.
  - Compare evidence from the various sources, determining timelines and chronology of events.

- Reconstruct the event by:
  - Recovering deleted files.
  - Sequences of events.
  - System activity.
- This is usually conducted in a controlled environment such as a lab, but field triage is now also possible thanks to advances in hardware write-blockers and forensic software.

- **PRESENTATION OF FINDINGS AND INTERPRETATION AND ANALYSIS OF THE EXAMINATION**
  - When evidence is lacking, well-trained, experienced investigators will often be called upon to give their opinion, or interpret and analyze the examination and present these findings in non-technical terms. It can be very difficult to explain technical concepts to non-technical audiences. Most judges, lawyers, CEOs, or board members are not technical. It is imperative that CISSPs are able to explain things using non-technical terms and analogies and metaphors (e.g., a computer stores information like a filing cabinet does).
  - Findings may be considered secret or as confidential information. If done under the auspices of the legal department or outside counsel, they're also likely to be privileged.

Computer Forensics

- Key components
  - Crime scenes
  - Digital evidence
  - Non-criminal cases

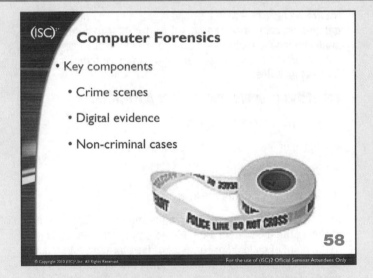

58

- **COMPUTER FORENSICS** – Computer forensics is not some piece of software or hardware. It is a set of procedures and protocols which are:
  - Methodical.
  - Repeatable.
  - Defensible.
  - Auditable.

- NOTE: One area that has traditionally been lacking in most organizations is proper evidence handling and management.
- **CRIME SCENE** – The computer crime scene is often harder to define than a physical crime scene – it may be a computer, a network, or disbursed across many countries and machines.
- **DIGITAL EVIDENCE** – Computer forensics will include all domains in which the evidence or potential evidence exists in a digital or electronic form, whether in storage or on the wire.
- **CIVIL SUITS AND NON-CRIMINAL CASES** – Computer forensics is also used in civil suits, such as:
  - Divorce.
  - Breach of contract.
  - Dissolution of corporation or partnerships.
  - Embezzlement.
  - Personal injury.
  - Litigation, etc.
  - NOTE: Digital forensics is also required in many workplace investigations that may not be criminal in nature, but may be a breach of corporate ethics or acceptable behavior.

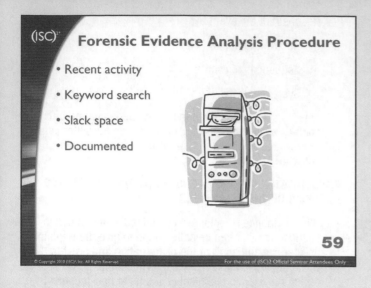

Forensic Evidence Analysis Procedure

- Recent activity
- Keyword search
- Slack space
- Documented

59

- **FORENSIC EVIDENCE ANALYSIS PROCEDURE** – When analyzing the target drive, first reduce the amount of data to be analyzed by comparing known good hash values with the files on the drive and focusing on files that do not match known good hashes.

- **RECENT ACTIVITY** – Analyze the subject user's profile/environment for recent activity. Examples include:

  - Opened files.

  - Web browsing history.

  - Email activity.

  - Personal data areas.

- **KEYWORD SEARCH** – Establish the best possible keyword search database using information about the suspected activity and search the drive for keyword evidence.

- **SLACK SPACE** – Recover data from unallocated or slack space on the drive for additional information.

- **DOCUMENTED** – The entire process of analyzing a drive, searching for evidence, and cataloging that evidence should be well documented by the forensic analyst. The process and evidence is usually made available during discovery, so it needs to be reproducible.

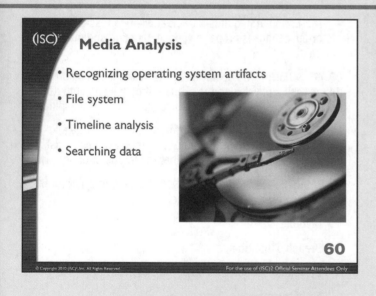

Media Analysis

- Recognizing operating system artifacts
- File system
- Timeline analysis
- Searching data

60

- **MEDIA ANALYSIS** – Media analysis is the disciplined and detailed process of searching a drive for information. The analyst needs to understand and be able to explain several aspects of the operating system and its file system. This process includes:

- **RECOGNIZING OPERATING SYSTEM ARTIFACTS:**

  - Operating system artifacts.

  - Types of files created as the system runs.

  - Where they should be.

  - What their contents are likely to be.

- **FILE SYSTEM** – Understanding, analyzing, and possibly reconstructing the file system itself based on the state that it is in at the point of collection. The type of file storage system used by the operating system will also affect the tools that can be used for analysis.

- **TIMELINE ANALYSIS** – Being able to construct a likely timeline analysis based on the three file times:

  - Modified.

  - Accessed.

  - Created.

  - NOTE: It is often helpful to create a chronology of what activities were running concurrently on the system.

- **SEARCHING DATA** – Searching through data files that applications create and being able to interpret that data.

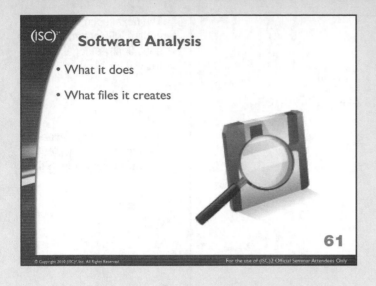

- **SOFTWARE ANALYSIS** – There are two broad categories involved in software analysis:

- **WHAT IT DOES** – First, the software itself must be analyzed in order to see what it does when it executes. In the case of potentially malicious software, the analyst needs to monitor disk and network activity in order to determine the software's activity. It may very well be that the computer user had no idea that this software was running.

- **WHAT FILES IT CREATES** – Second, software must be analyzed in order to determine:

  - What types of files it creates.

  - Where it creates them.

  - How data is arranged in those files.

- Cases often hinge on proving "someone did something" such as accessing a website or sending an email. Analysts may be asked to duplicate or prove that the evidence collected actually comes from a given software application and they may, therefore, need to reproduce the same information in order to show that they recovered what they claim to have recovered.

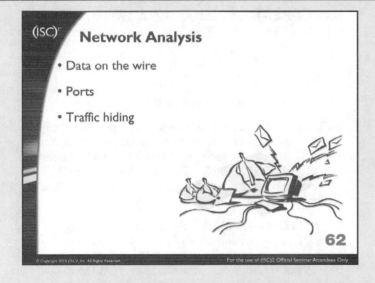

- **DATA ON THE WIRE** – Network analysis is:

  - Collecting data on the wire.

  - Dissecting the data based on the protocol being used.

  - Then being able to read the data in the network stream.

- **PORTS** – Clients and servers communicate over known and designated ports, and based on the traffic analysis and data presentation, the analyst should be able to determine what type of communication is taking place.

- **TRAFFIC HIDING** – Data collected on the network should be compared with network ports in use on either end of the communication. The ports used on the systems should be visible – not hidden from someone running commands that show network status on either system. If administrators on the systems cannot see the network ports that are in use from network analysis on the system itself, there may be root kit software on the system hiding traffic flow.

Domain Agenda

- Computer Crime and International Legal Issues

  - Liability and Privacy Issues

- Incident Management

- Forensic Investigation

- **Compliance**

63

- The next section of the course will look more specifically at legal issues related to:

  - Liability.

  - Negligence.

  - Protection of privacy and personally identifiable information (PII).

Compliance

- Knowing legislation
- Following legislation

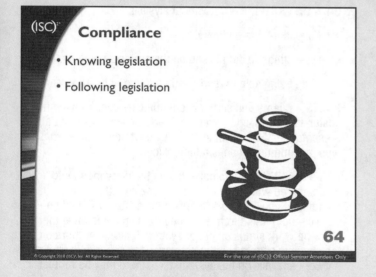

64

- **COMPLIANCE** – Compliance is a state of being in accordance with:

  - Established guidelines.

  - Specifications.

  - Legislation or the process of becoming so.

  - NOTE: For the security professional, compliance usually refers to behavior in accordance with legislation, such as the United States' Can Spam Act of 2003, the Sarbanes-Oxley Act (SOX) of 2002, HIPAA (United States Health Insurance Portability and Accountability Act of 1996), or the Gramm-Leach-Bliley Act (GLBA) of 1999.

- **KNOWING AND FOLLOWING LEGISLATION** – Ignorance of the law is not an acceptable excuse for noncompliance. The organization, and in particular security professionals, should be aware of the legislation that affects their job. Professionals must ensure compliance and that the requirements of the legislation are being met.

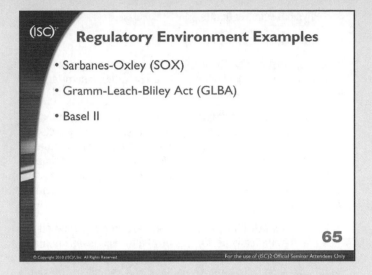

SARBANES-OXLEY (SOX) – Is meant to enhance corporate governance through measures that will strengthen internal checks and balances and, ultimately, strengthen corporate accountability. Impact on IT, security, and audit: Section 302 requires the CEO and CFO to personally sign off on the appropriateness of the firm's financial statements. Section 404 covers attestation of financial reporting controls and Section 409 calls for more frequent reporting.

GRAMM-LEACH-BLILEY ACT (GLBA) FINANCIAL MODERN-IZATION ACT OF 1999 – At the heart of GLBA is protecting the privacy of consumer information held by financial institutions. Financial institutions are prohibited from disclosing their customers' account numbers to non-affiliated companies when it comes to:

- Telemarketing.
- Direct mail marketing.
- Email.
- Other marketing.
- **ANOTHER PROVISION PROHIBITS "PRETEXTING" –** The practice of obtaining customer information from financial institutions under false pretenses. Impact on IT, security, and audit: Firms must attest, on an annual basis, that all their subcontractors and vendors have the appropriate processes in place to maintain the security of financial data. Many vendors use a SAS 70 to fulfill this requirement. Another major impact of GLBA is the requirement to use dummy or sanitized rather than live customer data for system testing.

- **BASEL II –** Is about regulatory harmony in the international banking community on questions of capital adequacy. Auditors (supervisors) are empowered by part 2 #722, which states that "Supervisors are expected to evaluate how well banks are assessing their capital needs relative to their risks and to intervene, where appropriate."

REFERENCES:

http://www.itcinstitute.com/Research/displayReg.aspx?ID=66 – SOX
http://www.itcinstitute.com/Research/displayReg.aspx?ID=66 – GLB
http://www.privacyrights.org/fs/fs8a-hipaa.htm – HIPAA
http://www.privcom.gc.ca/aboutUs/index_e.asp
http://www.bis.org/publ/bcbs107.htm

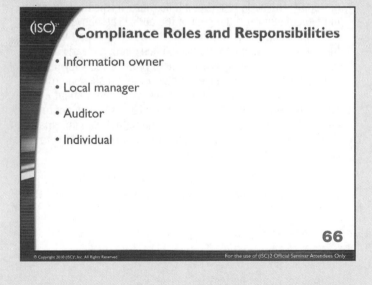

- **COMPLIANCE ROLES AND RESPONSIBILITIES –** An important part of legislation is the need to identify the persons responsible for ensuring and reporting on compliance with the legislative requirements.

- **INFORMATION OWNER –** Perhaps the person with the greatest single responsibility for compliance, the information owner, sets out the classification levels and access controls for each piece of sensitive information.

- **LOCAL MANAGER –** The local manager is responsible for ensuring that the personnel in his or her area are complying with policy and providing oversight for privacy-related procedures.

- **AUDITOR –** The auditor provides verification of risks and the compliance environment as a third-party observer. The auditor provides reports to senior management that indicate control weaknesses or areas of inadequate compliance.

- **INDIVIDUAL –** Each individual bears some responsibility for following the policies and procedures put in place to protect information. Whether the individual is a user, customer, or business partner, he or she may be liable for failure to protect information adequately.

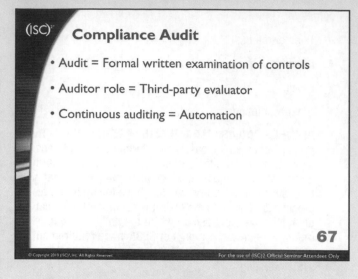

Compliance Audit

- Audit = Formal written examination of controls
- Auditor role = Third-party evaluator
- Continuous auditing = Automation

67

- **AUDIT –** An audit means that an internal or outside organization is conducting a formal written examination of one or more crucial components of the organization. The most common examinations a security professional will encounter are:

  - Financial audits.

  - Physical security audits.

  - Information security audits.

- Compliance audits are typically performed on a regular basis. This can vary by organization, but can be annual, semi-annual, quarterly, or even ad-hoc.

- **AUDITOR ROLE –** The major role in the audit process is that of the auditor. The auditor compares the stated policy with the actual controls in place. Any policy and control that does not match is considered to be a gap or a finding. All findings are reported to senior management and regulatory bodies for remediation. It is up to management to budget resources for compliance.

- **CONTINUOUS AUDITING –** Continuous auditing is a method used to automatically perform control and risk assessments on a more frequent basis. Continuous auditing changes the audit paradigm from periodic reviews of a sample of transactions to ongoing audit testing of 100 percent of the transactions. Continuous audit involves the local manager in monitoring the controls and doing a level of local audit and reporting.

REFERENCE:
http://www.theiia.org/guidance/technology/gtag/gtag3/

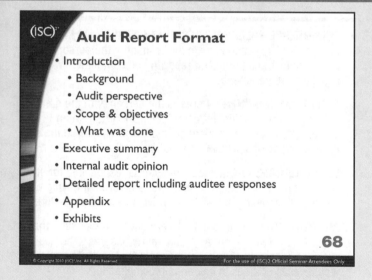

Audit Report Format

- Introduction
  - Background
  - Audit perspective
  - Scope & objectives
  - What was done
- Executive summary
- Internal audit opinion
- Detailed report including auditee responses
- Appendix
- Exhibits

68

- **AUDIT REPORT FORMAT –** The output from an audit is the audit report. The audit report can take many forms depending on the type of audit and the goal of the audit. The above are the common sections of an audit report. The audit report will have the sections outlined on the slide. Each section clearly states the information that is appropriate to present the information that is important to disclose. The information section provides general information about the purpose and environment of the audit. The executive summary provides an overview appropriate for senior managers without providing detailed information. The detailed information and findings are found in the remaining sections of the audit.

- The audit report must be approved and signed by the appropriate company officials as well as the entity performing the audit. These people typically are:

  - Senior management.

  - Audit manager.

  - Auditor him or herself.

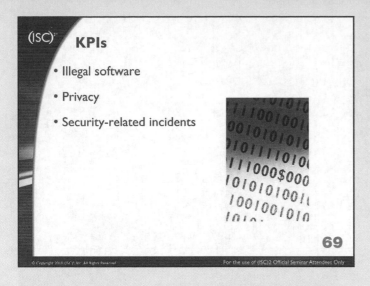

KPIs

- Illegal software
- Privacy
- Security-related incidents

69

- **KPIs** – Key performance indicators are metrics or quantifiable measurements, agreed to beforehand, that reflect the critical success factors of an organization or process and are different for every organization.

- **ILLEGAL SOFTWARE** – This is a topic that many organizations fight daily. Naturally, the standard must be to never have illegal software on any system. However, that standard is going to be difficult to achieve and will often take time. Therefore, senior management may establish a timeline with milestones to accomplish the desired end-state. KPIs could be established by management to demonstrate that the milestones are being met.

- **THE USE OF A KPI HAS TWO MAJOR PURPOSES:**

  - First, it will help improve the software inventory process in your environment. By having such KPI you may understand process weakness in your environment related to software inventory (on servers and desktops, etc.).

  - The second benefit of this KPI is management awareness. Quantifying the amount of legal software may spin off into other projects:

    - Reducing the amount of illegal software and minimizing legal exposure.

    - The need for more general-user awareness with respect to software piracy.

    - Understanding the lack of controls in the environment that can lead to controls improvement.

    - Containment of the proliferation and deployment of illegal software, etc.

- **PRIVACY** – Privacy related incidents can also be measured with KPI. KPI for privacy-related incidents discovered in your environment can be represented as the number of privacy incidents occurring over a 30-day period.

- **SECURITY-RELATED INCIDENTS** – Security-related incidents can be measured with KPI and described in the same way as privacy-related incidents.

Domain Summary

- This domain reviewed the areas a CISSP candidate should know regarding:

  - International Legal Issues

  - Incident Management

  - Forensic Investigation

  - Compliance

70

Security Transcends Technology
(ISC)²
71
© Copyright 2010 (ISC)², Inc. All Rights Reserved.

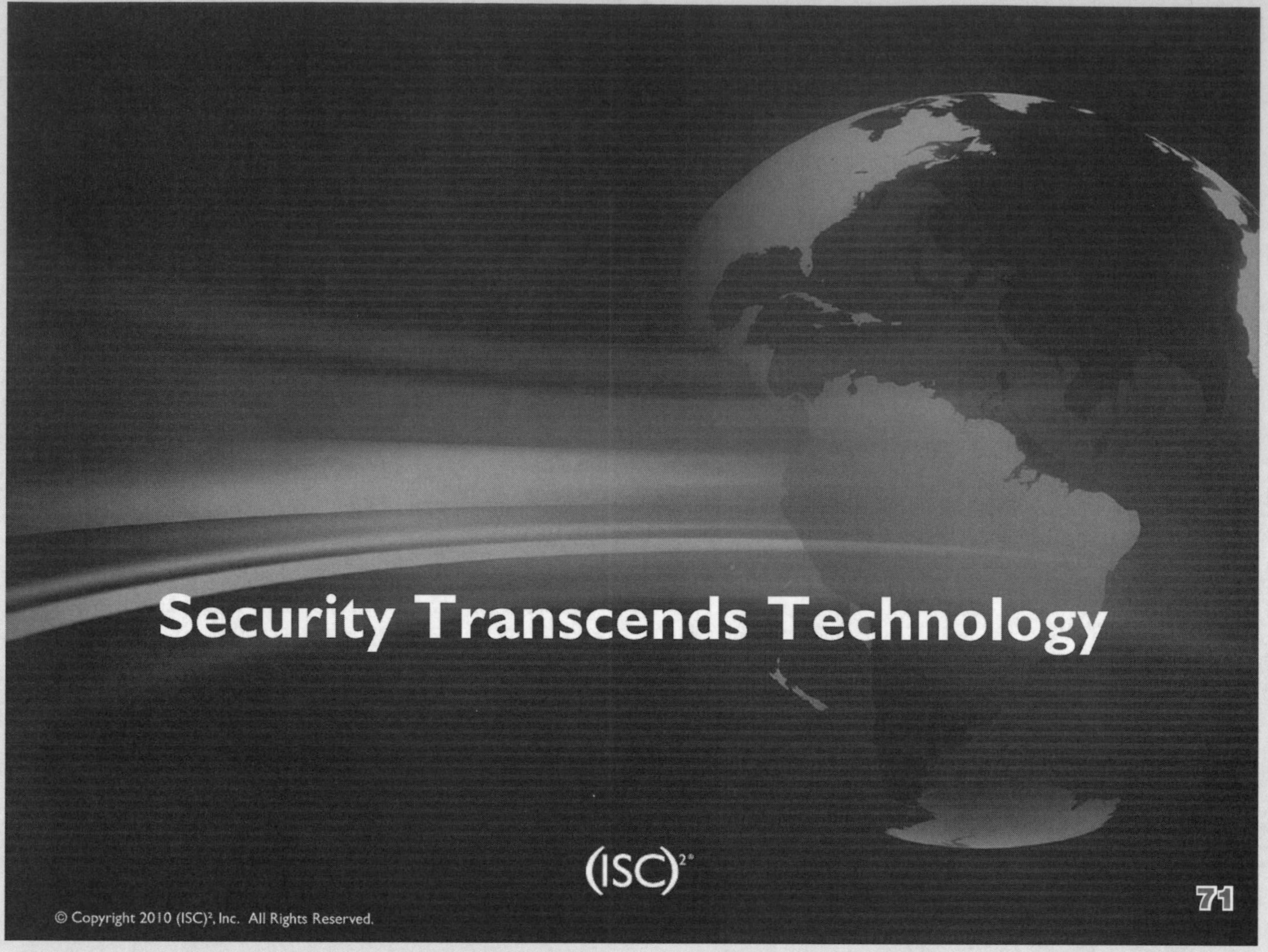

Review Questions

LEGAL, REGULATIONS, INVESTIGATIONS, AND COMPLIANCE

1. **Chain of custody is a legal term that deals with evidence**

   A. investigation and follows evidence through its life cycle.

   B. handling and follows evidence through its life cycle.

   C. identification and analysis and follows evidence through its life cycle.

   D. protection from contamination and follows evidence through its life cycle.

2. **What does the Wassenaar Arrangement cover?**

   A. It specifies all controlled dual-use goods, including encryption products and products that use encryption utilities, and how those can be used and exported.

   B. It specifies all controlled goods, like encryption products and products that use encryption utilities, and how those can be developed.

   C. It specifies all dual-use goods, including encryption products and products that use encryption utilities, and how those can be used and exported.

   D. It specifies how controlled dual-use goods, including encryption products and products that use encryption utilities, should be developed and maintained.

3. **What is the role of the auditor?**

   A. The auditor checks the effectiveness of the controls implemented by the organization in terms of design and implementation.

   B. The auditor ensures that the controls comply with COBIT (Control Objectives for IT).

   C. The auditor checks that controls comply with ISO (International Standards Organization) 27001:2005, Annex A (Controls Section).

   D. The auditor compares the stated policy with the actual controls in place.

4. **Which of the following BEST describes what compliance should be, in accordance with**

   A. the law, organizational rules, and industry standards.

   B. guidelines, specifications, and legislation.

   C. standards, regulations, and guidelines.

   D. the relevant International Standards Organization (ISO) standards.

5. **The difference between compliance and conformance is**

   A. compliance requires changing attitude and belief to match those of the group. Conformance is following group rules.

   B. compliance refers to a person being influenced by the group and changing his/her attitudes and/or beliefs, while the main point of conformance is the achievement of some specified task.

   C. conformance requires changing attitude and belief to match those of the group. Compliance is following group rules.

   D. compliance requires conformance. Conformance does not require compliance.

6. **To satisfy the requirements of International Standards Organization (ISO) 27001:2005, an organization being assessed must provide**

   A. evidence of compliance with the requirements.

   B. evidence of conformance to the requirements.

   C. evidence of effective implementation of requirements.

   D. a detailed statement of applicability (SOA) and scope of the information security management system (ISMS).

7. **What are the three (3) categories of computer forensics?**

   A. Investigation of media, network traffic, and software.

   B. Investigation of data, processes, and computer systems.

   C. Investigation of data, systems, and people.

   D. Investigation of crime scene, evidence, and suspects.

8. **What does it mean "work by order of volatility" when investigating evidence?**

   A. Some computer evidence is volatile. It can disappear or be affected more easily than physical evidence, therefore more volatile evidence should be investigated before less volatile evidence.

   B. All computer evidence is volatile. It can disappear or be affected more easily than physical evidence, therefore more volatile evidence should be investigated before less volatile evidence.

   C. Evidence that can evaporate (spilled alcohol) must be investigated before solid evidence is investigated.

   D. Volatile evidence includes evidence that is potentially harmful to the organization, such as a negative effect on reputation, and should therefore be handled before other evidence.

9. **Which of the following BEST describes the steps to be answered to prove chain of custody?**

   A. Who, why, where, and how

   B. Who, what, how, and when

   C. Who, what, when, where, and how

   D. Who, what, when, which, and how

10. **Why is it important to make two copies of investigated media?**

   A. To have a control copy in the event that the working copy is damaged.

   B. So there is a backup in case the original media is contaminated during the investigation.

   C. So that the investigator can make a hash of the original media and compare it to the copy he or she investigates.

   D. It is mandated by criminal forensic laws in most countries.

11. **Why is computer evidence usually considered "hearsay"?**

   A. It is not. Computer evidence is admissible in court, while "hearsay" is not.

   B. Because it is a statement made where the evidence is presented by a person.

   C. Because it does not prove that the suspect committed the crime for which he or she is accused.

   D. Because the presenter of the evidence is merely telling what a tool or device "says."

12. **Which of the following is most likely to result in admissible evidence?**

   A. If the evidence was collected and analyzed using accepted forensics tools.

   B. If the presenter can demonstrate clear knowledge of how the system creates the records and how the tools are used.

   C. If the evidence was collected using tools from the "Helix" toolkit.

   D. If the presenter can provide a "chain of custody."

13. **What is the role of a judge in common law versus civil law?**

   A. In common law, the judge applies the law as it is written in the common law book (hence the name "common" law).

   B. In common law, rulings made by judges become the core of the law. In civil law, the judge will rule based on the formal code.

   C. In common law, the judge deals with criminal cases. In civil law, the judge deals with civil litigation.

   D. In common law, the judge can sometimes play an active part in the inquisitorial process. In civil law, he or she acts more in the capacity of legal "referee" and cannot "take sides."

14. **What is the main difference between "computer crime" and "traditional crime"?**

   A. A computer crime is a crime where the computer is the target of the crime or where a computer is used to commit the crime.

   B. Traditional crime does not deal with computers. Computer crime deals only with computers.

   C. Computer crime deals with intangible assets and evidence. Traditional crime deals with tangible assets and evidence.

   D. There is no difference. The same laws and principles apply to both.

15. **When would a patent be considered less desirable than a trade secret?**

   A. When the asset involved needs to have the highest degree of legal protection possible.

   B. When the asset involved is an expression of an idea, rather than the idea itself.

   C. When confidentiality outweighs the legal protection afforded by a patent.

   D. When the asset involved needs to be protected in the United States as well as in the European Union.

16. **What is the difference between "freeware" and "public domain"?**

   A. "Freeware" is free for use as software and can be used for any purpose. "Public domain" can only be used for public, non-private implementations.

   B. "Freeware" is free for use, but the author still maintains copyright. "Public domain" is not copyrighted.

   C. "Freeware" provides free or very low cost software for a limited trial period or functionality. "Public domain" provides the full software indefinitely.

   D. "Freeware" cannot be used by corporations, only individuals. "Public domain" can be used by anyone.

17. **What is the difference between "due care" and "due diligence"?**

   A. Due care can be equated to doing the right thing and due diligence to ensuring that due care actions are effective.

   B. Due diligence can be equated to doing the right thing and due care to ensuring that due diligence actions are effective.

   C. Due care means executing careful actions. Due diligence means executing them quickly.

   D. Due care requires acting in due diligence.

18. **What is the definition of "negligence"?**

    A. Forgetting to perform an activity, which then results in harm to someone.

    B. Direct causation of harm to someone else, as opposed to indirect or proximate causation.

    C. Acting carelessly in public areas, but with little effect on or notice by others.

    D. Acting without care or failing to act as a reasonable and prudent person would under similar circumstances.

19. **What is the correct sequence of steps to follow when performing incident response?**

    A. Triage, investigation, analysis, containment, and tracking.

    B. Triage, investigation, containment, analysis, and tracking.

    C. Triage, containment, analysis, investigation, and tracking.

    D. Detection, classification, containment, analysis, and tracking.

20. **What is the most important guideline to provide to incident investigators?**

    A. Do not exceed your knowledge or capabilities.

    B. Always use the professional forensic tools designed for this specific task.

    C. Act quickly. Evidence is volatile.

    D. Any mistake you make can destroy the evidence, or at least make it inadmissible.

Notes

(ISC)² — Legal, Regulations, Investigations, and Compliance

Operations Security

1

Domain Agenda

- **Operator and Administrator Security**

  - **Monitoring of Special Privileges**

  - Misuse of Resources

  - System Recovery

- Resource Protection

  - Environmental Issues and Controls

  - Media Management

2

Control Over Privileged Entities

- Review of access rights
- Supervision
- Monitoring/audit

3

- **CONTROL OVER PRIVILEGED ENTITIES** – Because personnel with privileged access pose a higher level of risk to an organization, it is important to have adequate controls in place to prevent either intentional or accidental breaches of the security of the organization.

- **REVIEW OF ACCESS RIGHTS** – Access permissions for those personnel with privileged access should be reviewed frequently to ensure they are appropriate and necessary for their job requirements.

- **SUPERVISION** – All personnel with privileged access should go through a rigorous hiring and review process to ensure that they are suitable for a position of trust and have the necessary education and qualifications.

- **MONITORING/AUDIT** – A supervisor of personnel with privileged access as well as internal auditors should routinely review violation reports, job schedules, and changes made to systems in order to ensure that changes are not being made without proper approval and adherence to the change control process.

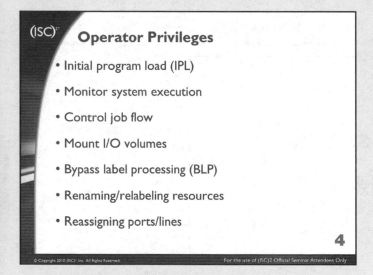

Operator Privileges

- Initial program load (IPL)
- Monitor system execution
- Control job flow
- Mount I/O volumes
- Bypass label processing (BLP)
- Renaming/relabeling resources
- Reassigning ports/lines

4

- **OPERATOR PRIVILEGES** – The organization's data flows through the operator's hands. Some studies have indicated that 70 percent of all security breaches come from insider abuse of privilege. Controls must be in place to reduce the opportunity for a breach, or to detect and respond effectively if a breach does take place. Examine the controls on data flows at each point in the operator's actions. The operator's duties and responsibilities consist of:

- **INITIAL PROGRAM LOAD (IPL)** – Initializing computer operations (IPL – initial program load); starting a system program with required system software; and operating the computer system as directed.

- **MONITORING SYSTEM EXECUTION** – Observing operation of equipment, control panels, error lights, verification printouts, error messages, and faulty output. Recording job completion times, error codes, escalating problems. Monitoring computer and network systems using operating systems utilities; interpreting console messages from system software or applications programs, and performing required actions.

- **CONTROL JOB FLOW** – The operator regulates the execution of jobs – ensuring that jobs are run in the correct sequence, have adequate resources available, and are completed correctly.

- **MOUNT I/O VOLUMES** – Jobs may require tapes or other resources to be loaded or available. Printers may require paper to be replaced. Jobs may require a higher priority to ensure timely completion.

- **BYPASS LABEL PROCESSING (BLP)** – When reading a tape, the system can be told to read the tape without checking the label on the tape. This can circumvent the security protection on the tape. Therefore, it is important that we ensure backup operators do not permit BLP which can give someone the ability to bypass the security controls.

- **RENAMING/RELABELING RESOURCES** – Files, directories, and programs can all be renamed. This is useful for creating backup copies or uploading multiple versions. However it can also mask the true content of the file or directory.

- **REASSIGNING PORTS/LINES** – The operator can divert output to another device, or reassign a process to another location. This can be used to bypass equipment failure or divert output to a more convenient location, but may also divert sensitive output to an insecure area.

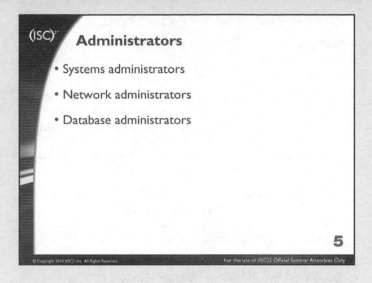

- **ADMINISTRATORS** – There are many types of administrators on an organization's networks and systems. They are the custodians responsible for the daily operation of the systems, networks, etc. Administrators have high levels of permission and their activities should be carefully monitored, recorded, and access levels reviewed on a periodic basis.

- **SYSTEMS ADMINISTRATORS** – System administrators should only be given access to the systems they directly manage.

- **NETWORK ADMINISTRATORS** – Network administrators should only be given access to the network devices they directly manage.

- **DATABASE ADMINISTRATORS** – Of course, database administrators should only have administrative rights for their database servers.

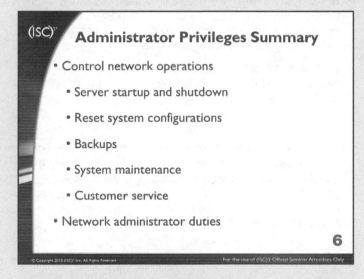

- **DATA BACKUPS.**
- **SYSTEM MAINTENANCE:**
  - Applying operating system updates and configuration changes.
  - Installing and configuring new hardware/software.
  - Adding/deleting/modifying user account information, resetting passwords, etc.
  - Documenting the configuration of the system.
  - Tuning system performance.
- **CUSTOMER SERVICE:**
  - Answering technical queries.
  - Security.
  - Troubleshooting any reported problems.
  - Keeping the network up and running.
- **NETWORK ADMINISTRATORS** – A particular type of information administrator responsible for layer three devices and below. Security responsibilities include:
  - Configuring and maintaining routing tables.
  - Configuring and maintaining MAC address tables.
  - Configuring and maintaining IDS and IPS.
  - Review of network access logs and alerts.

- **CONTROL NETWORK OPERATIONS** – A system administrator's responsibilities typically include:
  - **SERVER STARTUP AND SHUTDOWN:**
    - File systems, databases, and applications.
    - File permissions.
    - Boot sequence.
  - **SYSTEM CONFIGURATIONS RESET:**
    - Time.
    - Date.
    - Passwords.

Backup Types

- File image
- System image
- Data mirroring
- Electronic vaulting
- Remote journaling
- Database shadowing
- Redundant servers
- Standby services

7

- **FILE IMAGE** – Backup software that creates disk image files with exact, byte-by-byte copies of a hard drive, partition, or logical disk. These drive image files can be created on the fly and stored in a variety of places, including various removable media. At any time, data from the images may be restored onto the original disks, any other partitions, or even on a hard drive's free space.

- **SYSTEM IMAGE** – The contents of the hard disk, including the operating system and installed applications. Copying system images from one computer to another is the fastest way to populate new hardware because copying pre-installed ap-

plications is much faster than installing them.

- **DATA MIRRORING** – Is the replication of data on separate disks in real time to ensure continuous availability, currency, and accuracy (i.e., RAID Level 1).

- **ELECTRONIC VAULTING** – Is the bulk transfer of backup data over communications facilities. It can simplify the backup process and provide timelier offsite "operational" data protection. This process can be facilitated with a "host-to-host" or "channel extension" connection and typically serves to reduce (but not eliminate) the exposure to loss of data.

- **REMOTE JOURNALING** – Delivers real-time database data integrity by capturing and transmitting the journal and transaction log data offsite as they are created. This solution interacts with the standard database journal and logging facilities in many databases.

- **DATABASE SHADOWING** – Reduces recovery time from a database failure by using a database restore and roll-forward process, using a backup and the journals to enable recovery without data loss.

- **REDUNDANT SERVERS** – Keep a redundant idle server available for failover in case of a failure of the primary server. This provides fault tolerance by having one or more entire systems available in case the primary one crashes.

- **STANDBY SERVICES** – Provide recovery of most critical applications in a matter of minutes through guaranteed access to an alternate processor.

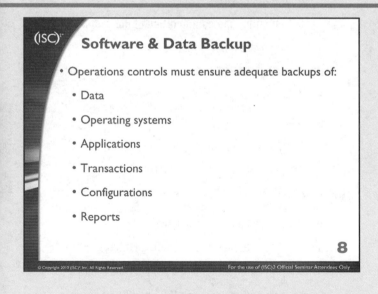

Software & Data Backup

- Operations controls must ensure adequate backups of:
  - Data
  - Operating systems
  - Applications
  - Transactions
  - Configurations
  - Reports

8

- **OPERATIONS CONTROLS MUST ENSURE ADEQUATE BACK-UPS OF** – All types of system, application, and transactional data, as well as system configuration files. Documentation must be backed up in order to allow for system recovery in the event of a failure.

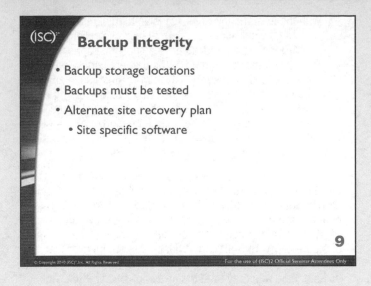

Backup Integrity

- Backup storage locations
- Backups must be tested
- Alternate site recovery plan
  - Site specific software

9

- **BACKUP STORAGE LOCATIONS** – Backups should be kept onsite, offsite, and possibly near-site. An onsite backup is valuable to restore a deleted file or recover from a virus, but an offsite is necessary for recovery in the event of fire or large scale disaster. A near-site backup stored, for example, in another building on campus may be good enough for fire but not suitable for a natural disaster.

- **BACKUPS MUST BE TESTED** – To ensure that they are usable and complete and so as to fully understand, for example, what software and procedures would be required to get the system operational from a bare-metal machine.

- **ALTERNATE SITE RECOVERY PLAN** – Recovery planning must include an offsite backup of all data required to rebuild the system. The recovery plan must also address the need to encrypt those backups, how to access them when required, and the steps for restoring the system.

  - **SITE SPECIFIC SOFTWARE** – Some software is restricted to only work on a registered CPU or at a certain location, so arrangements must be made with the vendor to permit the recovery of operations at an alternate site with different equipment.

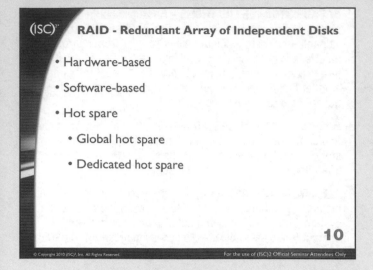

- **RAID - REDUNDANT ARRAY OF INDEPENDENT DISKS –** RAID can be used for several purposes depending on the implementation. It can speed up the read/write operation for data stored on disk drives and/or provide backup capability to recover data in the event of a disk drive failure.

- **HARDWARE-BASED RAID –** Requires a RAID controller (often a PCI expansion card or motherboard capability) that provides an interface between the host and the storage disks. The interface may be a high-speed SCSI, a network attached storage, or fiber. The controller is responsible for the management of the disks as well as the calculation of parity bits where needed. A hardware implementation often includes hot-swappable disks to allow for data recovery with no system downtime.

  - **A HARDWARE IMPLEMENTATION OF RAID –** Requires at a minimum a special-purpose RAID controller. On a desktop system, this may be a PCI expansion card or a capability built in to the motherboard. In larger RAIDs, the controller and disks are usually housed in an external multi-bay enclosure. The controller links either directly or through a network fabric to the host computer(s) with one or more high-speed SCSI fiber channel connections. It can also be accessed as network attached storage. This controller handles the management of the disks and performs parity calculations (needed for many RAID levels). This option tends to provide better performance and makes operating system support easier. Hardware implementations also typically support hot swapping, which allows failed drives to be replaced while the system is running. In rare cases, hardware controllers become faulty. This can result in data loss. Hybrid RAIDs have become increasingly popular with the introduction of inexpensive hardware RAID controllers. The hardware is a normal disk controller that has no RAID features, but does have a boot-time application that allows users to set up RAIDs that are controlled via the BIOS. Modern operating systems require specialized RAID drivers that will make the array look like a single block device. Since these controllers actually do all calculations in software rather than hardware, they are often called "fakeraids." Unlike software RAID, these "fakeraids" typically cannot span multiple controllers.

- **SOFTWARE-BASED RAID –** Is handled by the operating system through the normal drive controller. It can be faster than hardware-based RAID, but it reduces CPU performance. This option is often used for high-transaction volume systems and OLTP, or online transaction processing. Another disadvantage of a pure software RAID is that depending on the disk that fails and the boot arrangements in use, the computer may not be able to be rebooted until the array has been rebuilt. One major exception is when the hardware implementation of RAID incorporates a battery backed-up write-back cache, which can speed up applications such as OLTP database servers. In this case, if there is a crash, the hardware RAID implementation flushes the write cache to secure storage to preserve data at a known point. The hardware approach is faster than accessing the disk drive but is limited by RAM speeds, the rate at which the cache can be mirrored to another controller, the amount of cache, and how fast it can flush the cache to disk. For this reason, battery-backed caching disk controllers are often recommended for high transaction rate database servers. In the same situation, the software solution would be limited to no more flushes than the number of rotations or seeks per second of the drives. With a software implementation of RAID, the operating system manages the disks of the array through the normal drive controller.

- **HOT SPARE –** Both hardware and software versions may support the use of a hot spare, which is a pre-installed drive that can immediately (and almost always automatically) replace a failed drive. This reduces the mean-time-to-repair period during which a second drive failure in the same RAID redundancy group might result in loss of data.

  - **GLOBAL HOT SPARE –** A hot spare that is a backup for any physical disk in the array that fails.

  - **DEDICATED HOT SPARE –** A hot spare that is a backup for a specific disk in the array.

REFERENCES:

http://www.acnc.com/04_01_00.html

http://www.eecs.berkeley.edu/Pubs/TechRpts/1987/5853.html

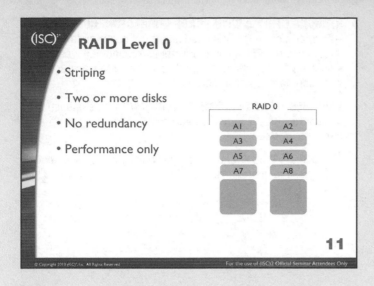

- **STRIPING** – Stripes the data across several disks allowing for a faster read and write speed. It does not provide backup or redundancy and is, therefore, not useful for high integrity systems or high-availability applications.

- **TWO OR MORE DISKS** – The data are broken into blocks, which are then written to separate disks. Ideally, each disk will have a separate disk controller.

- **NO REDUNDANCY** – Since RAID 0 does not provide any redundancy or parity bits, it is not fault tolerant and should not be used on mission-critical systems. RAID 0 is less reliable than independent disks.

- Usable disk storage is the sum of all the disk capacities. For example, five 100GB drives would yield 500GB of usable space.

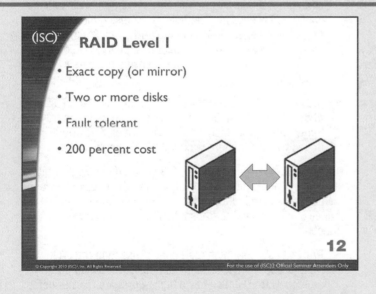

- **EXACT COPY (OR MIRROR)** – Also called mirroring, is popular because of its simplicity and high level of reliability and availability.

- **TWO OR MORE DISKS** – Mirrored arrays consist of two or more disks. Each disk in a mirrored array holds an identical image of user data. A RAID Level 1 array may use parallel access for a high transfer rate when reading, but more commonly, RAID Level 1 array members operate independently and improve performance for read-intensive applications although at a relatively high inherent cost.

- **FAULT TOLERANT** – This is a good entry-level redundant system, since only two drives are required. Disk duplexing, which is a variation of disk mirroring, requires the drives to be on separate disk controllers so that the data can be accessed if one of the disks or controllers goes bad. RAID 1 provides 100 percent redundancy of data, so data can simply be copied onto a replacement disk in the event of a disk failure.

- Usable disk storage is equal to the size of the smallest disk. Two mirrored disks, one 100GB and one 200GB, would yield a mirrored capacity of 100GB of usable space.

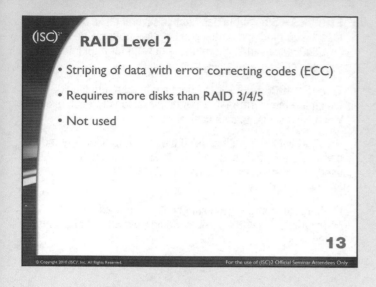

RAID Level 2

- Striping of data with error correcting codes (ECC)
- Requires more disks than RAID 3/4/5
- Not used

13

- **STRIPING OF DATA WITH ERROR CORRECTING CODES (ECC)** – This form of RAID is not used and is not commercially viable. It creates a hamming code for error correction and was designed for systems that required very high data transfer rates with simultaneous error correction.

- **REQUIRES MORE DISKS THAN RAID 3/4/5** – To establish a basic array, RAID 2 requires many more disks than the other methods of RAID.

- **NOT USED** – Raid 2 requires so many disks that it is almost never used in operations.

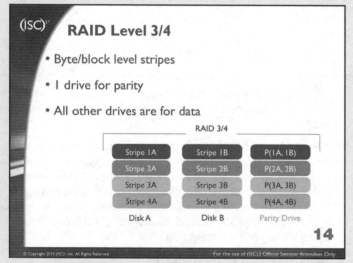

RAID Level 3/4

- Byte/block level stripes
- I drive for parity
- All other drives are for data

RAID 3/4		
Stripe 1A	Stripe 1B	P(1A, 1B)
Stripe 2A	Stripe 2B	P(2A, 2B)
Stripe 3A	Stripe 3B	P(3A, 3B)
Stripe 4A	Stripe 4B	P(4A, 4B)
Disk A	Disk B	Parity Drive

14

additional disk failures. Also, a RAID 3 array can improve the throughput of read operations by allowing reads to be performed concurrently on multiple disks in the set.

- At best, the RAID 3 transaction rate is only equal to that of a single disk drive and the amount of actual disk space consumed is always a multiple of the disk's block size times the number of disks in the array, which can lead to wastage of space. The controller design is fairly complex and very difficult and resource intensive to do as a "software" RAID.

- Usable disk storage is calculated by multiplying the size of the smallest disk by the number of disks in the array, minus one disk (which is the parity drive). Five 100GB drives would therefore yield 400GB of usable space.

- **RAID LEVEL 4** – Is similar to RAID 3 in that it uses parity bits stored on a single disk to protect data. RAID Level 4 array's member disks are independently accessible and its performance is more suited to transaction I/O than to large file transfers.

  - RAID 4 has a very high read data transaction rate. A low ratio of ECC (parity) disks to data disks results in greater efficiency. RAID 4 also has a high aggregate read transfer rate.

  - As with RAID 3, usable disk storage is calculated by multiplying the size of the smallest disk by the number of disks in the array, minus one disk (which is the parity drive). Five 100GB drives would, therefore, yield 400GB of usable space.

  - RAID 4 exhibits poor transaction write performance due to a bottleneck on the parity disk. That is one reason RAID 5 is more popular.

- **RAID LEVEL 3** – Adds redundancy of information in the form of storing parity on a parallel access striped array, which permits regeneration and rebuilding in the event of a disk failure. One stripe of parity protects the corresponding stripes of data on the remaining disks. RAID Level 3 provides a high transfer rate and high availability at an inherently lower cost than mirroring. Its transaction performance is poor, however, because all RAID Level 3 array member disks operate in lockstep.

  - RAID 3 has very high read and write data transfer rates. Any disk failure will have an insignificant impact on throughput. RAID 3 ensures that if one of the disks in the striped set (other than the parity disk) fails, its contents can be recalculated using the information on the parity disk and the remaining functioning disks. If the parity disk itself fails, the RAID array is not affected in terms of I/O throughput, but the array no longer has protection from

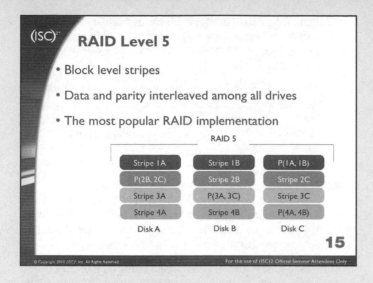

- **BLOCK LEVEL STRIPES** – Stripes the data and the parity bits across the disk array.

- **DATA AND PARITY INTERLEAVED AMONG ALL DRIVES** – It provides redundancy and the ability to recover lost data due to disk failure through the calculation of the parity bit.

- **THE MOST POPULAR RAID IMPLEMENTATION** – It provides low cost redundancy and has, therefore, become the most popular RAID implementation.

- As with RAID Levels 3 and 4, usable disk storage is calculated by multiplying the size of the smallest disk by the number of disks in the array, minus one disk (which is the lost space used for parity). Five 100GB drives would, therefore, yield 400GB of usable space.

- RAID 5 is more popular than RAID 4 because it provides better write performance on random I/O.

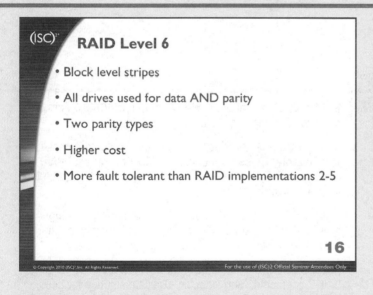

- **BLOCK LEVEL STRIPES** – Provides protection against double disk failures and against failures while a single disk is re-building.

- **ALL DRIVES USED FOR DATA AND PARITY** – RAID 6 does not have a performance penalty for read operations, but it does have a performance penalty on write operations due to the overhead associated with the additional parity calculations.

- **TWO PARITY TYPES** – RAID 6 is essentially an extension of RAID Level 5 that allows for additional fault tolerance by using a second, independent, distributed (two-dimensional) parity scheme. As with RAID 5, data are striped on a block level across a set of drives, and a second set of parity is calculated and written across all the drives. RAID 6 provides extremely high data-fault tolerance and can sustain multiple, simultaneous drive failures. RAID 6 is a perfect solution for mission-critical applications.

- **HIGHER COST** –

  - RAID 6 has a very complex controller design and the controller overhead to compute parity addresses is extremely high. It yields very poor write performance.

  - RAID 6 is infrequently used due to the higher costs involved. RAID 5 with hot spares is more cost effective than RAID 6 and almost as reliable.

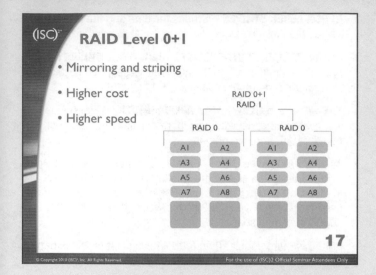

RAID Level 0+1

- Mirroring and striping
- Higher cost
- Higher speed

17

mum of four hard drives, however, and adding an extra hard drive to one stripe requires that an additional hard drive be added to the other stripes to balance out storage among the arrays.

- RAID 0+1 is not as robust as RAID 1+0 and cannot tolerate two simultaneous disk failures unless they are from the same stripe. Once a single disk fails, each of the mechanisms in the other stripe becomes a single point of failure. Once the single failed mechanism is replaced, all the disks in the array must participate in rebuilding the data.

- **HIGHER COST** – A single drive failure will cause the whole array to become, in essence, a RAID Level 0 array. It is very expensive and has high overheads. All drives must move in parallel to properly track lowering sustained performance. It has very limited scalability at a very high inherent cost.

- **HIGHER SPEED** – RAID 0+1 is implemented as a mirrored array, the segments of which are RAID 0 arrays. RAID 0+1 has the same fault tolerance as RAID level 5 and has the same overhead for fault tolerance as mirroring alone. Multiple stripe segments allow for high I/O rates. It is an excellent solution for sites that need high performance but are not concerned with achieving maximum reliability.

- **MIRRORING AND STRIPING** – Used for both replicating and sharing data among disks. The difference between RAID 0+1 and RAID 1+0 is the location of each RAID system: In RAID 1+0, stripes are mirrored.

  - The advantage of RAID 0+1 is that when a hard drive fails in one of the Level 0 arrays, the missing data can be transferred from the other array. This requires a mini-

---

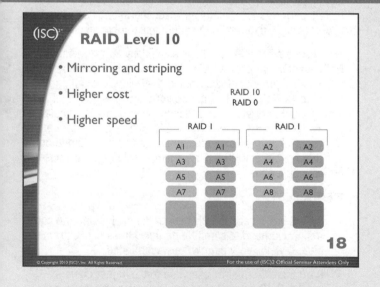

RAID Level 10

- Mirroring and striping
- Higher cost
- Higher speed

18

- **RAID LEVEL 10** – All but one drive from each RAID 1 set can fail without damaging the data.

- **MIRRORING AND STRIPING** – RAID 10 is implemented as a striped array whose segments are RAID 1 arrays with RAID 1 level tolerance. RAID 10 has the same overhead for fault tolerance as mirroring alone.

- **HIGHER COST** – RAID 10 is very expensive and yields high overhead. It has very limited scalability at a very high inherent cost.

- **HIGHER SPEED** – The high I/O rates are achieved by striping RAID 1 segments. It provides an excellent solution for sites that would have otherwise gone with RAID 1, but need an additional performance boost.

- Usable disk storage is equal to the sum of the individual RAID 1 sets.

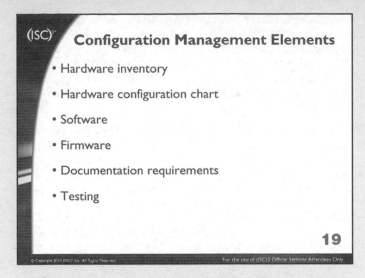

Configuration Management Elements

- Hardware inventory
- Hardware configuration chart
- Software
- Firmware
- Documentation requirements
- Testing

19

- **CONFIGURATION MANAGEMENT** – Definition – To maintain the systems' integrity with respect to the approved settings. Configuration management includes the hardware, software, firmware, and documentation of an automated system throughout the system life cycle. Configuration management ensures that all system baselines are maintained. If the baseline is changed via the change control process, then all related systems are changed.

- **HARDWARE INVENTORY** – Most organizations lack a hardware inventory of what equipment they have, who has ownership or possession of it, and which departments or systems are using it. This is a serious gap in a security program. In the event of a fire, equipment failure, or theft, this lack of documentation may result in extended loss of operations and poor response.

- **HARDWARE CONFIGURATION CHART** – It is essential to have an up-to-date map or layout of the configuration of the hardware components to ensure that all systems are configured according to the baseline, that all work on a system or network has been properly reviewed, and that correct changes are being made without allowing any bypass of security features. One study alleges that half of all network failures are caused by poor cabling records!

- **SOFTWARE LICENSING MANAGEMENT** – Software licensing management ensures the organization is legally compliant with its software licensing and eliminates the financial (and other) risks of noncompliance. It saves money on software purchases and planning. Productivity is increased and costs are reduced by eliminating surplus purchases and deployment costs.

- **DOCUMENTATION REQUIREMENTS** – Documentation of all systems, applications, and configurations should be kept up to date and all changes to documentation should be reviewed and approved. In addition, no change to a system or network should be approved without the accompanying documentation being prepared and submitted.

  - **FORMAT** – Documentation of all systems should include the normal transaction volume expected for the system, the description of the system or application, the owner, all changes made to date, the scheduling of the job runs, and how to respond to any errors on the system.

  - **COPIES** – A copy of all documentation should be kept both onsite and offsite, usually at the backup or alternate site for use in the event of a disaster.

- **TESTING** – Both functionality and security must be tested before production systems are updated. Testing can be done at worst via blue screen and at best via QA with full regression.

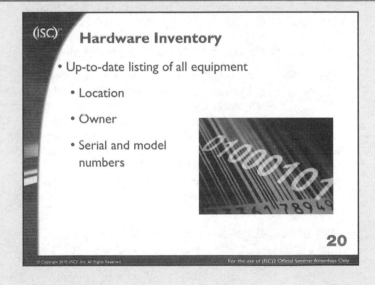

Hardware Inventory

- Up-to-date listing of all equipment
  - Location
  - Owner
  - Serial and model numbers

20

- **HARDWARE INVENTORY** – It is important to have a list of all equipment that the administrator is responsible for. This is required both for recovery needs in the event of theft or fire, but also for proper asset management – to ensure that patches, antivirus, and other tools are maintained. Some of the important items to include in the inventory are the location where the equipment (or its owner) resides; the name of the person who has responsibility for the equipment (especially when the equipment is portable); and the model and serial number of the equipment.

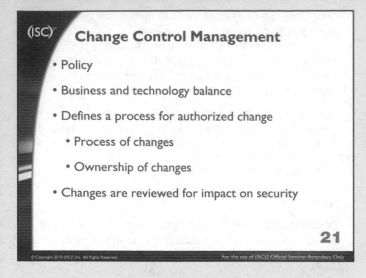

Change Control Management

- Policy
- Business and technology balance
- Defines a process for authorized change
  - Process of changes
  - Ownership of changes
- Changes are reviewed for impact on security

21

- **DEFINITION –** Change control management is the management of security features and supporting assurances, through the control of changes made to hardware, software, firmware, documentation, test fixtures, and test documentation of an automated system. It begins during developme nt and is conducted throughout the operational life of a system. It is a part of risk management with respect to systems and technology.

- **CHANGE CONTROL MANAGEMENT –** Is the process of developing a planned approach to controlling change in an environment that includes the involvement of the security department. The objective is to maximize the collective benefits for all people involved in the change and minimize the risk of failure when implementing the change. Change control is the means for maintaining system integrity.

- **POLICY –** Change control policy mandates that changes must be approved, documented, and made via an authorized process.

- **BUSINESS AND TECHNOLOGY BALANCE –** To be effective, change management should be multi-disciplinary, touching all aspects of the organization. It should allow the business to change as needed. A business should not be constrained to the point of being inflexible and unable to adopt new technologies, improvements, and modifications, or other changes as needed.

- **DEFINES A PROCESS FOR AUTHORIZED CHANGE –** Change management requires a written policy that defines all roles, responsibilities, and procedures related to change management, and approved by the CIO/IT director and the business information security manager. Change management procedures and standards are communicated to define the techniques and technologies to be used throughout the enterprise in support of the change management policy. Change management can be either "reactive," in which case management is responding to changes in the business environment (that is, the source of the change is external – i.e., changes in regulations, customer expectations, supply chain), or "proactive," where the change request is initiated by management in order to achieve a desired goal or benefit (that is, when the source of the change is internal – i.e., adoption of new technology). Change management can be conducted on a continuous basis, on a regular schedule (such as an annual review, or "release" basis where many small changes are incorporated into one larger change), or when deemed necessary on a program-by-program basis.

- **CHANGES ARE REVIEWED FOR IMPACT ON SECURITY –** A change is a time of risk for a business because it may circumvent security features previously built into a system, result in outage or system failure, or may require extensive retraining and learning new systems.

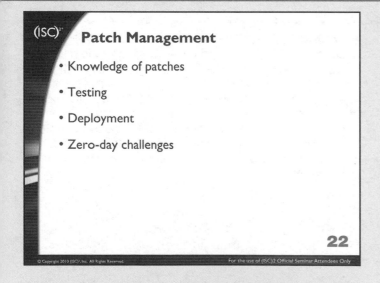

Patch Management

- Knowledge of patches
- Testing
- Deployment
- Zero-day challenges

22

- **PATCH MANAGEMENT –** The methodical application of vendor-related updates and security enhancements. Patch management can be thought of as faster change control.

- **KNOWLEDGE OF PATCHES –** Vendors frequently release modifications and security patches to their systems and applications. Administrators must keep informed about all of the software in their environment. Automation is the only way to have an accurate inventory of organizational software. The large quantity of patches can be burdensome to most administrators.

- **TESTING –** Vendor patches have been known to have flaws or to affect other system components, or prevent them from functioning. All patches should, therefore, be tested before they are implemented or "rolled out" to production. This may require an isolated system that can be used to test the patch.

- **DEPLOYMENT –** The rollout or deployment of patches needs to be coordinated to ensure that all systems are patched properly and in a timely manner. This is often done by "pushing" the changes out to the systems automatically, or in some cases, by checking machines as they log in to ensure that they are up to date with the various patches and antivirus signature files. Except for the fact that patch management deployments are typically pre-approved by policy, since patch management is a part of change management, it is subject to the same requirements.

- **ZERO-DAY CHALLENGES –** Security patch management is often a short cycle process. When a security vulnerability is discovered by a vendor (whether the vendor has made it public or not), vendors often come out with a patch very quickly. Deploying security patches puts the organization in a race with its adversaries. Organizations must deploy the patch, keep the machines stable, and verify that the patch does not adversely affect the environment, while adversaries are reverse engineering the patch to define the system's weakness, build an exploit, search for targets, and take advantage of the vulnerability.

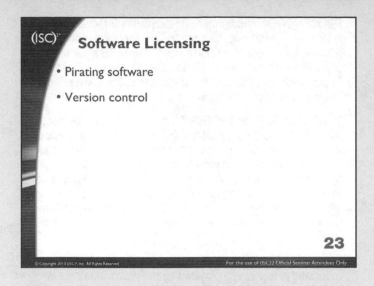

- **PIRATING SOFTWARE** – Care must be taken to ensure that the organization is using software in accord with the End User License Agreements (EULAs) that are agreed to during the installation process. This includes ensuring that software is only installed on the appropriate number of machines, and that the organization does not use pirated software or not have licenses for each user.

- **VERSION CONTROL** – Closely linked with patch management and applications development, version control ensures that all team members are using compatible products and ones that have the latest security updates applied.

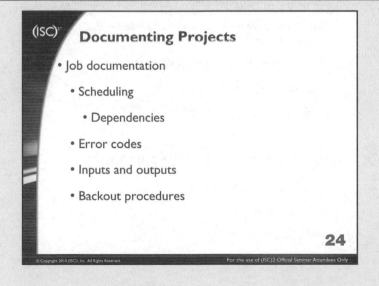

- **JOB DOCUMENTATION** – Every job should be documented. This is important for continuity and possible staff changes. The job should list when the job must be run – which jobs must be completed first (end of month processing must be done after the end of the last day processing); what error codes the job may return and how to deal with them; as well as a list of the inputs and outputs the job depends on. Finally the job documentation should outline the procedures to follow in event of job failure – how to clean out corrupted files and purge residual data elements.

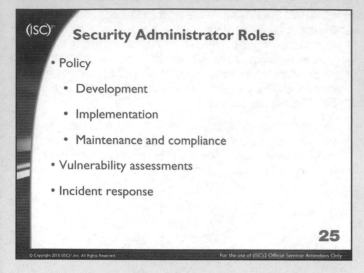

- **SECURITY ADMINISTRATOR ROLES** – The security administrator monitors the system and reports problems from the perspective of security. In this management structure, the security administrator will work closely with the system manager. In many organizations, the roles of security administrator and systems administrator are combined. This poses additional risk.

- **POLICY** – When management develops, implements, maintains, and monitors compliance through policy, the policy must address the potential for harm from a trusted insider such as security administrators. It is more likely that control will be maintained and understood if these capabilities and privileges are specifically discussed in the functional policy.

- **VULNERABILITY ASSESSMENT** – As a function by the security administrator is a delicate task, balancing the need to know the weaknesses in systems with the use of that knowledge. Security administrators will collect the data and use it to protect systems by applying the correct patch. Users should not have access to this capability. IDS/IPD systems should warn when vulnerability assessment activities are being performed because unauthorized use of vulnerability assessment is a threat.

- **INCIDENT RESPONSE** – Allows the security administrator to expend resources as dictated by the policy. This entails spending money, decreasing availability, investigation, and possibly communicating outside the organization. These activities require management to delegate clearly, and require security administrators to understand the power they have.

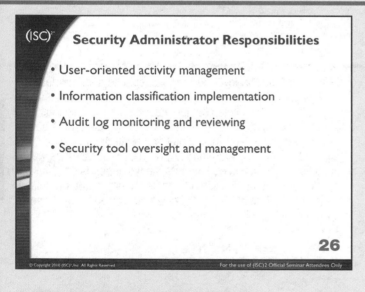

- **USER-ORIENTED ACTIVITY MANAGEMENT:**
  - Setting user clearances.
  - Creating security profiles.
  - Setting passwords.
  - Setting access permissions for users.

- **INFORMATION CLASSIFICATION IMPLEMENTATION:**
  - Setting file-sensitivity labels.
  - Setting access permissions for files and equipment.
  - Setting security characteristics (devices and communications channels).

- **AUDIT LOG MONITORING AND REVIEWING:**
  - Reviewing audit data.
  - Setting access permissions.
  - Setting security profiles.

- **SECURITY TOOL OVERSIGHT AND MANAGEMENT:**
  - Antivirus management.
  - Firewall configuration.
  - IDS/IPS settings.

Domain Agenda

- Operator and Administrator Security
  - Monitoring of Special Privileges
  - **Misuse of Resources**
  - System Recovery
- Resource Protection
  - Environmental Issues and Controls
  - Media Management

27

Misuse Prevention

Threats	Countermeasures
Personal Use	Acceptable use policy, workstation controls, web content filtering, and email filtering
Theft of Media	Appropriate media controls
Fraud	Balancing of input/output reports, separation of duties, and verification of information
Sniffers	Encryption and policy

28

- **PERSONAL USE –**

  - **ACCEPTABLE USE POLICY –** To ensure the proper personal use of workstations, organizations need to develop an acceptable use policy that emphasizes appropriate usage. The policy should address topics such as what kind of applications users may run, what kind of data they may store, what they may surf on the Internet, what type of activity is strictly forbidden, and what consequences will result if the policy is violated.

  - **WORKSTATION CONTROLS –** Organizations should implement comprehensive security and controls to mitigate risks due to misuse or inappropriate use. Organizations should consider an enterprise-wide, standard-build workstation rollout that locks down and baselines system capabilities, an implementation of role-based access control, a centralized automated antivirus solution, a patch and update management system, software metering, a monitoring system, and an enterprise backup solution that also includes backing up the workstations.

- **WEB CONTENT FILTERING –** Helps organizations enforce corporate Internet usage policies; allows control of access to non-business related websites; protects organization, staff, and network assets; and provides tools to monitor web usage. Filtering out non-business content leads to increased employee productivity, increased network efficiency, minimizes bandwidth costs, avoids workplace issues caused by objectionable content, and helps protect the organization from legal liabilities. The web filtering solution typically has a categorized database of various website categories, a self-learning capability to catch new websites, and usually comes with a granular policy manager with real-time monitoring and managing controls.

- **EMAIL FILTERING –** Solutions filter the content based on organizational policies and preferences. Email filtering allows the organization to limit bandwidth consumption, provide spam control, block file attachments likely to contain malicious software, control viruses and worms, and enforce email usage policies. Email filtering protects organizations from leaking confidential information and limits the size and type of email attachments, which helps prevent serious attacks such as denial of service.

- **THEFT OF MEDIA –** Can lead to the compromise of sensitive data and may result in legal liability. Appropriate media controls such as inventory, labeling, secure storage, and disabling ports that could be used to improperly transfer data, are used to protect sensitive information whether it is on computer printouts, portable memory, or CDs.

- **FRAUD PREVENTION –** Fraud prevention is provided through tasks such as balancing input and output reports, separation of duties, and verification of information with originating documents and departments.

- **SNIFFERS –** The best defense against the use of sniffers is data encryption. The organization should also have a clear policy regarding the possession and use of any sniffing tools.

Domain Agenda

- Operator and Administrator Security

  - Monitoring of Special Privileges

  - Misuse of Resources

  - **System Recovery**

- Resource Protection

  - Environmental Issues and Controls

  - Media Management

29

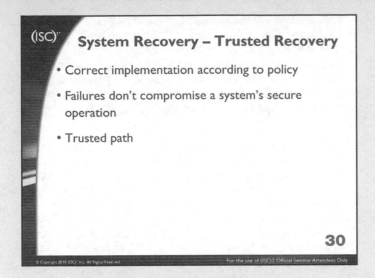

System Recovery – Trusted Recovery

- Correct implementation according to policy
- Failures don't compromise a system's secure operation
- Trusted path

30

- **SYSTEM RECOVERY – TRUSTED RECOVERY –** As defined in the Trusted Computer Security Evaluation Criteria, the assurance control objective is that:

- "Systems that are used to process or handle classified or other sensitive information must be designed to guarantee correct and accurate interpretation of the security policy and must not distort the intent of that policy. Assurance must be provided that correct implementation and operation of the

policy exists throughout the system's life cycle."

- This objective affects trusted recovery in two important ways. First, the design and implementation of the recovery mechanisms and procedures must satisfy the life-cycle assurance requirements of correct implementation and operation. Second, the system's administrative procedures and recovery mechanisms should ensure correct enforcement of the system security policy in the face of system failures and discontinuities of operation.

- **TRUSTED PATH –** It is only possible to perform administrator or management functions for many systems through a trusted channel or trusted path. A trusted path is a secure link from the management console directly to the equipment, often to an administrator port on the device. This provides a level of protection, since the person desiring to change any administrative settings must have physical access to the management console or equipment itself. In the mainframe world, the operator console is on a trusted path and usually hardwired directly to the mainframe itself and not attached to any other networks. A trusted path is a mechanism by which a person at a terminal can communicate directly with the trusted computing base (TCB). This mechanism can only be activated by the person or the TCB and cannot be imitated by untrusted software.

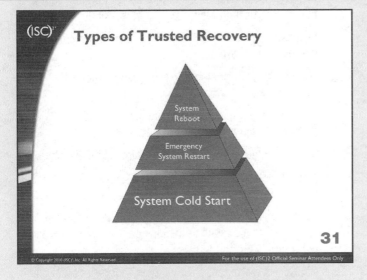

Types of Trusted Recovery

System Reboot

Emergency System Restart

System Cold Start

31

- **TYPES OF TRUSTED RECOVERY –** There are three general categories of operating systems' responses to failures: (1) system reboot, (2) emergency system restart, and (3) system cold start.

  - **SYSTEM REBOOT –** Is performed after shutting down the system in a controlled manner in response to a TCB (trusted computing base) failure. For example, when the TCB detects that space in some of its critical tables has been exhausted, or finds inconsistent object data structures, it

will close all objects, abort all active user processes, and restart with no user process in execution. Before restart, however, the recovery mechanisms will make a best effort to correct the source of inconsistency and, occasionally, the mere termination of all processes frees up some important resources thus allowing restart. Note that system rebooting is useful when the recovery mechanisms can determine that TCB and user data structures affecting system security and integrity are in a consistent state.

  - **EMERGENCY SYSTEM RESTART –** Is done after a system fails in an uncontrolled manner in response to a TCB or media failure. In such cases, TCB and user objects on nonvolatile storage belonging to processes active at the time of TCB or media failure may be left in an inconsistent state. The system will enter maintenance mode, automatically perform recovery, and the system will restart with no user processes in progress after bringing up the system in a consistent state.

  - **SYSTEM COLD START –** Takes place when unexpected TCB or media failures take place and the recovery procedures cannot bring the system to a consistent state. TCB and user objects may remain in an inconsistent state following attempts to recover automatically. Intervention of administrative personnel will be required in order to bring the system to a consistent state from maintenance mode.

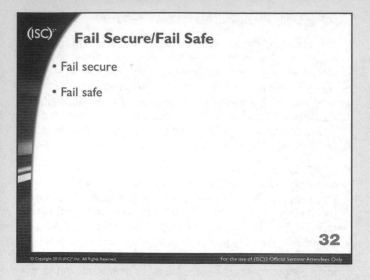

Fail Secure/Fail Safe

- Fail secure
- Fail safe

32

- **FAIL SECURE** – It is important that when a system fails, it fails in a secure manner rather than leaving everything open. Should firewall software crash, for example, all traffic should be disallowed rather than allowed. Fail Closed is a synonym for Fail Secure – in the event of a failure, the system reverts to a closed or secure condition. A system that fails soft (or fails open) is one that remains open and permits traffic in the event of a failure.

- **FAIL SAFE** – Please note that the above definitions are open to debate. The explanation used above is the analogy of the access control system on a door – does it fail open – allowing traffic through, or fail closed and prohibit all traffic. This is the opposite of the analogy of an electrical circuit such as a circuit breaker – when it "trips" it "opens" the electrical path and stops all current flow (traffic). For this reason it may be better to use the terms "fail safe" and fail soft rather than the terms fail open or fail closed.

Fault Tolerance

- Hardware failure is planned for
- System recognizes a failure
- Automatic corrective action
- Standby systems
  - Cold – Configured, not on, lost connections
  - Warm – On, some lost data or transactions (TRX)
  - Hot – Ready - failover

33

- **FAULT TOLERANCE** – A fault-tolerant system is designed to keep running even after a fault has occurred. Fault-tolerant features in early network operating systems included mirrored disks, where both disks read and wrote the same information. If one disk failed, the other kept running in "failover" mode. This fault tolerance was expanded to disk duplexing, in which the disks and disk controllers were duplicated. These redundant components not only provided fault tolerance, but also improved performance, since disk reads could come from either disk. (Writes still had to be performed by both disks.) Fault-tolerant systems must provide more than just disk failover, however.

- **SOME OTHER EXAMPLES OF REDUNDANT SYSTEMS INCLUDE THE FOLLOWING:**
  - RAID disk systems that combine multiple hard drives into fault-protected arrays.

- Deployment of redundant servers.
- Primary server mirrored to secondary server.
- Fail over or roll over to secondary servers in the event of a failure. Server fault tolerance can be warm or hot.
- Installation of redundant components (power supplies, I/O boards, and so on).
- Multiple servers clustered to minimize problems if any of the servers fail.
- Alternate pathing and load balancing that improve throughput and provide redundant links.
- Multiple data centers to protect against local disasters.
- **STANDBY SYSTEMS** – Cold, Warm, and Hot refer to the readiness of standby systems.
  - **COLD** – A cold standby model would provide a configured spare, but would result in the loss of all connections and delay due to startup time
  - **WARM** – A warm model would be a "hot spare" that could fail over but would still lose some data or transactions that were in process at the time of the primary failure.
  - **HOT** – A hot model has redundant and complete failover capability that would assume processing with little or no process or transaction loss in the event of a failure of the primary equipment.

REFERENCE:
http://www.aldex.co.uk/continuity.html

Domain Agenda

- Operator and Administrator Security

  - Monitoring of Special Privileges

  - Misuse of Resources

  - System Recovery

- **Resource Protection**

  - **Environmental Issues and Controls**

  - Media Management

34

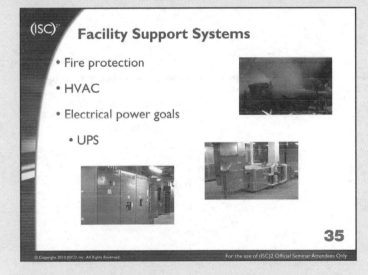

Facility Support Systems

- Fire protection
- HVAC
- Electrical power goals
  - UPS

35

- **FACILITY SUPPORT SYSTEMS –** The operations group may not be responsible for the maintenance of facilities and safety equipment, but they are frequently responsible to monitor, and report, on any facilities-related issues. They must watch for problems that could affect the operations of the information systems equipment or allow unauthorized access to secure areas.

- **FIRE PROTECTION –**

  - **PREVENTION, DETECTION, & SUPPRESSION**

    - Classes of fires (A, B, C, etc.)

    - Have suppression agents such as water, carbon dioxide, FM-200 (the industry recognized replacement for Halon 1301), etc., on hand. Install alarms and sensors (i.e., ion-based or optical smoke detectors), and fixed, or rate-of-rise temperature sensors.

    - Data centers require particularly sensitive alarms. Instead of commercial-grade fire alarms, data centers should have devices that signal the early stages of a fire

through optical or chemical sensors that may sound an alarm before a fire even starts. Many data centers are now using VESDA (Very Early Smoke Detection Apparatus) devices for fire detection. A fire normally goes through four stages of development: incipient (pre-combustion), visible smoke, fast flaming, and heat. Conventional smoke detectors are only able to detect smoke when the fire has reached the visible smoke phase. A VESDA device continuously samples the air in the facility and runs it through laser-powered detectors, which allow it to detect smoke even before the human eye can notice it, during the incipient stage of fire development

- **HVAC –** Heating, ventilation, and air conditioning systems maintain appropriate humidity and temperature controls as well as a contaminant-free air supply.

  - Monitoring systems can detect abnormal data center temperatures, humidity, or other factors. Monitoring devices alert you to a potential problem before there is a disruption in service.

  - Ideally, HVAC systems will have backup power and be isolated from the rest of the building. Nonetheless, it is important to have proper fans and cooling systems in place to mitigate against potential HVAC system failure, as well as provide adequate air flow to mitigate the masses of hot air that can build up toward the ceiling, where rack-mounted servers may be located.

- **ELECTRIC POWER GOALS –** Provide clean and steady power for data centers and include UPS (uninterruptible power supply) surge protectors and protection from transient noise, etc.

  - Ensure that a proper electrical infrastructure is in place, and have this validated by a certified electrician.

  - Mission-critical data centers should have alternate power sources such as emergency generators, as well as a minimum 24-hour fuel supply.

Facility Support Systems (cont.)

- Water
- Communications
- Alarm systems

36

- **WATER –** Protect against water and humidity damage. Water can damage or destroy the data center through flooding, rain, snow, and condensation. Protect against flooding by ensuring that the data center is properly insulated against pipe leaks or toilet or sink overflows from an upper floor or neighboring room. The data center should not be located below grade level if there is any risk of flooding. The roof must be properly insulated, water-proofed, and designed so that it is unable to accumulate snow or rain.

- **COMMUNICATIONS –** The data center may require redundant links and failover communication lines in order to provide communications and network capability if the primary links are lost. Always have a backup communications channel for critical communications networks.

- **ALARM SYSTEMS –** Monitoring systems require reliable communications and alert systems in order to notify personnel of an incident or problem.

Domain Agenda

- Operator and Administrator Security

  - Monitoring of Special Privileges

  - Misuse of Resources

  - System Recovery

- **Resource Protection**

  - Environmental Issues and Controls

- **Media Management**

37

protected in such a way that they are not physically or visually accessible to persons who do not have a need to know. For example, they might be secured in a locked container, office, or other restricted access area. Magnetic media must be handled carefully to protect against contamination or damage from other sources such as magnets.

- **STORING** – Provide secure storage and environmental protection from heat, humidity, liquids, dust, smoke, and magnetism.

- **DECLASSIFYING AND DESTROYING** – When storage media must be destroyed or declassified, the action should be undertaken by an authorized staff member in the presence of a witness. In the most sensitive cases, a certificate of declassification should be completed and sent to the departmental security authority. This certificate should include:

  - A description of the medium (type, manufacturer, model, serial number).

  - The original and final classification and intended destination of the medium.

  - The reason for declassification.

  - A description of the declassification procedure, detailing, as appropriate, the degausser used, the identification of overwriting software, or the destruction process.

  - The names and signatures of the departmental staff members carrying out and witnessing the activity.

- **MARKING** – All media that contains sensitive or classified information should be clearly labeled both electronically and physically. This marking should be written or stamped in plain style bold type, or by using bar codes.

- **LABELING** – Object labeling refers to the marking of the classification on magnetic media (files).

- **HANDLING** – Everyone is responsible for ensuring that records containing sensitive or classified information are safeguarded at all times. Information and records must be

---

- All media storage locations need to be as well protected as the primary site.

- USB-based devices such as thumb drives, hard drives, and MP3 players deserve special consideration. They have fast transfer rates, high capacity, and are easily concealed and/or lost. They can often be hidden inside other devices such as toys, watches, knives, pens, wrist bands, and wallets. Establish policies on the use of USB-based storage devices that include use, access, monitoring, labeling, and encryption.

- **TAPES** – Tapes are still a relatively cheap way to store large amounts of data and easily move it to offsite locations. Tapes have a limited lifetime that includes the acceptable number of times a tape can be used. The operations staff needs to ensure that tapes are not used beyond their acceptable lifespan.

- **ENCRYPTION** – Any time that sensitive information is taken offsite, it should be encrypted to protect against loss or theft of equipment. Many countries now require this under privacy protection laws (Japan).

- **RETRIEVAL** – Transport of storage media is a time of risk for the organization – the media may be lost, stolen, or damaged, so care must be taken to facilitate safe transportation of the media in a timely manner.

- **DISPOSAL** – Every organization should have a media disposal policy – especially for media that had contained sensitive data. This will be seen in more depth on the following slides.

- **MEDIA MANAGEMENT** – Information assets include valuable or sensitive information whether written, verbal, or electronic. All forms of media must be protected from misuse, disclosure, and accidental erasure.

  - Onsite magnetic media should be maintained and protected by the operations center tape librarians.

  - Write-protect rings or read-only settings should be used on tapes or other media that must be protected from overwriting.

  - Offsite and/or alternate site storage media also requires physical, technical/logical, and administrative access controls.

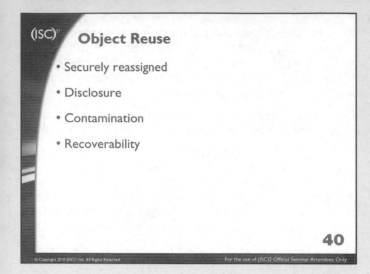

Object Reuse

- Securely reassigned
- Disclosure
- Contamination
- Recoverability

40

© Copyright 2010 (ISC)², Inc. All Rights Reserved.   For the use of (ISC)2 Official Seminar Attendees Only

- **OBJECT REUSE** – Reassigning of a storage medium (i.e., page frame, disk sector, magnetic tape) that once contained data or objects belonging to another process to a new process, or subject. As defined by A Guide to Understanding Data Remanence in Automated Information Systems: "The requirement

ultimately derives from observations made during the early penetration testing experiences that systems typically did not clear a user's working memory when the user completed a session. Thus, when memory was reassigned to another user, the information placed in it by the previous user was now available to the new owner of the scratch space. Often, the disclosure was inadvertent: The second user had not intended to obtain the information suddenly made available. However, it also meant that a malicious (or just curious) user could browse through the system, obtaining scratch space and looking for items of interest (the equivalent of rummaging through the trash)."

- **SECURELY REASSIGNED** – No residual data is available to the new subject.

- **DISCLOSURE** – Inappropriately revealing information to a subject.

- **CONTAMINATION** – Reducing integrity below acceptable levels.

- **RECOVERABILITY** – There are numerous digital forensic and data recovery tools available that can recover data from previous used objects.

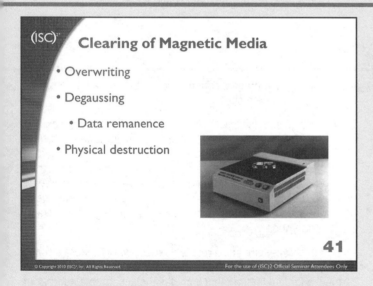

Clearing of Magnetic Media

- Overwriting
- Degaussing
  - Data remanence
- Physical destruction

41

© Copyright 2010 (ISC)², Inc. All Rights Reserved.   For the use of (ISC)2 Official Seminar Attendees Only

- **OVERWRITING** – One method of clearing data from magnetic media is to overwrite the existing data with several "passes" of 1s, 0s, and random values. There are several government-approved tools available for this purpose. Unless dealing with media that once contained very sensitive data, an overwriting program is sufficient to secure against the risk of object reuse. NIST SP 800-88 provides guidance and is intended for both government and industry (www.csrc.nist.gov).

- **DEGAUSSING** –

  - Data is stored in magnetic media (hard drive, floppy disks, and magnetic tape) by forcing magnetic domains to change their magnetic alignment in the direction of an applied magnetic field.

  - Degaussing, commonly called erasure, leaves the domains in random patterns with no preference to orientation,

thereby rendering previous data unrecoverable. However, some domains may not be properly randomized even after degaussing. The retained information is commonly called magnetic remanence. Proper degaussing will ensure that there is insufficient magnetic remanence to reconstruct the data.

- A degausser is a device that can generate a magnetic field for degaussing magnetic storage media. Erasure via degaussing may be accomplished in two ways: In AC-powered erasure, the media is degaussed by applying an alternating field that is reduced in amplitude over time from an initial high value, whereas in DC-powered erasure, the media is saturated by applying a unidirectional field. This can also be accomplished by employing a permanent magnet.

- **DATA REMANENCE** – Is the residual physical representation of data remaining on media after the data has been in some way erased. After storage media is erased, it may still retain some physical characteristics that allow data to be reconstructed. Without the application of data-removal procedures, inadvertent disclosure of sensitive information is possible should the storage media be released into an uncontrolled environment. Protection against data remanence can be achieved by degaussing, overwriting, data encryption, and media destruction. Over a period of time, certain practices have been accepted for the clearing and purging of storage media.

- **PHYSICAL DESTRUCTION** – There is no totally secure method of erasing extremely sensitive data that has been stored on magnetic media. For that reason, the only way to dispose of magnetic media that has contained very sensitive media is to physically destroy the media itself.

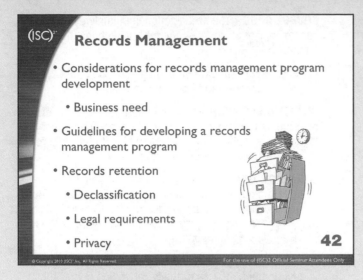

Records Management

- Considerations for records management program development
  - Business need
- Guidelines for developing a records management program
- Records retention
  - Declassification
  - Legal requirements
  - Privacy

42

- **CONSIDERATIONS FOR RECORDS MANAGEMENT PROGRAM DEVELOPMENT -**

  - Length of time during which records have operational, legal, fiscal, or historical value.

  - Length of time during which records are considered active and must be maintained in the primary filing area.

  - Point at which records can reasonably be transferred to a secondary storage facility.

  - Method of records disposal or disposition.

  - Procedures for operating the program and ensuring compliance.

  - The relationship between records retention and other aspects of the records management (RM) program such as archives for microfilm, filing, data processing, and historical records.

- **GUIDELINES FOR DEVELOPING A RECORDS MANAGEMENT PROGRAM -**

  - Obtain top management support.

- Establish a program coordinator for the development and operation of the records management program.

- Gather information from data custodians about all information handled within the organization.

- Review records to determine their operational, legal, fiscal, and historical value and retention requirements.

- Provide for the disposition of the original and duplicate copies in the records retention schedule.

- Include all forms of media in the retention and disposition schedule.

- Ensure that all legal requirements with which the organization must comply are reviewed.

- Protect, handle, and destroy records in the appropriate manner as identified in the records management policy.

- Consider other storage formats that may be better than original documents or files (i.e., scanning documents).

- Coordinate with legal counsel to ensure that designated files are cleared from litigation proceedings.

- **RECORDS RETENTION –** A records retention and disposition program is a component of an organization's records management program that:

  - Declassifies when data no longer requires protection.

  - Defines the length of time that records must be kept.

  - Outlines the procedures for the transfer, storage, and final disposition of records.

  - Conforms to the legal requirements required by industry or regulatory agencies.

  - Protects stored data from unauthorized access.

  - Note that the records retention policy will change in response to the business needs of the organization.

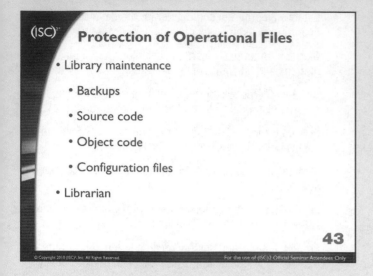

Protection of Operational Files

- Library maintenance
  - Backups
  - Source code
  - Object code
  - Configuration files
- Librarian

43

- **LIBRARY MAINTENANCE** – All organizations need to carefully protect their production programs and applications as well as their data.

  - **BACKUPS** – Operating systems, tables, directories, configuration files, transaction files, databases, and data files must all be backed up.

- **SOURCE CODE** – The organization should always have a secure copy of all source code for applications that is kept offsite.

  - Application software should be kept up to date with vendor patches and licensing control.

- **OBJECT CODE** – Executables and other object code must be protected from misuse or alteration, and care must be taken to ensure that the source and object code, where applicable, are of the same version.

- **CONFIGURATION FILES** – Operations personnel and administrators need to keep copies of all configuration files for communications channels, firewalls, IDS, DBMS, directories, etc., so that equipment can quickly be returned to service following component failure.

- **LIBRARIAN** – Although this term is used primarily in a mainframe environment, the role of the librarian is a part of the duties of many system administrators. The librarian is the sole person with write-access privileges to the main system files, backups, and application libraries. This person is responsible for implementing all changes to production systems. This role should never be filled by a developer or the person initiating the change request.

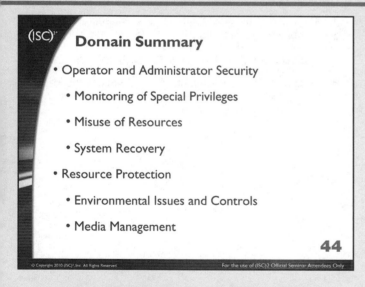

Domain Summary

- Operator and Administrator Security
  - Monitoring of Special Privileges
  - Misuse of Resources
  - System Recovery
- Resource Protection
  - Environmental Issues and Controls
  - Media Management

44

- **OPERATOR AND ADMINISTRATOR SECURITY** – These individuals have high-level access to system files, data, equipment, and networks. This requires special controls and monitoring to protect the systems from accidental or intentional failure.

- **RESOURCE PROTECTION** – The protection of hardware, software, and media against system failure and threats from internal or external intruders. Controls must be in place to preserve integrity even when modifications to the configuration of these resources are made. Operations security is part of implementing the principle of due diligence during the life cycle of an information system or the network on which it resides.

Security Transcends Technology
(ISC)²
45
© Copyright 2010 (ISC)², Inc. All Rights Reserved.
For the use of (ISC)2 Official Seminar Attendees Only

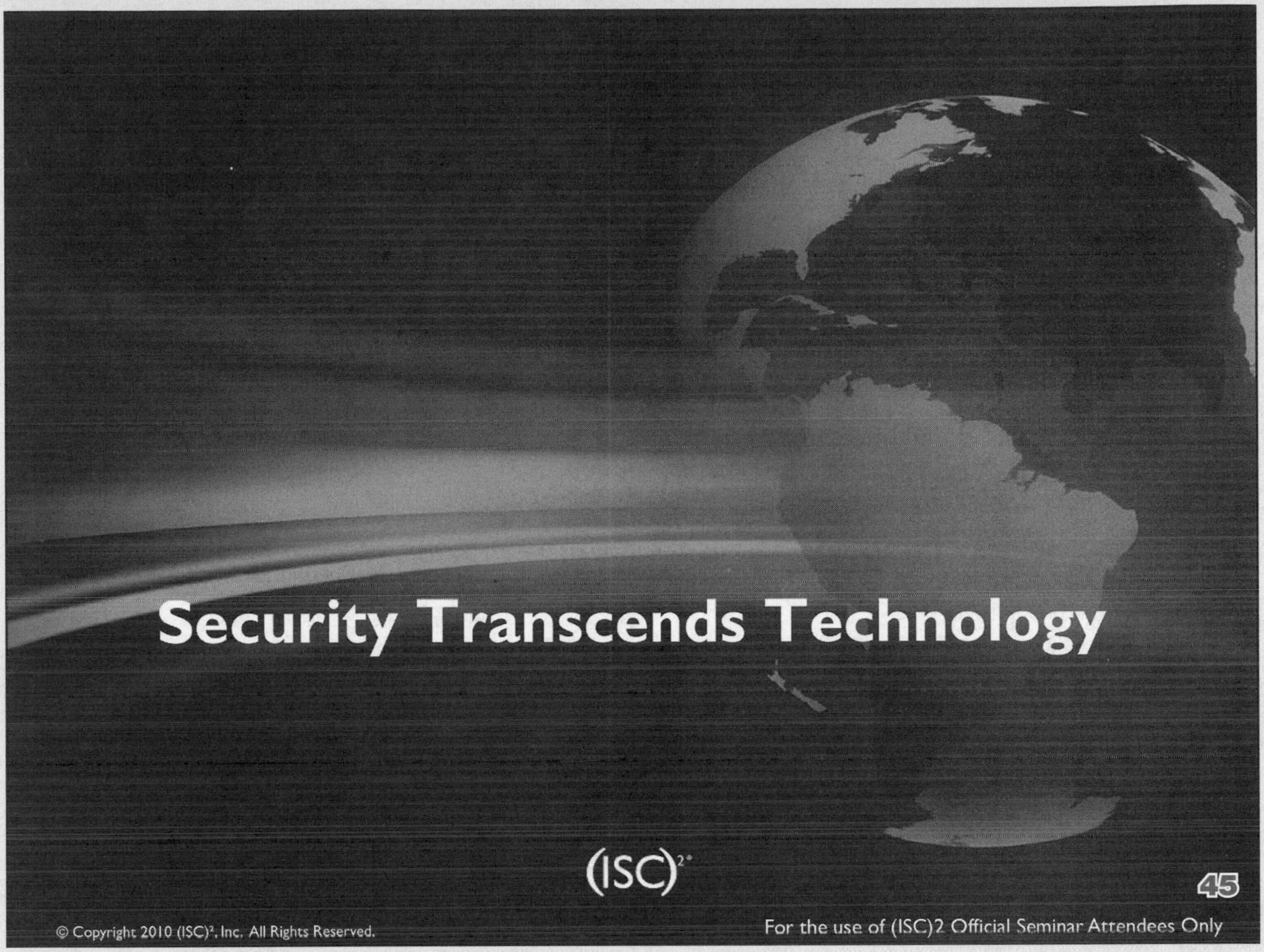

Review Questions

OPERATIONS SECURITY

1. Due to a software bug and a reload of the firewall, the firewall has lost its complete configuration. After that happened, all firewall ports are shut down. This is commonly referred to as

   A. secure configuration.
   B. fail secure.
   C. fail open.
   D. fail soft.

2. The BEST way to control users with elevated system privileges is with

   A. clear job descriptions.
   B. thorough hiring procedures.
   C. constant supervision.
   D. rotation of duty.

3. Which RAID (redundant array of independent disks) configuration offers the usable disk storage as the sum of all disk capacities?

   A. RAID 0
   B. RAID 1
   C. RAID 3
   D. RAID 6

4. Which RAID (redundant array of independent disks) configuration offers the lowest cost redundancy?

   A. RAID 0
   B. RAID 1
   C. RAID 5
   D. RAID 6

5. The temperature in the data center has risen. It has been observed that the primary and backup air conditioning units are malfunctioning. When contacted, the vendor maintenance staff advises that it will take one (1) hour before anyone can arrive. What step should be taken?

   A. Power down the complete system and all of the peripheral devices.
   B. Do nothing until the vendor maintenance staff arrives.
   C. Power down only the peripheral devices.
   D. Follow your business continuity plan's procedures.

6. Security administrator responsibilities include reviewing audit log data, setting access permissions, conducting vulnerability assessments, and

   A. setting file-sensitivity labels.
   B. reassigning ports/lines.
   C. mounting I/O volumes.
   D. configuration management.

7. Media management practices include media marking, labeling, handling, storing,

   A. recovery, and destroying.
   B. declassifying, and recovery.
   C. declassifying, and destroying.
   D. reviewing, and backup.

8. Which of the following backup types is the replication of data on separate disks in real time?

   A. File image
   B. System image
   C. Data mirroring
   D. Database shadowing

9. Storage area network (SAN) is BEST defined as

   A. disk drives connected to a separate optical network for the use of servers.
   B. disk drives connected to a separate optical network for the use of clients.
   C. disk drives connected to the same network as all clients and servers for the use of servers.
   D. disk drives connected to the same network as all clients and servers for the use of all.

10. Network administrator responsibilities include

    A. performing backups of data.
    B. applying operating system updates and configuration changes.
    C. resetting of time/date and network/operating system passwords.
    D. configuring traffic priority controls on devices.

11. Backup integrity is assured with

    A. backup planning.
    B. backup reporting.
    C. backup verification.
    D. backup execution.

12. A hot spare redundant array of independent disks (RAID) disk is used to

    A. reduce the mean time to repair period for the first drive failure in the same RAID.
    B. reduce the mean time to repair period for the second drive failure in the same RAID.
    C. reduce the mean time to repair period for both first and second drive failure in different RAIDs.
    D. reduce the mean time to repair period for the first drive failure in the different RAID.

13. Which of the following tasks is the responsibility of the librarian?

    A. Managing the symmetric key recovery system.
    B. Determining who has access to the data.
    C. Determining the classification of data.
    D. Ensuring availability of data.

14. A review of an operator's shift logs can be identified as which type of control?

    A. Preventive
    B. Detective
    C. Recovery
    D. Deterrent

15. Policy should state only approved users should possess or use a network sniffer. Of the following groups, who would normally be included in the list of approved users?

    A. Network administrator
    B. Security administrator
    C. Application developer
    D. System administrator

16. An application program has aborted. The application developer requests permission to have access to the data center in order to process a program report. What action should be taken?

    A. Grant access and provide him or her with a computer console.
    B. Grant access and assign him or her an operator to provide assistance.
    C. Advise the developer to resubmit his or her program and to make the necessary steps to have it processed.
    D. Refuse the request.

17. Network attached storage (NAS) is BEST defined as

    A. a group of disks connected to a separate network used by all servers.
    B. a group of disks connected to the same network used by all clients and servers.
    C. a group of disks connected to a separate network used by all clients.
    D. a group of disks connected to the same network used by all servers.

18. What is the MOST secure way to dispose of information on a read/write CD (RW-CD)?

    A. Sanitize the RW-CD using multiple overwrites with a standardized, evaluated software utility.
    B. Format the RW-CD.
    C. Degauss the surface of the RW-CD.
    D. Physically destroy the RW-CD.

19. Personnel security checks should be conducted with assistance from the

    A. physical security office.
    B. senior management.
    C. audit division.
    D. human resources department.

20. Change control procedures include request, impact, assessment, approval, build and test,

    A. verify, and implement.
    B. implement, and monitor.
    C. back up, and verify.
    D. back up, and implement.

Notes

Physical (Environmental) Security

(ISC)²

1

(ISC)²

Domain Agenda

- **Physical Security Threats and Controls**

- Perimeter Security

- Building and Inside Security

- Secure Operational Areas

2

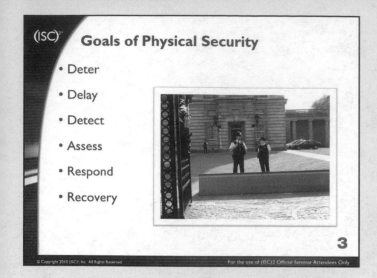

GOALS OF PHYSICAL SECURITY – Physical security counter-measures use barriers, entry and search controls, intrusion detection systems, and various types of alarm assessment. When properly combined with organizational practices and procedures, they are intended to deter, delay, detect, assess, and appropriately respond to an unauthorized activity. When possible, it is always best to deter threats. However, should deterrence fail, we want to delay them long enough to detect their actions, launch the appropriate response, and respond before they can damage our information systems and the data on them. Notice the layering of security in this photo.

- **DETER** – Convince the threat agents not to attack.

- **DELAY** – If they do decide to attack, we want to delay them long enough to detect the attack and respond to block it before damage to the information system or information occurs.

- **DETECT** – We need to have the ability to detect the attack. We can't delay forever so our ability to detect the attack is important and must be timely.

- **ASSESS** – There is an old saying that the first report is almost always wrong. Once detected, we need time to assess the method of the attack, the target, and what should be done.

- **RESPOND** – Take the appropriate actions without overreacting. This is often very difficult and should be covered in the incident response plan.

- **RECOVERY** – Recovery is the process of getting back to normal operating condition – repairing the damage, addressing the vulnerabilities, and applying the lessons learned to prevent, or respond more effectively to, future incidents.

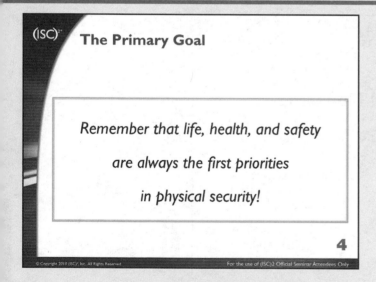

Threats to Physical Security

- Natural/environmental
  - Utilities
- Circumstantial
- Human-made/political events

5

- **NATURAL/ENVIRONMENTAL** – Disasters are fairly easy to understand, but often very hard to predict and to counter. Looking into the history of your area will give you a good start. Natural or environmental threats might include earthquakes, floods, storms, hurricanes, fires, etc.

  - **UTILITIES** – Threats may include communication outages, power outages, etc. Backup sources for power, water, and communications can minimize these potential risks. Don't forget about possible problems with sewage systems which can be particularly troublesome to deal with in an operational environment and can quickly endanger workers' health – which we never want to do.

- **CIRCUMSTANTIAL** – Many times the threats to an organization may not be the result of anything it has done wrong. Perhaps the threat is due to a fire or break-in at a neighboring building, a strike at a critical point in the supply chain, a radical change in markets, or an adverse reaction to an environmental issue. In these cases, the organization must have contingency plans, be prepared to execute appropriate physical security measures, and protect the assets of the organization effectively.

- **HUMAN-MADE/POLITICAL EVENTS** – Explosions, vandalism, theft, terrorist attacks, strikes, activism, riots, etc. These are also difficult to deal with. They require thorough preventative planning and having a good incident response plan already in place.

REFERENCE:

Kallhoff, Justin (2007) Physical Security Threats, http://www.giac.org/resources/whitepaper/physical/287.php

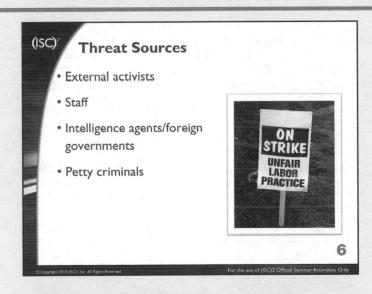

Threat Sources

- External activists
- Staff
- Intelligence agents/foreign governments
- Petty criminals

ON STRIKE UNFAIR LABOR PRACTICE

6

- **THREAT SOURCES** – Threats can come from many angles and the security professional must be prepared to protect against any type or vector of attack. Many threats may come from opportunity. If potential attackers or employees find a weakness to exploit, they may take advantage of that opportunity, even if they had not previously been planning to do something wrong. Physical security requires all-around vigilance and continuous attention to suspicious behavior or abnormal activity.

- **EXTERNAL ACTIVISTS** – Many threat sources are external. The physical threat comes from unruly citizens in the area, activists protesting against a sensitive issue, or action taken against other firms or governments located in close geographic proximity. Unfortunately unrest can lead to mobs and

vandalism, so in many cases the controls must include barriers, monitoring, and obvious security protection.

- **STAFF** – Most staff are trustworthy and will follow policy and guidelines, but when an opportunity presents itself – such as unguarded equipment or lack of surveillance – or an employee is angry or upset, a staff member may exploit the situation and steal or do damage to the assets of the organization.

- **INTELLIGENCE AGENTS/FOREIGN GOVERNMENTS** – The most skilled hackers in the world are employed by governments. Working for intelligence agencies, the military, or trade associations, these hackers are highly educated, have access to the latest equipment, and have the time to patiently probe for vulnerabilities in competing companies, governments, or military systems.

- **PETTY CRIMINALS** – Theft of equipment, vandalism, and damage to property are usually the acts of petty, small-time criminals. Lacking in skill, and often with little planning, most of these criminals take advantage of opportunities that present themselves.

Threat Sources and Controls

Threat	Controls
• Theft	• Locks
• Espionage	• Background checks
• Dumpster diving	• Disposal procedures
• Social engineering	• Awareness
• Shoulder surfing	• Screen filters
• HVAC access	• Motion sensors in ventilation ducts

7

- **HERE ARE SOME EXAMPLES OF PHYSICAL THREATS AND THEIR ASSOCIATED COUNTERMEASURES:**

  - **THEFT** – Countermeasures include strong access controls, Intrusion Detection Systems, locked doors, key control, and bag checks.

  - **ESPIONAGE** – Countermeasures include good hiring processes, background checks, good internal controls, and job rotation.

  - **DUMPSTER DIVING** – Countermeasures include proper disposal policy and procedures and layered controls with periodic checks.

  - **SOCIAL ENGINEERING AND SHOULDER SURFING** – Countermeasures include employee awareness programs and training, random spot checks, and screen filters to prevent improper observation.

  - **HVAC ACCESS** – Countermeasures include section lockdowns to control access, and smoke or IDS sensors.

REFERENCE:

Rutgers (2007) Social Engineering, http://rusecure.rutgers.edu/students/topics/social-engineering

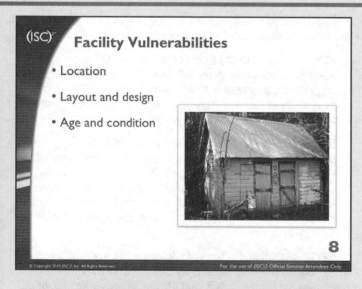

Facility Vulnerabilities

- Location
- Layout and design
- Age and condition

8

- **FACILITY VULNERABILITIES** – It is difficult, if not impossible, to secure some facilities. They simply are not suitable for very sensitive operations or to support critical services.

- **LOCATION** – Care must be given to the location of a facility. If it is in a flood plain, subject to storms or other threats, more precautions have to be taken. Factors such as proximity to an airport, major roadway, or train line must be considered in relation to physical protection. Risks from explosion, chemical spills, high crime area, and weather must be addressed in the security plan. Proximity to other buildings – or a building that is shared with other tenants – also affects physical security.

- **LAYOUT AND DESIGN** – A facility often contains public, semi-private, and protected areas. The physical security must be built around protection of areas that contain sensitive data, systems, or support utilities. Electrical panels, wiring closets, printers, and general office space should be protected from casual persons gaining access; and media storage, server rooms, cash handling departments, and executive areas must be closely protected. It is important to ensure that the physical security of an area is not easily bypassed by back doors or alternate stairways. A complicated floor plan may be more difficult to secure than a simple one, and care must always be taken to ensure that an adequate number of emergency exits are clear and available.

- **AGE AND CONDITION** – Older buildings were often built to lower safety standards and may contain more combustible or deteriorating building materials. Infestations from termites, dry rot, poor quality electrical wiring, or rusted plumbing are all common problems in an older facility.

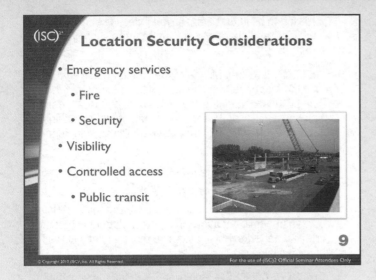

Location Security Considerations

- Emergency services
  - Fire
  - Security
- Visibility
- Controlled access
  - Public transit

9

- **LOCATION SECURITY CONSIDERATIONS** – Most security professionals work in facilities that already exist, but if the CISSP is involved in choosing or building a new facility, there are security concerns that should be addressed from the beginning stages.

- **SITE SECURITY CONSIDERATIONS** – Where is the building located? How should it be built? What is nearby? Consider-

ations will include proximity to an airport, highways, military bases, emergency support systems, and local crime rates. Consider as well the likelihood of natural disasters in a particular location. Each of these will have a different effect on security plans. Although an airport nearby provides easy access for travel, there is also the possibility that a plane could land short of the runway and hit the building, or that air traffic noise will make employees unhappy.

- **EMERGENCY SERVICES** – A secure facility or one that deals with hazardous chemicals should consider the availability of emergency services in its site plan. Having police, fire, or ambulances able to respond quickly may be a critical part of disaster management.

- **VISIBILITY** – Should the facility be well marked with clear signage – or kept rather low-key? Should the facility be clearly visible or located behind trees, a hill, or other obstruction?

- **CONTROLLED ACCESS** – Is it hard to control access for most locations in a city? Is it desirable to have a very remote location? Is the ability of staff to reach the location via public transport a consideration?

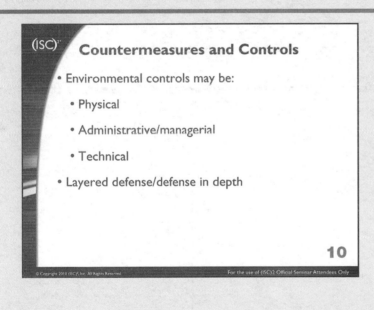

Countermeasures and Controls

- Environmental controls may be:
  - Physical
  - Administrative/managerial
  - Technical
- Layered defense/defense in depth

10

- **COUNTERMEASURES AND CONTROLS** – A strong control environment will include various types of controls and layers or series of controls. As seen through this domain, these controls may be physical in nature – locks and lighting; administrative – policy, separation of duties; or, technical – passwords, backups, and audit logs.

- **LAYERED DEFENSE** – Layered defense is a core physical security principle. Physical security should never depend on one layer of control or a single point of access, or failure. As will be seen through this domain, physical security is instituted at every layer of the facility, from the perimeter to the building entrance and through to sensitive internal areas.

Crime Prevention Through Environmental Design (CPTED)

- Principle of deterring crime through managing the potential crime scene
- Territoriality
  - Restricted access
- Surveillance
  - Monitoring
- Access control
  - Entrances

11

- **CRIME PREVENTION THROUGH ENVIRONMENTAL DESIGN –** Considerable research has gone into the relationship between incidents and frequency of crime, and the environment the crime was committed in. For example, fraud is found more commonly in organizations with poor controls or a seeming attitude among executives to spend money carelessly. This relationship may indicate steps that can be taken to actually reduce crime through the environmental factors in the area. Three factors are key to the reduction in crime.

- **TERRITORIALITY –** Possession, ownership, a sense of separation – all of these are factors in restricting a person from doing something inappropriate. A sense that "this is our area, this is our responsibility" often causes employees to be watching more diligently for actions that affect "their" area and much more likely to take action if they see something wrong.

  - **RESTRICTED ACCESS –** Part of the concept of territoriality is to restrict access to only those individuals who have a reason to be in that area. Anyone else is seen to be an "outsider" and, therefore, subject to more suspicion and monitoring.

- **SURVEILLANCE –** Perhaps one of the biggest deterrents to crime is the fear of getting caught. If people know that they are being watched, perhaps even recorded, and that the organization has a policy of prosecuting or taking action against inappropriate behavior, they may think more carefully before doing something wrong.

  - **MONITORING –** The very presence of a guard force or an obvious camera placement may deter crime.

  - **OPEN AREAS –** Well-lit areas and ensuring that debris or other garbage is not allowed to accumulate may hinder criminal behavior. Having signage that indicates surveillance is also good.

  - **DISCRETE OFFICES –** Employees who handle sensitive data or work on sensitive systems should be located in secure areas with proper access controls. Such offices may need to be TEMPEST protected to prevent the leakage of emanations out of the area.

- **ACCESS CONTROL –** All sensitive areas should be located behind adequate access controls. No one should just be able to "wander through" areas that contain sensitive data.

  - **ENTRANCES –** Entrances should be monitored, protected behind layers of control, and well-lit.

  - **VISITORS –** All visitors should be identified, and only allowed into private areas with an appropriate level of escort.

REFERENCE:

http://www.aic.gov.au/documents/9/E/8/%7B9E810185-7D54-4480-8EEC-D92D84C3FB36%7Dcpted.pdf

---

Domain Agenda

- Physical Security Threats and Controls

- **Perimeter Security**

- Building and Inside Security

- Secure Operational Areas

12

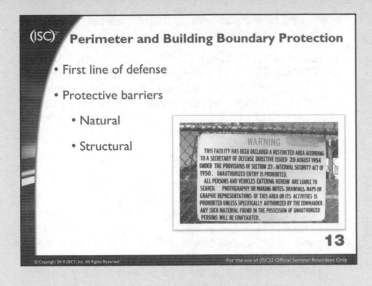

Perimeter and Building Boundary Protection

- First line of defense
- Protective barriers
  - Natural
  - Structural

WARNING

THIS FACILITY HAS BEEN DECLARED A RESTRICTED AREA ACCORDING TO A SECRETARY OF DEFENSE DIRECTIVE ISSUED 20 AUGUST 1954 UNDER THE PROVISIONS OF SECTION 21, INTERNAL SECURITY ACT OF 1950. UNAUTHORIZED ENTRY IS PROHIBITED.

ALL PERSONS AND VEHICLES ENTERING HEREON ARE LIABLE TO SEARCH. PHOTOGRAPHY OR MAKING NOTES, DRAWINGS, MAPS OR GRAPHIC REPRESENTATIONS OF THIS AREA OR ITS ACTIVITIES IS PROHIBITED UNLESS SPECIFICALLY AUTHORIZED BY THE COMMANDER. ANY SUCH MATERIAL FOUND IN THE POSSESSION OF UNAUTHORIZED PERSONS WILL BE CONFISCATED.

13

- **FIRST LINE OF DEFENSE** – The perimeter security controls are the first line of defense and are usually located as far as possible from the main buildings. They should delay an intruder long enough for security personnel to react appropriately. Signage alone may stop individuals who don't REALLY want to get inside.

- **PROTECTIVE BARRIERS** – These can be either natural or structural:

  - **NATURAL** – Location in terrains that are difficult to cross (deserts, mountains).

  - **STRUCTURAL** – Devices such as fences, gates, bollards, and facility walls.

REFERENCE:
http://www.globalsecurity.org/military/library/policy/army/fm/3-19-30/ch4.htm

---

Fences

- May be restricted by local regulations
- Inspections
- Parking should not be allowed near fences

14

ever, can be used by attackers to alleviate this threat.

- **MAY BE RESTRICTED BY LOCAL REGULATIONS** – Whether or not the organization can install a fence or wall may depend on local regulations regarding aesthetics or neighborhood standards. Fences often cannot be used where they might affect the appearance of the area.

- **INSPECTIONS** – Fences require regular maintenance. Animals may burrow under the fence or the earth may wash out leaving the fence unstable and providing easy access for an intruder.

- **NO PARKING SHOULD BE ALLOWED NEAR FENCES** – Do not allow vehicles to be parked near the fence, since they could be used to assist a person in climbing over, or damaging the fence.

REFERENCE:
Chain Link Fence Manufacturers Institute Security Fencing Recommendations, http://www. associationsites.com/page.cfm?usr=clfma&pageid=887

- **FENCES** – Fences are used to enclose security areas and designate property boundaries. They should meet specific gauge and fabric specifications. High-security areas may need a "top guard" such as barbed wire or concertina wire. The following provides some generally accepted fence heights and the level of protection they provide:

  - **1 METER/3-4 FEET** – Will deter casual trespassers.

  - **2 METERS/6-7 FEET** – Too high to climb easily.

  - **2.5 METERS/8 FEET** – Will delay the determined intruder.

  - Top guard will add 2-3 feet, and will deter access by severely cutting the intruder. A blanket, or mattress, how-

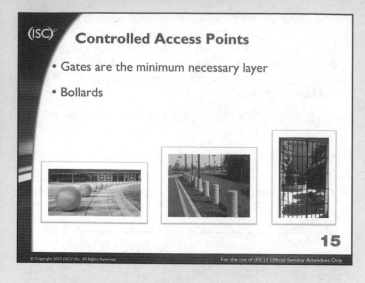

Controlled Access Points

- Gates are the minimum necessary layer
- Bollards

15

- **CONTROLLED ACCESS POINTS** – By definition, gates provide access through fences. Fences are barriers. The more access points through the barriers, the greater the number of access points for intruders. Gates obviously provide a necessary function, but also add to our security concerns. Access control points must be managed and controlled. They may potentially weaken our overall security.

- **GATES ARE A PRIMARY CONTROL RELATED TO A FENCE OR WALL** – The portions of a wall or fence system that control entrance and/or egress by persons or vehicles and complete the perimeter of the defined area. The gates provide controlled access through the fence and a point of observation for monitoring traffic onto the facility.

- **BOLLARDS** – Bollards are a permanent or retractable post used to deter vehicle-based attacks, such as vehicles ramming into or stopping near buildings. They come in a variety of sizes and shapes depending on their use. Retractable bollards are designed for use in traffic control. Lighted bollards can be used for lighting controls along parks, paths, and sidewalks. Few products have changed over the past few years as much as the bollard. From a concrete pole stuck in the ground, these security devices have evolved into functional works of art. Although aesthetics are important, the main reason for bollards is to control traffic and protect property.

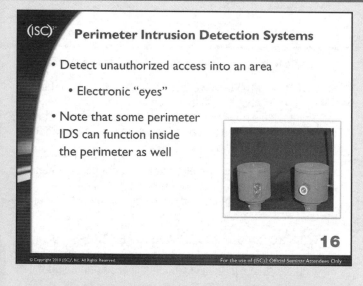

Perimeter Intrusion Detection Systems

- Detect unauthorized access into an area
  - Electronic "eyes"
- Note that some perimeter IDS can function inside the perimeter as well

16

- **PERIMETER INTRUSION DETECTION SYSTEMS** – These come in many forms. They can be external to the facility, manually operated, electronic, unmanned, etc. – the application will vary depending upon the value of the resource. Some perimeter sensors can detect intrusion across or under a land boundary or through a physical barrier, such as a chain link fence. Some use sound and pressure to detect motion, and many of them can be used to trigger lighting around your perimeters. The problem with many is that they can be triggered by non-adversarial activities such as animals, wind, etc.

- **CHARACTERISTICS OF DIFFERENT SPACE PROTECTION/INTRUSION DETECTION DEVICES:**

  - **PHOTOELECTRIC** – Active Infrared beam that triggers an alarm when the beam is broken.

  - **ULTRASONIC** – Ultrasound energy bounces off of the floors, walls, and objects. The receiver detects a "foreign" signal change caused by the intruder and sounds the alarm.

  - **MICROWAVE** – Receiver diode picks up transmitted and "bounced" energy waves in an enclosure. Intruder disrupts the waves and activates the alarm.

  - **PASSIVE INFRARED** – Objects radiate infrared with the heat of their bodies. Detector notes the change and triggers an alarm.

  - **PRESSURE SENSITIVE** – Detects pressure on the sensor or surrounding area.

  - **SOUNDS AND VIBRATION** – Microphones and other monitoring equipment are used to detect changes in sound or listen in to a facility.

  - **ELECTRICAL CIRCUITS** – Used to detect open windows or doors – many work on magnetic switches that close the electrical circuit when the window is opened and moves the magnet away from the electrical switch.

  - **MOTION SENSORS** – Most motion sensors work on Passive Infrared technology. Various types may autodial an emergency number, sound an alarm, or trigger lights when they sense motion.

- Note that some of these perimeter intrusion detection systems can also be used for "inside of the perimeter" protection.

REFERENCE:

DOE-M-5632.1c-1 Chapter VI – Protection Element: Intrusion Detection Systems – http://www.fas.org/irp/doddir/doe/m5632_1c-1/m5632_1c-1_c6.htm

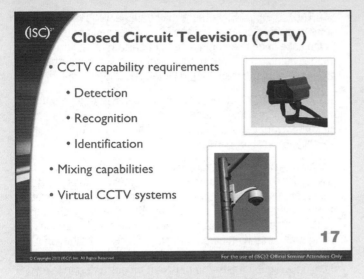

Closed Circuit Television (CCTV)

- CCTV capability requirements
  - Detection
  - Recognition
  - Identification
- Mixing capabilities
- Virtual CCTV systems

17

- **CLOSED CIRCUIT TELEVISION (CCTV) –** CCTV is a television transmission system that uses cameras to transmit pictures to connected monitors via a wired or wireless transmission medium. Many CCTV camera types can be monitored from more than one location, including over the Internet or over a corporate network.

- CCTV adds an excellent tool to our security arsenal, but it should not be seen as the "only" security device. Important considerations for CCTV cameras are blind spots, motion detection systems, and workplace privacy issues.

- **CCTV CAPABILITY REQUIREMENTS –** The CCTV system must meet these three requirements:

  - **DETECTION –** The ability to detect the presence of an object or activity.

  - **RECOGNITION –** The ability to determine the type of object or activity it detects (i.e., theft, medical, fire, etc.).

  - **IDENTIFICATION –** The ability to determine the object's details (a camera required to identify a person must have a high quality lens, transmission, monitoring, and storage media).

- **MIXING CAPABILITIES AND DETECTION METHODS –** Adding camera features such as infrared and thermal detection can greatly increase capability. This allows the strength of each system to supplement the weaknesses of the other types of camera while minimizing the costs that would be required to install additional cameras, lighting, or sensors.

- **VIRTUAL CCTV SYSTEMS –** Fake systems that are installed as a deterrent control. The very presence of a camera may deter inappropriate activity. However, it is good to note that the organization may be subject to legal repercussions if users think they are safe, since the area is being monitored while in fact it is not.

REFERENCE:

Pros and Cons of CCTV (Legal Report, July 2006) http://www.securitymanagement.com/library/cops_surveillance0706.pdf

---

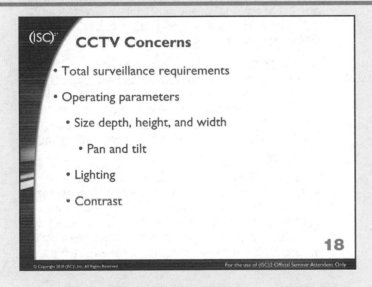

CCTV Concerns

- Total surveillance requirements
- Operating parameters
  - Size depth, height, and width
    - Pan and tilt
  - Lighting
  - Contrast

18

- **TOTAL SURVEILLANCE REQUIREMENTS –** Understand the facility's total surveillance requirements in order to develop a cost-effective and efficient system. This allows the system to be engineered and installed in a manner that maximizes the coverage with minimum equipment.

- **OPERATING PARAMETERS –** A camera must be installed with the correct lens (wide-angle, normal, zoom) and the correct angle (do not invade privacy), as well as a good quality transmission media (a good camera with a poor quality cable will result in poor quality images). The installers and operators must implement a system that is compatible with the environment (the effect of lighting or the sun on the camera at different times of the day/year), the effect of aperture and zoom on

depth of field, and the need to monitor the images effectively.

- **SIZE DEPTH, HEIGHT, AND WIDTH –** The size of the area to be monitored – depth, height, and width – makes a major difference in what lens and other components to select. The aspect ratio of CCTV cameras is normally 4:3 (horizontal: vertical). The area to be monitored will determine camera selection (camera focal length, angle of view, etc.), placement, and the number of cameras.

  - **PAN AND TILT –** Some cameras are designed to pan horizontally across a large area or are required to tilt vertically up and down in order to provide more precise coverage or monitoring. The operator must be careful not to leave the camera in a position that doesn't allow it to monitor activity in some area.

- **LIGHTING –** Proper lighting is important. Different lamps and types of lighting will provide various levels of effectiveness and a variety of lighting techniques should be employed to provide the most effective CCTV system. The location, direction, and intensity of the lighting will directly affect the CCTV system's performance.

- **CONTRAST –** Having sufficient contrast between the object and background is another important consideration in selecting the right components. Contrast is the noticeable difference between black and white in a picture. If the two extremes look like gray and off-white, the contrast is not good. A gray scale can be used to check the CCTV monitor's ability to reproduce good contrast.

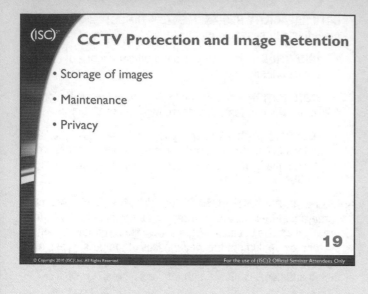

CCTV Protection and Image Retention

- Storage of images
- Maintenance
- Privacy

19

- **STORAGE OF IMAGES** – There may be legal requirements to store or discard camera images for or after a set time period. In the case of an investigation it is important to secure the images as quickly as possible to avoid overwriting or theft. All access to stored media should be logged and controlled.

- **MAINTENANCE** – A camera and its associated equipment needs maintenance – cleaning, replacement of tapes or storage media, protection of cabling, and lubricating the pan and tilt mechanisms, to name a few.

- **PRIVACY** – Capturing images can result in violations of privacy for some individuals. Operators must be aware of the requirements to protect the "expectation of privacy" of people being monitored and not do anything that would violate the rights of those individuals, including discussing the actions being monitored with unauthorized persons. Operators of CCTV systems must be trained and reminded of their obligations on a regular basis and must not be permitted to take any copies of CCTV images – this may include the need to ban camera phones in the monitoring area.

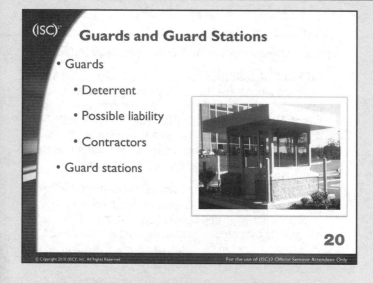

Guards and Guard Stations

- Guards
  - Deterrent
  - Possible liability
  - Contractors
- Guard stations

20

- **GUARDS** – Guards are expensive controls (pay, cost of training, retirement, etc.), but can provide a unique capability to our security efforts: providing reasoned, discriminating, and measured responses to changing situations. Guards are an invaluable asset in emergencies, but if not properly selected and trained, they can also be a major liability. Guards must be motivated and attentive. If they are bored or distracted by TVs, computer games, surfing the Internet, etc., they can provide a false sense of security to the organization.

  - **DETERRENT** – Guards can act as deterrents and provide a flexible security and safety response in the event of an intrusion.

  - **POSSIBLE LIABILITY** – Guards who can be convinced to "make exceptions" are a liability, as are guards who use their position as a cover for malicious acts. In some

cases, the presence of guards may provide personnel with a false sense of being protected, whereas the guard may not be able to take any direct action to protect an individual in trouble. Note that guards can be the object of social engineering.

- **CONTRACTORS** – Guards are frequently contractors who do not work directly for the organization they are protecting. Some of the concerns with hiring of contractors is the need to ensure that they have been properly "vetted" prior to hiring. The duties of the guards should be clearly written down and the procedures they are to follow must be defined and enforced.

- **GUARD STATIONS** – For many of the reasons mentioned above, guard stations can be a mixed blessing. Almost every soldier in the world has been trained to determine the presence of guards, their patterns, to scope out guard station locations, and the techniques to use to bypass them. This training information is also readily available on the Internet for those with less valid reasons for needing these skills.

  - In high-threat environments, guard stations are constructed with bulletproof walls, doors, or windows. Ensure that there are clear sight lines and access to main doors, etc.

- Questions to consider when deciding on a security force:

  - Is it more cost-effective to hire guards or to contract out?

  - Are the guards certified or licensed?

  - Should the guards be armed or unarmed?

REFERENCE:
http://www.globalsecurity.org/military/library/policy/army/fm/3-19-30/ch9.htm

Domain Agenda

- Physical Security Threats and Controls

- Perimeter Security

- **Building and Inside Security**

- Secure Operational Areas

21

Building Entry Points

- Doors

- Windows

- Loading ramps

- Elevator shafts

- Ventilation ducts

- Crawlspaces

- Sewage or steam lines

22

- **BUILDING ENTRY POINTS** – Obviously a prime responsibility of a physical security program is to limit unauthorized access to a building. Many organizations struggle with good building entrance security. This is in part since there are often many entrances to the building, some areas which are commonly accessed by outsiders – such as loading docks, reception, utility rooms; and some areas which are not commonly used as entrances – such as windows, elevator shafts, and ventilation ducts.

- The security professional needs to ensure complete security of all possible entry points. This is especially difficult in shared facilities where there may be common rooms for utilities, a common attic space, crawlspace or basement that extends across multiple tenants, or where there are tunnels or steam lines that join buildings together.

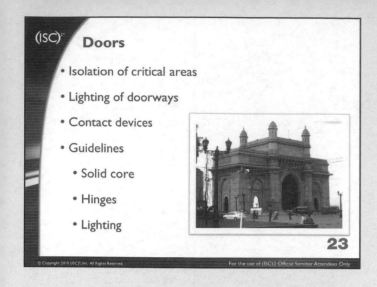

Doors

- Isolation of critical areas
- Lighting of doorways
- Contact devices
- Guidelines
  - Solid core
  - Hinges
  - Lighting

23

- **DOORS** – Doors play a key role in a physical security program. Consider all of the following:

- **ISOLATION OF CRITICAL AREAS** – Critical areas must be isolated from the general public and employee traffic. Security doors combined with CPTED (Crime Prevention through Environmental Design) can help by selecting areas "off the beaten path" for critical areas such as server rooms.

- **LIGHTING OF DOORWAYS** – Lighting, particularly around doorways, plays a major deterrent role in security efforts.

- **CONTACT DEVICES (SWITCHES)** – Doors can be controlled by contact devices. If doors can be remotely controlled by computer-controlled switches after the correct identification and authentication has occurred, so much the better. A guard with a switch that opens doors can be problematic, since the guard may be subject to intimidation or social engineering. Contact alarms can also signal if a door is blocked open.

  - **NOTE: PROTECTION OF HUMAN LIFE IS THE TOP PRIORITY** – Security plans must not result in undue risks to people, particularly during emergencies.

- **GUIDELINES:**

  - Doors should be solid core. Hollow-core doors provide little security; they are easily breached and provide a very limited barrier to fire.

  - Doors should not open out except as required by building codes. Exterior doors that open out should have sealed (welded) hinge pins and dog bolts (pins on the hinge side of the door that extend into the doorframe) so that they can't be removed.

  - Door locks should provide both daytime locks (such as push-button locks while the room is occupied), and 24-hour locks (such as deadbolts for after business hours).

  - Door hinges should be fixed to the frames with a minimum of three hinges per door.

  - Door frames should be permanently fixed to the adjoining wall studs.

  - Doors should have the same fire-resistance rating as adjacent walls.

  - Emergency exit doors must be clearly marked with emergency exit signs and equipped with panic bars to permit rapid egress.

  - Decide which doors are to be monitored or alarmed.

  - Ensure that doors can provide entry and exit in an emergency especially in the event of a power failure or fire.

- It is important to note that some emergency exits will not have any outside hardware. That allows the door to be used as an emergency exit only and will not permit unauthorized access into the facility.

Access and Visitor Logs

- Identification/sign in and out
- Temporary badges
- Vehicles
- Escort

ACME Explosives

DATE:_____   Entrance:_____

Name	Company	Name of Person Visiting	Time In	Time Out

24

© Copyright 2010 (ISC)², Inc. All Rights Reserved.   For the use of (ISC)2 Official Seminar Attendees Only

- **ACCESS AND VISITOR LOGS** – Both access logs and visitor logs are in common use in most corporate environments. These capture common information about visitors to a facility, including information about who is sponsoring their visit. Logs are often kept at a guard location at the entrance to a secure area or facility and visitors are not allowed access until their admission is approved and logged. They should be stored in a safe location for review at a later date, should that prove necessary.

- **IDENTIFICATION** – Prior to allowing access, visitors should be required to show a valid ID and declare the area and person they are intending to visit. Some facilities may require visitors to be registered in advance and approved prior to arrival.

- **SIGN IN AND OUT** – At many facilities, each visitor and employee is required to sign in and out (often by swiping a badge). This tracks who was in the building at any point in time and may be important in case of fire or other adverse incident.

- **TEMPORARY BADGES** – There are computer-based logs that can also interact with other systems, for example capturing an image to print on a disposable badge. Such systems are handy for repeat visitors as information only needs to be entered once; subsequent visits simply require a valid ID to access the saved information. Any time a temporary badge is issued it should be tracked and recovered at the end of the visit.

  - For very secure locations, other measures are usually employed for access control and logging, including electronic location-specific monitors and access locks. Some of these systems log the whereabouts of individuals on an ongoing basis via an ID unique to that individual.

- **VEHICLES** – Vehicles entering a secure area should be checked and registered. It may be preferable to direct visiting vehicles to a separate location away from employee parking. Vehicles needing access to a large compound or base should have an identification and authorization sticker that indicates where they are permitted to drive and park.

- **ESCORT** – Any visitor entering a secure area should be escorted by a knowledgeable employee. If a vendor is working on equipment, attending meetings, or accessing protected areas, he or she should not be left unsupervised.

Turnstiles and Mantraps

- Tailgating/piggybacking

Turnstile

Delta Turnstile Controls

External Mantrap
Kouba Systems

25

© Copyright 2010 (ISC)², Inc. All Rights Reserved.   For the use of (ISC)2 Official Seminar Attendees Only

- **TURNSTILES AND MANTRAPS** – Both turnstiles and mantraps have been a cost-effective method of controlling access and limiting traffic flow for hundreds of years. They can work with little or no guard oversight or intervention.

  - **TURNSTILES** – The function of a turnstile or a mantrap can be as simple as limiting access or traffic flow through the use of an access card, restricting entry to unauthorized personnel, or sounding an alarm. Some allow only one-way passage, and track or count all people entering and exiting.

- **TAILGATING/PIGGYBACKING** – Before the electronic era, it was difficult to get mantraps to effectively prevent "tailgating" (wherein one person sneaks in behind another). Some modern systems handle tailgating quite well in an automated fashion by physically limiting entry to one person at a time.

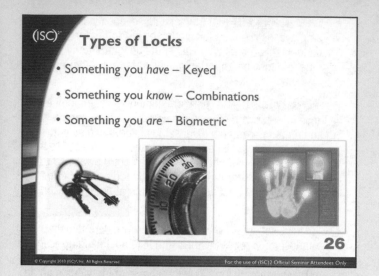

Types of Locks

- Something you *have* – Keyed
- Something you *know* – Combinations
- Something you *are* – Biometric

26

- **SOMETHING YOU HAVE** – Keyed/Key card. Keyed locks come in the following form factors: cylindrical locksets, dead-bolts, mortise, drop-bolt, rim-cylinder, and unit. The deadbolt is thought to be the most secure. (A deadbolt is a bolt inserted into the frame of a door for added security. To be most effective, the bolt of the latch should be applied so that the bolt slides into the door-casing frame or into a keeper firmly attached to the doorframe.) A key card is considered "something you have," but it is computer controlled. Key cards come in the following form factors: Magnetic-Stripe, Proximity, Laser, Smart, and Bar Code. The main benefit of key cards is more immediate key management; the main drawback is cost.

- **SOMETHING YOU KNOW** – Dial or combination locks. The lock contains wheels and a dial-face. The more wheels, the better the protection. Those with four or more wheels offer higher penetration resistance; those with three or fewer wheels can

be opened by listening to the sound of the wheels and by the feel of the dial. Combination locks are opened by using a sequence of numbers in a specific order. Combination locks can be push-button (whether mechanical or computer-controlled) or dial combinations. Keypads were originally in fixed positions, but this caused uneven wear. Digital push-button locks are sometimes called cipher locks. Digital keypads can now be programmed to show random placement of keypad data; instead of the #1 always being in the upper left corner, for example, it can be placed anywhere on the digital display.

- **SOMETHING YOU ARE** – Biometric. Computer controlled central databases of biometric data can limit the impersonation or theft that may occur with keyed or combination locks. Any form of biometrics for access control can be applied to controlling a point of entry.

- In large installations, all lock systems may be controlled from a common access console. New access cards must be set by the console and the system will restrict access according to policy. For example, smart locks are designed to permit only authorized people into certain doors at certain times. (An example is the key system used in some hotels, where the key is a plastic card that is programmed at a central computer to permit the guest access to a specific door.)

REFERENCES:

http://www.usgs.gov/usgs-manual/handbook/hb/440-2-h/440-2-h-ch6.html

http://www.globalsecurity.org/military/library/policy/army/fm/3-19-30/ch8.htm#pgfld-1024523

http://www.globalsecurity.org/military/library/policy/army/fm/3-19-30/ch6.htm#pgfld-1024523

IMAGE:

http://officeimages.microsoft.com/i/0000/MB/j0309/j0309599.gif

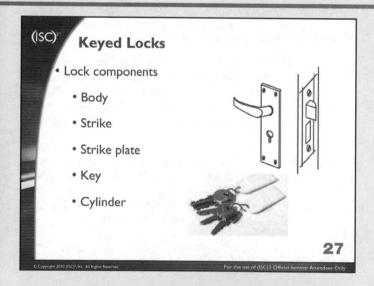

Keyed Locks

- Lock components
  - Body
  - Strike
  - Strike plate
  - Key
  - Cylinder

27

- **KEYED LOCKS** – Keyed locks are the most common and acceptable way to secure areas and property. They keep honest people out, but unauthorized people who wish to gain access can often force them, pick locks, or duplicate keys. Locks should, therefore, be used in combination with other controls to provide reliable security. They should be considered delay devices rather than foolproof barriers to entry.

- **LOCK COMPONENTS** – Most locks have similar components. Depending on the quality of the lock, these parts may be more or less robust, but they work together to provide protection:

  - **BODY** – The lock body is the metal casing that encloses the cylinder and holds the protruding bolt that actually fastens the door.

  - **STRIKE/STRIKE PLATE** – The strike and strike plate form a separate rectangular metal piece that is inserted into the door jam. The strike plate contains the "strike" (the slot that receives the matching bolt attached to the lock body). It's important to remember that if the door jamb is not strong and securely fastened to the door frame, the door can be forced – regardless of how strong the lock is.

  - **KEY** – The key matches the tumblers in the lock's cylinder and releases them from the locked position.

  - **CYLINDER** – The cylinder accepts the key and causes the bolt to move in or out of its receptacle in the strike.

REFERENCES:

http://www.usgs.gov/usgs-manual/handbook/hb/440-2-h/440-2-h-ch6.html

http://www.globalsecurity.org/military/library/policy/army/fm/3-19-30/ch8.htm#pgfld-1024523

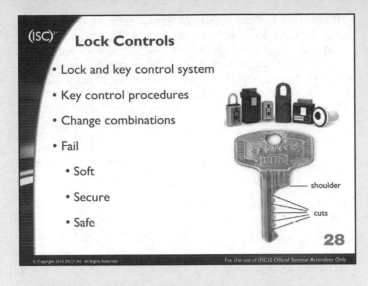

Lock Controls

- Lock and key control system
- Key control procedures
- Change combinations
- Fail
  - Soft
  - Secure
  - Safe

shoulder

cuts

28

- **LOCK AND KEY CONTROL SYSTEM** – The effective use of locks and keys is dependent upon effective key control systems.

- **KEY CONTROL PROCEDURES** – Proper procedures for key control should be implemented and documented. Accurate records must be maintained to include:

  - Who has access to the keys.
  - To whom the keys are issued.
  - Key inventory (sign out, destruction).

- Unused locks should be securely stored.

- The default settings on all locks should be changed.

- **CHANGE COMBINATIONS** – At specific times or under specific circumstances:

  - Every twelve months.
  - When possibly compromised.
  - When a facility member who knows the combination leaves.

- When a power failure occurs, what is the reaction of the electronic lock?

  - **FAIL-SOFT** – The lock is unlocked.
  - **FAIL-SECURE** – The lock is locked.
  - **FAIL-SAFE** – The lock is in a state that protects human life. In the event of an emergency, the lock will allow people to exit the building rather than secure the facility and allow no traffic to pass through the door.
  - (Note that these terms originally applied to the reaction of software.)

REFERENCES:
http://www1.od.nih.gov/oma/manualchapters/management/1415/
http://www.fas.org/irp/nsa/rainbow/tg004.htm

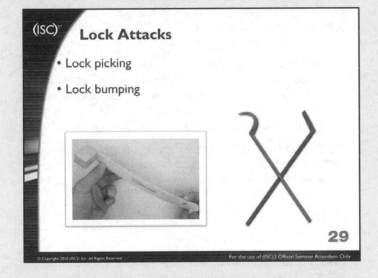

Lock Attacks

- Lock picking
- Lock bumping

29

- **LOCK PICKING** – Basic picking tools are the tension wrench and the pick. Although intended for use by professionals as part of their business, they are also found in the hands of those who have no lawful use for them. The tension wrench turns the lock's key plug and helps find the locking tumblers, while the pick is used to move the binding tumblers, one at a time, to the shear line. When all tumblers are aligned properly with the shear line, the lock opens. Locks are "pick-resistant," not "pick-proof." Complex, automated lock-picking tools have kept pace with newer, better locks.

- **LOCK BUMPING** – Lock bumping involves cutting a key to the maximum depth on all cuts and hammering the key with a "Tomahawk" (a flexible hammer, pictured above) to transfer maximum force to all of the pins so that they jump into the open position. More expensive locks tend to be more susceptible to this technique due to the stronger materials used in the manufacturing of these locks.

REFERENCE:
Blaze, Matt (2004) Safecracking for the computer scientist, www.crypto.com/papers/safe-locks.pdf

IMAGE:
http://www.toool.nl/bumping.pdf

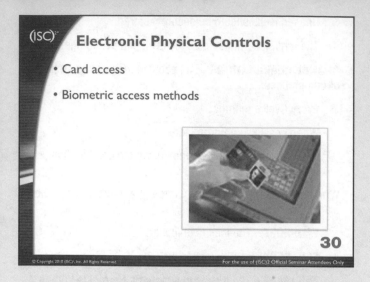

ELECTRONIC PHYSICAL CONTROLS
- Card access
- Biometric access methods

30

- **BIOMETRIC ACCESS METHODS** – Fingerprint, retina scans, signature dynamics, voice recognition, hand geometry. In the physical security domain, biometric locks are frequently used for identification, not authentication. The biometric device identifies applicants from a list of known, approved entrants, and permits them access. In technical biometric implementations, the biometric device is commonly used for authentication – to validate that the applicants are who they say they are.

REFERENCE:

Ryan Hay (2003) Physical Security: A Biometric Approach, http://www.sans.org/reading_room/whitepapers/physcial/1325.php

- **ELECTRONIC PHYSICAL CONTROLS** – These are discussed at length in the Access Control Domain, but we will discuss them here in terms of physical access control. When combined with other access control mechanisms, electronic physical controls form multi-factor systems that increase reliability and reduce the possibility of error. Combining all of these access methods with the presence of security guards allows for the best of all worlds. Be careful of providing guards with the ability to by-pass these systems – remember that guards are susceptible to social engineering.

- **CARD ACCESS** – Smart cards, Magnetic Stripe cards, Proximity cards.

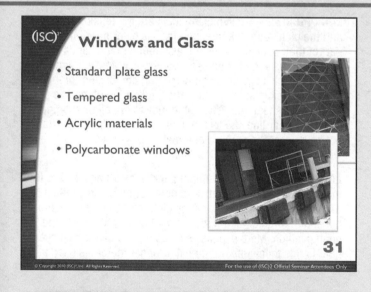

Windows and Glass
- Standard plate glass
- Tempered glass
- Acrylic materials
- Polycarbonate windows

31

fragments when broken. Because of the way in which it shatters, tempered glass must be pre-cut to the exact size of the window. Tempered class is often seen in automobile windows.

- **ACRYLIC MATERIALS** – Standard acrylics are not as strong as polycarbonate acrylics, but they are more resistant to breakage than plate glass. The disadvantages to acrylics are that they burn and produce toxic fumes. They also scratch fairly easy and can become hazy or yellow over time.

- **POLYCARBONATE WINDOWS** – These are very expensive and typically used only for high-security areas. Glass and polycarbonate combinations combine the best qualities of glass and acrylics. They are made from plastic that is significantly stronger than standard acrylic of the same thickness. They are resistant to abrasion, chemicals, fires, and are even anti-ballistic (bullet resistant).

- **OTHER WINDOW CONSIDERATIONS** – Use shatter-resistant, laminated glass of a minimum thickness (based on the risk assessment). Windows should be installed in fixed frames so that the windowpanes cannot be removed from the outside. Window frames must be securely anchored to the wall.

- **WINDOWS** – Windows can provide unauthorized access and be quite dangerous in the event of windstorm or explosion. Care must be taken in the type of glass used, and the types of locks and alarms deployed.

- **STANDARD PLATE GLASS** – The most common type of window is standard plate glass. It is easy to cut standard plate glass to fit a window. Standard plate glass can shatter into dangerous jagged shards if broken. This is a particularly dangerous problem during an explosive blast, earthquake, or a windstorm as the flying glass adds to the blast effects and can be just as deadly.

- **TEMPERED GLASS** – Is five to seven times more break-resistant than plate glass and shatters into small, less dangerous

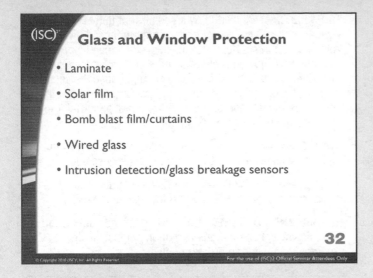

Glass and Window Protection

- Laminate
- Solar film
- Bomb blast film/curtains
- Wired glass
- Intrusion detection/glass breakage sensors

32

- **SOLAR FILM** – Solar film provides protection from sunlight and the stress that extra heat would place on the air conditioning system.

- **BOMB BLAST FILM** – Is used to stop flying glass from causing injuries in the event of an explosion. The film or curtain will hold the glass together or contain it, so that it does not fly into the area and injure personnel.

- **WIRED GLASS** – Is a laminate glass with wire between the sheets of glass – this can prevent a person from breaking the glass to gain entry since the wire will also provide a barrier to access.

- **INTRUSION DETECTION/GLASS BREAKAGE SENSORS** – Can be placed on the glass or window frame to detect glass breakage or the opening of a window. These should be used in a layered defense model and monitored at a central location.

- **GLASS AND WINDOW PROTECTION** – If the organization has high-security needs, windows can be alarmed, contain steel wire mesh, or be protected by steel bars. Windows that can be opened by employees (other than during emergencies) add risk: If this practice is accepted by management, a compensating control (such as a person walking around to ensure an unoccupied office does not have an open window) is appropriate – even during daylight hours.

- **LAMINATE GLASS** – Uses a plastic sheet between several layers of tempered glass. The laminate is a very strong form of protection and will hold the glass together in the event of glass breakage.

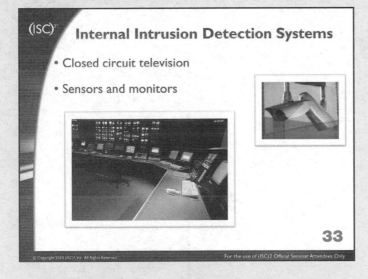

Internal Intrusion Detection Systems

- Closed circuit television
- Sensors and monitors

33

protected. CCTV has the added value of providing an audit trail with recorded footage.

- **SENSORS AND MONITORS** – Motion detectors and sound, heat/infrared, and pressure sensors are common and can be used individually or in combination for increased security. Microwave, ultrasonic, and photoelectric sensors are also common. Highly secure facilities will have electronic badges integrated with state-of-the-art access control systems and monitoring equipment.

- **INTRUSION DETECTION SYSTEMS (IDS)** – Many of the concepts that apply to Logical Intrusion Detection for systems and networks also apply for physical intrusion detection. Some of the same tools used for Perimeter Intrusion Detection can be used internally as well. Regardless of the tools, it takes effective planning to create a system that is effective yet unobtrusive.

- **COMMON TOOLS FOR INTERNAL INTRUSION DETECTION SYSTEMS INCLUDE:**

  - **CLOSED CIRCUIT TELEVISION (CCTV)** – (Discussed previously.) Common in high traffic areas, at entrances and exits, in highly secure locations, or in cash-handling areas. If using wireless, ensure that the transmission is properly

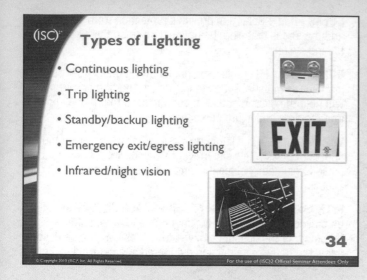

Types of Lighting

- Continuous lighting
- Trip lighting
- Standby/backup lighting
- Emergency exit/egress lighting
- Infrared/night vision

34

- **TRIP LIGHTING** – Activated by a sensor that detects activity such as movement or heat. If the trigger point is activated, the light will illuminate. Note that these systems can be prone to nuisance tripping by pranksters and can also be used by intruders to create several false alarms that cause the security team to respond to various entry points. Granting that it may not be possible to monitor every entry point, an intruder may be able to gain access by doing this.

- **STANDBY/BACKUP LIGHTING** – Lighting with a battery supply that is automatically turned on when power goes out.

- **EMERGENCY EXIT/EGRESS LIGHTING** – Lighting that indicates where exits are located and the way to the exit.

- **INFRARED/NIGHT VISION LIGHTING** – Infrared lighting can assist in low light conditions and augment closed circuit TV cameras to monitor an area at night.

REFERENCES:

http://www.globalsecurity.org/military/library/policy/army/fm/3-19-30/ch5.htm

U.S. National Electrical Code 700-16

International: 2000 International Bldg. Code, International Standards Organization, & International Maritime Organization

IMAGE:

With permission of PNA Group, Oakville, Ontario

- **CONTINUOUS LIGHTING** – This is the most common form of lighting. It consists of a series of fixed lights arranged to continuously flood a given area during hours of limited visibility. Glare lighting uses the glare of lights to inhibit intruders' vision across the selected area. Flood lighting directs the light in a particular direction or toward a particular location.

  - **CRITICAL AREAS AROUND BUILDINGS** – Install lighting at least 8 feet (2.4 meters) above the ground with illumination of 2 foot candles/lumens.

Domain Agenda

- Physical Security Threats and Controls

- Perimeter Security

- Building and Inside Security

- **Secure Operational Areas**

35

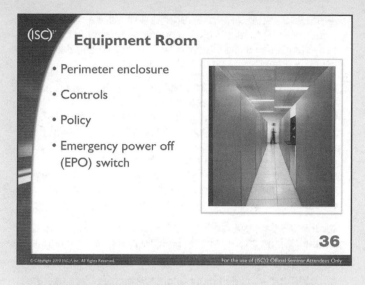

Equipment Room

- Perimeter enclosure
- Controls
- Policy
- Emergency power off (EPO) switch

36

walls are of sufficient strength and height – reaching not just to the ceiling, but (in the case of drop or false ceilings) to the structure above.

- **CONTROLS** – For critical equipment rooms are electronic controls, access locks, and monitoring equipment.

- **POLICY** – Policies and procedures must be developed to deal appropriately with employees, visitors/guests, and maintenance workers. Business continuity (also known as disaster preparedness) must also be given serious consideration: The BCP must accommodate ongoing continuity during an emergency as well as ongoing security and data and resource integrity.

- **EPO SWITCH** – In case of flooding, fire, or other hazardous condition, server rooms frequently have an EPO switch that will enable the operators the opportunity to rapidly cut off all power to the equipment room if needed. Such switches should be protected, labeled, and located in a safe but accessible area.

- **EQUIPMENT ROOM** – Physical security is accomplished by having proper design, adequate access controls, and intrusion detection. The physical design of the facility incorporates power, air conditioning, floor space, perimeter enclosure (walls), fire control, and the associated security controls and equipment. Many of these aspects are covered in other sections.

- **PERIMETER ENCLOSURE** – Is often overlooked, particularly when retrofitting a current space (such as a hall closet) for equipment operation. Care must be taken to ensure that the

---

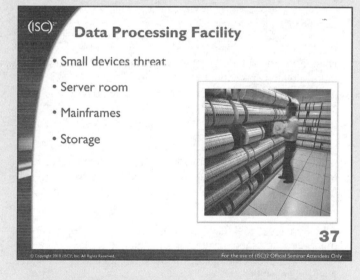

Data Processing Facility

- Small devices threat
- Server room
- Mainframes
- Storage

37

PROLIFERATION OF SMALL, SOPHISTICATED ELECTRONIC DEVICES – A digital camera (even a cell phone with camera) or a USB drive can easily compromise the integrity of the building or critical data. It is difficult to guard against malicious activity from a trusted employee in a cost-effective way, although security monitoring devices (video in particular), or the perceived surveillance with video (dummy camera housings) often inhibit malicious activity. Placing cameras (or dummy housings) in open, difficult to access places contributes to the overall security of a facility.

- **SERVER ROOM** – The main processing of the organization and the primary data storage area is often a server room. The most important requirements for these rooms are space, power, air conditioning, access control, and security monitoring.

- **MAINFRAMES** – Most personnel who have access to the server room have access to the mainframe and all of the other equipment to which it is connected. While most mainframes have logical security measures – RACF (Resource Access Control Facility, an IBM Mainframe Access Control Software), Login IDs, and Passwords, etc. – there is often little physical security once a trusted person gains access. Proper monitoring and access control are, therefore, essential.

- **STORAGE** – Primary storage and media backups must be stored in a secure environment as well. For large operations, this usually means storing offsite as a precaution against a disaster at the processing facility. If a company does use offsite storage, security must also be maintained during all media handling and transport.

- **DATA PROCESSING FACILITY** – The data processing facility is often enclosed in a larger complex offering general office space to many different departments. A current trend with corporations that operate large data centers is to build specifically hardened specialized buildings for core data systems and storage. All of the topics of physical security are pertinent to the data processing facility; all methods discussed herein can and should be employed to keep the facility secure. Methods and procedures will vary greatly depending upon the level of security required and the capital budget expended.

- **A VERY REAL THREAT IN TODAY'S ENVIRONMENT IS THE**

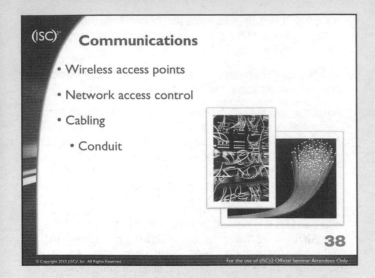

WIRELESS ACCESS POINTS (WAPs) – These are particularly vulnerable due to their exposed positions throughout a facility. They should be solidly attached and the device and its connectivity properly managed.

NETWORK ACCESS CONTROL (NAC) – Provides access and validity control of system and networked devices. Basic NAC functions include validating software and release levels (Firewall, Antivirus, Anti-Spam, etc.) and providing login security to the device and the network. "Enterprise NAC" devices can disable unused ports (also a base function with many smart switches) on telecommunications equipment and manage some functions of corporate security policy (such as login credentials).

CABLING – Cables are often run through wiring closets and conduit. Wiring closets should be locked to prevent a person from tapping onto a line, or re-routing cabling.

CONDUIT – Conduit can protect wiring from damage or tampering. Conduit can be pressurized to detect unauthorized penetration and stop water from leaking into a hole in the conduit.

COMMUNICATIONS EQUIPMENT – Equipment rooms encompass much more than server or mainframe rooms. Modern networks require routers, switches, access points, and plenty of wire to route communications from one system to another, or from the workplace desk to the server. These areas are typically less secure than mainframe server facilities and are consequently far easier to breach. A well-placed tap on a switch could compromise the environment as much as any other kind of breach. Again, proper access control and monitoring is imperative.

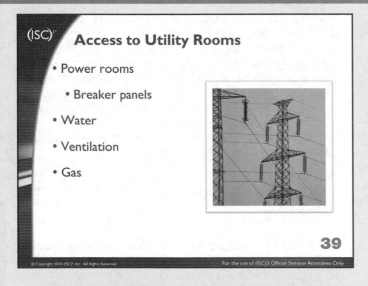

the room as well as proper signage and training for personnel who access those areas.

WATER – Water can do a lot of damage in a very short time – whether a broken pipe, faulty valve, or flooding from outside, there should be precautions in place to detect water leakage and protect equipment. The main shut-off value for the facility should be labeled and, quite possibly locked, with an emergency access key in a glass breakage box nearby.

VENTILATION – Equipment can generate a lot of heat and needs a stable operating environment. Ventilation ducts can provide access for personnel or other contaminants. Therefore, smoke and motion detectors should be placed in large ventilation ducts and plenums.

GAS – Facilities that use gas for heating, manufacturing, or other purposes should have gas sensors and protection in case of leakage. A main shut-off value should be labeled and easily accessible.

UTILITY AND POWER ROOMS – These are not as critical in terms of losing data, but are just as critical to ongoing operations. Malicious manipulation of utilities and the power supply could force the facility into a backup state, and likely affect many of your electronic controls and monitoring systems. A power outage allows for easier intrusions into otherwise protected areas and greater ease in injecting covert network or data monitoring probes.

POWER ROOMS AND BREAKER PANELS – Power rooms, including rectifiers, backup power generating equipment, Uninterruptible Power Supply units (UPS), batteries, and power transfer switches should be protected with restricted access. Proper safety and fire equipment should be located in

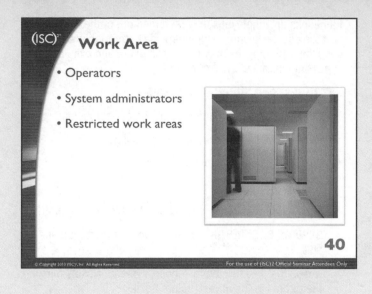

Work Area

- Operators
- System administrators
- Restricted work areas

40

- **WORK AREAS** – Keeping a work area safe is important for both the computing environment and for its employees.

- **OPERATORS AND SYSTEM ADMINISTRATORS** – Operators and system administrators should be subject to multiple checks and balances in order to ensure that the proper personnel are accessing the computing environment as required. Use appropriate access controls and monitoring equipment; recorded video (CCTV), for example, provides an excellent historical log of not just personnel access, but also of their actions while in view of the lens.

- **RESTRICTED WORK AREAS** – With many systems, physical access means administrator level access. For example, the operator console in a mainframe environment is a trusted path that provides high level access to the system and the ability to execute commands that may not be able to be executed from anywhere else. It is, therefore, important to have areas that are **RESTRICTED WORK AREAS** – designed to restrict access to the most valuable areas to the select few who need this access. Again, this can be accomplished with the right implementation of access controls and monitoring, including access credentials, ID cards and card readers, proximity cards, RFID (radio-frequency identification) sensors, Biometric locks, and access logs.

Equipment Protection

- Inventory
- Locks and tracing equipment
- Data encryption
- Disabling I/O ports

41

- **EQUIPMENT PROTECTION** – This is another layer of physical security. LAN infrastructure equipment (routers, switches, wireless access points) may be physically dispersed throughout a facility, or may be centrally located within a wiring closet or server room. Portable equipment (laptops or PDAs, also known as personal data assistants) often accompany the traveling user. A comprehensive security strategy will incorporate individual components regardless of their location.

- **INVENTORY** – Having a physical count of equipment along with its location, configuration, I/O (input/output) port utilization, and backup procedures will make management easier when you run across a piece you don't recognize, or have to execute a business continuity plan. Operational policy should dictate keeping a current inventory and storing it in a safe place.

- **LOCKS AND TRACING EQUIPMENT** – Portable (or easily moved) equipment should be properly secured either in a docking bay with a cable and lock, or within a rack. Very portable equipment (PDAs or laptops) should have an operating system-enabled timeout. Tracing software or other inventory control products can help maintain the integrity of the network and systems and can also identify rogue hardware.

- **DATA ENCRYPTION** – Many industries (such as the Payment Card Industry – Data Security Standard (PCI-DSS)) and corporations require data encryption and some governmental standards dictate it. Many multinational organizations employ specialized encryption devices for the parts of their network that reach into suspect areas. Encryption on portable devices is just as important – even when the devices are used in theoretically "trusted" areas. Laptops or PDAs are easily lost or stolen, but there is commonly available software that will encrypt some or all of the data on these devices.

- **DISABLING I/O PORTS** – USB ports are very handy for interconnectivity of devices, and are often available today even when traditional parallel or serial ports are not. With the proliferation of inexpensive, small, and very powerful data storage devices that utilize USB or IEEE1394 (Firewire) ports, however, it is important to incorporate the acceptable use of these ports into your security policy. Device hardware ports can usually be disabled within the operating system by the administrator.

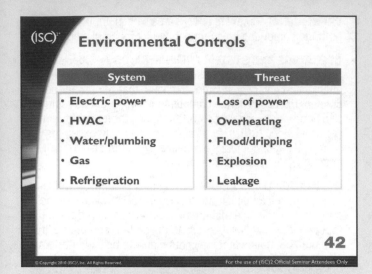

Environmental Controls

System	Threat
• Electric power	• Loss of power
• HVAC	• Overheating
• Water/plumbing	• Flood/dripping
• Gas	• Explosion
• Refrigeration	• Leakage

42

- **ENVIRONMENTAL CONTROLS –** Infrastructure Support Systems include electrical power, water/plumbing, steam lines, gas lines, heating, ventilation, refrigeration, and sewage. All of these are out of the security professional's direct control. What the security professional can do, however, is consider the impact to the information systems if one or more of these systems are interrupted. This topic is discussed in detail in the BCP domain, but for now, understand that these can have an impact on physical security. For example, if the sewage system backs up, employees may be forced out of the building, or if the cooling system fails to provide comfortable working conditions, employees may prop open doors and exits thereby bypassing entrance and exit controls.

- **KEY THREATS TO SUPPORT SYSTEMS –**

  - **POWER LOSS –** Disruption/stoppage of operations.

  - **HVAC FAILURE –** Overheating/overcooling.

  - **WATER –** Flooding/dripping.

  - **GAS LEAKS –** Explosion.

  - **FIRE –** Damage and destruction of facilities/equipment.

  - **SEWAGE BACKUP/BREAKAGE –** Work areas uninhabitable.

  - Notice that key threats to support systems closely mirror the threats to the infrastructure itself.

- An environment should maintain the optimum operational conditions for information systems: clean air free of contaminants and relative humidity between 40-60 percent (though some facilities prefer 45-55 percent). Low humidity can cause electrostatic discharge and high humidity causes condensation and corrosion. The ambient temperature should be between 20-22°C or 70-74°F. (Recommended temperature setting is mostly for the comfort of operators and users.)

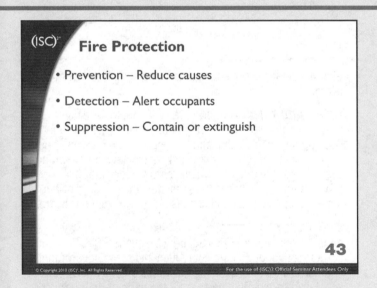

Fire Protection

- Prevention – Reduce causes

- Detection – Alert occupants

- Suppression – Contain or extinguish

43

- **FIRE PROTECTION –** Prevention, detection, and suppression combine to form "fire protection." Life safety issues include communications, alarms, routes of exit, and refuge areas.

- **PREVENTION –** Reduces causes of fire by:

  - Using fire-resistant materials for walls, doors, and furnishings.

  - Reducing the amount of combustible material in the facility.

  - Providing fire-prevention training to employees.

  - Conducting fire drills on all shifts.

- **DETECTION –** Alerts personnel to the presence of a fire before it becomes a more serious problem. Several types of detectors are available:

  - Ionization-type smoke detectors detect charged particles in smoke.

  - Optical (photoelectric) detectors react to light blockage caused by smoke.

  - Fixed or rate-of-rise temperature sensors – Heat detectors that react to the heat of a fire.

  - A combination of these will provide the most effective means of detecting a fire.

- **SUPPRESSION –** Extinguishing and containing a fire so as to minimize damage:

  - Carbon Dioxide (CO_2) extinguishers provide a colorless, odorless chemical that displaces oxygen in the air.

  - Inert gases such as Argon and products such as FM200 are alternatives to Halon.

  - Water Sprinkler Systems – But note that water can conduct electricity and may compound the problems in computer rooms.

  - "Pre-action" or "dry-pipe" system – Water is held back by a valve and is released when the sensor activates. The pipes then fill with water and the sprinkler system engages. In computer rooms and areas with electrical equipment, this allows for the systems to be shut down before the water is released (and in fact, many of these systems are wired into the power systems for the computer equipment to ensure this happens).

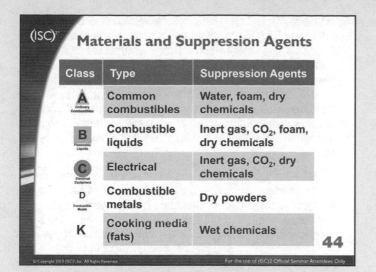

- **CLASS A – COMMON COMBUSTIBLE MATERIALS** (e.g., wood, paper, cloth, rubber, and plastics) that can act as fuel and are found in non-specialized operating areas. The following fire extinguishing agents are approved for Class A combustibles:

  - Water
  - Multipurpose dry chemical (ABC)
  - Halon Replacement

- **CLASS B – CLASS B COMBUSTIBLES INCLUDE FLAMMABLE AND COMBUSTIBLE LIQUIDS** (e.g., oils, greases, tars, oil-based paints, and lacquers), **FLAMMABLE GASES, AND FLAMMABLE AEROSOLS SUCH AS THOSE FOUND IN SPRAY CANS.** The following fire extinguishing agents are approved for Class B combustibles:

  - Carbon dioxide
  - Multipurpose dry chemical (ABC)
  - Halon Replacement

- **CLASS C – CLASS C COMBUSTIBLES ARE ENERGIZED ELECTRICAL EQUIPMENT WHICH, WHEN DE-ENERGIZED, WOULD BE CLASSIFIED AS CLASS A OR B COMBUSTIBLES.** The following fire extinguishing agents are approved for Class C combustibles:

  - Carbon dioxide
  - Multipurpose dry chemical (ABC)
  - Halon Replacement

- **CLASS D – CLASS D COMBUSTIBLES ARE COMBUSTIBLE METALS SUCH AS MAGNESIUM, THORIUM, POTASSIUM, OR SODIUM METALS.** Class D combustibles present special fire safety and extinguishing problems. Dry powders are used to extinguish Class D combustibles.

- **CLASS K – CLASS K COMBUSTIBLES ARE COOKING MEDIA SUCH AS VEGETABLE OR ANIMAL OILS AND FATS.** This class of combustibles requires extinguishing agents that are specifically listed and labeled for use on Class K fires. Wet chemicals are used to extinguish Class K combustibles.

- **A WAY TO REMEMBER EACH:**

  - **A**SH
  - **B**OIL
  - **C**URRENT
  - **D**RIVE
  - **K**ITCHEN

REFERENCES:

http://www.lbl.gov/ehs/pub3000/CH12.html

http://www.lbl.gov/ehs/pub3000/CH12.html#sec127

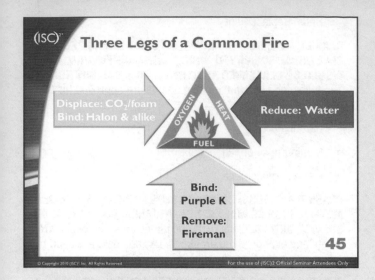

Three Legs of a Common Fire

Displace: CO_2/foam
Bind: Halon & alike

OXYGEN   HEAT

Reduce: Water

FUEL

Bind:
Purple K

Remove:
Fireman

45

portant as CO_2 will remain in lower levels such as open pits and areas below grade, thus necessitating the ventilation of such areas prior to re-entry. These systems are best for unattended facilities, but if they are used in manned areas, a delay should be installed providing time for personnel to exit the area. Gas masks give no protection as the problem with CO_2 is the resultant lack of oxygen. Gaseous carbon dioxide is 1.5 times denser than air. Therefore, it will be found in greater concentrations at floor level and affect the ability of people to breathe.

- **WATER** – The fire protection and insurance industries support the use of water as the primary fire extinguishing agent for all business environments, including those dependent on information systems. If the electrical power can be cut to a computing facility, a water sprinkler will not usually cause much damage to the equipment. A water misting system is an even better choice as it will often extinguish a fire without the water even contacting the equipment.

- **PURPLE K** – A dry powder used by the fire department that binds with solid objects at the point of combustion to limit the fire's access to the fuel.

- **THE LEGS OF A FIRE ARE FUEL, HEAT, AND OXYGEN** – All three are required for combustion to occur. Removing one of these factors will stop the fire. CO_2 and foam reduce access to oxygen, water reduces temperature, and gas (Halon/Halon substitutes) interferes with chemical reaction between elements.

- **CO_2** – Is colorless, odorless, and potentially lethal in that it lowers the concentration of oxygen in the air making it unable to support life. High concentrations of CO_2 can displace oxygen, and cause death if inhaled. This is especially im-

REFERENCES:

Hopkins, Mark (2002) Planning Your Fire Suppression System,
http://palimpsest.stanford.edu/byorg/abbey/an/an26/an26-1/an26-102.html
http://www.lbl.gov/ehs/pub3000/CH12.html

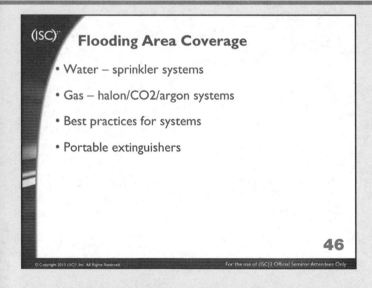

Flooding Area Coverage

- Water – sprinkler systems

- Gas – halon/CO2/argon systems

- Best practices for systems

- Portable extinguishers

46

- **BEST PRACTICES FOR SYSTEMS INCLUDE:**

  - **ZONES OF COVERAGE** – Smoke detectors, fire alarm systems, and permanent suppression systems are usually divided into zones of coverage in order to maximize the effectiveness of the detection, response, and suppression systems.

  - **TIMED RELEASE** – Most permanent suppression systems are designed with a timed release that will alert staff to an impending discharge of the system, which will allow them to evacuate the facility or even override the system if it turns out to be a minor incident or false alarm.

  - **HVAC OFF BEFORE ACTIVATION** – The HVAC system should close all ventilation ducts upon activation of the fire alarm.

  - **SPRINKLERS** – Water offers conventional sprinkler heads with water at the sprinkler head and released when the heat of the fire breaks a solder joint or glass bulb. Some sprinklers hold the water back and only fill the pipes when an alarm sounds. These are called "dry pipe" systems.

- **FLOODING AREA COVERAGE** – The suppression agent is discharged through installed pipes designed to distribute the suppressant and extinguish the fire.

- **WATER** – Sprinkler systems include the following components: source (water supply), pipes (delivery), and heads (distribution).

- **GAS** – Halon/CO2/Argon systems include the following components: enclosed space for the gas to stay concentrated, automated sealed doors, personnel warning system, source of gas, pipes, and heads.

- **PORTABLE EXTINGUISHERS** – Used to minimize fire damage. Portable extinguishers are filled with approved/applicable suppression agents and should be located within 50 feet of any piece of electrical equipment as well as at all exits. Portable extinguishers should be clearly marked, located in an area with an unobstructed view, easily reached, operable by personnel of average size and strength, and inspected quarterly. Note, however, that personnel should not attempt to extinguish the fire unless it is safe to do so. It is usually best to get the people out and let the professional firefighters fight the fire.

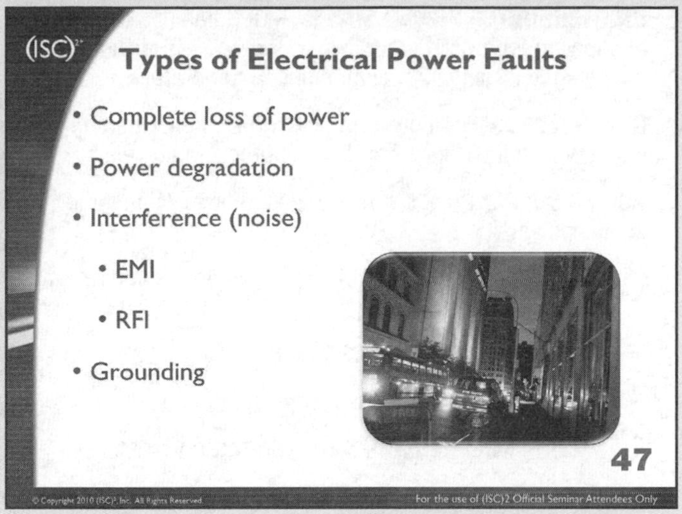

Types of Electrical Power Faults

- Complete loss of power
- Power degradation
- Interference (noise)
  - EMI
  - RFI
- Grounding

47

- **COMPLETE LOSS OF POWER -**
  - **BLACKOUT** – A prolonged loss of commercial power.
  - **FAULT** – Momentary loss of power.
- **POWER DEGRADATION –**
  - **BROWNOUT** – A reduction of voltage by the utility company for a prolonged period of time.
  - **SAG/DIP** – A short period of low voltage.
  - **SURGE** – A sudden rise in voltage in the power supply.

- **TRANSIENTS** – Line noise that is superimposed on the supply circuit, typically caused by a fluctuation in power.
- **IN-RUSH CURRENT** – The initial surge of current required when there is an increase in power demand. This can cause breakers to trip/fail.
- **ELECTROSTATIC DISCHARGE** – A power surge generated by a person or device contacting another device and transferring a high voltage shock.
- **INTERFERENCE (NOISE)** – A natural occurrence that happens when unwanted signals are generated in circuits that are in close proximity. Normally, engineers place filters in their equipment to handle the noise generated internally. However, as more and more equipment is placed in a site, "noise" from one device can affect another. If this happens, the best resolution is to shield or separate the pieces of equipment causing it.
  - EMI and RFI are types of noise that must be understood, identified, and dealt with by information security professionals.
  - **ELECTROMAGNETIC INTERFERENCE (EMI)** – Caused by motors, lightning, low humidity, etc.
  - **RADIO FREQUENCY INTERFERENCE (RFI)** – Created by components of electrical systems. Caused by electric cables, fluorescent lighting, truck ignition, etc.
- **GROUNDING** – Many power problems and errors on communications lines in a facility are caused by poor grounding of electrical equipment or alternate power generators.

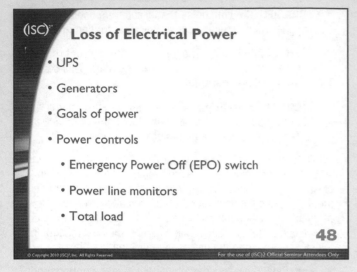

Loss of Electrical Power

- UPS
- Generators
- Goals of power
- Power controls
  - Emergency Power Off (EPO) switch
  - Power line monitors
  - Total load

48

- **LOSS OF ELECTRICAL POWER** – A clean and steady electrical power supply is a necessity in order to ensure business continuity. Any outage or malfunction in electrical power can result in serious damage, such as loss of data, equipment breakdown, or work interruptions. In this respect, it is essential to have power generation equipment that can be engaged prior to a planned outage or activated when an actual outage of primary power occurs. This equipment should be sized to carry the maximum load of the facility (including air conditioning). It is also good to have a spare generator available in case one fails. Ensure that critical power feeders and switch facilities are properly protected from physical destruction. Depending on budgets and critical business operations, an organization might choose which equipment and workstations should have a backup power, and which ones are not critical and, therefore, may not seriously impact business operations in the event of a failure.

- **UNINTERRUPTED POWER SUPPLY** – UPS has had a goal of allowing for orderly shutdown of systems. That trend is changing to issuing start commands to generators.

- **GENERATORS** – For long-term power loss, generators or engines with their fuel offer days of alternate power.

- **POWER SUPPLY GOALS** – The goal is to have "clean and steady power":

  - **DEDICATED FEEDERS** – Different "feeder" lines from electrical substations.

  - **ALTERNATE POWER SOURCE** – Generators, batteries.

  - **ACCESS CONTROLS** – Locked power panels.

  - **SECURE BREAKER AND TRANSFORMER ROOMS**

  - **SURGE SUPPRESSORS**

  - **ELECTRICAL FACILITIES** separated from Data Center, so that power fluctuations in other parts of the facility do not affect the data center.

  - **FLY WHEEL OR KINETIC ENERGY WHEEL** – A specific type of power storage system.

- **POWER CONTROLS** -

  - **EPO** – Have an Emergency Power Off (EPO) switch that allows someone to shut down the power.

  - **POWER LINE MONITORS** – Install a power line monitor that detects and records fluctuations in voltage.

  - **TOTAL LOAD** – Ensure there is enough backup battery power to conduct an orderly shutdown to avoid data loss or device damage.

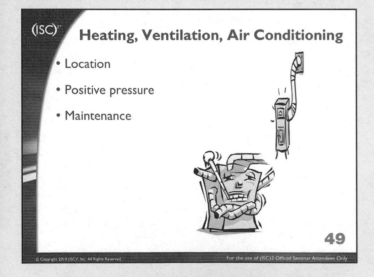

Heating, Ventilation, Air Conditioning

- Location
- Positive pressure
- Maintenance

49

- **HEATING, VENTILATION, AND AIR CONDITIONING (HVAC)** – Controls for IT equipment must be separate from those for the building at large and protected to ensure that they are not accidentally adjusted for human comfort.

- **HVAC CONTROL CONSIDERATIONS** –

  - **LOCATION** -

    - Independence of the data center air conditioning system from the rest of the building.

  - Access controls.

- **POSITIVE PRESSURE** – Applying greater air pressure and circulation than is needed within an enclosed space, thereby constantly forcing air leakage out of that enclosed space. This ensures that air is constantly being forced from the environmentally controlled (quality, humidity, temperature, etc.) area to areas that are not environmentally maintained. This is a concept that is common in fire control systems and biological engineering (negative pressurization). Note, too, that variance in the amount of room pressure may indicate an unauthorized physical breach.

- **APPROPRIATE MAINTENANCE OF** -

  - Temperature

  - Humidity levels

  - Air quality

  - Documented maintenance procedures

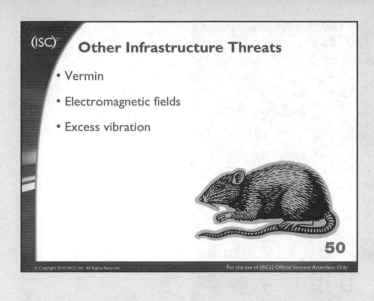

Other Infrastructure Threats

- Vermin
- Electromagnetic fields
- Excess vibration

50

- **VERMIN** – Other factors that can affect a data processing facility include rodents, termites, squirrels, or burrowing animals that may chew on wires, damage electrical lines, or pose a health risk to the staff.

- **ELECTROMAGNETIC FIELDS** – Data lines can be affected by neighboring equipment, power lines, or poor grounding. The electromagnetic fields given off by equipment and power lines can "bleed" onto the data lines, causing errors and even damaging equipment attached to the lines. In such areas, shielded cable should be used and precautions taken to avoid power line imbalances or low humidity conditions that could lead to static or other faults.

- **EXCESS VIBRATION** – Excessive vibration may come from many causes, including earthquake, trains, or public transport systems, and poorly installed equipment. In places where a lot of vibration can occur, racks should be mounted on flexible footings or the server room floor designed to move with the building and absorb the effect of the movement without jarring the equipment.

Domain Summary

- The security professional should be aware of the threats, risks, and countermeasures for each of these areas:

  - Physical Security Threats and Controls

  - Perimeter Security

  - Building and Inside Security

  - Secure Operational Areas

51

Security Transcends Technology

Review Questions

PHYSICAL SECURITY

1. The six (6) goals of physical security are

   A. protect, delay, detect, assess, respond, and recover.
   B. deter, delay, detect, assess, respond, and recover.
   C. protect, delay, detect, assess, respond, and react.
   D. deter, delay, detect, assess, respond, and react.

2. The union representing many of the employees who work for your coal supplier goes on strike. This type of threat is best categorized as

   A. natural/environmental.
   B. utilities.
   C. circumstantial.
   D. human-made/political events.

3. Five (5) examples of successful countermeasures for theft include

   A. strong access controls, intrusion detection systems, locked doors, key control, and bag check.
   B. strong access controls, anti-phishing software, locked doors, key control, and bag check.
   C. identification and authentication, intrusion detection systems, locked doors, key control, and bag check.
   D. identification and authentication, anti-phishing software, locked doors, key control, and bag check.

4. Environmental controls are grouped into three (3) distinct categories:

   A. Layered, administrative/managerial, and technical.
   B. Physical, layered, and technical.
   C. Physical, administrative/managerial, and layered.
   D. Physical, administrative/managerial, and technical.

5. An approach to physical security that delves into the relationship between incidents and frequency of crime, and the environment the crime was committed in, is known as

   A. defensible space – crime prevention through urban design (CPTUD).
   B. the layered approach.
   C. crime prevention through environmental design (CPTED).
   D. creating defensible space through superior design and analysis (CDSTSDA).

6. You have been directed to assist with determining the minimum height of a fence which will encircle the building that houses your company's data center. The desire is to deter trespassers and to delay determined intruders. What is the minimum recommended height of the fence?

   A. 1.0 meter/~ 3.0 feet
   B. 2.0 meters/~6.0 feet
   C. 2.5 meters/~8.0 feet
   D. 3.0 meters/~10 feet

7. Which type of intrusion detection system (IDS) is BEST described as an active beam of light that triggers an alarm when the beam is broken?

   A. Electrical circuits
   B. Motion sensor
   C. Ultrasonic
   D. Photoelectric

8. Closed circuit television (CCTV) systems must meet which of the following requirements?

   A. Mixing capabilities, recognition, and identification
   B. Detection, recognition, and identification
   C. Detection, recognition, and mixing capabilities
   D. Detection, identification, and mixing capabilities

9. Which of the following statements BEST describes the relationships between guards and a cost benefit analysis?

   A. Guards are inexpensive and provide a unique capability by providing reasoned, discriminating, and measured responses to changing situations.
   B. Guards are inexpensive and do not provide a unique capability by providing reasoned, discriminating, and measured responses to changing situations.
   C. Guards are expensive and do not provide a unique capability by providing reasoned, discriminating, and measured responses to changing situations.
   D. Guards are expensive and provide a unique capability by providing reasoned, discriminating, and measured responses to changing situations.

10. **Doors play a critical role in a physical security program. Best business practice guidelines for doors include solid core open**

    A. inward if permitted by law, minimum of three (3) hinges, and the same fire resistance rating as the adjoining walls.

    B. outward if permitted by law, minimum of three (3) hinges, and the same fire resistance rating as the adjoining walls.

    C. inward if permitted by law, minimum of three (3) hinges, and a 25 percent greater fire resistance rating as the adjoining walls.

    D. outward if permitted by law, minimum of three (3) hinges, and a 25 percent greater fire resistance rating as the adjoining walls.

11. **Which statement below BEST describes the attributes of the entry control mechanism?**

    A. Both turnstiles and mantraps are considered a cost-prohibitive method of controlling access and generally do not work without guard oversight or intervention.

    B. Both turnstiles and mantraps are considered a cost-effective method of controlling access but generally do not work without guard oversight or intervention.

    C. Both turnstiles and mantraps are considered a cost-prohibitive method of controlling access even though they can work with little or no guard oversight or intervention.

    D. Both turnstiles and mantraps are considered a cost-effective method of controlling access and can work with little or no guard oversight or intervention.

12. **Which type of lock is BEST described as a "keyed" lock?**

    A. A deadbolt lock

    B. A combination lock

    C. A cipher lock

    D. A dial lock

13. **Which statement below BEST describes the attributes associated with the various types of locks?**

    A. Combination locks are the most common and acceptable way to secure areas and property even though they are only considered a delay device rather than foolproof barrier to entry.

    B. Keyed locks are the most common and acceptable way to secure areas and property even though they are only considered a delay device rather than foolproof barrier to entry.

    C. Combination locks are an unacceptable way to secure areas or property because they are only considered a delay device rather than foolproof barrier to entry.

    D. Keyed locks are an unacceptable way to secure areas or property because they are only considered a delay device rather than foolproof barrier to entry.

14. **When a power failure occurs, locks can be thought of as being in one of several states. Which state is BEST described as the one which is designed to protect human life and allows people to exit a building rather than secure the facility?**

    A. Fail-over

    B. Fail-soft

    C. Fail-secure

    D. Fail-safe

15. **Which one of the following is BEST for exterior windows that will be used in high-security areas?**

    A. Standard plate glass

    B. Tempered glass

    C. Acrylic materials

    D. Polycarbonates

16. **What class of fire suppression agent should be used on energized electrical equipment?**

    A. Class A

    B. Class B

    C. Class C

    D. Class D

17. **Why is it important to properly identify individuals before entering their facility access in the visitor log?**

    A. To prevent imposters from using fake IDs.

    B. To ensure only authorized people are allowed into the facility.

    C. To create a temporary visitor badge for them.

    D. To prevent inaccurate information from being entered into the visitor log.

18. **General best practices for fire protection systems include**

    A. heat transfer, timed release, HVAC off before activation, and sprinklers.

    B. zones of coverage, timed release, HVAC off before activation, and sprinklers.

    C. heat transfer, timed release, HVAC on before activation, and sprinklers.

    D. zones of coverage, timed release, HVAC on before activation, and sprinklers.

19. **Motors placed and used in close proximity to computers and peripherals are likely to cause which type of interference?**

    A. TEMPEST

    B. Electromagnetic interference (EMI)

    C. Radio frequency interference (RFI)

    D. Defensive interference (DI)

20. **Heating, ventilation, and air conditioning (HVAC) systems used within data processing facilities (DPF)**

A. must be separate from those used for the common building and protected to ensure that they are not accidentally adjusted for human comfort.

B. must be separate from those used for the common building but controlled from within the DPF to allow for temperature and humidity adjustments for human comfort.

C. should be the same systems used for the common building and protected to ensure that they are not accidentally adjusted for human comfort.

D. should be the same systems used for the common building but controlled from within the DPF to allow for temperature and humidity adjustments for human comfort.

Notes

(ISC)² — Physical (Environmental) Security

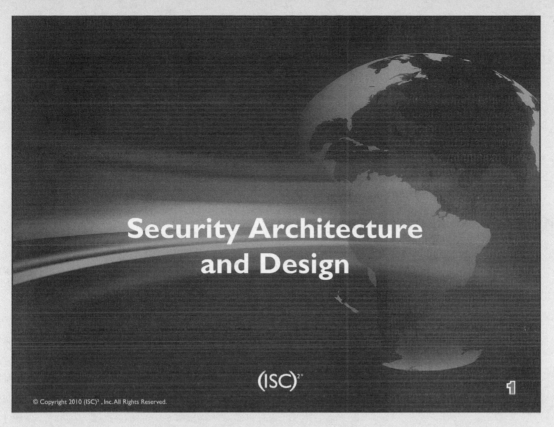

Security Architecture
and Design

(ISC)²*

© Copyright 2010 (ISC)² , Inc.All Rights Reserved.

- The Security Architecture and Design domain addresses the high-level and detailed processes, concepts, principles, structures, and standards used to define, design, implement, monitor, and secure/assure: operating systems, applications, equipment, and networks. It addresses the technical security policies of the organization, as well as the implementation and enforcement of those policies. Architecture and design must clearly address the design, implementation, and operation of those controls used to enforce various levels of confidentiality, integrity, and availability to ensure effective operation and compliance (with governance and other drivers).

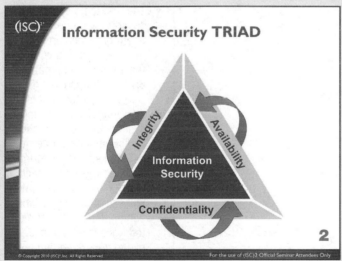

- **INTEGRITY** – Accuracy of processing by the TCB is assumed by all who use its resources. Both management and implementers are concerned with the level of trust they can have in the veracity and accuracy that a system will provide. This level of trust is achieved through testing and evaluation of products. Among the models that directly address integrity are Biba and Clark & Wilson.

- **CONFIDENTIALITY** – The architecture and design will enforce the protection of the secrecy or privacy of information. The Bell-LaPadula model is the main confidentiality model.

- The application of availability, integrity, and confidentiality is driven by security architectures. CISSPs are often asked to define a problem in terms of availability, integrity, or confidentiality and may find that abstracting the problem in terms of a model is helpful in defining or describing the main issue.

- **AVAILABILITY** – Stakeholders typically want as much processing power as possible so as to solve their problems as quickly as possible. The trusted computing base (TCB) will deliver within the limitations of the security architecture and the physical implementation. Although none of the traditional models addresses availability, availability is addressed through the redundancy and continuity of the operations provisions built into the design of modern systems and networks.

Domain Agenda

- System and Component Security

- System Design Principles

- Security Models

- Information Systems Evaluation Models

- Security Frameworks

3

- This is the agenda for this domain. We will discuss each of these in detail on the following slides.

Domain Agenda

- **System and Component Security**

  - **Definitions and Key Concepts**

  - Architecture Components

- System Design Principles

- Security Models

- Information Systems Evaluation Models

- Security Frameworks

4

- The first topic addressed is "System and Component Security." Since architecture is concerned with the integration of many diverse components into a working, interoperable, and mutually supporting system, the security specialist must be concerned with the security strengths and weaknesses in each individual component. We will examine many of the components that make up today's systems with an eye to understanding how to use them effectively to build security into our systems and networks.

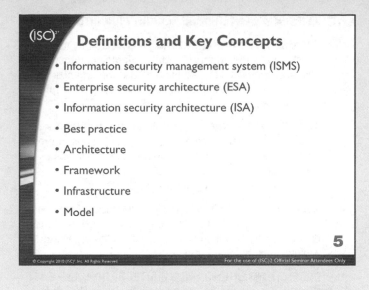

- **INFORMATION SECURITY MANAGEMENT SYSTEM (ISMS)** – One of the most popular frameworks in the world today, ISMS sets a standard for addressing security throughout the development, deployment, and implementation schedule.

- **ENTERPRISE SECURITY ARCHITECTURE (ESA)** – Enterprise security architecture (ESA) includes all areas of security for an organization: leadership, strategy, organizational structure, planning, design, implementation, and operations.

- **INFORMATION SECURITY ARCHITECTURE (ISA)** – Another term from the ISO/IEC 27002. High-level description of how security requirements are structured.

- **BEST PRACTICE** – A well-recognized and accepted approach to designing, developing, managing/monitoring, and enhancing processes, often codified into a standard.

- **ARCHITECTURE** – A high-level perspective of how business requirements are to be structured and aligned with technology and processes in a comprehensive and manageable way.

- **FRAMEWORK** – A defined approach to the process used to achieve the goals of an architecture, based on policy, and reflecting the requirements and expectations of the various stakeholders.

- **INFRASTRUCTURE** – The integrated building blocks that support the goals of the architecture.

- **MODEL** – A security model outlines how security is to be implemented within the organization.

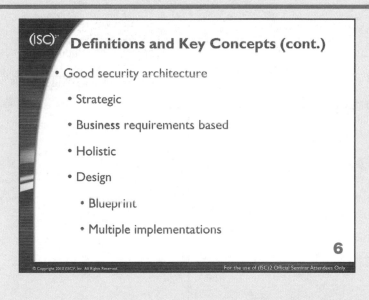

- **STRATEGIC** – It provides a long-range perspective that is less subject to tactical changes in technology. It is specific to the goals of the organization, but not so detailed that technical constraints limit the ability of the organization to be flexible or adopt new technologies.

- **BUSINESS REQUIREMENTS BASED** – The core requirement for a successful architectural effort is to truly understand both the business and security requirements and design a system that meets those requirements. This requires a balance between functionality and security, a consideration of cost and technology, and the realization of the effect of security on the end-user experience.

- **HOLISTIC** – It shifts from an IT-centric to a business-centric security process to more effectively manage risk. It also addresses business drivers, legal requirements, threat scenarios, and design, and ensures they are operationally integrated with the overall IT architecture, business processes, and business culture.

- **DESIGN** – Architecture produces the design of the system based on the requirements.

  - **BLUEPRINT** – Functional definition for the integration and development of technology infrastructure into the business process.

  - **MULTIPLE IMPLEMENTATIONS** – Flexibility due to location and business constraints is required to address business needs.

Definitions and Key Concepts (cont.)

- Benefits of a good security architecture
  - Consistently manage risk
  - Reduce the costs of managing risk
  - Accurate security-related decisions
  - Promote interoperability, integration, and ease of access
  - Provide a frame of reference

7

- **BENEFITS OF AN ENTERPRISE SECURITY ARCHITECTURE –**
  - **CONSISTENTLY MANAGE IT RISK –** Consistently manage IT risk across the enterprise while leveraging industry best practices. This is enabled because the organization is working from the same architecture based on a holistic point of view.
  - **REDUCE THE OVERALL COSTS OF MANAGING RISK –** Reduce the overall costs of managing IT risk and improve flexibility by implementing common security solutions across the enterprise because decisions are based on a total view providing long-term interoperability.
  - **ACCURATE SECURITY-RELATED DECISIONS –** Allow decision makers to make better and quicker security-related decisions across the enterprise because the organization is viewed as a single entity.
  - **PROMOTE INTEROPERABILITY, INTEGRATION, AND EASE OF ACCESS –** Promote interoperability, integration, and ease of access while effectively managing risk.
  - **PROVIDE A FRAME OF REFERENCE –** Provide a frame of reference for guidance to other organizations interacting with the enterprise.

Domain Agenda

- **System and Component Security**

  - Definitions and Key Concepts

  - **Architecture Components**

- System Design Principles

- Security Models

- Information Systems Evaluation Models

- Security Frameworks

8

- Now that we have looked at some of the key concepts and definitions, we will look at some of the components of architecture.

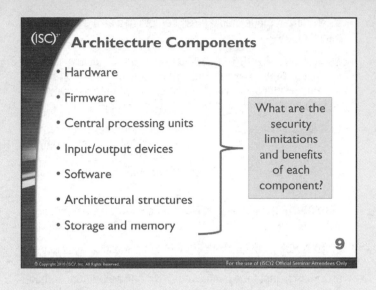

- Security architects bring together many system components, including hardware and software, in an effort to provide basic security services including:

- **ARCHITECTURE:**

  - Maintaining integrity of the computing processes.

  - Controlling access to system resources and data.

  - Providing consistent and predictable computing services.

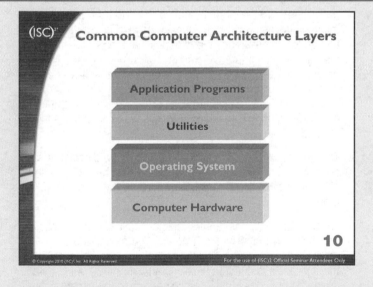

- **ARCHITECTURE LAYERS –** These are the computer system layers. The user interacts with data and the network resources through applications. The applications sit on top of the utilities and operating system. The operating system provides management of the computer hardware resources.

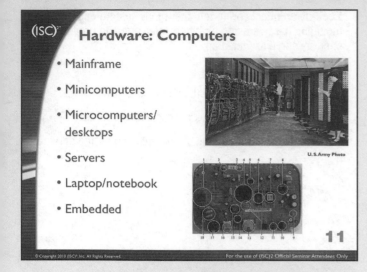

Hardware: Computers

- Mainframe
- Minicomputers
- Microcomputers/ desktops
- Servers
- Laptop/notebook
- Embedded

U.S.Army Photo

11

© Copyright 2010 (ISC)², Inc. All Rights Reserved.   For the use of (ISC)2 Official Seminar Attendees Only

- **MAINFRAME** – Historically, the word "mainframe" described a metal-framed, room-size computer. Today, a mainframe is a large, highly fault-tolerant, multiuser computer engineered to run without interruption for long periods of time. It typically has one operating system designed specifically for that particular hardware. One of the earliest mainframes was the ENIAC housed at the Army Research Laboratory in Maryland. Mainframes clearly provide a very centralized platform with separate peripherals such as disks.

- **MINICOMPUTER** – A smaller system, often seen as the little brother to a mainframe, but frequently still architected into

a centralized model. Most large servers can also be called minicomputers.

- **MICROCOMPUTERS/DESKTOPS** – Also known as a micro-computer. These may take many forms, such as free-standing towers, desktops, or blades. Desktops have many synonyms, including "personal computer" or "workstation."

- **SERVERS** – The term servers can represent many different types of devices. Usually servers provide storage and computing services for users who are connected to them. They are typically larger, more fault-tolerant computers, usually serving more than one user.

- **LAPTOP/NOTEBOOK** – A self-contained, portable computer with a battery.

- **EMBEDDED** – Computers built into other devices. Typically single purpose, real-time computers. They are by far the most prevalent computer system. Today we find computers embedded into many of the products we use. We are also seeing them being embedded into the human body to address some medical problems.

- From a security perspective, each security risk must be addressed individually.

- Shown are the ENIAC and an embedded ADSL modem router.

REFERENCE:
http://ftp.arl.mil/ftp/historic-computers/

Hardware: Mobile Devices

- USB storage
- Portable hard drives
- PDAs and mobile phones

12

© Copyright 2010 (ISC)², Inc. All Rights Reserved.   For the use of (ISC)2 Official Seminar Attendees Only

- **MOBILE DEVICES** – Perhaps one of the greatest challenges faced by the security professional today is the proliferation of mobile devices. Many types of devices are on the market that can contain immense amounts of corporate data. This provides a great benefit to the business in the ability to port data from one site to another, but also presents the risk of data being carried outside of a secure area. This opens the organization up to the risk of data loss when a device is lost or stolen.

- The security architect must find ways to allow devices to connect in a secure manner and ensure that the policies and encryption tools are in place to protect the data from unauthorized access.

- These mobile devices require special security consideration because they may frequently connect outside of the enterprise from less-trusted environments. It is also noteworthy that there is a distinction between an external portable hard drive that provides highly mobile storage and a personal data assistant/smartphone that provides mobile processing.

- Security of the data on these devices is very important and is often accomplished with cryptography.

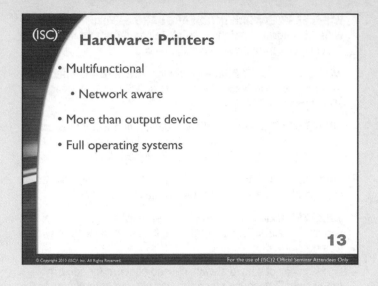

Hardware: Printers

- Multifunctional
  - Network aware
- More than output device
- Full operating systems

13

- **PRINTERS** – Today's printers can be directly attached to the network, support removable media, intelligently communicate with users, and provide multiple services such as scanning and faxing. Networked, intelligent printers are served directly from internal, often proprietary, operating systems. These operating systems can have their own vulnerabilities, and because they are only thought of as office equipment, often go unpatched. Networked printers can suffer from denial of service attacks and can also be compromised and subsequently turned into an attack platform.

- From a security perspective, these printers present many of the same risks as other computers on our networks. However, software such as desktop firewalls and antivirus do not exist to protect them. Therefore, network printers must be carefully monitored for unusual activity.

Hardware: Communication Devices

- Modem
- Network interface card (NIC)

14

- **COMMUNICATION DEVICES** – Hardware that allows computers to exchange data either via wireless or wired media. Some examples are:

- **MODEM** – A device that converts signals from digital to analog so that computers can communicate with each other over analog telephone lines. Modem connections are sometimes compromised by war-dialing and eavesdropping.

- **NETWORK INTERFACE CARD (NIC)** – The interface device that enables computers to communicate over various media. The NIC provides the interface between the computer and the communications media (cable, wireless, optical). Anytime a computer is connected to a network it may become the target of a range of attacks through the network, including denial of service (DoS), IP spoofing, man-in-the-middle, viruses, and worms.

- These provide security concerns as neither provide significant security capability and instead provide access into our networks and critical machines.

Hardware: Wireless

- Wireless network interface card
- Wireless access point
- Wireless Ethernet bridge
- Wireless router
- Wireless range extender

15

- **WIRELESS NETWORK INTERFACE CARD** – Expansion card with an integrated antenna; it links a computer to a network access point transceiver via radio waves.

- **WIRELESS ACCESS POINT** – A bridge device that connects to computers wirelessly and then to an adjacent, wired local area network (LAN).

- **WIRELESS ETHERNET BRIDGE** – Connects a wired network to a wireless network. Two wireless bridges may be used to connect two wired networks over a wireless link.

- **WIRELESS ROUTER** – A device that integrates a wireless access point with an IP router and an Ethernet switch.

- **WIRELESS RANGE EXTENDER** – A wireless range extender (or wireless repeater) can increase the range of an existing wireless network.

- Wireless devices have always caused concern for security professionals because these devices allow a potential attacker a point of attack without gaining physical access to the network. In earlier times the strategy was to disallow these in our networks. That of course was a flawed strategy as users gain increased productivity from these devices and they have become a critical part of any network.

Firmware: Pre-Programmed Chips

- ROMs (read-only memory)
- PROMs (programmable read-only memory)
- EPROMs (erasable programmable read-only memory)
- EEPROMs (electrically erasable, programmable, read-only memory)
- Field programmable gate arrays (FPGAs)
- Flash chips
- Embedded system

16

- **FIRMWARE** – Firmware is software that is permanently (or semi-permanently) embedded in hardware and typically provides low-level services and/or control of hardware. Firmware is typically executed on a microcontroller, and can be stored in a number of different devices, including those listed on the slide.

- **EXAMPLES OF FIRMWARE INCLUDE:**
  - 3-D rendering services in graphic cards.
  - Soft-modem services on PCI cards.
  - TCP/IP communication stacks in printers, cable modems, and hubs.

- Some types of firmware are upgradable (PROMs, EPROMs, EEPROMs, flash), while others are not (ROMs).

- **UNAUTHORIZED UPDATING OR MODIFICATION** – Access to a firmware chip may result in unauthorized modifications or updates. This requires change control procedures and physical protection of chips.

- **EMBEDDED SYSTEM** – An embedded system is one or more dedicated functions as part of a complete device, often including hardware and machinery.

- From a security perspective, each of these contain software on the chips that control how the chip performs its function. If compromised, this software could cause the chip to perform in a manner that would reduce or even bypass our security measures.

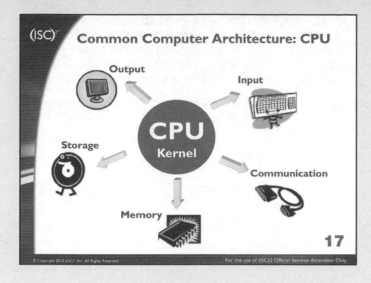

Common Computer Architecture: CPU

- **COMMON COMPUTER ARCHITECTURE: CPU** – The CPU is the heartbeat of a system. It controls primary processing, interaction with peripheral devices, organization of memory, and control over networking operations. The CPU also does logging, error detection, power on self-tests, and handles application interfaces.

- From a security perspective, security of a single centralized CPU is easier than that of a distributed computing model in that the processing power is located in a single place and less vulnerable to attack. However, one must always be mindful of things such as:

  - Denial of service attacks.

  - Mobile code.

  - Scalability.

  - Transparency.

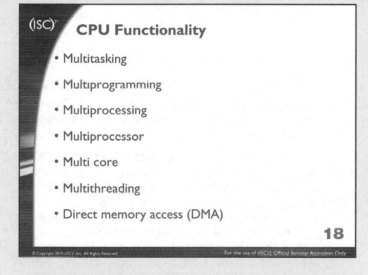

CPU Functionality

- Multitasking
- Multiprogramming
- Multiprocessing
- Multiprocessor
- Multi core
- Multithreading
- Direct memory access (DMA)

- **MULTITASKING** – Concurrent performance/interleaved execution of two or more tasks.

- **MULTIPROGRAMMING** – Interleaved execution of two or more programs by a processor.

- **MULTIPROCESSING** – Simultaneous execution of two or more programs by a computer. Parallel processing by two or more processors of a multiprocessor.

- **MULTIPROCESSOR** – Computer with two or more processors having common access to main storage.

- **MULTI CORE** – Two processors on a single chip.

- **MULTITHREADING** – Allows several processes to share the same resource. A thread that is running on a system will give up CPU cycles to other threads when it is waiting for a response or other long latency activity to complete. This is used in conjunction with multiprocessing, but it is not the same, since multiprocessing usually uses multiple resources, not just the sharing of one resource such as multithreading.

- **DIRECT MEMORY ACCESS (DMA)** – Direct memory access allows a hardware device to access system memory directly over a DMA channel without having to go through the CPU. This is used in multiprocessing systems, and for graphics and sound cards. The CPU cannot be used to enforce system security when peripherals are given direct access to memory, thus protection of memory is typically provided outside the CPU in the motherboard chipset.

- **CPU FUNCTIONALITY** – CPUs have come a long way in the past few years. Modern systems can handle many tasks at once and dual- and quad-core processors have greatly increased operational speeds. This supports the efficient, high-performance requirements of business users. Today's high-performance computers may contain multiple processors that share system resources but provide extremely high-performance response and capability. Since all of these features involve collaboration by the operating system (OS) to provide resources to multiple applications and processes, there should be consideration of isolating processes operating at different levels of privilege or integrity to prevent one process from compromising another, possibly more critical, process. Especially important is the protection of memory storage areas and the residual data which might be accessible in those memory segments.

REFERENCE:
http://www.answers.com/topic/multiprogramming

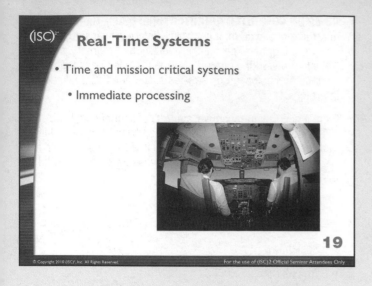

- **REAL-TIME SYSTEMS** – Real-time systems are ones that support mission critical services such as flight controls, and alarm and monitoring sensors. Such systems are not just designed for high availability, or rapid response, but they require immediate reaction and response to conditions.

- Such systems must be designed with high levels of tolerance, failover, and processing speed.

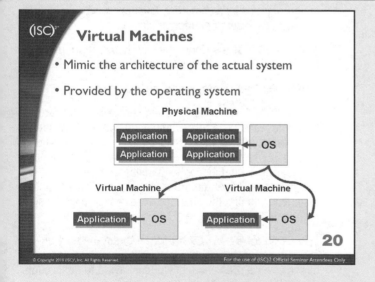

- **VIRTUAL MACHINES** – The actual system is referred to as the "real machine" while created environments are known as "virtual machines."

- **MIMIC THE ARCHITECTURE OF THE ACTUAL SYSTEM** – When an application runs on a computer, it thinks it is the only program running and it does not necessarily know that it is sharing resources with several other types of programs, applications, and processes. This simplifies the issues that programmers need to be concerned about when writing an application. The application, thinking it is the only one executing, needs to be presented with an environment that reflects this type of reality. This is done through virtual machines and virtual memory.

- **PROVIDED BY THE OPERATING SYSTEM** – The operating system creates a virtual environment (virtual machine) for the application to work in and allots it a segment of virtual memory. Another application could have its own virtual machine and virtual address segment and the two would not know that each other even existed. This way the two applications do not interact with each other's data in memory or step on each other's toes while being executed by the CPU. It is a very orchestrated, controlled, and timed event-oriented atmosphere.

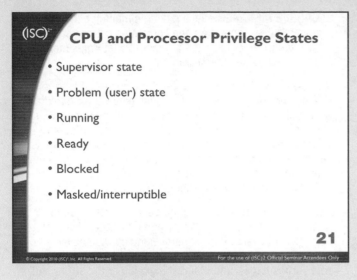

CPU and Processor Privilege States

- Supervisor state
- Problem (user) state
- Running
- Ready
- Blocked
- Masked/interruptible

21

- **CPU AND PROCESSOR PRIVILEGE STATES** – A system can be operating in several different operational modes depending upon the tasks it is carrying out. These modes protect the system by not allowing unprivileged users and processes to access privileged commands.

- **SUPERVISOR STATE** – The supervisor state is used to execute a system's programs. To run in supervisor state, a user needs a userid/password with special privileges. When operating in the supervisor state, a program can access the entire system and execute both privileged and non-privileged instructions.

- **PROBLEM STATE** – Is intended for application programs and only non-privileged instructions are executed. This is sometimes called user state or program state.

- **RUNNING** – CPU is executing.

- **READY** – CPU is idle either because there is no input or it is waiting for another process to run.

- **BLOCKED** – Unable to run until an external event occurs, typically waiting for input.

- **MASKED/INTERRUPTIBLE** – If the masked bit is not set, interrupts are disabled (masked off) – known as IRQs in systems. IRQ = Interrupt Request Queue.

- Keep in mind that the CPU privilege level has nothing to do with operating system users. Whether you're root, administrator, guest, or a regular user, it does not matter. All user code runs in ring 3 and all kernel code runs in ring 0. Due to restricted access to memory and I/O ports, user mode can do almost nothing to the outside world without calling on the kernel. It can't open files, send network packets, print to the screen, or allocate memory. User processes run in a severely limited sandbox set up by the controls in ring 0. That's why it's impossible, by design, for a process to leak memory beyond its existence or leave open files after it exits. All of the data structures that control such things – memory, open files, etc. – cannot be touched directly by user code; once a process finishes, the sandbox is torn down by the kernel. That's why our servers can have 600 days of uptime – as long as the hardware and the kernel don't fail, stuff can run forever. With this in mind, it is clear that from a security perspective, user code must ALWAYS process within its assigned sandbox and NEVER be allowed to directly access the CPU ring 0 code.

REFERENCES:
ISBN: 0130131429388 p61
http://duartes.org/gustavo/blog/post/cpu-rings-privilege-and-protection

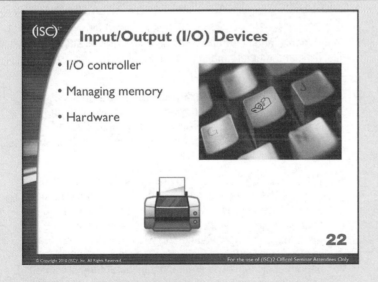

Input/Output (I/O) Devices

- I/O controller
- Managing memory
- Hardware

22

- **INPUT/OUTPUT (I/O) DEVICES** – One of the critical functions of a system is interprocess communications. This involves locating and relocating data and instructions between a number of storage facilities. The communication process itself must be performed in a consistent manner to ensure that access to data is protected whether it is at rest or being transferred within the system.

- **I/O CONTROLLER** – The I/O controller is responsible for moving data in and out of memory.

- **MANAGING MEMORY** – An element of managing the I/O devices and thus managing memory is through swapping or paging files.

- **HARDWARE** – Hardware must support paging and segmentation.

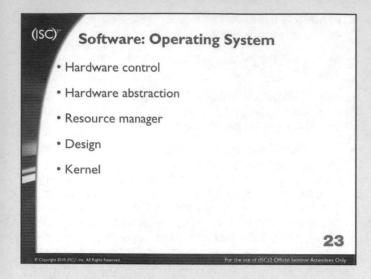

Software: Operating System

- Hardware control
- Hardware abstraction
- Resource manager
- Design
- Kernel

23

- **RESOURCE MANAGER** – As a resource manager, the operating system provides more than one competing user or program access to the limited amount of processor, storage, memory, and I/O to the computer system.

- **DESIGN** – Operating systems were originally designed for every specific set of hardware. However, now we have middleware and other ways of accessing and moving information, and even operating programs written for different operating systems. As mentioned earlier, the operating system is responsible for providing a good deal of our security. As each operating system does this task differently, it can increase our residual risk when we allow these cross-platform activities.

- **KERNEL** – The security kernel function of the operating system is to provide the security functionality and control necessary to ensure that resources and operations execute correctly without overwriting each other, accessing the wrong areas or resources, and maintaining a log of the errors and activities on the system. The security kernel consists of several components – software, firmware, and hardware, and represents all the security functionality of the operating system.

- **HARDWARE CONTROL** – Operating systems perform low-level control of hardware for a computerized system.

- **HARDWARE ABSTRACTION** – Operating systems are extensible programs designed to abstract the hardware features for programmers, and to offer simple interfaces for reading and writing data.

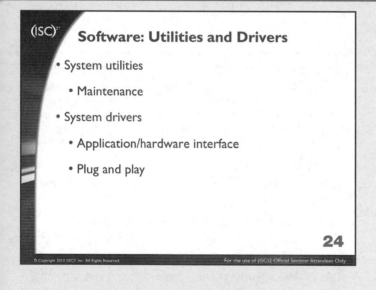

Software: Utilities and Drivers

- System utilities
  - Maintenance
- System drivers
  - Application/hardware interface
  - Plug and play

24

- **SOFTWARE UTILITIES AND DRIVERS** – Most hardware and system components operate through the use of utilities and drivers. They represent the interface that is used to enable the functionality of the system for the user or application.

- **SYSTEM UTILITIES** – System utilities are used for system maintenance and operation. They provide services such as file, disk, and memory management, and testing and error handling.

- **SYSTEM DRIVERS** – System drivers are the interface between equipment and the system or application that is using the equipment. The drivers are written for a specific piece of equipment but may be called or accessed by many different applications or operational environments.

  - **PLUG AND PLAY** – Older equipment required manual settings of switches, jumpers, and configurations during the installation process. This allowed the equipment to be configured for its operational environment. Most equipment today can be installed and will run without any user-required configuration. This is called plug and play. Most operating systems will automatically detect the presence of new equipment and search for the appropriate drivers.

- From a security perspective, it is very important to ensure that all utilities and drivers come from known, trusted sources and are fully tested prior to being introduced into the production environment. Testing helps reduce the risk that malware could be introduced through these types of software.

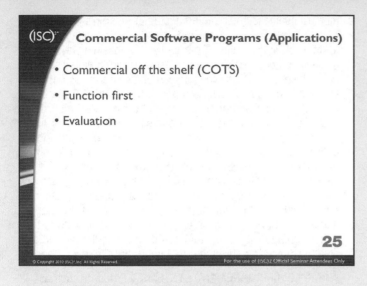

Commercial Software Programs (Applications)

- Commercial off the shelf (COTS)
- Function first
- Evaluation

25

- **VENDOR SOFTWARE,** also called commercial off the shelf (COTS), is developed to meet a specific need, such as serving a particular vertical market, or providing a specific piece of software infrastructure, such as that necessary for a web server. There are more than 25,000 software vendors that make fixed products for larger markets.

- **FUNCTION FIRST** – Unless the software is inherently a security-focused application (such as a firewall), attention will first be devoted to functionality. Security is usually an afterthought.

- **EVALUATION** – When evaluating third-party applications, make sure to consider the information security aspects of the application, such as:

  - Authentication methods.

  - Audit capabilities.

  - Separation of duties, at times implemented through roles, within the application.

  - Integrity constraints within the supporting database.

  - Edit checks and error reporting.

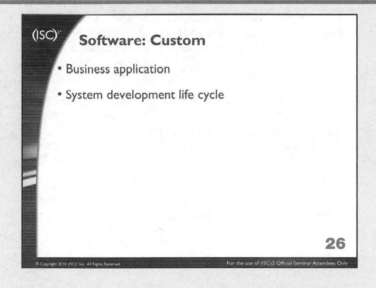

Software: Custom

- Business application
- System development life cycle

26

- Not including the vendors who will customize their own COTS (such as SAP will do to fit an organization they have sold the product to), there are just as many pieces of custom software as there are environments. Every organization uses some form of scripting or interpreted code and many organizations employ their own software developers.

- **BUSINESS APPLICATION** – No two businesses do every process in the same way and in order to achieve a competitive edge, organizations automate some of their business applications.

  - Customized software is the solution used as a natural progression from manual processes to automation of tasks.

- **SYSTEM DEVELOPMENT LIFE CYCLE** – A major cause for architectural failure is not having a well thought-out system development life cycle strategy as an organization moves from simple scripts to major software and systems development teams.

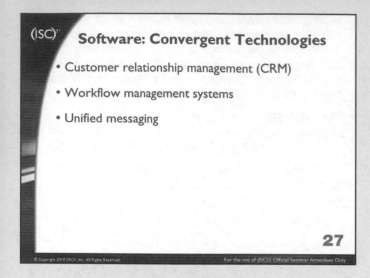

SOFTWARE: CONVERGENT TECHNOLOGIES – A prime objective for many organizations is to combine IT systems together in order to provide more seamless service to the user. Instead of switching between different systems, each one providing a different service, one larger application will bring together the functionality of several systems. This is seen at the application layer using CRM products, at the network layer using federated identity management, and at the database level using data warehouses and data mining.

CUSTOMER RELATIONSHIP MANAGEMENT (CRM) – In modern business, maintaining customer loyalty is paramount to long-term success. A customer relationship management (CRM) system is designed to track all the possible ways that a business communicates with a customer (often called "touchpoints") so that the relationship can be as interactive with the customer as possible. Common entries into a CRM are requests for information that come in over the web, an order placed by a customer, purchase of a candidate customer list, or a list of customers produced from a merger or acquisition. CRM systems usually contain extensive information brought together from various system and customer or business interface points on customer habits, including website activity, phone calls, and purchase history. This information would be very valuable to a competitor. If an external attacker can penetrate a CRM system, he or she will be able to acquire this rich information, as would an unauthorized insider who was able to collect data through direct query access to a database.

WORKFLOW MANAGEMENT SYSTEMS – Products such as Microsoft's SharePoint and IBM's Lotus Notes are used to provide a collaborative managed work environment that can be accessed by multiple users. This allows all the users to work together on a common platform and yet track the activities of each person, as well as provide protection against different people working on different versions of the documents or work product.

UNIFIED MESSAGING – UM was designed to allow different technologies to work together – for example being able to fax to a PDA, access the Internet over a television, etc.

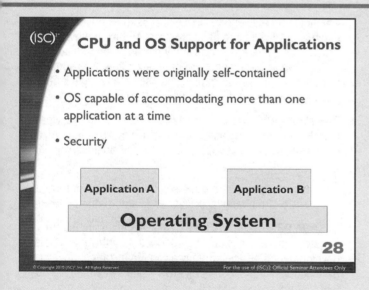

APPLICATIONS WERE ORIGINALLY SELF-CONTAINED – Applications were originally self-contained, independent entities that were written for specific operating system platforms. Because of this, programmers could write specifications that directly addressed certain hardware functions.

CAPABLE OF ACCOMMODATING MORE THAN ONE APPLICATION AT A TIME – Some operating systems were capable of multiprogramming, or accommodating more than one application at a time, through interleaving or multitasking of instructions using time slots.

SECURITY – The security in this scenario is reinforced by the OS, since the OS has the ability to control the activity of the applications and ensure that one or more application threads do not affect another.

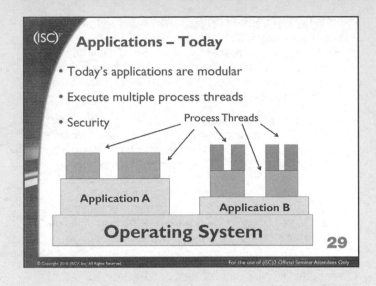

- **TODAY'S APPLICATIONS ARE MODULAR** – Applications today are designed to be modular, portable, and efficient. Many, if not most, of today's programs are composed of many individual modules, programs, or processes that are separately written and work together to fulfill the overall objective of the application. These may be called modules or process threads. Threads are the smallest sets of code which can be scheduled for processing by the scheduling service of a processor or multiprocessor system. A thread is defined as "pieces of code." A modern browser for example has a small component of central code that accesses more than 1,000 other process threads.

- **EXECUTE MULTIPLE PROCESS THREADS** – Multithreading capabilities permit the operating system to appear to simultaneously execute multiple process threads (even within separate applications), thus increasing system performance.

- **SECURITY** – The security problems lie in the fact that these independent sections are frequently written by someone else and may be malicious. The module may also be used in a way that was not intended by the author. The modules or threads will often communicate directly and not involve the OS. This prevents the operating system from being able to manage the activity of the process threads.

REFERENCE AND DIAGRAM:

Secrets and Lies, Bruce Schneier page 162. ISBN 0-471-25311-1

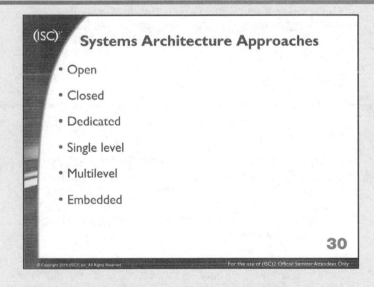

- **OPEN SYSTEMS** – Standards-based interfaces. Many of today's systems use standard interfaces and support standardized protocols. Most of these are designed for client/server environments. While open systems' approaches are often considered vulnerable to attack, their open nature often results in a more robust set of security features.

- **CLOSED SYSTEMS** – Proprietary interfaces. Many older systems used proprietary interfaces, and implementations were customized for a specific application's environments. Interoperability was sacrificed to achieve uniqueness and obscurity, an illusion that security through obscurity works.

- **DEDICATED SYSTEMS** – Single level of processing permitted. In military applications, this often means that only personnel holding the designated security clearance are granted access to the system.

- **SINGLE LEVEL SYSTEMS** – Like early generation PCs running DOS and early Windows OS, these systems permit users to execute any instruction available.

- **MULTILEVEL SYSTEMS** – Processing at two levels is permitted through some form of user authentication and authorization (i.e., user and administrator). These are most common today and are designed to permit the system to be accessed by users holding different levels of privilege.

- **EMBEDDED SYSTEMS** – A single purpose computer typically programmed to perform a dedicated function.

- Note: Open and closed are not references to security! A closed system is not necessarily more secure.

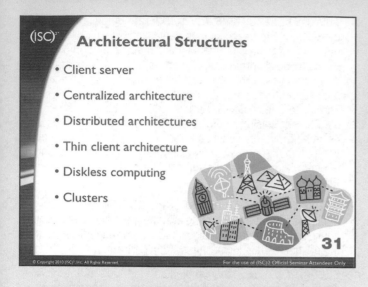

Architectural Structures

- Client server
- Centralized architecture
- Distributed architectures
- Thin client architecture
- Diskless computing
- Clusters

31

DISTRIBUTED ARCHITECTURES – Decentralized architectures, including client/server and today's network-based environments, require adherence to standards-based interfaces and protocols. From a business enablement standpoint, these architectures are the most flexible and accessible, but can become quite complex to design and manage.

THIN CLIENT ARCHITECTURE – Thin client is another form of architecture, which removes most client functions from the desktop workstation and moves them rather to the server and, thereby, provides a centralized approach to access control. While this may reduce user functionality and freedom, thin client approaches reduce many of the vulnerabilities common in today's heterogeneous PC environment. For example, all the data is stored on central hardware so there is only one place that the data must be protected when at rest.

DISKLESS COMPUTING – Diskless computing is closely related to thin client with one major difference. Thin client systems do all the processing at a central server and only use the local workstation for presentation and GUI (graphical user interface) commands. Diskless workstations boot off of a network drive but then do some processing on the local machine. The hard drive (if it exists on the local system) is not used for local booting of the system or storage of data.

CLUSTERS – Clusters are a group of servers working together – for load balancing, grid computing, or to meet high-availability requirements.

- From a security perspective, centralized and thin client architectures provide significant security advantages as the security controls can be managed at one point. Diskless computing provides much of this same advantage. Client server and distributed architecture provide some of the most expensive and challenging security issues as the attacker has many more potential points of entry directly to the processes and the data.

- **ARCHITECTURAL STRUCTURES** – There are several generations of system architectures which permit different approaches to security enforcement while supporting a variety of business requirements.

- **CLIENT SERVER** – The term client server is very generic and can be used in many architectures. It refers to a system where a central server, or group of servers, provides service (data storage, processing, networking, etc.) to a user who accesses the server through a network. The entire web can be considered one form of client server network, as can a traditional mainframe that used a central CPU accessed from remote terminals.

- **CENTRALIZED ARCHITECTURE** – Centralized architectures, common in mainframe-based environments, permit centralized control and enforcement of security policies, including a number of physical security measures to restrict access to the computing facilities. A closed or proprietary set of functions limits accessibility.

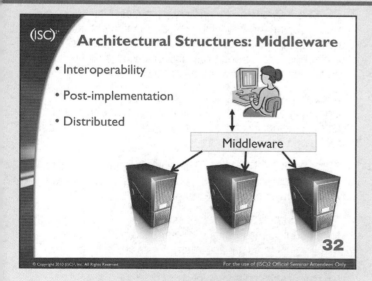

Architectural Structures: Middleware

- Interoperability
- Post-implementation
- Distributed

Middleware

32

data from multiple systems and combine it onto one screen or function for the user.

- Middleware was commonly used by database vendors to allow applications written for a competitor's database to interoperate with their own products. Mainframe applications utilize middleware to expand services across business applications and increase their ability to be ported from one type of system to another.

- More recent uses of middleware center on distributed communication capabilities such as those found in the Common Object Request Broker Architecture (CORBA), Distributed Component Object Model (DCOM), and Enterprise JavaBeans (EJB). These types of middleware services provide extensive application-messaging services for heterogeneous networked environments.

- There are several security considerations with middleware. However, the one we should remember is that the middleware provides functionality and could provide vulnerabilities within the code as well as backdoors that may bypass access controls.

REFERENCE:
http://middleware.internet2.edu/

- Middleware is a software-based architecture structure that provides translation or communication services for applications. Middleware is typically used to extend the capability of applications by allowing them to interact with other applications or services with which they were not originally designed to interoperate. This allows a user application to receive input

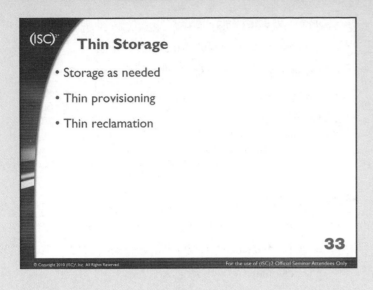

- **THIN STORAGE** – It is expensive to maintain enough backups and storage for large corporate systems. The traditional methods of backup were direct attached storage (DAS) or storage attached networks (SANs).

- **STORAGE AS NEEDED** – The challenge was to have storage where it was needed, when it was needed, and not to have empty storage sitting around in case it would be needed later, nor to have one system overfull and others underutilized. The answer was to build out the capacity of a SANs but only allocate it to the servers when it was needed, instead of building it out and pre-allocating to the servers.

- **THIN PROVISIONING** – Provision only as needed.

- **THIN RECLAMATION** – Reclaim unused storage when no longer required.

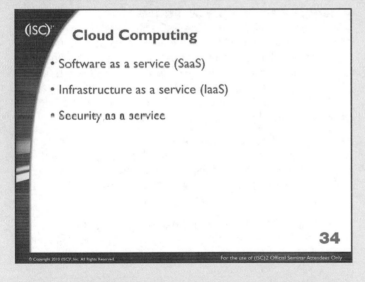

the user is accessing email stored on the Gmail cloud), Hotmail, and Salesforce. The user organization pays for its usage levels.

- **SOFTWARE AS A SERVICE (SAAS)** – Software as a service is the provisioning of an application over the Internet. The software resides on Internet-based servers provided by the vendor instead of on the local machines or network. Salesforce is an example of Saas.

- **INFRASTRUCTURE AS A SERVICE (IAAS)** – Infrastructure as a service provides a remote IT infrastructure that can be used to support business operations without the business building its own servers, networks, and infrastructure.

- **SECURITY AS A SERVICE** – In the past, managed security service providers managed security on behalf of clients. The clients had little to do with the day-to-day configuration and monitoring of their security, instead that was a function of the MSSP. Security as a service is more like cloud computing and the other "as a Service" offerings. It provides security services (antivirus, key management, etc.) over the web but is different from MSSP, since it usually is administered by the local client over a secure connection to the service provider.

- The security considerations for these offerings include the quality of the offerings, the ability of the provider to meet the service level agreements, and the lack of direct control of the customer.

- **CLOUD COMPUTING** – Cloud computing is a generic term used to describe the provisioning of computer services over the Internet (the cloud). Many companies (Amazon, Google, etc.) now offer software and other services over Internet links (such as a VPN or simple browser) that can be accessed from anywhere in the world by a subscriber. Users log into the application using a simple client on their local machine and can access the services located on a virtual server managed by the vendor. Examples include Gmail (when logging into Gmail,

Service-Oriented Architecture

35

- Service-oriented architecture (SOA) is a global mesh of collaborative services. The services offered are independent of each other, but have well-defined interfaces designed for reuse. Security is provided by encryption and authentication.

- **TECHNOLOGY BENEFITS:**

  - More flexible architecture.

  - Integration of existing applications.

- Improved data integration.

- Supports business process management.

- Facilitates enterprise portal initiatives.

- Speeds custom application development.

- **SECURITY ISSUES** – A system that relies on distributed processing must have adequate bandwidth and high availability. The coordination of servers and processes often requires a short response time in order to complete the processes correctly.

- **BUSINESS BENEFITS:**

  - More effective integration with business partners.

  - Supports customer-service initiatives.

  - Enables employee self-service.

  - Streamlines the supply chain.

  - More effective use of external service providers.

  - Facilitates global sourcing.

REFERENCE:
Information Security Management Handbook, Sixth Edition, Volume 2

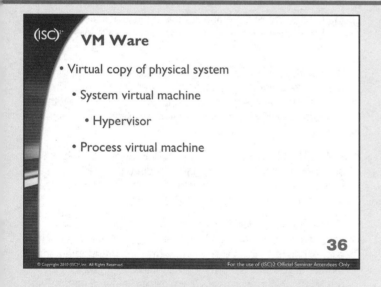

VM Ware

- Virtual copy of physical system

  - System virtual machine

    - Hypervisor

  - Process virtual machine

36

- **VIRTUAL COPY OF PHYSICAL SYSTEM** – As seen earlier in the domain, a virtual machine is a representation of a physical system. It is designed to provide an abstract operating environment that is isolated from the actual physical system. This allows the physical system to support several different operating environments (such as various operating systems) and also to protect the physical environment from being altered by activity within the virtual environment.

  - **SYSTEM VIRTUAL MACHINES** – A system virtual machine is a complete operating environment that can support user needs and multiple environments. It is usually configured using a **HYPERVISOR** to interface between the physical and virtual environments.

  - **PROCESS VIRTUAL MACHINES** – Process virtual machines are systems that are dedicated to supporting one process or program.

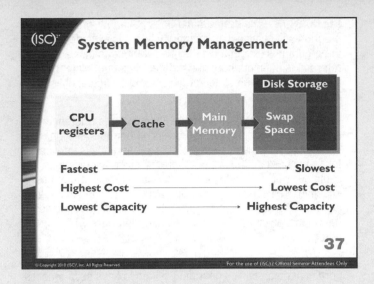

- **SYSTEM MEMORY MANAGEMENT** – A memory management function is required to manage the flow of data between resources. The operating system should be the only function that can directly address these resources, requiring all other processes (including applications) to be explicitly mapped to assigned memory areas through some symbolic referencing scheme. One cost-performance issue would be the relative costs of cache and main memory.

REFERENCES:
http://www.memorymanagement.org/
http://lwn.net/Articles/253361/
http://docs.hp.com/en/5965-4641/ch01s03.html

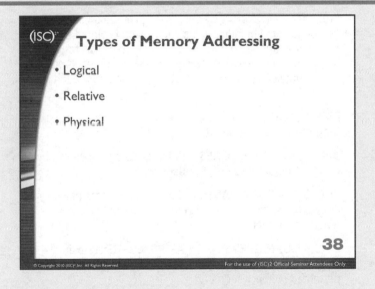

- **THREE TYPES OF MEMORY ADDRESSING** – There are three basic types of memory addresses. A memory manager function allocates memory storage segments of application processes through logical or relative (offset) addressing. This is actually performed by a memory mapper function. Since applications should not directly address physical memory, the operating system, through the memory mapper, is responsible for accessing instructions or data requested by the application.

- **LOGICAL** – Refers to a memory location that is independent of the current assignment of data to memory. Requires a translation to the physical address.

- **RELATIVE** – Address expressed as a location relative to a known point.

- **PHYSICAL** – The absolute address or actual location.

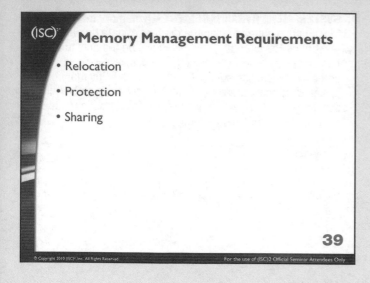

- **RELOCATION** – The programmer does not know where the program will be placed in memory when it is executed. While the program is executing, it may be swapped to disk and returned to main memory at a different location. Memory references must be translated in the code to an actual physical memory address.

- **PROTECTION** – Processes should not be able to reference memory locations in another process without permission. The operating system is in charge of this and it really is impossible for us to check addresses in programs, since the program could be relocated by the operating system itself without us knowing. We have to trust the operating system in how it does all of this. This is known as "process isolation," which is how the OS makes sure that processes don't interfere with each other.

- **SHARING** – Allows several processes to access the same portion of memory. The operating system allows each process (person) access to the same copy of the program rather than having his or her own separate copy.

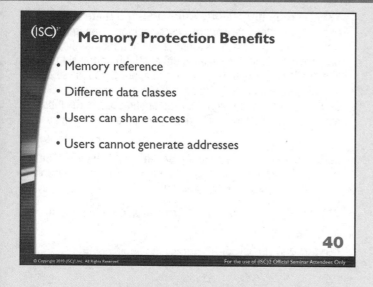

- **MEMORY PROTECTION BENEFITS** – Since the goal is protection of data, the memory areas where data is stored (permanently or temporarily) must also be protected. This requires monitoring and checking the status of memory resources by the security components of an OS before and after each access.

- **MEMORY REFERENCE** – Every memory reference is checked for protection requirements.

- **DIFFERENT DATA CLASSES** – Different data classes can be assigned different levels of protection.

- **USERS CAN SHARE ACCESS** – Two or more users can share access to the same memory segment with potentially different access rights.

- **USERS CANNOT GENERATE ADDRESSES** – Users cannot generate an unpermitted address or gain access to an unpermitted memory segment.

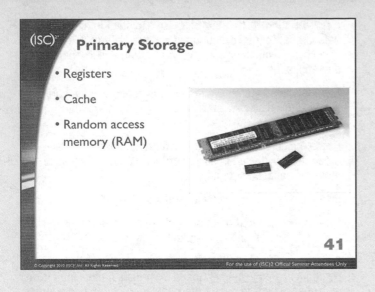

- **PRIMARY STORAGE** – This is the memory directly accessible by the CPU and with the highest response speed.

- **REGISTERS** – Registers are very high-speed storage structures built into the CPU chip set and are often used to store timing and state information for the CPU to maintain control over processes. These are called dedicated registers.

- **CACHE** – Cache is the very fast memory directly on the CPU chip body. It is not upgradeable. There are three types of cache. Level 1 is nearly always on the CPU chip. Level 2 may or may not be on the CPU chip. Level 3 is generally off-chip. Not all systems have a level 3 cache.

  - As you move farther from the CPU, you increase memory latency which makes the CPU wait longer for data and instructions whenever they aren't in cache (refer back to Slide 37).

- **RANDOM ACCESS MEMORY (RAM)** – RAM is the main memory of the system and is provided through chips inserted into slots on the motherboard. Most peripheral devices, such as printers, also have RAM. Data stored in RAM is much faster to access than data located on a hard drive. The greatest risk with RAM is that the data stored on RAM will be lost once the machine is powered off.

IMAGE:

Samsung high-density memory chip.

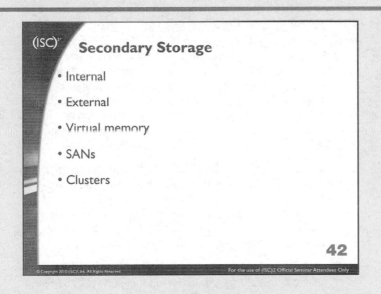

- **SECONDARY STORAGE** – Secondary storage is accessible to the CPU but usually with a longer delay than primary storage. There are many types of secondary storage available today – from hard drive to flash drives and from tapes to DVDs.

- **INTERNAL VERSUS EXTERNAL** – As its name suggests, some memory is internal to the machine and considered a part of the machine configuration. Other memory is portable and designed to be added or removed as required. This would include flash or USB drives, or external hard drives.

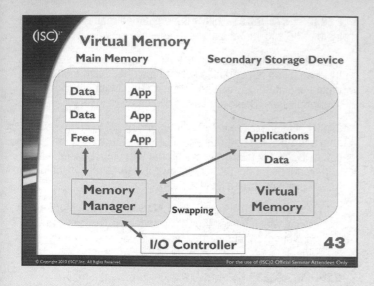

- **EXTENDS APPARENT MEMORY** – In a system to accommodate larger program execution space than is possible using only physical memory, and involves paging and swapping operations.

- A virtual memory (VM) system usually deals with memory blocks of fixed size as units for paging. These are known as pages.

- Pages are generally 4 or 8KB in length. The page size is determined by the addressing hardware of the machine (the memory management unit).

- Swapping and paging can be used interchangeably.

- Swap space is a portion of the disk (backing store) reserved for the memory pages that are swapped to disk.

- Page fault is an exception when accessing VM, usually resulting in a page being fetched from disk. A page fault is an exception occurring during the translation of a virtual address to a physical address. "Page fault" usually means an access to a page that has been paged out and thus requires fetching from disk before use (it can also mean invalid page fault or protection fault).

- Memory mapping (aka file mapping) is the technique used to map a portion of a device to a memory page.

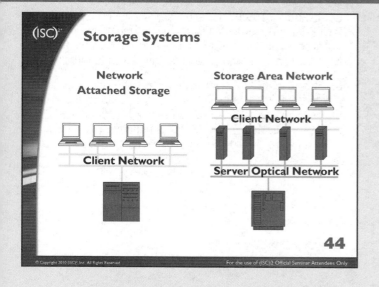

- **NETWORK ATTACHED STORAGE (NAS)** – Is a simple, cost-effective solution to the challenge of having limited hard drive space spread among many devices on the client network. NAS offers economies of scale for small- to medium-sized organizations by providing a common storage area for all devices on the network to share. The security drawback is that the use of the primary network for both production processing and for backup and data storage can lead to network performance issues.

- **STORAGE AREA NETWORK (SAN)** – Is a complex, expensive solution to offer large capacity storage for servers over high-speed (usually fiber) links. The SAN uses its own network for data backup and sharing and alleviates the burden on the production network. This solution also provides for secondary servers and other business continuity solutions.

- The use of shared storage can assist the organization in managing data security and better version control through common document storage. However, it also presents additional security risks through potentially allowing users of the network unauthorized access to data which isn't theirs. A user may also be able to monitor network traffic and see data in transit.

REFERENCE:
ISBN 0130130559, Toigo

Blade Systems

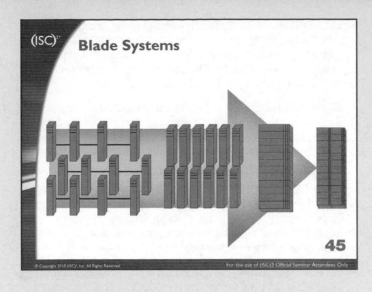

45

- A blade server is a server chassis housing multiple thin, modular electronic circuit boards, known as server blades. The blades are literally servers on a card, containing processors, memory, integrated network controllers, an optional fiber channel host bus adaptor (HBA), and other input/output (IO) ports. Each blade typically comes with one or two local ATA or SCSI drives. For additional storage, blade servers can connect to a storage pool facilitated by a network-attached storage (NAS), fiber channel, or iSCSI storage-area network (SAN).

- Blade servers allow more processing power in less rack space, simplifying cabling, storage, networking, and reducing power consumption.

- Blade servers simplify management through server consolidation and resource centralization. They also provide the ability to cluster servers or support virtualization. Virtualization allows for better use of physical assets by granting applications the ability to tap into, or access, physical assets as required.

REFERENCE:
www.blade.org/techovr.cfm

Domain Agenda

- System and Component Security

- **System Design Principles**

- Security Models

- Information Systems Evaluation Models

- Security Frameworks

46

- At a platform level, security architecture defines the structure of the hardware and software components that provide basic security services.

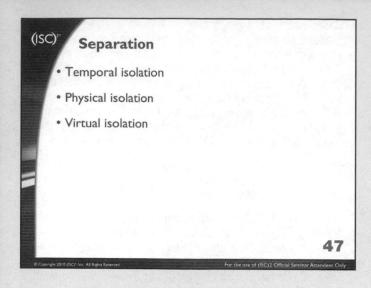

- **SEPARATION** – A core security concept is the principle of separation. One of the easiest ways to protect an asset is to restrict access to it. Some of the ways to address the principle of separation in an architecture are through temporal, physical, and virtual isolation.

- **TEMPORAL ISOLATION** – As also addressed in the Access Control domain, temporal isolation is accomplished through time limits. A person cannot access an area of the building, or an area of the network, or an application outside of certain authorized hours.

- **PHYSICAL ISOLATION** – Physical isolation refers to separating out sensitive areas from common access, such as setting up compartmentalized areas or secure rooms. Physical isolation is used within individual systems to protect sensitive components from compromise.

- **VIRTUAL ISOLATION** – Virtual isolation protects against malicious activity by not permitting a process to execute outside of a strict set of boundaries.

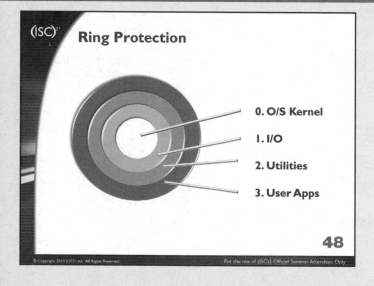

- **RING PROTECTION** – Is based on the Honeywell Multics Operating System architecture. It is portrayed by a set of segments in concentric numbered rings. The ring number determines the access level.

- A procedure assumes its appropriate ring number when executing. This prohibits a process from unregulated execution of commands at higher levels of privilege.

- A subject may access a service at its level or higher.

- A program may call services residing on the same or a more privileged ring.

- A program may only access data that resides on the same ring, or a less privileged ring.

- Ring "0" contains the kernel functions of the operating system and must, therefore, be rigorously protected.

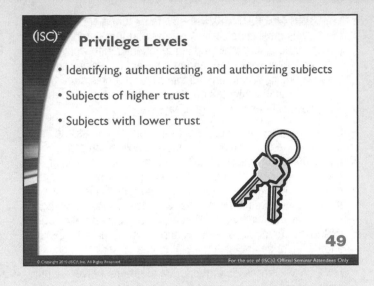

- **IDENTIFYING, AUTHENTICATING, AND AUTHORIZING SUBJECTS** – Is usually done by first designating (classifying) certain resources (or groups of resources) into protection levels, and then mapping specific rights to subjects (or groups of subjects) based on trust (subjects were described on Slide 55).

- **SUBJECTS OF HIGHER TRUST** – Can access more system instructions and operate in privileged mode.

- **SUBJECTS WITH LOWER TRUST** – Can access a smaller portion of system instructions and operate only in user mode.

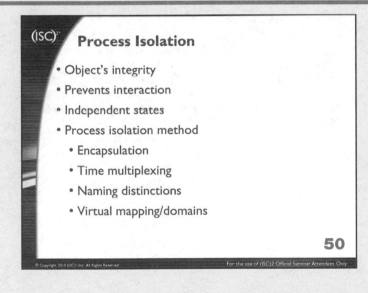

- **OBJECT'S INTEGRITY** – Preserves object's integrity and subject's adherence to access controls.

- **PREVENTS INTERACTION** – Prevents objects from interacting with each other and their resources.

- **INDEPENDENT STATES** – Actions of one object should not affect the state of other objects.

- **PROCESS ISOLATION METHODS INCLUDE:**

  - **ENCAPSULATION OF OBJECTS** – Objects, data, and functions are packaged together or encapsulated. Because an object includes the functions for operating on it, the details of how it is implemented can be hidden.

  - **TIME MULTIPLEXING OF SHARED RESOURCES** – Assigning specific time slots for processing the information within a system using time division multiplexing.

  - **NAMING DISTINCTIONS** – Using distinctive naming conventions to distinguish between different processes.

  - **VIRTUAL MAPPING** – Mapping information objects to virtual locations to ensure applications can find their data.

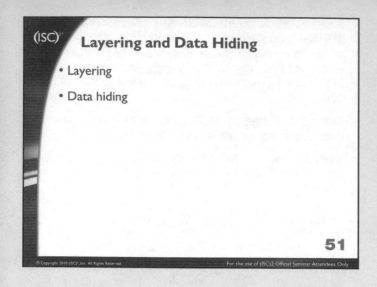

- **LAYERING AND DATA HIDING** – Systems that meet certain trust levels must supply mechanisms that force processes (and, therefore, different kinds of functionality) to work independent of each other and at different layers of a system. This requires a structured and hierarchical architecture that has basic functionality taking place at lower layers and more complex functions at the higher layers.

- Layering further separates processes and resources and adds modularity to the system. The different layers can communicate, but only through defined interfaces that uphold the integrity of the system. In some instances, processes at different layers cannot be allowed to communicate and are, therefore, not supplied with interfaces that would allow them to interact with each other. This process is called **DATA HIDING:** The data at one layer is hidden because the subjects at another layer do not even know the data exists.

- **LAYERING** – Processes that operate at different layers within a system must communicate through interfaces. Layers can be divided by functionality or security. The OSI model is an example of layering through dividing the communications process into several individual activities, each happening at different layers of the OSI stack.

- **DATA HIDING** – If a process does not have an interface with a process at a different layer, it cannot communicate and will, therefore, not have access to the data on the different layer. Hiding can prevent unauthorized disclosure or threats to integrity.

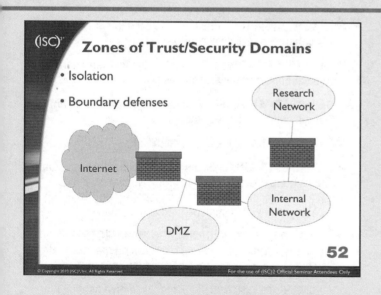

- **ZONES OF TRUST** – Some areas of a network may need to be more trusted than others. This will depend on issues such as sensitivity of data to be processed, trust of users, availability, and network performance. Separating out zones of trust – whether in a network example as shown here, or in a geographic example – is one way to protect areas that require a higher level of security. Between each zone should be access control defense and monitoring.

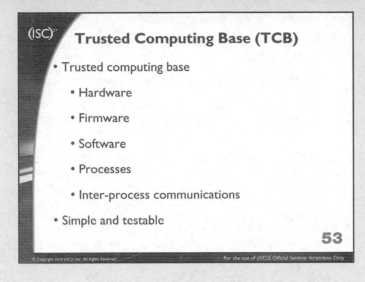

- **TRUSTED COMPUTING BASE** – Includes all the components and their operating processes and procedures that ensure that the security policy of the organization is enforced. The TCB includes the reference monitor, hardware, software, inter-process communications, and human factors that make up a security solution, and whose failure would lead to a security breach.

- **SIMPLE AND TESTABLE** – The TCB must be simple enough that it can be verified to be functioning correctly and completely.

REFERENCE:

http://www.unet.univie.ac.at/aix/aixbman/admnconc/tcb.htm

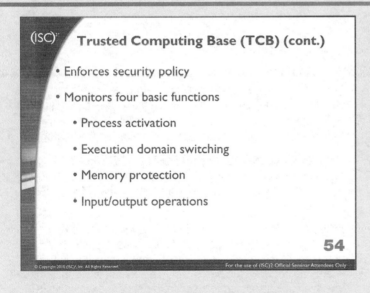

- **ENFORCES SECURITY POLICY** – The TCB must be able to enforce security policy regardless of user input and be protected from interference or tampering.

- **MONITORS FOUR BASIC FUNCTIONS** –

  - **PROCESS ACTIVATION** – In a multiprogramming environment, activation and deactivation of processes create the need for a complete change of registers, file access lists, process status information, and other pointers, much of which is security sensitive.

  - **EXECUTION DOMAIN SWITCHING** – Processes running in one domain often invoke processes in other domains to obtain data or services. The TCB must ensure that all processes are regulated and only able to access data in accordance with security policy.

  - **MEMORY PROTECTION** – Because each domain includes code and data stored in memory, the TCB must monitor memory references to ensure confidentiality and integrity for each domain.

  - **INPUT/OUTPUT OPERATIONS** – In some systems, software is involved in the transfer of characters to the I/O operation. This process connects a user program in the outermost domain with the I/O operation in the innermost. This cross-domain connection must be monitored.

- The TCB also includes components that control how any resource (object) is handled (protected).

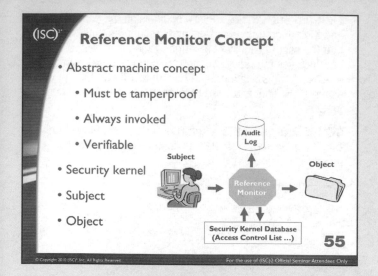

Reference Monitor Concept

- Abstract machine concept
  - Must be tamperproof
  - Always invoked
  - Verifiable
- Security kernel
- Subject
- Object

55

- The rules for the reference monitor are:
  - Must be tamperproof, i.e., protected from unauthorized modification.
  - Must always be invoked and be impossible to bypass.
  - Must be small enough to be verifiable as correct through analysis and tests or other assurance methods.

- **SECURITY KERNEL** – The hardware, firmware, and software elements of a trusted computing base (TCB) that implement the reference monitor. The security kernel components of an operating system perform various protection tasks designed to control and monitor system events and prevent things from occurring that might disrupt normal execution or threaten the stability of the system or any of its resources. In addition, the kernel functions are designed to:

  - Check every access.
  - Enforce least privilege.
  - Verify acceptable (appropriate) usage through authorization concept.

- **SUBJECT** – Active entities – Include users, programs, processes, logon identifiers.

- **OBJECT** – Passive entities – Include files, programs, instructions, data, hardware.

REFERENCE:

http://citeseer.ist.psu.edu/cache/papers/cs/14684/ftp:zSzzSztaurus.cs.nps.navy.milzSzpubz-
SzirvinezSz99zSzwise99_RMCUnifySecEd.pdf/the-reference-monitor-concept.pdf

- **REFERENCE MONITOR CONCEPT** – In the early days of data processing, the term "operating system" had not yet emerged. The control functions in a computing system were custom designed to provide operators with the ability to "monitor" the status of execution. Special program routines were created to handle error handling, alarms, queuing tasks, and job sequencing. In some cases, the operator would monitor indicator lamps and other displays to manage and troubleshoot various anomalies during processing cycles.

- **ABSTRACT MACHINE CONCEPT** – The concept of the reference monitor is as an abstract machine that is regulating all access on the system and enforcing security controls.

  - The reference monitor enforces (mediates) access relationships between all subjects and objects based on privilege and "need to know."

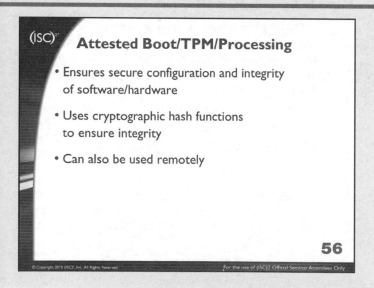

Attested Boot/TPM/Processing

- Ensures secure configuration and integrity of software/hardware
- Uses cryptographic hash functions to ensure integrity
- Can also be used remotely

56

- **ATTESTED BOOT/TRUSTED PROTECTION MODULES (TPM)** – The ideal location for security is at the lowest level – just like the foundation for a physical building, the lower levels of a system are the most critical to the overall security infrastructure.

- **ENSURES SECURE CONFIGURATION AND INTEGRITY OF SOFTWARE/HARDWARE** – The TPM was developed to ensure the integrity of a system by locating a chip (the TPM) on the motherboard of a CPU.

- **USES CRYPTOGRAPHIC HASH FUNCTIONS TO ENSURE INTEGRITY** – Using cryptographic hashes and public key infrastructure, the TPM could ensure that a machine and software had not been tampered with. This meant assurance that the system was booted in a secure manner and would also ensure the integrity of a process running on the machine. For example, conditions could be put in to prevent the user from modifying an application, printing a secure document, etc.

- **CAN ALSO BE USED REMOTELY** – It is also possible to ensure the correct configuration of a remote entity using the TPM and attested boot principles. If the remote unit is altered or the software modified, a remote entity would notice the alteration due to the change in the hash values of the software and hardware at the modified site.

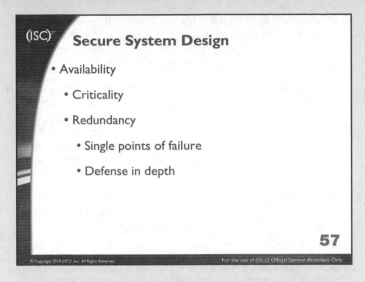

Secure System Design

- Availability
- Criticality
- Redundancy
  - Single points of failure
  - Defense in depth

57

© Copyright 2010 (ISC)², Inc. All Rights Reserved.   For the use of (ISC)2 Official Seminar Attendees Only

- **AVAILABILITY** – A system must be designed to meet business needs – including transaction loads, error handling, response times, and effective controls. This requires sufficient bandwidth, CPU cycles, memory, and efficient data flow.

  - **CRITICALITY** – The data and function of some systems is more time-critical to the organization than that of other systems. The design of the system must ensure that the critical processes can run effectively

- **REDUNDANCY** –

  - **SINGLE POINTS OF FAILURE** – Critical system components and networks must be designed to avoid single points of failure. This can be accomplished through redundancy, failover, and error detection.

  - **DEFENSE IN DEPTH** – Defense in depth will ensure that the security of the system cannot be circumvented just through one vulnerability. As we know, the advantage of the defense in depth is that we have layered controls to protect our data.

- **SECURE SYSTEM DESIGN** – The end result of architecture should be the development of a design that meets the organization's needs. The design can then be passed to developers and technicians to build and implement.

Domain Agenda

- System and Component Security
- System Design Principles
- **Security Models**
- Information Systems Evaluation Models
- Security Frameworks

58

© Copyright 2010 (ISC)², Inc. All Rights Reserved.   For the use of (ISC)2 Official Seminar Attendees Only

- Each model is based upon a mathematical formula. CISSPs don't need to know the math, but there are many original documents that contain the math and the transforms. The core summary documents are Technical Report 79-91 INTEGRITY IN AUTOMATED INFORMATION SYSTEMS prepared for the National Computer Security Center (NCSC) and Morrie Gasser's book, Building a Secure Computer System.

- The graphic is intended to show the security issue that the models address, but of course many of the concepts also overlap.

- Some models were designed specifically for a particular implementation, such as Lipner for Microsoft® Windows®.

- There are varying thoughts on the accuracy and efficacy of the models. However, this is normal, since whenever an attempt is made to summarize

- **MODEL ORGANIZATION** – The security models demonstrate the theoretical application of security problems in a computer environment. Each model was developed as a solution to a security problem – integrity issues, confidentiality requirements, or support for real-world business problems.

- To understand the models, we need to know which problem the model was trying to solve. It helps to ask "What kind of problem is this?" Once the problem is defined, we start to understand the logic and purpose of the models themselves. Once we understand the model, we can use that model to build a solution to a real-world problem. It helps to frame the solution using a model, irrespective of whether one is building a single tool (such as Multics) or a group of tools to be applied to a business problem. Conditions that must be met are then set forth in the models.

a complex theorem, some detail will have to be overlooked. It is important for the CISSP to know the purpose and value of the models and how they provide an architectural foundation for modern business and security implementations.

REFERENCES:

http://www.iwar.org.uk/comsec/resources/standards/rainbow/C-TR-79-91.htm

http://nucia.unomaha.edu/library/gasserbook.pdf

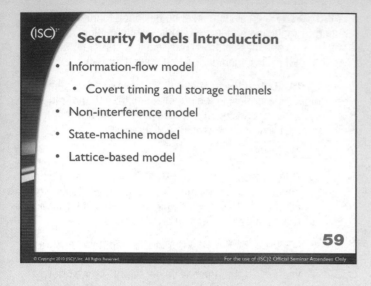

Security Models Introduction

- Information-flow model
  - Covert timing and storage channels
- Non-interference model
- State-machine model
- Lattice-based model

59

- **FUNDAMENTAL MODELS** – Simple statements about the need for a security property to be addressed in a system can be represented by a model. These four models make fundamental statements that are present in many models:

- **INFORMATION-FLOW MODEL** – Tracks the movement of information from one object to another so that movement of sensitive data to an unprotected area will be identified. A covert channel is the release of information in violation of security policy. The information-flow model specifically addresses the issue of covert channel analysis; no other model addresses this.

- **NON-INTERFERENCE MODEL** – Is based upon rules to prevent processes (subjects) that are operating in different domains from affecting (interfering with) each other in violation of security policy.

- **STATE-MACHINE MODEL** – Is an abstract mathematical model where state variables represent the system state. The transition functions define system movements between states (Bell-LaPadula and Biba are examples).

- **LATTICE-BASED MODEL** – Is a hierarchical model defining access control privilege levels. Each subject and object would be defined in a level of the lattice with a least upper boundary and greatest lower boundary.

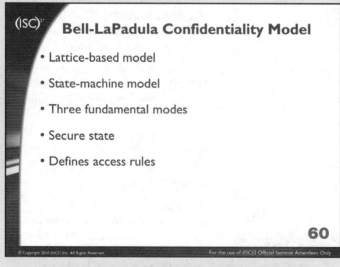

Bell-LaPadula Confidentiality Model

- Lattice-based model
- State-machine model
- Three fundamental modes
- Secure state
- Defines access rules

60

(lattice) based model with dominance relationships between the higher and lower security levels. It can be called a state-machine model that addresses the state of confidentiality.

- **THREE FUNDAMENTAL MODES OF ACCESS** – Read only, write only, or read and write.

- **SECURE STATE** – BLP defined the notion (concept) of a secure state.

  - Access is only permitted in accordance with security policies.

  - A secure state is maintained when rules are security preserving.

  - Transactions move the system from one secure state to another secure state.

- **DEFINES ACCESS RULES** – For giving subjects access to objects.

  - Dominance relation: clearances of subjects related to classifications of objects.

  - Discretionary security property: Only specific subjects are authorized for a particular mode of access.

  - Data is allowed to flow up only: prevents unauthorized disclosure of confidential information.

- **BELL-LaPADULA CONFIDENTIALITY MODEL (BLP)** – The authors of this model are David Bell and Leonard LaPadula of Mitre Corporation. This model is designed to address confidentiality only. It is interesting to note that this model does not address need to know. This formed the basis for TCSEC (the Orange Book). BLP is an informational flow model because it is concerned with data flowing between levels.

- **LATTICE-BASED MODEL** – This is a lattice-based model meaning that the model is described using rows and columns.

- **STATE-MACHINE MODEL** – Bell-LaPadula is a hierarchical

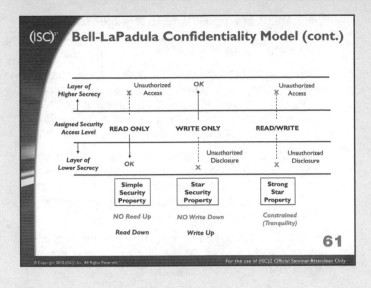

- **BELL-LaPADULA CONFIDENTIALITY MODEL** – Let's assume there are three layers of secrecy or sensitivity regarding our data: the layer our data reside in, a layer of higher secrecy, and a layer of lower secrecy.

  - The **SIMPLE SECURITY PROPERTY** says that if you have read capability, you can read data at your level of secrecy and the level below it, but you cannot read data at a higher layer of secrecy. (Otherwise you would be reading secrets you are not entitled to read.)

  - The **STAR PROPERTY** says that if you have write capability, you can write data at your level of secrecy, you can write your secret data to a higher layer of secrecy without compromising the secrecy of the data, but you must not write your secret data to a lower layer of secrecy. (Otherwise you would be divulging your secrets to others who might not be entitled to see them.) Writing to a level you can't read creates a type of covert channel because if you can't read what you write, you know that there is a higher level of secrecy in the system. To prevent this type of inference attack you may actually be writing to more than one level.

  - The **STRONG STAR PROPERTY** says that if you have both read and write capabilities, you are restricted to read and write your data at your level of secrecy, but you cannot read and write to levels of higher or lower secrecy. (Otherwise you would have the problems described above.) This is sometimes referred to as the constrained or tranquility property.

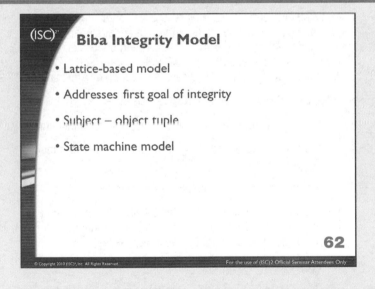

- **BIBA INTEGRITY MODEL** – Biba's model was published in 1977 and because Ken Biba was convinced that external integrity was the only issue, it only addresses external integrity. He argued that internal integrity threats could be adequately dealt with through testing. Model to address integrity: Unauthorized users cannot make modifications.

- **LATTICE-BASED MODEL** – Based on hierarchical lattice of integrity levels.

- **ADDRESSES FIRST GOAL OF INTEGRITY** – By preventing unauthorized subjects from making modifications.

- **SUBJECT - OBJECT TUPLE** – Mathematical dual of confidentiality policy. Defines the "access tuple": subject & object – Set of subjects (active, information processing) – Set of objects (passive, information repository). This defined relationship between subjects and objects.

- **STATE-MACHINE MODEL** – As with BLP, this too is a state machine model.

- The claim that this model is a mathematical dual of the BLP confidentiality policy is a reference to the fact that Biba described the model in a form of predicate calculus, a first order logic that so precisely defines the relations between subjects and objects that the policies defining the relationships are virtually mathematical.

- Biba is an informational flow model because it is concerned with data flowing between levels.

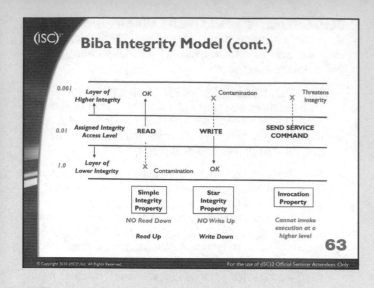

- **ASSUME THERE ARE THREE LAYERS OF ACCURACY OR INTEGRITY REGARDING DATA** – The layer data resides in a layer of higher accuracy and a layer of lower accuracy.

  - **SIMPLE INTEGRITY PROPERTY** – Says that if you have read capability, you can read data at your level of accuracy as well as at a higher layer of accuracy, but you cannot read in data from a lower layer of accuracy. (Otherwise you would risk contaminating the accuracy of your data.)

  - **STAR INTEGRITY PROPERTY** – Says that if you have write capability, you can write data at your level of accuracy as well as to the level below it, but you cannot write your data to a higher layer of accuracy. (Otherwise you would risk contaminating the data at that higher layer.)

  - **INVOCATION PROPERTY** – Preventing a user from taking advantage of, i.e., invoking, the powers of a more privileged user.

- Notice that this diagram is the exact opposite of the Bell-LaPadula model. To help you remember this model, call it the "Read Up – Write Down" model.

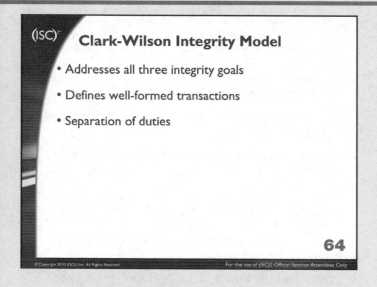

- Published in 1987 by David Clark and David Wilson, the Clark-Wilson model adds a focus on authorized user's unauthorized acts and to internal integrity threats. This model asks the question "Does the software do what it is supposed to do?" This model was designed to address commercial applications.

- **ADDRESSES ALL THREE INTEGRITY GOALS –**

  - Preventing unauthorized users from making modifications.

  - Preventing authorized users from making improper modifications.

  - Maintaining internal and external consistency.

- **DEFINES WELL-FORMED TRANSACTIONS –** A well-formed transaction is one that only permits changes to data if it meets the conditions of the three integrity rules.

  - Preserve/ensure internal consistency.

  - User can manipulate data only in ways that ensure internal consistency.

- **SEPARATION OF DUTIES –**

  - Operation is divided into subparts.

  - Different entity executes each part.

  - Ensures external consistency (data represents real world).

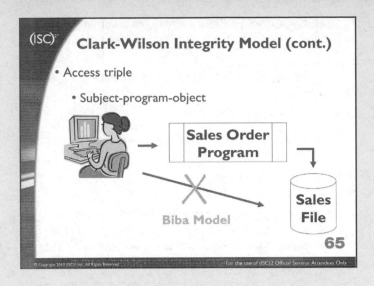

- **CLARK-WILSON INTEGRITY MODEL** – This slide shows the difference between Biba and Clark-Wilson. A subject's access is controlled by his or her authorization to execute a program that would allow the user to make changes to data. Data integrity is ensured, since unauthorized users cannot execute the program (first integrity rule) and authorized users can access the different programs. But the programs will only allow them to make changes in accordance with the rules of integrity (separation of duties). The model ensures that a transaction is evaluated or authenticated by another, thus enforcing separation of duties.

- **ACCESS TRIPLE** – Defines the subject–program–object relationship known as an "access triple." This relationship forces a user making a change to data to comply with the restrictions built into the program, thereby preventing user error or intentional inappropriate manipulation of the data.

- **INTEGRITY ENFORCED BY BINDING** – Integrity is enforced by subject/user-to-program and program-to-object/data binding, which creates separation of duties and ensures that only authorized transactions are performed.

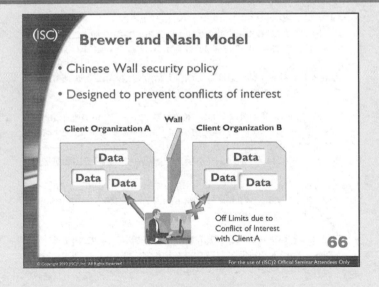

- **BREWER AND NASH MODEL** – Allows for the separation of competitors' data within the same integrated database. Published in 1989.

- **CHINESE WALL SECURITY POLICY** – Defines the rules for separation and develops a set of rules over time. The rules change as the users make decisions that cause conflicts of interest.

- **DESIGNED TO PREVENT CONFLICTS OF INTERESTS** – Individuals are only allowed to access data that is not in conflict with data they have accessed previously. For example: If a user accesses one company's data, the competitor's data can automatically be deemed off-limits.

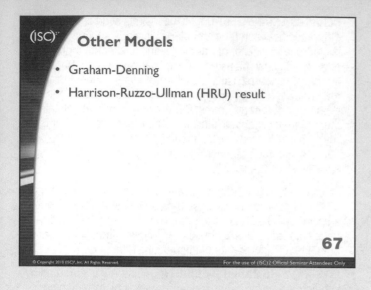

Other Models

- Graham-Denning
- Harrison-Ruzzo-Ullman (HRU) result

67

- **GRAHAM-DENNING MODEL** – Introduces a formal concept of protection rules which operate on primitive rights listed below.
  - Formal system of protection rules (create, delete, grant, revoke).
  - Primitive rights:
    - Create object, create subject, delete object, delete subject.
    - Read access rights, delete access rights, transfer access rights.
- **HARRISON-RUZZO-ULLMAN (HRU) RESULT** – A more granular variation of the Graham-Denning model. This model restricts the commands which are available to alter access rights or permissions.

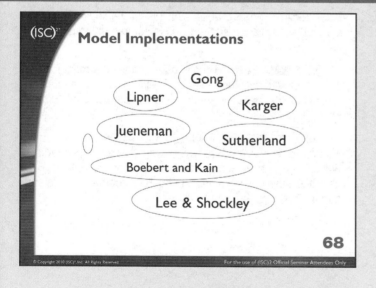

Model Implementations

Gong
Lipner
Karger
Jueneman
Sutherland
Boebert and Kain
Lee & Shockley

68

- **KARGER AND GONG** combine the advantages of capabilities (protection domains and performance) and ACLs (control over propagation and revocation of access rights) to provide protection. Karger's model allows for dynamic separation of duties, but Gong's model is simple, implementable, and more efficient for static separation of duties.
- In 1982, **LIPNER** started looking at computer security in a new way. He recommended that primary emphasis be placed on categories, and only minor emphasis be placed on levels. This has come to be know as **"GROUP PERMISSIONS OR ROLES."**
- **LEE AND SHOCKLEY** independently developed implementations of the Clark-Wilson model using Biba integrity categories and (partially) trusted subjects.
- **JUENEMAN** developed a defensive detection scheme that is based on mandatory and discretionary integrity controls, encryption, checksums, and digital signatures.
- **BOEBERT AND KAIN** developed a matrix-based set of access permissions that reviewed the sensitivity of the subject and object, and allowed actions prior to granting the user access to modify data. It was an implementation of mandatory access control.
- **SUTHERLAND** was an integrity model based on state. The model would map out a change of state from the initial to the current state. It would detect information flow over covert channels.
- All of the above are excerpts from Technical report 79-91 and the Handbook of Information Security Management.

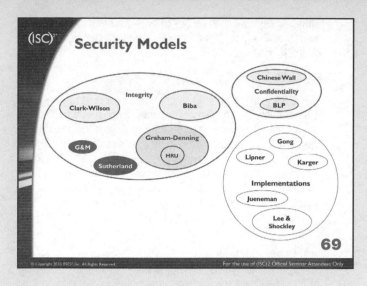

- Now that we have studied these models, it is important to note which ones are integrity and confidentiality models.

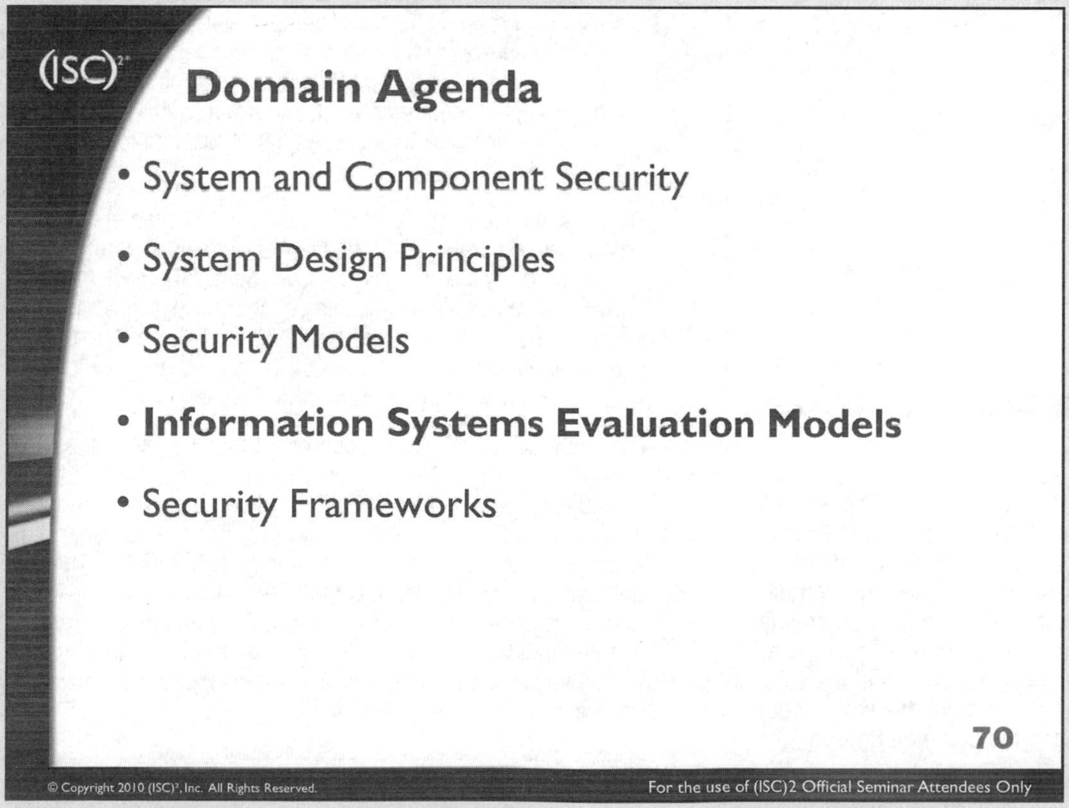

Domain Agenda

- System and Component Security

- System Design Principles

- Security Models

- **Information Systems Evaluation Models**

- Security Frameworks

70

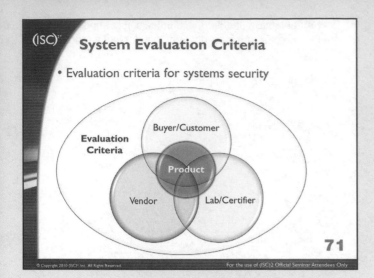

System Evaluation Criteria

- Evaluation criteria for systems security

71

- **EVALUATION CRITERIA** – Evaluation criteria set standards for the evaluation of the security functionality for a system. The perspective of all three major participants in the process of manufacturing, certifying, and purchasing secure equipment must be addressed. In order to ensure that the purchaser is buying a product that will meet the security requirements the purchaser needs, the participants may employ a certification scheme to evaluate the products being considered for

purchase against a common set of evaluation criteria that measures all the products against a standard benchmark for functionality and assurance.

- **EVALUATION ROLES:**

  - **BUYERS** want to be able to compare products of equal functionality and assurance to make choices that fit their business needs. It is difficult to separate specifications from marketing when looking at vendor material or claims. Since buyers cannot be experts in evaluating all products, they request that vendors apply for certification of their products. By having enough purchasing power, buyers can dictate what certification level a vendor's product must attain in order to be considered for purchase.

  - **SELLERS** want their product performance claims to have validity. The increased costs the sellers incur for certifying their products is passed on to the buyers.

  - **LABS** want to maintain their ability to certify products and attract more vendor business, so they must test the products in a fair and cost-effective manner.

- All of these parties are doing business in an international setting and need to ensure that the certifications performed in one country are valid in another.

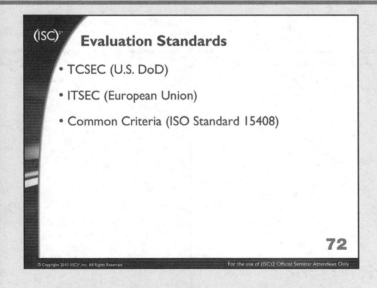

Evaluation Standards

- TCSEC (U.S. DoD)
- ITSEC (European Union)
- Common Criteria (ISO Standard 15408)

72

- The history of certification bodies for certification (testing) and accreditation starts with the United States Department of Defense (DoD) and the Trusted Computer System Evaluation Criteria (TCSEC) in 1985. Other countries built their own certification standards, but these were not widely adopted. International harmonization began with the development of an international criteria, or Information Technology Security Evaluation Criteria (ITSEC), by several countries in the European Union (EU). The standard used around the world today for security product evaluation is the Common Criteria.

- **TCSEC (ORANGE BOOK)** – Was created to provide a means of evaluating protection elements in a system which preserved confidentiality. Functional elements were the only set of crite-

ria. The concept of a Trusted Computing Base (TCB) was used to define the required functionality.

  - **TRUSTED NETWORK INTERPRETATION (TNI (RED BOOK))** – Was an extension of the Orange Book that permitted evaluation of communications networks consisting of multiple systems, and added integrity and availability to functional requirements. It extended system-security evaluation criteria to address typical communications networks.

- **ITSEC (EU)** – Was a result of the integration of several national criteria and separately identified functional and assurance requirements by using a dual-rating scheme. The goal was to derive a more flexible and usable set of criteria to suit both government and commercial needs. ITSEC was intended to enable vendors to have products evaluated in one country and have the evaluation accepted in all other participating countries.

- **COMMON CRITERIA** – Each document has its advantages and disadvantages. Due to its primary focus on confidentiality, TCSEC was found to be too rigid for most non-defense organizations; ITSEC, on the other hand, was found to be not rigid enough. ITSEC, however, was not universally adopted. The publication of the Common Criteria as ISO/IEC 15408 was the first international standard for product evaluation criteria and it is commonly used today because it allows more flexibility for the vendor/consumer to define at a granular level how secure they need the system to be.

REFERENCE:
The Common Criteria Introduction document.

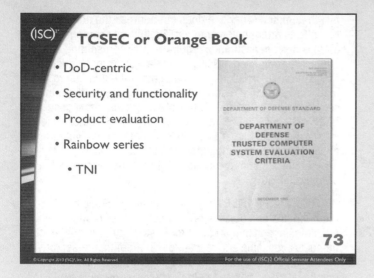

TCSEC or Orange Book

- DoD-centric
- Security and functionality
- Product evaluation
- Rainbow series
  - TNI

73

- **DOD-CENTRIC** – The TCSEC was first issued by the National Computer Security Center (NCSC) in 1983 and then updated in December 1985 by the U.S. Department of Defense (DoD). The major goals of the publication were to give DoD personnel direction in choosing products based upon both trust (assurance) and functionality, to give product designers direction on what large organizations wanted from products, and to give evaluators direction in performing assessments.

- **SECURITY AND FUNCTIONALITY** – "The functional requirements identified the system's technical features and capabilities, like access control lists and classification labels. The assurance requirements identified specific activities that had to be performed and documents that had to be written to help provide confidence that the system worked correctly. At the low end, assurance requirements focused on testing and ba-

sic documentation, while at the high end they involved formal proofs of security properties.

- **PRODUCT EVALUATION** – The TCSEC defined an ordered set of evaluation levels (C1, C2, B1, B2, B3, A1) in which the lowest level evaluation combined low assurance with limited functional requirements. Higher assurance systems had to provide richer sets of predefined security functions as well as higher assurance through more stringent test, review, and analysis requirements. Note that the statement above is missing D level because this is the default level of any unevaluated product.

  - This rigid document compelled complete compliance with requirements in order to achieve a particular rating. Since it was developed by the military for the military, these were acceptable conditions. Vendors were seeking product certifications under TCSEC through 2000.

  - ITSEC and Common Criteria (CC) displaced the TCSEC over time as the main certification tool, but the Defense Information Systems Agency (DISA) for the DoD still makes reference to TCSEC in its evaluations of networks.

- **RAINBOW SERIES** – TCSEC was a part of the Rainbow Series of books dealing with security topics (so named since each book had a different color of cover).

  - **TNI** – Other books in that series included TNI (Trusted Network Interpretation) which applies security concepts to networks, and books dealing with passwords, access control, and physical security, to name a few.

REFERENCE:

http://csrc.nist.gov/nissc/2000/proceedings/papers/032.pdf

IMAGE:

Luis F. Gonzalez, picture

ITSEC

- International origin
- ITSEM
- Assurance
- Functionality

Information Technology Security Evaluation Criteria (ITSEC)

74

- **INTERNATIONAL ORIGIN** – In May 1990, France, Germany, the Netherlands, and the United Kingdom published the Information Technology Security Evaluation Criteria (ITSEC) based on existing work done in all of these countries. ITSEC was developed after widespread international review. The latest version is 1.2.

- **ITSEM** – The IT Security Evaluation Manual (ITSEM), a companion document to the ITSEC, describes how a product should be evaluated.

- ITSEC breaks assurance (E) and functionality (F) into separate ratings.

- **ASSURANCE** – There are seven ascending correctness/assurance levels: E0 to E6. Evaluations of correctness assess whether the security enforcing functions and mechanisms are implemented correctly. Correctness is addressed in construction for both the development process and the development environment.

- **FUNCTIONALITY** – The five functionality classes F-C1, F-C2, F-B1, F-B2, and F-B3 form a hierarchy because they were derived from the functionality requirements of the hierarchical TCSEC classes. Traditionally, the F rating starts at 1 and ends at 5. Each one of these classes addresses some or all of the following: identification, authentication, access control, accountability, audit, object reuse, integrity, and reliability.

REFERENCES:

ISBN: 0471978442 p 155

http://www.ssi.gouv.fr/site_documents/ITSEC/ITSEM-uk.pdf, Page 17

IMAGE:

ISBN 92-820-3004-8 – Catalogue number: CD-71-91-502-EN-C – © ECSC-EEC-EAEC, Brussels Luxembourg, 1991

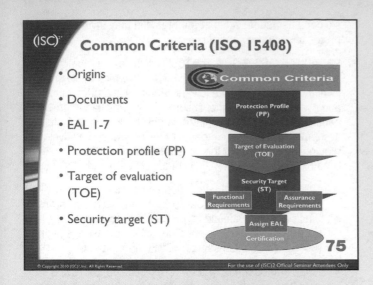

Common Criteria (ISO 15408)

- Origins
- Documents
- EAL 1-7
- Protection profile (PP)
- Target of evaluation (TOE)
- Security target (ST)

75

- **ORIGINS** – The CC was born from the existing European, U.S., and Canadian criteria (ITSEC, TCSEC, and CTCPEC respectively). The current version 3.1R1 was published in September 2006. It has been adopted by the International Organization for Standardization as ISO 15408, but Australia, New Zealand, Canada, France, Germany, Japan, the Netherlands, Spain, the United Kingdom, and the United States maintain the original copyright.

- **DOCUMENTS** – There are four document parts: Part 1: Introduction and general model; Part 2: Security functional requirements; Part 4: Security assurance requirements; and CEM v3.1: Common Evaluation Methodology. The introduction specifies which methodology is suitable for a particular environment.

- **EAL 1-7** – The evaluation assurance level or EAL is a measure of the confidentiality, integrity, and availability that is assigned

by the Common Criteria. It does not address the administration efforts after implementation. Evaluation assurance level (EAL) is a set of assurance requirements representing a point on the CC predefined assurance scale from 1 to 7, which ranges from informal (expressed in natural language) to formal (expressed in a restricted syntax language with defined semantics based on well-established mathematical concepts). EAL1 is the most basic and EAL7 is the most stringent and most expensive. Higher EAL levels do not mean a higher level of security, they only mean that the claimed security assurance of the target of evaluation (TOE) has been more extensively validated.

- **PROTECTION PROFILE (PP)** – A general set of security requirements and objectives for a category of products which meet similar consumer needs for IT security. These PP documents are reusable and reasonable in meeting the security objectives of the general product description. PPs point to functional standards and help the buyer write a clear RFP.

- **TARGET OF EVALUATION (TOE)** – A set of software, firmware, and/or hardware to be evaluated, possibly accompanied by guidance.

- **SECURITY TARGET (ST)** – Contains the IT security objectives and requirements of a specific, identified TOE and defines the functional and assurance measures offered by that TOE to meet stated requirements.

- Independent parties write a basic set of rules (PP). Each vendor describes how his or her product (TOE) adheres to the rules (ST). A lab hired by the vendor verifies adherence to the rules (certification).

REFERENCES:

http://www.niap-ccevs.org/cc-scheme/

http://www.commoncriteriaportal.org/public/consumer/index.php?menu=2

CC Part 1 V3.1R1 page 37.

Comparison of Evaluation Levels

Common Criteria	US TCSEC	European ITSEC
–	D: Minimal Protection	EO
EAL 1	–	–
EAL 2	C1: Discretionary Security Protection	E1
EAL 3	C2: Controlled Access Protection	E2
EAL 4	B1: Labeled Security Protection	E3
EAL 5	B2: Structure Protection	E4
EAL 6	B3: Security Domains	E5
EAL 7	A1: Verified Design	E6

76

- This chart provides a comparison of the common evaluation schemes. Comparison is associated with assurance levels only.

REFERENCE:

http://www.commoncriteriaportal.org/

Domain Agenda

- System and Component Security

- System Design Principles

- Security Models

- Information Systems Evaluation Models

- **Security Frameworks**

77

- **THERE ARE MANY SECURITY FRAMEWORKS AVAILABLE –** Each one designed to incorporate security functionality into systems design and implementation. They all address business needs, security needs, and regulation and compliance issues.

- Frameworks provide us with a way of looking at our security features and mapping them to business requirements.

ISO 7498-2

- Defined secure communications

- NOT an implementation

78

- **ISO 7498-2 –** From ISO: Provides a general description of security services and related mechanisms, which can be en-sured by the Reference Model, and of the positions within the Reference Model where the services and mechanisms may be provided.

- **DEFINED SECURE COMMUNICATIONS –** Extends the field of application of ISO 7498 to cover secure communications between open systems. Adds to the concepts and principles included in ISO 7498 but does not modify them.

- **NOT AN IMPLEMENTATION –** ISO 7498-2 is not an implemen-tation specification, nor a basis for assessing the confor-mance of actual implementations.

- ISO 7498-2 takes the traditional seven-layer OSI model and maps it to a two-layer functional model which provides IT security professionals a way to look at the OSI model in a functional view.

REFERENCE:

http://www.iso.org/iso/iso_catalogue/catalogue_tc/catalogue_detail.htm?csnumber=14256

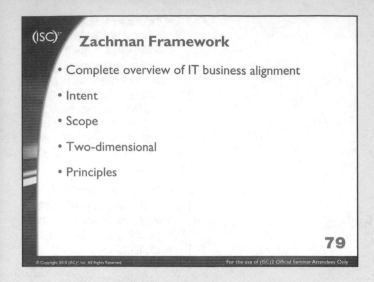

Zachman Framework

- Complete overview of IT business alignment
- Intent
- Scope
- Two-dimensional
- Principles

79

- **ZACHMAN** – Originally conceived by John Zachman at IBM in the 1980s, the framework is now a de facto world standard for expressing the basic elements of an enterprise architecture (EA). This EA is a total architecture and does not just focus on security.

- **COMPLETE OVERVIEW OF IT AND BUSINESS ALIGNMENT** – The purpose of the Zachman framework is to link technology projects back to specific goals.

- **INTENT** – The Zachman Framework is influenced by principles of classical architecture that establish a common vocabulary and set of perspectives for describing complex enterprise systems. This influence is reflected in the set of rules that govern an ordered set of relationships that are balanced and orthogonal. By designing a system according to these rules, the architect can be assured of a design that is clean, easy to understand, balanced, and complete in itself. The Zachman Framework provides the blueprint, or architecture, for an organization's information infrastructure.

- **SCOPE** – The Zachman Framework describes a holistic model of an enterprise's information infrastructure from six perspectives: planner (ballpark view), owner, architect, designer, builder, and the working system. The focus is on ensuring that all aspects of an enterprise are well organized and exhibit clear relationships that will ensure a complete system regardless of the order in which they are established.

- **TWO-DIMENSIONAL** – In a two-dimensional view, the rows represent perspectives in detail while the columns represent models of abstraction in interpreting the details.

- **PRINCIPLES** – By defining clear architectural design principles, Zachman ensures that any tailored or extended implementation will be equally well built as long as the designer and builder continue to follow the rules.

REFERENCES:
http://www.zifa.com/
http://www.research.ibm.com/journal/sj/263/ibmsj2603E.pdf

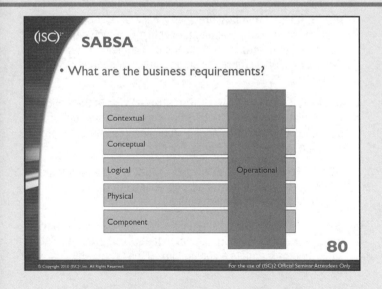

SABSA

- What are the business requirements?

Contextual
Conceptual
Logical
Physical
Component

Operational

80

- **SHERWOOD APPLIED BUSINESS SECURITY ARCHITECTURE (SABSA)** is a risk-driven enterprise security architecture (ESA) framework that operates under the premise that everything flows from the business requirements. The diagram and design starts at the highest level – contextual – and flows down to the lowest level – component. At each layer, the questions who, what, where, why, when, and how must be answered.

REFERENCE:
http://www.sabsa-institute.org/the-sabsa-method/what-is-sabsa.aspx

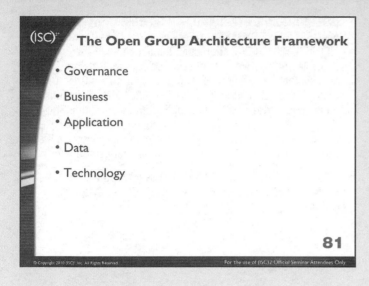

- **THE OPEN GROUP ARCHITECTURE FRAMEWORK (TOGAF)** – Is a framework for enterprise architecture which provides a comprehensive approach to the design, planning, implementation, and governance of an enterprise information architecture. The architecture is typically modeled at four levels or domains: business, application, data, technology. A set of foundation architectures is provided to enable the architecture team to envision the current and future state of the architecture.

REFERENCE:

http://www.opengroup.org/architecture/

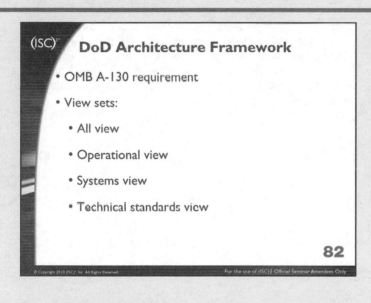

- **OMB A-130 REQUIREMENT** – All major U.S. government Department of Defense (DoD) weapons and information technology system procurements are required to develop an enterprise architecture and document that architecture using the set of views prescribed in the DoDAF. While it is clearly aimed at military systems, it has broad applicability across the private, public, and voluntary sectors around the world and represents only one of a large number of systems architecture frameworks.

- **VIEW SETS** – DoDAF views are organized into four basic view sets: overarching all view (AV), operational view (OV), systems view (SV), and the technical standards view (TV). Only a subset of the full DoDAF view set is usually created for each system development.

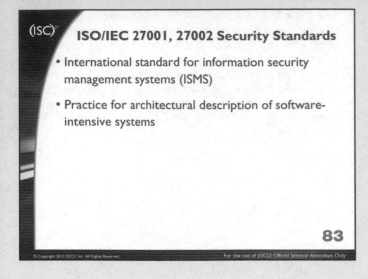

ISO/IEC 27001, 27002 Security Standards

- International standard for information security management systems (ISMS)

- Practice for architectural description of software-intensive systems

83

- **INTERNATIONAL STANDARD FOR INFORMATION SECURITY MANAGEMENT SYSTEMS (ISMS)** – From the ISO website: "ISO/IEC 42010:2007 addresses the activities of the creation, analysis and sustainment of architectures of software-intensive systems, and the recording of such architectures in terms of architectural descriptions. ISO/IEC 42010:2007 establishes a conceptual framework for architectural description and defines the content of an architectural description. Annexes provide the rationale for key concepts and terminology, the relationships to other standards, and examples of usage."

- **PRACTICE FOR ARCHITECTURAL DESCRIPTION OF SOFTWARE-INTENSIVE SYSTEMS** – ISO 27002 is the code of pratice.

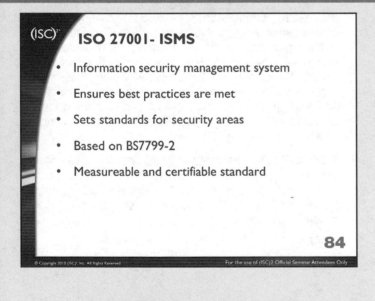

ISO 27001- ISMS

- Information security management system

- Ensures best practices are met

- Sets standards for security areas

- Based on BS7799-2

- Measureable and certifiable standard

84

- **ISMS** – One of the most popular frameworks in the world today, ISMS sets a standard for addressing security throughout the development, deployment, and implementation schedule. It divides security into 11 major areas and provides a mechanism for an organization to be certified as compliant with the standard.

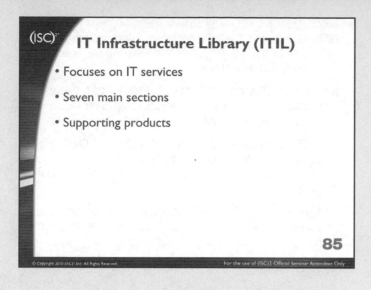

IT Infrastructure Library (ITIL)

- Focuses on IT services
- Seven main sections
- Supporting products

85

- **FOCUSES ON IT SERVICES** – "ITIL (the IT Infrastructure Library) is essentially a series of documents that are used to aid the implementation of a framework for IT Service Management. This customizable framework defines how Service Management is applied within an organization. It also aligns with the international standard, ISO 20000."

- **SEVEN MAIN SECTIONS** – The 'library' itself comprises seven distinct sets: Service Support; Service Delivery; ICT Infrastructure Management; Planning To Implement Service Management; Applications Management; The Business Perspective; and Security Management. Within these sets are the specific descriptions and definitions of the various ITIL disciplines."

- **SUPPORTING PRODUCTS** – The widespread adoption of the ITIL guidance has encouraged organizations worldwide, both commercial and non-proprietary, to develop supporting products as part of a shared ITIL philosophy. It is often used to complement the CobiT framework.

REFERENCE:
http://www.itlibrary.org

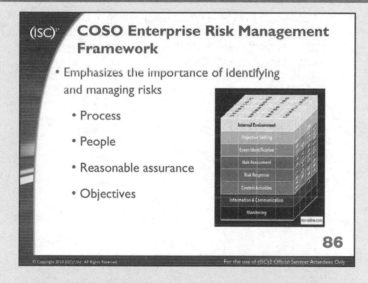

COSO Enterprise Risk Management Framework

- Emphasizes the importance of identifying and managing risks
  - Process
  - People
  - Reasonable assurance
  - Objectives

86

- **COMMITTEE OF SPONSORING ORGANIZATIONS (COSO)** – Describes a unified approach for evaluation of internal control systems that management has designed to provide reasonable assurance of achieving corporate mission, objectives, goals, and desired outcome, while adhering to laws and regulations. Allows the company to accurately report successes and outcomes to the public and interested third parties. COSO serves as a common basis for management, directors, regulators, academics, and others to better understand enterprise risk management, its benefits and limitations, and to effectively communicate about enterprise risk management.

- **EMPHASIZES THE IMPORTANCE OF IDENTIFYING AND MANAGING RISKS** – The enterprise risk management (ERM) COSO framework emphasizes the importance of identifying and managing risks across the enterprise. The framework consists of eight components. The COSO methodology considers four elements as a part of its security objective:

  - **PROCESS** – Internal control is a process. It is a means to an end, not an end in itself.

  - **PEOPLE** – Internal control is effected by people. It's not merely policy manuals and forms, but people at every level of an organization.

  - **REASONABLE ASSURANCE** – Internal control can be expected to provide only reasonable assurance, not absolute assurance, to an entity's management and board.

  - **OBJECTIVES** – Internal control is geared to the achievement of objectives in one or more separate but overlapping categories.

REFERENCE:
http://www.coso.org/audit_chop.htm

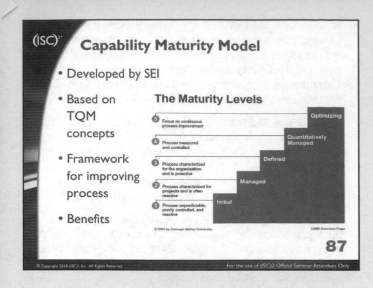

- **DEVELOPED BY SEI** – The Software Engineering Institute (SEI) is a federally funded research and development center sponsored by the U.S. Department of Defense and operated by Carnegie Mellon University.

- **BASED ON TOTAL QUALITY MANAGEMENT (TQM) CONCEPTS** – The maturity of an organization is developed through a program of continuous improvement and better controls.

- **FRAMEWORK FOR IMPROVING PROCESS** – The CMMI provides a framework through a set of measurable criteria that an organization would follow to demonstrate a higher level of maturity.

- **BENEFITS** – The CMMI Product Suite provides the latest best practices for product and service development and maintenance.

REFERENCE:

http://www.sei.cmu.edu/cmmi/general/general.html

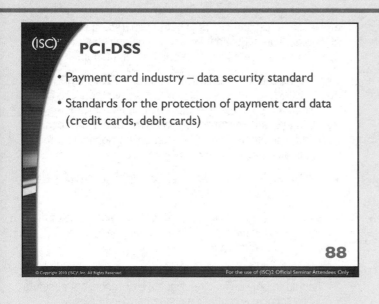

- **PCI-DSS** – Sets the standard for the handling of credit and debit cards and the protection of cardholder data. This is examined in more detail in the Legal, Regulations, Investigations, and Compliance domain.

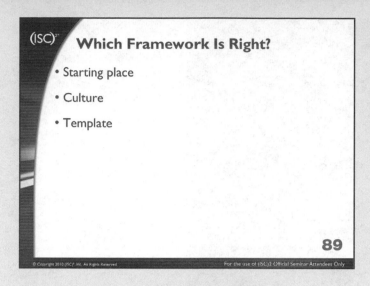

- **WHICH FRAMEWORK IS RIGHT?** There is no "right" framework for every organization; each organization should choose the one that it can be comfortable with. The framework is a starting place for a customized ISMS. Since these templates are commonly used by organizations, it is possible to hire staff or contractors who already have experience working with the templates, and the templates can be used to provide a framework for the restructuring and changes required as two organizations merge.

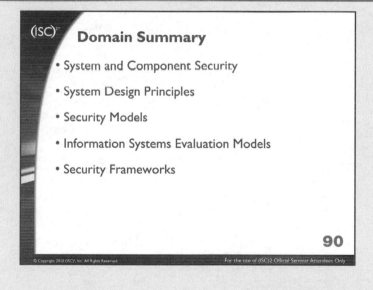

- Here are the topics covered in this important domain. We have covered the basic components of system security, the design principles, and frameworks. Additionally, we have covered the very important areas of information system evaluation models (Common Criteria is the current system) and the security models. At this point, you should have a working knowledge of each area.

Security Transcends Technology

(ISC)²·

91

Review Questions

SECURITY ARCHITECTURE AND DESIGN

1. What type of central processing unit (CPU) functionality allows simultaneous execution of two or more programs by one or more processors?

   A. Multithreading
   B. Multiprocessor
   C. Multiprocessing
   D. Multitasking

2. What computer component organizes memory, logging, and error detection?

   A. Central processing unit (CPU)
   B. Registers
   C. Input devices
   D. Output devices

3. What central processing unit (CPU) operational mode processes data for an application and allows less access to some resources?

   A. Supervisor state
   B. Limited state
   C. Problem state
   D. Semi-privileged state

4. What type of system architecture supports standardized interfaces and protocols, rather than proprietary and customized applications?

   A. Embedded
   B. Open
   C. Closed
   D. Single level

5. What network architectural structure is more secure, removes client functions, and primarily supports processing and storage at a centralized location?

   A. Clusters
   B. Diskless computing
   C. Thin client
   D. Distributed

6. Which of the following software is best described as being distributed, providing translation or communications, and expanding applications and services?

   A. Middleware
   B. Firmware
   C. Operating system
   D. Cloud computing

7. Which of the following is the combination of all hardware, firmware, and software responsible for enforcing the security policy and serves as a protection mechanism within a computer system?

   A. Reference monitor
   B. Security kernel
   C. Computer operating system
   D. Trusted computer base

8. Which of the following security models addresses preventing unauthorized users from making modifications, preventing authorized users from making improper modifications, and maintaining internal and external consistency?

   A. Bell-LaPadula
   B. Biba
   C. Clark-Wilson
   D. Brewer and Nash

9. What Lattice model is characterized by Read "Down" and No Write "Down"?

   A. Access control matrix
   B. Clark Wilson
   C. Bell-LaPadula
   D. Biba

10. Which of the following security models PRIMARILY protects confidentiality?

    A. Brewer and Nash
    B. Clark-Wilson
    C. Graham-Denning
    D. Karger and Gong

11. What fundamental security model is based upon rules to prevent subjects that are operating in different domains from affecting each other?

    A. Information flow
    B. Non-interference
    C. Lattice
    D. State machine

12. What type of memory storage is the fastest, highest cost, and lowest capacity?

    A. Cache
    B. Main memory
    C. Swap space
    D. Central processing unit (CPU) registers

13. **What cloud computing service offers support to business operations without the organizations building their own servers and networks?**

A. Software as a service (SaaS)

B. Security as a service

C. Infrastructure as a service (IaaS)

D. IT as a service (ITaaS)

14. **A framework that provides a comprehensive approach to the design, planning, implementation, and governance of an enterprise and typically modeled at four levels – business, application, data, and technology – is**

A. the Open Group Architecture Framework (TOGAF).

B. the Sherwood Applied Business Security Architecture (SABSA).

C. the Zachman Framework.

D. the Department of Defense Architecture Framework (DoDAF).

15. **An international information security standard and framework that addresses security throughout all phases is called what?**

A. Information Security Management System (ISMS)

B. IT Infrastructure Library (ITIL)

C. Enterprise Risk Management (ERM)

D. Capability Maturity Model (CMM)

16. **Which one of the following Common Criteria components outlines a general and industry set of security requirements for a category of products?**

A. Target of evaluation (TOE)

B. Security target (ST)

C. Protection profile (PP)

D. Certification and accreditation (C&A)

17. **Which of the following set of security evaluation ratings can be described as methodically designed, tested, and reviewed; and, apply mandatory access control and labeled security protection, respectively.**

A. EAL 2, C1

B. EAL 4, B1

C. EAL 3, C2

D. EAL 5, B2

18. **What protection ring level provides access to the system components and contains utilities and file system drivers?**

A. Ring 0

B. Ring 1

C. Ring 2

D. Ring 3

19. **To create virtual memory on a computer, two different types of memory must be combined. They are**

A. primary storage and random access memory (RAM).

B. Level I (L1) cache and secondary storage.

C. random access memory (RAM) and secondary storage.

D. video random access memory (VRAM) and secondary storage.

20. **What type of memory addressing uses absolute addresses?**

A. Logical

B. Relative

C. Physical

D. Virtual

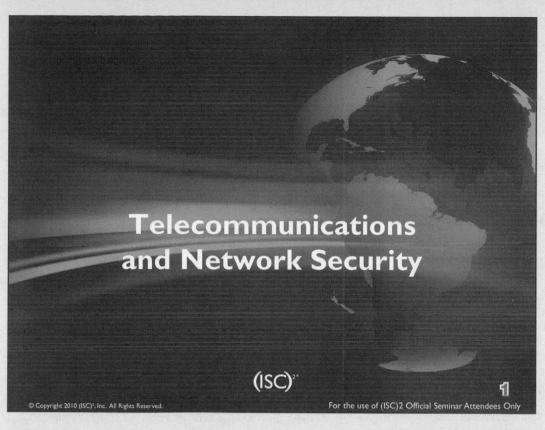

- From the CISSP® CBK®: The Telecommunications and Network Security domain encompasses the structures, transmission methods, transport formats, and security measures used to provide integrity, availability, authentication, and confidentiality for transmissions over private and public communications networks and media.

- In today's global marketplace, being able to communicate quickly, safely, and efficiently is mandatory. The candidate is expected to demonstrate an understanding of network and communications security as it relates to:

- Voice communications.

- Local area, wide area, and remote access data communications.

- Internet/Intranet/Extranet security in terms of firewalls, routers, and TCP/IP.

- Preventative, detective, and corrective communications-security management and techniques.

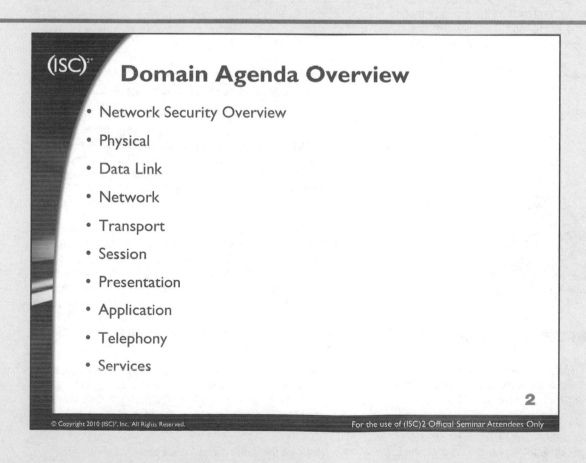

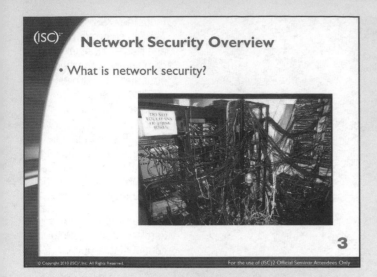

and systems from attacks and not simply rely on perimeter defense. This includes resilience, redundancy, and error correction. The carrier also ensures the integrity and confidentiality of its networks through link encryption and error correction. The availability requirements are usually provided through redundant facilities such as mesh or SONET networks.

- This domain covers only the basics of networking in order to give a foundational understanding of network security issues. Although it is impossible to cover all attacks, threats, and other network-based scenarios in a short course, the CISSP should nonetheless have a solid understanding of all network security issues and risks – and in many cases may require more in-depth knowledge in order to execute his or her job responsibilities. There are excellent books and Internet resources available for supplemental learning.

- Network security is a cornerstone for business operations because network connectivity can be a make-or-break problem for business operations. Networks provide an easy and consistent venue of attack, and network security is critical to the business, since a failure in network protection (such as theft, loss of data, or system failure, etc.) can lead to business failure or bankruptcy. A well-designed and protected network provides a business with a stable foundation.

- In smaller organizations, IT security is a task often handed to the network manager, but it can also be a career path in and of itself. Controlling a network is like air superiority in battle – more often than not it will be a decisive factor. On the other hand, network security is not the totality of IT security. Having a firewall (like wearing a seatbelt) is a good starting point but is not the end of the matter. Network security needs to be built from the inside out.

IMAGE:

www.flickr.com

- **WHAT IS NETWORK SECURITY? NETWORK SECURITY** encompasses the **STRUCTURES, TRANSMISSION METHODS, TRANSPORT FORMATS, AND SECURITY MEASURES** used to provide **INTEGRITY, AVAILABILITY, AUTHENTICATION,** and **CONFIDENTIALITY** for transmissions over **PRIVATE** and **PUBLIC** communications networks and media. As always in IT security, the primary objectives are preservation and protection of confidentiality, integrity, and availability. Network security is particularly important because of its complexity, and also because the network is the central communications medium in most organizations.

- It is important to differentiate between security controls at the carrier, or network provider level, and the customer configuration, or corporate network level. Attacks are executed daily against both. The customer network is composed of the local area network infrastructure, as well as the infrastructure that attaches to and traverses the carrier-provided network. Customers must ensure that they have protected their networks

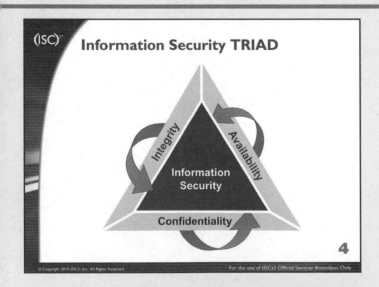

- **INFORMATION SECURITY TRIAD** – The Telecommunications and Network Security domain addresses all three goals of the AIC TRIAD: availability, integrity, and confidentiality.

- **AVAILABILITY** – "Availability" is the up-time (versus downtime) of a component or group of components. Availability (whether of the customer network or the supplier network as a whole) is now a standard measurement in the IT and network space and

is often included in service level agreements (SLAs).

- CISSPs look for single points of failure, where (based upon business needs) the non-redundant components can be reinforced. Redundancy often has to be engineered into a system at the network, application, and/or processor level, and this can include backup and redundant hardware, networks, applications, and data replication, all of which is related to disaster recovery and business continuity.

- **INTEGRITY** – The integrity and protection of data in transit is a critical element of successful business and e-commerce transactions. Data must be error-free, and sent to the intended location, and the network needs to support this. While messages can sometimes be modified at the higher network layers (i.e., within applications), networks can be set up to provide robustness or resilience against interception and change of a message through attacks such as man-in-the-middle or replay attacks.

- **CONFIDENTIALITY** – Networks (particularly when wireless) are vulnerable to sniffing. Because the network is the carrier of almost all digital information within a corporation, it is an attractive target; sensitive data must, therefore, be protected while in transit.

- Note that the same controls that provide confidentiality also often protect integrity.

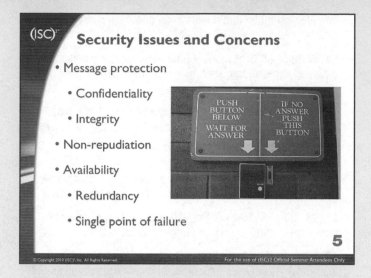

Security Issues and Concerns

- Message protection
  - Confidentiality
  - Integrity
- Non-repudiation
- Availability
  - Redundancy
  - Single point of failure

5

- **MESSAGE PROTECTION –** Telecommunications security is focused on the protection of data in transport. This includes the protection of message data from unauthorized disclosure and modification.

- **NON-REPUDIATION** is the assurance that a specific author actually did create and send a specific item to a specific recipient, and that it was successfully received. With assurance of non-repudiation, the sender of the message cannot later credibly deny having sent the message, nor can the recipient credibly claim not to have received it.

  - Effective non-repudiation is accomplished through the use of digital signatures, created by encrypting a SHA-256 hash with the private key of the originator.

- Another alternative (though not the digital signature standard (DSS)) is MD5 as covered in the Internet RFC1321: "The [MD5] algorithm takes a message of arbitrary length as input, and produces 128-bit 'fingerprint' or 'message digest' as output. It is believed to be computationally infeasible to produce two messages that have the same message digest, or to produce any message having a given pre-specified target message digest. The MD5 algorithm is intended for use in digital signature applications, where a large file must be 'compressed' in a secure manner before being encrypted with a private (secret) key under a public-key cryptosystem such as RSA."

- **REDUNDANCY** is very important if systems are to remain highly available. A redundant component remains in standby and will take over the workload when another component fails or has to be taken down for maintenance. Redundant components can include network components, LAN switches, gateways, authentication systems, servers, etc., and often also incorporate data replication. They are often kept in proximity to the primary device and provisioned and configured in the same way. In the realm of redundant networks, it is common for organizations to have one primary network of one technology (perhaps a private MPLS network) and a redundant system of another (perhaps across the Internet or utilizing ISDN). In these cases, organizations will typically maintain geographically diverse data centers incorporating replicated databases and applications to guard against cataclysmic local disasters.

IMAGE:

www.static.flickr.com

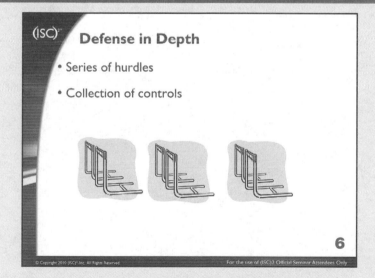

Defense in Depth

- Series of hurdles

- Collection of controls

6

- **SERIES OF HURDLES –** Defense in depth applies to any asset worth protecting. In the realm of IT and networks, it refers to layering the security tools and methods, often varying numerous parameters between layers, in an effort to restrict non-authorized users from penetrating more than the outer layers. For example, a bank's defense in depth might include:

  - Physical barriers outside its building to prevent vehicles from crashing through its vulnerable areas.

  - Locks on its doors and windows.

- Video feed to an offsite security team.

- An alarm system.

- A caged area prior to entry to or exit from a vault.

- A heavy steel vault door (often of secret, proprietary design).

- Complex multiple key combination and timed locks.

- **COLLECTION OF CONTROLS –** Any one of these alone has its vulnerabilities and can be circumvented. When taken together as a holistic system, however, breaking in becomes much more difficult and requires significantly greater resources.

- A common IT and network infrastructure is to have a firewall to protect against unauthorized users from public access networks, an intrusion detection system (IDS or IPS) to validate and monitor the usage of authorized or unauthorized personnel, application and/or system login credentials, and encryption of confidential data. For remote user access across an untrusted or public network, it is also common to have login and password protection with two-factor authentication (such as an RSA token) through the firewall. Some companies also choose to use different vendors (hardware devices or service providers) for the various layers.

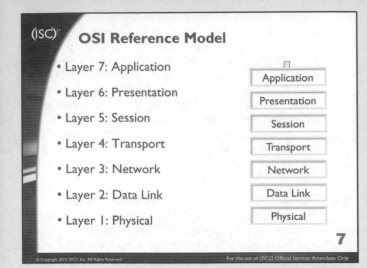

- The OSI (open system interconnect) model was first defined and published as an international standard (ISO/IEC 7498-1) in 1984. Its last revision was in 1994. Although complex, it has provided a practical and widely accepted way to describe network engineering. In practice, some layers (such as the presentation layer) have proved to be less crucial to operations, while others (e.g., the network layer) have required a more specific security structure. There are a number of applications that overlap layer boundaries. Certain network architectures are better described by splitting Layer 2, while at present, Layers 5 and 6 aren't always used. They are nonetheless necessary and may be used for added functionality later on, such as for DRM (digital rights management) in Layer 6.

- **LAYER 7: APPLICATION LAYER** – Describes the structure, interpretation, and handling of information.

- **LAYER 6: PRESENTATION LAYER** – Describes the presentation of information and does syntax conversion such as ASCII/EBCDIC.

- **LAYER 5: SESSION LAYER** – Describes the handshake between applications, such as the authentication or sign-on process.

- **LAYER 4: TRANSPORT LAYER** – Using protocols such as TCP and UDP, the transport layer describes data transfer between applications and provides flow control and error detection and correction.

- **LAYER 3: NETWORK LAYER** – Describes data transfer between networks using protocols such as Internet Protocol (IP).

- **LAYER 2: DATA LINK LAYER** – Describes data transfer between machines, e.g., via an Ethernet connection.

- **LAYER 1: PHYSICAL LAYER** – Describes the networking hardware such as network interfaces and cabling, as well as the way to transmit bits and bytes of data whether as electrical pulses, radio waves, or light.

- **STRENGTHS** -

  - Established, widely-accepted model.

  - Published as an ISO standard.

  - Flexible and generic.

- **WEAKNESSES** -

  - Generally considered complex.

  - Layer definition too coarse on the lower layers, too detailed on the upper layers.

REFERENCE:

http://www.cisco.com/univercd/cc/td/doc/cisintwk/ito_doc/introint.htm#wp1020580

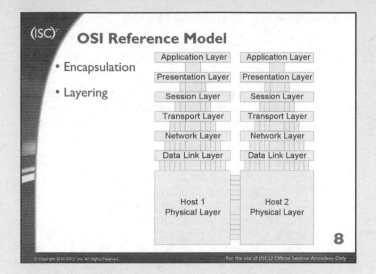

OSI Reference Model

- Encapsulation
- Layering

Application Layer — Application Layer
Presentation Layer — Presentation Layer
Session Layer — Session Layer
Transport Layer — Transport Layer
Network Layer — Network Layer
Data Link Layer — Data Link Layer

Host 1 Physical Layer — Host 2 Physical Layer

8

- **OSI REFERENCE MODEL** – When an application transmits data over a network, the data enters the top layer and moves to each successive lower level (i.e., "moves down the stack") until it is transmitted over the network at Layer 1. The remote host receives the data at Layer 1 and moves it to successively higher layers (or, "up the stack") until it reaches Layer 7 and then passes it to the application on the host.

  - It is important to see how this works. Each layer at the originating host performs operations on the data that will be required by its same layer at the final destination or perhaps by some intermediate hosts that will forward the packet. Layer 3 on Host 1, for instance, communicates with Layer 3 on Host 2, but in doing so encapsulates the information it is passing to Layer 3 of the remote host location with header and trailer information that will instruct Layer 3 at the far end what the data represents and how to deal with the received packet.

- However, the communications travel through each layer of the stack, so the output of Layer 3 at the originating point is sent on its way via Layer 2. Layer 2 will do its operations and send the packet onward via Layer 1. When the packet is received at the far end, Layer 2 will remove the header and trailer information used to encapsulate the packet that was sent to it from the originating point, and pass the data on to Layer 3.

- **ENCAPSULATION** – Is the process of wrapping the data using headers and, sometimes, trailers before sending it on to the next lower protocol in the stack. As the data flows through the protocol stack, each layer builds on the previous layer's encapsulation and adds its own header information. As the data travels up the stack at the other end, the opposite happens. Each layer removes the header information meant for it, reads it, and passes the rest up to the next layer until the data get to the application that can process them properly. Note also that we can see here a major source of security troubles in the making. If the boundaries between the protocol stacks are not properly checked, then data could be overwritten, resulting, for instance, in a change of payload.

- **LAYERING** – The key aspect of a layering model is the separate function of each layer. Each layer has a separate purpose that it plays in the communications operation. Each layer can do its work independent of the other layers, thereby modularizing the communications operation. A layer can be changed without having to completely redo the communications operation.

  - Normally, this segregation is not entirely opaque and access to data from other layers is possible with a little effort, so layering in itself is not sufficient to serve as a security model. However, it can form the basis of a security architecture – it is entirely possible to build a layered security model on a layered network model.

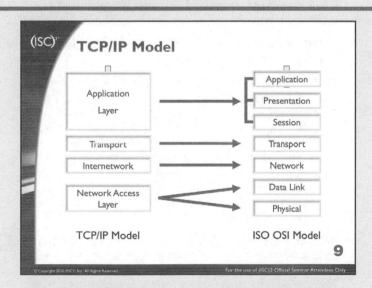

TCP/IP Model

Application Layer → Application
                    Presentation
                    Session
Transport → Transport
Internetwork → Network
Network Access Layer → Data Link
                       Physical

TCP/IP Model — ISO OSI Model

9

- **THE TCP/IP MODEL FUNCTIONS LIKE THE OSI MODEL** – The TCP/IP model is similar to the OSI model, but has a simpler structure. It is designed to describe the TCP/IP stack. As with the OSI model, data that is transmitted on the network enters the top of the stack, and each layer (except for the physical layer) encapsulates information for its peer on the remote host and places information at the beginning (header), and sometimes the end (trailer), of the message it receives from the layer above it. On the remote host, each layer removes the encapsulating headers and trailers from the packet and then passes the message upward. Each layer

processes messages in a modular fashion, without concern about the function of the other layers that are processing the message.

- **THE TCP/IP MODEL SUPPORTS THE TCP/IP PROTOCOL** – The network, or Internet (Internetworking) layer, includes everything that is required to move data between networks. It corresponds to the IP protocol, but also ICMP and IGMP. In terms of the OSI model it corresponds to Layer 3. The host to host (transport) layer includes everything required to move data between applications. It corresponds to the TCP and UDP protocols. In terms of the OSI model, it corresponds to Layer 4.

- **THE APPLICATION LAYER IS UNIQUE** – The application layer covers everything specific to a session or application, or in other words, everything relating to the data payload. It corresponds to Layers 5 through 7 of the OSI model.

- **STRENGTHS -**

  - **SIMPLER** than OSI model.

  - **ALIGNED** with TCP/IP protocol.

- **WEAKNESSES –**

  - Its network-centric view doesn't describe the function of the application layer in enough detail.

REFERENCES:
http://www.protocols.com/pbook/tcpip1.htm
http://www.redbooks.ibm.com/abstracts/gg243376.html

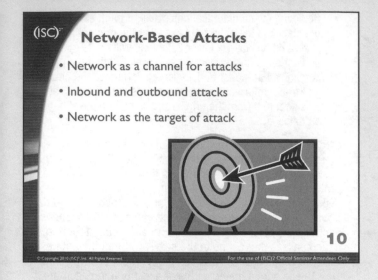

- **"Passive attacks"** wiretap or eavesdrop on data flows using spyware.

- Attacks such as man-in-the-middle attacks intercept data streams.

- **NETWORK AS A CHANNEL FOR ATTACKS** – This is the most frequent network security threat today. For example, viruses exploit networks in order to spread without actually breaching the security of the network itself.

- **NETWORK AS THE TARGET OF ATTACK** – Although some attacks have affected the functionality and performance of the Internet, to date, no attacker has yet managed to take control over any significant portion of the Internet. The development of botnets, however, is making this possibility more likely. On the other hand, attacks directed at a particular network's availability, or one of its other services (particularly security devices), are common. These include denial of service (DoS) attacks, distributed denial of service attacks (DDoS) or attempts to breach a firewall or router.

  - **DENIAL OF SERVICE (DOS) ATTACK** – The easiest attack to carry out against a network. Overloads the network through excessive traffic.

  - **DISTRIBUTED DENIAL OF SERVICE ATTACK** – Overloading the victim's network using a network (botnet) of compromised machines that will launch an attack on command.

- **NETWORK-BASED ATTACKS** – Network-based attackers have a range of motives and attack methods.

  - Threat agents may be external or internal.

  - Attackers may be motivated by profit or gain, recognition (ego), revenge, etc.

  - "Active attacks" change or damage systems. They exploit vulnerabilities, infiltrate networks, launch malicious code, or deny service.

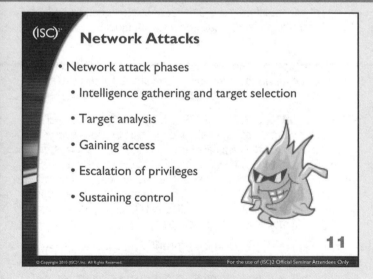

- **NETWORK SECURITY AND RISKS** – A CISSP should know the types of attacks that pertain to the various models such as TCP/IP and OSI, as well as to the layers within each model. A CISSP should also understand the various steps that can be taken to prevent, detect, and respond to an attack.

- **NETWORK ATTACKS** – Are one of the most common threats faced by an organization today.

- **ATTACK TREES** – Security attacks are formally described as attack-tree models. Attack trees are based upon the goal of the attacker, the risk to the defender, and the vulnerabilities of the defense systems. They form a specialized form of decision tree that can be used to formally evaluate system security. The network security specialist should consider all possible routes that may lead to a successful attack – this is sometimes called misuse modeling as well, but the intention is to ensure that the entire range of possible attack avenues have been identified and addressed.

- **PATH OF LEAST RESISTANCE** – The methodology shown describes common steps that an attacker would take in order to successfully traverse the attack tree toward his or her target. The attacker's path may depend on the nature of the attacker. Is she or he opportunistic, or prepared? Is the goal to maximize damage, or to proceed with minimal impact until the attacker has the time and funds to proceed further? In many cases (depending on the motivation and purpose of the threat agent) the hacker will take the easiest route to the attack. The network security specialist may prevent many attacks just by making an attack too expensive, too time consuming, or too difficult.

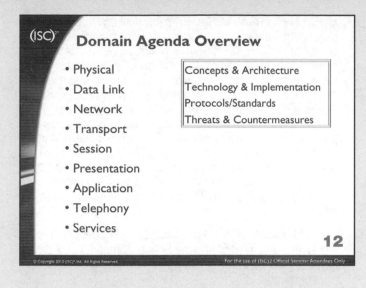

Domain Agenda Overview

- Physical
- Data Link
- Network
- Transport
- Session
- Presentation
- Application
- Telephony
- Services

Concepts & Architecture
Technology & Implementation
Protocols/Standards
Threats & Countermeasures

12

- Each section of this domain is divided by OSI layer and then by topic focus. A CISSP will address each layer and ask:

  - What concepts and architectures are present at this layer?

  - What technologies and implementations span this layer?

  - Are there protocols at this layer that are in use by the organization?

  - Are there controls in place to address the threats at this layer?

- A CISSP must understand each of these issues from the perspective of both the defender and an attacker. By taking on the role or mindset of an attacker, a CISSP can better defend his or her organization. The OSI model is universally accepted as a tool by which to organize information-technology concepts. This course is structured by the technical description offered by the OSI model, which gives a structure for designing security architecture identifying which areas of a network might be exposed to attacks and vulnerabilities. As protocol design does not always happen according to the OSI model, there will occasionally be ambiguity as to which layer to best map a protocol to, and consequently, whether a protocol or component is being addressed in the correct layer.

- The telephony and service sections have been added to highlight topics that do not fit neatly into the OSI model but are nonetheless very important to CISSPs.

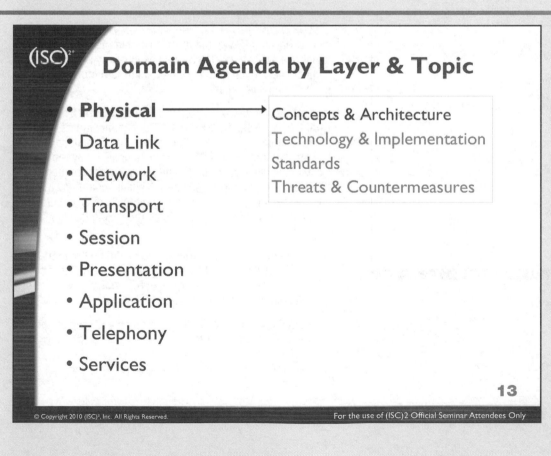

Domain Agenda by Layer & Topic

- **Physical** ———→ Concepts & Architecture
- Data Link
- Network
- Transport
- Session
- Presentation
- Application
- Telephony
- Services

Technology & Implementation
Standards
Threats & Countermeasures

13

- The concepts and architecture at the physical layer consist of analog and digital communications, as well as layout, or network topology.

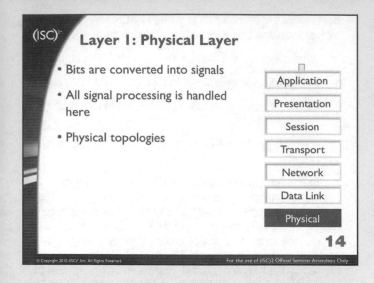

- **LAYER 1: PHYSICAL LAYER** – The physical layer describes the networking hardware, the format of the communications as electrical signals and bits, bytes, or optical pulses, as well as network interfaces and cabling. "Cabling" includes traditional cable, wireless connections, the network topology and layout of different networks and the different physical components that support this infrastructure. Although many types of hardware (such as cables, connectors, and modems) operate primarily at the physical layer, routers and switches operate at several layers, typically the network layer (for routers) and the data link layer (for switches). Not all hardware will be a Layer 1 device, nor do all signals need to be electrical: A signal can be anything from a flash of light to a number on a piece of paper.

- **BITS ARE CONVERTED INTO SIGNALS** – Bits from the data link layer are converted into the signals appropriate for the physical medium that will carry them, and transmitted on a physical circuit.

- **ALL SIGNAL PROCESSING IS HANDLED HERE** – Since signals depend on the transmitting media, all signal processing happens on this layer.

- **PHYSICAL TOPOLOGIES** – Are defined at this layer.

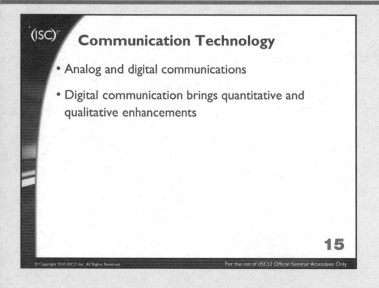

- **ANALOG AND DIGITAL COMMUNICATIONS** – Analog technology is widespread, even today. It is used in the public switched telephone network (PSTN) as well as in nearly all wireless technologies. Much of today's digital infrastructure is built upon analog components.

- **DIGITAL COMMUNICATIONS BRING QUANTITATIVE AND QUALITATIVE ENHANCEMENTS** – The enhancements from digital technology are a result of higher throughput capability (which in the case of DSL was accomplished by reusing existing analog infrastructure and removing the frequency filters and other restrictions used in analog communication), a better signal-to-noise ratio and fault tolerant error correction, and the ability to immediately process digital signals in a computer.

  - Packet switched networks would be difficult to implement using purely analog technology. The move to digital communication has opened the door to a whole new class of telecommunications networks.

  - Digital communication makes it much easier to do integrity checking and protection.

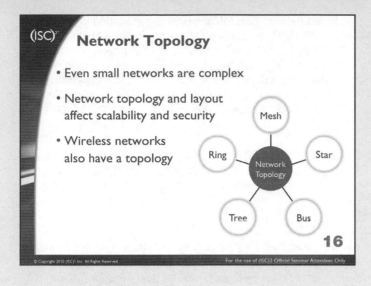

- **EVEN SMALL NETWORKS ARE COMPLEX** – The network topology defines which devices are crucial to network security, whether there are single points of failure (and consequently, whether controls are properly located).

- **NETWORK TOPOLOGY AND LAYOUT AFFECT SCALABILITY AND SECURITY** – Although the primary consideration at the physical layer typically has to do with physical parameters such as the layout of buildings or the distance between the areas that must be connected together, the topology and layout will also have an effect on scalability and security. The layout of the physical layer affects the higher layers (starting with the data link layer) and will determine how easy or hard it will be for the network operator to seal off parts of the network that have been compromised, or for an attacker to traverse the network. Most of these (except mesh and sometimes star) are broadcast-based which impacts authentication, integrity, and confidentiality.

- **WIRELESS NETWORKS ALSO HAVE A TOPOLOGY** – The topology of wireless networks becomes even more important as increasing numbers of office LANs become wireless. A peer-to-peer wireless network has the same characteristics as a mesh network.

REFERENCE:
http://www.ciscopress.com/articles/article.asp?p=25188&seqNum=3

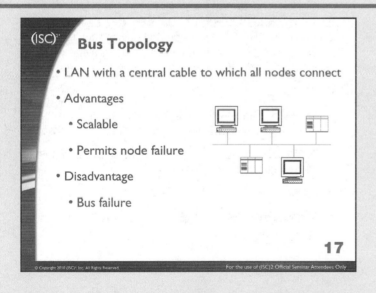

- **LAN WITH A CENTRAL CABLE (BUS) TO WHICH ALL NODES (DEVICES) CONNECT** – All nodes transmit directly on the central bus. Each node listens to all of the traffic on the bus and processes only the traffic that is addressed to it. This topology relies on the data link layer to determine when a node can transmit a frame on the bus without "colliding" with another frame that is already on the bus.

- **ADVANTAGES** –

  - **SCALABLE** – Adding and removing nodes from the bus is simple.

  - **PERMITS NODE FAILURE** – Failure of a single node will not affect the rest of the network.

- **DISADVANTAGE** –

  - **BUS FAILURE** – A bus failure will leave the network inoperable.

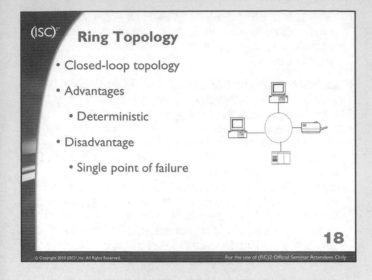

Ring Topology

- Closed-loop topology
- Advantages
  - Deterministic
- Disadvantage
  - Single point of failure

18

- **CLOSED-LOOP TOPOLOGY** – Data is transmitted in one direction on simple rings (though two-ringed infrastructures such as FDDI, or fiber distributed data interface, can transmit in both directions). Each device can only receive data from its upstream neighbor and can only transmit to its downstream neighbor. Rings typically use coaxial or fiber-optic cables. Rings can be used as a LAN or as a network backbone.

- **ADVANTAGES** -

  - **DETERMINISTIC** – Since rings use tokens to control traffic flow, the flow's transmission rate is stable and one can predict the maximum time that a node will have to wait before it can transmit.

- **DISADVANTAGE** –

  - **SINGLE POINT OF FAILURE** – Simple rings have a single point of failure. If one node fails, the entire ring fails. Some rings (such as FDDI) use dual rings for failover.

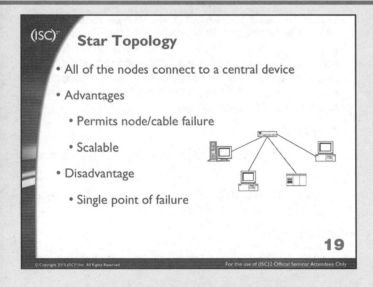

Star Topology

- All of the nodes connect to a central device
- Advantages
  - Permits node/cable failure
  - Scalable
- Disadvantage
  - Single point of failure

19

- **ALL OF THE NODES CONNECT TO A CENTRAL DEVICE** – Each node is connected directly to a central device such as a hub, switch, or router. Modern LANs usually employ a star topology because of considerations of scale and manageability.

- **ADVANTAGES** –

  - **PERMITS NODE/CABLE FAILURE** – The failure of a node, or cable to a node, will not affect the rest of the network.

  - **SCALABLE** – A star network is very flexible; it is simple to add or remove nodes as needed.

- **DISADVANTAGE** -

  - **SINGLE POINT OF FAILURE** – If the central device fails, the network fails.

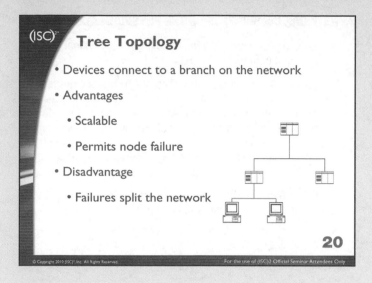

- **DEVICES CONNECT TO A BRANCH ON THE NETWORK –** Rather than to a central bus. Devices often connect through a switch.

- **ADVANTAGES –**

  - **SCALABLE –** Adding or removing a node is easy.

  - **PERMITS NODE FAILURE –** A node failure will not affect the rest of the network.

- **DISADVANTAGE –**

  - **FAILURES WILL SPLIT THE NETWORK –** A cable failure (or a switch failure, if the switch controls the connection to a branch) will "cut off" a branch of the tree causing loss of connectivity for all the nodes downstream from the point of failure.

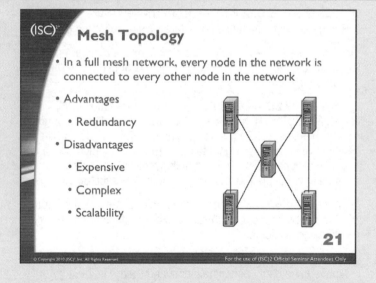

- **EVERY NODE IN THE NETWORK IS CONNECTED TO EVERY OTHER NODE IN THE NETWORK –** A full mesh network, however, is usually too expensive to run. A partial mesh can be employed instead, in which only selected nodes (typically the most critical) are connected in a full mesh and the remaining nodes are connected to a few devices. As an example, core switches, firewalls, routers, and their hot-standbys are often all connected to ensure as much availability as possible.

- **ADVANTAGES –**

  - **REDUNDANCY –** Mesh networks provide a high level of redundancy. The failure of any node or combination of nodes or cable links will not affect the operations of the remainder of the network.

  - Note: Another benefit of mesh is its lower latency (a full mesh has no latency due to intermediate nodes/routers).

- **DISADVANTAGES –**

  - **EXPENSIVE –** A lot of cable is required for a mesh network.

  - **COMPLEX –** It is complex to set up and administer.

  - **SCALABILITY –** Connecting new nodes or removing old ones is expensive and difficult.

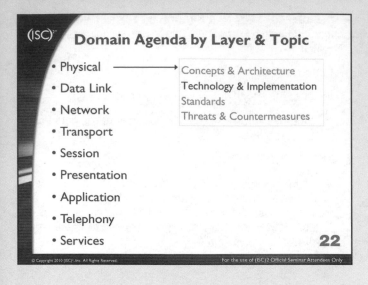

- **NETWORK COMPONENTS ON THE PHYSICAL LAYER ARE:**

  - **WIRED** – Choosing the best cabling for a physical network can be a complicated task.

  - **WIRELESS** – Wireless networks use frequency ranges and encryption and authentication technologies not commonly found on a wired network. Discussion of wireless networks might arguably have belonged in the data link layer. However, because they form the basis for the physical layer in the same fashion as a cable, they are covered here.

  - **EQUIPMENT** – There are various pieces of equipment used at this level, including hubs and patch panels.

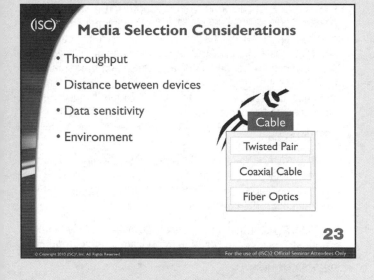

- **CABLE SELECTION CONSIDERATIONS** – Here are some parameters that should be considered when selecting cables:

- **THROUGHPUT** – The rate of data transmission. Fiber optic cables, for example, are designed for hauling an incredible amount of data at once.

- **DISTANCE BETWEEN DEVICES** – The degradation or loss of signal quality (attenuation) in long runs of cable is an ongoing problem, especially if the signal is at a high frequency. The time required for a signal to travel (the propagation delay) may also be a factor. A bus topology that uses collision detection may not operate correctly if the cable is too long.

- **DATA SENSITIVITY** – What is the risk of someone intercepting the data? Fiber optic cables, for example, make data interception very difficult.

- **ENVIRONMENT** – It's a cable-unfriendly world: Cables may have to be bent upon installation, and there can be a great deal of electromagnetic interference due to motors and older lighting ballasts as well. Cables in an environment with a lot of interference may have to be shielded, which increases the cost of installation.

REFERENCES:
http://www.ciscopress.com/articles/article.asp?p=102304
http://www.d-m.com/tutorial.htm

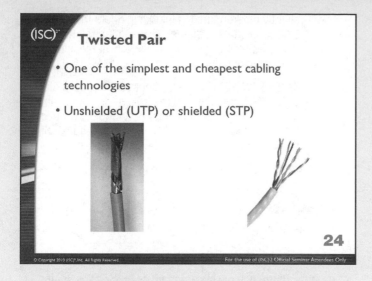

Twisted Pair

- One of the simplest and cheapest cabling technologies

- Unshielded (UTP) or shielded (STP)

24

- **ONE OF THE SIMPLEST AND CHEAPEST CABLING TECH-NOLOGIES** – Twisted pair has been a popular choice for many years, although it has significant drawbacks from a security perspective because it is easy to tap into and can be subject to various kinds of environmental stress.

- **UNSHIELDED (UTP) OR SHIELDED (STP)** – The choice will depend on whether the environment is subject to mechanical stress and electromagnetic interference.

- **UNSHIELDED (UTP)** – Pairs of copper wires are twisted together to reduce electromagnetic interference and crosstalk. Each wire is insulated with a fire-resistant material, such as Teflon. The twisted pairs are surrounded by an outer jacket that physically protects the wires. The quality of cable (and, therefore, the application for which it's appropriate) is determined by the number of twists per inch, the type of insulation, and the conductive material used. To intercept transmitted data, an intruder can install a tap on the cable or monitor the radiation from the wire. UTP may, therefore, not be a good choice for transmitting very sensitive data, or in an environment with excessive electromagnetic (EMI) or radio frequency interference (RFI). Despite its drawbacks, UTP is so commonly used that CAT-5 or CAT-5e cables are stocked in many grocery stores. UTP is inexpensive, can be easily bent during installation, and in most cases, the risk from the above drawbacks is not enough to justify the choice of more expensive cables.

- **SHIELDED (STP)** – Shielded twisted pairs are pairs of insulated twisted copper enclosed in a protective jacket. They are similar to UTP except that STP uses an electrically grounded shield that surrounds the bundle of twisted pairs, thereby protecting the electronic signals from outside interference and from eavesdropping by intruders.

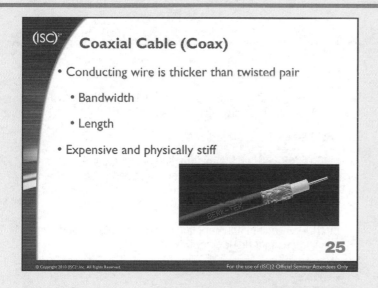

Coaxial Cable (Coax)

- Conducting wire is thicker than twisted pair

  - Bandwidth

  - Length

- Expensive and physically stiff

25

- **COAXIAL CABLE (COAX)** – Uses a central conductor that is surrounded by an insulator and then a grounding braid of wire.

- **CONDUCTING WIRE IS THICKER THAN TWISTED PAIR** – The conducting wire is much thicker than twisted pair and can, therefore, support greater bandwidth and longer cable lengths. The superior insulation protects coaxial cable from electronic interference such as EMI and RFI, and the shielding makes it harder for an intruder to monitor the signal with an antenna, or to install a tap.

- **EXPENSIVE AND PHYSICALLY STIFF** – The cable is expensive and mechanically "stiff." Coaxial cable is typically used for specialized applications such as cable TV.

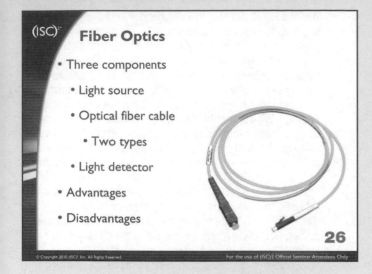

Fiber Optics

- Three components
  - Light source
  - Optical fiber cable
    - Two types
  - Light detector
- Advantages
- Disadvantages

26

- **THREE COMPONENTS –** Fiber optic cables consist of three components: a light source, an optical cable, and a light detector. They use glass or plastic fibers to transmit light. Optical fiber is made from a very thin glass or plastic fiber surrounded by a cladding designed to reflect transmitted light back into the fiber, and the cladding itself is further covered by a protective sheath.

  - **LIGHT SOURCES –** There are two types of light sources:

    - Light emitting diodes (LEDs).

    - Diode lasers.

  - **OPTICAL FIBER CABLE –**

    - **MULTIMODE FIBER –** Wherein light is transmitted in

slightly different modes (paths) in fibers that are about 50-100 microns in diameter. Due to the relatively large diameter, light disperses excessively in medium and long cable lengths.

  - **SINGLE MODE FIBER –** Is about 10 microns in diameter. As the name implies, the transmitted light will take a direct path down the center of the fiber. This allows for greater bandwidth and longer cable lengths. Single mode is suitable for carrier backbones.

- **LIGHT DETECTOR –** Converts the light signal back into an electrical signal.

- **ADVANTAGES –**

  - High bandwidth.

  - Immune to EMI and RFI.

  - Difficult (though possible) to tap, as fiber optics do not emit energy from the cable and wiretapping, therefore, requires physical manipulation, which makes it easier to detect.

- **DISADVANTAGES –**

  - Expensive.

  - Difficult to install.

REFERENCES:
http://www.cableorganizer.com/
http://www.corningcablesystems.com/web/college/fibertutorial.nsf/introfro#3
http://www.fiber-ed.com/fiberguide.htm

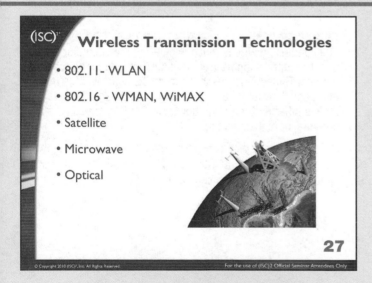

Wireless Transmission Technologies

- 802.11 - WLAN
- 802.16 - WMAN, WiMAX
- Satellite
- Microwave
- Optical

27

- **802.11 –** WLAN – From the wired network to station, wireless local area networks.

- **802.16 –** WMAN – From the neighborhood to station, wireless metropolitan area networks, or WiMAX®.

- **SATELLITE –** From orbit to station.

- **MICROWAVE –** High bandwidth, line of sight, point-to-point communications that require licensing. Used in two forms for communications: terrestrial (ground to ground) and satellite (ground to orbiter to ground).

- **OPTICAL –** High bandwidth, line of sight, point-to-point communications that do not require licensing.

REFERENCE:
http://computer.howstuffworks.com/wireless-network3.htm

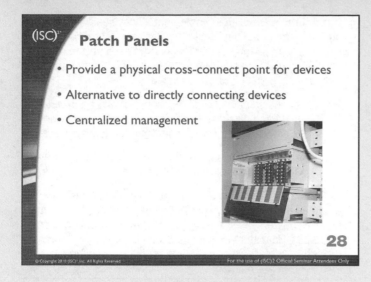

- PROVIDE A PHYSICAL CROSS-CONNECT POINT FOR DEVICES
– The advantage of a patch panel is that devices located in different places can be managed and connected at one central point, which permits the network manager to quickly make changes to the network configuration without running new cables. Anybody who has ever looked at a patch panel knows that they can be complex and require careful management. Managing a patch panel requires thorough mapping of connections; even moderately sized data centers have many interconnected devices such as switches, routers, servers, workstations, and even test equipment.

- ALTERNATIVE TO DIRECTLY CONNECTING DEVICES – Devices are connected to the patch panel and patch cables are then used to interconnect the devices. "Wireless" patch panels (panels without the connecting wires or patch cords) are also available.

- CENTRALIZED MANAGEMENT – Changes to the topology of the network can be made at a central location simply by moving the patch cables.

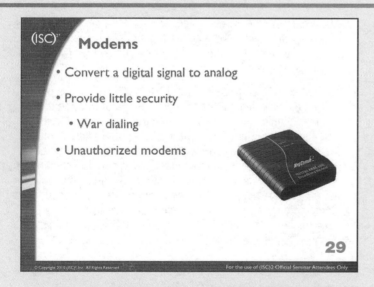

tials before network connections can be established. Three basic methods to restrict dial-up remote access are:

- RESTRICTED ACCESS – Wherein the modem only accepts incoming calls from locations on an approved list.

- CALLER ID – The modem checks each caller's telephone number against an approved list.

- CALLBACK – Wherein callers identify themselves (e.g., with passcodes or caller ID) and the server terminates the connection and calls the user back at a pre-determined phone number. (Note that this scheme does not usually require further authentication!)

- WAR DIALING – While modems allow legitimate users remote access to networks from almost anywhere, they can also be used as a portal into the network by an attacker. Using automated dialing software, an attacker can dial the entire range of phone numbers used by the company in order to identify lines connected to modems. If the host to which the modem is attached has a weak password, the attacker may be able to gain easy access to the network. Worse yet, if voice and data share the same network, both voice and data may be compromised.

- UNAUTHORIZED MODEMS – Illegitimate modems connected to a network are a special problem, and can be used for unauthorized inbound or outbound connections.

- CONVERT A DIGITAL SIGNAL TO ANALOG – A modem is a device that can both modulate and demodulate signals (and in fact the word "modem" is short for "MOdulate-DEModulate). Modems are connected to users' computers, and convert their digital signals into analog signals that can then be carried over a traditional phone line and vice versa.

- PROVIDE LITTLE SECURITY – Modems may use caller recognition to identify an incoming call, but require further credentials before network connections can be established. Three

Hubs and Repeaters

- Hubs
  - Used to implement a physical star/logical bus topology
  - All devices can read and potentially modify the traffic of other devices
- Repeaters
  - Allow greater distances between devices

30

- **HUBS** – Hubs are used to implement a "physical" star topology, since all of the devices in the star connect to the hub. Essentially, hubs retransmit signals from each port to all other ports. This makes a star-hub a "logical" bus type of topology. Hubs have significant disadvantages:

  - All connected devices will receive each other's broadcasts, potentially wasting valuable resources, processing irrelevant traffic, or exposing information to disclosure.

  - If the hub becomes inoperable, then the connected devices will not have access to each other or other networks.

- **REPEATERS** – As the distance between the sender and receiver increases, the signal's quality will degrade due to attenuation. Repeaters boost the signal, thereby allowing greater distances. Repeaters may be used on all types of networks, including wireless, fiber optic, and traditional cabling.

REFERENCES:

http://www2.edc.org/cope/networkprimer/primch5.pdf
http://www.ifs.com/Training/Network1/NetworkingWebinar1R1blue.swf

---

Wireless Access Points (WAPs)

- Access point (AP)
- Multiple input/multiple output (MIMO)

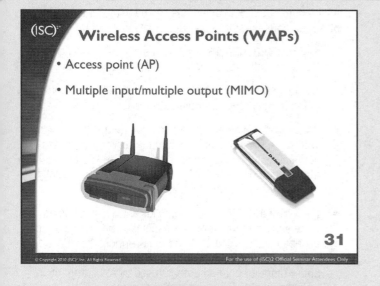

31

- **ACCESS POINTS** – Wireless access points are the points at which wireless signals are converted into wired signals, and signals are converted from one physical media type (radio waves) to another (typically copper).

- **MULTIPLE INPUT/MULTIPLE OUTPUT (MIMO)** – Access points started as a single input and single output, but through the use of technologies such as multiple frequencies and multiple antennas, MIMO (multiple input/multiple output) has increased the capacity of wireless networks to approach that of wired networks. MIMO uses multiple antennas at both the sending and receiving ends, and transmits different signals on each antenna. This avoids some of the interference experienced by single antenna units and increases performance and message quality. MIMO takes advantage of multipath signals as opposed to being hampered by them.

REFERENCE:

www.intel.com/support/wireless/sb/cs-025345.htm

IMAGE:

http://www.dlink.com/products/?pid=656 (Image of D-Link Dual Band N Wireless Adaptor)

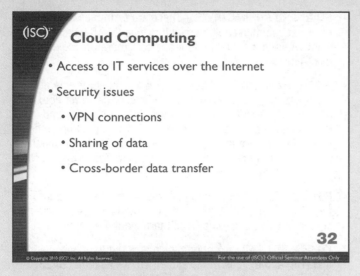

Cloud Computing

- Access to IT services over the Internet
- Security issues
  - VPN connections
  - Sharing of data
  - Cross-border data transfer

32

- **CLOUD COMPUTING** – Cloud computing is the provisioning of IT services over a cloud, the Internet. The term cloud is based on the depiction of the Internet as a cloud in many diagrams. Some of the services provided over the cloud are data storage, software, security, communications, etc. An organization can use Internet-based services for a large part of its IT infrastructure needs and just connect to services using minimal equipment and with very little local infrastructure.

- **SECURITY ISSUES** – Since the services are being provided by a third party, the issue of trust is a major concern. Most of the larger third parties (Amazon, Google, IBM, Symantec, etc.) offering services over the Internet have quite secure systems and are following best practices for remote access and data protection.

- **VPN CONNECTIONS** – Since data is being transmitted over an insecure channel (the Internet), it is important to ensure that secure VPNs are used for anyone accessing secure data or services via the cloud.

- **SHARING OF DATA** – Data is being stored at a third-party location. This is always a concern in the event that the third party is breached, suffers employee misuse, is served notice under a court order for release of information, or does not isolate data of one company adequately from another.

- **CROSS-BORDER DATA TRANSFER** – Cloud services are provided over the Internet and it may be a challenge to ensure that regulations regarding cross-border transmission of traffic are being followed. Many cloud services vendors provide separate services in various countries to address this.

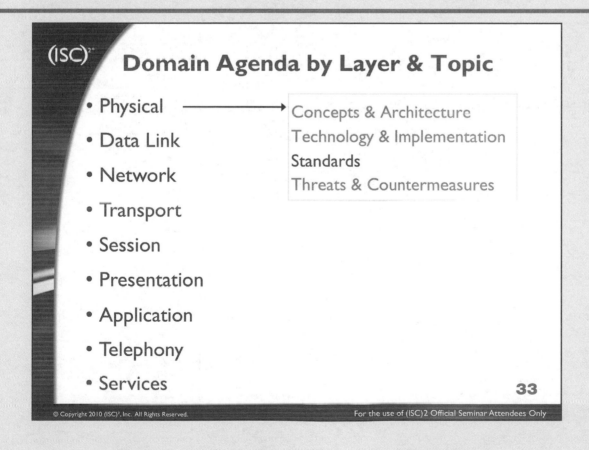

Domain Agenda by Layer & Topic

- Physical   ⟶   Concepts & Architecture
- Data Link   Technology & Implementation
- Network   Standards
- Transport   Threats & Countermeasures
- Session
- Presentation
- Application
- Telephony
- Services

33

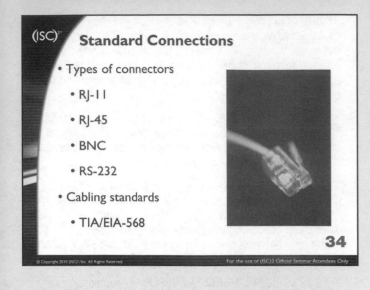

Standard Connections

- Types of connectors
  - RJ-11
  - RJ-45
  - BNC
  - RS-232
- Cabling standards
  - TIA/EIA-568

34

- **STANDARD CONNECTIONS** – These are examples of some of the most common cable connectors. The RJ-45 typically has eight wires to the RJ-11's four and can, therefore, connect more lines.

- **BNC** – The British Naval Connector is a connector between solid core copper segments. The solid core cable for coaxial is a standard RG-58 and RG-59. These different cables and the BNC connectors associated with them define the impedance: either 50 ohms for thin-net, or 75 ohms for cable television media. The original name for the connector was Bayonet Neill Concelman after the inventors.

- **RS-232** – Is used in computer serial ports. It is a standard for serial binary data signals connecting a DTE (data terminal equipment) to DCEs (data circuit terminating equipment).

- **TIA/EIA-568** – The Telecommunications Industry Association (TIA) and the Electronic Industries Association (EIA) 568 define: the maximum length of cable allowable to the patch panel or wiring closet, where and how cable should be run, and the wiring patterns for connectors and crossovers.

REFERENCE:
http://www.amphenolconnex.com/products/bnc.asp

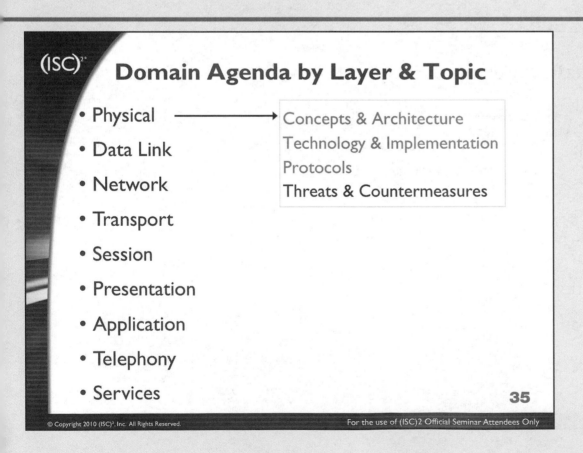

Domain Agenda by Layer & Topic

- Physical   →   Concepts & Architecture
- Data Link   Technology & Implementation
- Network   Protocols
- Transport   Threats & Countermeasures
- Session
- Presentation
- Application
- Telephony
- Services

35

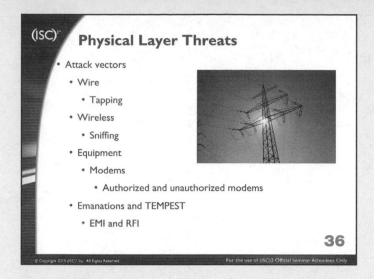

Physical Layer Threats

- Attack vectors
  - Wire
    - Tapping
  - Wireless
    - Sniffing
  - Equipment
    - Modems
      - Authorized and unauthorized modems
  - Emanations and TEMPEST
    - EMI and RFI

36

- **ATTACK VECTORS** – Adversaries will often try to attack physical security first. Once the physical layer is breached, it is very difficult for any other access control to successfully prevent access.

  - **WIRE** – Copper wire can be attacked by cutting, tapping, or TEMPEST (radio frequency (RF) emanations) collection.

  - Optical fiber cabling can be attacked by cutting and tapping.

- **WIRELESS** –
  - Both wired and wireless technologies are susceptible to sniffing (the collection of signals).

  - Wireless can be attacked by jamming, interception, or other forms of resource (e.g., bandwidth) exhaustion.

- **EQUIPMENT** – Equipment can be attacked because of weak authentication, by shutting down, or disturbing/degrading the signal, by reprogramming, and by tapping.

  - Unauthorized modems can be detected by scanning equipment, and threats can be reduced by disabling them, or by controlling access to dial tone services.

  - Authorized modems are susceptible to war dialing (a reconnaissance attack which will yield operating system, owner, or location information).

  - Outbound modem vulnerabilities such as caller ID spoofing coupled with call forwarding can be reduced with the use of authentication and hardware.

- **EMANATIONS AND TEMPEST** – Electromagnetic interference (EMI)/radio frequency interference (RFI) can be used to disturb/degrade the signal. This threat can be reduced by shielding.

REFERENCES:

http://www.simson.net/clips/academic/2001.Wardial.pdf
http://www.timberlinetechnologies.com/products/dialup.html

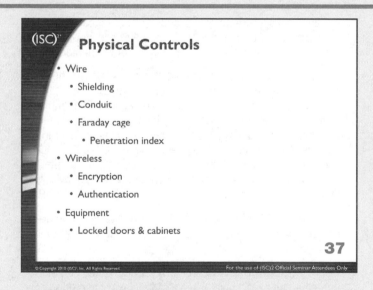

Physical Controls

- Wire
  - Shielding
  - Conduit
  - Faraday cage
    - Penetration index
- Wireless
  - Encryption
  - Authentication
- Equipment
  - Locked doors & cabinets

37

- **WIRE** – Controls over physical wiring include:

  - Shielding.

  - Using conduit to reduce the threat of cutting, or using pressurized conduit to detect a breach.

  - A Faraday cage (named for physicist Michael Faraday) is a device used to block or contain radio and electromagnetic signals. It generally consists of a thin sheet or mesh of conducting material enclosing a particular space. The conducting material redistributes electromagnetic fields along the surface of the cage, thus preventing external signals from penetrating, and blocking internal signals from leaking out of the enclosure. Faraday cages have a number of security related applications, including shielding buildings, and spaces, from unwanted data leakage, protecting resources against electrical damage, and shielding RFID-based technologies from leakage and eavesdropping. The effectiveness of a Faraday cage is a function of the type and the thickness of materials out of which it is constructed. (NOTE: Faraday cages are a physical control for wireless networks. Encryption and authentication are technical controls.)

    - The penetration index is the measurement of how strong a signal is depending on where signal strength is measured relative to the source. This is used to place sensitive processes into secure areas where a signal will not be strong enough to penetrate to the outside world.

- **WIRELESS** – Wireless signal controls include encryption and authentication.

- **EQUIPMENT** – Equipment should be placed behind locked doors, enclosed in cabinets, and shielded.

REFERENCES:

Engineering Electromagnetics, Nathan Ida, ISBN: 0387201564
http://www.phlink.com/Education/AskExperts/ae176.cfm

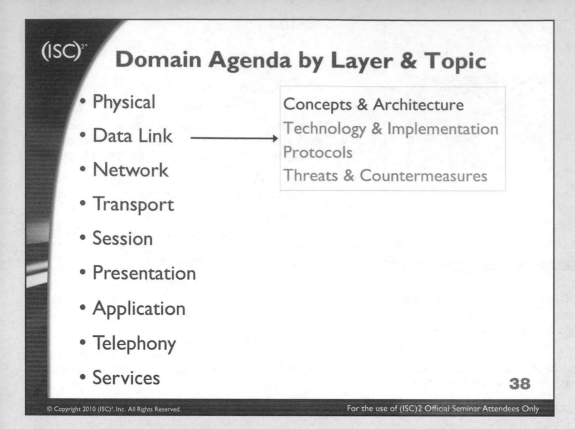

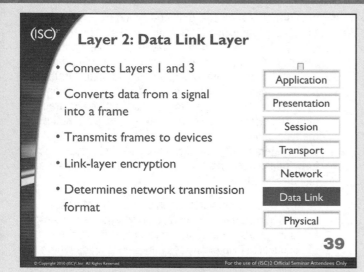

Ethernet's 48-bit hardware address is often called a "MAC address" as a reference to the name of this sub-layer. This is the portion that interfaces with the physical media.

- **CONVERTS DATA FROM A SIGNAL INTO A FRAME** – The data link layer prepares the packet that it receives from the network layer to be transmitted on the network. The data link layer ensures that the information that it exchanges with its peers is error-free. If the data link layer detects an error in a frame, it will request that its peer resends it. The data link layer converts information from the higher layers into bits in the format expected for each networking technology, e.g., Ethernet, token ring, etc.

- **TRANSMITS FRAMES TO DEVICES** – Using hardware addresses, this layer transmits frames to devices that are physically connected.

- **LINK-LAYER ENCRYPTION** – Link-layer encryption can be implemented at this layer. Note that link layer encryption only protects the information between two connected devices; to encrypt information between end-nodes using link layer encryption, the information must be decrypted and re-encrypted at each device along the path. The quality of the encryption of many of the intermediate devices may be out of the control of the owners of the two end-nodes.

- **DETERMINES NETWORK TRANSMISSION FORMAT** – The data link layer must know what type of physical medium it is connected to and must format the frames through fragmentation and reassemble accordingly, with attention to consequent limitations such as the maximum size of each frame.

- **CONNECTS LAYERS 1 AND 3** – The data link layer connects computers to physical networks and passes information between the physically adjacent devices. The OSI model is sometimes seen as too coarse on the lower layers. The Institute of Electrical and Electronics Engineers (IEEE), for example, defines the data link layer as divided into two sub-layers:

  - **LOGICAL LINK CONTROL (LLC)** – Manages connections between two peers, and provides error and flow control and control bit sequencing. This is the link that faces back toward the computer.

  - **MEDIA ACCESS CONTROL (MAC)** – Transmits and receives frames between peers. Logical topologies and hardware addresses are defined at this sub-layer. An

Local Architecture Security

- Perimeter-based security
  - The "egg" concept of security
    - Hardened outside defenses
    - Lack of internal defenses?
- Security domains
  - Internal layers of defense
  - Isolating networks within the organization

40

- **LAYERED SECURITY** – Network security, like most other security, must be layered with defense in depth and a series of hurdles or obstacles that the attacker would need to overcome in order to breach security.

- **PERIMETER-BASED SECURITY** – One of the early approaches to network security was to protect the perimeter of the network – to defend the gateways that allowed access in and out of the network. The internal network was often considered "trusted" and left relatively unprotected. The attackers were on the outside and all the attention was on keeping them out. This approach ignored the problem of the malicious insider. Today, defense must be both external and internal and layers of defense must be set up, starting with a very secure perimeter, but extending into every layer of the internal network right down to the component and end-equipment level.

- Provide controlled entry to and from network perimeters; in other words, use secure controls to interconnect networks at their perimeter entry points. The decision to permit or deny predefined traffic is done via ACLs. A boundary router, for example, can forward permitted traffic to and from secure gateways and networks. Boundary routers primarily control routes that external hosts can use to reach internal ones. However, they should also act as part of an organization's security perimeter by filtering external traffic that should not be allowed to enter the internal network. For example, boundary routers may prevent external packets from the finger service from entering the internal network (because finger service is used to gather information about hosts). A key function of perimeter security is the prevention of inbound or outbound IP spoofing attacks. If boundary routers are used, spoofed IP addresses wouldn't be routable across the network perimeter.

- **SECURITY DOMAINS** – As seen in the Security Architecture domain, it is wise to separate internal systems and networks from each other. This isolation helps prevent network overload through unnecessary data traversing network segments that it doesn't need to be on, protects sensitive information from being available to personnel who do not need access to it, and allows greater control and assurance of compliance for privacy.

  - **ISOLATING NETWORKS** – The isolation of networks can be done via virtual LANS (VLANs), switches, and geographic separation. Many military organizations also separate secret from unclassified networks and color code the cables and equipment to ensure that networks are not unwittingly cross-connected.

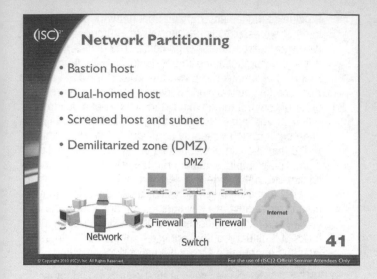

- **NETWORK PARTITIONING** – Segmenting networks into domains of trust is an effective way of enforcing security policies. Controlling what traffic is forwarded between segments will go a long way to protecting an organization's critical digital assets from malicious and unintentional harm. Network partitioning can be done with routers, firewalls, switches, VLANs, etc.

- **BASTION HOST** – A bastion host is a computer system that is usually located in a place on the network that is vulnerable to attack (usually because it is exposed to an untrusted network) and is, therefore, designed and configured to be highly secured. Bastion hosts serve as a gateway between a trusted and untrusted network, and, like a gatekeeper, serves to give limited access to authorized external users. For instance, a bastion host at an Internet gateway could allow external users to transfer files to it via the FTP protocol, which would permit files to be exchanged with external hosts without granting them access to the internal network. If an organization has a network segment that contains sensitive data, the organization can control access to the network segment by requiring

that all access be from the bastion host. In addition to isolating the network segment, the bastion host can be configured to force users to authenticate to the bastion host which will help audit access to the sensitive network segment. For example, if a firewall limits access to the sensitive network segment, then allowing access to the segment only from the bastion host will eliminate the need for allowing many hosts access to that segment.

- An application-level gateway is a type of "bastion host" because it is a designated system that is specifically armored and protected against attacks.

- **DUAL-HOMED HOST** – A dual-homed host is a host with two network connections, each on a separate network. Provided that the host controls or prevents the forwarding of traffic between networks, it can be an effective measure for isolating a network.

- **SCREENED HOST AND SUBNET** – Partitioning can also be called screening. A screened subnet is network partitioning along IP logical boundaries. Screening a subnet can be done as granularly as a single host.

- **DEMILITARIZED ZONE (DMZ)** – A demilitarized zone (DMZ), also known as a screened subnet, allows an organization to give external hosts limited access to public resources such as a company website without granting them access to the internal network. Typically, the DMZ is an isolated subnet attached to a firewall (when the firewall has three interfaces – internal, external, and DMZ, this configuration is sometimes called a three-legged firewall). Because external hosts by design have access to the DMZ (albeit controlled by the firewall), organizations should only place hosts and information that are not sensitive in the DMZ. DMZ networks function as a small and isolated network positioned between the untrusted network and the private network. Typically, systems on the untrusted network and some systems on the private network can access a limited number of services on the DMZ. Generally, an additional security device (such as firewall or router) provides access control from the trusted LAN to the DMZ.

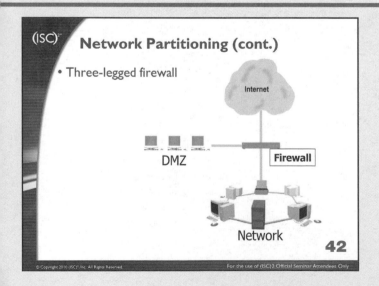

- **THREE-LEGGED FIREWALL** – A type of DMZ implementation. The firewall is configured with a third network interface, usually for the DMZ. The DMZ segment allows both internal and external users to access common servers. It does not allow external users to access non-DMZ resources.

  - **DISADVANTAGES –**

    - Single point of failure.

    - No defensive depth.

    - Often chosen for less cost and complexity – but managing firewall rules can be very complex. In the single device configuration shown here, the firewall should be made a stateful-inspection rather than a packet-filter device for additional security.

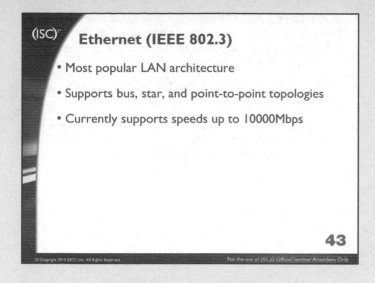

Ethernet (IEEE 802.3)

- Most popular LAN architecture

- Supports bus, star, and point-to-point topologies

- Currently supports speeds up to 10000Mbps

43

- **MOST POPULAR LAN ARCHITECTURE** – Ethernet, which is defined in the IEEE 802.3 standard, played a major role in the rapid proliferation of LANs in the 1980s. The architecture was flexible, relatively inexpensive, and it was easy to add and remove devices from the LAN. It is still the most popular LAN architecture. With the exception of full-duplex Ethernet, the architecture uses CSMA/CD. This protocol allows devices to transmit data with a minimum of overhead (compared with Token Ring), resulting in an efficient use of bandwidth. However, since devices must retransmit when more than one device attempts to send data on the medium, too many re-transmissions due to collisions can cause serious throughput degradation.

- **SUPPORTS BUS, STAR, AND POINT-TO-POINT TOPOLOGIES** – The physical topologies that are supported by Ethernet are the bus, star, and point-to-point, but the initial logical topology was a bus. The Ethernet standard supports coaxial cable, unshielded twisted pair, and fiber optics.

- **CURRENTLY SUPPORTS SPEEDS UP TO 10000 MBPS** – Ethernet was originally rated at 10Mbps. To meet the growing demand for more bandwidth, 100Base-TX (100Mbps over twisted pair) and 100Base-FX (100Mbps over multimode fiber optics) were defined. When the demand for bandwidth grew even further, 1000Base-T was defined for unshielded twisted pair, and 1000Base-SX and 1000Base-LX were defined for fiber optics. These standards support 1000Mbps. Today the standard is 10000 or 10Gig Ethernet.

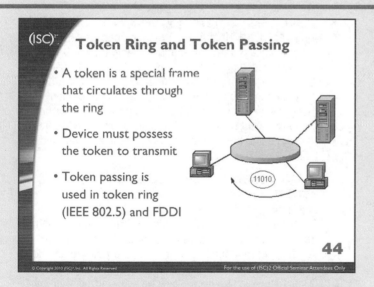

Token Ring and Token Passing

- A token is a special frame that circulates through the ring

- Device must possess the token to transmit

- Token passing is used in token ring (IEEE 802.5) and FDDI

11010

44

- **A TOKEN IS A SPECIAL FRAME THAT CIRCULATES THROUGH THE RING** – Token passing takes a more orderly approach to media access. With this access method, only one device may transmit on the LAN at a time, thus avoiding collisions and re-transmissions. Transmission control is provided by a "token" that circulates to all devices around the ring at a fixed rate of speed.

- **DEVICE MUST POSSESS THE TOKEN TO TRANSMIT** – Once in its possession, the device replaces the token with a frame containing the message to be transmitted, and sends the frame to its neighbor. As each device receives the frame it will relay it to its neighbor until the frame reaches the intended recipient. That device will copy the message, modify the frame

to signify that the message has been received, and transmit the frame on the network. Once the frame reaches its original sender, the sender will remove it.

- **TOKEN PASSING IS USED IN TOKEN RING (IEEE 802.5) AND FDDI** – FDDI is a token passing architecture that uses two rings. Because FDDI employs fiber optics, it was designed to be a 100Mbps network backbone. Only one ring (the primary) is used; the other one (secondary) is used as a backup. Information in the rings flows in opposite, or "counter-rotating," directions.

  - **DEVICES THAT ARE ON THE FDDI RING FALL INTO FOUR CATEGORIES:**

    - **SINGLE ATTACHMENT STATION (SAS)** – A device that connects to the primary ring only. These are not expected to remain online.

    - **SINGLE ATTACHMENT CONCENTRATOR (SAC)** – Used as a concentrator to connect SAS devices to the primary ring.

    - **DUAL ATTACHMENT STATION (DAS)** – A device that connects to both rings.

    - **DUAL ATTACHMENT CONCENTRATOR (DAC)** – A device that attaches devices to both rings. SAS, SAC, and DAS devices connect to this device.

REFERENCE:
http://www.wildpackets.com/support/compendium/token_ring/overview

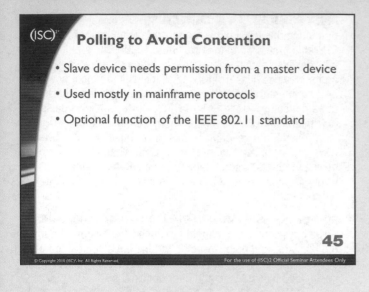

Polling to Avoid Contention

- Slave device needs permission from a master device
- Used mostly in mainframe protocols
- Optional function of the IEEE 802.11 standard

45

- **SLAVE DEVICE NEEDS PERMISSION FROM A MASTER DEVICE** – A network that employs polling avoids contention by allowing a device (a slave) to transmit on the network only when it is asked (polled) by a master device.

- **USED MOSTLY IN MAINFRAME PROTOCOLS** – Such as synchronous data link (SDLC).

- **OPTIONAL FUNCTION OF THE IEEE 802.11 STANDARD** – The point coordination function, an optional function of the IEEE 802.11 standard, uses polling as well.

Carrier Sense Multiple Access

- Only one device may transmit at a time
- There are two variations
  - Carrier sense multiple access with collision avoidance (CSMA/CA)
  - Carrier sense multiple access with collision detection (CSMA/CD)

46

- **ONLY ONE DEVICE MAY TRANSMIT AT A TIME** – When many devices are connected to a network, some form of control must be established to determine which device may transmit. Since there is not an inherent mechanism that determines transmission priority, all of the devices must compete for available bandwidth. CSMA is referred to as a **CONTENTION-BASED** architecture. CSMA is non-deterministic.

- **CARRIER SENSE MULTIPLE ACCESS WITH COLLISION AVOIDANCE (CSMA/CA)** – LANs using carrier sense multiple access with collision avoidance (CSMA/CA) require devices to announce their intention to transmit by broadcasting a jamming signal. When devices detect the jamming signal, they know not to transmit; otherwise there will be a collision. After sending the jamming signal, the device waits to ensure that all devices have received the signal and then broadcasts the frames on the media. 802.11 uses CSMA/CA.

- **CARRIER SENSE MULTIPLE ACCESS WITH COLLISION DETECTION (CSMA/CD)** – Devices on a LAN using carrier sense multiple access with collision detection (CSMA/CD) listen for a carrier before transmitting data. If another transmission is not detected, the data will be transmitted. It is possible for a station to transmit before another station's transmission has had enough time to propagate. If this happens, two frames will be transmitted simultaneously, and a collision will occur. Instead of all stations simply retransmitting their data (which will likely cause more collisions), each station will wait for a randomly generated interval of time before retransmitting. 802.3 uses CSMA/CD.

REFERENCE:
http://www.cs.ucdavis.edu/~aksoy/course/s06/Lectures/link(2.1).ppt

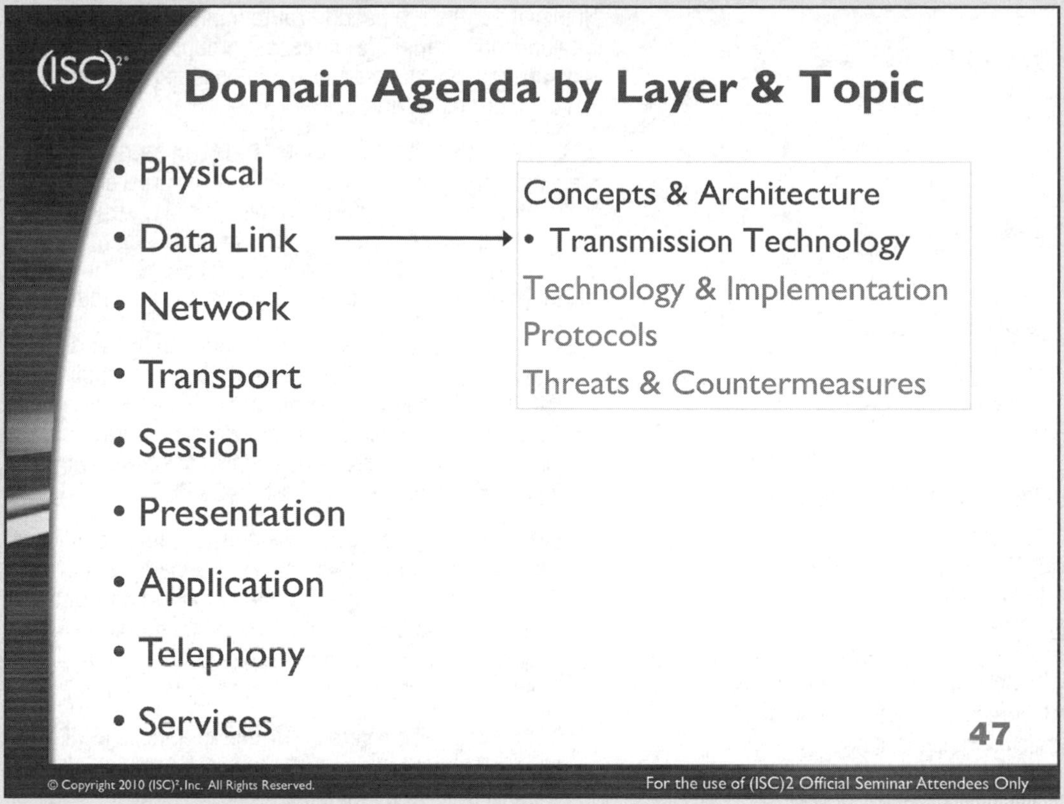

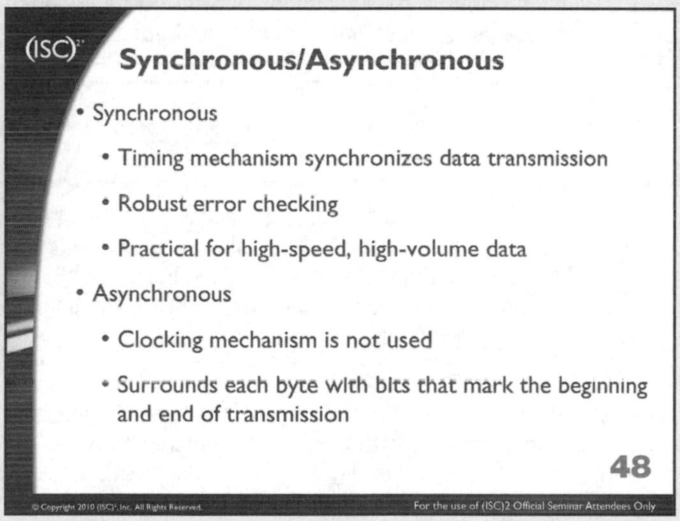

Domain Agenda by Layer & Topic

- Physical
- Data Link → Concepts & Architecture
  - • Transmission Technology
  - Technology & Implementation
  - Protocols
  - Threats & Countermeasures
- Network
- Transport
- Session
- Presentation
- Application
- Telephony
- Services

47

Synchronous/Asynchronous

- Synchronous
  - Timing mechanism synchronizes data transmission
  - Robust error checking
  - Practical for high-speed, high-volume data
- Asynchronous
  - Clocking mechanism is not used
  - Surrounds each byte with bits that mark the beginning and end of transmission

48

- **SYNCHRONOUS -**

  - **TIMING MECHANISM SYNCHRONIZES DATA TRANS-MISSION –** Synchronous communication uses a timing mechanism to synchronize the transmission of data between two devices. The communicating devices can use a clocking mechanism or the transmitting device can include timing information in the stream. When devices communicate synchronously, they transmit large frames of data which are accompanied by synchronizing bit pat-terns. This is much more efficient than the 3-bit overhead required for every byte in asynchronous transmissions.

  - **ROBUST ERROR CHECKING –** Error checking in synchro-nous communication is more robust than in asynchronous communication. For instance, the transmitting device can apply a cyclic redundancy checking (CRC) polynomial to a frame, and include the resulting value in the frame. CRC error checking will detect an erroneous transmission with high certainty.

  - **PRACTICAL FOR HIGH-SPEED, HIGH-VOLUME DATA –** Because of its minimal use of overhead, synchronous communication is much more practical for high-speed, high-volume data transfer than is asynchronous commu-nication.

  - **ASYNCHRONOUS –** In asynchronous communications, a clocking mechanism is not used. Instead, the sending device surrounds each byte with bits that mark the beginning and end of each byte as well as one bit for error control. For each byte, a start bit is sent to signal the start of a transmission. Next, the data byte is sent, followed by a parity bit (for error control), and then a stop bit to signal the end of transmission. Each byte, therefore, of data requires 3 bits of overhead. The receiving device strips off the overhead bits before sending the data up the communications stack. Modems and dumb terminals are examples of devices that use asynchronous communication.

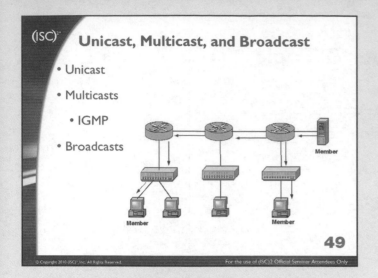

Unicast, Multicast, and Broadcast

- Unicast
- Multicasts
  - IGMP
- Broadcasts

49

© Copyright 2010 (ISC)², Inc. All Rights Reserved. For the use of (ISC)2 Official Seminar Attendees Only

- **UNICAST, MULTICAST, AND BROADCAST TRANSMISSIONS** – A transmission that is sent to one receiving host is called unicast, one that is sent to several is called a multicast, and for an unspecified number of hosts (for example, every device on a network) it is called a broadcast. Note that multicasts or broadcasts do not use reliable sessions, and there is, therefore, no guarantee of delivery with multicast or broadcast transmissions.

- **UNICAST** – Sending a message from one host to another.

- **MULTICASTS** – Are directed to a defined set of recipients. Public and private networks are being used more often than ever for streaming transmissions such as movies, videoconferences, and music. Unless there is a very small audience, unicast delivery is not practical because the multiple simultaneous copies of the large stream on the network at the same time can cause congestion. Delivery with broadcasts, on the other hand, would deliver to every host, whether or not it was interested in the stream. Multicast was designed to deliver a stream only to interested hosts.

- Multicast agents are used to route multicast traffic over networks and administer multicast groups. Each network and sub-network that supports multicasting must have at least one multicast agent.

- **INTERNET GROUP MANAGEMENT PROTOCOL (IGMP)** – Is used to manage multicasting groups, which are a set of hosts anywhere on a network that are interested in a particular multicast. Multicast agents are used to administer multicast groups. Hosts send IGMP messages to local agents to join and leave groups. There are three versions of the protocol:

  - **VERSION 1** – Multicast agents periodically send queries to hosts on their network to update their databases of multicast groups' membership. Hosts stagger their replies to prevent a storm of traffic to the agent. When a group ceases replying, agents will stop forwarding multicasts to that group.

  - **VERSION 2** – This version extends the functionality of version 1. It defines two types of queries: a general query to determine membership of all groups, and a group-specific query to determine the membership of a particular group. In addition, a member can notify all multicast routers that it wishes to leave a group.

  - **VERSION 3** – This version further enhances IGMP by allowing hosts to specify the sources from which they want to receive multicasts.

- **BROADCASTS** – Can have an unlimited number of recipients. A host can send a broadcast to everyone on its network or sub-network.

  - Because a single broadcast can result in hundreds or even thousands of packets on the network, intruders often leverage this to launch denial of service (DoS) attacks.

REFERENCE:
http://www.pms.ifi.lmu.de/mitarbeiter/ohlbach/multimedia/IT/IBMtutorial/3376c27.html

---

Circuit-Switched vs. Packet-Switched

- Circuit-switched
  - Dedicated circuit between endpoints
  - Endpoints have exclusive use of the circuit and its bandwidth
- Packet-switched
  - Data is divided into packets and transmitted on a shared network
  - Each packet can be independently routed on the network

50

© Copyright 2010 (ISC)², Inc. All Rights Reserved. For the use of (ISC)2 Official Seminar Attendees Only

- **CIRCUIT-SWITCHED** – Circuit-switched networks establish a dedicated circuit between endpoints. These circuits consist of dedicated switch connections. The endpoints have exclusive use of the circuit and its bandwidth. Neither endpoint will start communicating until the circuit is completely established. Carriers base the cost of using a circuit-switched network on the duration of the connection, which makes this

type of network cost-effective only for steady communication streams between the endpoints. Examples of circuit-switched networks are the traditional "plain old telephone service" (POTS), integrated services digital network (ISDN), and point-to-point protocol (PPP) leased lines.

- **PACKET-SWITCHED** – Packet-switched networks do not use a dedicated connection between endpoints. Instead, data is divided into packets and transmitted on a shared network. Networking devices will attempt to find the best path for each packet between its source and destination. Each packet contains meta-information so that it can be independently routed on the network. Since carriers base the cost of using a packet-switch network on the amount of data transmitted, such networks are appropriate for transmissions with significant idle time (i.e., **"BURSTY"** transmissions). Since each packet associated with a communication may travel a different path, the amount of latency (delay in processing associated with traversing the switches and routers) may vary. At some times the packets may arrive faster than others due to bandwidth availability. This variation in speeds causes jitter which is not really a problem with data, but can be a problem with streaming communications.

REFERENCE:
http://www.cisco.com/univercd/cc/td/doc/cisintwk/ito_doc/introwan.htm

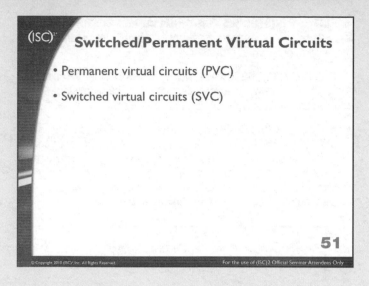

Switched/Permanent Virtual Circuits

- Permanent virtual circuits (PVC)
- Switched virtual circuits (SVC)

51

- **SWITCHED VS. PERMANENT VIRTUAL CIRCUITS** – Virtual circuits provide a connection between endpoints over high-bandwidth multiuser cable or fiber networks, which causes them to behave with similar performance characteristics (latency, bandwidth, routing) as if the circuit were a dedicated physical circuit.

- **PERMANENT VIRTUAL CIRCUITS** – The carrier configures the route to be used by the traffic through the packet-switched network when the circuit is purchased. Unless the carrier changes the routes to tune the network, respond to an outage, etc., routes will not change. Permanent virtual circuits thus have similar characteristics to circuit-switched networks.

- **SWITCHED VIRTUAL CIRCUITS** – The traffic routing is configured dynamically by the routers each time the circuit is used.

REFERENCE:

http://searchnetworking.techtarget.com/sDefinition/0,,sid7_gci214239,00.html

---

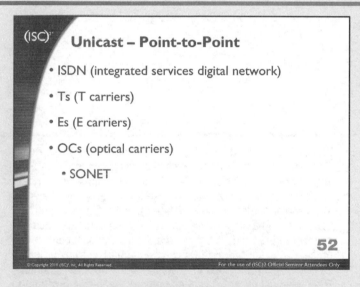

Unicast – Point-to-Point

- ISDN (integrated services digital network)
- Ts (T carriers)
- Es (E carriers)
- OCs (optical carriers)
  - SONET

52

- **ISDN** – Before the days of DSL and cable modems, users wanted remote access with higher bandwidth than dialup. ISDN provides such bandwidth by using a set of protocols and specialized equipment.

  - **TWO TYPES OF CHANNELS** – The B (bearer) channel for voice and data, and the "D" (delta) channel used for signaling and data.

  - **TWO VARIETIES** – BRI (basic rate interface) and PRI (primary rate interface). Some organizations use BRI ISDN as a low-cost backup for a leased line.

- **T CARRIER** – T1 carrier is a popular point-to-point communications method in North America and Japan. Using time division multiplexing, T1 multiplexes 24 channels over copper cable. In a 193-bit frame, each of the channels in a round robin transmits 8 bits (7 data and 1 control bit). One bit for synchronization is appended to the beginning of each frame.

  - Eight thousand T1 frames are transmitted every second, making the transmission rate 1.544 Mbit/s (8000 frames/sec x 193 bits/frame).

- Fractional T1 is available for organizations with a modest T1 budget. Customers may purchase fewer than 24 channels, which can be much less expensive than a full T1. Channels that are not purchased do not carry data.

- To meet the demand for more WAN bandwidth, multiple T1 channels are multiplexed into technologies with more throughput. In general, customers use T1 and T3. T3 refers to the basic speed of a fiber channel. Fractional T3 is available at a reduced cost for organizations that do not need all T3 channels. As with fractional T1, fractional T3 channels that are not purchased do not carry data.

- **"E" CARRIER** – Employs a similar concept as T-carrier. Using time division multiplexing, 30 channels take their turns transmitting 8 bits of data in a frame. E1 transmits at the same rate as T1 (8000 frames per second). The throughput for E1 is, therefore, 2.048Mbps.

- As with T-carrier, E1 channels are multiplexed into E-carrier technology with more bandwidth. Each successive E-carrier level contains four times as many channels as the previous one.

- Customers typically use E1 and E3, and fractional E-carrier lines are available for organizations that do not require the entire capacity of either.

- **OPTICAL CARRIER – T3; E3; SONET** – Optical carriers or OCs are specified optical speeds. Bandwidth is calculated in total Mbps and doesn't address overhead. Optical overhead using SONET is a constant 3.45 percent for any speed.

REFERENCES:

http://www.techfest.com/networking/wan/isdn.htm

http://www.mckerracher.org/isdn/

http://www.wildpackets.com/support/compendium/manual_appendices/nxT1_wan

X.25

- Suite of protocols for unreliable networks

- Has a strong focus on error correction

- Users and hosts connect through a packet-switched network

- Most organizations now opt for frame relay and ATM instead of X.25 for packet switching

53

- **SUITE OF PROTOCOLS FOR UNRELIABLE NETWORKS** – X.25 is a protocol developed for simple ("dumb") terminals and unreliable networks.

- **HAS A STRONG FOCUS ON ERROR CORRECTION** – Because networks were very unreliable when X.25 was developed, the protocol has a strong focus on error correction.

- **USERS AND HOSTS CONNECT THROUGH A PACKET-SWITCHED NETWORK** – X.25 allows users and hosts to connect through a modem to remote hosts via a packet-switched network. As with all packet-switched networks, the user's stream of data is subdivided into packets, and forwarded through the X.25 network to the destination host.

REFERENCE:
http://www.cisco.com/univercd/cc/td/doc/cisintwk/ito_doc/x25.htm

---

Frame Relay

- Network cloud of switches

- Customers share resources in the cloud

- The cloud is assumed to be reliable

- Customers are charged only for bandwidth used

54

- **NETWORK CLOUD OF SWITCHES** – The heart of a frame relay (FR) network is the FR cloud of switches on the carrier provider's premises. For example, a telephone company providing frame relay services would have frame relay switches in every major central office – all interconnected as a "cloud" of switches in a mesh-style network. Each customer would connect to the frame relay cloud at his or her local central office. Traffic sent from that customer would be transmitted as frames over the cloud of switches to the far end customer. As in a typical packet-switched network, each frame will find its way as seems best to it at the time of transmission. If the customers want a higher level of guaranteed service, they may purchase a permanent virtual circuit (PVC) to ensure that all their traffic follows a pre-defined path through the cloud of switches.

- **CUSTOMERS SHARE RESOURCES** – FR customers share resources in the cloud.

- **THE CLOUD IS ASSUMED TO BE RELIABLE** – The cloud does not require the error-correcting overhead of X.25 and because it is a mesh-style network, it has very high availability and is resistant to failure.

- **CUSTOMERS ARE CHARGED FOR USED BANDWIDTH ONLY** – Customers are billed according to their bandwidth usage.

REFERENCE:
http://www.cisco.com/en/US/tech/tk1330/tsd_technology_support_technical_reference_chapter09186a0080759833.html

Asynchronous Transfer Mode (ATM)

- ATM is connection-oriented
  - Uses virtual circuits
  - Guarantees QoS but not the delivery of cells
  - Types of virtual circuits

55

- **ATM IS CONNECTION-ORIENTED –** Asynchronous transfer mode (ATM) is a connection-oriented suite of protocols designed to transmit data, voice, and video over the same network at very high speeds (e.g., 155Mbps). This speed is made possible through the practice of fragmenting all data to flow over an ATM network into small, fixed-length 53-byte cells for all ATM traffic.

  - **USES VIRTUAL CIRCUITS –** Virtual circuits can be either permanent (virtual circuits remain active) or switched (virtual circuits are torn down after the connection is terminated).

  - **GUARANTEES QOS BUT NOT THE DELIVERY OF CELLS –** The ATM network guarantees certain performance characteristics such as bandwidth and availability, but it does not guarantee that every cell with be transmitted correctly.

  - **ALL VIRTUAL CIRCUITS ARE CLASSIFIED IN ONE OF THE FOLLOWING CATEGORIES –**

    - **CONSTANT BIT RATE (CBR) –** The circuit's cells are transmitted at a constant rate.

    - **VARIABLE BIT RATE (VBR) –** The circuit's cells are transmitted within a specified range. This is often used for "bursty" traffic.

    - **UNSPECIFIED BIT RATE (UBR) –** The circuit's cells "steal" bandwidth that is not being used by other circuits

    - **AVAILABLE BIT RATE (ABR) –** The circuit's throughput is adjusted based on feedback achieved by monitoring the available network bandwidth.

REFERENCE:
http://www.cisco.com/en/US/tech/tk39/tsd_technology_support_category_home.html

---

Multi-Protocol Label Switching (MPLS)

- Bandwidth management and scalability
- Permits traffic engineering
- Provides QoS and defense against network attacks
- Operates at Layers 2 and 3
- Operates over most other packet-switching technologies such as frame relay and ATM

56

- **BANDWIDTH MANAGEMENT AND SCALABILITY –** Multi-Protocol Label Switching (MPLS) provides bandwidth management and a scalable solution for network usage without the performance penalties of encryption.

- **PERMITS TRAFFIC ENGINEERING –** MPLS is an IETF-specified framework for the efficient routing and forwarding of traffic through a network to avoid congestion and obtain reliable performance.

- **PROVIDES QUALITY OF SERVICE (QOS) AND DEFENSE AGAINST NETWORK ATTACKS –** Traffic is routed with consistent performance by placing a label on each packet that will determine its priority and route through the network. This allows better transmission of higher priority traffic. It is important to note that MPLS does NOT encrypt traffic. If sensitive traffic is to be sent over an MPLS network, it must be encrypted before it enters the network.

- **OPERATES AT LAYERS 2 AND 3 –** MPLS operates with Layers 2 and 3. It is used with VPNs and over many of today's network technologies such as IP, frame relay, ATM, and Ethernet.

REFERENCE:
http://www.cisco.com/en/US/tech/tk436/tk428/tsd_technology_support_protocol_home.
  html http://www.iec.org/

Digital Subscriber Lines (DSL)

- Uses CAT-3 cables and the local telecom loop

  - Asymmetric digital subscriber line (ADSL)

  - Rate-adaptive DSL (RADSL)

  - Symmetric digital subscriber line (SDSL)

  - Very high bit-rate DSL (VDSL)

57

- **USES CAT-3 CABLES AND THE LOCAL TELECOM LOOP** – Telephone companies offer digital subscriber lines (DSL) that use CAT-3 cables and the local loop, in other words the line from the central office (CO) to the subscriber's home or office. The local loop is the weakest link of the PSTN but can support a relatively high transmission rate. Traditionally, all frequencies above 4 KHz are filtered to optimize the network for human speech. When the filter is removed from the line, the line has the capacity for frequencies as high as 1.1MHz, which is entirely adequate for the DSL's throughput needs.

- **DSL IMPLEMENTATIONS INCLUDE:**

  - **ASYMMETRIC DIGITAL SUBSCRIBER LINE (ADSL)** – Downstream transmission rates are much greater than upstream rates.

- **RATE-ADAPTIVE DSL (RADSL)** – The upstream transmission rate is automatically tuned depending on the quality of the line.

- **SYMMETRIC DIGITAL SUBSCRIBER LINE (SDSL)** – Uses the same transmission rate for upstream and downstream transmissions.

- **VERY HIGH BIT-RATE DSL (VDSL)** – Supports much higher transmission rates (e.g., 13Mbps downstream and 2Mbps upstream) than other DSL technologies.

- How does a home computer transmit at high speeds on a CAT-3 cable? The leading method is to use discrete multitone (DMT). The 1.1MHz bandwidth of the local loop is subdivided into 256 channels. Voice is transmitted over one channel; 250 channels are allocated for ADSL, and five unused channels help isolate ADSL and voice. Since downstream transmission is favored over upstream, many more channels are allocated for downstream. All channels are modulated by an ADSL modem before transmitting over the local loop. At the central office (CO), the ADSL channels are forwarded to a digital-subscriber-line access multiplexer (DSLAM), which demodulates the signal and sends the resulting bits to an ISP. DSL allows the users to remain connected to the Internet for much longer periods of time than would otherwise be possible. This is convenient for the user, but also increases the risk of attack. It is, therefore, imperative that PCs have a personal firewall, that vendor security patches are installed, and that dangerous and unused protocols are disabled.

REFERENCES:
http://electronics.howstuffworks.com/dsl.htm
http://www.pulsewan.com/data101/adsl_vdsl_basics.htm

Cable Modem

- PC Ethernet NIC connects to a cable modem

- Modem and head-end exchange cryptographic keys

- Cable modems increase the need to observe good security practices

58

- **CABLE MODEM** – Cable TV companies have physical networks direct to the home that allow cable providers to operate as ISPs and compete with telephone companies for interactive voice, video, and data services. Service speeds range from 256Kbps to 50Mbps.

- **PC ETHERNET NIC CONNECTS TO A CABLE MODEM** – The cable modem is a bridging device. Users connect their PC-Ethernet NICs to cable modems, which are connected via coaxial cable to the cable provider's network. As with DSL, cable modems allow home users to enjoy high-speed Internet connectivity.

- **MODEM AND HEAD-END EXCHANGE CRYPTOGRAPHIC KEYS** – Most major cable providers supply cable modems that comply with data-over-cable service interface specifications (DOCSIS), which helps ensure compatibility. To help protect the cable provider from piracy and its users from having data intercepted by other cable users, the modem and head-end exchange cryptographic keys. (Note: The head end is the core of the cable network.)

- **CABLE MODEMS INCREASE THE NEED TO OBSERVE GOOD SECURITY PRACTICES** – When a cable modem is powered on, it is assigned upstream and downstream channels. It then establishes timing parameters depending on how far it is from the head end. The cable modem then makes a dynamic host configuration protocol (DHCP) request for an IP address. Cable modem users must take the same precautions as DSL users by ensuring that PCs on the home network have a personal firewall, installing vendor security patches, and disabling dangerous and unused protocols.

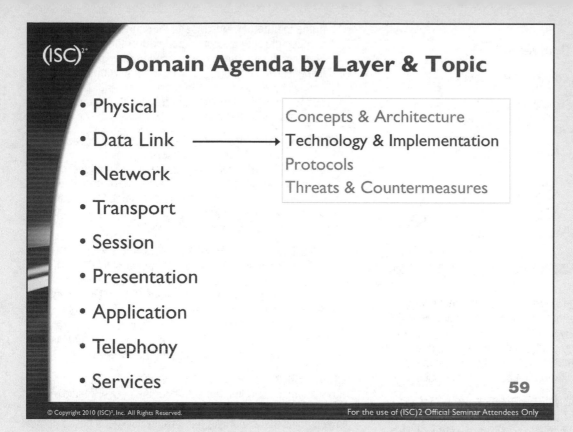

Domain Agenda by Layer & Topic

- Physical
- Data Link ⟶
- Network
- Transport
- Session
- Presentation
- Application
- Telephony
- Services

Concepts & Architecture
Technology & Implementation
Protocols
Threats & Countermeasures

59

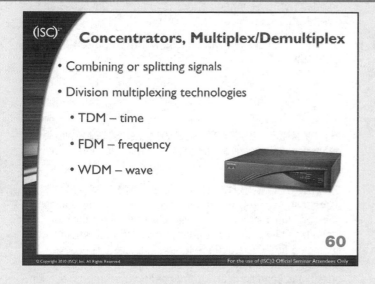

Concentrators, Multiplex/Demultiplex

- Combining or splitting signals
- Division multiplexing technologies
  - TDM – time
  - FDM – frequency
  - WDM – wave

60

- **CONCENTRATOR** – A concentrator combines channels together. This is often used to permit several remote access connections (SSL, IPSEC) to terminate on a network at the same time.

- **MULTIPLEX/DEMULTIPLEX** – Combining several signals into a single data stream is multiplexing. Splitting signals into data streams is demultiplexing. The division (or separation) of the signals being carried simultaneously can be done by time, frequency, or wave. Multiplexers are sometimes called concentrators. The technology name indicates the method used to multiplex the signals onto a common channel. For example, T1 systems multiplex 24 channels onto one pair of wires by giving each channel a separate time slice wherein it encapsulates the data it needs to send to the remote location.

IMAGE:

Image is of the CISCO 3000 VPN concentrator.

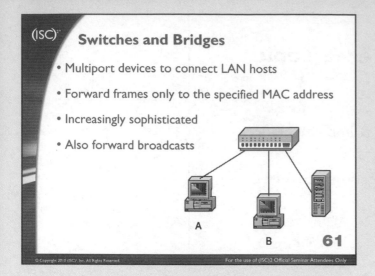

BRIDGES – While the use of bridges has been diminishing, their function has been incorporated into several higher-end devices, such as switches. As LANs grow in number of users, bandwidth utilization, and physical dimensions, they can reach thresholds that prevent them from further expansion. Bridges are one possible solution to both of these issues.

- **LAYER 2 DEVICES THAT FILTER TRAFFIC BETWEEN SEGMENTS BASED ON MAC ADDRESSES** – When a client PC on segment "A" transmits to a server on segment "A," the bridge will read the destination's MAC address and not forward the traffic to segments "B" and "C," thereby relieving them of unnecessary traffic.

- **CAN CONNECT LANS WITH UNLIKE MEDIA TYPES** – Bridges can connect LANs with unlike media types, such as a UTP segment with a segment that uses coaxial cable.

- **SIMPLE BRIDGES DO NOT REFORMAT FRAMES** – Bridges do not reformat frames, such as converting a token ring

frame to Ethernet. This means that only identical Layer-2 architectures can be connected with a simple bridge (i.e., Ethernet to Ethernet, etc.). Network administrators can use encapsulating bridges to connect dissimilar Layer-2 architectures, such as Ethernet to token ring. These bridges encapsulate incoming frames into frames of the destination's architecture.

- **SWITCHES** – Multiport devices to connect LAN hosts – Switches solve the same issues addressed by bridges in a different way. A basic switch is essentially a multiport device to which LAN hosts connect. Switches forward frames only to the device specified in the frame's destination MAC address, which greatly reduces unnecessary traffic. While a bridge connects networks, a switch connects hosts.

- **FORWARD FRAMES ONLY TO THE SPECIFIED MAC ADDRESS** – In this very simple LAN, client "A" transmits traffic to the server. When the switch receives the traffic, it relays it out the port to which the server is connected. Client "B" does not receive any of the traffic. Hubs, in contrast, would forward the traffic to client "B" as well. Note, however, that there are sophisticated attacks that can "trick" a switch (particularly if poorly configured) into sending traffic to client "B."

- **INCREASINGLY SOPHISTICATED** – Switches can perform more sophisticated functions to increase network bandwidth. Due to the increased processing speed of switches, there are now models that can make forwarding decisions based on IP address as well as prioritize types of network traffic (VoIP).

- **SECURITY MISCONCEPTIONS** – Switches do not, as many people incorrectly seem to think, provide confidentiality. Hackers can usually get around switches and monitor traffic on other ports. A common attack is to poison the cache and divert traffic in an unauthorized manner.

- Note that like hubs and bridges, **SWITCHES FORWARD BROADCASTS**.

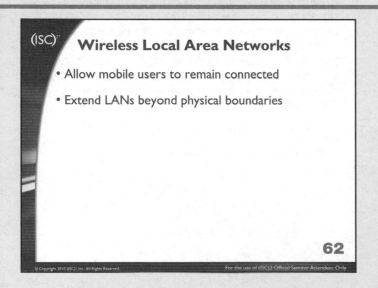

- **ALLOW MOBILE USERS TO REMAIN CONNECTED** – Wireless networks allow users to be mobile while remaining connected to a LAN.

- **EXTEND LANS BEYOND PHYSICAL BOUNDARIES** – Allow users to move freely within the range of the wireless access point and still maintain a connection. This solves the challenge faced by a physical Ethernet network that requires a cable and firm connection to maintain access. This does, however, present new security challenges in that it can be possible to connect to an internal network even from outside the physical building.

REFERENCES:

http://www.usr.com/education/net10.asp

http://cob.jmu.edu/choiyb/FALL%202004%20IT%20320/N5C05-PPT.ppt

http://searchsecurity.techtarget.com/loginMembersOnly/1,289498,sid14_gci1167653,00.html

http://searchsecurity.techtarget.com/general/0,295582,sid14_gci1169448,00.html?track=wsland2

Wireless Standards: IEEE 802.11

- 802.11b
- 802.11a
- 802.11g
- 802.11n (multiple input/multiple output)
- 802.11i (security)
- 802.16 (WiMAX)
- 802.15 (Bluetooth)
- Wireless multiplexing
  - OFDM/DSSS/FHSS (AFH)

63

- **802.11B** – This amendment to IEEE 802.11 was ratified in 1999. It continued the usage of CSMA/CA and direct sequence spread-spectrum (DSSS). The bandwidth was increased to 5.5Mbps and 11Mbps, and continued to support the original 1 and 2Mbps rates. There are 14 transmission channels in the 2.4GHz band, each 5MHz wide. Channel 14 is only used in Japan, and some countries limit usage to 11 bands. Use of DSSS ensured that transmissions were resilient to interference due to the number of "chips" used per broadcasted bit.

- **802.11A** – IEEE 802.11a was ratified in 1999. Since the 2.4GHz band specified in IEEE 802.11b was overused, resulting in increased problems from interference, this amendment offered the 5GHz band. IEEE 802.11a is not compatible with IEEE 802.11b. The higher frequency has the disadvantage of requiring more access points because the range is significantly reduced. This amendment employs orthogonal frequency-division multiplexing (OFDM), using 20MHz channels subdivided into 52 sub-carriers (48 are used for data). The maximum transmission speed is 54Mbps.

- **802.11G** – This standard was ratified in 2003 and combines the frequency band of 802.11b (2.4GHz) with the increased speed of 802.11a (54Mbps). IEEE 802.11g is fully compatible with IEEE 802.11b. Cards are available to compensate for the incompatibility of some of the standards. Both IEEE 802.11g and IEEE 802.11b are very popular.

- **802.11N (MULTIPLE INPUT/MULTIPLE OUTPUT)** – (MIMO) multiple input multiple output allows for more radios in a single form factor and greater range and throughput for the station's connection to the wired segment.

- **802.11I (SECURITY)** – Is the sixth amendment to the IEEE 802.11 (wireless) standard to add enhanced security features to support AIC. It has now been incorporated in the latest (2007) revision and is built into the 802.11 standard as the concept of RSN (robust security network). 802.11i was designed to address the shortcomings of WEP and WPA in securing wireless between the AP and endpoint (STA). 802.11i is based on the newer AES encryption algorithm, whereas the previous WEP and WPA used RC4. 802.11i is the recommended solution for wireless security. It is generally accepted that pre-RSNA technologies (such as WEP and WPA) do not offer sufficient security, meaning these should only be used either during migrations to an RSN or to support legacy devices that are not 802.11i/RSN-capable.

- **802.16 (WIMAX)** – This standard is for the last mile between

wired carriers and the customer. The commercial name for 802.16 is World Interoperability for Microwave Access (WiMAX®).

- **802.15 (BLUETOOTH)** – Bluetooth allows Bluetooth-enabled devices to communicate over a short distance without wires. The convenience of wireless exchange of information, cell phone earpieces without cables, etc., has become very popular. Today, Bluetooth technology can be found in electronics such as cell phones, PDAs, and laptops. In fact, the IEEE has adapted Bluetooth in the IEEE 802.15 standard. Unfortunately, the technology's security features are inadequate and to make matters worse, far too many owners of Bluetooth devices are unaware of the technology's vulnerabilities. Bluetooth devices are designed to communicate over a distance of 10 meters (30 feet), but longer ranges are possible. Class 1 Bluetooth devices contain a 100mW transmitter and have been known to bridge distances of up to one kilometer. Devices transmit at the 2.4GHz band using frequency hopping spread spectrum (FHSS).

- Attacks against Bluetooth are possible, since it does not have any cryptographic integrity protection. It has a proprietary encryption process, and a rather weak pairing authentication. Common attacks include:

  - **BLUE JACKING** – Allows an anonymous message to be displayed on the victim's device.

  - **BUFFER OVERFLOW** – An attacker can remotely exploit bugs in software on Bluetooth-enabled devices.

  - **BLUE BUG ATTACK** – An attacker can use the victim's cell phone to initiate calls.

- **WIRELESS MULTIPLEXING** – Is the ability to send many signals over the same media. WLAN offers three main options:

  - **DIRECT SEQUENCE SPREAD SPECTRUM (DSSS)** – Is a wireless technology that spreads transmissions over a larger frequency band, resulting in smaller amplitudes. The signal is consequently less susceptible to interference at any specific frequency. A pseudo-random noise code (PN code) is modulated with the signal during transmission. The sender and receiver's PN code generators are synchronized so that the PN code can be filtered out.

  - **FREQUENCY HOPPING SPREAD SPECTRUM (FHSS)** – Is a wireless technology that spreads its signal over rapidly changing frequencies. Each available frequency band is subdivided into sub-frequencies. Signals rapidly change ("hop") among these in a pre-determined order. Interference at a specific frequency will only affect the signal during that short interval. FHSS can, however, cause interference with adjacent DSSS systems. A sub-type of FHSS used in Bluetooth is adaptive frequency hopping spread spectrum (AFH)

  - **ORTHOGONAL FREQUENCY DIVISION MULTIPLEXING (OFDM)** – Is a signal that is subdivided into sub-frequencies bands. Each of these bands is manipulated so that they can be broadcast together without interfering with each other. The basic principle of OFDM is to split a high bandwidth transmission into several "slower" low bandwidth transmissions.

REFERENCES:

http://authors.phptr.com/tanenbaumcn4/samples/section04_04.pdf

http://www.wlana.org/pdf/highspeed.pdf

http://standards.ieee.org/getieee802/

- **PARAMOUNT TO THE SECURITY OF WIRELESS LANS** – Authentication is paramount to the security of wireless LANs. It is nearly impossible for an organization to hide its access points' signal from unauthorized users. Authentication should be the first line of defense. Several methods exist, starting from delegating authentication to higher layers (i.e., no authentication).

- **SERVICE SET IDENTIFIER (SSID)** – The SSID is the "name" given to the wireless access point. It is shipped with a default name that should be changed by the administrator. The WAP will usually be set to broadcast its SSID. This makes it easy for the person attempting to associate with a WAP to know which access points are available in the vicinity. Some admins prefer to turn off the SSID broadcast hoping that will provide a little more security.

- **OPEN SYSTEMS AUTHENTICATION (OSA)** – OSA is the most basic form of wireless authentication. The wireless client sends an encrypted frame containing its SSID to the access point. Upon successful authentication (matching SSIDs), the client is associated with the wireless LAN. The SSID is defined in IEEE 802.11 as the identification for the wireless LAN, not as an authentication mechanism. Wireless client cards can broadcast a probe to ask wireless LANs that receive the probe to respond with their SSID. Not broadcasting an SSID provides obscurity but not security. Notably, while OSA is called an authentication method it does not, in fact, provide any authentication at all. Using SSID for authentication is about as

secure as using a phone number to identify a caller. As a general precaution, one should not use SSIDs that can be easily identified. However, this is an obscurity measure, not one that provides security.

- **SHARED KEY AUTHENTICATION** – In shared key authentication, WEP is used to encrypt a shared secret between the access point and wireless client. Possession of the shared secret is proven in a challenge-response scheme. There is a serious flaw with the implementation of shared key authentication in WEP. An attacker can intercept the challenge and response, and recover the key stream. After the client identifies its MAC address to the access point, the access point responds with a frame containing a randomly generated challenge using the WEP key stream generator. The client responds with the challenge encrypted with WEP. If the access point decrypts the challenge and it is the same as the one that it sent to the client, the client is authenticated. The flaw in WEP is based on the use of exclusive ors (XORs) in the authentication.

- **MAC ADDRESS FILTERING** – Similar to SSID, a MAC address is an identifier, not an authentication token. Authenticating based on a MAC address is not very effective as it is very easy to spoof a MAC address.

- **EXTENSIBLE AUTHENTICATION PROTOCOL (EAP)** – EAP is defined in the IEEE 802.1X authentication framework. Supported authentication methods include:

  - **EAP-TLS (EAP, TRANSPORT LAYER SECURITY)** – Both the client and authentication server mutually authenticate over a TLS session with digital certificates. However, administrative overhead is increased.

  - **EAP-TTLS (EAP, TUNNELED TLS)** – Like EAP-TLS, digital certificates are used. However, to establish an encrypted tunnel, the authentication server only presents a certificate to the client. EAP-TTLS is easier to administrate than EAP-TLS, but the less robust client authentication makes EAP-TTLS less secure.

  - **EAP-PEAP (EAP, PROTECTED EAP)** – EAP-PEAP is similar to EAP-TLS. To establish an encrypted tunnel, the authentication server authenticates to the client with a digital certificate, and the client employs a non-digital certificate mechanism to authenticate to the server. EAP-PEAP is easier to administrate than EAP-TLS, but the lack of a client-side certificate makes it less secure than EAP-TLS.

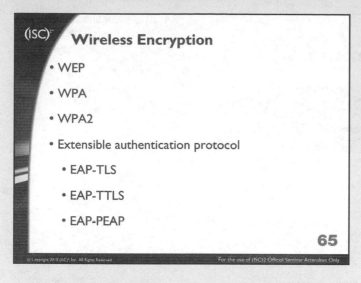

Wireless Encryption

- WEP

- WPA

- WPA2

- Extensible authentication protocol

  - EAP-TLS

  - EAP-TTLS

  - EAP-PEAP

65

- **WIRELESS ENCRYPTION** – Wireless signals transmit through the air and are easily subject to sniffing or modification. Several encryption techniques have been developed to protect wireless signals.

- **WIRED EQUIVALENT PRIVACY (WEP)** –

  - Wired equivalent privacy uses a shared secret between the client and access point.

  - WEP can now be cracked in three to 30 seconds with minimal tools and knowledge.

- **WI-FI PROTECTED ACCESS (WPA)** –

  - WPA was published as a stopgap measure after the weaknesses in WEP had become public and before publication of IEEE 802.11i.

  - WPA uses an improved implementation of RC4 with 128-bit keys. The initialization vector was expanded from 24 to 48 bits. WPA uses TKIP (temporal key integrity protocol) using a different key for each packet. Attacks against TKIP were published in late 2008.

  - WEP's CRC-32 checksum was replaced with a message integrity check, dubbed "Michael." Michael protects the packet's header and data and uses a frame counter to thwart replay attacks.

  - Another advantage of WPA is mutual authentication (i.e., both the client and network authenticate each other).

- **WI-FI PROTECTED ACCESS 2 (WPA2)** –

  - WPA2 is FIPS 140-2 compliant and implements the final IEEE 802.11i amendment to the 802.11 standard (as opposed to WPA, which only implements a subset of IEEE 802.11i).

  - RC4 was replaced by AES (advanced encryption standard), a stronger encryption algorithm. TKIP and Michael were replaced by CCMP (counter-mode/CBC-MAC protocol), which manages encryption keys and message integrity.

  - WPA2 supports IEEE 802.1X authentication, based on the extensible authentication protocol (EAP) framework. Instead of limiting the authentication to methods that may not be appropriate, the framework allows the authenticating partners to negotiate the authentication method during the authentication phase.

- **EXTENSIBLE AUTHENTICATION PROTOCOL (EAP)** – EAP is defined in the IEEE 802.1X authentication framework. Supported authentication methods include:

  - **EAP-TLS (EAP, TRANSPORT LAYER SECURITY)** – Both the client and authentication server mutually authenticate over a TLS session with digital certificates. However, administrative overhead is increased.

  - **EAP-TTLS (EAP, TUNNELED TLS)** – Like EAP-TLS, digital certificates are used. However, to establish an encrypted tunnel, the authentication server only presents a certificate to the client. EAP-TTLS is easier to administrate than EAP-TLS, but the less robust client authentication makes EAP-TTLS less secure.

  - **EAP-PEAP (EAP, PROTECTED EAP)** – EAP-PEAP is similar to EAP-TLS. To establish an encrypted tunnel, the authentication server authenticates to the client with a digital certificate, and the client employs a non-digital certificate mechanism to authenticate to the server. EAP-PEAP is easier to administrate than EAP-TLS, but the lack of a client-side certificate makes it less secure than EAP-TLS.

Wireless Encryption Summary

	802.1x Dynamic WEP	Wi-Fi Protected Access	Wi-Fi Protected Access 2
Access Control	802.1X	802.1X or Pre-Shared Key	802.1X or Pre-Shared Key
Authentication	EAP methods	EAP methods or Pre-Shared Key	EAP methods or Pre-Shared Key
Encryption	WEP	TKIP (RC4)	CCMP (AES Counter Mode)
Integrity	None	Michael MIC	CCMP (AES CBC-MAC)

66

- This table shows some of the characteristics of wireless encryption methods.

Domain Agenda by Layer & Topic

- Physical
- Data Link $\longrightarrow$
- Network
- Transport
- Session
- Presentation
- Application
- Telephony
- Services

Concepts & Architecture
Technology & Implementation
Protocols
Threats & Controls

67

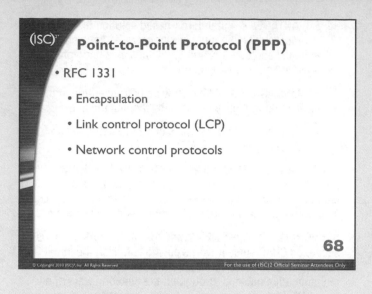

- **POINT-TO-POINT PROTOCOL** – The following is quoted directly from the RFC 1331:

  - The Point-to-Point Protocol (PPP) provides a standard method of encapsulating Network Layer protocol information over point-to-point links. PPP also defines an extensible Link Control Protocol, which allows negotiation of an Authentication Protocol for authenticating its peer before allowing Network Layer protocols to transmit over the link.

  - PPP is composed of three main components:

    - A method for encapsulating datagrams over serial links

    - A Link Control Protocol (LCP) for establishing, configuring, and testing the data-link connection

    - A family of Network Control Protocols (NCPs) for establishing and configuring different network-layer protocols.

  - The two authentication protocols for PPP are PAP and CHAP.

REFERENCE:

http://tools.ietf.org/html/rfc1331

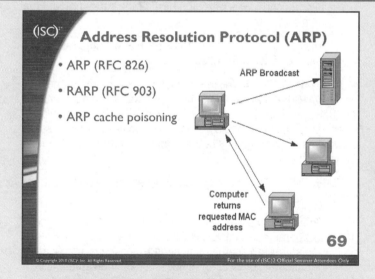

device's address, ARP first looks in its cache to see if the MAC address is already known. If it isn't, ARP sends out a broadcast asking all devices who know the answer to return the MAC address. The returned MAC address is added to the cache. Since ARP does not require authentication, an attacker could place bogus entries in the ARP cache (cache poisoning), to carry out a man-in-the-middle attack.

- **ARP (RFC 826)** – Is a generic address-resolution protocol, and was designed to be able to convert any network protocol address to any data-link address. Its use today is normally directed at resolving 802.x addresses to IP addresses.

- **RARP (RFC 903)** – Is used to map a device's IP address to its MAC address. It is sometimes used by diskless workstations to learn their own IP address.

- **ARP CACHE POISONING** – If a valid request is answered by an invalid authority, the client will rely upon the false data. If the valid answer arrives after the invalid answer, it will be too late. The table, or cache, stores entries locally on the client. Client resolution paths for MAC to IP are both permanent and temporary files on the system. If an adversary can put incorrect values in the file, adversaries can redirect the client to an inappropriate server. Since ARP is only for the local segment, the adversary must be resolving only locally compromised resources.

- **ADDRESS RESOLUTION PROTOCOL** – It is important to understand the risks of ARP, since ARP messages can be misused to misconfigure networks. The contents of the protocol responses are implicitly trusted by the receiving stations, making it easy for the "bad guys" to misuse this protocol.

  - ARP is used to resolve a Layer-3 IP address of a device with the device's Layer-2 MAC address. ARP tracks IP addresses and their corresponding MAC address in a dynamic table called an ARP cache. To determine a

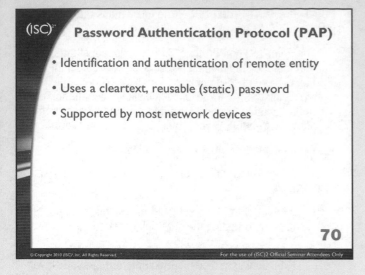

Password Authentication Protocol (PAP)

- Identification and authentication of remote entity
- Uses a cleartext, reusable (static) password
- Supported by most network devices

70

- **IDENTIFICATION AND AUTHENTICATION OF REMOTE ENTITY** – PAP (password authentication protocol, RFC 1334) – PAP is a simple, standards-based password protocol. A user's ID and password are transmitted at the beginning of an incoming call and then validated by the receiving equipment using a central PAP database. The PAP password database is encrypted, but PAP does not encrypt the user ID or password on the transmission line.

- **ADVANTAGES** – A standards-based solution that provides interoperability in a multivendor network, inexpensive to install and operate, and the database is encrypted to prevent password snooping.

- **DISADVANTAGES** – The password is transmitted in the clear, making it easy to snoop by tapping the line.
  - The reply is either an ACK or an NAK. There is no replay protection in PAP.

- **USES A CLEARTEXT, REUSABLE (STATIC) PASSWORD** – PAP provides node authentication using a cleartext, reusable (static) password. This makes it vulnerable to replay attacks. A compromised password will permit unauthorized access.

- **SUPPORTED BY MOST NETWORK DEVICES** – PAP is not as secure as CHAP, since it works only to establish the initial link. PAP is also more vulnerable to attack because it sends authentication packets throughout the network. Nevertheless, PAP is commonly used to log into remote hosts such as Internet service providers (ISPs).

REFERENCE:
http://h20331.www2.hp.com/Hpsub/downloads/WWAN-Security.pdf

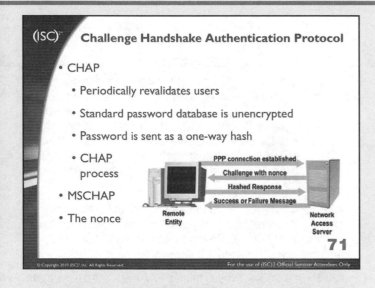

Challenge Handshake Authentication Protocol

- CHAP
  - Periodically revalidates users
  - Standard password database is unencrypted
  - Password is sent as a one-way hash
  - CHAP process
- MSCHAP
- The nonce

PPP connection established
Challenge with nonce
Hashed Response
Success or Failure Message

Remote Entity   Network Access Server

71

- **PERIODICALLY REVALIDATES USERS** – With a sophisticated challenge-handshake protocol using a non-replayable, challenge/response dialog. Periodic authentication will reduce the threat of session hijacking.

- **STANDARD PASSWORD DATABASE IS UNENCRYPTED** – Although the MSCHAP implementation stores one-way encrypted passwords.

- **PASSWORD IS SENT AS A ONE-WAY HASH** – Over the transmission link. As seen in the Cryptography domain, a hash value cannot feasibly be reverse engineered, making the sniffing of a password transmission valueless to the attacker.

- **THE CHAP PROCESS** –
  - Client connects to the network access server (NAS) and sets up a PPP link.

- The server sends a challenge, including a nonce. (See below.)

- The client sends a response to the challenge, including the user ID, and a one-way MD5 hash of the password and the nonce.

- The server computes the same hash and compares the value with what the client has sent.

- **MSCHAP** – MSCHAP (Microsoft CHAP) is a variation of the original CHAP standard done by Microsoft. Unlike the standard CHAP specification, in MSCHAP, the server stores a one-way encrypted hash of the user's password, instead of the password itself. This is much better from a security sense, but it is nonstandard.

- **THE NONCE** – The nonce is a general security feature used in CHAP and in other protocols.

- Definition from SearchSecurity TechTarget: In IT, a nonce is a parameter that varies with time, or as Ross Anderson states in Security Engineering, a nonce is simply a "number used once." A nonce can be a time stamp, a visit counter on a Web page, or a special marker intended to limit or prevent the unauthorized replay or reproduction of a file. Because a nonce changes with time, it is easy to tell whether or not an attempt at replay or reproduction of a file is legitimate; the current time can be compared with the nonce. If it does not exceed it, or if no nonce exists, then the attempt is authorized.

- Because hashing will always produce the same output if given the same input, the nonce is supplied by the server as a random value so as to "perturb" the input values to the hash. Thus, the same user ID/password can be hashed again and again, each time with a different nonce, thus precluding replay attacks.

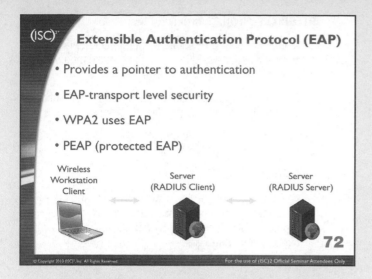

WPA2 USES EAP – As wireless becomes a de facto standard of station-to-station communication in many organizations, it will become a critical infrastructure component. Ever expanding uses of wireless will demand stronger authentication. EAP allows for adoption of new developments in authentication.

PEAP (PROTECTED EAP) – Designed to provide better security for EAP exchanges.

DIFFERENCES BETWEEN EAP-TLS AND PEAP – EAP-TLS requires that the user identity be transmitted in cleartext between the client and the EAP server in order to start the EAP exchange. PEAP (and EAP-TTLS (EAP Tunneled Transport Layer Security)) allows the EAP exchange to start by instead using a domain identifier in response to the EAP identity request packet. PEAP and EAP-TTLS protect the user's identity from eavesdroppers, whereas EAP-TLS does not. EAP-TLS requires server authentication through certificates, using either "key exchange public key (such as an RSA or Diffie-Hellman key exchange public key) or a signature public key (such as an RSA or DSS signature public key)." [quoted from RFC2716] EAP-TLS allows the server to request that the client authenticate itself via public signature key.

- PEAP uses the same TLS setup as EAP-TLS, requiring the server to authenticate via a public key, but provides for extended exchanges that define other client authentication mechanisms (including MS-CHAPv2, SecureID, or certificates via TLS). These extended exchanges are protected by the TLS tunnel and are, therefore, more secure than if they were used over an open channel. PEAP, therefore, is a logical extension of EAP-TLS, which defines a set of optional client exchanges as a replacement for a client certificate.

REFERENCE:
http://tools.ietf.org/html/rfc3748#section 3.2

- **EXTENSIBLE AUTHENTICATION PROTOCOL (EAP)** – EAP is an authentication framework typically (though not exclusively) used with wireless networks and point-to-point (PPP) connections. In its various forms, it is the official authentication mechanism for WPA and WPA2, the Wi-Fi protected access programs.

- **PROVIDES A POINTER TO AUTHENTICATION** – "EAP does not select a specific authentication mechanism at the PPP Link Control Phase, but rather postpones this until the Authentication Phase…. EAP may be used on dedicated links, as well as switched circuits, and wired as well as wireless links."

- **EAP-TLS TRANSPORT LEVEL SECURITY** – Transport level security (TLS) (as per the original RFC 2716 – this was incorrectly written as transport level security instead of transport layer security in the RFC) provides for mutual authentication, integrity-protected cipher suite negotiation and key exchange between two endpoints.

  - Mutual authentication is required when using EAP-TLS.

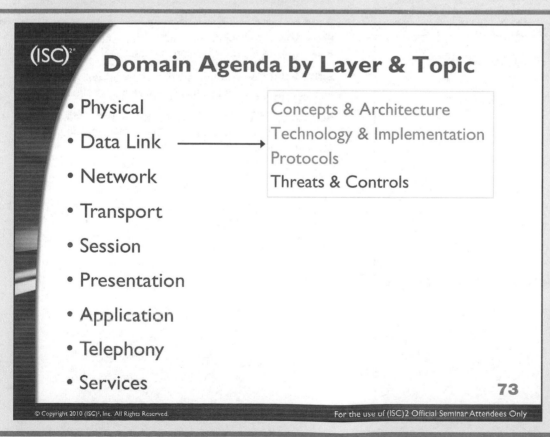

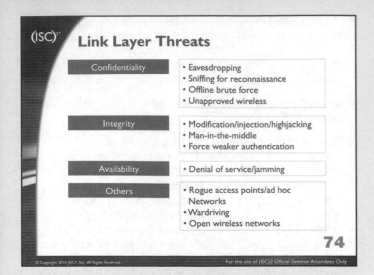

INTEGRITY – An attacker may try to:

- Modify or spoof EAP packets, inject packets into a communications session, or hijack an existing session.

- Convince the peer to connect to an untrusted network by mounting a man-in-the-middle attack.

- Disrupt the EAP negotiation in order to force the selection of a weak authentication method.

AVAILABILITY – An attacker may:

- Launch denial of service attacks by spoofing lower-layer indications or success/failure packets, or by replaying EAP packets, or by generating packets with overlapping Identifiers.

OTHER –

- Unapproved (rogue) wireless access points are a threat or uncontrolled network changes by users.

- Wardriving is the process of traveling around an area looking for wireless access points using high-gain antennas, scanning software (such as NetStumbler), and GPS devices. Wardrivers can create detailed maps of open Wi-Fi access points that are frequently posted to public websites. (Note that this technique should also be used in penetration testing.)

- **OPEN WIRELESS NETWORKS** – Unprotected WAPs that do not employ authentication or encryption may be used maliciously.

REFERENCE:
Directly from the http://tools.ietf.org/html/rfc3748#page-42

- **LINK LAYER THREATS** – All of the following were originally documented as EAP protocol threats in RFC 3748, but many can be applied to other link protocols and technologies as well.

- **AN ATTACKER WITH ACCESS TO THE LINK MAY CARRY OUT A NUMBER OF ATTACKS, INCLUDING THOSE ON:**

  - **CONFIDENTIALITY** – An attacker may:

    - Try to discover user identities by sniffing authentication traffic.

    - Attempt to recover the pass-phrase by mounting an offline dictionary or brute force attack.

    - Be an employee who installs unapproved (rogue), open wireless access points that do not conform to the security policy. Employee laptops may also be configured to allow file sharing or unauthenticated sessions.

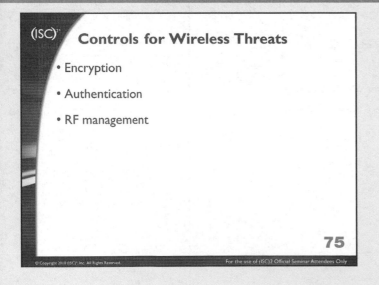

- **ENCRYPTION** – All wireless access points should use encryption to protect the transmission of data.

- **AUTHENTICATION** – Authentication protocols will ensure that only authorized users can use wireless access services.

- **RF MANAGEMENT** – Careful placement of WAP antennas can reduce the strength of the signal that is available outside of the authorized area.

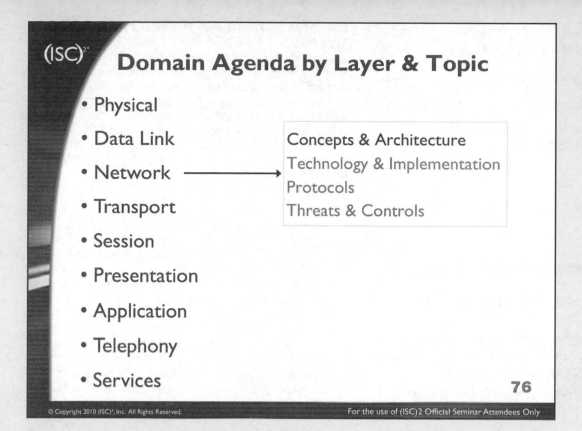

Domain Agenda by Layer & Topic

- Physical
- Data Link
- Network ⟶ Concepts & Architecture
            Technology & Implementation
            Protocols
            Threats & Controls
- Transport
- Session
- Presentation
- Application
- Telephony
- Services

76

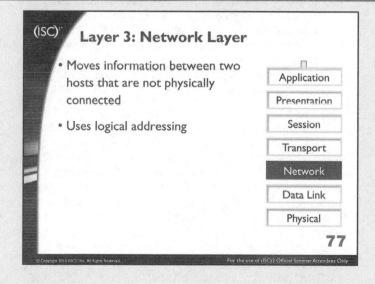

Layer 3: Network Layer

- Moves information between two hosts that are not physically connected
- Uses logical addressing

| Application |
| Presentation |
| Session |
| Transport |
| Network |
| Data Link |
| Physical |

77

- **LAYER THREE** – Network layer.
- **MOVES INFORMATION BETWEEN TWO HOSTS THAT ARE NOT PHYSICALLY CONNECTED** – While the data link layer is concerned with moving a data to the next physically connected device, the network layer moves information between two hosts that are not physically connected.
- **USES LOGICAL ADDRESSING** – Whereas the data link layer relies on hardware addressing, the network layer uses the logical addressing created when hosts were configured.

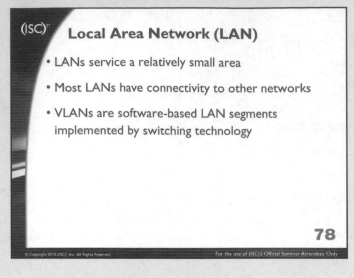

Local Area Network (LAN)

- LANs service a relatively small area

- Most LANs have connectivity to other networks

- VLANs are software-based LAN segments implemented by switching technology

78

- **LANS SERVICE A RELATIVELY SMALL AREA –** Such as a single building, one floor in an office, or a department.

- **MOST LANS HAVE CONNECTIVITY TO OTHER NETWORKS –** Via dialup or dedicated lines to the Internet, to other LANs via wide area networks (WANs), and so on.

- **VIRTUAL LOCAL AREA NETWORKS (VLANS) ARE SOFTWARE-BASED LAN SEGMENTS IMPLEMENTED BY SWITCHING TECHNOLOGY –** A VLAN is not a VPN. VLANs allow network administrators to use switches to create software-based LAN segments that can be defined based on factors other than physical location. Devices that share a VLAN communicate through switches without being routed to other sub-networks, which increases throughput and reduces overhead due to router latency (although as routers become faster, this is less of an advantage). Furthermore, broadcasts are not forwarded outside of a VLAN, which reduces congestion. Placing devices that often communicate with each other in the same VLAN allows them to do so more efficiently.

  - VLANs make networks easier to manage because they are not restricted to the physical location of devices. When a user or group of users changes physical location, network administrators can simply change the membership of ports within a VLAN. Similarly, when additional devices need to communicate with members of a VLAN, new ports can be easily added. VLANs can be configured based on switch port, IP subnet, MAC address, and protocols. Note that VLANs do NOT guarantee a network's security. Although it might seem that traffic can't be intercepted because communication within a VLAN is restricted to member devices, an attack known as "VLAN hopping" allows malicious users to see traffic from other VLANs.

Metropolitan Area Network (MAN)

- Optimization for city

- Uses wireless infrastructure, fiber optics, or Ethernet to connect sites together

- Still needs security

- Switched multi-megabit data service (SMDS)

- SONET/SDH

79

- **A METROPOLITAN AREA NETWORK, OR MAN,** is a computer network distributed over a large area such as a city.

- **OPTIMIZATION FOR CITY –** The IEEE 802 standard states that "a MAN is **OPTIMIZED** for a larger geographical area than is a LAN, ranging from several blocks of buildings to entire cities. As with local networks, MANs can also depend on communications channels of moderate-to-high data rates. A MAN might be owned and operated by a single organization, but it will usually be used by many individuals and organizations. MANs might also be owned and operated as public utilities. They will often provide means for Internetworking of local networks."

- **USES WIRELESS INFRASTRUCTURE, FIBER OPTICS, OR ETHERNET TO CONNECT SITES TOGETHER –** Metropolitan area networks typically use wireless infrastructure, optical fiber, or Ethernet connections to link their sites.

- **STILL NEEDS SECURITY –** On a MAN, each subscriber's traffic is encapsulated with a unique 802.1Q virtual LAN (VLAN) header and bridged over the MAN. If segregation of traffic with VLANs (or Q-in-Q) is not enough, organizations may decide to deploy firewalls or other devices at each endpoint for filtering and/or tunneling across the MAN. Additional security precautions must be taken in wireless-based MAN infrastructures due to the nature of the transmit method. A MAN may also call for link or transport encryption, authentication, and/or integrity protection, as the media typically leaves the physical control boundary so the data is susceptible to hijacking.

- **SWITCHED MULTI-MEGABIT DATA SERVICE (SMDS) –** SMDS is a high-speed, packet-switching data service. It is a connectionless, public data service that extends a local area network (LAN) or metropolitan or wide area network. SMDS uses fiber or copper-based media for data transmission. SMDS data units encapsulate entire IEEE 802.3, IEEE 802.5, and fiber distributed data interface (FDDI) frames. These older technologies are being replaced by Gigabit Ethernet and 10 Gigabit Ethernet – MetroE. SMDS implements two security features: source address validation and address screening. The source address validation checks that the PDU source address is assigned to the SNI. This prevents address spoofing. Address screening provides private virtual networks to subscribers that will exclude unwanted traffic.

- **SONET/SDH –** SONET/SDH refers to a group of fiber-optic transmission rates that are able to transport digital signals with different capacities. MANs are typically based on SONET, SDH, and wavelength division multiplexing (WDM) technologies.

REFERENCES:

IEEE 802 LAN/MAN Standards: http://grouper.ieee.org/groups/802/

History from Network World: http://www.networkworld.com/research/2001/1105feat.html

TechTarget MAN Articles: http://search.techrepublic.com.com/search/
   metropolitan+area+network.html

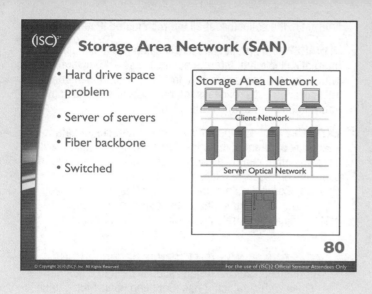

- **STORAGE AREA NETWORKS (SANS)** – Are used to provide a common storage area and a dedicated network for backup and common storage. The use of a dedicated separate network to back up data reduces congestion on the production network.

- **HARD DRIVE SPACE PROBLEM** – When users see more space, they will "need" more space. So as quickly as administrators would install new and larger storage in all servers, the users would fill those disks with more data.

- **SERVER OF SERVERS** – Instead of adding drives to the individual servers, the SANs solution consolidated the storage drives into a single large drive array.

- **FIBER BACKBONE** – Because servers are making requests on behalf of clients, all server-drive array connections must be fast: i.e., fiber optic.

- **SWITCHES** – Fiber channel switches (a Layer 2 device) are used to connect drive arrays and servers. Broadcasts are thus eliminated and congestion kept to a minimum.

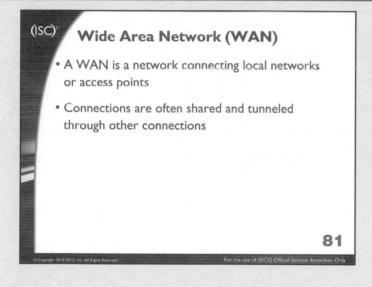

- **A WAN IS A NETWORK CONNECTING LOCAL NETWORKS OR ACCESS POINTS** – Because WAN connections are almost always outsourced to specialized providers, the security of the WAN connection is outsourced as well. It is very important for the IT security manager to establish clear contractual responsibilities and a sound service level agreement.

- **CONNECTIONS ARE OFTEN SHARED AND TUNNELED THROUGH OTHER CONNECTIONS** – Technologies used for WANs vary widely. From a network security perspective, their most important property is their ability to protect and separate traffic.

REFERENCE:

http://www.wildpackcts.com/support/compendium/manual_appendices/nxT1_wan

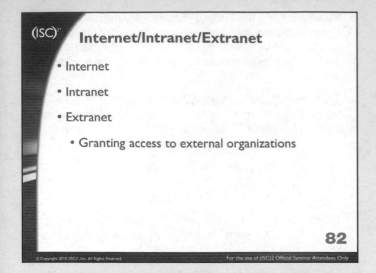

- **NETWORKS** – It takes a combination of various networks – Intranets, Extranets, and the Internet – to provide seamless service to an organization.

- **INTERNET** – In public perception, the Internet is a range of email and web-based applications. Technically, however, the Internet is the collective of all interconnected IP networks.

- **INTRANET** – An Intranet, loosely speaking, is a company's internal collection of Internet services, usually delivered over WAN lines and accessible only for the corporation in question. This collection of services is interconnected so as to allow information sharing and replication.

- **EXTRANET** – An extranet allows large quantities of data to be shared by different companies. Typically, one company will grant the other controlled access to an isolated segment of its own network so as to exchange information. Companies that share an Extranet do not have control of each other's security posture. To mitigate this, some companies demand that certain security controls are in place before granting access to an Extranet.

- **GRANTING ACCESS TO EXTERNAL ORGANIZATIONS** – Granting an external organization access to a network comes with significant risk. Both companies have to be certain that the controls, both technical and non-technical (i.e., contracts), effectively minimize the risk of unauthorized access to information. This includes preventing a business partner from accessing a third party's information.

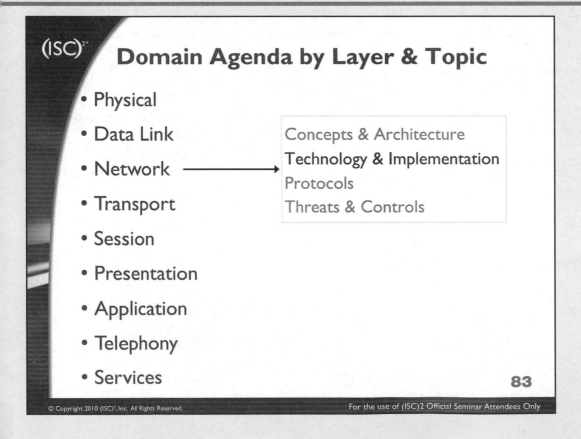

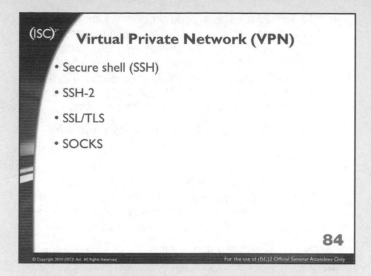

Virtual Private Network (VPN)

- Secure shell (SSH)
- SSH-2
- SSL/TLS
- SOCKS

84

- **SECURE SHELL (SSH)** – Users often want to log on to a remote computer. Unfortunately, most early implementations of remote access were designed for trusted networks. Protocols/programs, such as TELNET, RSH, and rlogin, consequently transmit without encryption, which allows traffic to be easily intercepted. Another problem with telnet (in addition to no encryption) is no integrity protection, which makes it susceptible to hijacking.

  - Secure shell (SSH) was designed as an alternative to these insecure protocols and allows users to securely access resources on remote computers over an encrypted tunnel. SSH's services include remote logon, file transfer, and command execution. It also supports port forwarding, which redirects other protocols through an encrypted SSH tunnel.

  - Many users protect less secure protocols such as X Windows and VNC (virtual network computing) by forwarding them through an SSH tunnel. The SSH tunnel protects the integrity of the communication by preventing session hijacking and other man-in-the-middle attacks. Another advantage of SSH over its predecessors is that it supports strong authentication. There are several alternatives for SSH clients to authenticate to an SSH server, including passwords and digital certificates. Keep in mind that authenticating with a password is still a significant improvement over the other protocols because the password is encrypted before transmission.

- **SSH-2** – There are two incompatible versions of the protocol: SSH-1 and SSH-2, though many servers support both

versions. SSH-2 has improved integrity checks (SSH-1 is vulnerable to an insertion attack due to weak CRC-32 integrity checking) and supports local extensions and additional types of digital certificates, such as Open PGP. SSH was originally designed for UNIX, but there are now implementations for other operating systems, including Windows, Macintosh, and OpenVMS.

- **SSL/TLS VPNS** – SSL VPNs are another approach to remote access that is gaining momentum. Instead of building a VPN around the IPSec and the network layer, SSL VPNs leverage SSL/TLS to create a tunnel back to the home office. Remote users can then employ a web browser to access applications that are in the organization's network. Even though users employ web browsers, SSL VPNs are not restricted to applications that use the HTTPS protocol. With the aid of plug-ins such as Java, users can access back-end databases and other non web-based applications. SSL VPNs have several advantages over IPSec. First, they are easier to deploy on client workstations because they only require a web browser and almost all networks permit outgoing HTTPS. Secondly, SSL VPNs can be operated through a proxy server. In addition, applications can restrict users' access based on criteria such as the network that the user is on. This is useful for building Extranets between several organizations. IPSec VPNs, on the other hand, grant direct access to a network. A user is usually given access to applications and devices as if he or she were physically at the office. This is a double-edged sword, however: Although authorized users will have access to many devices on the internal network, so will an intruder who can steal IPSec VPN access. Currently, SSL VPNs do not support network-to-network tunnels. A significant disadvantage of IPSec VPNs is that a VPN client must be installed and updated on every workstation.

- **SOCKS** – SOCKS is a popular circuit proxy server with several commercial and freeware implementations. Note that RFC 1928 does not require developers to include traffic encryption in their implementations. Users employ the SOCKS client to access a remote server. The client initiates a connection to the SOCKS proxy server, which accesses the remote server on behalf of the user. (A SOCKS server may require that a user authenticates before providing services.) If the implementation supports encryption, the server can act as a VPN, protecting the confidentiality of the traffic between the SOCKS and remote servers. Because SOCKS is concerned with maintaining a circuit, SOCKS can be used with almost any application. A key advantage of SOCKS and SSL VPNs is that unlike most other VPNs, they allow the use of proxy servers.

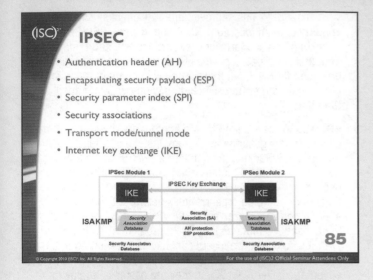

85

- **IPSEC AUTHENTICATION & CONFIDENTIALITY FOR VPNS** – IP security (IPSec) is a suite of protocols for communicating securely with IP by providing mechanisms for authentication and encryption. Implementation of IPSec is mandatory in IPv6 and many organizations are using it over IPv4 as well. IPSec can be implemented in two modes: one that is appropriate for end-to-end protection and one that safeguards traffic between networks. Standard IPSec only authenticates hosts with each other. If an organization requires users to authenticate, they will have to use a non-standard, proprietary IPSec implementation, or use IPSec over L2TP (Layer 2 tunneling protocol), which authenticates users and encapsulates IPSec packets. Since IPSec interprets the change of IP address within packet headers as an attack, NAT does not work well with IPSec. To resolve the incompatibility of the two protocols, NAT-transversal (a.k.a. "NAT-T") encapsulates IPSec within UDP port 4500 (see RFC 3948 for details).

- **AUTHENTICATION HEADER (AH)** – The authentication header is used to guarantee the identity of the sending node and ensure that the transmitted data has not been tampered with. Before each packet (headers + data) is transmitted, a hash value of the packet's contents is inserted in the last field of the AH. The hash calculation is based on a shared secret that the endpoints negotiate during the initial setup of the communications session. This initial communication sets up the "security association" between the two communicating parties. They also determine which hashing algorithm to use and a shared secret.

  - To help thwart replay attacks (when a legitimate session is retransmitted to gain unauthorized access), each packet transmitted during a security association is given a sequence number which is stored in the AH.

  - In transport mode, the AH is shimmed between the packet's IP and TCP header.

  - Note that the AH helps ensure integrity, not confidentiality. Encryption is implemented with the encapsulating security payload.

- **ENCAPSULATING SECURITY PAYLOAD (ESP)** – The encapsulating security payload encrypts IP packets for confidentiality and ESP also ensures the packet's integrity. ESP contains four sections:

  - **ESP HEADER** – Contains information showing which security association to use, and the packet sequence number. Like the AH, the ESP sequences every packet to thwart replay attacks.

- **ESP PAYLOAD** – The payload contains the encrypted part of the packet. If the encryption algorithm requires an initialization vector (IV), it is included with the payload. The endpoints negotiate what form of encryption to use when the security association is established. Because packets must be encrypted with as little overhead as possible, ESP typically uses a symmetric encryption algorithm.

- **ESP TRAILER** – May include padding (filler bytes) if required by the encryption algorithm, or in order to align fields.

- **AUTHENTICATION** – If used, this field will contain the integrity check value (hash) of the ESP packet. As with the AH, the authentication algorithm is negotiated when the endpoints establish their security association.

- **SECURITY PARAMETER INDEX (SPI)** – Is an arbitrary number assigned to an IPSec connection by the administrator to identify the connection.

- **SECURITY ASSOCIATIONS** – A security association (SA) establishes the credentials of the two communicating parties and defines the mechanisms that will be used to communicate. The SA is agreement on factors such as IPSec protocol(s) (AH, ESP), the mode of operation of the protocol(s) (transport or tunnel mode), cryptographic algorithms, cryptographic keys, and the lifetime of the keys. SA parameters are stored in security association databases (SADs). All SAs cover transmissions in one direction only. A second SA must be defined for two-way communication. Mechanisms that are defined in the SA include the encryption and authentication algorithms and whether to use the AH or ESP protocol. Deferring the mechanisms to the SA (as opposed to specifying them in the protocol) allows the communicating partners to use the appropriate mechanisms based on perceived risk.

- **TRANSPORT MODE/TUNNEL MODE** – Endpoints communicate with IPSec using either transport or tunnel mode. In transport mode, the IP payload is protected. This mode is primarily used for end-to-end protection, for example between a client and a server. In tunnel mode, the IP payload and its IP header are protected. The entire protected IP packet becomes a payload of a new IP packet and header. Tunnel mode is often used between networks, such as with firewall-to-firewall VPNs.

- **INTERNET KEY EXCHANGE (IKE)** – IKE (Internet key exchange) is the protocol IPSec uses to negotiate and establish authenticated keying materials for security associations (SAs). IKMP (Internet key management protocol) is the process that handles key management, within which IPSec uses IKE (ISAKMP/OAKLEY).

- Internet key exchange allows communicating partners to prove their identity to each other and establish a secure communication channel. IKE uses two phases:

- **PHASE 1:** The partners authenticate with each other, using one of the following:

  - **SHARED SECRET** – A key that is exchanged by humans via telephone, fax, encrypted email, etc.

  - **PUBLIC KEY ENCRYPTION** – The exchange of digital certificates.

  - **REVISED MODE OF PUBLIC KEY ENCRYPTION** – To reduce the overhead of public key encryption, a nonce is encrypted with the communicating partner's public key, and the peer's identity is encrypted with symmetric encryption, using the nonce as the key.

- **PHASE 2:** IKE establishes a temporary security association and secure tunnel to protect the rest of the key exchange.

- IPSP (IP security policy) stipulates the type of traffic (for example, from what source or to what destination) that is allowed to pass through the IPSec system, and the security mechanisms that should be applied to the traffic.

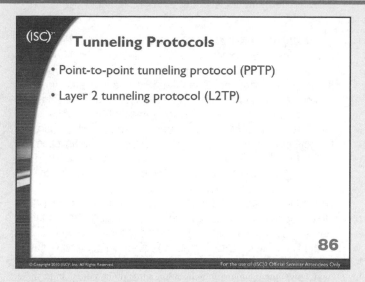

of its predecessor's weaknesses, such as using an improved version of MSCHAP for authentication, but PPTPv2 is still vulnerable to offline password guessing attacks. A key weakness of PPTP is the fact that it usually derives its encryption key from the user's password. This violates the cryptographic principle of randomness and can provide a basis for attacks. Password-based VPN authentication in general violates the recommendation to use two-factor authentication for remote access.

  - Note: Newer implementations of PPTP from Microsoft allow the use of digital certificates instead of passwords, but this is not implemented as often as passwords.

- **LAYER 2 TUNNELING PROTOCOL (L2TP)** – Layer 2 tunneling protocol (L2TP) is a hybrid of Cisco's Layer 2 Forwarding (L2F) and Microsoft's PPTP protocols. It allows callers over a serial line using PPP to connect to a remote network over the Internet. A dialup user connects to hls or her ISP's L2TP access concentrator (LAC) with a PPP connection, and the LAC encapsulates the PPP packets into L2TP and forwards it to the remote network's Layer 2 network server (LNS). At this point, the LNS authenticates the dialup user. If authentication is successful, the dialup user will have access to the remote network. The LAC and LNS may authenticate each other with a shared secret, but as RFC 2661 states, the authenticating is effective only while the tunnel between the LAC and LNS is being created. L2TP does not provide encryption and relies on other protocols (such as tunnel mode IPSec) for confidentiality.

- **POINT-TO-POINT TUNNELING PROTOCOL (PPTP) –** Point-to-point tunneling protocol (PPTP) is a VPN protocol that runs over other protocols. PPTP relies on generic routing encapsulation (GRE) to build the tunnel between the endpoints. After the user authenticates, typically with Microsoft Challenge Handshake Authentication Protocol Version 2 (MSCHAPv2), a point-to-point protocol (PPP) session is created and tunneled using GRE. PPTP came under much fire in the 1990s. Cryptographers announced weaknesses in the protocol, including flaws with MSCHAPv1 (the authentication protocol) and the encryption implementation, and the use of user passwords as keys. Microsoft released PPTPv2, which addressed many

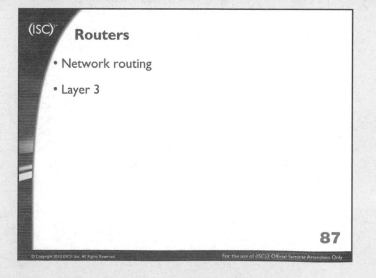

- The Internet is simply a collection of many interconnected networks or, in other words, an Internetwork.

- **NETWORK ROUTING –** Routing is the act of moving information across an Internetwork from a source to a destination. Routers use routing protocols to determine the optimal path from source to destination. The routing protocols assist a router in finding the best route from themselves to other points on the network. Sometimes those rules (protocols) may look for the shortest path, or, in other cases, the fastest.

- **LAYER 3 –** Routing and bridging might be described as similar except that bridging occurs at Layer 2 (the link layer) of the OSI reference model, whereas routing occurs at Layer 3 (the network layer).

- **FILTERING** – Firewalls filter traffic based on rule sets. Each rule instructs the firewall to block or forward a packet based on one or more conditions. For each incoming packet, the firewall will look through its rule set for a rule whose conditions apply to that packet, and block or forward the packet as specified in that rule.

  - **FILTERING BY ADDRESS** – Firewalls will often use the packet's source or destination address (or both) to determine whether the packet should be filtered/thrown out.

  - **FILTERING BY SERVICE** – Packets can also be filtered by service. The firewall inspects the service the packet is using (if the packet is part of the TCP or UDP protocol, the service is the destination port number) to determine if the packet should be filtered. For example, firewalls will often have a rule to filter the finger service to prevent an attacker from using it to gather information about a host.

- **ADDRESS AND SERVICE ARE OFTEN COMBINED IN RULES** – If the engineering department wanted to grant anyone on the LAN access to its web server, it could write a rule to forward packets whose destination address is the web server's and whose service is HTTP (TCP port 80).

- **STATIC PACKET FILTERING** – When a firewall uses static packet filtering, it examines each packet without regard to the packet's context in a session. With static packet filtering, packets are examined against static criteria: For example, packets with a port number of 79 (finger) can be blocked. Because of its simplicity, static packet filtering requires very little overhead. It also has a significant disadvantage, however: Static rules cannot be temporarily changed by the firewall to accommodate legitimate traffic. If a protocol requires a port to be temporarily opened, administrators have to choose between permanently opening the port, and disallowing the protocol.

- **STATEFUL INSPECTION OR DYNAMIC PACKET FILTERING** – Stateful inspection examines each packet in the context of a session, which allows it to make dynamic adjustments to the rules to accommodate legitimate traffic while blocking malicious traffic that would appear benign to a static filter. Consider the FTP protocol: A user connects to an FTP server on TCP port 21 and then tells the FTP server on which port to transfer files. Because the port can be any TCP port above 1023, if the FTP client tells the server to transfer files on TCP port 1067, the server will attempt to open a connection to the client on that port. A stateful inspection firewall would watch the interaction between the two hosts, and know that even though the required connection is not permitted in the rule set, it should be allowed because the connection is part of the FTP protocol. Static packet filtering, in contrast, would block the FTP server's attempt to connect to the client on TCP port 1067 unless a static rule were already in place. In fact, because the client could instruct the FTP server to transfer files on any port above 1023, a static rule would have to be in place to permit access to over 65536 ports.

- **PERSONAL FIREWALLS** – The firewalls that we've discussed so far protect a network or a segment of one. But what protects users from hosts that are behind the firewall? Following the principle of layered security (defense-in-depth), personal firewalls installed on workstations protect the user from all other hosts on the network. It is critical for home users with DSL or cable modem access to the Internet to have a personal firewall installed on every PC, especially if they do not have a firewall protecting their network. Because personal firewalls are employed by general users, they are easy to install and configure. Firewall rules are created with a non-technical interface that does not require expertise in networking or security. While they don't provide the flexibility of the best enterprise firewalls, they provide all of the essential functions of a firewall, such as stateful inspection, logging, etc.

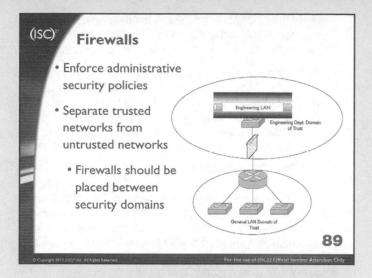

Firewalls

- Enforce administrative security policies
- Separate trusted networks from untrusted networks
  - Firewalls should be placed between security domains

Engineering LAN

Engineering Dept. Domain of Trust

General LAN Domain of Trust

89

- **ENFORCE ADMINISTRATIVE SECURITY POLICIES** – Firewalls are devices that enforce administrative security policies by filtering incoming and outgoing traffic and either permitting or denying the traffic from passing through the firewall based on a set of firewall rules.

- **SEPARATE TRUSTED NETWORKS FROM UNTRUSTED NETWORKS** – Firewalls are often thought of as things that only protect Internet gateways. While a firewall should certainly be placed at Internet gateways, there are other considerations that should be taken into account as well:

  - **FIREWALLS SHOULD BE PLACED BETWEEN SECURITY DOMAINS** – Firewalls should be placed between entities that have different trust domains. For instance, if an engineering department LAN segment is on the same network as general LAN users, there will be two trust domains: general LAN users, and engineers with access to the organization's intellectual property. Installing a firewall where the two trust domains meet would help protect the intellectual property from being accessed by the general LAN user population.

- **FIREWALLS WILL NOT BE EFFECTIVE RIGHT OUT OF THE BOX; RULES MUST BE PUT IN PLACE** – Firewall rules must be defined correctly and not inadvertently grant unauthorized access. As with all other hosts on a network, administrators must install patches to the firewall and disable all unnecessary services. Note as well that firewalls offer limited protection against vulnerabilities enabled by software on other hosts. For example a firewall is relatively ineffective to control threats related to web applications since the firewall will usually permit port 80 and 443 traffic.

- VLANs (or virtual LANs) are a method of separating traffic of different types that would otherwise share the same network. VLANS were never designed for security. Use VLANs sparingly on critical firewalls, since there have been numerous exploits against VLANS used to logically separate traffic. In addition, VLAN-enabled interfaces are inefficient because they need far more processing than regularly routed traffic. Most currently available firewalls support host-based VLANs. Many firewall vendors (i.e., Netscreen and Check Point) use virtual firewalls in some of their high-end chassis firewalls. High-end chassis firewalls allow you to create several virtual firewalls on the same chassis. You can apply virtual firewalls to specific VLANs – for example, if you want to firewall several VLANs, but you want different departments to manage the separate firewalls (e.g., in a government environment with several interconnect-

ed ministries), you can allocate separate firewalls for specific sets of VLANs.

- **FIREWALL RULES** – Firewall rules are used to define what traffic is permitted or denied access to the network. These rules are the implementation of the policy of the organization.

  - **STEALTH RULES** are used to protect the firewall itself from being attacked. A stealth rule forbids any access to the firewall from unauthorized hosts.

  - **CLEANUP RULES** are used as the last rule in the rulebase. They are used to drop and log any traffic that does not meet the rules preceding it.

  - **A SILENT RULE** is a rule to drop "noisy" traffic without logging it. Silent rules have a security function by reducing the volume of data in logs and by not responding to packets.

  - **"NEGATE RULES"** are used instead of "any rules" in that they do not grant full permissive access to the prescribed node or network. For example, if you are on the internal network, most administrators would create a rule that says Internal_net -> Any using HTTP (for browsing). But this rule also grants access to the firewall (that in some cases has a web administrative console) and the servers in the DMZ. It is better to use an Internal_Net -> Not DMZ or Firewall using HTTP.

  - **IMPLIED RULES** fire before the normal rule base and can be an exposure point. Implicit rules include allowing services such as ICMP, DHCP, SmartUpdate, DNS, and other related services. Because, in some instances, they can be configured as the "first" rule and, therefore, bypass any of the rules below it, it is important to review them.

- **IN ADDITION, IT IS IMPORTANT TO:**

  - Document and clearly communicate who is authorized to:

    - Install, de-install, and move firewalls.

    - Perform hardware maintenance and changes to physical configuration.

    - Make physical connections to the firewall.

  - Define procedures for:

    - Locating and securing firewalls by zone.

    - Securing console physical access.

    - Recovering in the event of physical damage.

    - Escalating in the event of firewalls tampering.

  - Ensure that the operating systems have been appropriately hardened.

  - Ensure that unnecessary services have been disabled.

  - Turn on operating system logging mechanism.

  - Use double intervention controls for critical functions (i.e., access to the operating system).

REFERENCES:

http://csrc.nist.gov/publications/nistpubs/800-41/sp800-41.pdf

http://www.networksecurityjournal.com/features/heighten-security-install-a-fire-wall-031407

http://www.cisco.com/univercd/cc/td/doc/product/iaabu/centri4/user/scf4ch3.htm

http://www.secmanager.com/Top_Ten_Tips_for_Managing_Your_Firewall

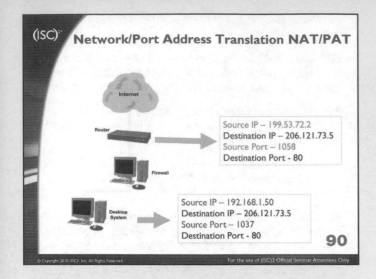

Network/Port Address Translation NAT/PAT

Source IP – 199.53.72.2
Destination IP – 206.121.73.5
Source Port – 1058
Destination Port - 80

Source IP – 192.168.1.50
Destination IP – 206.121.73.5
Source Port – 1037
Destination Port - 80

90

- **NETWORK ADDRESS TRANSLATION (NAT) –** Devices at Layer 3 can change the source address of each outgoing packet they handle to a different IP address. This is frequently done on traffic going from trusted to untrusted networks, such as from the internal LAN onto the Internet. The address of outgoing packets is changed from an internal address to the external address of the device doing the NATing.

- There are several applications where this is done, most notably to allow hosts with RFC 1918 addresses access to the Internet by changing their non-routable address to one that is routable on the Internet. This saves routable addresses and has the restriction that a host with a non-routable address cannot be reached directly from the Internet. Anonymity is another reason to use NAT. Many organizations don't want to advertise their internal IP addresses to an untrusted host and, thus, unnecessarily provide a hacker monitoring network traffic information about their network size or configuration.

- Network address translation, or "natting," occurs at Level 3 of the OSI and is typically performed at the router or firewall. It allows the use of two sets of IP addresses for resources – one for internal use and a different one for external use. Natting was developed as a solution to the problem of the limited number of IP addresses available in the IPv4 address space.

- **PORT ADDRESS TRANSLATION (PAT) –** An extension to NAT is to translate the **SOURCE** port number in the packet to a different unique value. Port translation allows the firewall to keep track of multiple sessions that are using NAT/PAT. This means that even though the firewall may be NATing connections from several internal systems, it is able to differentiate the traffic of one session from the others since each communications session would have a unique port number.

- **FOR EXAMPLE –** An organization has chosen to identify all the computers on its internal network with non-routable addresses such as the 10.0.0.0 range. This allows it to uniquely identify all internal machines, but would cause a problem if one of the internal machines wanted to request information from an external web server. When the traffic leaves the internal network toward the server, the firewall (which acts as the gateway to the Internet) changes the source IP address on the packet from the internal machine to the firewall's own, routable IP address. Then the reply from the web server will be routed to the firewall, which can then filter the traffic and forward it internally to the internal non-routable address of the original requester.

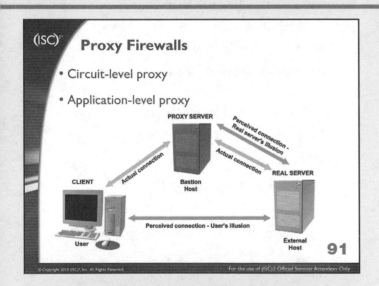

Proxy Firewalls

- Circuit-level proxy
- Application-level proxy

91

- **PROXY FIREWALLS –** A proxy firewall communicates to untrusted hosts on behalf of the hosts that it protects. It forwards traffic from trusted hosts, creating the illusion to the untrusted server that the traffic originated from the proxy firewall thus hiding the trusted hosts from potential attackers. Proxy servers are often placed at Internet gateways so as to hide the internal network behind a single IP address and to prevent direct communication between internal and external hosts.

- **CIRCUIT-LEVEL PROXY –** A circuit-level proxy creates a conduit through which a trusted host can communicate with an untrusted one. This type of proxy does not inspect any of the traffic that it forwards and therefore adds very little overhead to the communication between the user and untrusted server.

- **APPLICATION-LEVEL PROXY –** An application-level proxy relays the traffic from a trusted host running a specific application to an untrusted server. An application-level proxy can support only one protocol. Web proxy servers are a very popular example of application-level proxies. The most significant advantage of application-level proxies is that they analyze the traffic for malicious packets and can restrict some of the application's functionality. Application-level proxies add overhead because they scrutinize the traffic they forward. Application-level proxies are also able to direct client requests to a server that is running a program dealing with external servers on behalf of internal clients.

- Proxy services can provide separation of trusted (internal) networks from untrusted (external) networks. Conceptually, outsiders are not allowed to "talk" directly to private nodes. Because the proxy hides all internal hosts behind it, intruders can't map the IP addresses and size of the internal network as easily as they could otherwise.

- Because firewalls utilizing proxy services make a distinct physical separation between your local network and the Internet, they are a good choice for high-security requirements. However, because an actual program must analyze the packets and make decisions about access control, these types of firewalls tend to reduce network performance. In other words, firewalls utilizing proxy services are significantly slower than those utilizing packet filtering. If you plan to use proxy services, use the fastest processors available for the computer that will be hosting the proxy server.

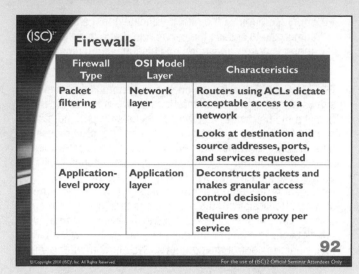

Firewalls

Firewall Type	OSI Model Layer	Characteristics
Packet filtering	Network layer	Routers using ACLs dictate acceptable access to a network Looks at destination and source addresses, ports, and services requested
Application-level proxy	Application layer	Deconstructs packets and makes granular access control decisions Requires one proxy per service

92

- **FIREWALLS** – This chart provides a good overview of firewall categories.

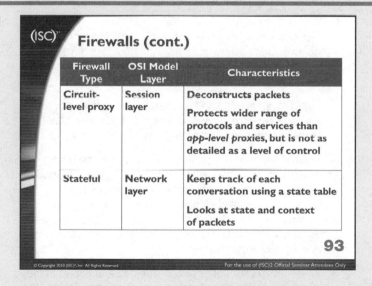

Firewalls (cont.)

Firewall Type	OSI Model Layer	Characteristics
Circuit-level proxy	Session layer	Deconstructs packets Protects wider range of protocols and services than *app-level proxies*, but is not as detailed as a level of control
Stateful	Network layer	Keeps track of each conversation using a state table Looks at state and context of packets

93

- In a way, the **END SYSTEMS** section should be called Beginning Systems because most of the topics here are the reason networks exist – to allow the systems listed to exchange information. Because the information on these devices is the crown jewel of the network, they are highly susceptible to harm. Much could be written about protecting these systems; the following merely presents the highlights.

- **SERVERS AND MAINFRAMES –** Servers and mainframes are repositories of information, much of which is critical to an organization's mission, employees, and clients. The information held supports critical business processes, customer databases, and intellectual property. Information on these hosts is protected by an ever-growing number of international, national, and local security and privacy regulations. Because of the importance of the information and the accessibility of servers and mainframes on a network, servers and mainframes will always be at risk. Although people often imagine that intruders are nameless, faceless, and external, they are actually more often insiders. Note, too, that malicious activity is not always the greatest threat – human error is just as dangerous. Due to the importance of the information held on servers and mainframes, it is vital that organizations minimize the risk posed. The following are a few important controls.

  - Owners should only grant the access required for personnel to perform their duties, log such access sufficiently so as to support forensic investigation, and regularly review logs. Because the failure of an application can increase the risk to other applications on the same host, companies should not run multiple applications on the same physical or virtual machine. For instance, a compromise of a low-risk application (which may not be rigorously protected) could allow an intruder access to a high-risk application on the same server. Similarly, the failure of a development instance of an application could corrupt production, particularly if they share the same database.

  - Sensitive data should be encrypted with strong encryption algorithms. Network traffic between client and servers/mainframes should be also be encrypted.

  - Risks from remote access should be reduced through strong authentication and disabling remote administration ability.

  - Controls discussed previously (such as firewalls) should be used to help ensure that only authorized clients can access the servers and mainframes.

  - Verify (perhaps with digital certificates) that clients are authorized to access the server and that a middleware server is not an attacker's machine masquerading as middleware.

- **OPERATING SYSTEMS –** An operating system is the layer of software that serves as an interface between the application and the hardware. It services requests for peripherals on behalf of the users and interfaces with the central processing unit. Security is an integral and critical function of the operating system. Operating systems also provide mechanisms by which to improve the availability of information, such as redundant arrays of independent disks (RAID) and computer clusters. Regardless of the applications that are running on a computer, the operating system will always be a target of attack because a compromised operating system will allow an intruder to control the computer. System/computer owners should, therefore, always remove unnecessary targets of attack (such as dangerous or unused services) and install security patches as soon as it is feasible.

- Operating systems implement access controls to help ensure that only authorized users access resources.

- **NOTEBOOKS/LAPTOPS/TABLET PCS –** Notebooks, laptops, and tablet PCs have the same problems as workstations, but suffer additional security issues because of their portability: They can easily be stolen or lost, thereby potentially disclosing sensitive information.

  - These machines are not protected by the organization's firewall when attached to another network, such as a home network or wireless hotspot. There is a significant danger that users might unintentionally be infected with malicious code when attached to another network and unleash it on the organization when the notebook returns to the office.

  - The above risks can be partly mitigated with technical controls, such as ensuring that all notebooks have personal firewalls and antivirus software with current signatures, and also by encrypting sensitive files and disks.

  - Users must be educated on the additional dangers posed by using these machines, and alerted to the additional responsibilities that come with their use.

- **WORKSTATIONS –** Workstations are computers that users physically log into, and are typically used as clients. As with all network devices, they are potential targets of attack. Some of the vulnerabilities are similar to those of servers (e.g., unpatched operating systems and unnecessary network services) and in fact, some workstation operating systems provide server functionality.

  - Workstation user behavior can threaten a network. Some users forget that they do not "own" their workstation, and freely engage in dangerous behavior, such as downloading from untrusted sites, chatting using instant messaging, or leaving their office with their workstation logged in but unprotected.

  - It is also common for users to underestimate the sensitivity of the information on their workstation and, therefore, underestimate the importance of protecting it.

  - Organizations should consider not granting administrator rights to workstation users.

  - As with other end systems, software updates must be

installed as soon as possible, unnecessary and dangerous services must be disabled, and antivirus software and personal firewalls should be installed.

- **SMARTPHONES** – Smartphones are a combination of a PDA and a cell phone. While they offer the convenience of both devices, they also share both devices' security problems.

  - A smartphone's subscriber identity module (SIM) can be cloned and used to steal personal information from the card.

  - A thief can use the cellular capabilities of a smartphone to email stolen information or pictures while still on the victim's premises.

  - As with PDAs, the best defense is to encrypt sensitive information on the smartphones, protect the computer ports that can be used to download information, and educate users on how to recognize and stop theft.

- **PERSONAL DIGITAL ASSISTANTS** – Personal digital assistants can store confidential and private information, yet many models do not include sufficient controls (such as strong encryption) to protect the contents in the event the device is stolen or lost. A thief can easily steal information by downloading it to a PDA from an unprotected computer. Note, too, that PDAs with camera attachments can be used to take unauthorized photographs. To help reduce the risk of confidential information walking out of the office on a PDA, computer ports (where PDAs are attached to computers to download information) should be physically and logically protected.

- **NETWORK ATTACHED STORAGE (NAS)** – Is an endpoint dedicated to shared hard drive space for clients of the network. A NAS device is typically a single-purpose appliance with minimal configurable options. The greatest risks for NAS systems are availability and the theft of stored data. These systems require physical and logical controls to mitigate risk.

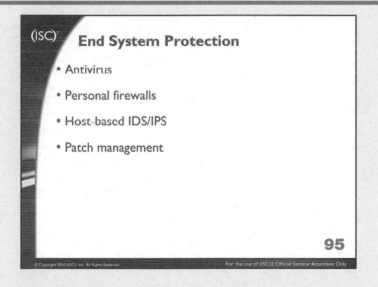

- **END SYSTEM PROTECTION** – This domain focuses on protecting the network, but it must be remembered that the security professional will also carefully protect the end systems that are connected to the network. Some common end system protective measures are listed here.

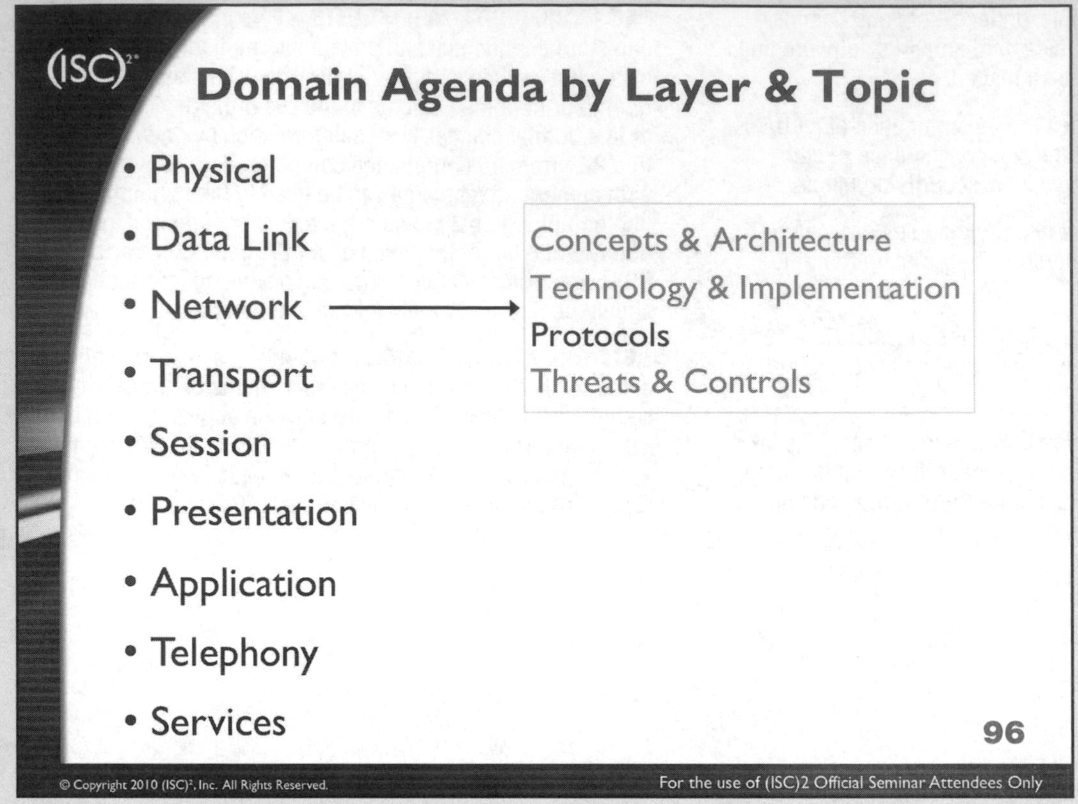
(ISC)²
Domain Agenda by Layer & Topic
• Physical
• Data Link
• Network
• Transport
• Session
• Presentation
• Application
• Telephony
• Services
Concepts & Architecture
Technology & Implementation
Protocols
Threats & Controls
96
© Copyright 2010 (ISC)², Inc. All Rights Reserved.
For the use of (ISC)2 Official Seminar Attendees Only

- The protocol section covers Internetworking, testing, routing, virtual private networking, and tunneling.

- **ROUTING PROTOCOLS** – Use algorithms to help routers determine the best path for traffic through networks. They operate at Layer 3 and populate the routing table on the routers.

- **ROUTING INFORMATION PROTOCOL (RIP)** – RIP is a dynamic routing protocol designed for small networks. Routers in a RIP network regularly merge their view of the network by exchanging their routing table with their neighbors. The routing path is chosen based on the number of hops. RIP has several shortcomings:

  - Routers exchange their entire route table every 30 seconds (by default), which can cause network congestion.

  - RIP cannot route to a network or host that is more than 15 hops away.

  - RIP only works in classful networks. In other words, RIP cannot be used in networks with different subnet masks.

  - **ROUTING TABLE COMPROMISE** – There is no way for a router to verify the trustworthiness of a route update that it receives from its neighbors. This means that attackers can manipulate route tables with bogus route updates.

  - RIP version 2 (RIPv2) was implemented to address some of RIP's limitations. For example, RIPv2 can be used in a network with different subnet masks. Also, routers authenticate with each other, originally with a plaintext password, and later, using RFC 2082, keyed MD5 authentication.

- **VIRTUAL ROUTER REDUNDANCY PROTOCOL (VRRP)** – Organizations that require networks with high availability cannot tolerate critical routers as single points of failure. The most acceptable option is for a secondary router to automatically take the place of a failed router (i.e., failover). VRRP supports automatic failover. First of all, a virtual router is configured. The virtual router looks like a physical router to the rest of the network. A primary and at least one secondary router are then configured alongside the virtual router. The primary router performs all of the routing on behalf of the virtual router. If the primary router fails, one of the secondary routers will automatically perform the routing for the virtual router. As long as hosts forward packets to the virtual router, it will not matter which physical router is doing the work. Primary and secondary routers are often placed in separate data centers in order to improve resilience in the case of disaster.

- **OPEN SHORTEST PATH FIRST (OSPF)** – OSPF is an intra-AS (interior gateway) routing protocol, although it is capable of sending and receiving routes to and from other ASs. OSPF is based on the shortest path first (SPF) algorithm, which is sometimes referred to as the Dijkstra algorithm. As with IGRP (described below), OSPF was created in the mid-1980s in response to RIP's increasing inability to serve large, heterogeneous Internetworks.

- **EXTERIOR GATEWAY PROTOCOL (EGP)** – EGP was one of the first routing protocols to communicate between networks that were under the control of different administrators.

- **BORDER GATEWAY PROTOCOL (BGP)** – BGP was developed as a replacement for EGP and is the routing protocol employed on the Internet. It is very robust and scalable. To achieve scalability at this level, BGP uses many route parameters (called attributes) to define routing policies and maintain a stable routing environment. In addition to BGP attributes, BGP uses CIDR to reduce the size of the Internet routing tables.

- **INTERMEDIATE SYSTEM-TO-INTERMEDIATE SYSTEM (ISIS)** – ISIS is a classless, hierarchical, vendor-neutral routing protocol.

- **INTERIOR GATEWAY ROUTING PROTOCOL (IGRP)** – IGRP is a vendor-proprietary routing protocol and provides stable routing tables for large networks and the ability to change routing due to transmission errors or changes in the topology.

- **ENHANCED INTERIOR GATEWAY ROUTING PROTOCOL (EIGRP)** – EIGRP is an enhanced version of IGRP that allows for faster updates of routing data.

REFERENCES:

http://www.oreillynet.com/

http://tools.ietf.org/html/rfc904

http://www.cisco.com/en/US/tech/tk365/technologies_white_paper09186a00800c8ae1.shtml

http://www.cisco.com/univercd/cc/td/doc/product/software/ios100/eigrp/36545.htm

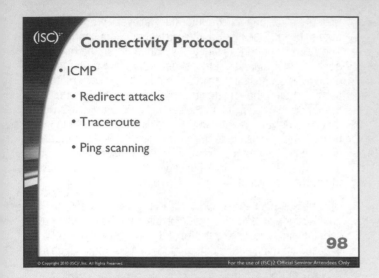

Connectivity Protocol

- ICMP
  - Redirect attacks
  - Traceroute
  - Ping scanning

98

- **ICMP REDIRECT ATTACKS** – A router may send a legitimate ICMP redirect to a host to tell it to use a different, more effective default route. However, an attacker can also send an ICMP redirect to a host telling it to use the attacker's machine as the default route. The attacker will then forward all of the redirected traffic to a router so that the victim will not know that his/her traffic has been intercepted. This is a good example of a man-in-the-middle attack. Another attack is that some operating systems will crash if they receive a storm of ICMP redirects.

- **TRACEROUTE** – Traceroute is a diagnostic tool that displays the path a packet traverses between the source and destination hosts.

- **PING SCANNING** – Ping scanning is a basic network mapping technique which helps narrow the scope of a planned attack. An attacker can use one of many tools that can be downloaded from the Internet to ping all of the addresses in a range. If a host replies to a ping, the attacker knows that a host exists at that address.

REFERENCE:
http://www.pms.ifi.lmu.de/mitarbeiter/ohlbach/multimedia/IT/IBMtutorial/3376c24.
   html#icmp

- **INTERNET CONTROL MESSAGE PROTOCOLS (ICMP)** – Is used for the exchange of control messages between hosts and gateways and is used for diagnostic tools such as ping and traceroute. ICMP is a valuable tool for network administrators trying to troubleshoot networks, but it can also be leveraged for malicious behavior, including man-in-the-middle and denial of service attacks. Many ICMP based problems occur because ICMP messages are unauthenticated.

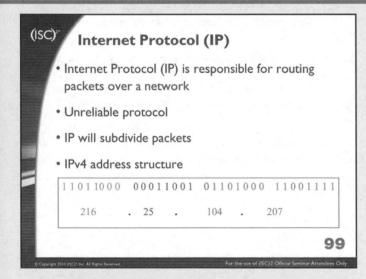

Internet Protocol (IP)

- Internet Protocol (IP) is responsible for routing packets over a network
- Unreliable protocol
- IP will subdivide packets
- IPv4 address structure

| 11011000 | 00011001 | 01101000 | 11001111 |
| 216 . | 25 . | 104 . | 207 |

99

- **INTERNET PROTOCOL (IP)** – For the common user, IP is probably best known for its ability to route information globally, although in most cases a user will be more familiar with DNS addresses and URLs.

- **INTERNET PROTOCOL (IP) IS RESPONSIBLE FOR SENDING PACKETS OVER A NETWORK** – From the source to the destination host(s).

- **UNRELIABLE PROTOCOL** – IP is an unreliable protocol in that it does not guarantee that packets arrive error-free or in the correct order. (This task is left to protocols on higher layers.)

- **IP WILL SUBDIVIDE PACKETS** – Into **FRAGMENTS** when a packet is too large for a network.

- **IPV4 ADDRESS STRUCTURE** -
  - Each octet will have a value between 0 and 255, although 0 and 255 are not used for hosts. (0 is usually reserved to refer to the entire sub-network (see below) and 255 is used for broadcast addresses.)
  - Hosts are distinguished by the IP addresses of their network interfaces.
  - The address is expressed as four octets separated by dots ("."), for example 216.25.104.207.
  - Each address is subdivided into two parts: the network number and the host. The network number assigned by an external organization represents the organization's network. The host represents the network interface within the network.

REFERENCE:
http://www.protocols.com/pbook/tcpip2.htm#IP

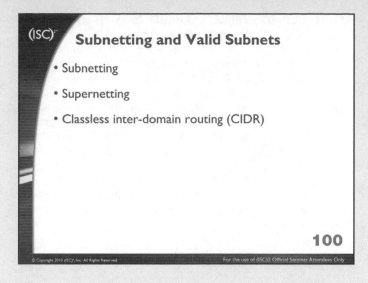

Subnetting and Valid Subnets

- Subnetting
- Supernetting
- Classless inter-domain routing (CIDR)

100

- **SUBNETS** – Networks are typically subdivided into separately routed subnets. Subnets are described by a subnet mask such as 255.255.255.0.

- **SUBNETTING** – The logical division of large network address ranges into small logical networks. Internet service providers (ISP) are in control of large blocks of IP addresses and offer smaller blocks of addresses to customers for reasons of address conservation. This process is typically done along octet or class boundaries.

- **SUPERNETTING** – The logical aggregation of several small network address ranges. This solves two problems – the inability of routing tables to represent several networks with a single entry, and it addresses the exhaustion of Class B network addresses.

- **CLASSLESS INTER-DOMAIN ROUTING** – Supernetting is also called CIDR – classless inter-domain routing.

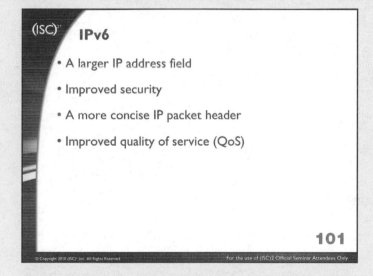

IPv6

- A larger IP address field
- Improved security
- A more concise IP packet header
- Improved quality of service (QoS)

101

- **IPV6** – After the explosion of Internet usage in the mid-1990s, IPv4 began to experience serious growing pains. It was obvious that the massive usage of the Internet was stretching the protocol to its limit. The most obvious problems were a shortage of unallocated IP addresses and serious shortcomings in security. (Note that IP Version 5 was an experimental real-time streaming protocol.) IPv6 is a modernization of the IPv4 protocol and includes:

- **A LARGER IP ADDRESS FIELD** – IPv6 addresses are 128 bits, which supports 2128 hosts. Suffice it to say that there will never be a shortage of IPv6 addresses. Computing how many hosts will be supported by IPv6 and comparing it with some other large constant (such as the number of grains of sand on a beach) will be left as an exercise for the curious.

- **IMPROVED SECURITY** – IPSec must be implemented in IPv6. This will help ensure the integrity and confidentiality of IP packets and allow communicating partners to authenticate with each other.

- **A MORE CONCISE IP PACKET HEADER** – Hosts will require less time to process each packet, which will result in increased throughput.

- **IMPROVED QUALITY OF SERVICE** – This will help services obtain the appropriate share of a network's bandwidth.

- The slow process of converting to IPv6 has already begun. Public IPv6 networks, such as 6Net and 6Bone, are accepting additional networks to connect to their IPv6 network. Since there are always stragglers, it will probably take a long time for every network to convert to the new protocol, but, if recent history is an indicator, the vast majority of networks will convert in a relatively small interval of time.

REFERENCE:
http://www.protocols.com/pbook/tcpip2.htm#IPv6

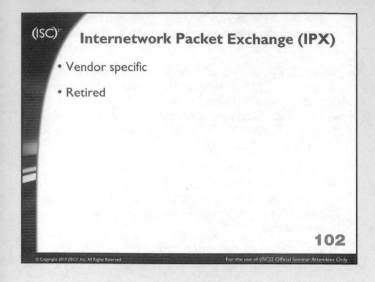

Internetwork Packet Exchange (IPX)

- Vendor specific
- Retired

102

- **INTERNETWORK PACKET EXCHANGE (IPX)** – Is the original NetWare, Network layer (Layer 3) protocol used to route packets through an Internetwork. IPX is a connectionless datagram-based network protocol and as such, is similar to the Internet Protocol found in TCP/IP networks. Novell IPX network addresses must be unique. These addresses are represented in hexadecimal format and consist of two parts: a network number and a node number. The IPX network number (assigned by the network administrator) is 32 bits long. The node number, which is usually the media access control (MAC) address for one of the system's network interface cards (NICs), is 48 bits long. IPX uses the services of a dynamic distance-vector routing protocol (routing information protocol [RIP]) or a link-state routing protocol (NetWare link-state protocol [NLSP]).

- **RETIRED** – The use of IPX is declining now as more networks migrate to TCP/IP-based protocols.

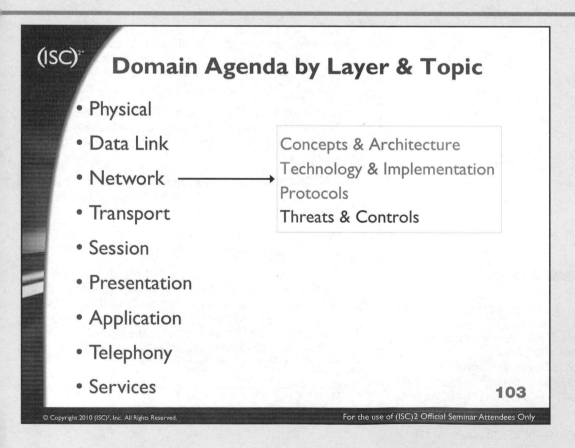

Domain Agenda by Layer & Topic

- Physical
- Data Link
- Network ⟶
- Transport
- Session
- Presentation
- Application
- Telephony
- Services

Concepts & Architecture
Technology & Implementation
Protocols
Threats & Controls

103

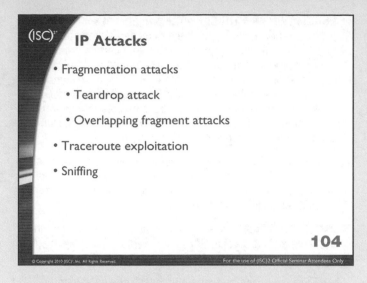

- **IP FRAGMENTATION ATTACKS –** Most IP fragmentation attacks were designed to cause some form of denial of service to a system and have been "fixed" through the deployment of patches. In most cases the attacker was taking advantage of flaws in the Internet Protocol related to the fragmentation and reassembly of packets being sent.

  - **TEARDROP ATTACK –** IP packet fragments arc constructed by the attacker so that when the target host attempts to reconstruct the packet, it calculates a negative number for the fragment length. If the target host's IP stack does not compute a reasonable fragment length, the host may crash or become unstable. This problem can be fixed with a vendor patch.

- **OVERLAPPING FRAGMENT ATTACKS –** Are used to subvert packet filters that only inspect the first fragment of a fragmented packet. The technique involves sending a harmless first fragment that will satisfy the packet filter, and then sending other packets that overwrite the first fragment with malicious data thereby bypassing the packet filter and being accepted by the victim host. A solution to this problem is for TCP/IP stacks to refuse to permit fragments to overwrite each other.

- **TRACEROUTE EXPLOITATION –** Traceroute can be used maliciously to map a victim network and learn about its routing. In addition, tools such as Firewalk use techniques similar to traceroute to enumerate a firewall rule set.

- **SNIFFING THE WIRE –** Listening on the wire, or sniffing, can be used by network administrators to analyze problems with communications. When adversaries sniff, however, the action is called eavesdropping.

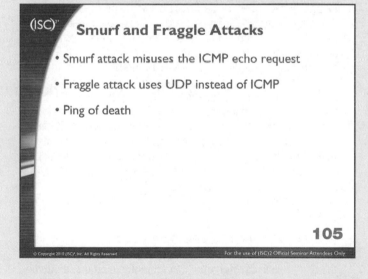

- **SMURF ATTACK MISUSES THE ICMP ECHO REQUEST –** The intruder sends an ICMP echo request with a spoofed source address of the victim to a network's broadcast address. The victim will be overwhelmed by the ICMP echo replies.

- **FRAGGLE ATTACK USES UDP INSTEAD OF ICMP –** The attacker sends a UDP packet on port 7 with a spoofed source address of the victim. The victim host will be overwhelmed by the responses from the network.

- **PING OF DEATH –** This is an attack based on a misconfigured ICMP packet that is 64 Kb in size. An improperly patched host receiving a ping of death packet may crash, leading to a denial of service. Amazingly, an enormous number of operating systems will crash or become unstable upon receiving an ICMP echo greater than the legal packet limit of 65,536 bytes. Before the ping of death became famous, the source of the attack was difficult to find because many system administrators would ignore a harmless looking ping in their logs.

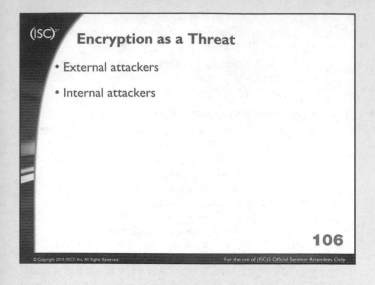

- **ENCRYPTION AS A THREAT** – The primary network-layer protection mechanisms available to us depend on our ability to inspect packets, filter traffic, and reject certain protocols. This is fine when traffic is in the clear, but when traffic is encrypted, it becomes impossible to enforce these controls. By using the same techniques the good guys use to provide confidentiality for traffic, the bad guys can prevent their traffic from being identified as malicious and get through the various controls and protections on the enterprise.

- **EXTERNAL ATTACKERS** – External attackers utilize various methods to plant encrypted backdoors that will allow them access into the enterprise and can use improperly configured services as encrypted tunnels.

- **INTERNAL ATTACKERS** – Internal attackers utilize commonly available tools (SSL, TLS, SSH) to encrypt traffic so as to subvert controls. Examples of available tools include:

  - Trojans/viruses that set up an encrypted backdoor.

  - Tunnels set up to get to "home" computers.

  - Tunnels set up to use company resources for personal pursuits.

  - Tunnels set up to protect criminal or improper behavior.

  - Compromised servers that provide SSL/TLS connections.

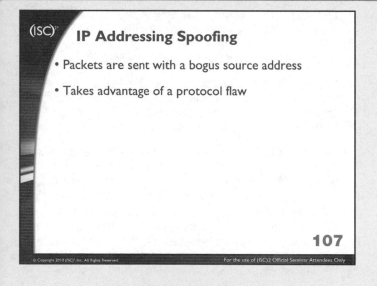

- **PACKETS ARE SENT WITH A BOGUS SOURCE ADDRESS** – Spoofed addresses can be used to abuse the three-way handshake required to start a TCP session. Under normal circumstances, a host offers to initiate a session with a remote host by sending a packet with the SYN option, the remote host responds with a packet with the SYN and ACK options, and the handshake is completed when the initiating host responds with a packet with the ACK option. If the source address of the requesting host is spoofed, the SYN ACK never reaches the true source and the handshake cannot complete. When the attacker arranges for several of these connections to be requested and leaves the handshakes uncompleted, the system may become clogged with half-open connections and consequently become unable to respond to legitimate connections.

- **TAKES ADVANTAGE OF A PROTOCOL FLAW** – Spoofing and SYN flooding take advantage of a protocol flaw. To mitigate the risk of a successful attack, vendors have released patches that reduce the likelihood that the limit of uncompleted handshakes is reached. Security devices such as firewalls can also block packets that arrive from an external interface with an internal network source address.

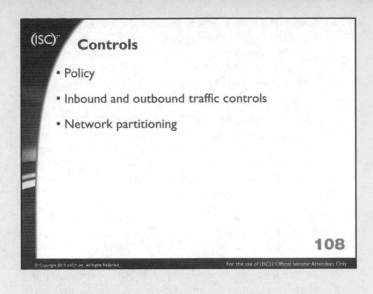

- **POLICY** – Not all access and traffic can be limited by technical means. Policies and deterrents against inappropriate network activity can be an effective tool.

- **INBOUND AND OUTBOUND TRAFFIC CONTROLS** – IDS, IPS, and/or firewalls are reasonable controls for packet-based attacks.

- **NETWORK PARTITIONING** – Dividing the network into smaller physical and logical segments will support filtering. Smaller segments allow for greater granularity in access rules.

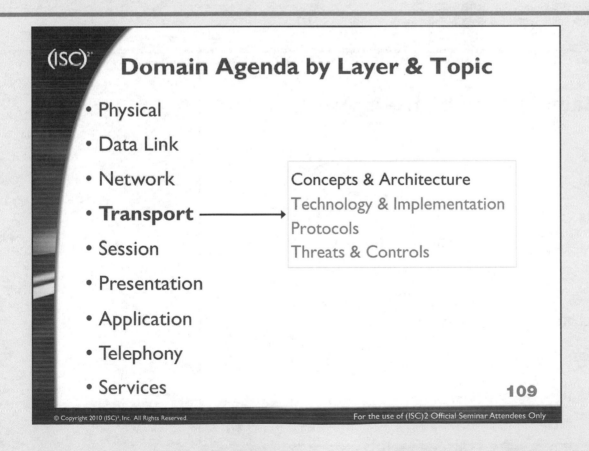

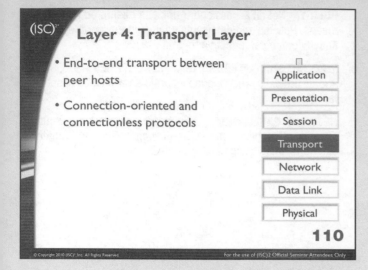

Layer 4: Transport Layer

- End-to-end transport between peer hosts

- Connection-oriented and connectionless protocols

| |
| Application |
| Presentation |
| Session |
| Transport |
| Network |
| Data Link |
| Physical |

110

- **LAYER 4: TRANSPORT LAYER** – The transport Layer provides data communication between hosts and is concerned with the information payload. It relies on Layer 3 correctly addressing (routing) information, while deferring any process-related handling such as authentication to Layers 5 and above.

  - The transport layer is commonly implemented as part of an integrated stack with Layer 3 (TCP/IP stack). Layer 4 offers two principal types of communication:

    - A connection-oriented mode, where information delivery is guaranteed and flow control and error recovery are provided.

    - A connectionless mode where, due to concerns such as performance, no such guarantee is required.

- Attacks on Layer 4 seek to manipulate, disclose, or prevent delivery of the payload as a whole. This might happen by reading the payload (as in a sniffer attack) or changing it (as in a man-in-the-middle attack). While service can be disrupted on other layers as well, the transport layer has become a common attack ground.

- **END-TO-END TRANSPORT BETWEEN PEER HOSTS** – The transport layer creates an end-to-end transmission path between peer hosts. (Reminder: The data link layer ensures that no data is lost, the network layer ensures data is fragmented into transmittable packets, and the transport layer ensures that correct order is maintained.)

- **CONNECTION-ORIENTED AND CONNECTIONLESS PROTOCOLS** – User datagram protocol (UDP) and transmission control protocol (TCP) are the best-known and most important transport layer protocols in the TCP/IP suite. UDP does not ensure that transmissions are received without errors and is therefore classified as a connectionless, unreliable protocol. This does not mean that UDP is poorly designed, but rather that error checking will be done by the application, not by the UDP protocol.

  - Connection-oriented reliable protocols such as TCP ensure integrity by providing error-free transmission. These protocols divide information from multiple applications on the same host into segments to be transmitted on a network.

  - Note that connection-oriented versus connectionless is not another split layer but rather a different type of implemented functionality.

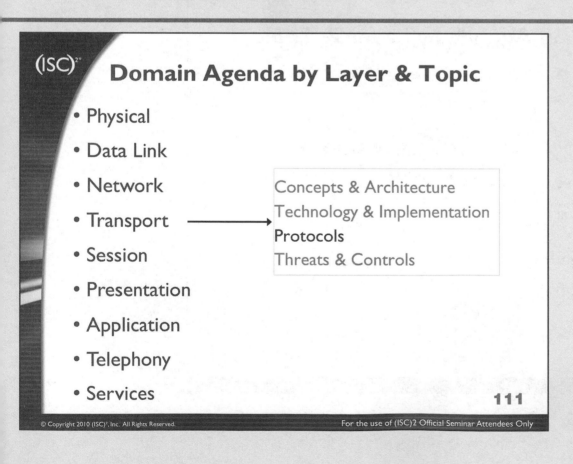

Domain Agenda by Layer & Topic

- Physical
- Data Link
- Network
- Transport ⟶
- Session
- Presentation
- Application
- Telephony
- Services

Concepts & Architecture
Technology & Implementation
Protocols
Threats & Controls

111

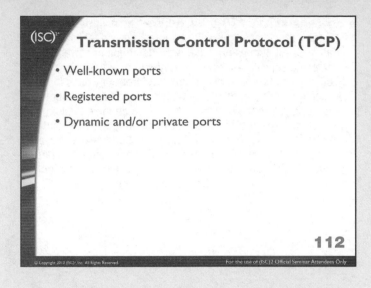

- **TRANSMISSION CONTROL PROTOCOL (TCP)** – The Transmission Control Protocol provides connection-oriented data management and reliable data transfer. TCP and UDP map data connections to port numbers. TCP and UDP port numbers are managed by the Internet Assigned Numbers Authority (IANA). There are 65,536 ports, and they are structured into three ranges:

- **WELL-KNOWN PORTS** – Ports 0 through 1023 are known as the well-known ports. Ports in this range are assigned by IANA and on most systems can only be used by privileged processes and users.

- **REGISTERED PORTS** – Ports 1024 through 49151 can be registered with IANA by application developers but are not assigned by IANA.

- **DYNAMIC AND/OR PRIVATE PORTS** – Ports 49152 through 65535 can be freely used by applications. A typical use for these ports is the initiation of return connections.

REFERENCE:
http://www.cs.virginia.edu/~cs458/material/Redbook-ibm-tcpip-Chp5.pdf

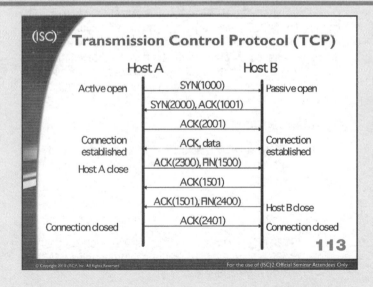

- **TRANSMISSION CONTROL PROTOCOL (TCP) SESSION** – This slide shows the establishment, data transfer, and disconnection of a TCP session. As can be seen, TCP establishes a "connected" session through a three-way handshake, ensures flow control and data receipt through the use of ACKs, and uses a "graceful close."

- The initial packet's SYN ("synchronize," or open request) bit set transmits the initial sequence number for its side of the connection. The initial sequence numbers are random. All subsequent packets have the ACK ("acknowledge") bit set. Note the acknowledgment of the FIN ("final") bit and the independent close operations.

- If Host A does not respond to Host B's SYN/ACK, Host B will be holding a half-open session, using resources. This is a SYN flood attack if done repeatedly.

REFERENCE:
Firewalls and Internet Security: Repelling the Wily Hacker, William R. Cheswick, Steven M. Bellovin, Aviel D Rubin (2nd Edition) Addison-Wesley Professional Computing Series I

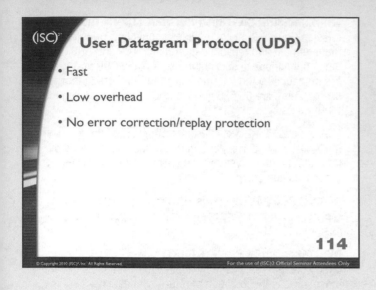

- **USER DATAGRAM PROTOCOL (UDP)** – The user datagram protocol provides a lightweight service for connectionless data transfer. It does not have error detection or correction. The same considerations for port numbers as described for TCP apply to UDP. UDP also omits the three-way handshake which removes communication startup latency. A number of protocols within the transport layer have been defined on top of UDP as a result of technical development, thereby splitting the transport layer in two. Protocols stacked between Layers 4 and 5 include real-time protocol (RTP) and real-time control protocol (RTCP), MBone (a multicasting protocol), reliable UDP (RUDP), and stream control transmission protocol (SCTP).

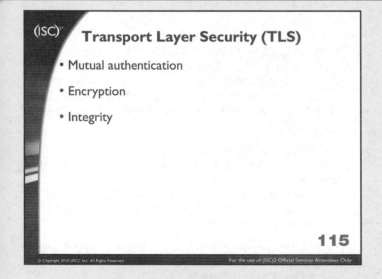

- **TRANSPORT LAYER SECURITY (TLS)** – TLS was based on SSL version 3 and first appeared in RFC 2246 as a way of providing security for HTTP traffic. The current version of TLS, version 1.1, is RFC 4346. It protects against attacks such as a man-in-the-middle, and provides message integrity through the use of hashed MACing. While the name indicates that this is a transport-layer protocol, it also provides compression and encryption and could therefore also be considered a Layer 6 protocol.

  - **FUNCTIONS OF TLS –**

    - **MUTUAL AUTHENTICATION –** Of server and client (although client authentication is seldom used in practice).

    - **ENCRYPTION –** Encrypted connections, extensible via algorithms implemented on both client and server.

    - **INTEGRITY –** TLS supports several versions of hash functions and message authentication codes (MAC) to ensure message integrity

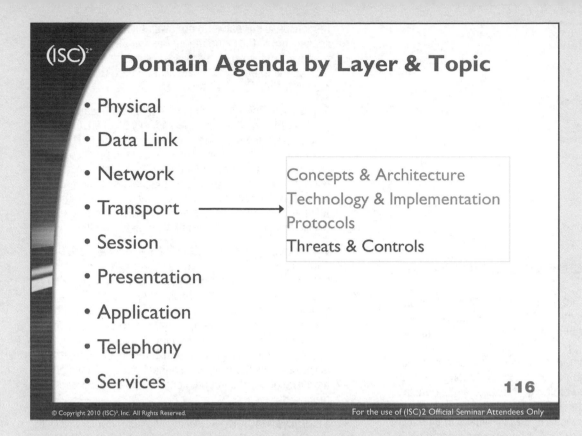

Domain Agenda by Layer & Topic

- Physical
- Data Link
- Network
- Transport →
- Session
- Presentation
- Application
- Telephony
- Services

Concepts & Architecture
Technology & Implementation
Protocols
Threats & Controls

116

Attacks

- SYN flood
- Denial of service

117

- **SYN FLOOD** – An attacker can also launch a denial of service attack by sending a flood of the initial packets with the **SYN** option, but not replying to the **SYN** and **ACK** that comes back from the victim system. If the attacker sends a storm of such packets, as above, the victim may reach the limit of uncompleted ("half-open") three-way handshakes, and refuse other legitimate network connections.

- **DENIAL OF SERVICE** – A SYN flood attack is a denial of service attack against the initial handshake in a TCP connection. Many new connections from faked, random IP addresses are opened in short order, overloading the target's connection table. Controls include tuning of the operating system parameters (the size of the backlog table) according to vendor specifications. Another solution (which requires modification to the TCP/IP stack) are SYN cookies, which enclose a cookie in the SYN/ACK from the recipient. The originator responding with the third part of the handshake will return the cookie with its ACK. The absence of the correct cookie would alert the recipient to an illegitimate packet.

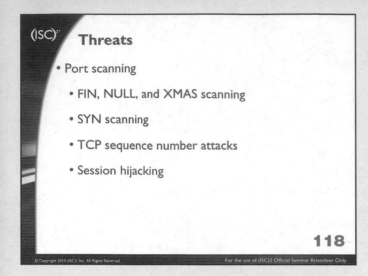

Threats

- Port scanning
  - FIN, NULL, and XMAS scanning
  - SYN scanning
- TCP sequence number attacks
- Session hijacking

- **PORT SCANNING** – Is the act of probing for TCP services on a machine. It is performed by establishing the initial handshake for a connection. While not in itself an attack, it allows an attacker to test for the presence of potentially vulnerable services on a target system. Port scanning can also be used for fingerprinting an operating system by evaluating response characteristics such as the timing of a response, the details of the handshake, etc. Protection from port scanning includes restriction of network connections, i.e., by means of a host-based or network-based firewall, or by defining a list of valid source addresses at the application level.

  - **FIN, NULL, AND XMAS SCANNING** – In FIN scanning, a request to close a connection is sent to the target machine. If no application is listening on that port, a TCP RST or an ICMP packet will be sent. This attack only works on UNIX machines. (Windows machines behave in a slightly different manner, deviating from RFC793 (always responding to a FIN packet with an RST), thereby rendering recognition of open ports impossible.) FIN is a stealth scan. Note that firewalls operating in stealth mode (i.e., suppressing responses to FIN packets) are available. NULL and XMAS scans work in the same manner as the FIN scan, except that in a NULL scan, no flags are set on the initiating TCP packet and in the XMAS scan, several (FIN, URG, and PSH) are set (or "lit," as in a Christmas tree).

- **SYN SCANNING** – As traditional TCP scans became widely recognized and, therefore, increasingly blocked, various stealth scanning techniques were developed. In TCP half-scanning (also known as TCP SYN scanning), no complete connection is opened; instead only the initial steps of the handshake are performed. This makes the scan harder to recognize (for instance, it won't show up in application log files). It is, however, possible to recognize and block TCP SYN scans with an appropriately equipped firewall.

- **TCP SEQUENCE NUMBER ATTACKS** – TCP sequence numbers are transmitted within data packets in order to detect and correct data packet loss. If the transmission of a packet is not reported back as successful, the packet will be retransmitted. These sequence numbers can be predicted and fake packets with the correct sequence number can be introduced into the data stream by an eavesdropping third party. One use of this class of attack is session hijacking. Protection mechanisms based on better randomization of sequence numbers have been proposed.

- **SESSION HIJACKING** – Session hijacking (for example, a man-in-the-middle attack) is the unauthorized insertion of packets into a data stream. Hijacking is normally based on sequence number attacks, where sequence numbers are either guessed or intercepted. The attacker sniffs or intercepts packets, removes legitimate packets from the data stream, and replaces them with his or her own. Both sides of the communication would then be communicating with the attacker. Controls against IP spoofing can be executed on Layer 3. As TCP sessions only perform an initial authentication, application layer encryption can be used to protect against man-in-the-middle attacks.

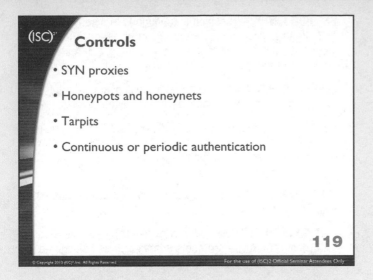

Controls

- SYN proxies
- Honeypots and honeynets
- Tarpits
- Continuous or periodic authentication

119

- **HONEYPOTS AND HONEYNETS** – Are effective means of assessing what is really occurring in the network. They also provide controls and potentially discourage would-be intruders from returning. Honeypots are typically placed within a network infrastructure and are intended to draw malicious traffic to them and away from legitimate systems. They advertise themselves as easy targets in order to detect and deflect malicious attackers. They often appear as legitimate business machines, though they are frequently hardened specifically so as to entice and then ensnare attackers. A honeynet is a type of honeypot built with multiple systems. Many organizations have begun to use honeypots and honeynets to identify, quantify, and qualify types of traffic (particularly malicious traffic) on the Internet, in order to disseminate the information and to fabricate tools and procedures to counteract the attacks.

- **TARPITS** – Are similar to honeypots and honeynets in that they appear to be "easy targets" to attackers. Tarpits entice hackers by presenting legitimate looking systems that they will spend time attempting to crack. It is particularly useful against spamming and network (port) scanning.

- **SYN PROXIES** – Limit the number of open and abandoned connections to a critical server by intercepting the initial three-way handshake operation and establishing the initial connection between the SYN proxy and the originator. The SYN proxy only passes the connection to the true recipient if the three-way handshake completes properly. Incomplete transmissions will be dropped before they reach the recipient.

- **CONTINUOUS OR PERIODIC AUTHENTICATION** – Limits session hijacking at the transport layer. Since session hijacking attacks the connection/session data rather than the credentials, continuous/periodic authentication throughout the session limits the duration of the hijack.

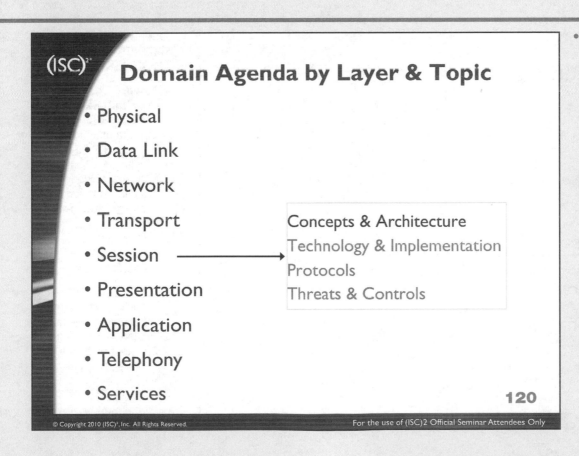

Domain Agenda by Layer & Topic

- Physical
- Data Link
- Network
- Transport
- Session → Concepts & Architecture
  Technology & Implementation
  Protocols
  Threats & Controls
- Presentation
- Application
- Telephony
- Services

120

- **LAYER 5: SESSION LAYER** – Provides a logical, persistent connection between peer hosts. The session layer includes several different types of services, some of which are interdependent. One of its most basic functions is to provide directory services, which allows for the identification of objects between hosts. The session layer also allows for remote procedure calls (where objects can be communicated between hosts) and for access services (important for the higher layers) such as NFS, which allows one to access and manipulate objects on another host.

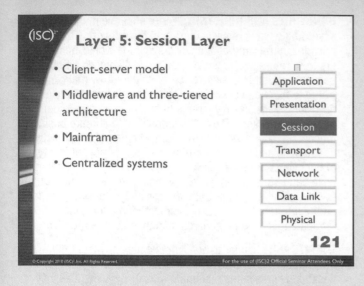

Layer 5: Session Layer

- Client-server model
- Middleware and three-tiered architecture
- Mainframe
- Centralized systems

Application
Presentation
Session
Transport
Network
Data Link
Physical

121

- **SESSION LAYER** – A session is analogous to a conversation that allows applications to exchange information. The session layer is responsible for creating, maintaining, and tearing down the session.

- **CLIENT-SERVER MODEL** – Spreads the session among many machines and in some cases, across many networks.

- **MIDDLEWARE AND THREE-TIERED ARCHITECTURE** – Many implementations are designed to spread the workload of a complex process to specialized computers within a larger network of computers.

- **MAINFRAME** – Keeps the sessions local, unless remote terminals are implemented.

- **CENTRALIZED SYSTEMS** – Allow for control of the session. RADIUS and TACACS+ protocols enable remote connection through which a session can be established with the local server.

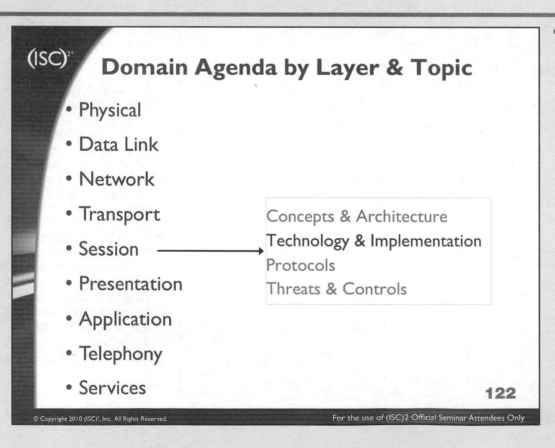

Domain Agenda by Layer & Topic

- Physical
- Data Link
- Network
- Transport
- Session →
- Presentation
- Application
- Telephony
- Services

Concepts & Architecture
Technology & Implementation
Protocols
Threats & Controls

122

- **SOME EXAMPLES OF TECHNOLOGIES AT THE SESSION LAYER ARE:**

  - **JAVA REMOTE METHOD INVOCATION (JAVA RMI)** – Enables programmers to create distributed-Java technology-based to Java-technology-based applications, wherein remote Java objects can be invoked from other Java virtual machines, even if on different hosts.

  - **MICROSOFT .NET** – Provides a framework that allows objects to interact with one another without being on the same machine.

REFERENCE:
http://java.sun.com/javase/technologies/core/basic/rmi/index.jsp

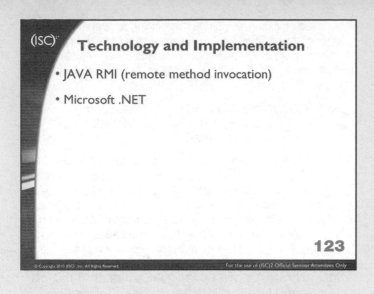

Technology and Implementation

- JAVA RMI (remote method invocation)
- Microsoft .NET

123

- **JAVA** – Java is both a program and a platform. As a program, it is simpler to use than C++ and usually requires less code. Java is an object-oriented, portable, and secure language. Java runs on most machines through the use of the Java platform that permits Java bytecode to run on nearly all hardware platforms.

- **JAVA RMI (REMOTE METHOD INVOCATION)** – Allows a program running on one Java virtual machine to invoke methods running on another JVM.

- **MICROSOFT .NET** – The Microsoft .NET Framework is a software framework that can be installed on computers running Microsoft Windows operating systems. It includes a large library of coded solutions to common programming problems and a virtual machine that manages the execution of programs written specifically for the framework. The .NET Framework is a Microsoft offering and is intended to be used by most new applications created for the Windows platform.

REFERENCE:
Oracle and Microsoft websites

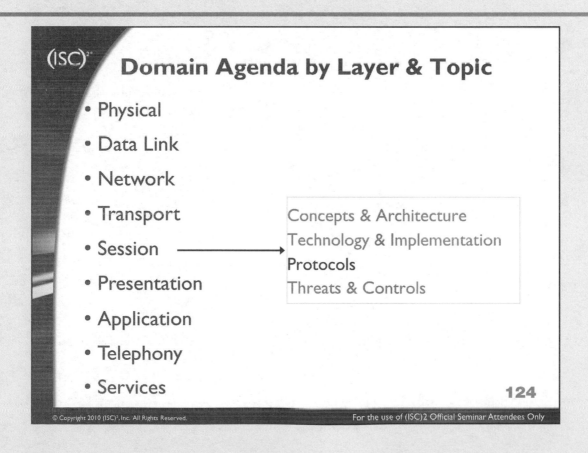

Domain Agenda by Layer & Topic

- Physical
- Data Link
- Network
- Transport
- Session →
- Presentation
- Application
- Telephony
- Services

Concepts & Architecture
Technology & Implementation
Protocols
Threats & Controls

124

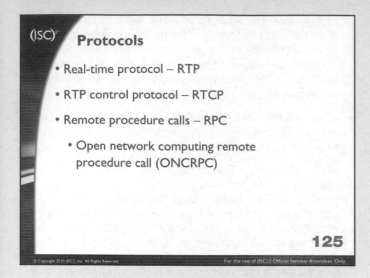

Protocols

- Real-time protocol – RTP
- RTP control protocol – RTCP
- Remote procedure calls – RPC
  - Open network computing remote procedure call (ONCRPC)

125

© Copyright 2010 (ISC)², Inc. All Rights Reserved.   For the use of (ISC)2 Official Seminar Attendees Only

---

- Due to the widespread use of the TCP/IP protocol suite which combines session, presentation, and application layers into one monolithic application layer, there are very few protocols that operate only at the session layer.

- **REAL-TIME PROTOCOL (RTP) –** Provides end-to-end delivery services for data with real-time characteristics, such as interactive audio and video. Those services include payload type identification, sequence numbering, time-stamping, and delivery monitoring. Applications typically run RTP on top of UDP to make use of its multiplexing and checksum services. Both protocols contribute parts of the transport protocol functionality.

- **RTP CONTROL PROTOCOL (RTCP) –** Is used to monitor the quality of service (QoS) and to communicate information about the users during a session.

- **REMOTE PROCEDURE CALLS –** Remote procedure calls (RPC) execute objects across hosts. The core service of RPC is a "portmapper." Any client wishing to avail himself or herself of services provided by an RPC server will obtain access through this portmapper, which will then redirect the client to the TCP port on which the actual application providing the service is running. There are several (mutually incompatible) services in this category, such as Distributed Computing Environment RPC (DCE RPC) and **OPEN NETWORK COMPUTING RPC** (ONC RPC, also referred to as SunRPC or simply RPC). Common Object Request Broker Architecture (CORBA) and Microsoft Distributed Component Object Model (DCOM) can be viewed as RPC type protocols. RPC services are not typically limited to Layer 5.

REFERENCE:
http://tools.ietf.org/html/rfc3550

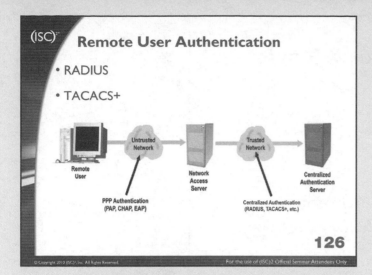

Remote User Authentication

- RADIUS
- TACACS+

Remote User → Untrusted Network → Network Access Server → Trusted Network → Centralized Authentication Server

PPP Authentication (PAP, CHAP, EAP)

Centralized Authentication (RADIUS, TACACS+, etc.)

126

- **REMOTE USER AUTHENTICATION** – A major issue with implementing authentication controls in network environments is trying to ensure only the correct people or processes are gaining access and preventing replay attacks. (In a replay attack, the attacker captures access control authentication credentials off the wire and tries to play them back at a later time.) The two techniques used to prevent this type of attack are:

  - Time stamps in the credentials. The credentials will not work outside of the specified period of time (Kerberos).

  - A nonce in the credentials, which is a random number only used once (parts of Kerberos as well as many of the other protocols).

- Another major issue with any authentication system is the susceptibility to password-guessing attacks. As we learned in the Access Control domain, any password-based (one-factor) authentication system is vulnerable to a brute-force password guessing attack. Only two-factor systems can really address this risk. This typically means token cards, or smart cards with digital certificates, or biometrics.

- Here is how the next set of protocols fits together: The remote user connects to the network access server (NAS) using PPP and one of the PPP authentication methods is used to authenticate either the user or the node. The NAS can't typi-

cally perform the authentication, and instead uses a centralized access control protocol to submit the query to a central database where the user authentication actually takes place. The PPP authentication protocols (PAP, CHAP, and EAP) are used to establish the link between the remote user on the untrusted network and the NAS, and the centralized access control protocols (RADIUS, TACACS+, etc.) are used over the trusted network (from the NAS to the centralized authentication server).

- **REMOTE AUTHENTICATION DIAL-IN USER SERVICE (RADIUS)** – RADIUS is an authentication protocol used mainly in networked environments such as Internet service providers (ISP), or for similar services requiring single sign-on for Layer 3 network access and scalable authentication combined with an "acceptable" degree of security. RADIUS also provides support for consumption measurements such as connection time. RADIUS authentication is based on the use of simple username/password credentials. These credentials are encrypted by the client using a shared secret with the RADIUS server. RADIUS is vulnerable to a number of cryptographic attacks as well as replay attacks. RADIUS also suffers from a lack of integrity protection due to the fact not all fields are encrypted when transmitted. Nonetheless, within its usual scope of deployment, RADIUS is generally considered to be sufficiently secure. An ISP in particular will want to balance the risk of unauthorized access (and theft of bandwidth) with deployment cost: Because RADIUS is relatively easy to deploy and is supported by a large number of devices in the market, the resulting cost reduction may well offset the ISP's risk. Conversely, RADIUS may not be sufficiently secure when higher levels of security are needed. In these cases, one would take advantage of the added security offered by VPNs or IPSec.

- **TACACS+** – TACACS+ (terminal access control access control system +) is an authentication protocol similar in purpose to RADIUS, except that it separates out the authentication and authorization functions instead of combining them like RADIUS does. TACACS+ also uses TCP for communication instead of UDP like RADIUS. TACACS+ is a CISCO proprietary product.

REFERENCES:

http://publib.boulder.ibm.com/infocenter/pseries/v5r3/index.jsp?topic=/com.ibm.aix.security/doc/security/radius_server.htm

http://www.untruth.org/~josh/security/radius/radius-auth.html

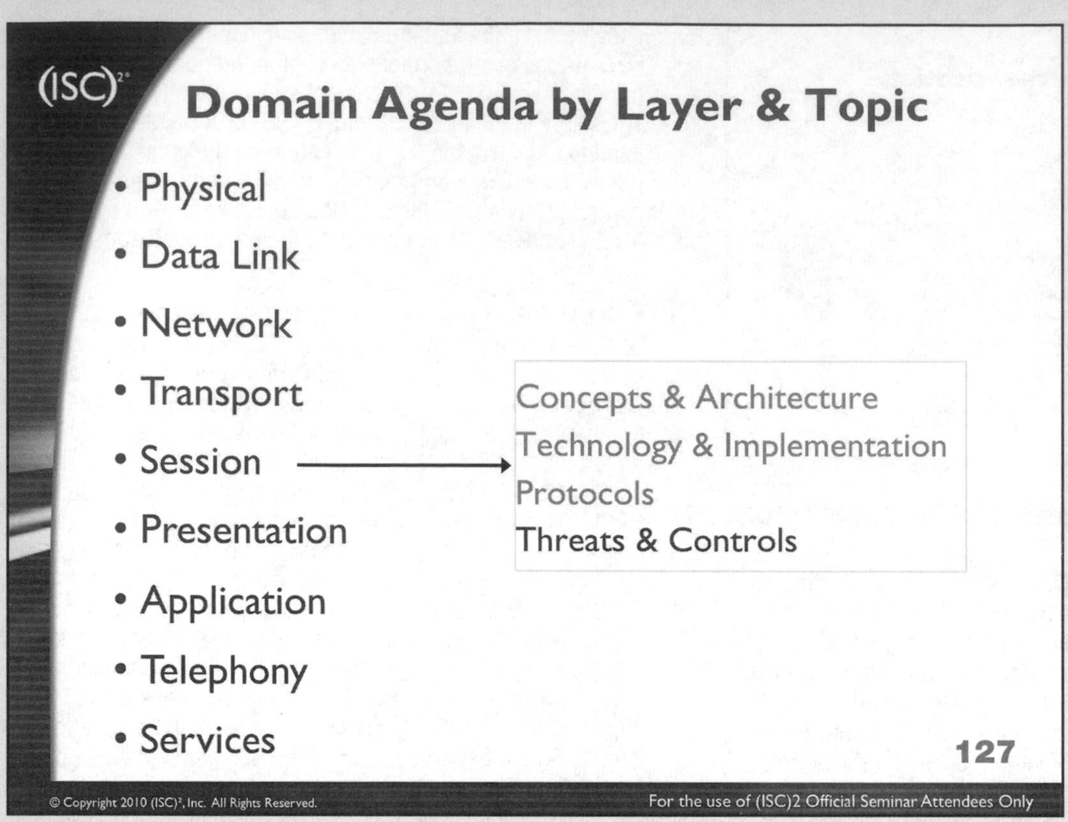

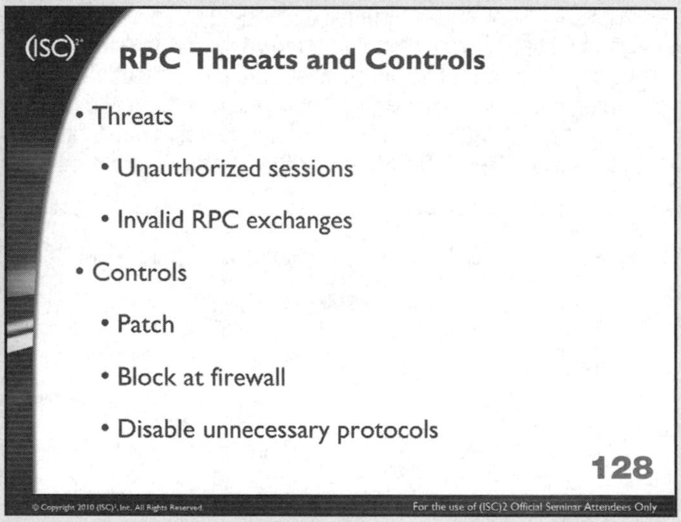

Domain Agenda by Layer & Topic

- Physical
- Data Link
- Network
- Transport
- Session → Concepts & Architecture
  Technology & Implementation
  Protocols
  Threats & Controls
- Presentation
- Application
- Telephony
- Services

127

RPC Threats and Controls

- Threats
  - Unauthorized sessions
  - Invalid RPC exchanges
- Controls
  - Patch
  - Block at firewall
  - Disable unnecessary protocols

128

- **THREATS -**
  - **UNAUTHORIZED SESSIONS** – Security problems with RPC include its weak authentication mechanism as well as an implementation problem: Portmapper will normally run under administrative privileges and can be quickly leveraged for privilege escalation by an attacker.
  - **INVALID RPC EXCHANGES** – Attackers can subvert the RPC process and reveal sensitive information about a responding host, or cause a DoS.
- **CONTROLS -**
  - **PATCH** – Updating software to remove known weaknesses.
  - **BLOCK AT FIREWALL** – Because RPC is seldom required in a WAN environment, filtering is a good option.
  - **DISABLE UNNECESSARY PROTOCOLS** – Session protocols can be turned off for some hosts. Note that good configuration management is required for control of services.

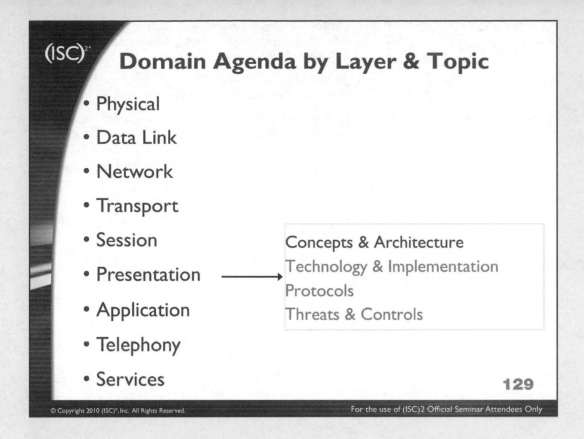

Domain Agenda by Layer & Topic

- Physical
- Data Link
- Network
- Transport
- Session
- Presentation →
- Application
- Telephony
- Services

Concepts & Architecture
Technology & Implementation
Protocols
Threats & Controls

129

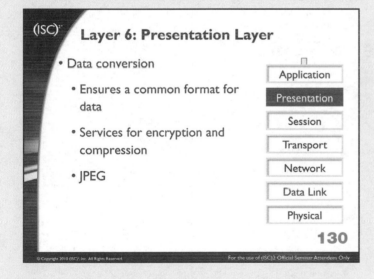

Layer 6: Presentation Layer

- Data conversion
  - Ensures a common format for data
  - Services for encryption and compression
  - JPEG

| Application |
| Presentation |
| Session |
| Transport |
| Network |
| Data Link |
| Physical |

130

- **ENSURES A COMMON FORMAT FOR DATA –** This layer might be more appropriately called the representation layer. Applications communicating over a network may use incompatible character sets, such as ASCII and Unicode. This layer ensures that the peer applications use a common format when representing data between hosts.

- **SERVICES FOR ENCRYPTION AND COMPRESSION –** This layer can provide services for the encryption and compression of network data, although these services may be performed by other layers or by the application itself. Functionality directly affecting the representation of data (such as digital rights management) can be incorporated into Layer 6.

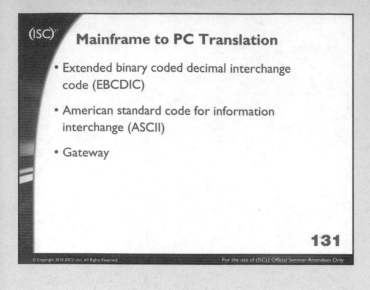

Mainframe to PC Translation

- Extended binary coded decimal interchange code (EBCDIC)
- American standard code for information interchange (ASCII)
- Gateway

131

- **EBCDIC** – Extended Binary Coded Decimal Interchange Code (EBCDIC) is a mainframe encoding scheme used primarily on IBM® AS/400.

- **ASCII** – American Standard Code for Information Interchange (ASCII) is a personal computer encoding scheme.

- **GATEWAY** – A gateway is specialized equipment used to translate presentation-layer protocols. This gateway is often improperly confused with a "default gateway," which is the client-side description of a router used to exit a LAN.

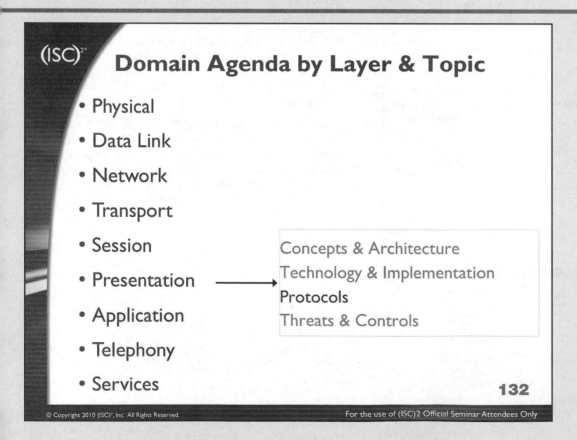

Domain Agenda by Layer & Topic

- Physical
- Data Link
- Network
- Transport
- Session
- Presentation →
- Application
- Telephony
- Services

Concepts & Architecture
Technology & Implementation
Protocols
Threats & Controls

132

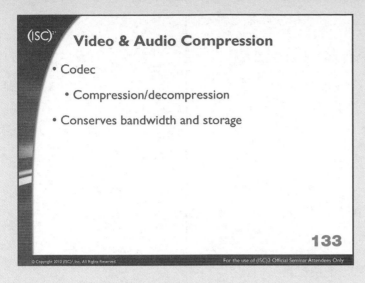

- **VIDEO AND AUDIO COMPRESSION –** Compression algorithms are closely tied to protocols. The main goal of compression algorithms is to conserve bandwidth and storage; for example, the data on a single music CD is equal to 600Mb of storage space and its equivalent after compression is an order of magnitude smaller, i.e., 60Mb. Compressing data has its drawbacks, however, depending on the algorithm used and the ratio chosen, since the quality of the playback can be significantly worse.

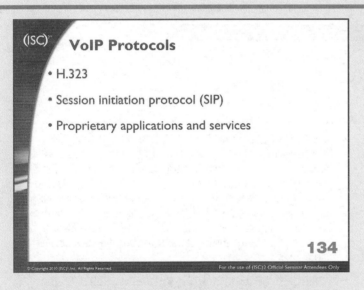

- **H.323 –** Developed by The International Telecommunication Union (ITU), H.323 was the original specification for voice over data networks. It has been largely replaced by SIP.

- **SESSION INITIATION PROTOCOL (SIP) –** SIP is a protocol designed to manage multimedia connections. It is not a comprehensive protocol suite, and leaves much of the actual payload data transfer to other protocols (e.g., real-time transport protocol (RTTP)). A number of phone companies have begun offering SIP services to end users.

  - SIP has been included in applications such as Microsoft Windows Messenger, and open source clients have been developed. SIP is designed to support digest authentication structured by "realms" similar to HTTP, although basic username/password authentication was removed from the protocol as of RFC 3261.

- SIP also provides integrity protection through MD5 hash functions and supports a variety of encryption mechanisms, such as TLS. Privacy extensions to SIP, including encryption and caller ID suppression, have been defined in extensions to the original SIP as defined in RFC 3325. While SIP, which has been closely modeled after HTTP, is a peer-to-peer application by design, it is possible to proxy it and thereby build a scalable and manageable public infrastructure.

- SIP does not work with network address translation (NAT), as it will always be impossible for at least one client to address the other, because outgoing IP headers are changed from private (non-routable) LAN addresses to the router's routable IP address. This result is a target conflict between network security and VoIP operation that must be resolved in a secure manner, e.g., by building a gateway in the form of a session controller. This controller can act as a proxy for SIP sessions (although it won't necessarily act as proxy for some of the streaming protocols carrying the actual voice information). On a related note, a SIP client is also a server and can receive requests from other machines. This is a general risk for the machine to which the software is deployed, and as with any server software, there is a risk of security gaps (such as buffer overflows) that can be exploited over the network.

- **PROPRIETARY APPLICATIONS AND SERVICES –** i.e., Skype: An online telephony/voice over IP application that offers clearing points with the public switched telephony network (PSTN). While the protocol is proprietary, its basic architecture has been published by the vendor, as well as by independent analysis. From a security perspective, Skype's peer-to-peer architecture is its most important feature. Any Skype client can turn into a so-called "super node," i.e., it will serve as a gateway for communication from other clients.

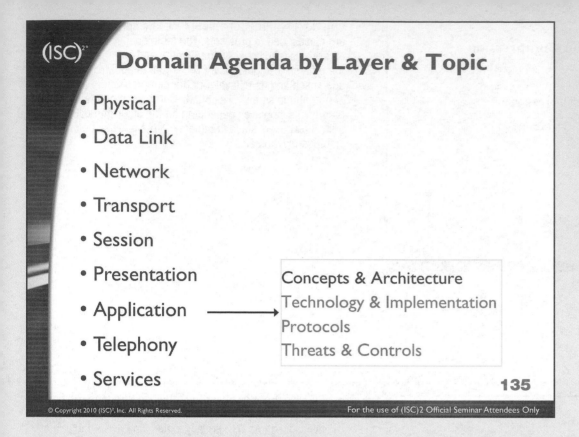

Domain Agenda by Layer & Topic

- Physical
- Data Link
- Network
- Transport
- Session
- Presentation
- Application → Concepts & Architecture
  Technology & Implementation
  Protocols
  Threats & Controls
- Telephony
- Services

135

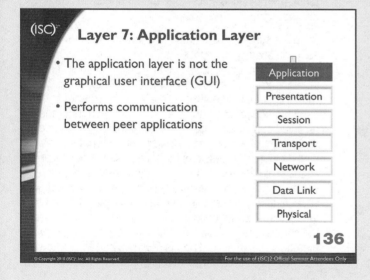

Layer 7: Application Layer

- The application layer is not the graphical user interface (GUI)

- Performs communication between peer applications

| Application |
| Presentation |
| Session |
| Transport |
| Network |
| Data Link |
| Physical |

136

- **THE APPLICATION LAYER IS NOT THE GRAPHICAL USER INTERFACE (GUI)** – It is important to remember this, particularly when an application has the same name as a Layer 7 protocol. For example, FTP protocol is a Layer 7 entity; the GUI is a separate function. The perfect opposing example is *NIX systems with no GUI installed that can still run all of the application-layer protocols. The Layer 7 protocol and the GUI can be installed at the same time, but they are not at the same layer.

- **PERFORMS COMMUNICATION BETWEEN PEER APPLICATIONS** – This layer is the application's portal to network-based services (e.g., determining the identity and availability of remote applications). When an application or the operating system transmits or receives data over a network, it uses the services from this layer.

Domain Agenda by Layer & Topic

- Physical
- Data Link
- Network
- Transport
- Session
- Presentation
- Application → Concepts & Architecture
  Technology & Implementation
  Protocols
  Threats & Controls
- Telephony
- Services

137

Implementations

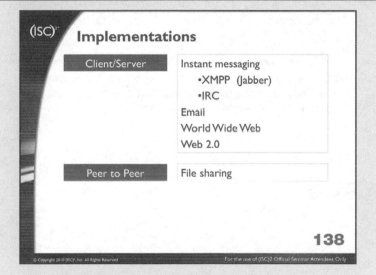

Client/Server	Instant messaging
	• XMPP (Jabber)
	• IRC
	Email
	World Wide Web
	Web 2.0
Peer to Peer	File sharing

138

- **CLIENT/SERVER –** Client requests are fulfilled by a central server(s) that does the bulk of the processing and leaves the client free to do end-user related tasks.

  - **INSTANT MESSAGING –** "Chat"/Text-messaging: Started as an informal method of brief communication between two or more people, but some organizations use IM for critical business applications.

    - **XMPP (FORMERLY CALLED JABBER) –** Extensible messaging and presence protocol is an open, XML-based protocol used in instant messaging and maintaining contact (buddy) lists. It is also compatible with most VOIP implementations.

    - **IRC –** Internet relay chat – IRC is used for Internet chatting and group conferencing.

  - **EMAIL –** Electronic mail is a store-and-forward technology. A client composes a message, sends the message

to a server, the server stores the message, forwards the message to another server, and the recipient retrieves the message. Mail can be composed on full-featured clients or text-only clients. Breaking the email process down allows CISSPs to identify actions to be taken at key junctures in the process.

- **WORLD WIDE WEB –** Developed by Tim Berners-Lee, at CERN in March 1989. A way to publish and organize related information so that it can be found quickly. "Hypertext allows documents to be linked into 'live' data so that every time the link is followed, the information is retrieved."

- **WEB 2.0 –** Is using the web as a platform for business where applications and customers leverage the benefits of the Internet for business instead of running traditional business applications on top of the Internet. It is noteworthy that WEB 2.0 is a new approach to using the web, not a new technology. WEB 2.0 represents the movement toward embracing the Internet as a tool and building on the connectivity, computational, and interactive possibilities the web permits rather than just running static systems and using a website as a simple information repository.

- **PEER TO PEER -**

  - **FILE SHARING –** Having every user install a floppy disk or other media reader on a workstation was originally thought to be wasteful. With the low cost of equipment today, that idea has faded away. Users do not need to keep a copy of a file when they can simply share it and may decide to operate under a policy of "what's mine is yours." This has led to users overstepping their authority, and the abuse of intellectual property laws.

REFERENCES:
http://www.w3.org/History/1989/proposal.html
http://www.oreillynet.com/pub/a/oreilly/tim/news/2005/09/30/what-is-web-20.html

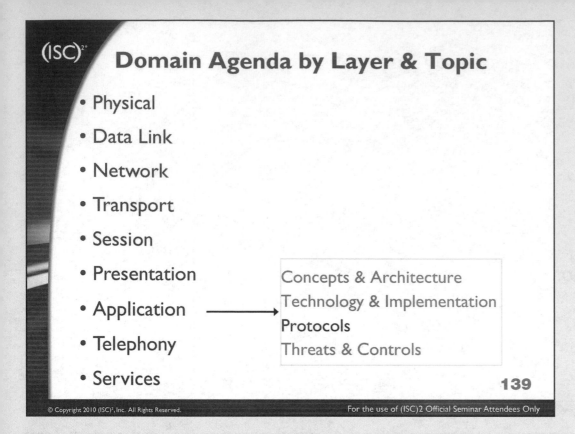

Domain Agenda by Layer & Topic

- Physical
- Data Link
- Network
- Transport
- Session
- Presentation
- Application $\longrightarrow$
- Telephony
- Services

Concepts & Architecture
Technology & Implementation
Protocols
Threats & Controls

139

Protocol Examples

FTP	File transfer protocol
RSH	Remote shell
IMAP	Internet message access protocol
IRC	Internet relay chat
MIME	Multipurpose internet mail extensions
POP3	Post office protocol (version 3)
Rlogin	Remote login in UNIX systems
SOAP	Simple object access protocol
SSH	Secure shell
TELNET	Terminal emulation protocol

140

- This is a short list of the most frequently used application-layer protocols and is drawn from the hundreds of application-layer protocols available.

- **SYNCHRONOUS MESSAGING -**

  - **INSTANT MESSAGING (IM)** – Instant messaging systems can be categorized into three general classes: peer-to-peer networks, brokered communication, and server-oriented networks. Most chat applications do offer additional services beyond their text messaging capability, for instance, screen sharing, remote control, exchange of files, voice and video conversation, etc. Some applications allow command scripting. VOIP is also converging with IM technology.

  - **INTERNET RELAY CHAT (IRC)** – RFC 2810 to 2813 – IRC was developed as a text-based communication system and was arguably the first of the widely deployed chat systems on the Internet. Communication is organized into public discussion groups ("channels") as well as private messaging between individual users. IRC is a client-server-based network. The server's role is to directly or indirectly send or relay a message from client to client. IRC is still popular in academia but elsewhere has lost its dominant position to commercial services. IRC is unencrypted and is, therefore, an easy target for sniffing attacks.

- **ASYNCHRONOUS MESSAGING -**

  - **SIMPLE MAIL TRANSFER PROTOCOL (SMTP)** – RFC 2821 – A server-to-server, store-and-forward protocol for electronic mail over the Internet. SMTP is pervasive and used for practically all mail routing outside of closed application networks (such as Lotus Notes). SMTP is a client-server protocol, using port 25/TCP; information on mail servers for Internet domains are managed through DNS (in Mail exchange, or MX records). While SMTP takes a fairly simple approach toward authentication, it is fairly robust in the way that it deals with unavailability: The SMTP server will try to deliver email over a pre-configured period of time. From a protocol perspective, SMTP's main shortcomings are its non-existent authentication and its lack of encryption.

  - **POST OFFICE PROTOCOL (POP)** – RFC 1939 – A client-to-server email protocol that operates in a "download and delete" approach. While SMTP addresses the task of sending and receiving email on a server, POP allows clients to access email from a server. Widely implemented in its current (and probably last) version 3 (or "POP3"), it nonetheless offers only basic functionality, such as username/password authentication and unencrypted transmission. Modern email clients, therefore, rely on encryption through TLS to provide secure transmission in order to protect the confidentiality and integrity of a message. Once downloaded onto a client, email is only protected by the client's operating system security.

  - **INTERNET MESSAGE ACCESS PROTOCOL (IMAP)** – RFC 3501 – IMAP offers functional enhancements over POP, including concurrent access from different clients to different mailboxes and the ability to synchronize email to a client from a server. IMAP offers native support for encrypted authentication as well as encrypted data transfer. If forced by the server, IMAP will support plaintext transmission.

  - **NETWORK NEWS TRANSFER PROTOCOL (NNTP)** – RFC 3977 – Network news was one of the first discussion systems on the Internet, pre-dating web-based discussion forums and loosely modeled after former dialup "mailbox" electronic discussion systems. It has been largely replaced by HTTP thread-based discussions.

- **REMOTE COMMUNICATION SERVICES** – While the services described in this section are present in many UNIX operations, and when combined with NFS and NIS provide users with seamless remote working capabilities, they will form risky combinations if not properly administered. Because all are built on mutual trust, they can be misused to obtain access, and horizontally and vertically escalate privileges in an attack. Their authentication and transmission capabilities are insecure by design and they have, therefore, been retrofitted (X11) or replaced altogether (TELNET and rlogin by SSH).

- **TCP/IP TERMINAL EMULATION PROTOCOL (TELNET)** – TELNET is a command-line protocol designed to give command-line access to another host. TELNET's original domain was the world of UNIX servers, where a TELNET server is still standard equipment. (Whether it should in fact be enabled is another question, but in small LAN environments, TELNET is still widely used.) There are now Windows implementations as well. Because it is a fairly low-level TCP implementation, a TCP client can be used to emulate other protocols. TELNET offers little security (authentication is limited to username/ password, and there is no encryption) and indeed its use poses serious security risks in untrusted environments. Once an attacker has obtained logon credentials at any level, he or she can easily escalate privilege levels because the attacker cannot only transfer data to and from a machine, but can also execute commands. TELNET servers run under system privileges and are, therefore, attractive targets in and of themselves because exploits on the server pave the way to system privileges. TELNET should, therefore, not be used over the Internet or on Internet-facing machines. In fact, the standard hardening procedure for any Internet-facing server should include disabling its TELNET service. (Note that under UNIX systems, TELNET normally runs under the name telnetd). TELNET also lacks integrity protection, so it is susceptible to hijacking.

- **REMOTE LOGIN (RLOGIN), REMOTE SHELL (RSH), REMOTE COPY (RCP)** – In its most generic form, rlogin is a protocol used for granting remote access to a machine, typically a UNIX server. Similarly, RSH grants direct remote-command execution, while RCP copies data from or to a remote machine. If an rlogin daemon (rlogind) is running on a machine, rlogin access can be granted either by a central configuration file or by a user configuration. If by a user configuration, a user will be able to grant access that is not permitted by the system administrator. Although they are relying on different daemons (rshd), the same mechanism applies to RSH and RCP. Authentication can be considered host/IP address-based. While rlogin grants access based on user ID, this is not in fact verified; i.e., the ID the remote client claims to possess is taken for granted if the request comes from a trusted host. The rlogin protocol transmits data without encryption and is, therefore, susceptible to eavesdropping and interception. The rlogin protocol is of limited value; its main benefit (remote access without supplying a password) is really its main drawback. It should only be used in trusted networks, if at all. SSH for rlogin, RSH, and RCP are secure replacements.

- **X WINDOW SYSTEM (X11)** – The X Window system is a comprehensive environment for remote control and display of applications. While its original realm is the world of UNIX workstations, it also has implementations for other operating systems such as Windows and Mac OSX. X Window is a server that runs on the user's client and is used to display graphics and send local events such as mouse clicks back to the client (the remote machine). The X Window system's core functionality is also its key risk: X Window allows remote administration and remote display of graphics. If the server is not adequately configured, any client on the Internet can, for instance, use it to display graphics on an attached console. This may sound humorous at first (and in fact it has been the subject of many lab pranks!) but is also possible to use an open X Window server for eavesdropping, screen shots, and key logging. The X Window system is built on unencrypted communication. This can be addressed by using lower-layer encryption or by tunneling the X Window system through (for instance) SSH. The X Window system should only be used in trusted environments, for instance, in a LAN-based UNIX cluster because it's simple security model can be used to subvert and compromise other, stronger authentication mechanisms. Internet-facing servers should never run X11.

- **VIDEO AND MULTIMEDIA** – Telephony is being augmented with video and application sharing to provide a richer, more interactive experience. There are many vendors vying for market share. Note, however, that the purchasing choices that are made today may lock an organization into a technology that will soon be superseded.

- **FILE TRANSFER PROTOCOL (FTP)** – Before the advent of the World Wide Web and the proliferation of HTTP (which made the web successful), FTP was "the" protocol used to publish or disseminate data over the Internet. In its early days, the usual way to use FTP was in a non-firewalled environment from a UNIX command shell. The protocol reflects some of the early design decisions made to support this environment, even though it is now typically used via dedicated FTP clients or web browsers. Unlike HTTP, FTP is a stateful protocol. FTP requires two communication channels: one control channel on port 21 under TCP over which state information is exchanged, and a data channel on port 20 through which payload information is transmitted. In its original form, FTP authentication is simple: Username/password authentication, credentials and data are all transmitted in cleartext. The protocol is, therefore, subject to guessing or stealing of credentials, man-in-the middle attacks, and sniffing. While this can be addressed by the use of encryption on underlying layers, it is a severe drawback as additional effort is required for secure configuration and additional requirements to support encryption have to be met by the client.

- **TRIVIAL FILE TRANSFER PROTOCOL (TFTP)** – TFTP is a simplified version of FTP that is used when authentication isn't needed and quality of service is not an issue. TFTP runs on port 69/UDP and should, therefore, only be used on trusted networks of low latency. In practice, TFTP is used mostly in LANs for the purpose of pulling packages, e.g., booting up a diskless client.

- **HYPERTEXT TRANSFER PROTOCOL (HTTP)** – The HTTP protocol, originally conceived as a stateless, stripped-down version of the FTP protocol, was developed at the European Organization for Nuclear Research CERN in order to support the exchange of information in hypertext markup language (HTML). As HTTP transmits data in cleartext and generates a great deal of logging information on web servers and proxy servers as it does so, the data can be readily captured and used for com-

petitor intelligence, industrial espionage, and other illegitimate activities. As a general rule, HTTP proxy servers should not allow queries from the Internet. Best practice is to separate application gateways (sometimes implemented as reverse proxies) from the proxy for web browsing, as these have very different security levels and levels of business importance. If possible, it is best to implement the application gateway as an application proxy rather than as an HTTP proxy. When these proxies are unauthenticated, they are said to be "open" proxies. The data from the http protocol can have passive or active content, and filtering this content can be difficult.

- **HTTP OVER TLS (HTTPS)** – It is important to note that for most applications, the security offered through the use of HTTP over TLS is little more than protection against eavesdropping, and that this protection depends on the strength of encryption jointly supported by both client and server. Most web browsers support DES encryption, which is not very strong. Authentication is still based on username/password credentials. HTTPS is susceptible to man-in-the-middle attacks, DNS spoofing, etc. It is broadly supported and is – incorrectly – thought to be a "secure" solution. In fact, it is the de-facto standard for online retailers who offer encrypted connections for their ordering and credit card billing systems. Its very popularity has lulled users into a false sense of security.

- **SECURE HYPERTEXT TRANSFER PROTOCOL (S-HTTP)** – Whereas HTTPS protocol relies on an underlying TLS or SSL tunnel to protect its connection, S-HTTP is an enhancement to HTTP 1.1 and aims to manage encryption entirely on the application layer. S-HTTP is designed to co-exist with HTTP and can, for example, use the same port. A server will distinguish an S-HTTP request from an HTTP request by header information. S-HTTP goes hand in hand with security extensions to HTML. S-HTTP is a highly flexible protocol that allows negotiation and renegotiation of encryption mechanisms and security policies. Through its integration into the client/server requests, S-HTTP is more resilient than HTTPS and is less susceptible to man-in-the-middle attacks and known plaintext attacks. Applications can be selective about which parts of a request to encrypt and thereby enhance performance as necessary. S-HTTP is now obsolete.

- **PROXIES** – A proxy server acts on behalf of the user by making the request for services such as FTP and HTTP. If the administrator controls the proxy server, he or she can limit or filter traffic based upon every factor of the connection. If the user is allowed to use external proxy servers, then the administrators cannot control traffic. External proxy servers typically encrypt all traffic to and from the user. External proxy servers typically are used for privacy of the user and do not require accounts. This anonymous proxy or open proxy is a threat to the organization.

REFERENCE:

http://www.phptr.com/articles/article.asp?p=169578&rl=1

Domain Agenda by Layer & Topic

- Physical
- Data Link
- Network
- Transport
- Session
- Presentation
- Application $\longrightarrow$
- Telephony
- Services

Concepts & Architecture
Technology & Implementation
Protocols
Threats & Controls

144

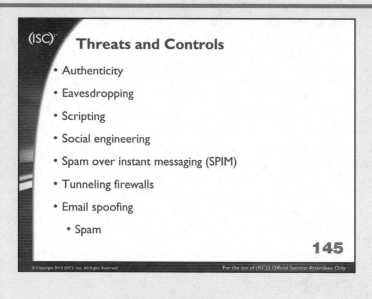

Threats and Controls

- Authenticity
- Eavesdropping
- Scripting
- Social engineering
- Spam over instant messaging (SPIM)
- Tunneling firewalls
- Email spoofing
  - Spam

145

- As of September 2007, the OSVDB.org recognized more than 15,000 stable **VULNERABILITIES**, 20,000 new ones, and more than 10,000 **EXPLOITS**. This is just a well-known list of the most common threats. Each of these threats has also been addressed at other points in the course.

- **CONTROLS** are based on a good risk-management policy. If a risk associated with a particular application-layer protocol is deemed to be too high, the protocol can be replaced. Patches and updates will be available (and must be applied in a timely manner) for protocols that have vendor or community support.

Domain Agenda by Layer & Topic

- Physical
- Data Link
- Network
- Transport
- Session
- Presentation
- Application
- Telephony →
- Services

Concepts & Architecture

Technology & Implementation

Protocols

Threats & Controls

146

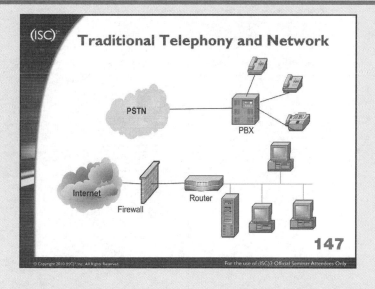

Traditional Telephony and Network

147

- **TRADITIONAL TELEPHONY AND NETWORK LAYOUTS –** Traditionally, we have had two distinct networks:

  - Data networks.

  - Analog voice network (PSTN = public switched telephone network).

- Technology has now enabled us to merge the two. We are now using network technology to carry data as well as voice applications on IP networks. Note that if the networks are not separate and distinct, we will assume that we are using an IP network and call it voice over IP (VoIP).

Mobile Telephony – Cellular Service

- Analog
  - Advanced mobile phone service (AMPS)
- Digital
  - Global service for mobile communications (GSM)
    - EDGE (enhanced data rate for GSM evolution)
  - General packet radio service (GPRS)
- Data

148

- **MOBILE TELEPHONY** or cellular telephone services are radio and wired transmissions using local low-powered towers, public-switched telephone networks (PSTNs), mobile telephone switching offices (MTSOs), and mobile subscriber units (MSUs).

- **ANALOG** – The first mobile technology was analog. It was insecure, expensive, and prone to errors. The first service was called advanced mobile phone service (AMPS).

- **DIGITAL SERVICE** was first introduced using GSM, and other standards such as CDMA and PCS. Digital services have traded ideas and advanced rapidly over the past 20 years. Since GSM is a specification defining functions and interface requirements, without limiting vendors to a particular hardware platform, it has the highest acceptance and should supplant earlier, entrenched technologies.

- **GLOBAL SERVICE FOR MOBILE COMMUNICATIONS (GSM)** –
  - The most common deployment of mobile telephony in Europe, South America, North America, and Southeast Asia.
  - Digital signal from phone to towers for low bandwidth usage.
  - Customer advanced services: SMS, Facsimile, voice-mail, call forwarding, etc.
  - Well-optimized bandwidth of 13Kbps per encoded call.
  - Uses narrowband time division multiple access (TDMA).
  - Note that GSM specifications define the functions and interface requirements in detail, but do not address the hardware.
  - **EDGE** – Provides approximately three times the data speed of GPRS systems.

- **GENERAL PACKET RADIO SERVICE (GPRS)** – Is the advanced services functionality based on GSM, and provides mobile Internet services.

- **DATA** – VoIP is becoming the norm and other data such as email, live video, and transaction processing are a part of all mobile communications.

REFERENCES:

http://www.iec.org/online/tutorials/gsm/
http://www.iec.org/online/tutorials/acrobat/cell_comm.pdf
http://www.eventhelix.com/RealtimeMantra/Telecom/
http://www.gsmworld.com/technology/gprs/index.shtml
http://www.3gamericas.org/English/index.cfm

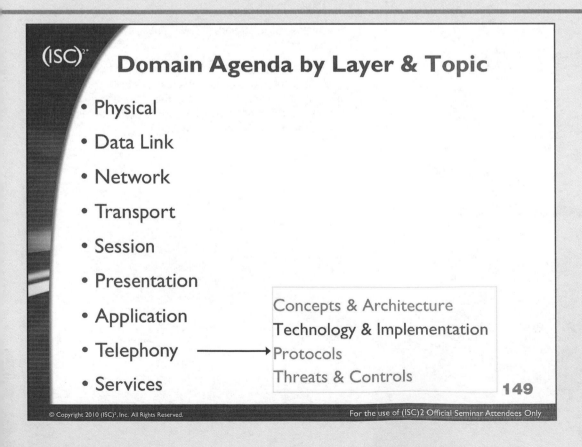

Domain Agenda by Layer & Topic

- Physical
- Data Link
- Network
- Transport
- Session
- Presentation
- Application
- Telephony ⟶ Concepts & Architecture
  Technology & Implementation
  Protocols
  Threats & Controls
- Services

149

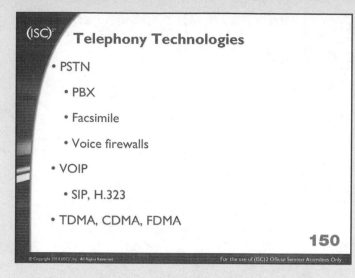

Telephony Technologies

- PSTN
  - PBX
  - Facsimile
  - Voice firewalls
- VOIP
  - SIP, H.323
- TDMA, CDMA, FDMA

150

- **PSTN** – The publicly switched telephone network (sometimes referred to as POTS – the plain old telephone service) is a global network of interconnected switches that process telephone calls and signaling through a series of switches and trunking media. The telephone number dialed directs the establishment of a connection through the various switches. Originally the PSTN was circuit-based communications, but now uses packet-based connections for data transmission.

  - **PBX** – Private branch exchange is the installation of a telephone switch at a customer premises. This switch will direct calls to the appropriate extension and manage all incoming and outgoing telephone calls.

  - **FACSIMILE** – FAX is a half-duplex communications device (it can send and receive but not at the same time) used to transmit the scan of a document to a remote location. This

can lead to serious information leakage problems.

- **VOICE FIREWALLS** – Voice firewalls are an emerging technology used to monitor and control voice communications, usually within a large organization.

- **FREQUENCY DIVISION MULTIPLE ACCESS (FDMA) –**

  - FDMA is only used in analog cellular.

  - Subdivides a frequency band into sub-bands and assigns an analog conversation to each sub-band.

- **TIME DIVISION MULTIPLE ACCESS (TDMA) –**

  - TDMA multiplexes several digital calls (voice or data) at each sub-band by devoting a small time-slice in a round robin to each call in the band.

  - Two sub-bands are required for each call; one in each direction between sender and receiver.

- **CODE DIVISION MULTIPLE ACCESS (CDMA, CDMA2000, WIDEBAND CDMA) –**

  - CDMA is a spread-spectrum wireless technology that is mainly used for cellular technology. Like DSSS, it spreads each call over a large frequency band and is tagged with a pseudo-random noise code to differentiate between the calls.

  - CDMA2000 offers an improved capability of 10 times the number of calls, and a transmission rate of 153.6Mbps. CDMA2000 is a registered trademark of Telecommunications Industry Association (TIA-USA) in the United States.

  - Wideband CDMA (or WCDMA) uses a wider band than CDMA, which increases the throughput of the carrier. Another important point about WCDMA is that it is used in UMTS for 3G networks by legacy GSM carriers.

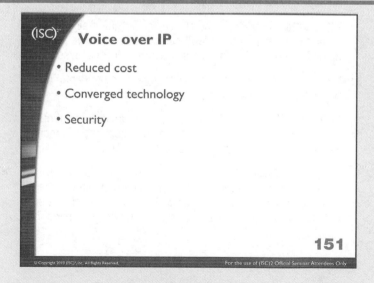

Voice over IP

- Reduced cost
- Converged technology
- Security

151

- **VOICE OVER IP (VOIP) –** While the ability to transmit voice over Internet connections has existed for a long time, the widespread acceptance of broadband Internet access for business and home has only recently created a viable market for voice over IP solutions. Telephone networks are also used to carry Internet dialup traffic, but now this is moving to DSL and other solutions that replace traditional corporate telephony networks.

- **CONVERGED TECHNOLOGY –** Allows one network to provide

both voice and data services. A VoIP solution also integrates well with other corporate IT systems allowing customer support systems to be readily available for call center personnel, for example.

- **SECURITY –** While the benefits (such as negligible connection cost, a comparable initial investment, and a larger degree of configurability) are obvious, VoIP networks are vulnerable to new security risks. They can be attacked by viruses, hacked, and are dependent on electric power at all communication endpoints. VoIP systems are also significantly more complicated and need higher levels of expertise to operate. Questions of interconnectivity and interoperability for public services need to be addressed. It is still unclear from a legal perspective whether VoIP networks should be regulated in the same way as the public switched telephone network (PSTN).

  - VoIP needs gateways to public emergency services. Law enforcement also needs VoIP access, and although this is important from a public policy perspective, it raises security concerns. (Backdoors introduced could be exploited by third parties, for example.)

  - Deployment of VoIP services may raise security concerns for its carrier network, for instance with regards to enabling secure interconnectivity with other VoIP applications. Finally, all VoIP installations must have a form of independent, backup communication channel in case of a disaster or network outage.

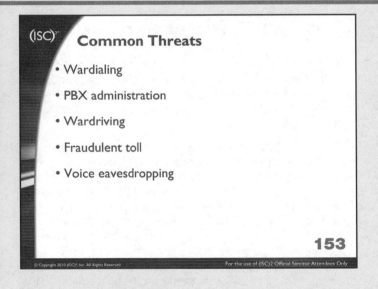

Domain Agenda by Layer & Topic

- Physical
- Data Link
- Network
- Transport
- Session
- Presentation
- Application
- Telephony   →   Concepts & Architecture
- Services

Concepts & Architecture
Technology & Implementation
Protocols
Threats & Controls

152

Common Threats

- Wardialing
- PBX administration
- Wardriving
- Fraudulent toll
- Voice eavesdropping

153

- **WARDIALING** – Wardialing uses products such as Phone Sweep to dial large blocks of numbers. This is intended to help the attacker find unprotected modems that may lead to an access control breach.

- **PBX ADMINISTRATION** – As always, one of the main problems is the failure to change default passwords or remove privileges from staff who do not require admin-level access.

- **WARDRIVING** – Driving through an area trying to detect unprotected wireless access points.

- **FRAUDULENT TOLL** – Making large numbers of fraudulent long distance calls from an unprotected telephony connection. This can cost tens of thousands of dollars within a few hours.

- **VOICE EAVESDROPPING** – Since most networks are using packet-switched media for telephony communications, there is an increased risk of someone with a network sniffer being able to capture all the packets associated with your baggage.

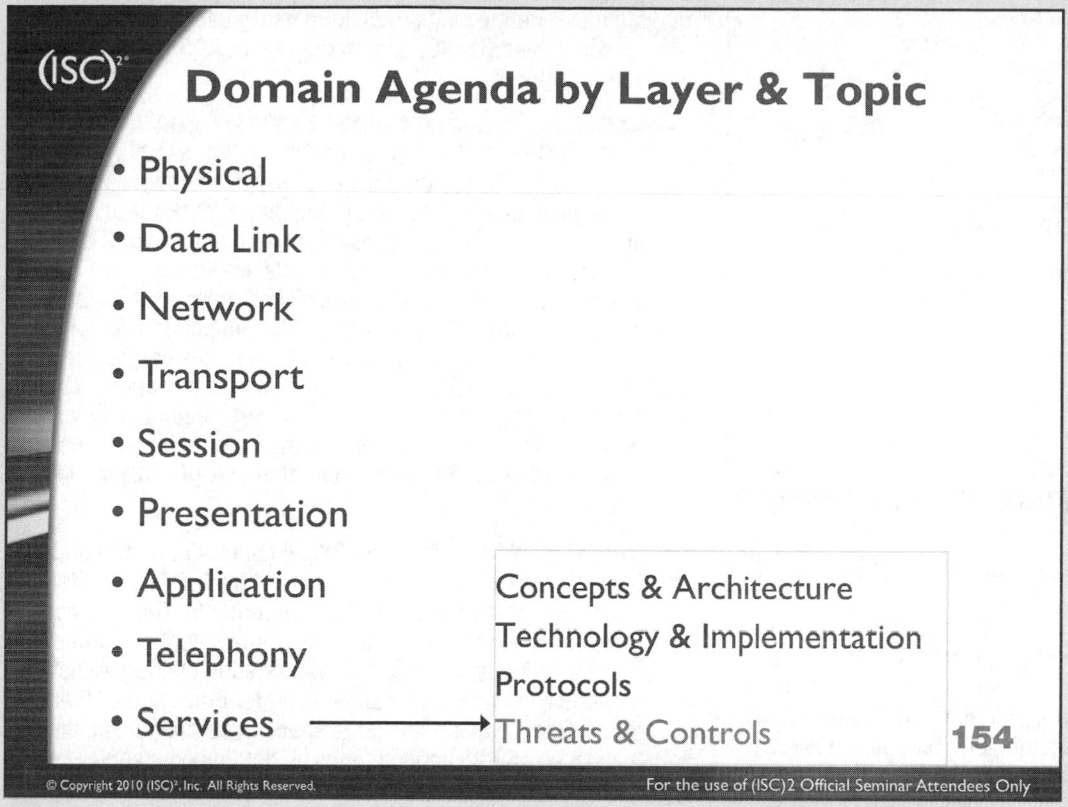

Domain Agenda by Layer & Topic

- Physical
- Data Link
- Network
- Transport
- Session
- Presentation
- Application
- Telephony
- Services ⟶

Concepts & Architecture
Technology & Implementation
Protocols
Threats & Controls

154

- For the service section, concepts and architecture, technology and implementation, and protocols all blend together.

- **DOMAIN NAME SERVICE (DNS) –** DNS is one of the most prominent and visible of the network services below the application layer because of its role in email, WWW addresses, and URLs (uniform resource locators), all of which are now ubiquitous. DNS has, therefore, become a prominent target of attack, aggravating the problem of the pre-existing weaknesses in the protocol. By manipulating DNS, it is easy to divert, intercept, or prevent the vast majority of end-user communications without having to resort to attacking any end-user devices. DNS is a distributed, hierarchical database. Its central element is a set of hierarchical name (domain) trees, starting from a so-called "top level domain" (TLD). A number of so-called "root servers" manage the authoritative list of TLD servers. In order to resolve any domain name, each domain name server in the world must hold a list of these root servers. Various extensions to DNS have been proposed that would enhance DNS's functionality and security. Because of its caching architecture, DNS possesses a remarkable degree of robustness, flexibility, and scalability. On the other hand, DNS does not enforce data consistency and integrity, its built-in authentication mechanisms are weak, and the management of the global DNS infrastructure has become a subject of political and economic controversy, while the objects it manages (domain names) are often the subject of local and global trademark disputes.

- **LIGHTWEIGHT DIRECTORY ACCESS PROTOCOL (LDAP) –** LDAP is a client-server based directory query protocol loosely based on X.500, commonly used for managing user information. Unlike DNS, LDAP is not used to manage or synchronize data per se. Back-ends to LDAP can be directory services such as NIS, Lotus Notes, Microsoft Exchange, etc. LDAP provides only weak authentication based on hostname resolution and it is, therefore, easy to subvert LDAP security by breaking DNS. Furthermore, LDAP communication is transferred in cleartext and is, therefore, trivial to intercept. One way to address the issues of weak authentication and cleartext communication is by deploying LDAP over SSL, which provides authentication, integrity, and confidentiality. Although various other extensions to LDAP have been proposed in order to address these shortcomings, they have not been widely accepted. This might be because LDAP was meant to be simple and building (for example) a strong authentication and encryption framework around it could make it more complex. Note, however, that Microsoft Active Directory does address these issues through its use of Kerberos. LDAP is also the basis of Microsoft's Active Directory Service (ADS) whose authentication is based on Kerberos. Applications such as

Microsoft NetMeeting are making heavy use of LDAP for this reason. Unlike NetBIOS (its predecessor), ADS is fully TCP/IP and DNS based.

- **NETWORK BASIC INPUT OUTPUT SYSTEM (NETBIOS) –** The NetBIOS API was developed in 1983 by IBM. NetBIOS was later ported to TCP/IP (NetBIOS over TCP/IP, also known as NetBT); however, implementations running on top of NetBEUI or IPX are still in use. NetBIOS is susceptible to a number of attacks. Exploiting the fact that its credentials are static, a user can be brought to delivering his or her credentials by tricking his or her host into setting up a NetBIOS connection with a host under an attacker's control. NetBIOS services can be used for information collection (they will disclose information on users, hosts, and domains). NetBIOS ports have become popular targets of attacks for Internet worms. Circulating exploits rely on weaknesses in the implementation of NetBIOS, not in the protocol itself.

- **NETWORK INFORMATION SERVICE (NIS/NIS+) –** NIS and NIS+ are directory services developed by Sun Microsystems, which are mostly used in UNIX environments. They are commonly used for managing user credentials across a group of machines, for instance, a UNIX workstation cluster or client/server environment, but can be used for other types of directories. NIS is using a flat name space in so-called domains. It is based on RPC and manages all entities on a server (NIS server). NIS servers can be set up redundantly through the use of so-called slave servers.

  - **NIS –** Is known for a number of security weaknesses.

    - The fact that NIS does not authenticate individual RPC requests can be used to spoof responses to NIS requests from a client. This would, for instance, enable an attacker to inject fake credentials and, thereby, obtain or escalate privileges on the target machine.

    - Retrieval of directory information is possible if the name of an NIS domain has become known or is guessable, as any client can associate himself or herself with an NIS domain.

    - Conversely, the fact that an NIS server is an attractive target of attacks cannot be considered a weakness of NIS as such; it is in fact an architectural issue with all client/server platforms.

    - A number of guides have been published on how to secure NIS servers. The basic steps here are to secure the platform an NIS server is running on, to isolate the NIS server from traffic outside of a LAN, and to configure it in a way that limits the probability for disclosure of authentication credentials, especially system privileged ones.

  - **NIS+ –** Authentication and authorization concepts in NIS+ are more mature, they require authentication for each access of a directory object. However, NIS+ authentication in itself will only be as strong as authentication to one of the clients in a NIS+ environment, as NIS+ builds on a trust relationship between different hosts. The most relevant attacks against a correctly configured NIS+ network are aimed at its cryptographic security. NIS+ can be run at different security levels. However, most levels available are irrelevant for an operational network.

REFERENCE:
http://www.ehsco.com/reading/19961215ncf1.html

Configuration Services

- Simple network management protocol (SNMP)

- Dynamic host configuration protocol (DHCP)

- Network time protocol (NTP)

- Finger user information protocol

156

- **SIMPLE NETWORK MANAGEMENT PROTOCOL (SNMP)** – SNMP is a protocol designed to manage network infrastructure. While its basic architecture is a fairly simple client server architecture with a relatively limited set of commands, managing a network via SNMP is anything but simple, and there are important security issues associated with SNMP. SNMP architecture consists of a management server (called "manager" in SNMP terminology) and a client (or "agent"), which is usually installed on network devices such as routers and switches. SNMP allows the manager to retrieve ("get") values of variables such as routing tables, or performance monitoring information from the agent, as well as to "set" these variables and remotely adjust the configuration of the device. While SNMP has proven to be remarkably robust and scalable and its near omnipresence suggests a high degree of resilience against common attacks, it does have a number of clear weaknesses. Some of them are by design; others are subject to configuration parameters. The most easily exploited SNMP vulnerability is probably a brute-force attack on default or easily guessable passwords. Given the scale of deployment and the frequent relative inexperience of network administrators, this is certainly a realistic scenario. The effect is potentially severe, but with proper administrator education, the risk is easily mitigated.

- **DYNAMIC HOST CONFIGURATION PROTOCOL (DHCP)** – According to RFC 2131: "The Dynamic Host Configuration Protocol (DHCP) provides a framework for passing configuration information to hosts on a TCP/IP network. DHCP is based on the Bootstrap Protocol (BOOTP), adding the capability of automatic allocation of reusable network addresses and additional configuration options." DHCP assigns IP addresses and other configuration information to hosts.

- **NETWORK TIME PROTOCOL (NTP)** – NTP is a protocol that synchronizes computer clocks in a network. This can be extremely important for operational stability (for instance, under NIS), but also for maintaining consistency and coherence of audit trails, for instance, in log files. Simple network time protocol (SNTP) is a variant of NTP and offers a less resource-consuming, but also less exact form of synchronization. From a security perspective, our main objective with NTP is to prevent an attacker from changing time information on a client or a whole network by manipulating its local time server. NTP can also be configured to restrict access based upon IP address. From NTP version 3 onward, cryptographic authentication is also available. At present, this is based upon symmetric encryption, but this will be replaced by public key cryptography in NTP version 4. In order to make a network robust against accidental or deliberate timing inaccuracies, a network should have its own time server and possibly a dedicated, highly accurate clock. As a standard precaution, a network should never depend on one external time server alone, but synchronize with several, trusted time sources so that the manipulation of a single source will have no immediate effect. In order to detect de-synchronization, standard logging mechanisms can be used with NTP to ensure synchronicity of time stamping.

- **FINGER USER INFORMATION PROTOCOL** – "Finger" is an identification service that allows a user to obtain information about whether another user is logged in, as well as the user's last login time. The "fingered" user can have information from two files in his or her home directory displayed: the ".project" and the ".plan" file. Finger was developed as early as 1971 and is also implemented as a UNIX daemon, "fingered." For all practical purposes, the finger protocol has become obsolete. Its use should be restricted to situations where no alternatives are available. Its decrease in popularity is due to the facts that:

  - It has been the subject of a number of security exploits.

  - It raises privacy and security concerns and can easily be abused for social engineering attacks.

  - The user's self-actuation (an important social aspect in early UNIX networks) happens on web pages today.

REFERENCES:

FRC 2131

http://tools.ietf.org/html/rfc2131

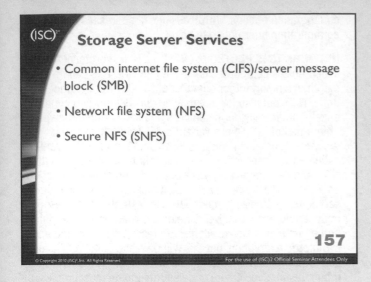

Storage Server Services

- Common internet file system (CIFS)/server message block (SMB)
- Network file system (NFS)
- Secure NFS (SNFS)

157

- **COMMON INTERNET FILE SYSTEM (CIFS)/SERVER MESSAGE BLOCK (SMB)** – CIFS/SMB is a file-sharing protocol prevalent on Windows systems. The (free) "Samba" project is the UNIX/Linux implementation. SMB was originally designed to run on top of the NetBIOS protocol, but it can also be run directly over TCP/IP. CIFS is capable of supporting user-level and tree/object-, or share-level security. Authentication can be performed via challenge/response, as well as by the transmission of credentials in cleartext. This second provision has been added largely for backward compatibility in legacy Windows environments. The main attacks against CIFS are based upon obtaining credentials by sniffing for cleartext authentication or via cryptographic attacks.

- **NETWORK FILE SYSTEM (NFS)** – Network file system is a client-server, file-sharing system common to the UNIX platform. It was originally developed by Sun Microsystems, but has implementations on all common UNIX platforms including Linux, as well as on Microsoft Windows. NFS has been revised several times.

- **SECURE NFS (SNFS)** – NFS offers secure authentication and encryption on the basis of secure RPC, which is based on DES encryption. In contrast to standard NFS, secure NFS (or rather secure RPC) will authenticate each RPC request. This increases latency for each request as the authentication is being performed and also introduces a light performance premium, mainly paid for in terms of computing capacity. Secure NFS uses DES-encrypted time stamps as authentication tokens. If server and client do not have access to the same time server (see NTP section), the server and client will have to be resynchronized.

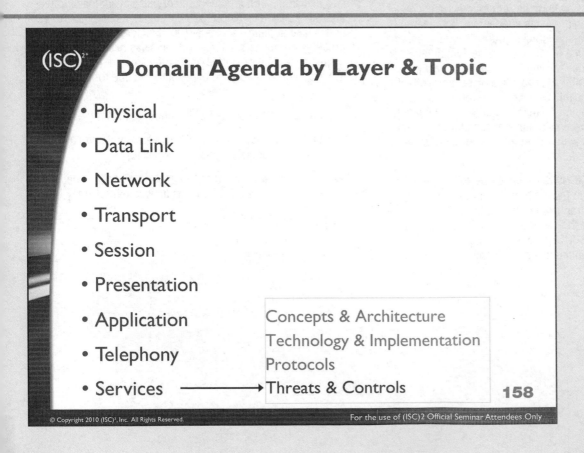

Domain Agenda by Layer & Topic

- Physical
- Data Link
- Network
- Transport
- Session
- Presentation
- Application
- Telephony
- Services ⟶

Concepts & Architecture
Technology & Implementation
Protocols
Threats & Controls

158

DNS Threats

- Spoofing
- Query manipulation:
  - Hosts file manipulation
  - Social engineering
- Information disclosure
- Domain litigation
- Cybersquatting

159

- **DNS SPOOFING** – In order to resolve a domain name query such as mapping a web server address to an IP address, the user's workstation will query the local DNS server. If the query response is falsified, the returned data could resolve to a site containing malware or other attacks.

- **MANIPULATION OF DNS QUERIES** – Technically, the following two techniques are only indirectly related to DNS weaknesses. However, it is worth mentioning them in the context of DNS as they seek to manipulate name resolution in other ways:

  - **MANIPULATION OF THE HOSTS FILE** – This is a technique used by a number of viruses. A hosts file (for instance, /etc/hosts on many UNIX machines, C:\Windows\I386\Hosts on Windows XP) is the resource first queried before a DNS request is issued. It will always contain the mapping of the host name localhost to the IP address 127.0.0.1 (loop back interface, as defined in RFC 3330) and potentially to other hosts as well. The virus will add addresses of antivirus software vendors with invalid IP addresses to the hosts file in order to prevent download of virus pattern files.

  - **SOCIAL ENGINEERING** – These techniques will not try to manipulate a query on a technical level, but can trick the user into misinterpreting a DNS address displayed in an email or in a web-browser address bar. One way to achieve this in email or HTML documents is to display a link in text where the actual target address is different from the one displayed. Another way to achieve this is the use of non-ASCII character sets (for instance, Unicode – ISO/IEC 10646 – characters) that nonetheless look like ASCII (i.e., Latin). This may become an increasingly popular technique with the popularization of internationalized domain names.

- **INFORMATION DISCLOSURE** – Smaller corporate networks do not split naming zones; in other words, the names of hosts that are accessible only from an Intranet may be visible from the Internet. While knowing a server name will not enable anyone to access it, this knowledge can aid and facilitate preparation of a planned attack because it provides an attacker with valuable information on existing servers, network structure, and, for instance, details such as organizational structure or server operating systems (if the OS is part of the host name). Businesses should operate split DNS zones wherever possible and refrain from using telling naming conventions for their machines. In addition, a domain registrar's database of administrative and billing domain contacts (Who is database) can be an attractive target for information and email harvesting.

- **DOMAIN LITIGATION** – Domain names are subject to trademark risk and may consequently become temporarily unavailable or permanently lost. For the business in question, the consequences can be equivalent to the loss of its whole Internet presence in an IT-related disaster. If a business has reason to be concerned about trademarks, or has concerns about any kind of a domain name issue, it should put contingency plans into place. These might include setting up a second domain unrelated to the trademark in question (e.g., based on the trademark of a parent company) that can be advertised on short notice, if necessary.

- **CYBERSQUATTING AND ILLEGITIMATE USE OF SIMILAR DOMAINS** – This can be done by using common misspellings or representing the same second-level domain under a different top-level domain. The only way to protect a business from this kind of fraud is to register the most prominent "adjacent" domains, or to engage in trademark litigation as necessary. A residual risk will always remain, relating not only to public misrepresentation but also to potential loss or disclosure of email.

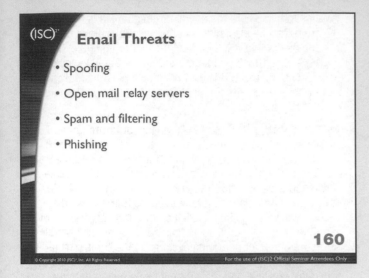

Email Threats

- Spoofing
- Open mail relay servers
- Spam and filtering
- Phishing

160

to blacklist (refuse) all email from the associated hosts. While using blacklists has its merits, it is risky to use them as an exclusive indicator. Blacklists are typically run by private organizations and individuals according to their own rules. They sometimes disappear overnight and in any case, can rarely be held accountable for the way they operate their lists.

- **SPAM** – Spam, or unsolicited commercial email (UCE), benefits from the low cost of email as opposed to phone calls or letters. It can be sent in massive amounts with little additional cost and a low risk of retribution. Over the years, sending spam has become a professional and highly profitable business. This means that spammers are highly organized and structured. In general, spam is not limited to email; it can also occur in newsgroups, web logs ("blogs"), or instant messaging. Spam often promotes illegitimate or fraudulent businesses and shady websites. It is often crafted so as to trick the recipient into thinking that he or she is either being personally addressed, or that he or she has accidentally received an important email intended for someone else. Spam is less of a security problem than it is a problem of acceptable use; however, it does rely on illegitimate (and security-breaching) means for its distribution. It is almost always sent with invalid (faked) sender addresses. Since spam is not welcome and the majority of providers have acceptable use policies in place that disallow sending UCE, spammers have to resort to (illegitimate) distribution and redistribution of their emails and hiding their origins. Note that spam can be sent through open mail relays. Spam is increasingly sent via virus-infected, backdoored hosts, or "Zombie networks." This is possible when a security breach is exploited, whether by the spammer or otherwise.

- **EMAIL SPOOFING** – As SMTP does not possess an adequate authentication mechanism, email spoofing is extremely simple and can be done with a simple TELNET command to port 25 of a mail server and by issuing a number of SMTP commands. Email spoofing is frequently used in order to hide the identity of a spammer, in which case the purported sender is also a victim of spam. The most effective protection against this is the social one, where the recipient can confirm or simply ignore implausible email.

- **OPEN MAIL RELAY SERVERS** – An open mail relay server is an SMTP server that allows inbound SMTP connections for domains it doesn't serve (i.e., for which it doesn't possess a DNS MX record). An open mail relay is generally considered a sign of bad system administration. Open mail relays are a principal tool for the distribution of spam because they allow attackers to hide their identity. There are a number of blacklists for open mail relay servers, and these can be used by an administrator

- **PHISHING** – This is a form of social engineering where the desired victim is tricked into taking an action (usually going to a webpage) and providing sensitive data.

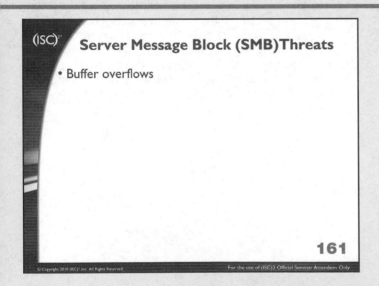

Server Message Block (SMB) Threats

- Buffer overflows

161

- **SERVER MESSAGE BLOCK (SMB)** – According to the Internet Storm Center statistics, server message block is still the top service being scanned on the Internet today. If PCs are listening, they are vulnerable to more than 94 exploits.

- **BUFFER OVERFLOWS** – Buffer overflows in SMBs lead to remote execution of code, information disclosure, and many other vulnerabilities.

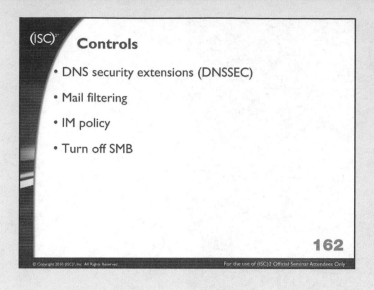

- **DNS SECURITY EXTENSIONS (DNSSEC)** – DNSSEC was designed to protect the Internet from DNS cache poisoning. It provides origin authentication of DNS data, data integrity, and authenticated denial of existence. It has not been implemented because it does not have backward compatibility with DNS. It can be interesting to follow the exploit exposed by Dan Kaminsky in the summer of 2008 which led to a very rapid deployment of patches for DNS servers.

- **MAIL FILTERING** – See previous discussion.

- **IM POLICY** – An organizational offering of IM services can vastly reduce most IM threats.

- **TURN OFF SMB** – Unless you need to share files on local PCs, turning off SMB will significantly reduce adversaries' ability to compromise the machine. Some applications still require SMB to be turned on.

REFERENCE:

DNSSEC: http://www.dnssec.net/

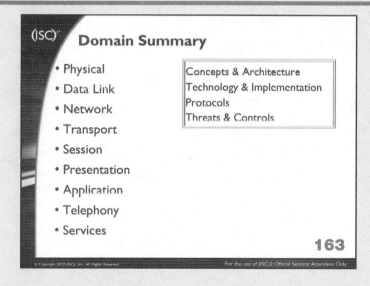

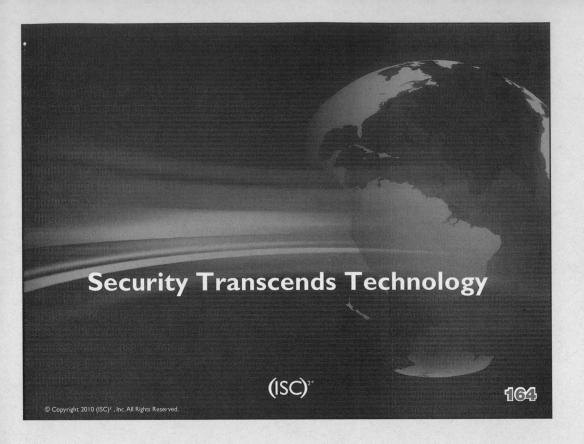

Security Transcends Technology

164

Review Questions

TELECOMMUNICATIONS AND NETWORK SECURITY

1. Cloud computing involves accessing software and data across the Internet on servers managed by a third-party supplier. Cloud computing arrangements increase availability, offer greater scalability, and

   A. increase confidentiality.
   B. increase the opportunity for attack.
   C. increase integrity.
   D. eliminate the need for data encryption.

2. Which of the following is the correct sequence of the open systems interconnect (OSI) model layers, starting with the layer closest to the end user?

   A. Application, session, network, and physical
   B. Application, network, session, and physical
   C. Presentation, network, transport, and physical
   D. Presentation, transport, network, and physical

QUESTIONS 3-7 refer to the following information:

Every Monday, the London branch of a manufacturing company sends its weekly sales figures for the prior week to corporate headquarters in Seattle. It is imperative to use the most secure method of data transmission.

3. You are in charge of deciding what technology to use for this data transfer. The BEST alternative is

   A. X.25 protocol.
   B. a permanent virtual circuit (PVC).
   C. a virtual private network (VPN).
   D. an optical carrier-class (OC-class) carrier.

4. Your boss is confused about the merits of RIP (routing information protocol) and OSPF (open shortest path first). You explain that

   A. RIP is preferable because variable length subnet masks (VLSMs) are supported in all versions.
   B. OSPF is preferable because it is more flexible and inherently more secure.
   C. RIP is preferable because OSPF is only used in smaller networks.
   D. RIP is preferable because it is more flexible and inherently more secure.

5. London is one of a number of small branch offices, and there is no local authentication server. The employees must, therefore, authenticate to a domain controller at the corporate office. The best method of authentication involves

   A. a dial-up virtual private network (VPN).
   B. establishing a private virtual circuit (PVC) to forward the request.
   C. a Windows server running routing and remote access (RRAS) configured as a remote authentication dial in user service (RADIUS) client.
   D. synchronous optical network (SONET).

6. You advise the use of Layer 2 Tunneling Protocol (L2TP) virtual private networks (VPN) for people working outside of the branch offices or headquarters because

   A. a L2TP VPN is automatically encrypted. This removes the responsibility of remembering to encrypt from the shoulders of employees and enables them to focus on their jobs.
   B. data entering the enterprise is encrypted and will pose no internal danger.
   C. you can chose to use Encapsulating Security Payload (ESP) with Internet protocol security (IPSec) when you set up the VPN to make the remote communication more secure.
   D. full-disk encryption makes the use of VPNs unnecessary.

7. The head office has decided to use Kerberos for network authentication. The company has a number of remote offices scattered across the country. What problems might this present?

   A. Kerberos is time sensitive in its default configuration.
   B. Kerberos logons are sent in plaintext.
   C. If the central key distribution center (KDC) fails, then all logons will fail.
   D. The key distribution center (KDC) retrieves passwords from the security accounts manager (SAM).

8. Which of the following is a service which supplies Internet protocol (IP) addresses to workstations?

   A. DHCP (Dynamic Host Configuration Protocol)
   B. NIS (Network Information Service)
   C. DNS (Domain Name Service)
   D. LDAP (Lightweight Directory Access Protocol)

9. **Which statement is TRUE concerning Internet protocol (IP)V4 and IPV6 security?**

   A. IPV6 is less secure than IPV4. IPV6 allows every node to have its own IP address. IPV4 allows shielding private addresses behind public addresses.

   B. IPV6 is less secure than IPV4. Although there is still a centralizing body, it is now international and terrorist organizations may now get IP addresses.

   C. IPV6 is more secure than IPV4. IPV6 mandates the use of Internet protocol security (IPSec).

   D. IPV6 is more secure than IPV4. Only enterprises that have been governmentally approved may use it.

10. **You are a CISSP working for a small corporation with responsibility for providing security advice to the Internet technology (IT) department. Your primary concern for training all employees in the company on security awareness is defending against**

    A. denial of service.

    B. malware.

    C. social engineering.

    D. botnets.

11. **Bot-herding has become an extremely lucrative business and causes extraordinary damage both to individuals and enterprises. The BEST method to prevent your computer from becoming a victim is**

    A. ensuring that your internal Internet protocol (IP) address is not exposed.

    B. turning off your computer when it's not being used.

    C. being careful about clicking on email links or links on unfamiliar websites.

    D. not using social networking, such as MySpace, Facebook, etc.

12. **The PRIMARY disadvantage of combining data and voice networks is that**

    A. it's expensive to implement and maintain.

    B. as a result, there will be poor voice quality regardless of quality of service (QoS) labels.

    C. a distributed denial of service (DDoS) can disable all communication.

    D. joining voice and data networks allows for greater protection using firewalls.

13. **Which of the following BEST describes asynchronous transfer mode (ATM)?**

    A. A point-to-point technology to ensure speed and reliability.

    B. A connectionless suite of protocols for transmitting data, voice, and video at high speeds.

    C. An old military technology that is slow, but robust with respect to error-checking.

    D. A technology that is no longer used.

14. **Which of the following authentication protocols periodically re-validates users, keeps its standard password database unencrypted, and sends passwords as one-way hashes?**

    A. Password authentication protocol (PAP)

    B. Challenge-handshake authentication protocol (CHAP)

    C. Terminal access controller access control system (TACACS+)

    D. Internet protocol security (IPSec)

15. **When using the secure socket layer (SSL) protocol, the symmetric session key is encrypted by the client using**

    A. a client-generated pre-shared key.

    B. the server's private key.

    C. the server's public key.

    D. the client's previous session key.

16. **File transfer protocol (FTP) and multipurpose Internet mail extensions (MIME) are protocols that operate at which open system interconnect (OSI) layer?**

    A. Layer 7 (application)

    B. Layer 6 (presentation)

    C. Layer 4 (transport)

    D. Layer 3 (network)

17. **What is one of the methods used to protect a domain name server (DNS)?**

    A. Spoofing

    B. Split DNS zones

    C. Cache poisoning

    D. Registration hijacking

18. **What is the PRIMARY objective of a firewall?**

    A. To monitor network traffic.

    B. To protect trusted networks from less trusted networks.

    C. To filter based on protocols.

    D. To look at destination and source addresses, ports and services requested and determine what is authorized.

19. **Which of the following BEST describes why a network administrator would use a packet-sniffer?**

    A. To read any unencrypted traffic.

    B. To determine whether firewalls are working properly.

    C. To look for illicit activity.

    D. To monitor network traffic.

20. Which of the following is a connection-oriented protocol?

A. Transmission control protocol (TCP)
B. User datagram protocol (UDP)
C. Internet control message protocol (ICMP)
D. Post office protocol 3 (POP3)

Notes

(ISC)² — Telecommunications and Network Security

Index

References are to domain and page number (e.g., VII.92 refers to page 92 in Domain 7.)

A

B

Backdoor attacks, II. 8, II.20, II.22, II.26, II.27, II.34
Background checks, V.8
Backups
  business continuity planning and, III.16–III.17
  for databases, II.39
  integrity of, VII.5
  for network security, X.43
  of operational files, VII.24
  testing of, VII.5
  types of, VII.4
Backup storage locations, VII.5
Balancing, transaction processing and, II.15
Bandwidth, compression and, X.75
Basel II regulations, VI.35
Baselines, definition of, V.19
BASIC (Beginner's All-Purpose Symbolic Instruction Code), II.13
Bastion hosts, X.22
Battery power, VIII.26
BCP. See Business Continuity Planning
Behavior of computer criminals, VI.21
Bell-LaPadula model, IX.1, IX.30, IX.32
Best practices, definition, IX.3
BGP (border gateway protocol), X.55
Biba model, IX.1, IX.30, IX.31, IX.34
Biometric authentication methods
  accuracy of, I.15
  behavioral, I.14
  description, I.14
  dynamic types, I.14
  physiological, I.14
  selection criteria, I.14
  static types, I.14
  system access using, I.14
Birthday Paradox, IV.48
Bits, X.8
Bitstream imaging, VI.30
Blackouts, power failures and, VIII.25
Blade servers, IX.23
Blind testing, for penetration, I.40
Block ciphers, IV.16–IV.17, IV.24
Blowfish cipher, IV.28
Blue bug attacks, X.33
Blue jacking, X.33
Blueprints. See Security blueprints
Bluetooth, IV.16, X.33
Board level executives, V.5
Boards of directors, V.5
Bollards, VIII.8
Bomb blast film, VIII.17
Boot sector infectors, II.30
Border gateway protocol (BGP), X.55
Botnets, II.24
Boundary routers, X.21
Breach of duty, VI.2
Breakage, threats from, VIII.22
Breaker panels, VIII.20
Brewer and Nash Model, IX.33
Bribery, attacks and, IV.48
Bridges and network security, X.32

British Naval Connectors (BNCs), X.18
Brittleness, IV.8
Broadband wireless, X.85
Broadcast transmissions, X.26
Brownouts, VIII.25
Brute-force attacks, IV.45
BS 25999, III.2
Budgets
  business continuity plans and, III.6, III.7
  disaster recovery plans, III.11
  risk management and, V.22
Buffer overflow, II.13, X.33, X.92
Building entry points, VIII.11–VIII.18
Build Security In (BSI), II.4
Built-in security, II.3–II.4
Bus failure, X.9
Business analysis, III.5
Business Continuity and Disaster Recovery Planning
  activation of plans, III.22
  activity continuity options, III.16
  assessing awareness and training levels, III.30–III.31
  assessing training, III.30–III.31
  BCM lifecycle, III.5
  benefits of, III.10
  contents, III.23–III.24
  disaster recovery phase, III.22
  embedded, III.30, III.31
  emergency response procedures, III.21
  equipment room security and, VIII.19
  estimating continuity requirements, III.13, III.24
  feedback phase, III.28, III.30
  incident readiness and response, III.12
  incident response teams, III.26
  initiation of, III.7
  maintaining arrangements, III.18
  master plans, III.19
  plan development, III.5, III.10–III.24
  plan implementation, III.26
  plan management, III.25–III.28
  processing agreements, III.18
  recovery alternatives, III.17
  recovery strategies, III.13–III.18
  rehearsals, III.5, III.29
  resource consolidation, III.24
  risk assessments, III.5
  risk management and, III.9
  rounds, IV.17
  sources of information, III.2
  strategy for, III.5
  system evaluation criteria, IX.35
  testing arrangements, III.29
  testing of backup methods, VII.5
  testing the program, III.29–III.30
  test types, III.29
Business Continuity Institute (DCI), III.2
Business Continuity Management, III.5–III.6
Business Continuity Planning (BCP), III.1–III.33
  activation of plans, III.22
  assessing awareness and training levels, III.30–III.31
  creating the plan, III.18–III.24
  critical disaster timelines, III.16

CISSP Review Seminar Questions, Answer Key

ACCESS CONTROL		BUSINESS CONTINUITY AND DISASTER RECOVERY PLANNING		ISGRM		OPERATIONS SECURITY		SECURITY ARCHITECTURE	
1.	C	1.	D	1.	D	1.	B	1.	C
2.	B	2.	B	2.	C	2.	D	2.	A
3.	A	3.	B	3.	C	3.	A	3.	C
4.	C	4.	A	4.	B	4.	C	4.	B
5.	B	5.	B	5.	A	5.	D	5.	C
6.	A	6.	B	6.	D	6.	A	6.	A
7.	C	7.	C	7.	A	7.	C	7.	D
8.	B	8.	C	8.	A	8.	A	8.	C
9.	D	9.	D	9.	B	9.	A	9.	C
10.	A	10.	B	10.	D	10.	D	10.	A
11.	B	11.	D	11.	B	11.	C	11.	B
12.	A	12.	A	12.	B	12.	B	12.	D
13.	B	13.	D	13.	A	13.	D	13.	C
14.	D	14.	B	14.	C	14.	B	14.	A
15.	A	15.	D	15.	A	15.	A	15.	A
16.	B	16.	D	16.	C	16.	C	16.	C
17.	C	17.	B	17.	B	17.	B	17.	B
18.	D	18.	A	18.	A	18.	D	18.	C
19.	B	19.	A	19.	A	19.	D	19.	C
20.	R	20.	A	20.	C	20.	B	20.	C

APPLICATION DEVELOPMENT SECURITY		CRYPTOGRAPHY		LRIC		PHYSICAL SECURITY		TELECOM-MUNICATIONS	
1.	C	1.	D	1.	B	1.	B	1.	B
2.	B	2.	C	2.	A	2.	C	2.	A
3.	D	3.	B	3.	D	3.	A	3.	C
4.	B	4.	A	4.	B	4.	D	4.	B
5.	A	5.	A	5.	C	5.	C	5.	C
6.	B	6.	D	6.	B	6.	B	6.	C
7.	C	7.	B	7.	A	7.	D	7.	C
8.	A	8.	A	8.	A	8.	B	8.	A
9.	D	9.	C	9.	C	9.	D	9.	C
10.	C	10.	C	10.	A	10.	A	10.	C
11.	A	11.	D	11.	D	11.	D	11.	B
12.	C	12.	B	12.	B	12.	A	12.	B
13.	A	13.	A	13.	B	13.	B	13.	B
14.	C	14.	D	14.	A	14.	D	14.	B
15.	D	15.	C	15.	C	15.	D	15.	C
16.	C	16.	B	16.	B	16.	C	16.	A
17.	B	17.	D	17.	A	17.	D	17.	B
18.	D	18.	B	18.	D	18.	B	18.	B
19.	A	19.	A	19.	B	19.	B	19.	D
20.	B	20.	B	20.	A	20.	A	20.	A